Money and Exchange in Europe and America, 1600–1775
A HANDBOOK

D1597584

The Institute of Early American History and Culture
is sponsored jointly by The College of William and Mary in Virginia
and The Colonial Williamsburg Foundation.

"Exchange is the Rudder of the ship of Trafficke. . . .
Money may well be compared to the Compasse."

GERARD DE MALYNES (1622)

Money and Exchange
in Europe and America, 1600–1775

A HANDBOOK

John J. McCusker

Published for the Institute of Early American History and Culture
Williamsburg, Virginia
by The University of North Carolina Press
Chapel Hill

Scribner Public Library
Scribner, Nebraska 68057

The quotation opposite the title page is from Gerard de Malynes,
Consuetudo, vel Lex Mercatoria, or, The Ancient Law-Merchant (London, 1622), 60–61.

Quotations from crown-copyright records in the Public Record Office, London,
appear with the permission of the Controller of H.M. Stationery Office.

Copyright © 1978 by John J. McCusker
All rights reserved
Manufactured in the United States of America
Library of Congress Catalog Card Number 76-54774

Library of Congress Cataloging in Publication Data

McCusker, John J.
  Money and exchange in Europe and America, 1600–1775.

  Bibliography: p.
  Includes index.
  1. Money–Tables, etc. 2. Money–United States–History–
Colonial period, ca. 1600–1775. 3. Money–Europe–History.
I. Institute of Early American History and Culture, Williamsburg, Va.
II. Title.
HG219.M33   332.4'5'0212   76-54774
ISBN 0-8078-1284-6
ISBN 0-8078-4367-9 (pbk.)
95 94 93 92 91   6 5 4 3 2

For Diana, John III, Patrick, and Margaret

Preface

In the course of my own research I often needed to be able to reduce various values in local currencies to a common denominator. I thus began to collect and compile exchange rate quotations. This handbook shares the results of my researches to date. I present it with a twofold hope: first, that the materials herein, though imperfect, may be of use to others; second, that the imperfection of what follows may provoke others to dig further into the subject. I also hope that readers in the former category will not condemn me too harshly for the quite real gaps and mistakes in my own work and that those in the latter category will share with me the fruits of their own labors.[1] If enough new data are assembled, there is a possibility of a second, revised edition of the handbook.

Money and exchange rates are not subjects about which many people—archivists, awarders of research grants, wives, colleagues, or publishers—can muster much enthusiasm. However vital such data might be to a rational analysis of a variety of topics in social and economic history, their complexity and their "dryness" allow us to ignore them. The result has been no end of confusion for the history of the seventeenth and eighteenth centuries. For this reason I am grateful to those who have supported me in this study.

There are many to thank. The staffs of libraries and archives in which I worked provided the raw materials for this handbook. The Institute of Early American History and Culture, the General Research Board of the University of Maryland, the American Philosophical Society, the Kress Library of Business and Economics in the Baker Library of the Graduate School of Business Administration of Harvard University, the Smithsonian Institution, the Council on Research in Economic History, the Department of History of University College, London, and the Institute of United States Studies of the University of London have aided my research and writing with fellowships and grants-in-aid. John P. Ravilious and Rondai L. Ravilious helped me in the last stages of the preparation of the book for the press. Grace J. Myles carefully typed the final draft. The editor, visiting editor, and associate editor of publications for the Institute of Early American History and Culture, Norman S. Fiering, David L. Ammerman, and Joy Dickinson Barnes, provided advice and assistance. Jacob M. Price, Stuart Bruchey, John M. Hemphill, Ronald Hoffman, Joseph A. Ernst, and Walter Rundell, Jr., read various versions of the text. Each was kind enough to point out and to correct a "few and light mistakes," in the words of William Hughes on the errata leaf to his book *The*

---

1. Material can best be sent to me in care of the Institute of Early American History and Culture, P.O. Box 220, Williamsburg, Virginia, 23185. It will be helpful if data are sent in their original, uncompiled form with full citations as to their source.

Man of Sin, or a Discourse of Popery (London, 1677). ''There may be others like, and some mispointings, but not to trouble the intelligent reader.''

Finally I acknowledge my greatest debt to those to whom I have dedicated this book, especially my dear wife, Diana. Without her encouragement and effort, particularly her patient typing and retyping of text and tables, this handbook would still be a sheaf of yellow pages.

Contents

Illustrations

Money and Exchange in Europe and America, 1600–1775
A HANDBOOK

Chapter 1

Money, Rates of Exchange, and Bills of Exchange: An Introduction

"The various coins which have circulated in America,
have undergone different changes in their value,
so that there is hardly any which can be considered as a general standard,
unless it be Spanish dollars."[1]

The purpose of this handbook is to provide sufficient information of a technical and statistical nature to allow the reader to convert a sum stated in one money into its equivalent in another money. It is limited in time to the colonial era before the American Revolution; it is limited in territory to the Atlantic world. Since there were six European colonial powers with some sixty to seventy colonies in the Western Hemisphere, and since almost every one of them, colony as well as mother country, had a different currency, the task, intellectually and mechanically, is not a simple one—for reader or writer. Yet contemporaries not only lived with this system, they prospered within it. Merchants of Baltimore and Philadelphia could juggle the current sale prices of their grain in Barbados, Guadeloupe, and Lisbon and make the best choice.

Owners of slave ships in Liverpool planned the voyages of their vessels aware of the costs and returns in Africa, the West Indies, and North America. Any of us today who wish to understand the seventeenth or the eighteenth century cannot know less than those whom we study; we need to appreciate how people of the time related to one another at this level as at all others. We need to know something about money and exchange. The purpose of this book is to make the acquisition of that knowledge as painless as possible.

Alexander Justice, writing in 1707, stated that "money in general is divided into two sorts, imaginary and real."[2] Real

1. Sec. of Finance Robert Morris to president of Congress, 15 Jan. 1782, in Jared Sparks, ed., *The Diplomatic Correspondence of the American Revolution*, XII (Boston, 1830), 91.

2. [Alexander Justice], *A General Treatise of Monies and Exchanges* (London, 1707), 1. See also J[ean] Boizard, *Traité des monoyes, de leurs circonstances et dépendances*, new ed. (Paris, 1711), 6. Henry Callister, Chester River, Md., merchant and tobacco planter, once commented: "Our money . . . is imaginary, and will forever fluctuate with the course of exchange." To [William] Carmichael, 30 Apr. 1761, Henry Callister Letter Books, 1741–1766, fol. 400, Callister Family Papers, 1741–1788, Maryland Diocesan Archives of the Prot-

Figure 1. Some Common European Silver and Gold Coins. (From Thomas Snelling, *A View of the Coins at This Time Current Throughout Europe* [London, 1766], from plates 1, 2, 9, 12, and 13, engraved by J. Lodge; courtesy of the Kress Library of Business and Economics, Graduate School of Business Administration, Harvard University, Boston.)

Great Britain

France

Denmark

Netherlands

Spain

Portugal

Key to the coins (shown obverse and reverse):

Great Britain
1. Shilling of George II (silver)
2. Shilling of George III (silver)

France
3. Petit ecu, or half ecu blanc, worth three livres tournois (silver)
4. Louis d'or (gold)

Netherlands
5. Gulden or florijn (silver)
6. Ducatoon (silver)

Denmark
7. Krone—the four-mark piece (silver)

Spain
8. Pisatreen (silver)
9. Peso, or piece of eight, clipped and worn, called a "cob" (silver)
10. Peso, or piece of eight, pillar type, from the Mexico City mint (silver)
11. Doblon, or pistole (gold)

Portugal
12. Cruzado (silver)
13. Moeda (gold)
14. Dobra de quatro escudos—the "Johannes" (gold)

money then was almost without exception coin minted from copper, silver, and gold. Imaginary moneys, also called moneys of account, were notational devices used in the counting-house and on the exchange. Some moneys of account, as we might expect, incorporated units common to real money, since one of the important functions of moneys of account was to reconcile disparate coin into national monetary systems. We can best understand moneys of account if we consider that the Royal Mint of Great Britain produced no coin equivalent to the "pound" until the nineteenth century. The pound was an imaginary unit, equal to twenty shillings. Silver shillings were minted, however, as was a gold guinea worth twenty-one shillings. Today, of course, the British pound is a form of real money (as well as money of account), and the guinea is no longer real but is sometimes used as a money of account in rarified circumstances. One buys a Rolls-Royce not with plebian pounds but with patrician guineas. Alexander Justice's distinction is an important one to remember, because goods were bought and sold by coin but books were kept and exchange transactions negotiated in moneys of account.

Tables 1.1 and 1.2 indicate something of the basic gold and silver coins in use in the Atlantic world in the seventeenth and eighteenth centuries. These lists are not exhaustive; each of the sources drawn on incorporated several times the number of coins set down here. Yet colonial documents rarely mention coins other than the ones in these tables, although

contemporaries knew some of them by different names. The French louis d'or was sometimes called the "French guinea"; the Portuguese dobra de quatro escudos, or peça, the "Johannes" or "Joe"; the German reichsthaler, the Danish rigsdaler, and the Dutch rijksdaalder, all the "rixdollar"; the Dutch leeuwendaalder, the "lion dollar" or even the "dog dollar"; the Spanish peso de plata, or piastra, the "piece of eight" or the "cob"; the real, the "bit"; and so on.[3] (Some of these coins are pictured in fig. 1, pp. 4–5.) A dictionary, preferably Murray's *Oxford English Dictionary* or Littré's *Dictionnaire de la langue française*, will serve to supply the proper name for most such coins.[4] A recourse to the tables will then give the approximate value in sterling of any coin once during the

3. See John Mair's comment, written in 1768, that the most common coins in the West Indies and North America were the real, the dollar, the pistole, the moidore, the Johannes, the guinea, and the double doublon, or four-pistole piece. Mair, *Book-keeping Modernized: or, Merchant-Accounts by Double Entry, According to the Italian Form*, "8th" ed. (Edinburgh, 1800), 350. See also Clarence P. Gould, *Money and Transportation in Maryland, 1720–1765*, Johns Hopkins University Studies in Historical and Political Science, Ser. XXXIII, no. 1 (Baltimore, 1915), 21–25; Edward Channing, *A History of the United States* (New York, 1905–1925), II, 498–499; W. T. Baxter, *The House of Hancock: Business in Boston, 1724–1775*, Harvard Studies in Business History, X (Cambridge, Mass., 1945), 15. For the piece of eight see also Robert Chalmers, *A History of Currency in the British Colonies* (London, [1893]), 390. For the lion or dog dollar see Gov. Col. Nathaniel Blakiston, at Maryland, to Board of Trade, 25 May 1701, C.O. 5/715, fols. 188v–189r, Public Record Office. (A key to these abbreviations for materials in the P.R.O. is incorporated in the Bibliography.) For a more systematic treatment of all of this, see Raphael E. Solomon, "Foreign Specie Coins in the American Colonies," in Eric P. Newman and Richard G. Doty, eds., *Studies on Money in Early America* (New York, 1976), 25–42. Note especially what he says about the "Joe," *ibid.*, 36–37.

4. James A. H. Murray *et al.*, eds., *The Oxford English Dictionary: Being a Corrected Re-Issue . . . of a New English Dictionary on Historical Principles* (Oxford, 1933); E[mile] Littré, *Dictionnaire de la langue française* ([Paris], 1956–1958).

estant Episcopal Church, Maryland Historical Society, Baltimore. See also Fernand P. Braudel and Frank C. Spooner's chapter, "Prices in Europe from 1450 to 1750," in E. E. Rich and C. H. Wilson, eds., *The Cambridge Economic History of Europe*, IV:*The Economy of Expanding Europe in the Sixteenth and Seventeenth Centuries* (Cambridge, 1967), 378–386.

seventeenth century and at three times during the eighteenth century and its comparative content in fine silver in terms of English assay weight (one pennyweight equals 1.55571 grams) and Dutch assay weight (one aas equals 4.806252 centigrams).[5] Just as these weights provided the mechanism for determining the value of each of the coins relative to sterling, so also can they be used in a similar determination of their value relative to any other money. One should also refer to the discussion of the various moneys of account in chapter 2, below.

The premier coin of the Atlantic world in the seventeenth and eighteenth centuries was the Spanish peso, or piastra—the piece of eight that in the seventeenth century came to be called the dollar and that later became the basic unit of the monetary system of the United States.[6] First minted in 1497, it was, in William Graham Sumner's words, "destined to serve as [the] universal money" of Europe and the Western Hemisphere.[7] We have only the vaguest idea of how many

were in circulation at any one time, but we do know, for instance, that in the ten years from 1766 to 1776 the Casa de la Moneda in Mexico alone coined 203,000,000 pieces of eight, more than 20,000,000 a year worth £4,567,500 sterling annually.[8] At a guess, perhaps as many as one-half of the coins in use in the colonies were pieces of eight.[9] The intrinsic value of the piece of eight continued almost unaltered for four hundred years.[10] In 1702 Sir Isaac Newton, as master of

5. Horace Doursther, *Dictionnaire universel des poids et mesures anciens et modernes, contenant des tables des monnaies de tous les pays* (Amsterdam, 1965 [orig. publ. Brussels, 1840]), 30, 250, 382. See also *De Koopman, of weekelyksche bydragen ten opbouw van Neederlands koophandel en zeevaard* (Amsterdam), I (nos. 16 and 17, [17 and 24 Dec. 1766]), 128, 132. This weekly commercial newspaper, edited by Gerrit Bom, appeared at Amsterdam from 1766 to 1776 and is usually bound in six volumes. I used the set in the Kress Library of Business and Economics, Graduate School of Business Administration, Harvard University, Boston. See also H[ajo] Brugmans, "De Koopman: Mercurius als spectator," *Jaarboek van het Genootschap Amstelodamum*, X (1912), 61–135. Brugmans was able to date the individual issues from advertisements placed in the *Leydse Maendagse Courant* (Leiden).

6. Chalmers, *History of Currency*, 391, says the 1690s for the origin of the name "dollar," but see J. H. Lefroy, ed., *Memorials of the Discovery and Early Settlement of the Bermudas or Somers Islands, 1515–1685* (London, 1877–1879), I, 240–247.

7. Sumner, "The Spanish Dollar and the Colonial Shilling," *American*

Historical Review, III (1897–1898), 609, translating Aloïss Heiss, *Descripcion general de las monedas hispano-cristianas desde la invasion de los Arabes* (Madrid, 1865–1869), I, 137 (q.v.).

8. Report of viceroy of New Spain, 31 Aug. 1793, as cited in Eduardo Arcila Farías, *El siglo ilustrado en América: Reformas economicas del siglo XVIII en Nueva España* (Caracas, Venezuela, 1955), 265–266, 269. A more systematic answer to this question can be developed using, among other things, materials assembled in the "Report, Together with Minutes of Evidence and Accounts from the Select Committee on the High Price of Gold Bullion," Great Britain, House of Commons, *Sessional Papers*, 1810, III (*Reports*), no. 349, 273ff. A useful general discussion is Pierre Vilar, *Or et monnaie dans l'histoire, 1450–1920* (Paris, 1974).

9. "In the West Indies, there is more Spanish money than of any other sort." [Justice], *General Treatise of Monies*, 91. Later in the century Alexander Hamilton estimated that on the eve of the American Revolution about a quarter of the money in the British continental colonies was in specie. If half of that were in pieces of eight, some 4,000,000 dollars (£900,000 sterling), or fewer than two per person, were in circulation there in the early 1770s. Hamilton to Morris, 30 Apr. 1781, in E. James Ferguson *et al.*, eds., *The Papers of Robert Morris, 1781–1784*, I (Pittsburgh, Pa., 1973), 35. According to Hamilton, there was a total of 30,000,000 dollars (£6,750,000 sterling) of specie and paper in circulation. This was the equivalent of about £2.70 sterling per person.

10. Sumner, "Spanish Dollar," *AHR*, III (1897–1898), 609, again translating Heiss, *Descripcion general de las monedas*, I, 137. "If we disregard the laws of 1642 and 1686 as domestic only, the dollar, as a world-coin, fell, between 1497 and our own times, according to actual tests (assuming that it started in 1497 at the standard of the law) from 394.29 grains of pure silver to 370.95 grains, or 5.9 per cent." Sumner, *ibid.*, 617. See also Chalmers, *History of Currency*, 392–393.

the Mint, reported that the standard Mexican piece of eight assayed at seventeen pennyweight (dwt.), nine grains (gr.), three mites (mi.) troy standard weight.[11] From 1601 to 1816 the ounce troy (oz. t.) of sterling silver was worth 5s 2d (25.8p, or "new pence") at the official English rate, making the standard piece of eight worth 53.9d, or 4s 6d (22.5p) sterling.[12] While newly minted coin remained fairly constant in its value, coin in circulation varied considerably in its worth, and contemporaries preferred, when they could, to take the piece of eight by weight rather than by "tale" (i.e., by count). Thus the continuing interest in the price per ounce of fine silver of sterling standard (see tables 1.3 and 1.4).

The concern that led people like Governor Thomas Culpeper of Virginia to prefer "the price sett on the ounce" since "that is certain, and not on the peece" arose from significant variations in the condition of coin.[13] These variations were induced partly by wear and partly by the propensity of individuals to cheat one another. One could "clip" a coin by shaving, filing, or cutting metal from its edges. A favorite technique was to cut a coin into not quite two halves by shaving a thin strip from the center. One could also "sweat" a coin by chemically leaching out some of its metallic content. The result was a "profit" for the cheaters and a debased coinage for everyone.[14] This is of interest to us for several reasons. It explains the reluctance of merchants and others to accept coins by tale, and it tells us the reason for the continuing concern about the weight of coins, a concern that gave rise to tables of assay weights such as those in tables 1.1 and 1.2. Also, the problem of underweight coinage reinforced the desirability of a money of account with which all of these coins, full-weight or not, could be equated. In repayment of a debt of, let us say, £100 sterling, the onus was on the debtor to produce enough coin of sufficient weight of metal to equal the sum owed. But in transactions satisfied by coin a certain ambiguity was present. This was especially true in the French West Indies, where the law insisted that all coin be accepted by tale at its face value no matter what its weight or condition. We will see more about the reasons for this below. Suffice it to say here that in the French West Indies the law had the added effect of turning the coin into the money of account, at least for exchange transactions. Finally, problems with coins created a climate in which people more readily accepted paper money, since paper money proclaimed its value on its face.

These problems with money, real and imaginary, obviously caused difficulties as the residents of a country tried to establish their own indigenous currency, but such difficulties

11. "The values of several forreign coynes," enclosure in Officers of the Mint to the Treasury, 17 July 1702, T. 1/80, fol. 330r, P.R.O., and in W. A. Shaw, ed., *Select Tracts and Documents Illustrative of English Monetary History, 1626–1730* (London, 1896), 140. See also Officers of the Mint to the Treasury, 9 Dec. 1703, copy in C.O. 323/5, fol. 161r–v.

12. Albert Feavearyear, *The Pound Sterling: A History of English Money*, ed. E. Victor Morgan, 2d ed. rev. (Oxford, 1963), 435. See also [William Douglass], *A Discourse concerning the Currencies of the British Plantations in America* (1739), [ed. Charles J. Bullock], American Economic Association, Economic Studies, II (New York, 1897), 300n. For monetary purposes, the ounce troy is divided into 20 pennyweight of 24 grains, each of which equals 20 mites; it is the equivalent of 31.103477 metric grains. Doursther, *Dictionnaire universel*, 161, 284, 368, 382; Ronald Edward Zupko, *A Dictionary of English Weights and Measures from Anglo-Saxon Times to the Nineteenth Century* (Madison, Wis., 1968), 73, 113, 119. All currencies have been expressed in decimalized notation in this handbook as an aid to calculations. See "A Note on Style," below in this chapter, and Appendix 1.

13. Culpeper's remarks on his "Instructions," 20 Sept. 1683, C.O. 1/48, fol. 59v.

14. Gould, *Money in Maryland*, 25–27. See also the "extract of a letter from a gentleman at New York dated the 4th of March, 1772, to his friend in Quebec," *Quebec Gazette*, 28 May 1772.

TABLE 1.1. **Basic Silver Coins of Europe and Their Relative Value in the Seventeenth and Eighteenth Centuries**

Origin and Denomination	Value in English Money, 1651 (Pounds Sterling) 1	After Sir Isaac Newton's Assay Report, 1702		Approximate Value, 1766 (Pounds Sterling) 4	Comparative Content in Fine Silver, 1781	
		Standard Weight (Dwt.) 2	Value (Pounds Sterling) 3		Weight (Dutch Azen) 5	Value (Pounds Sterling) 6
Amsterdam						
Ducatoon of 63 stuivers	£0.28	21.16	£0.27	£0.29	641.70	£0.28
Rijksdaalder of 50 stuivers	£0.23	16.86	£0.22	£0.23	506.90	£0.22
Leeuwendaalder of 42 stuivers		14.10	£0.18	£0.19	423.00	£0.19
Gulden (florijn) of 20 stuivers		[6.72]	[£0.09]	£0.09	200.00	£0.09
Hamburg						
Reichsthaler		17.72	£0.23	£0.25	532.00	£0.23
Thaler				£0.13	286.00	£0.12
Mark				£0.07	143.00	£0.06
Copenhagen						
Rigsdaler				£0.22	530.70	£0.23
Krone (4-mark piece)		10.47	£0.14	£0.14	311.00	£0.14
France						
Ecu of 60 sous tournois	£0.23	17.46	£0.23			
Ecu blanc, post-1726, of 6 livres				£0.26	557.53	£0.24
One-half ecu (crown of exchange)				£0.13	276.80	£0.12
England						
Crown	[£0.25]		[£0.25]	£0.25	579.30	£0.25
Shilling	[£0.05]		[£0.05]	£0.05	114.00	£0.05

TABLE 1.1 (Continued): Silver Coins

Origin and Denomination	Value in English Money, 1651 (Pounds Sterling)	After Sir Isaac Newton's Assay Report, 1702		Approximate Value, 1766 (Pounds Sterling)	Comparative Content in Fine Silver, 1781	
		Standard Weight (Dwt.)	Value (Pounds Sterling)		Weight (Dutch Azen)	Value (Pounds Sterling)
	1	2	3	4	5	6
Scotland, before 1707						
£3 piece			[£0.23]			
£2 piece			[£0.15]			
Mark of 13s 4d Scottish	£0.06		[£0.06]			
Spain						
Peso de plata antigua (piece of eight)						
Pre-1728	£0.23	17.38	£0.22		532.00	£0.23
1728–1772				£0.23	507.72	£0.22
Post-1772					499.94	£0.22
Peseta de vellon (pistareen) of 4 reales				£0.05	103.00	£0.04
Real de vellon				£0.01		
Portugal						
Cruzado		11.15	£0.14		331.00	£0.14
Cruzado, after 1747				£0.13	276.00	£0.12
Tostão				£0.03		

TABLE 1.2. **Basic Gold Coins of Europe and Their Relative Value in the Seventeenth and Eighteenth Centuries**

Origin and Denomination	Value in English Money, 1651 (Pounds Sterling) 1	After Sir Isaac Newton's Assay Report, 1702		Approximate Value, 1766 (Pounds Sterling) 4	Comparative Content in Fine Gold, 1781	
		Standard Weight (Dwt.) 2	Value (Pounds Sterling) 3		Weight (Dutch Azen) 5	Value (Pounds Sterling) 6
Amsterdam						
Ryder	£1.10			£1.28	190.58	£1.26
Ducat		2.38	£0.48	£0.48	71.33	£0.47
Hamburg						
Ducat			[£0.44]	£0.47	71.80	£0.47
Copenhagen						
Ducat of 15 marks		2.38	£0.48	£0.48		
Current ducat of 12 marks				£0.37	57.40	£0.38
France						
Louis d'or						
Pre-1726	£0.73	4.31	£0.86	£0.84	128.80	£0.85
Post-1726				£1.02	154.34	£1.02
England						
Guinea			[£1.03]	£1.05	159.42	£1.05
Spain						
Pistole (doblon)						
Pre-1722	£0.74	4.31	£0.86		128.38	£0.86
Post-1722				£0.83	127.90	£0.84

TABLE 1.2 (Continued): Gold Coins

Origin and Denomination	Value in English Money, 1651 (Pounds Sterling) 1	After Sir Isaac Newton's Assay Report, 1702		Approximate Value, 1766 (Pounds Sterling) 4	Comparative Content in Fine Gold, 1781	
		Standard Weight (Dwt.) 2	Value (Pounds Sterling) 3		Weight (Dutch Azen) 5	Value (Pounds Sterling) 6
Portugal						
Pre-1722						
Moeda	£1.27	6.86	£1.37	£1.35	205.20	£1.35
Post-1718						
Cruzado					20.25	£0.13
Pre-1720						
Dobrão					1,026.00	£6.76
Post-1722						
Dobra de 8 escudos				£3.60	547.25	£3.60
Dobra de 4 escudos (peça, "Johannes")				£1.80	273.63	£1.80
Escudo				£0.45	68.41	£0.45

Notes and Sources: **TABLES 1.1** and **1.2**

1651: "The Par of the Sylver [and Gold] coynes," [18 Nov. 1651], S.P. 18/16, fols. 213–218, Public Record Office, and in W. A. Shaw, ed., *Select Tracts and Documents Illustrative of English Monetary History, 1626–1730* (London, 1896), 86–90. On 14 May 1652 it was proposed to the Committee of the Mint that this booklet be printed. S.P. 18/24, pt. 1, fol. 40r.

1702: Officers of the Mint to the Treasury, 17 July 1702, and enclosure, "The values of several forreign coynes," T. 1/80, fols. 328r, 330r–v, P.R.O., and in Shaw, ed., *English Monetary History*, 136–147. Contemporary reprintings of Sir Isaac Newton's report (with some additions, q.v.) include *The Real or Intrinsic Par of Exchange, between London and the Cities on which Negotiations in Bills are usually made; Calculated from the Actual Assays made at the Mint, by the Accurate Sir Isaac Newton, of the Several Foreign Coins* (London, 1731); *Sir Isaac Newton's Table of the Assays, Weights and Values of most Foreign Silver, and Gold Coins* (London, 1740); J[ohn] Millan, *Coins, Weights and Measures, Ancient and Modern, of All Nations, Reduced into English* ([London], 1747), [20]; [Thomas Slack], *The British Negociator: or, Foreign Exchanges Made Perfectly Easy* (London, 1759), [246]–254; and [Timothy Cunningham], *The Law of Bills of Exchange, Promissory Notes, Bank-Notes and Insurances* (London, 1760), 373–379. The first two of these (the second is a later edition of the first) clearly seem to be the work of their publisher, Robert Willock. The only

Notes and Sources: **TABLE 1.2 (Continued)**

known copies of either of these two broadsides are in the Goldsmiths Library, University of London. The copy of the second broadside is close-cropped and without an imprint; we can date it from the entry in the bibliography of Jürgen Elert Kruse, *Allgemeiner und besonders Hamburgischer Contorist*, 3d ed., I (Hamburg, 1766), 465.

1766: Thomas Snelling, *A View of the Coins at This Time Current throughout Europe* (London, 1766), 1, 2, 8, 9, 12, 13.

1781: Samuel Ricard, *Traité général du commerce*, [ed. Tomás Antonio de Marien y Arróspide] (Amsterdam, 1781), II, 66, 77–78, 105, 126–127, 150, 287–298. The comparative value of silver in sterling (table 1.1, col. 6) is based on the shilling at 114 as. worth 12d sterling. The comparative value of gold (table 1.2, col. 6) is based on the guinea at 159.42 as. worth 21s sterling. See also, for Spain, Tomás Antonio de Marien y Arróspide, *Tratado general de monedas, pesas, medidas y cambios de todas las naciones, reducidas á las que se usan en España* (Madrid, 1789), xxxiv–xli. See also, for Scotland, Newton to Treasury, 16 Feb. 1709/10 and 21 Sept. 1717, T. 1/120, fol. 163r, and T. 1/208, fols. 204–205, and in Shaw, ed., *English Monetary History*, 150, 170; [Alexander Justice], *A General Treatise of Monies and Exchanges* (London, 1707), 92–93; and Henry Hamilton, *An Economic History of Scotland in the Eighteenth Century* (Oxford, 1963), 433. For Portugal see also J[oaquín] Ferraro Vaz, *Catálogo das moedas portuguesas: Portugal continental, 1640–1948* (Lisbon, 1948), 22, 33, 45, 56, 68, and *passim*; and A[ugusto] C. Teixeira de Aragão, *Descripção geral e historica das moedas cunhadas em nome dos reis, regentes e governadores de Portugal* (Lisbon, 1874–1880), *passim*. Also useful are such books as Robert Friedberg, *Gold Coins of the World, Complete from 600 A.D. to 1958: An Illustrated Standard Catalogue with Valuations* (New York, [1958]).

TABLE 1.3. Price of Sterling Silver in Bars at London, 1680–1716

(Pence Sterling per Ounce Troy)

Year	Jan.	Feb.	Mar.	Apr.	May	June	July	Aug.	Sept.	Oct.	Nov.	Dec.	Average
1680		62.50											62.50
1681					62.00								62.00
1682													
1683													
1684													
1685													
1686													
1687													
1688													
1689						62.00							62.00
1690													
1691										63.50			63.50
1692	63.75												63.75

TABLE 1.3 (Continued): Sterling Silver at London (Pence per Ounce)

Year	Jan.	Feb.	Mar.	Apr.	May	June	July	Aug.	Sept.	Oct.	Nov.	Dec.	Average
1693													
1694													
1695	64.50	65.00	66.50	67.00	63.00	69.00	73.00	74.00	77.00	74.00	75.00	77.00	70.42
1696	71.00	71.00		62.00			61.50	62.00	62.00	62.00	61.50	63.00	64.25
1697	62.00	61.50	60.50	60.00		61.25		61.12		61.50			61.14
1698													
1699													
1700													
1701											66.50		66.50
1702													
1703													
1704													
1705													
1706													
1707													
1708													
1709													
1710													
1711													
1712													
1713			66.00										66.00
1714													
1715													
1716							66.00						66.00

Notes and Sources: **TABLE 1.3**

  1680–1716: London price currents as listed in Appendix 2, below.

  1695–1697: *A Collection for Improvement of Husbandry and Trade* (London), 18 Jan. 1694/95–31 Dec. 1697 (the figure nearest the middle of the month).

TABLE 1.4. **Price of Sterling Silver in Bars at London, 1698–1775**

(Pence Sterling per Ounce Troy)

Year	Jan.	Feb.	Mar.	Apr.	May	June	July	Aug.	Sept.	Oct.	Nov.	Dec.	Average
1698	63.25	62.00	61.00										62.08
1699													
1700													
1701													
1702													
1703													
1704													
1705													
1706													
1707													
1708													
1709													
1710													
1711													
1712													
1713													
1714													
1715													
1716													
1717													
1718			66.50	65.00	65.00	65.12	65.50	65.50	65.00	64.50	65.38	65.25	65.48
1719	65.12	65.00	64.75	64.00	63.50	64.00	64.00	64.12	64.50	65.50	66.00	65.00	64.62
1720	65.00	65.50	65.00	64.75	64.50	64.50	64.75	67.00	67.00	65.00	65.00	65.50	65.29
1721	66.00	65.75	65.50	66.00	66.00	65.50	64.50	64.50	64.00	64.00	64.00	64.00	64.98
1722	64.00	64.00	64.00	64.00	64.00	64.00	64.00	64.00	64.00	64.00	64.75	64.75	64.12
1723	64.50	64.50	64.50	64.50	63.50	63.25	64.00	63.25	63.25	63.50	63.62	63.62	63.83
1724	63.62	63.50	63.50	63.50	63.50	63.50	63.50	63.44	63.44	63.44	63.44	63.44	63.48

TABLE 1.4 (Continued): Sterling Silver at London (Pence per Ounce)

Year	Jan.	Feb.	Mar.	Apr.	May	June	July	Aug.	Sept.	Oct.	Nov.	Dec.	Average
1725	63.50	63.50	63.50	63.50	63.50	63.50	63.50	63.50	63.50	63.50	63.50	66.00	63.71
1726	66.00	64.50	64.00	64.00	64.00	64.00	64.00	64.00	64.00	64.00	64.00	64.00	64.21
1727	64.00	64.00	64.00	64.00	64.00	64.00	63.25	63.25	63.25	63.25	63.25	63.25	63.62
1728	63.25	64.50	64.50	64.50	64.50	64.50	64.50	64.50	64.50	65.50	65.50	65.50	64.65
1729	65.50	65.50	65.50	65.50	65.50	65.50	65.50	65.50	65.50	65.50	65.50	65.50	65.50
1730	65.50	65.50	65.50	65.50	65.00	65.00	65.00	64.50	65.00	65.00	65.00	65.00	65.12
1731	65.00	65.00	65.00	65.00	64.50	64.25	65.00	64.50	64.25	64.00	63.75	63.56	64.48
1732	63.75	63.75	64.06	64.06	64.06	64.06	64.19	64.31	64.31	64.44	64.75	64.75	64.21
1733	64.75	64.75	64.75	64.44	64.25	64.25	64.25	64.12	64.31	64.25	64.25	63.88	64.35
1734	62.50	63.00	63.25	63.25	63.12	63.12	62.75	62.75	62.75	62.75	62.75	62.75	62.90
1735	62.75	62.75	62.62	63.00	62.88	63.12	63.12	63.25	63.25	63.12	63.12	63.12	63.01
1736	63.12	63.25	63.38	63.50	63.62	63.62	63.75	64.00	64.12	63.12	64.25	64.12	63.65
1737	64.00	64.06	64.12	64.25	64.38	65.25	65.25	65.75	65.50	64.50	64.12	64.00	64.60
1738	63.75	63.75	64.00	64.38	64.44	64.44	64.44	64.44	64.44	64.88	64.88	65.00	64.40
1739	65.00	65.00	65.00	65.25	65.25	65.25	65.25	65.25	65.25	65.25	65.25	65.38	65.20
1740	65.50	66.00	66.50	65.50	65.50	66.50	66.50	67.00	67.00	67.00	67.25	67.50	66.48
1741	67.75	67.50	67.50	67.50	67.50	67.50	67.50	67.50	67.50	67.50	67.50	67.50	67.52
1742	67.50	67.50	67.50	67.50	66.25	66.31	66.50	66.50	66.50	66.50	66.50	66.75	66.82
1743	66.75	66.75	66.75	66.75	66.75	66.50	66.50	66.50	66.50	66.50	66.50	66.50	66.60
1744	67.50	68.00	68.00	67.50	67.25	67.25	66.50	66.00	65.75	65.75	68.25	68.25	67.17
1745	68.25	67.25	67.25	67.25	67.25	67.25	67.25	66.25	66.50	66.50	64.00	63.00	66.50
1746	63.00	63.00	64.25	63.50	63.50	64.00	64.00	64.50	64.50	64.50	64.50	65.50	64.06
1747	65.50	65.50	65.50	65.50	65.00	65.00	65.00	65.00	65.50	65.50	65.50	65.50	65.33
1748	65.00	65.00	65.50	64.00	64.00	64.00	64.00	64.00	64.00	64.00	64.00	64.00	64.29
1749	64.00	64.00	65.25	65.25	65.25	64.50	64.50	64.00	64.50	64.50	64.50	64.50	64.56
1750	64.50	64.50	64.50	64.50	64.50	64.50	64.50	64.00	65.25	65.50	66.00	66.62	64.91
1751	65.00	64.81	64.50	64.75	64.75	64.88	64.75	64.69	65.25	65.69	65.75	65.75	65.05
1752	65.75	65.75	65.75	65.88	66.12	66.00	66.12	66.44	66.44	66.50	66.62	66.75	66.18

TABLE 1.4 (Continued): **Sterling Silver at London** (Pence per Ounce)

Year	Jan.	Feb.	Mar.	Apr.	May	June	July	Aug.	Sept.	Oct.	Nov.	Dec.	Average
1753	66.75	66.75	66.75	66.88	66.81	66.81	66.88	66.88	67.06	67.38	67.25	67.19	66.95
1754	66.75	66.88	66.31	66.44	65.88	65.75	66.06	66.62	66.38	65.75	65.69	65.50	66.17
1755	65.00	64.25	64.50	64.88	64.12	64.38	64.38	64.88	64.28	64.38	64.50	65.00	64.55
1756	65.00	64.50	64.50	64.62	64.62	64.50	64.25	64.00	63.75	63.75	63.50	63.50	64.21
1757	63.25	63.38	63.50	63.62	63.75	65.00	65.38	65.38	64.75	64.62	64.12	64.88	64.30
1758	64.62	64.75	66.75	67.00	67.50	67.50	67.75	67.75	68.25	67.25	67.62	67.62	67.03
1759	68.00	68.00	68.25	68.00	67.00	67.50	67.00	67.25	66.00	66.50	66.06	66.50	67.17
1760	66.75	66.38	66.75	66.62	66.38	66.38	66.50	67.00	67.25	67.62	67.75	69.00	67.03
1761	68.75	68.75	68.75	68.75	69.50	69.00	69.00	68.75	67.38	67.25	66.25	66.25	68.20
1762	67.00	67.50	68.50	67.75	67.50	66.00	66.00	66.00	64.50	64.50	64.75	65.00	66.25
1763	65.75	65.50	66.62	67.00	68.00	66.50	66.50	68.50	66.00	64.50	64.75	63.25	66.07
1764	64.25	64.00	63.38	63.50	63.50	63.50	63.50	63.50	63.75	63.50	63.50	63.50	63.62
1765	64.00	64.50	64.25	64.25	64.25	64.75	64.75	64.75	65.25	65.50	66.00	65.75	64.83
1766	66.00	66.50	66.50	66.50	66.75	67.00	67.25	67.00	67.00	67.25	67.25	67.25	66.85
1767	67.25	67.25	67.00	67.12	67.50	67.00	66.75	66.50	66.50	66.50	66.25	66.00	66.80
1768	65.50	65.50	66.00	67.00	66.75	66.25	65.75	66.25	66.25	66.25	66.50	67.50	66.29
1769	67.50	66.75	66.50	67.00	67.00	67.00	67.00	67.50	67.75	67.75	67.75	67.75	67.27
1770	67.75	67.75	67.75	68.00	68.00	68.00	68.00	67.50	67.50	67.38	67.25	67.00	67.66
1771	67.00	67.00	67.50	68.00	67.50	67.25	67.25	67.25	67.25	67.25	67.50	67.75	67.38
1772	68.00	68.00	68.00	68.00	68.25	68.25	66.00	65.25	65.25	65.00	64.50	64.00	66.54
1773	64.50	64.75	64.75	64.75	63.75	63.50	63.75	63.50	63.50	63.50	63.25	62.25	63.81
1774	62.50	62.50	62.50	63.00	64.00	62.75	62.50	62.75	63.75	64.00	64.00	64.00	63.19
1775	64.00	64.25	64.50	65.00	65.00	64.25	63.75	63.50	64.00	64.25	64.25	65.00	64.31

Notes and Sources: **TABLE 1.4**

1698–1775: *The Course of the Exchange* (London), 1698–1775. See the discussion below in the initial section to chap. 2 and n. 10, chap. 2. See also the price of fine silver in bars in gulden per mark for 1683, 1686, and 1719–1914 at Amsterdam in N. W. Posthumus, *Inquiry into the History of Prices in Holland* (Leiden, 1946–1964), I, 23*–25*, 394–395.

1718: *Freke's Prices of Stocks, &c.* (London), 14 Mar., 15 Apr. 1718. Edited by John Freke. From the copy in the British Library (press mark: 713.h.2,3).

were compounded enormously when it became necessary to effect an exchange between one currency and another. The question then became, How much must I give in my own money to obtain any given sum in another money? That is, What is the rate of exchange?

The rate of exchange is the ratio of the value of two currencies; it is the expression in one money of a sum of equal value in another money. The mechanisms involved in effecting any exchange were formalized ones in Europe in the seventeenth century, and they quickly became so in the colonies. Thus, while exchange could theoretically be accomplished on any monetary basis acceptable to the people involved, in practice exchange and the rate of exchange used moneys of account. We can recognize several modes of monetary exchange in the seventeenth and eighteenth centuries.

The classical distinction between *cambium minutum*, or the exchange of coins, and *cambium per litteras*, exchange by bills, does not concern us here.[15] We are exclusively involved with exchange by bills in this handbook. More pertinent is the distinction between inland and overseas exchange. Both are important, the latter more so than the former. Overseas exchange by means of bills of exchange was of two types: foreign exchange and colonial exchange. European businessmen exchanged with one another by each buying a bill in his own country and paying a sum in his own money of account for the delivery in another country of an equivalent sum in the money of account of that country. This was a foreign exchange transaction; it involved two different moneys of account. Colonies, by contrast, used the same money of account as the mother country. A colonial exchange transaction consisted of paying some premium in colonial currency for the delivery of a certain sum in the metropolis or vice versa. Thus colonial rates of exchange were usually expressed as a percentage of colonial currency.

Inland exchange between two separate places was one of two types of domestic exchange transactions that were common in the seventeenth and eighteenth centuries; an understanding of both types is needed to use this handbook most profitably to compare prices and the like. The second variety of domestic exchange involved two different moneys in the same place. It occurred in parts of Europe and in at least one colony, where the existence of more than one version of the money of account required an exchange between them. In Hamburg, Amsterdam, and elsewhere, the semiofficial bank money, or banco, was worth more than the current money. The difference could be expressed in two ways: as the percentage advance on bank money for current money or as the percentage discount from current money for bank money. Either way, it was called the agio, reflecting its origin in Italian banking. Somewhat surprisingly, a dual money of account operated in Maryland in the 1740s and 1750s.[16]

While conversion from bank money to current money was an exchange transaction and while the agio was very much a rate of exchange, economic historians have not in the past discussed them in these terms. Domestic exchange has

---

15. Raymond de Roover, *Gresham on Foreign Exchange: An Essay on Early English Mercantilism with the Text of Sir Thomas Gresham's Memorandum for the Understanding of the Exchange* (Cambridge, Mass., 1949), 94–95.

16. The agio in Maryland fluctuated over time. Other colonies sometimes had more than one money of account at the same time. Massachusetts with Old Tenor, Middle Tenor, and New Tenor is probably the premier example, but the ratio of each of these was fixed by law and unvarying in practice. Maryland is unique among colonies, much to the consternation of those who have studied her economic history.

more traditionally meant inland exchange. It began to develop in the middle of the seventeenth century. According to Raymond de Roover, all bills of exchange were foreign bills "until the eve of the English Civil War, when the London goldsmiths began to discount 'inland,' or domestic bills."[17] In practice this meant that a bill of exchange could now be drawn in Liverpool for payment in London but that it yielded something less than its face value. More will be said about all of this below.

A record of each of these four types of exchange somewhere included an indication of the rate at which the exchange was transacted. Every quotation in the series of these rates assembled in this handbook is the product of such a transaction. Some of them were compiled by contemporaries;[18] some have been compiled by economic historians who have recognized the need for such series; and others are compiled here for the first time. Each rate of exchange—that is, the price paid in one currency to buy a precise amount of another currency—comes to us from the marketplace and represents a response to the laws of supply and demand. There were, to be sure, attempts by government to influence the rate of exchange; laws establishing the par of exchange are the most obvious of such devices.[19] But we gain a clearer understanding of the processes involved in negotiating a bill of exchange if we think of the transaction as the purchase of money and if we think of the rate of exchange as the price paid.

One bought a bill of exchange in order to satisfy an obligation in some distant place. Perhaps the closest common analogy to the bill of exchange is the check. A check is, in fact, a bill of exchange drawn on a bank. We can imagine a person living today in New York or Paris approaching an acquaintance with an account in a London bank and offering to pay him or her in dollars (or francs) for a check drawn on that account. If one did this, perhaps debating a bit over how many dollars to pay for a check for £100, one would come very close to doing what people did in the eighteenth century. The amount finally agreed upon could provide the basis for determining the modern rate of exchange. It was just that kind of bargaining over the price of a bill of exchange that was one cause of fluctuations in the rate of exchange. By the seventeenth century the bill of exchange was already a financial instrument with a long history, and the era that concerns us here can be seen as a plateau in the history of foreign exchange practices with no basic changes in the method of exchange until after 1775.[20] An understanding of these methods is important for what follows.

17. De Roover, *Gresham on Foreign Exchange*, 95. See also *ibid.*, 105, and his citation to Abbott Payson Usher, *The Early History of Deposit Banking in Mediterranean Europe*, I (Cambridge, Mass., 1943), 98–109.

18. [Timothy Cunningham], *The Law of Bills of Exchange, Promissory Notes, Bank-Notes and Insurances* (London, 1760), 386–387. Cunningham often issued the first edition of his books anonymously and then put his name on the title page of the second and later editions.

19. Paul Einzig, *The History of Foreign Exchange* (New York, 1962), *passim*.

20. See Raymond de Roover, *L'évolution de la lettre de change, XIVe–XVIIIe siècles* (Paris, 1952), *passim*; Einzig, *Foreign Exchange*, 113, 125; Braudel and Spooner, "Prices in Europe," in Rich and Wilson, eds., *Cambridge Economic History*, IV, 386–391. See also J. Milnes Holden, "Bills of Exchange during the Seventeenth Century," *Law Quarterly Review*, LXVII (1951), 230–248; J. G. Sperling, "The International Payments Mechanism in the Seventeenth and Eighteenth Centuries," *Economic History Review*, 2d Ser., XIV (1961–1962), 446–468. A standard if somewhat older textbook treatment of much of this is Albert C. Whitaker, *Foreign Exchange*, 2d ed. (New York, 1933). A most interesting book, with actual examples of bills of exchange, is *The Bill on London; or, the Finance of Trade by Bills of Exchange*, 3d ed. (London, [1964]), published for Gillett Brothers Discount Co. Ltd.

The extensive legal literature on bills of exchange as negotiable instruments is neatly epitomized in Joseph Chitty, *A Treatise on the Law of Bills of Exchange, Checks on Bankers, Promissory Notes, Bankers' Cash Notes, and Banknotes* (London, 1799), which quickly became the authority on the subject and

The usual buying and selling of a bill of exchange involved four parties: the drawer, the drawee, the payer, and the payee.[21] The payer (buyer) of the bill of exchange approached the drawer (seller) and asked him to instruct his correspondent (the drawee) to deliver a sum of money to the person (the payee) designated by the payer.[22] The drawer of the bill parted with it in return for goods or services or local money or whatever he felt he needed and the payer was willing to provide. The moneys that he instructed the drawee to pay out were from a credit balance held for him by the drawee. If the drawer were a merchant, the credit balance might well have been established through the sale of his goods by the drawee as his agent. The bargain having been struck, the

drawer gave the payer several copies of the bill of exchange, known as a "set," in order to insure against loss in the mails; the payment of any one of them canceled the others, of course. The payer mailed each bill separately to the payee, who then presented one of them to the drawee. After a customary period of time (called the "usance"), stipulated in the bill, the drawee remitted the stated sum to the payee. An illustration might make all of this a bit clearer.[23]

Let us suppose that Benjamin Franklin in Philadelphia had had goods shipped him to the value of £100 sterling from Thistlethwayt and Jones of London, purveyors of kites. The account had been duly rendered and was now payable. Franklin had several options. He might choose to assemble a quantity of goods for shipment to England, where they would be sold by an agent and the net moneys earned paid to his creditors. But that entailed a great deal of work and expense in finding and buying the proper cargo for sale in London, shipping it, arranging for its sale by an agent, paying him a commission fee, paying freight and insurance costs, and worrying about the safe arrival and timely sale of the goods. Alternatively, Franklin might try to gather sufficient gold and silver coin in Philadelphia and send it all to London directly to his creditor. But then again there was the bother, the freight costs, the insurance charges, and even more worry. Most likely, instead of these other options, he would approach a large Philadelphia mercantile house with connections in London and buy a bill of exchange.[24] Franklin, the payer in

---

went through numerous editions in the 19th century. Of particular interest for us are the American editions incorporating state and federal case law prepared by Joseph Story from the 2d London edition and published at Boston and Philadelphia in 1809. A valuable parallel study, used by Chitty, is Robert J. Pothier, *Traité du contrat de change, de la négociation qui se fait par la lettre de change, des billets de change, et autres billets de commerce* (Paris and Orleans, 1763); there was a ʼ.d edition dated 1773. See also J. Milnes Holden, *The History of Negotiable Instruments in English Law* (London, 1955).

21. Some of the standard contemporary English-language discussions of the mechanics (and the technicalities) of the bill of exchange, all of which went through several editions, are: Gerard de Malynes, *Consuetudo, vel Lex Mercatoria, or, the Ancient Law-Merchant* (London, 1622); John Marius, *Advice concerning Bills of Exchange* (London, 1651); Wyndham Beawes, *Lex Mercatoria Rediviva: or, the Merchant's Directory* (London, 1752); [Cunningham], *Law of Bills of Exchange*; and [Timothy Cunningham], *The Merchant's Lawyer: or the Law of Trade in General* (London, 1761). See also de Roover, *Gresham on Foreign Exchange*, 94–172.

22. Exchange brokers grew up as financial intermediaries, one of whose functions was to eliminate the competitive disadvantage in which by definition the initiator of the transaction found himself. Einzig, *Foreign Exchange*, 122–123. London had a "well organized and highly competitive" exchange market by the end of the 17th century. T. S. Ashton, *An Economic History of England: The Eighteenth Century* (London, [1955]), 188. For the continental colonies, see below, chap. 3, n. 22.

23. There are examples of bills of exchange in Stuart Bruchey, ed., *The Colonial Merchant: Sources and Readings* (New York, [1966]), 193, and Warren M. Billings, ed., *The Old Dominion in the Seventeenth Century: A Documentary History of Virginia, 1606–1689* (Chapel Hill, N.C., 1975), 185.

24. See Philip L. White, *The Beekmans of New York in Politics and Commerce, 1647–1877* (New York, 1956), 382–384. See also Einzig, *Foreign Exchange*, 129.

our example, could have turned to Willing and Morris as a drawer, and offered to buy from them £100 sterling of their balance in the hands of their London correspondent, Thomas Willing, as the drawee.

Precisely how much Franklin offered Willing and Morris for the £100 sterling payable in London depended on several considerations. During the late colonial period the par of exchange—the comparative value of the moneys of account of Pennsylvania and England based on the price in each for the Spanish piece of eight—was 1⅔ (1.6667) to 1. That is to say, the piece of eight had a value of 7s 6d (37.5p) in Pennsylvania currency and 4s 6d (22.5p) in sterling and thus £166.67 Pennsylvania money was the legal equivalent of £100 sterling at par. Par for other English colonies ranged from parity (1 to 1) to as high as 7 to 1 and more. But par was only a benchmark; the commercial rate of exchange fluctuated around par in response to still other considerations.

The bill of exchange was, in one sense, an order to pay a specified sum at some future date and hence was a loan involving an element of interest. Thus the bill rate could and did vary with the maturity date of the bill. We can see this in the case of Franklin's arrangement with Willing and Morris. By giving them the £167 immediately, Franklin in effect lent Willing and Morris that sum subject to repayment in London sometime later. Bills had to be paid within a certain period after they were presented by the payee to the drawee. The period—the usance of the bill—depended largely on custom. New York bills on London were usually drawn to be paid from thirty to forty days after "sight"; Virginia bills were drawn at sixty days. European custom varied in a similar fashion. And depending on the locale, a few days of grace might be added. All this, plus the time required by the post,

meant that Willing and Morris had the use of Franklin's money for perhaps three months. Franklin could, then, expect to pay something less than par for his £100 sterling, the difference being understood in part as a kind of interest on the loan. Bills drawn at longer sight, therefore, cost even less.[25]

25. In the larger, more sophisticated mercantile centers, the payee might choose not to wait for his money. He could endorse the accepted bill over to a third party, who would give the payee in cash something less than the face value of the bill (the difference being, effectively, interest on the loan of the money). In the early 17th century one author called this "abating for the interest for the time and . . . according to the rate"; we know it as "discounting." See Malynes, *Consuetudo, vel Lex Mercatoria*, 98–99; Baxter, *House of Hancock*, 31. Later, in the 19th century, "'usance' no longer determined the maturity of bills but was the basis of calculating the difference between market quotations and actual amounts paid for bills." Einzig, *Foreign Exchange*, 171. As an example of discounting at London in the 18th century we have the following. In the fall of 1770 Christopher Champlin of Newport, R.I., sent bills drawn at 3, 8, and 12 months sight to Hayley and Hopkins of London. Champlin apparently asked that, after acceptance, the bills be sold at a discount and that the proceeds be immediately credited to his account. He wanted a rate of no more than 4%. The firm responded that all the bills had been accepted and would be paid in due course but that it was "impossible to discount them at four per cent. Bills not exceeding 2 months may be always discounted here at 5 per cent but not under; but when they are so long as 4, 8, and 12 months they cannot possibly be gott done even at 5 per cent. They must therefore remain till they are due before they can go to your credit." In the meantime Hayley and Hopkins would continue to bill Champlin's account for interest on the outstanding balance due. Hayley and Hopkins to Champlin, 8 Dec. 1770, in [Worthington C. Ford, ed.], *Commerce of Rhode Island, 1726–1800* (Massachusetts Historical Society, *Collections*, 7th Ser., IX–X [Boston, 1914–1915]), I, 355. (Ford identified himself as the editor of these volumes, *ibid.*, II, vi.) The journal of Joshua Johnson, the London partner of the Annapolis, Md., firm of Wallace, Davidson, & Johnson, "contains examples of accepted bills of exchange with less than 30 days to run [being] used as cash to pay debts without discount." Jacob M. Price, "Joshua Johnson in London, 1771–1775: Credit and Commercial Organization in the British Chesapeake Trade," in Anne Whiteman *et al.*, eds., *Statesmen, Scholars and Merchants: Essays in Eighteenth-Century History Presented to Dame Lucy Sutherland* (Oxford, 1973), 165n.

The reputation of the drawer and drawee of the bill of exchange also influenced the price. This was so because not all bills were paid as contracted. It sometimes happened that a drawee could not or would not honor a bill drawn upon him. Such unpaid bills, accompanied by a formal "protest," would be returned to the payer by the payee. Franklin would have had some legal redress in such a case, including the award of a sum for damages and of another sum for interest from the date of protest. Yet the inconvenience alone of having to start the process all over—not to mention any problems caused with his creditor—were enough to induce some to pay a higher cost in the beginning to insure that this did not happen.

The final and most important influence on the commercial rate of exchange was the state of the market for bills of exchange. Here, of course, the laws of supply and demand were at work. More sellers than buyers, and the price would decline; more buyers than sellers, and the price would rise. Supply and demand itself hinged upon several considerations, the most significant being the state of the balance of payments between the two places where buyer and seller lived. An imbalance in the current account regularly tended to increase the demand for, and decrease the supply of, bills for merchants in the deficient community—and therefore to increase their cost.

Three related mechanisms worked to dampen any extreme fluctuations in the bill rate caused by alterations in supply and demand. Imbalances in bilateral relationships regularly resulted in the resort to a third party; Thomas Mun spoke of how "the farther about will prove the nearest way home, if it come at last with good profit."[26] Exports of com-

modities to a third intermediary created credits there to be drawn on, either by buying other commodities there for shipment to and sale in the country in question or by negotiating bills there on the other country. The relationship between the British continental colonies and the West Indies is a classic example of such a multilateral arrangement to overcome the problems of direct trade between the continental colonies and the mother country. Third-party bills or third-party goods provided only two of the alternatives, however; the other was even more sophisticated.

When the price of bills rose too high, one could revert to shipping bullion or specie. This was true in the colonies, but it was even truer in Europe, where international exchange arbitrage was much more practiced. There was great concern over the point at which it became more profitable to export or import gold or silver than to buy bills; this was called the "gold point" (or the "specie point").[27] Convenient, pocket-size handbooks such as Thomas Collett's were published in aid of such considerations.[28]

On balance, in Europe multilateral trade and indirect exchange worked to keep the commercial rate of exchange near or below par and rarely high enough to make it more profitable to ship specie than to negotiate a bill.[29] By contrast, in

26. Mun, *England's Treasure by Forraign Trade; or, the Ballance of Our*

Forraign Trade Is the Rule of Our Treasure (Oxford, 1928 [orig. publ. London, 1664]), 48. Mun probably wrote between 1635 and 1641. De Roover, *Gresham on Foreign Exchange*, 151.

27. Ashton, *Economic History of England*, 189–190; Einzig, *Foreign Exchange*, 128–129, 144–145.

28. *Tables for Standard Gold and Silver, Compared with the Courses of Exchange* (London, 1731). See also de Roover, *L'évolution de la lettre de change*, 129–134, and his example from Malynes, *Consuetudo, vel Lex Mercatoria*, 372.

29. Ashton, *Economic History of England*, 190–191; Einzig, *Foreign Exchange*, 151. But see H. E. S. Fisher, *The Portugal Trade: A Study of Anglo-Portuguese Commerce, 1700–1770* (London, 1971), 20–22.

the colonies the bill rate fluctuated much more widely than in Europe and had a certain tendency to stand above par. The greater costs of shipping specie no doubt played a major role in creating this distinction.[30] A similar difference arose for many of the same reasons. European exchange rates tended to fluctuate more in unison than did colonial rates, obviously an effect of the more closely related European economy and the more highly developed exchange arbitrage.[31]

30. See Richard Cantillon, *Essai sur la nature du commerce en général* (written ca. 1734, orig. publ. 1755), ed. and trans. Henry Higgs (London, 1931), 250–253; and Joseph Albert Ernst, *Money and Politics in America, 1755–1775: A Study in the Currency Act of 1764 and the Political Economy of Revolution* (Chapel Hill, N.C., 1973), 15–16n. For a somewhat different view see Curtis P. Nettels, *The Money Supply of the American Colonies before 1720*, University of Wisconsin Studies in the Social Sciences and History, No. 20 (Madison, Wis., 1934), 181.

31. See de Roover, *Gresham on Foreign Exchange*, 129, 137; and Sperling, "International Payments Mechanism," *Econ. Hist. Rev.*, 2d Ser., XIV (1962), 456–460. Such factors were not perfect in their effect and sometimes allowed for significant gaps to develop in exchange transactions. See, e.g., tables 3.1 and 3.2, below. Moreover, a slight difference existed as a matter of course. In the 16th century the exchange rate at London on Antwerp was regularly 4d (1.7p) higher than the same rate at Antwerp; late in the 17th century the rate was 1d (0.4p) to 1.5d (0.6p) higher at Paris on London; and in the 1760s and 1770s the rate at Lisbon on London averaged 1d (0.4p) more than at London. For Antwerp see de Roover, *Gresham on Foreign Exchange*, 142–143, citing both the "Memorandum Prepared for the Royal Commission on the Exchanges," 1565, from R. H. Tawney and Eileen Power, eds., *Tudor Economic Documents* (London, 1924), III, 349, and Thomas Wilson, *A Discourse upon Usury* (1572), ed. R. H. Tawney (London, 1925), 306–307. See also J. D. Gould, *The Great Debasement: Currency and the Economy in Mid-Tudor England* (Oxford, 1970), 88. For Paris see the statement in *The Course of the Exchange between London and Paris before the Revolution; or, a Demonstration That Our Bullion Was Then Exported upon the Balance of Our Trade with France* (London, 1713). This was reprinted in *A Collection of Petitions Presented to the Honourable House of Commons against the Trade with France* (London, 1713), 3–11. For Lisbon see tables 2.34 and 2.35, below. See also Lucy S. Sutherland, *A London Merchant, 1695–1774* (Oxford, 1933), 30. For Ireland, see the discussion below in chap. 2.

It is to the discovery, compilation, and presentation of the bill rate, or rate of exchange for bills of exchange—what I call the commercial rate—that this handbook is devoted. The sources of the quotations are varied and will be discussed in some detail in each chapter. In general, for Europe they tend to be from printed materials, especially contemporary financial and commercial newspapers; for the colonies they are largely from manuscript letters, account books, and the like, belonging to planters and merchants. It was not always possible to find data for every place for every year, and the result is the all-too-frequent reliance on something less than quotations of the commercial rate of exchange. The best surrogate is, naturally, the par of exchange. The margin of error in estimating the bill rate at par is equal to the average variation from par of the commercial rate. Sometimes the variation from par was rather large. Thus the preference for the commercial rate of exchange.

Where research has provided some quotations of the commercial rate of exchange, these are compiled and presented in tabular form. Daily figures, sometimes as many as twenty to thirty per month, are averaged for the monthly figures;[32] yearly figures are, in turn, the mean of the twelve months. When the data are incomplete, care has been taken not to give undue weight in computing these averages to what

32. When data are complete month after month, year after year, the central tendency for the month is assumed to have approximated the value at mid-month. Thus the monthly figures extracted from *The Course of the Exchange* (for silver in this chapter; for the exchange on Dublin, Hamburg, Amsterdam, Paris, Cadiz, and Lisbon in the next chapter) are the figures for the 14th, 15th, 16th, or 17th of the month, with a preference for the 14th over the 17th when both are available. See Arthur Harrison Cole, *Wholesale Commodity Prices in the United States, 1700–1861* (Cambridge, Mass., 1938), I, 17–18; and Earl J. Hamilton, *War and Prices in Spain, 1651–1800*, Harvard Economic Studies, LXXXI (Cambridge, Mass., 1947), 109.

Scribner Public Library
Scribner, Nebraska 68057

merely happens to be available. In such instances a monthly mean is calculated from the means for each third of the month (centered on the fifth, fifteenth, and twenty-fifth of the month), and a yearly mean from the means of the four quarters. Sometimes in the tables a figure is italicized (e.g., table 3.1, below); this indicates that it is an estimate calculated as a straight-line interpolation on the bracketing quotations.[33] The constructed figure is incorporated into all other computations. Sometimes in the tables a figure is inserted in square brackets; this indicates that the original source ascribed it to the year only without specifying the month. Each chapter presents a series of tables establishing the monthly exchange rate for each place. The last chapter presents summary tables comparing the annual figures from the preceding chapters. The summary tables offer the capability of converting a value in most any currency to its equivalent in any other currency.

The open format of the resulting tables should serve two functions. The lack of data in many of them will reinforce the user's awareness of the incomplete basis for the annual averages in these and in the summary tables. It should inspire caution in their use. The blank spaces might also prod the reader to collect and compile additional data to fill the gaps. Given this format he or she can do just that directly on the page.

The following example shows how to use these tables and illustrates, as well, that this handbook—for all the labor of the author in preparing it and of the reader in understanding it—permits us merely to catch up with where people were two hundred years ago. In the spring of 1766, when flour sold at Baltimore for 14s (70p) a bushel, William Lux, a merchant there, wrote his friend Colonel Robert Tucker at Norfolk, Virginia, about the comparative markets for flour: "We have a vessel from Lisbon [which] left it the first of April. American flour [sold there for] 2800 [réis per bushel] which altho a price by which much prophet is not to be expected will however save us from losing and [is] much preferable to 13/9 at Barbados."[34] Lux obviously had at his command sufficient information to equate all of these different prices and to make an intelligent choice among the alternatives available to him. We can at least compare the various prices in this calculation; through reference to tables 2.34, 3.8, and 4.1, below, we can reduce all three prices to sterling.[35] As a result, we learn that Lux could have sold his flour at Baltimore for the equivalent of 8s 6d (43p) sterling, at Barbados for 10s 2d (51p) sterling, and at Lisbon for 15s 6d (78p) sterling. Lux's preference for the Lisbon market was well founded, even if a sale price some 82 percent higher than at Baltimore would not yield, in his estimate, "much prophet."

A Note on Style

In compiling data for these tables and in performing these computations, certain conventions have been followed that

33. See Myron B. Fiering, "On the Use of Correlation to Augment Data," *Journal of the American Statistical Association*, LVII (1962), 20–32; Milton Friedman, "The Interpolation of Time Series," *ibid.*, 729–757.

34. Lux to Tucker, 4 June 1766, Letter Book of William Lux, 1763–1768, New-York Historical Society, New York City. A transcript of the letter book forms an appendix to Pamela Satek, "William Lux of Baltimore: Eighteenth-Century Merchant" (M.A. thesis, University of Maryland, 1970).

35. The price at Baltimore, 14s (70p) divided by the average exchange rate for the year expressed as a percentage, 1.6399, equals 8s 6.4d (42.7p) sterling. The price at Barbados, 13s 9d (68.75p), divided by the average exchange rate expressed as a percentage, 1.35, equals 10s 2d (50.9p) sterling. The price at Lisbon, 2$800 réis, times the average exchange rate reduced to pounds (66.53d x 2.8 ÷ 240 x 100) equals 15s 6.25d (77.6p) sterling.

need to be made explicit. For ease of computation all currencies have been decimalized. Thus the English pounds (£), shillings (s), and pence (d) are expressed as pounds (£) and "new pence" (p); £1 13s 0d becomes £1.65, or 165p (see Appendix 1). Mentions in the text of amounts in the original English denominations are usually given in both the pounds-shillings-pence form and in the decimalized equivalent, following in parentheses. All references to weights and measures involved in any computation have been expressed in their metric equivalents to facilitate comparison.[36]

Neither of these conventions has been applied to quotations, which generally have been left intact, with certain exceptions. In order to make quotations more comprehensible, guidelines have been followed that basically conform to the "expanded" method of editing manuscripts outlined in the *Harvard Guide to American History*.[37] Original spelling has been retained, except that double letters have been dropped ("ffowler" becomes Fowler); the runic thorn has been replaced by its modern equivalent, "th" (thus "y^e" becomes "the"); and abbreviations and contractions have been silently expanded. Superior letters have been lowered to the line, and the letters omitted in the original have been supplied if the result of lowering the letters was an abbreviation or if the missing letters were in the middle of the word ("p^r c^t" becomes "per cent"). A modern spelling inserted in brackets supplements an unrecognizable word. Words printed in italics

or in all capital letters have been rendered in lower case roman type, unless the writer clearly intended emphasis. In a departure from the expanded method, the original capitalization has not been retained; most capital letters have been lowercased.

There are particular problems with dates for a work such as this. The "New Style," or Gregorian, calendar promulgated in 1582 did not replace the "Old Style," or Julian, calendar at the same time in all of the countries studied herein. France, Spain, and Portugal adopted the reforms before the end of 1582, and Holland in 1583; but Denmark and Hamburg did not follow until 1700, Great Britain and Ireland only in 1752, and Sweden in 1753.[38] Before 18 February 1699/1700 there was a difference of ten days between the two calendars and, from then until 17 February 1800, a difference of eleven days. Thus we have the classic instance in the Glorious Revolution of William of Orange leaving Holland on 11 November 1688 New Style and reaching England on 5 November 1688 Old Style. More to the point here, English price currents of the period often repeated the course of the exchange at Amsterdam. Even one who thinks he is aware of these calendar quirks can sometimes be puzzled by a report from Amsterdam dated 25 May 1696 in *Proctor's Price-Courant* of 21 May 1696.

The impact of these calendar differences upon this study extends not only to the collection of data but also to their

36. See my articles "Weights and Measures in the Colonial Sugar Trade: The Gallon and the Pound and Their International Equivalents," *William and Mary Quarterly*, 3d Ser., XXX (1973), 599–624; and "Les équivalents métriques des poids et mesures du commerce colonial aux XVIIe et XVIIIe siècles," *Revue française d'histoire d'Outre-Mer*, LXI (1974), 349–365.

37. Frank Freidel and Richard K. Showman, *Harvard Guide to American History*, rev. ed. (Cambridge, Mass., 1974), I, 25–36.

38. John J. Bond, *Handy-Book of Rules and Tables for Verifying Dates with the Christian Era*, [2d ed.] (London, 1875), 91–101; H[ermann] Grotefend, *Taschenbuch der Zeitrechnung des deutschen Mittelalters und der Neuzeit* (1898), ed. Th[eodor] Ulrich, 10th ed. (Hanover, 1960), 26–27. But cf. Beawes, *Lex Mercatoria Rediviva*, 448, and Mair, *Bookkeeping Modernized*, 366, both of which state that Denmark continued to use the Old Style calendar for exchange transactions well into the 18th century. This seems doubtful. See also Freidel and Showman, *Harvard Guide*, I, 23–25.

compilation and presentation. The tables that follow group data into months and years as specified in the original source. Therefore the average for the London-Amsterdam exchange rate might vary a bit depending on whether the source of the quotation is Amsterdam or London. The same would be true of the Philadelphia–St. Domingue exchange rate, since colonies followed their mother country in this as in most else. Usually such variations, provided we have sufficient data even to detect them, possess no statistical significance. Thus there has been no attempt to adjust for the ten- or eleven-day variation arising from the use of different calendars, in any of the computations made in this handbook.

Other related problems with dating have required appropriate adjustments. The Julian calendar recognized 25 March as the first day of the new year; the Gregorian calendar changed this to 1 January. Beginning in about the last quarter of the seventeenth century, Englishmen and others using the Julian calendar began to refer to the days between 1 January and 25 March by both the old and the new year. The practice was not widespread until the eighteenth century, and the London price currents of the 1690s, for instance, do not regularly use this convention. Nevertheless, it is used throughout this handbook. What contemporaries called 12 February 1696 and what we today would recognize as 12 February 1697, is herein designated 12 February 1696/97. The Quakers of Pennsylvania (and elsewhere) used arabic numerals to indicate the month rather than employ its pagan name. Since March was the first month of the new year for them until 1752, this too is a potential source of confusion. A letter dated "11.11.11." at Philadelphia we must recognize as having been written on 11 January 1711/12.[39] It should also be made explicit that the year used herein is always the calendar year January through December.

Finally, a caveat. While a great deal of care has been taken in the collection and compilation of these data, the results are not surprisingly inexact. The imperfections in the original information, the necessity of sometimes gross interpolations, the use of the statistically vital but always specious average: all of these should warn users of this handbook that they do not have an instrument of precision in their hands. The most that we can hope is that the margin of error is reasonably small. The figures offered below provide an acceptably approximation of reality. We can ask for little more.

39. With the rest of the English world, Quakers in the colonies after 1752 altered their calendar and began to use January as the first month of the year. Thus "11.11.61" meant 11 Nov. 1761. Private communication from J. William Frost, director of the Friends Historical Library, Swarthmore College, Swarthmore, Pa., 17 Sept. 1974. See also Bond, *Handy-Book for Verifying Dates*, 113–114.

Chapter 2

European Exchange on London

"Exchange is often fluctuating,
[it] rises and falls in proportion to
the exigencies of trade, and necessities of such
who want to make remittances."[1]

The course of the exchange between the major European commercial centers is a subject of some interest in itself, but for the purposes of this handbook, it is only a means to an end. In order to convert prices in one colonial currency into their equivalent in another currency, it is necessary to go indirectly by way of each colony's mother country. To compare the wholesale price for molasses at Surinam and Philadelphia, one must convert the Surinam price to its equivalent in Dutch current money, then to sterling, and finally to Pennsylvania pounds, shillings, and pence. Or vice versa. Thus this chapter begins the book by establishing in so far as possible the rate of exchange between the major colonial powers of seventeenth- and eighteenth-century Europe.[2]

All European exchange rates were quoted in terms of national moneys of account: pounds sterling for London, ecus of three livres tournois for Paris, milréis for Lisbon, and so forth. The specification of these moneys of account, their units, and their relationship to gold and silver coins are summarized in tables 1.1 and 1.2. Other material from chapter 1, such as the discussion of the bank money (banco) and current money of places like Amsterdam and Hamburg, is also relevant to what follows. If one is to use the tables in this handbook to convert prices or wages from one currency to another, knowledge of these interrelationships is vital.

Par, "the proportion that the imaginary monies of any country bear to those of another,"[3] will also concern us here for two reasons. First, for Europe par tended to be the upper limit of the commercial rate of exchange. Second, for those periods when we have no data on the commercial rate of

1. [Gertrude MacKinney and Charles F. Hoban, eds.], *Votes and Proceedings of the House of Representatives of the Province of Pennsylvania, Dec. 4, 1682–Sept. 26, 1776* (Samuel Hazard *et al.*, eds., *Pennsylvania Archives*, 8th Ser., I–VIII [Harrisburg, Pa., 1931–1935]), III, 2468–2469.

2. See Paul Einzig, *The History of Foreign Exchange* (New York, 1962). The revised edition of 1970 merely adds four chapters to bring his discussion up-to-date.

3. [Alexander Justice], *A General Treatise of Monies and Exchanges* (London, 1707), 4. See also J. D. Gould, *The Great Debasement: Currency and the Economy in Mid-Tudor England* (Oxford, 1970), *passim*.

Figure 2. The Royal Exchange, London, 1729. (Drawn and engraved by Sulton Nicholls and printed in Edward Oldenburgh, *A Calculation of Foreign Exchanges* [London, 1729]; courtesy of the Kress Library of Business and Economics, Graduate School of Business Administration, Harvard University, Boston.)

This building was the second of three on the same site; it was constructed after the original exchange was destroyed in the Great Fire (1666), and it burned, in turn, in 1838. The building took the form of the first structure, constructed (1564–1570) by Sir Thomas Gresham, with a quadrangular court surrounded by colonnades. In the center of the courtyard is a statue of Charles II in the classical style, and atop the bell tower is a large gilded weathervane in the shape of a grasshopper (Gresham's crest).

exchange, we tend to fall back on the par of exchange as a surrogate for the commercial rate.

Before we resort to par, we can employ another device of some importance to fill the gaps in data. The indirect negotiation of a bill of exchange, a technique used by merchants in the eighteenth century to make remittances to places not usually dealt with on their own exchange, provides the historical precedent for constructing some data series in a similar fashion. We are able, for instance, to estimate the London-Paris exchange rate during the War of the Spanish Succession by calculating the London-Amsterdam-Paris rate. The potential exists for many other similar calculations.

The sources for the series of tables in this chapter are nearly all of the same genre: the commercial and financial newspaper in its seventeenth-century form, the price current. Printed price currents seem to have appeared first at Antwerp, Hamburg, and Amsterdam as early as the 1580s;[4] they no doubt had their origin in the *mercuriales*, the weekly market price lists for grain.[5] The best-known price currents today are those of Amsterdam, if only because N. W. Posthumus has collected over two thousand of them and published the materials he extracted from them in the *Inquiry into the History of Prices in Holland*. Among these materials are exchange rate quotations at Amsterdam, and they have been turned to good use in what follows. The first of London's price currents did not appear until the 1660s; from the beginning they too

published the course of the exchange.[6] By 1695 three price currents were being distributed in London, as well as a somewhat more general commercial newspaper, *A Collection for Improvement of Husbandry and Trade*.[7] All four publications supplied information on prices and bill rates. At that point London was ready for a more specialized financial newspaper that would cater in greater detail to one part of the audience for the price currents. John Castaing's timing was faultless.

In March 1697, Castaing, a London stockbroker, founded *The Course of the Exchange, and Other Things*, a single-page, semiweekly financial newspaper that was the direct ancestor of the *Financial Times* and the *Wall Street Journal*. Castaing

---

4. V. Vázquez de Prada, *Lettres marchandes d'Anvers* (Paris, [1958–1964]), I, 131, IV, 265–266; Richard Ehrenberg, *Das Zeitalter der Fugger: Geldkapital und Creditverkehr im 16. Jahrhundert* (Jena, 1896), II, 23–24; N. W. Posthumus, *Inquiry into the History of Prices in Holland* (Leiden, 1946–1964), I, xix–xxx.

5. Micheline Baulant[-Duchaillut] and Jean Meuvret, *Prix des céréales extraits de la Mercuriale de Paris (1520–1698)* (Paris, 1960–1962), I, 1 *et seq.*

6. Jacob M. Price, "Notes on Some London Price-Currents, 1667–1715," *Econ. Hist. Rev.*, 2d Ser., VII (1954–1955), 240–250. Appendix 2, below, lists the extant numbers of all London price currents known to have begun publication prior to 1730. Price currents were an important tool of the merchants, who referred to them and who mailed them, apparently post free, to their customers. See, e.g., James Claypoole, at London, to William Chase, at Hamburg, 28 Mar. 1682, in Marion Balderston, ed., *James Claypoole's Letter Book, London and Philadelphia, 1681–1684* (San Marino, Calif., 1967), 103; earl of Bellomont, at New York, to Board of Trade, 22 June 1700, C.O. 5/1044, fol. 85r, Public Record Office; and Lascelles and Maxwell, at London, to Gedney Clarke, at Barbados, 5 Nov. 1757, Lascelles and Maxwell Letter Book, 1756–1760, fol. 148, Wilkinson and Gaviller, Ltd., Papers, Vol. VII, as noted in Richard Pares Transcripts, Box IV, Rhodes House Library, University of Oxford.

7. Published at London from 30 Mar. 1692 through 24 Sept. 1703 by John Houghton (1640–1705), an apothecary; dealer in tea, coffee, and chocolate; and fellow of the Royal Society. See James E. Thorold Rogers, *The First Nine Years of the Bank of England: An Enquiry into a Weekly Record of the Price of Bank Stock from August 17, 1694, to September 17, 1703* (Oxford, 1887), v–xx. All 583 numbers of the original can be seen if one consults successively the collections of the British Library, the Goldsmiths Library of the University of London, and the Bodleian Library, Oxford. The later reprint of Houghton, ed. R. Bradley (London, 1727–1728), omits all prices, exchange rates, and the like. The issues for 1 Jan. 1694/95–31 Dec. 1697 provide considerable data for the tables in this chapter.

published the paper for the next thirty years; it continued through the nineteenth century as the organ of the Stock Exchange and is still published today as *The Stock Exchange Daily Official List*.[8] Each issue included several kinds of information important to those on the Royal Exchange: the latest quotations for the major stocks; the price of gold and silver; offering prices and other information about lotteries, annuities, and the like; even the prices of dye and woolen cloth. And, of course, first on the page was the exchange on some fifteen European cities.[9] *The Course of the Exchange* is necessarily at the heart of a great deal of research in the economic history of the eighteenth century,[10] and it is the most important source for the tables that follow in this chapter.

8. James Stewart *et al.*, eds., *British Union-Catalogue of Periodicals* (London, 1955–1958), dates the initial number as 26 Mar. 1697; there have been several changes of title. Castaing first advertised its availability on 12 Mar. 1696/97, however: "J. Castaing at Jonathan's Coffee-House delivers the Course of Exchange, the Price of Bank-Notes, Bank-Stock East India Stock, and other things every Post-Day, for 10s. per Annum." *A Collection for Improvement of Husbandry and Trade* (London), No. 241, 12 Mar. 1696/97. Castaing had previously run advertisements for his services as a broker, and he continued to run them concurrently with this newer one for some time—e.g. *ibid.*, No. 128, 11 Jan. 1695, and others. See Price, "Notes on Price-Currents," *Econ. Hist. Rev.*, 2d Ser., VII (1954–1955), 240–250; and T. S. Ashton, *An Economic History of England: The Eighteenth Century* (London, [1955]), 188. At the end of the 18th century Johann Georg Büsch, an important authority on economic matters, could still write "Ich kenne Castaings Papers nicht" in his essay "Auszug aus der am 3ten April 1797 von der Londoner Bank-Direction angestellten Befragung über den Wechsel-cours zwischen London und Hamburg," in Büsch, *Sämtliche Schriften über Banken und Münzwesen*, [ed. Christoph D. Ebeling] (Hamburg, 1801), 736.

9. For an exposition of the contents of the 11 June 1706 number, see [Justice], *General Treatise of Monies*, 2d pagination, 31–51. See also [Timothy Cunningham], *The Law of Bills of Exchange, Promissory Notes, Bank-Notes and Insurances* (London, 1760), 386–387.

10. *The Course of the Exchange* has not been widely used by economic historians, in part because it has not been readily available. Only in 1955 was

a nearly complete series located in the Stock Exchange, London; it has recently been deposited in the Guildhall Library, London. The series has been microfilmed for the years 1698 to 1810, and copies of the film can be seen in the British Library; the Goldsmiths Library, University of London; and the McKeldin Library, University of Maryland. The only major gap in this series is the complete omission of any issues for Mar. through Dec. 1697. A two-month gap (14 Jan.–17 Mar. 1721) can be repaired by reference to the set in the British Library for the years 1720 to 1755 (36 vols.; press mark: C. 108.ee.2). Another, shorter run for the 18th century can be found in the Kress Library of Business and Economics in the Baker Library, Graduate School of Business Administration, Harvard University, Boston.

The data published in *The Course of the Exchange* were accurate quotations of the current rates of exchange and prices of stocks. When we can compare them with rates and prices published elsewhere, there are no significant variations. See, e.g., the London price currents listed below in Appendix 1, *Freke's Prices of Stocks, &c.* (London, 1716–1722), or, more important, *Lloyd's List* (London, 1734–). These and others, might simply have copied Castaing's figures, but even in so doing they proclaimed his reliability. More direct evidence of the reputation of *The Course of Exchange* was offered in a deposition before the Court of Exchequer in 1743 by Robert Shergold, a broker himself and then one of the publishers of the newspaper as successor to Castaing. In the case *Lewis* v. *Sawbridge*, rising out of the South Sea Bubble of 1720, Shergold brought along to court the bound office copy of the paper for that year as evidence of the price of shares. (This volume still exists as the first one in the set in the British Library. See the endorsement on the flyleaf by Charles Taylor, deputy remembrancer in the Court of Exchequer.) Shergold testified that "the manner of collecting the prices . . . entered in the said papers was by the observations and inquirys of the said Mr. Castaing his clerk or bookkeeper among the dealers in the said several publick stocks." He went on to state that "the said papers were of good credit and esteem among the persons who usually bought and sold stocks." E. 134, 17 Geo. II, Michaelmas No. 7, P.R.O. If Castaing (and, by implication, Shergold) correctly quoted prices of shares from one end of the Royal Exchange, we can reasonably assume that they correctly quoted exchange rates from the other end.

I know of only four previous uses of *The Course of the Exchange*. The first quotation each month of the rate on Hamburg, Lisbon, and Paris for the period 1718 to 1736 was extracted and printed in "An Account of the Market Prices of . . . Gold . . . Silver . . . and the Courses of Exchange," 1718–1736, 1746–1811, Great Britain, House of Commons, *Sessional Papers*, 1810–1811, X (*Accounts and Papers*), no. 43. (See also "Information Respecting the Prices of Gold and Silver Bullion, and Rates of Exchanges," 1736–1746, *ibid.*, no. 146.)

England, Scotland, and Ireland

Not surprisingly, the convenience of settling accounts by the use of bills of exchange made them as important to the internal trade of the British Isles as they were to its European trade. Moreover, at the beginning of the eighteenth century, both Scotland and Ireland were still foreign countries for exchange purposes. The Act of Union in 1707 ended this condition for Scotland and altered its exchange relationship with London from a foreign to an inland basis. But Ireland remained a place for which one negotiated bills on the Royal Exchange, and Castaing quoted the exchange rate on Dublin from the first.

All of the British Isles shared the same money of account, if not always the same real money. The basic coins of England and Wales are set out in tables 1.1 and 1.2, pp. 9–13;[11] about those of Scotland and Ireland there is further comment below. But all three countries, as well as all of England's colonies,

kept their accounts in terms of pounds, shillings, and pence. Table 2.1 specifies the inner relationships of the several denominations of the money of account they employed. All exchange at London was effected using the money of account although on several different bases. Table 2.2 indicates the essential elements of the exchange at London (that is, the terms in which exchange transactions were negotiated there); the exposition of this table is the fundamental task of this chapter.[12]

There was no course of exchange at London for inland bills of exchange despite their importance for the internal trade of the nation; nor do we have any quotations of the inland rates of exchange.[13] We would expect these rates to be small, given the integrated economy of the nation and the comparative ease of arbitrage transactions. Merchants and others elsewhere in England—and after 1707 in Scotland—regularly bought bills on London. And because there was usually a greater demand in, say, Bristol for bills on London than there was at London for bills on Bristol, a small differential regularly existed in London's favor.[14] Not only was this "rate of exchange" low by nature, but the Bank of England seems to have worked to keep it that way, as we will see in the case of Scotland. The normal charge for inland bills was 1 or 2 percent.[15]

Ashton, *Economic History of England*, 253, printed the first Jan. quotation on Hamburg for the years 1700 to 1720 and 1747 to 1800. P. G. M. Dickson, *The Financial Revolution in England: A Study in the Development of Public Credit, 1688–1756* (New York, 1967), 139, printed some security prices and the exchange on Amsterdam fortnightly in 1720. See also *ibid.*, 426, 488 and n, and opp. 490. H. E. S. Fisher, *The Portugal Trade: A Study of Anglo-Portuguese Commerce, 1700–1770* (London, 1971), 147, printed the first Jan. quotation on Lisbon and the annual average of the first monthly quotation for 1700 to 1770.

The figures published below are the quotations from the middle of each month—that of the 14th, 15th, 16th, or 17th of the month with the 14th preferred over the 17th when both were present. See chap. 1, n. 32, above, and Posthumus, *Prices in Holland*, I, 588. Certain gaps in the series have been filled by straight-line interpolation based on the two bracketing quotations.

11. Hereinafter, following the usual convention, the word "England" will refer to both England and Wales for the 17th and 18th centuries. Similarly, references after 1707 to "Great Britain" will mean all three of its constituent parts.

12. Information such as that presented in tables 2.1 and 2.2 is common to all contemporary discussions of the exchange. References to these works fill the notes to this chapter. See, e.g., n. 44, below. Thus tables such as these are not annotated.

13. On inland bills see Ashton, *Economic History of England*, 185–188.

14. [Justice], *General Treatise of Monies*, 55; John Mair, *Book-keeping Modernized: or, Merchant-Accounts by Double Entry, According to the Italian Form*, "8th" ed. (Edinburgh, 1800), 351.

15. See, e.g., Micah Shields, at Stockton-on-Tees, to a correspondent at

Merchants outside England were aware of the costs of negotiating inland bills and, therefore, hesitated to purchase bills payable in English cities other than London. Bills on the outports sometimes could not even be sold.[16] "Outport bills I am quite sick of," complained Stephen Bordley of Maryland in 1751.[17] When they could be sold, their lower price made them tempting, but unless one wanted payment in Exeter or Glasgow, the lower initial cost of the bill would easily be offset by the costs of having one's agent there negotiate an inland bill on London. As William Pollard, a Pennsylvanian, wrote in 1772, "Our excha[nge] is ruled by bills at 30 days on London but if a person wants a bill to remit to London and I can only draw on Liverpool, he will not take my bill, unless he has it lower than he can get a bill upon London for, and therefore I must either draw upon London sometimes or sell my bills lower by half or one per cent."[18] Pollard was fortunate; at other times and other places the difference was greater than "half or one percent."[19] Nearly everyone preferred to buy bills on London.

Distance from London influenced the rate of exchange within the British Isles, as did the political relationship of an area to England. Besides Ireland and Scotland, which will be discussed below, the only other area in the home islands that maintained a "foreign" exchange relationship with England was the Isle of Man. A Manx act passed in 1692 established a local currency by raising the value at which English coins circulated in the island in order to prohibit "any to go out of the Isle." The crown of 5s (25p) sterling was to pass at 5s 4d (26.7p) Manx currency, or at a rate of £106.67 Manx currency to £100 sterling. Four years later, in 1696, the House of Keys petitioned William Stanley, ninth earl of Derby and the island's lord, "that all crown pieces . . . by public consent be allowed to pass for 5s. 10d. [29.2p] a piece." Derby granted the petition and thereby set a par of exchange, £116.67 Manx currency to £100 sterling, which applied until 1840.[20] About the course of the exchange, again we have no knowledge.

Before 1707 Scotland had its own money of account denoted, as in England, in pounds, shillings, and pence but valued differently than English money.[21] This sometimes con-

---

Leith, 7 Feb. 1763, and to John Fry, [at London?], 17 Oct. 1763, Micah Shields Account and Letter Book, 1759–1777, Miscellaneous Manuscripts, Friends Historical Library, Swarthmore College, Swarthmore, Pa.

16. Bills on outports, in this instance Hull, were said to be "not so negotiable and by some rejected." Thomas Fearnley, at Fredrikshald, Norway, to John Holland and Company of Hull, 15 Sept. 1766, as quoted in H. S. K. Kent, *War and Trade in Northern Seas: Anglo-Scandinavian Economic Relations in the Mid-Eighteenth Century* (Cambridge, 1973), 51n.

17. Bordley to Jeremiah Chase, [at Baltimore?], 26 July 1751, Stephen Bordley Letter Books, 1727–1759, IV (1749–1752), 74, MS 81, Maryland Historical Society, Baltimore. See also Bordley to Chase, 22 Mar. 1749/50, *ibid.*, 15, and to William Perkins, [at London?], 7 Dec. 1757, *ibid.*, V (1756–1759), 52.

18. Pollard, at Philadelphia, to Peter Holme, at Liverpool, 16 May 1772, William Pollard Letter Book, 1772–1774, p. 26, Historical Society of Pennsylvania, Philadelphia.

19. See references in chap. 3, below.

20. A. W. Moore, *A History of the Isle of Man* (London, 1900), I, 414–416; Charles Clay, *Currency of the Isle of Man, from Its Earliest Appearance to Its Assimilation with the British Coinage in 1840* (Manx Society, *Publications*, XVII [Douglas, 1869]), 76, 90–91. John Feltham, *Feltham's Tour through the Isle of Man, in 1797 and 1798*, ed. Robert Airey (Manx Society, *Publications*, VI [Douglas, 1861]), 123, recorded that £100 English equaled £116 13s 4d Manx and £100 Manx equaled £97 17s 1d Irish. These were par values, of course.

21. See, in general, [Justice], *General Treatise of Monies*, 92–96; J. M. Henderson, *Scottish Reckonings of Time, Money, Weights and Measures*, Historical Association of Scotland Pamphlets, N.S., No. 4 ([Edinburgh], 1926), 8–10, 15–16.

fusing situation also existed in Ireland and in all of the British colonies in the Western Hemisphere. The difference in value meant, of course, that there was an exchange at London on Edinburgh. Prior to Union the accepted par of exchange was £1,300 Scottish to £100 sterling, although Sir Isaac Newton in 1710 argued that this was a bit imprecise and that "at their just value" it took £1,321 2s 0d Scottish to equal £100 sterling.[22] In 1601 the ratio was £1,200 Scottish to £100 sterling,[23] showing a devaluation over the century in terms of par, but we know little about the course of the exchange. Apparently, late in the seventeenth century, it was usually 10 to 12 percent below par,[24] suggesting a rate of exchange in the range of £1,450 Scottish to £100 sterling. In the midst of the English monetary crisis in 1696, the exchange reversed significantly, and the rate swung to a 15 percent premium,[25] or something like £1,125 Scottish per £100 sterling. A similar phenomena operated with regard to Ireland, as we shall see (table 2.3). What we can easily discover about real money in Scotland before 1707 is presented above in table 1.1, p. 10.

After 1707 Scotland's real money and its money of account were by law uniform with those of England.[26] Practice

in this instance was slow to follow the law: "Old Scots money . . . remained a money of account, especially in the country-side, and it was not until near the close of the eighteenth century that rents, prices of agricultural produce, and wages ceased to be expressed in Scots money."[27] Commerce and finance did, however, follow the lead of London, and exchange was effected on an inland basis. In times of financial stress when Scottish paper money tended to inflate slightly, the Bank of England would intervene to keep the rate at its usual level. It was to the nation's advantage to maintain such a situation, and even during the serious crisis occasioned by the failure of the Ayr Bank in 1772, such intervention kept the rate of exchange below 1 percent.[28]

Increasingly after 1707 more of Scotland's overseas exchange transactions were effected through London, a development enhanced by a standard national currency. But during the years before Union, Scotland maintained direct exchange relationships with several nations: "Viz. with France, by giving so many shillings Scots for the livre of 20 solses, and so with Spain, so many to a piece of 8, to Holland, so many for the guilder of 20 styvers, and so Dantzick, so many for the Polish guilder and to Sweden, so many for the dollar current, which is 30 styvers Swedish."[29] It is difficult to say how long

22. Isaac Newton, master of the Mint, to the Treasury, 16 Feb. 1709/10, T. 1/120, fol. 163r, P.R.O., and in W. A. Shaw, ed., *Select Tracts and Documents Illustrative of English Monetary History, 1626–1730* (London, 1896), 150. See also Newton to Treasury, 21 Sept. 1717, T. 1/208, fols. 204–205, and *ibid.*, 170.

23. Henderson, *Scottish Reckonings*, 16.

24. [Justice], *General Treatise of Monies*, 5, 93.

25. *Ibid.*, 5.

26. Act of 5 Anne, c. 27 (1706). All references in this book to English and British laws enacted before 1714 are to [Alexander Luders et al., eds.], *The Statutes of the Realm. Printed by Command of His Majesty King George the Third . . . from Original Records and Authentic Manuscripts* (London, 1810–1828). See also *Chronological Table of the Statutes Covering the Period from 1235 to the End of 1972* (London, 1973), an annual publication of H. M. Stationery Office, for the definitive calendaring and numbering of the statutes.

27. Henry Hamilton, *An Economic History of Scotland in the Eighteenth Century* (Oxford, 1963), 294.

28. Hamilton, *Economic History of Scotland*, 323. Between the end of 1761 and Apr. 1762 the exchange with London rose from 2% to 4.5% or 5% and fell again to 0.75%. *Ibid.*, 309–310. See also the evidence of James Mansfield, an Edinburgh banker, before the 1804 parliamentary committee on Irish monetary problems. Frank Whitson Fetter, *The Irish Pound, 1797–1826* (London, [1955]), 91.

29. [Justice], *General Treatise of Monies*, 94. But see also *ibid.*, 108; and T. C. Smout, *Scottish Trade on the Eve of Union, 1660–1707* (Edinburgh and London, 1963), 117–124. For bills in the Glasgow-Stockholm trade, see Jacob M. Price,

any of these direct contracts were maintained, but one French author, Thomas de Bléville, in 1760 quoted a Paris rate on Edinburgh that was separate from and 1.6 percent better than that on London.[30]

We have considerably more information, and some good data, about the London-Ireland exchange. The course of the exchange on Dublin is the first of several presented at length in this chapter (see tables 2.3 and 2.4). While exchange between London and Ireland was on a foreign basis, Ireland was under England's direct control during this entire period, and England dictated Irish monetary policy as it did other aspects of Irish life. In this way Ireland was indeed England's first colony.

Ireland had no mint and, therefore, no coin of its own. Its real money was English with a considerable admixture of foreign coin, amongst which Spanish silver and Portuguese gold played a major role. Ireland's money of account was English too—the usual pounds, shillings, and pence. The problems of the Irish economy, hamstrung in the service of the mother country, foreshadowed those of the continental colonies and created a chronic difficulty in the island's balance of payments, which was reflected in a perpetually depreciated value for Irish currency. Despite the impression created by shared coinage and the same money of account, Irish pounds were always worth less than English pounds.

England tried to limit the exchange on Ireland by legis-

lating the par of exchange. This was accomplished through regulations, proclamations, and laws that set the value in Ireland of English and foreign coin. As early as 1487 the English shilling was valued at 16d Irish currency, for a par of £133.33 Irish currency per £100 sterling. The same par is applied early in the seventeenth century, with a commercial bill rate of £130 quoted for 1622. A proclamation of 6 April 1637 sought to abolish the difference, but it is clear that within five years, and probably much sooner, coin in Ireland was again valued in excess of its sterling value. A proclamation of 20 January 1660/61 recognized an effective par of £105.56. This rate was reinforced twenty-two years later by another proclamation (6 June 1683) and stood as par until the important attempt to revalue Irish money, again by proclamation, on 25 March 1689. The value of the shilling in 1689 was set at 13d Irish; par, therefore, was £108.33 Irish per £100 sterling. It was moved still higher on 29 May 1695 to £116.67 and returned again to the 1689 level of £108.33 on 2 June 1701. Par was then to stay at this level until 1826, when, subsequent to the union of Ireland and Great Britain, a separate Irish money ceased to exist.[31] As usual, the commercial rate of exchange, or bill rate, fluctuated around the par of exchange and reflected changes in it.

31. The above is derived largely from James Simon, *An Essay towards an Historical Account of Irish Coins, and of the Currency of Foreign Monies in Ireland* (Dublin, 1749). Simon's study forms the foundations of almost everything else written on the subject; he has been usefully supplemented by: César Moreau, *The Past and Present Statistical State of Ireland* (London, 1827), 17–19; M. S. Dudley Westropp, "Notes on Irish Money Weights and Foreign Coin Current in Ireland," *Proceedings of the Royal Irish Academy*, XXXIII (1916), 43–72; Joseph Johnston, "Irish Coinage in the Eighteenth Century," *Hermethena: A Series of Papers on Literature, Science, and Philosophy*, LII (1938), 5–26; L. M. Cullen, *Anglo-Irish Trade, 1660–1800* (Manchester, 1968), 155–158. Fetter, *Irish Pound*, 19n, considers a rate at London of 109 to 109.5 as a better

"Multilateralism and/or Bilateralism: The Settlement of British Trade Balances with 'The North,' c. 1700," *Econ. Hist. Rev.*, 2d Ser., XIV (1961–1962), 254–274.

30. "Better" in the sense that 100 ecus purchased £13.54 in Edinburgh but only £13.33 in London. Thomas de Bléville, *Le Banquier et negociant universel, ou traité général de changes étrangers et des arbitrages, ou viremens de place en place* (Paris, 1760), I, 10.

The exchange rates quoted here are for Irish bills negotiated in London on Dublin. Obviously individuals in Ireland engaged in buying and selling bills too. Dublin was an early center for foreign exchange and seems to have maintained a certain prominence into the nineteenth century. But Belfast and Cork were also important, the former from as early as the 1670s. Late in the eighteenth century Waterford and Newry began to carry on direct exchange with London.[32] John Puget, the agent in London for the Bank of Ireland, gave evidence before Parliament in 1804 showing that the Dublin-London rate in Dublin "in general is from 1 to 1–½" percentage points lower than the rate in London.[33] Occasionally the difference was larger, as when in December 1770 the rate in London was as high as £109.20 while in Dublin it was only £106.75, a spread of two and a half points, or 2.3 percent.[34] Beginning in the 1790s, we have regular quotations of the rate on London in Dublin, Belfast, and Newry, and of the Dublin-Belfast inland rate, in the famous Irish Currency Report of 1804 and the Bullion Report of 1810.[35] Fortunately our quotations at London begin much earlier.

TABLE 2.1. Money of Account of Great Britain: Its Denominations and Their Relationships

Pound Sterling	Crown	Shilling	Pence	Farthing
1	4	20	240	960
	1	5	60	240
		1	12	48
			1	4

Although London was certainly the center for Irish exchange with foreign countries, Ireland, like Scotland, maintained some direct foreign exchange connections with countries other than England.[36] Even with France, Ireland's most important trading partner on the continent, such arrangements were irregular, however, despite the fact that negotiating bills

approximation of par for bills of exchange, given "the customary method of quoting exchange."

32. Cullen, *Anglo-Irish Trade*, 158–186, has a useful discussion of all of this.

33. Fetter, *Irish Pound*, 19n. See also Cullen, *Anglo-Irish Trade*, 175–176.

34. Cullen, *Anglo-Irish Trade*, 176.

35. Irish Currency Report: "Report, Minutes of Evidence, and Appendix, from the Committee on the Circulating Paper, the Specie, and the Current Coin of Ireland; and also, on the Exchange between That Part of the United Kingdom and Great Britain" (1804), Great Britain, House of Commons, *Sess. Papers*, 1810, III (*Reports*), no. 28, pp. 129–145, 154–156. Bullion Report: "Report, Together with Minutes of Evidence and Accounts from the Select Committee on the High Price of Gold Bullion," *ibid.*, no. 349, pp. 211–219.

The Currency Report went through five parliamentary editions in 1804, 1810, and 1826; I refer to the 1810 edition merely for convenience since it is in the same volume as the Bullion Report. The Bullion Report itself was printed twice in 1810, once in the parliamentary edition and again in a commercial edition. Both are divided into three sections: the report proper, testimony of witnesses ("minutes of the evidence"), and appended accounts. The report of the Bullion Committee has been published separately by Edwin Cannan, ed., *The Paper Pound of 1797–1821*, 2d ed. (London, 1925); the report of the Irish Currency Committee and selected testimony have been published by Fetter, *Irish Pound*. Neither reprint includes the exchange rate tables, although Fetter, *Irish Pound*, 129–130, does indicate where they were printed in the original edition.

36. Cullen, *Anglo-Irish Trade*, 161–166.

TABLE 2.2. The Course of the Exchange at London

On Amsterdam	£1 sterling,	for schellingen banco
Cadiz	for pence sterling,	1 peso de cambio
Copenhagen	£1 sterling,	for rigsdalers kurant
Dublin	£1 sterling,	for pounds Irish currency
Edinburgh, pre-1707	£1 sterling,	for pounds Scottish currency
Hamburg	£1 sterling,	for schilling-vls. banco
Lisbon	for pence sterling,	1 milréis
Paris	for pence sterling,	1 ecu of 60 sous tournois

Notes and Sources: **TABLES 2.1** and **2.2**
See n. 12 in this chapter.

directly was financially more favorable.[37] (In the North American continental colonies bills on Ireland also cost something less than bills on London, because of similar circumstances.) From France in 1760 the advantage to the merchant of Bordeaux or Paris was £2 per £100 negotiated.[38] Still, "there was little direct exchange dealing between Ireland and the continent."[39] All of which, of course, nicely establishes the validity of the indirect computation of exchange on Ireland made necessary for us by the data available.

Finally, bills drawn in London on the colonies were negotiated only occasionally, mostly during wartime when the army or the navy needed money in North America or the West Indies to purchase provisions or to pay troops. Even for this limited use of bills, we find little evidence. One reason is that there seems to have been difficulty locating anyone in London with sufficient credits in the colonies to draw against; London merchants preferred to bring such credits home in the form of colonial produce and in bullion. In one instance in the midst of the War of the Spanish Succession, complaint was made because bills on the colonies had to be drawn at forty, eighty, and even a hundred days after sight.[40] Perhaps the most important reason why bills were not used more frequently was the existence of a convenient and profitable alternative. The government simply shipped specie.

37. Louis M. Cullen, "An Ceangal Tráchtála idir Éire agus an Fhrainc, 1660–1800" (M.A. thesis, National University of Ireland, 1956), 83–91, as cited in Cullen, *Anglo-Irish Trade*, 161. See also [Justice], *General Treatise of Monies*, 108.

38. For the continental colonies see chap. 3 below. For France see Bléville, *Banquier et negociant universel*, I, 10.

39. Cullen, *Anglo-Irish Trade*, 161.

40. Lt. Gov. Thomas Handasyd, at Jamaica, to Board of Trade, 20 Nov. 1705, C.O. 138/11, p. 439.

TABLE 2.3. **Rate of Exchange: London on Dublin, 1613–1697**

(Pounds Irish Currency per £ 100 Sterling)

Year	Jan.	Feb.	Mar.	Apr.	May	June	July	Aug.	Sept.	Oct.	Nov.	Dec.	Average
1613													
1662		102.00	104.00										103.00
1663													
1664													
1665													
1666					105.00	106.00							105.50
1667													
1668													
1669													
1670													
1671												[115.00]	115.00
1672	[110.00]											[115.00]	112.50
1673													
1674													
1675													
1676													
1677													
1678													
1679										103.00			103.00
1680		109.00									107.50		108.25
1681					108.50		107.50						108.00
1682	111.00	108.50			108.00	107.50			107.50	106.00			107.75
1683	109.00	112.50			109.50			108.50		107.00			108.94
1684													
1685									108.00		109.00		108.50

TABLE 2.3. (Continued): London on Dublin (Pounds Irish Currency per £100 Sterling)

Year	Jan.	Feb.	Mar.	Apr.	May	June	July	Aug.	Sept.	Oct.	Nov.	Dec.	Average
1686												[107.00]	107.00
1687		114.00				105.86							109.93
1688													
1689													
1690													
1691	106.25									106.25			106.25
1692	106.25												106.25
1693			109.50										109.50
1694									106.50		105.00		105.75
1695	105.48	106.70	105.50	104.23	104.10	104.05	104.00	104.00					104.67
1696		98.00	103.75	107.08		109.50	115.50	114.00		116.00	115.50	116.00	109.94
1697	116.00	117.00	121.00	122.00	122.00	120.50	116.00	114.00	113.00	115.00	116.00	116.00	117.38

Notes and Sources: TABLE 2.3

Figures inserted in square brackets are assigned to that month arbitrarily; figures printed in italics are straight-line interpolations based on the two neighboring quotations.

1613: James Simon, *An Essay towards an Historical Account of Irish Coins, and of the Currency of Foreign Monies in Ireland* (Dublin, 1749), 44.

1662, 1666, 1672, 1679, 1686, 1687: L. M. Cullen, *Anglo-Irish Trade, 1660–1800* (Manchester, 1968), 178.

1671–1672: William Petty, *The Political Anatomy of Ireland* (1672) (London, 1691), 72, as reprinted in *The Economic Writings of Sir William Petty . . .* , ed. Charles Henry Hull (Cambridge, 1899), I, 185.

1680–1696: London price currents listed in Appendix 2, below.

1681–1683: Marion Balderston, ed., *James Claypoole's Letter Book, London and Philadelphia, 1681–1684* (San Marino, Calif., 1967), 40, 87, 116, 145, 164, 177–179, 186.

1687: Henry Ashurst, at London, to William Stewart, at Belfast, 30 June 1687, Letter Book and Account of Henry Ashurst, 1674–1701, fol. 55v, Deposited Deeds, Ashurst, c.1, Bodleian Library, Oxford.

1695–1697: *A Collection for Improvement of Husbandry and Trade* (London), 18 Jan. 1694/95–31 Dec. 1697 (the figure nearest the middle of the month).

TABLE 2.4. **Rate of Exchange: London on Dublin, 1698–1775**

(Pounds Irish Currency Premium per £100 Sterling)

Year	Jan.	Feb.	Mar.	Apr.	May	June	July	Aug.	Sept.	Oct.	Nov.	Dec.	Average
1698	16.50	19.00	18.75	18.00	16.00	15.00	16.75	16.75	16.50	15.75	15.00	15.50	16.62
1699	18.25	18.50	18.75	18.50	18.88	19.00	18.50	19.50	19.50	19.62	19.75	20.00	19.06
1700	22.00	23.00	22.50	22.50	22.00	20.75	19.50	18.75	18.62	20.00	20.88	21.00	20.96
1701	21.00	22.00	23.88	24.00	20.50	10.00	10.62	10.50	9.50	7.00	7.75	9.00	14.65
1702	9.12	9.25	10.00	9.88	10.00	11.50	11.62	10.38	7.88	7.75	8.50	9.38	9.60
1703	9.62	10.00	10.50	9.25	8.25	8.12	7.75	5.75	5.00	5.25	5.00	7.50	7.67
1704	9.50	8.50	7.00	6.25	6.50	7.00	6.75	5.75	6.00	7.00	7.12	9.00	7.20
1705	9.62	8.75	7.50	8.50	8.00	7.62	6.75	7.75	8.12	8.50	8.00	9.50	8.22
1706	9.38	8.75	8.88	8.75	8.25	8.12	8.00	7.88	7.25	7.25	7.00	8.00	8.13
1707	9.00	8.75	8.50	7.50	7.50	7.50	7.50	7.50	6.50	6.00	6.00	8.50	7.56
1708	8.50	8.00	8.00	9.00	10.00	9.00	9.00	8.75	8.00	8.00	8.50	10.00	8.73
1709	10.50	10.25	10.38	11.00	10.00	10.00	10.38	10.50	9.75	7.38	9.25	10.50	9.99
1710	10.50	10.50	11.00	10.50	9.00	8.75	8.75	7.00	6.00	5.50	5.75	7.00	8.35
1711	8.25	10.00	10.25	9.00	7.75	6.50	6.38	7.00	8.00	7.00	6.50	9.00	7.97
1712	9.75	9.00	8.00	9.25	9.00	8.38	8.25	8.25	8.25	7.25	6.50	9.62	8.46
1713	9.88	7.38	6.75	7.25	7.00	6.25	6.88	6.88	7.00	6.75	6.25	6.50	7.06
1714	7.50	7.25	7.25	7.38	7.38	7.25	7.75	7.69	7.88	5.00	7.00	8.00	7.28
1715	8.00	7.50	7.38	7.88	9.12	9.88	9.88	10.50	10.62	9.00	11.75	11.25	9.40
1716	10.50	11.75	9.50	9.75	10.88	10.81	10.00	8.00	9.12	9.50	9.75	10.62	10.02
1717	10.88	11.25	11.25	10.50	10.00	9.62	10.25	9.12	9.50	9.50	9.75	11.00	10.22
1718	11.31	11.50	11.69	11.25	9.50	9.75	10.38	10.81	10.81	10.75	11.50	13.50	11.06
1719	12.50	11.88	14.00	14.25	13.00	11.88	10.25	9.75	9.88	10.75	11.12	12.00	11.77
1720	12.50	12.50	12.50	14.50	12.12	11.38	12.88	13.50	12.25	15.00	12.00	12.00	12.76
1721	12.50	13.00	13.25	12.00	11.50	8.50	10.50	11.50	10.38	9.38	9.75	9.50	10.98
1722	10.62	10.88	10.75	11.50	11.25	10.75	10.25	9.12	9.25	9.75	10.75	11.12	10.50

TABLE 2.4 (Continued): London on Dublin (Pounds Irish Currency Premium per £ 100 Sterling)

Year	Jan.	Feb.	Mar.	Apr.	May	June	July	Aug.	Sept.	Oct.	Nov.	Dec.	Average
1723	11.00	11.00	11.00	10.25	9.25	10.62	10.56	11.00	11.50	11.38	11.25	11.31	10.84
1724	11.50	12.25	12.56	11.50	12.00	12.38	12.25	12.50	12.00	9.88	11.19	11.50	11.79
1725	11.28	11.25	11.25	10.88	10.31	10.25	10.00	9.25	9.44	9.00	9.88	10.50	10.27
1726	11.88	12.50	12.50	11.75	12.25	12.62	12.06	12.56	11.94	12.44	14.12	13.75	12.53
1727	15.25	14.12	11.75	13.50	13.75	12.50	12.00	11.75	9.75	10.94	11.19	11.12	12.30
1728	12.75	12.38	10.94	11.25	11.38	11.75	11.62	11.00	10.50	9.94	11.56	11.69	11.40
1729	12.38	10.44	11.25	12.00	11.12	11.56	11.62	11.00	10.50	9.94	11.56	11.69	11.26
1730	11.56	12.00	12.35	12.00	11.81	11.12	10.50	10.25	10.50	10.81	12.38	12.44	11.48
1731	12.06	11.94	11.56	10.62	10.69	11.69	10.50	10.56	10.75	10.06	11.19	11.06	11.06
1732	10.75	11.06	11.00	10.69	11.12	10.81	10.31	10.31	10.56	10.56	12.00	11.31	10.87
1733	11.50	11.81	11.94	12.00	11.06	10.56	10.19	10.69	12.25	12.12	12.75	11.31	11.52
1734	12.19	12.06	12.12	12.62	11.00	12.00	10.94	10.75	10.44	9.75	11.94	11.25	11.42
1735	11.75	12.25	11.81	11.25	11.50	11.38	11.56	11.88	11.94	11.44	12.38	12.06	11.77
1736	12.19	12.19	11.56	10.94	11.31	11.94	11.56	10.56	10.50	10.50	10.88	10.94	11.26
1737	10.75	10.75	10.50	10.44	10.25	10.19	10.00	9.75	9.00	9.00	8.31	8.25	9.77
1738	8.75	9.00	8.44	8.50	8.38	7.94	7.56	7.75	7.69	7.69	8.56	8.88	8.26
1739	9.00	8.94	8.94	8.94	9.25	9.50	9.19	9.50	8.50	8.19	8.94	8.50	8.95
1740	8.38	8.75	8.62	8.50	8.25	8.31	7.88	7.69	7.56	8.00	8.00	8.00	8.16
1741	7.88	8.44	9.00	8.94	8.75	8.88	9.50	9.62	10.38	9.12	9.94	10.56	9.25
1742	10.50	10.75	11.00	10.75	9.75	10.31	9.38	10.00	9.00	9.25	9.38	10.00	10.01
1743	10.25	9.75	9.38	9.25	8.31	8.00	7.88	7.38	8.00	8.19	8.25	8.00	8.55
1744	7.81	7.50	7.62	7.88	7.56	7.81	7.75	8.00	8.12	8.25	8.94	8.94	8.02
1745	8.75	9.25	9.50	9.75	10.12	10.94	10.00	9.44	10.50	11.50	9.38	9.25	9.86
1746	7.62	8.25	9.50	8.50	8.06	7.94	7.50	7.19	7.38	7.12	7.31	6.75	7.76
1747	7.31	7.44	6.94	7.12	7.50	7.69	8.00	8.38	8.19	7.75	8.75	9.00	7.84
1748	8.81	9.12	9.25	9.62	8.50	8.00	8.62	9.38	8.06	8.19	8.06	8.19	8.65
1749	8.44	8.81	8.88	8.62	7.94	8.00	8.50	8.00	7.94	8.12	8.00	8.00	8.27

TABLE 2.4 (Continued): London on Dublin (Pounds Irish Currency Premium per £100 Sterling)

Year	Jan.	Feb.	Mar.	Apr.	May	June	July	Aug.	Sept.	Oct.	Nov.	Dec.	Average
1750	8.25	9.00	9.50	9.00	9.00	9.12	9.06	9.25	9.50	9.75	9.50	9.69	9.22
1751	10.00	10.56	9.88	8.88	9.00	9.44	9.25	8.12	8.12	7.69	7.88	8.06	8.91
1752	7.99	7.88	7.94	8.25	7.75	7.75	8.12	7.94	7.81	8.38	8.94	9.00	8.15
1753	9.50	10.00	9.75	10.44	9.19	9.94	9.94	9.88	10.00	9.00	10.00	9.88	9.79
1754	10.62	10.50	10.81	10.00	9.75	9.50	9.00	9.62	9.00	9.25	8.88	9.38	9.69
1755	9.12	9.25	9.00	8.50	8.38	7.81	8.50	8.12	8.00	8.00	8.50	8.19	8.45
1756	8.50	9.06	8.94	8.69	8.38	8.56	8.75	8.12	7.88	7.94	8.00	7.75	8.38
1757	7.62	7.25	7.19	7.81	8.25	7.50	7.50	7.50	7.62	7.88	8.00	7.50	7.64
1758	7.56	7.50	7.12	7.50	7.75	7.50	7.94	8.38	8.44	8.69	9.25	9.81	8.12
1759	9.06	9.69	9.75	10.50	9.50	10.38	10.25	9.06	9.56	9.00	9.00	8.50	9.52
1760	8.75	9.50	9.25	8.81	8.38	8.00	8.62	8.12	7.62	7.62	7.38	7.00	8.25
1761	7.44	7.62	7.12	7.50	7.50	8.00	7.75	8.00	8.12	8.00	7.50	7.50	7.67
1762	8.12	8.00	7.44	8.31	8.25	7.75	8.69	8.25	7.62	8.12	7.75	7.88	8.02
1763	8.12	8.12	7.75	7.75	7.88	7.88	8.00	8.00	8.25	8.75	9.50	9.25	8.27
1764	9.25	9.00	9.25	8.69	9.00	9.19	9.12	9.25	9.25	8.88	9.00	9.00	9.07
1765	9.12	9.75	9.12	9.50	9.38	9.12	8.88	8.88	8.62	8.25	8.00	7.88	8.88
1766	7.88	8.12	8.12	9.00	8.62	8.62	8.88	9.44	9.44	9.75	8.62	8.62	8.76
1767	8.75	9.44	9.88	9.75	9.75	9.88	9.88	9.62	8.75	8.25	9.00	9.50	9.37
1768	9.00	8.50	8.38	8.00	8.31	8.38	8.50	8.38	8.38	8.44	8.62	8.00	8.41
1769	8.12	9.00	8.88	9.25	9.44	9.25	9.81	9.00	9.50	9.25	9.12	9.00	9.14
1770	9.88	10.00	10.25	10.25	10.62	10.62	10.25	10.00	9.75	9.38	10.38	9.00	10.03
1771	9.00	9.75	10.12	10.00	9.75	9.56	8.88	9.00	7.88	7.62	7.38	8.00	8.91
1772	8.75	8.75	8.12	8.75	9.62	8.50	9.25	9.62	9.50	9.25	9.44	10.00	9.13
1773	10.75	11.00	10.50	10.38	11.00	11.00	10.00	9.00	8.75	8.12	8.25	8.00	9.73
1774	8.31	8.00	8.00	8.25	8.00	8.12	8.38	8.38	7.75	7.62	7.88	8.00	8.06
1775	8.00	8.00	8.12	8.06	8.25	8.38	8.25	8.12	7.88	8.00	7.88	7.75	8.06

Notes and Sources: **TABLE 2.4**

1698–1775: *The Course of the Exchange* (London), 1698–1775. See the discussion above in the initial section of this chapter and in n. 10.

Amsterdam

The course of the exchange between London and Amsterdam takes a central place in this book not only because of the close and important financial connections between the two cities but also because of their pivotal location in the economy of all of Europe in the seventeenth and eighteenth centuries.[41] Amsterdam was also the seat of the West India Company, which controlled several West Indian colonies, and the locus of considerable trade with the New World. The exchange at Amsterdam functioned as a clearinghouse for commercial transactions linking the Atlantic and the Mediterranean with the North Sea, the Baltic, and beyond. Merchants in London or Lisbon who had accounts to balance in Stockholm or St. Petersburg, places for which it would be difficult to purchase bills in their own city, traditionally negotiated their bills by way of Amsterdam.[42] "London exchanges also with Denmark, Norway, Swedeland, Muscovy, Germany, Switzerland, Savoy etc.," wrote John Mair, "but it is commonly done by the way of Hamburg, Amsterdam, or Antwerp."[43] As a result we have the data to do the same thing. The course of the exchange between London and Amsterdam becomes for this handbook the first leg in numerous attempts to compute indirectly London's exchange with other places too.

Real money at Amsterdam consisted in a variety of gold and silver coins, the basic ones of which are set down in tables 1.1 and 1.2 (pp. 9–13). The unchanging metallic content of the gulden, or guilder, during the seventeenth and eighteenth centuries made Dutch money—with sterling—one of the soundest, most stable currencies in the world.[44] The

---

41. See Lucy S. Sutherland, *A London Merchant, 1695–1774* (Oxford, 1933), 37. Antwerp preceded Amsterdam in this role, and there are 16th-century exchange rate quotations on London at Antwerp. See Vázquez de Prada, *Lettres marchandes d'Anvers*, I, 267–305; Herman van der Wee, *The Growth of the Antwerp Market and the European Economy (Fourteenth-Sixteenth Centuries)* (The Hague, 1963), III, graph 33; and Gould, *Great Debasement*, 89. See also the information about exchange extracted from the memorandum book of Antwerp merchant Baltasar Andrea Moucheron (1577–1622) in Valentin Vázquez de Prada Vallejo, "Moneda y cambia internacionales a finales del siglo XVI y comienzos des XVII," *Studi in onore di Amintore Fanfani* (Milan, 1962), V, 727–734.

42. One can find occasional quotations of the direct rate, but series of these are rare. Two extremely uncommon series are: (1) a biweekly quotation of the rate at St. Petersburg on Amsterdam and London in the 1780s (and occasional quotations on Paris and Hamburg, 1781–1783 only), in *Changes de St. Petersbourg durant les années 1780, 1781, 1782, 1783 [et 1784, 1785, 1786, 1787]* ([St. Petersburg?], n.d.), two printed sheets removed from the papers of Edmund Charles Genêt, who served as the French chargé d'affaires at St. Petersburg until his expulsion in 1792, in the Rare Book Room, Library of Congress (the Genêt Papers are in the Manuscript Division, Lib. Cong.); (2) for the previous century, 40 random quotations of the rate of exchange at Archangel on Amsterdam, found by Simon Hart in the records of protested bills of exchange in the Notarieel Archief, Gemeentelijke Archiefdienst, Amsterdam, and extracted and printed by Hart in "Amsterdam Shipping and Trade to Northern Russia in the Seventeenth Century," *Mededelingen van de Nederlandse Vereniging voor Zeegeschiedenis*, XXVI (Mar. 1973), 30. For Russian moneys see S[tanisław] de Chaudoir, *Aperçu sur les monnaies russes et sur les monnaies étrangères qui ont cours en russie*, 3 vols. (St. Petersburg, 1836–1837), and A. G. Man'kov, *Le mouvement des prix dans l'état russe au XVI siècle* (Paris, 1957). This last book is a translation by G. Kruchevsky of the Moscow-Leningrad edition of 1951.

43. Mair, *Book-keeping Modernized*, 189. See also Ashton, *Economic History of England*, 190. For examples of this see Jacob M. Price, *The Tobacco Adventure to Russia: Enterprise, Politics, and Diplomacy in the Quest for a Northern Market for English Colonial Tobacco, 1676–1722* (American Philosophical Society, Transactions, N.S., LI, pt. 1 [Philadelphia, 1961]), 55, 58, and *passim*; and Kent, *War and Trade in Northern Seas, passim*.

44. Posthumus, *Prices in Holland*, I, liv–lvii. What follows hereafter in this and in subsequent sections is derived from a variety of contemporary handbooks on exchange, the most useful of which are Richard Hayes, *The Negociator's Magazine: or, the Exchanges Anatomiz'd* (London, 1719), in at least

money of account at Amsterdam was expressed in two inter-connected sets of moneys reflecting in their origin something of the divergent political and economic background of the area. Some prices were quoted in gulden, stuivers, and penningen; other goods were prices in ponden- , schellingen- ,

and grooten-Vlaamsch. The gulden was also called the florijn, or florin, and, as the basic silver coin after 1681, constituted the most important unit of both the real money and the money of account of Amsterdam. Table 2.5 expresses the interrelationships of the Dutch moneys of account.

The mercantile community of Amsterdam was served by the *Wisselbank van Amsterdam*, founded in 1609 and one of the oldest exchange banks in Europe and the first outside the Mediterranean.[45] The bank had several functions, including clearing bills of exchange, receiving deposits of money, and minting coin. In the process of carrying out these separate tasks, a difference in value arose between bank money (banco) and current money. All of the bank's transactions were entered into its books in bank money; at the same time everyday business used current money. The difference between the two, called the agio or the *opgelt*,[46] was expressed as the percentage premium on bank money for current money. Thus an agio of 4 percent meant that 104 guilders current money equaled 100 guilders banco. While the premium for bank money probably existed in the 1620s, we have no real mention of it until the late 1630s and early 1640s (see table 2.6).[47]

eleven 18th-century editions; Pierre Giraudeau, *La banque rendue facile aux principales nations de l'Europe* (Geneva, 1741), especially the new, revised edition of 1756; Jürgen Elert Kruse, *Allgemeiner und besonders Hamburgischer Contorist* (Hamburg, 1753), which went through three editions in 30 years; and Samuel Ricard, *Traité général du commerce* (Amsterdam, 1700), more particularly in the revised version edited by Tomás Antonio de Marien y Arróspide (Amsterdam, 1781). This "new edition" of Ricard's classic work is really a completely new book put together by Marien from the Giraudeau and Kruse editions of 1756 and 1766 and, probably, J. C. Nelkenbrecher's posthumous *Logarithmische Tabellen, zu Berechnung deren Wechselarbitragen, welche vor alle Handelsplätze in ganz Europa allgemein zind* (Könisberg, 1762), a book that was already in its 5th edition by 1781 (having been revised by M. P. B. Gerhart in 1769 along lines similar to Giraudeau and Kruse) and that was to become a standard 19th-century manual. Marien later republished his own work in translation as *Tratado general de monedas, pesas, medidas y cambios de todas las naciones, reducidas á las que se usan en España* (Madrid, 1789). There are many other such books, most of them more or less dependent on Ricard, Kruse, or Hayes, and I have not cited them for information common to them all (thus tables 2.5, 2.10, and the like are not specifically referenced).

An especially useful source for the Amsterdam exchange is Johannes Phoonsen, *Wissel-styl tot Amsterdam* (Amsterdam, 1676), which appeared in numerous editions, was translated into French by Jean Pierre Ricard (*Les loix et coutumes du change des principales places de l'Europe* [Amsterdam, 1715]), and was later revised and supplemented by Isaac Le Long, *Vervolg van de Wissel-styl tot Amsterdam* (Amsterdam, 1729). See also Jacques Le Moine de l'Espine, *Den koophandel van Amsterdam* (Amsterdam, 1694), which also went through a dozen editions by 1800. Later editions were edited by the same Isaac Le Long. The 2d edition of the French translation of Le Moine's work, *Le negoce d'Amsterdam* (Amsterdam, 1710), incorporated another useful study, Jacques Mondoteguy's *Traité des arbitrages* (Amsterdam, 1710). See Lucas Jansen, *"De koophandel van Amsterdam": Een critische studie over het koopmanshandboek van Jacques Le Moine de l'Espine en Isaac Le Long* (Amsterdam, 1946); Jansen reprints the 1694 edition of Le Moine's work on pp. 363–396.

45. J. G. van Dillen, "The Bank of Amsterdam," in J. G. van Dillen, ed., *History of the Principal Public Banks* (The Hague, 1934), 79–123. See also the important collection of essays by Büsch, *Sämtliche Schriften über Banken und Münzwesen*, [ed. Ebeling].

46. "Aggio, dat is opgelt van banckgelt." J[ohannes] Ph[oonsen], *Berichten en vertoogen raackende het bestier van den omslagh van de Wisselbanck tot Amsterdam* (Amsterdam, 1677), as reprinted in J. G. van Dillen, ed., "Een boek van Phoonsen over de Amsterdamsche Wisselbank," *Economisch-historisch jaarboek*, VII (1921), 37.

47. Van Dillen, "Bank of Amsterdam," in Van Dillen, ed., *Principal Public Banks*, 88–92; Posthumus, *Prices in Holland*, lvii–lx. See also Hayes, *Negociator's Magazine*, 2d ed. (London, 1724), 7–14; and William Banson, *The Complete Exchanger, Containing Tables of Exchange . . . from Great Britain to Holland*

TABLE 2.5. Moneys of Account of Amsterdam: Their Denominations and Their Relationships

Pond-Vlaamsch	Gulden (Florijn)	Schelling-Vlaamsch	Stuiver	Groot-Vlaamsch	Penning
1	6	20	120	240	1920
	1	3⅓	20	40	320
		1	6	12	96
			1	2	16
				1	8

For the purpose of this handbook the impact of the agio is significant. On the one hand, most foreign exchange transactions were negotiated in bank money, but some, notably on Denmark and Sweden, were not.[48] On the other hand, most commodities traded at Amsterdam were bought and sold at current money.[49] Obviously, if we are interested in converting exchange rates or commodity prices at Amsterdam into sterling, we must first determine if they were originally quoted in bank money or current money and, if in current money, convert them to bank money using the data for the agio in table 2.6. Failure to do this will result in an error of some 3 to 12 percent.[50]

Since the silver content of the gulden and the shilling was constant over this period, the par of exchange remained virtually unchanged at about 37 schellingen banco per £1 sterling.[51] At par £100 sterling equaled 1,111 gulden. Richard Hayes, in his handbook on exchange, provided numerous examples of the calculation of exchange transactions. For Amsterdam he asks us to convert 4,563 gulden current money into sterling; the exchange is at 32 schellingen and 5.75 grooten per £1, and the agio at 3.75 percent. Reducing current money to bank money first, we find that 4,563 gulden current divided by 1.0375 equals 4,398.07 gulden banco (4,393 gulden

___

(London, 1717), 133–134. Posthumus's reference is to the mercantile handbook compiled in the firm of Van Colen-de Groot of Antwerp, which its editor dates to 1643. See Jan Denucé, ed., *Koopmansleerboeken van de XVIᵉ en XVIIᵉ eeuwen in handschrift*, Verhandelingen van de Koninklijke Vlaamsche Academie voor Wetenschappen, Letteren en Schoone Kunsten van België, Klasse der Letteren en der Moreele en Staatkundige Wetenschappen, Jaargang III, no. 2 (Antwerp, 1941). According to this book the agio at that time (1643) was about 9% to 10%. *Ibid.*, 106, 112.

48. For Denmark and Sweden see Hayes, *Negociator's Magazine*, 202, 209. See also Eli F. Heckscher, "The Bank of Sweden in Its Connection with the Bank of Amsterdam," in Van Dillen, ed., *Principal Public Banks*, 179–180, who concludes that this shows that "it was the private banks—not the Bank of Amsterdam—who played the deciding part in the commercial transactions of western and northern Europe in the eighteenth century."

49. Posthumus, *Prices in Holland*, I, lvii–lviii, 1–32, 586. For a detailed contemporary analysis of Posthumus's source, the Amsterdam price currents, see P[aul] J. M[arperger], *Erläuterung der Holländischen und sonderlich der Amsterdamer waaren-, geld- und wechsel-preiss-couranten* ([Dresden], 172?). For this work see Hannelore Lehman, "Paul Jacob Marperger (1656 bis 1730), sin vergessener Ökonom der deutschen Frühaufklärung: Versuch einen Übersicht seiner Leben und Wirken," *Jahrbuch für Wirtschaftsgeschichte*, [XI] (1971), 153–157 (no. 86).

50. See Fernand P. Braudel and Frank C. Spooner's chapter, "Prices in Europe from 1450 to 1750," in E. E. Rich and C. H. Wilson, eds., *The Cambridge Economic History of Europe*, IV: *The Economy of Expanding Europe in the Sixteenth and Seventeenth Centuries* (Cambridge, 1967), 387–388.

51. See [Henri Desaguliers], *A General Treatise of the Reduction of the Exchanges, Moneys and Real Species of Most Places in Europe in Two Exact Tables*, trans. A[lexander] J[ustice] (London, 1704), table 9. Isaac Newton to Treasury, [Oct. 1712], T. 1/152, fol. 182r, and in Shaw, ed., *English Monetary History*, 162, 163; Hayes, *Negociator's Magazine*, 18; [Thomas Slack], *The British Negociator: or, Foreign Exchanges Made Perfectly Easy* (London, 1759), 97.

and 1 stuiver).[52] Through reference to table 2.5 we can determine that this sum equals 14,660.09 schellingen, which, divided by 32.479 schellingen per £1, equals £451.37 sterling.[53]

Tables 2.7, 2.8, and 2.9 print the monthly variations in the Amsterdam-London rate at Amsterdam and at London from 1609 to 1775 in terms of the value of £1 sterling in schellingen banco at Amsterdam. The mode of exchange between Amsterdam and other mercantile centers is set forth in table 2.10.

52. Hayes, *Negociator's Magazine*, 19–20. See also *ibid.*, 55; and *The Compleat Compting-House Companion; or, Young Merchant's and Tradesman's Sure Guide* (London, 1763), 32–33.

53. For examples of such negotiations involving trade with the continental colonies and including calculations involving agio, see the several letters from Jacob Henry Chabanel of Amsterdam to James Beekman of New York, 1764–1769, in Philip L. White, ed., *The Beekman Mercantile Papers, 1746–1799* (New York, 1956), II, 685–694. See, e.g., the letter of 29 May 1764, *ibid.*, 685, in which against a balance of fl. 5,026.12.8 "holland currency," Chabanel credits the proceeds of two sterling bills of exchange on London that Beekman has sent him—one for £200 sterling and another for £280 sterling.

£200 sterling, negotiated at "35 fl.[sic]11.3," yielded	fl. 2,155.10 banco
£280 sterling, negotiated at "36," yielded	fl. 3,031.— banco
	fl. 5,186.10 banco
agio 2¾	142.13
	fl. 5,329.3

Chabanel's arithmetic leaves a bit to be desired, but we can follow it just the same. He sold Beekman's first bill for 35 schellingen (not florijns), 11 grooten, and 3 penningen per £1 sterling, which should have yielded 2,157 florijns, or gulden (35.95 x 200 ÷ 3¹/₃); he credited Beekman with 2,155 gulden and 10 stuivers. Chabanel sold Beekman's second bill at 36 schellingen, for a yield of 3,024 gulden (36 x 280 ÷ 3 ¹/₃); this time he credited Beekman with too much, 3,031 gulden. All of this was in bank money; Chabanel converted it to currency by adding the agio at 2.75%, for a total of 5,329 gulden and 3 stuivers. Beekman then had a credit balance of 211 gulden and 10 stuivers current money. For another published series of calculations involving the agio, see David H. Kennett, "An English Merchant in Holland in 1737 and 1738," *Economisch- en sociaal-historisch jaarboek*, XXXV (1972), 148–186.

TABLE 2.6. **Agio on Amsterdam Bank Money, 1638–1775**
(Percentage Premium on Bank Money for Current Money)

Year	Jan.	Feb.	Mar.	Apr.	May	June	July	Aug.	Sept.	Oct.	Nov.	Dec.	Average
1638										0.50			0.50
1639													
1640													
1641													
1642													
1643													
1644													
1645													
1646													
1647													
1648								2.12	2.06	1.94	1.94		2.02
1649					2.31	2.69	2.62	2.44	3.25	3.00	1.62		2.53
1650	2.38	2.19	2.12	2.31	2.50								2.32
1651											3.06		3.06
1652								3.38					3.38
1653										2.00	1.88		1.94
1654		1.69	2.00	2.06	1.94				2.25	2.62	2.00		2.10
1655	2.42												2.42
1656						2.00							2.00
1657	2.62								3.38				3.00
1658													
1659													
1660										3.25			3.25
1661													
1662													

TABLE 2.6 (Continued): **Amsterdam Agio** (Percentage Premium for Current Money)

Year	Jan.	Feb.	Mar.	Apr.	May	June	July	Aug.	Sept.	Oct.	Nov.	Dec.	Average
1663					3.25								3.25
1664												3.06	3.06
1665										3.06			3.06
1666													
1667													
1668													
1669		3.75	3.56	3.44					3.75	3.75	3.75		3.65
1670													
1671				4.00	3.75								3.88
1672		3.75	3.44		4.00								3.80
1673													
1674	4.00					3.94	4.75	4.75	4.12	4.06	4.25		4.16
1675										3.81	3.50		3.66
1676				3.62						3.94			3.78
1677	4.00	4.31	4.31	4.19	3.75	3.75	3.75	3.75	3.38	3.50	5.50	3.38	3.96
1678								4.00	3.88	3.62	3.62		3.78
1679	4.50	3.69			3.75	4.00						4.50	4.16
1680			4.38				4.00	4.00	3.88	3.88	3.50		4.01
1681			3.50	3.50			3.75	3.75	3.50				3.58
1682		4.00		4.02			4.25	4.06	3.75	3.75		4.25	4.01
1683											4.00		4.00
1684		4.75	4.00			4.25	4.19	4.25	4.12	4.12		4.50	4.28
1685		4.25					4.25	4.25			4.25	4.25	4.25
1686	5.19	5.15	5.08	5.00	5.00	5.00	5.00	5.12	5.19	4.75	5.00	5.25	5.06
1687													
1688	4.75					5.25		5.31	5.25	5.44			5.18
1689		5.75	5.50		5.25	5.38							5.47

TABLE 2.6 (Continued): Amsterdam Agio (Percentage Premium for Current Money)

Year	Jan.	Feb.	Mar.	Apr.	May	June	July	Aug.	Sept.	Oct.	Nov.	Dec.	Average
1690													
1691						5.25	5.50					[5.50]	5.42
1692					5.47	5.50							5.48
1693	[12.50]	9.50			5.00		6.00	6.25					7.38
1694	5.00		4.75				4.69					4.75	4.77
1695		4.88		5.00		4.38	4.75				5.00		4.83
1696	5.00		4.81	4.78	4.62	4.88		4.77			4.62		4.76
1697					5.12			5.00		4.75	4.88	4.66	4.96
1698			4.75	4.62		4.75		4.75		5.00	5.19		4.82
1699		5.00			5.25	5.25	5.25						5.17
1700					4.82				4.50		4.75	4.50	4.65
1701	4.83			4.62	4.75		4.75	4.62					4.73
1702								3.00					3.00
1703							2.94	2.56	2.94				2.81
1704					2.50		2.75		3.00				2.69
1705					3.19			3.12		3.51			3.27
1706							5.56	5.31		5.62	5.69		5.54
1707	5.62												5.62
1708										4.88		4.81	4.84
1709		4.88		4.75	4.50	4.56	5.06	5.00	5.00			4.81	4.83
1710	4.88	5.00	4.88	4.75	4.50	4.56	4.75						4.76
1711													
1712													
1713													
1714								4.50					4.50
1715													
1716													
1717													

TABLE 2.6 (Continued): **Amsterdam Agio** (Percentage Premium for Current Money)

Year	Jan.	Feb.	Mar.	Apr.	May	June	July	Aug.	Sept.	Oct.	Nov.	Dec.	Average
1718					4.19		4.68	4.50		5.00			4.59
1719													
1720													
1721													
1722											5.25		5.25
1723							5.12	4.84	4.84	5.06	4.94	4.81	4.94
1724	4.62	4.62	4.88	4.75	4.62	4.56	4.56	4.56	4.50	4.25	4.50	4.38	4.57
1725	4.44	4.31	4.38	4.25	4.06	4.25	4.38	4.44	4.44	4.81	4.75	4.56	4.42
1726	4.50	4.53	4.75			4.94	4.88	5.00	5.06	5.06	5.12	4.81	4.88
1727	5.00	5.16	5.03	5.03	4.78	5.00	4.81	4.94	4.88	5.06	5.12	4.88	4.97
1728	4.88	4.88	4.94	4.75	4.88	4.75	4.62	4.62	4.75	4.75	4.88	4.75	4.79
1729	4.75	4.91	4.88	4.81	4.75	4.81	4.75	4.56	4.75	4.75	4.75	4.75	4.77
1730	4.75	4.62	4.75	4.69	4.62	4.50	4.44	*4.41*	4.38	4.62	4.62	4.50	4.58
1731	4.44	4.50	4.44	4.31	4.62	4.56	4.62	4.56	4.50	4.56	4.62	4.50	4.52
1732	4.44	4.44	4.50	4.38	3.88	3.75	3.75					3.88	4.02
1733						3.44	3.94		4.50		3.75		3.80
1734				4.56	4.12	4.56	4.50	4.56	4.50	4.56	4.59	4.00	4.44
1735	4.00	4.00	3.88	4.00	3.94	4.00	4.00	4.00	4.00	4.38	4.12	3.68	4.00
1736	3.81	3.94	4.00	4.00	3.75	3.88	3.94	3.88	3.88	3.94	4.00	3.75	3.90
1737	3.88	3.75	3.94	3.88	3.81	3.94	4.09	4.06	4.12	4.25	4.44	4.06	4.02
1738	4.00	4.12	4.31	4.31	4.31	4.44	4.44	4.38	4.50	4.78	5.00	4.81	4.45
1739	5.00	5.06	4.97	5.09	5.09	5.06	5.12	5.00	5.12	5.25	5.31	5.25	5.11
1740	5.25	5.38	5.44	5.38	4.81	5.12	5.12	5.12	5.25	5.19	5.38	5.31	5.23
1741	5.19	5.12	5.25	5.31	5.12	5.00	4.12	4.09	3.94	4.00	4.25	4.25	4.64
1742	4.44	3.94	4.22	4.25	4.12	4.31	4.38	4.50	4.75	4.75	4.75	4.75	4.43
1743	4.75	4.75	4.75	4.75	4.75	4.94	4.69	4.75	4.81	4.97	5.03	4.69	4.80
1744	5.00	4.88	4.69	4.81	4.94	5.03	4.94	4.94	4.72	4.81	4.62	4.94	4.86

TABLE 2.6 (Continued): **Amsterdam Agio** (Percentage Premium for Current Money)

Year	Jan.	Feb.	Mar.	Apr.	May	June	July	Aug.	Sept.	Oct.	Nov.	Dec.	Average
1745	5.00	5.00	5.00	4.94	5.00	4.94	4.94	4.94	5.00	4.61	4.88	4.94	4.93
1746	4.88	4.88	5.00	4.75	4.50	4.61	4.75	4.88	4.94	5.06	5.09	4.97	4.86
1747	5.00	4.88	4.88	4.94	4.75	4.75	4.75	4.75	4.12	3.50	4.69	4.75	4.65
1748	4.75	4.50	4.75	4.56	4.75	4.25	4.75	4.88	4.81	4.94	5.00	5.00	4.74
1749	5.06	5.12	5.12	5.12	4.25	4.12	4.25	4.19	4.38	4.62	4.75	4.75	4.64
1750	4.81	4.69	4.62	4.50	4.12	4.19	4.06	4.31	4.53	4.84	4.88	4.81	4.53
1751	4.75	4.75	4.81	4.75	4.75	4.75	4.88	4.88	5.00	5.06	5.12	5.12	4.88
1752	5.03	4.94	4.69	4.62	4.31	4.16	4.25	4.25	4.44	4.50	4.31	4.25	4.48
1753	4.25	4.38	4.75	4.62	4.50	4.69	4.50	4.62	4.88	4.88	4.69	4.75	4.63
1754	4.59	4.69	4.69	4.88	4.62	4.38	4.19	4.38	4.34	4.31	4.69	4.38	4.51
1755	4.31	4.34	4.44	4.38	4.00	4.06	3.88	3.62	4.38	4.25	4.31	4.25	4.18
1756	4.12	4.00	4.38	4.19	4.38	4.50	4.31	4.19	4.19	4.22	4.12	4.00	4.22
1757	3.94	3.94	3.88	3.88	3.38	3.69	3.88	3.56	3.69	3.88	3.75	3.62	3.76
1758	3.62	3.44	3.25	3.50	3.19	3.12	2.88	2.81	3.19	3.41	3.69	3.84	3.33
1759	2.62	3.00	2.69	2.62	2.12	1.75	1.88	2.00	2.00	2.44	2.12	2.00	2.27
1760	2.25	2.25	2.50	2.56	2.56	3.00	3.31	3.25	3.78	3.81	4.12	3.88	3.11
1761	3.88	4.69	4.94	4.50	4.75	4.34	4.44	4.50	4.38	4.38	4.75	4.81	4.53
1762	4.88	4.88	3.12	3.38	2.00	1.88	1.88	2.62	2.56	2.50	3.75	2.75	3.02
1763	2.22	2.00	2.00	2.06	1.62	1.75	2.00	1.88	3.00	3.38	3.25	3.12	2.36
1764	3.12	2.75	3.19	3.25	3.00	3.00	2.75	2.75	3.12	3.68	3.50	3.38	3.12
1765	3.38	3.38	3.62	3.62	3.38	3.50	3.38	3.56	3.94	4.44	4.38	4.50	3.76
1766	4.62	4.12	4.62	4.88	4.81	4.56	4.81	4.84	4.84	4.84	5.00	5.00	4.74
1767	4.81	4.62	4.88	4.81	4.88	4.75	4.38	4.62	4.75	4.88	4.88	4.88	4.76
1768	4.75	4.62	4.56	4.62	4.44	4.38	4.25	4.62	4.62	4.62	4.75	4.75	4.58
1769	4.94	4.69	4.88	4.94	4.69	4.88	4.94	4.69	4.94	4.81	5.00	5.00	4.87
1770	5.00	4.88	4.94	4.94	4.75	5.00	4.81	4.75	4.94	4.81	5.00	5.00	4.90
1771	5.00	4.75	4.69	4.75	5.00	5.00	4.81	4.81	4.81	4.81	5.16	5.00	4.88

TABLE 2.6 (Continued): **Amsterdam Agio** (Percentage Premium for Current Money)

Year	Jan.	Feb.	Mar.	Apr.	May	June	July	Aug.	Sept.	Oct.	Nov.	Dec.	Average
1772	5.00	4.88	5.00	4.94	4.81	4.44	4.62	4.88	4.38	4.88	4.38	4.75	4.75
1773	4.25	4.62	4.88	4.81	4.56	4.47	4.25	4.50	4.88	4.94	4.94	4.88	4.66
1774	4.91	4.56	4.75	4.81	4.62	4.62	4.62	4.62	4.75	4.81	4.81	4.88	4.73
1775	4.88	4.88	4.50	4.50	4.50	4.50	4.50	4.50	4.94	5.00	4.88	4.81	4.70

Notes and Sources: **TABLE 2.6**

Figures inserted in square brackets are assigned to that month arbitrarily; figures printed in italics are straight-line interpolations based on the two neighboring quotations.

1638–1701: J. G. van Dillen, ed., *Bronnen tot de geschiedenis der wisselbanken (Amsterdam, Middelburg, Delft, Rotterdam)*, Rijks geschiedkundige publicatiën, 59–60 (The Hague, 1925), I, 79–80, 115–117, 174–176, 188–190, 239, 241–242, 261–264, 311–312, II, 818–824, 932–936, 957–959.

1648–1775: N. W. Posthumus, *Inquiry into the History of Prices in Holland* (Leiden, 1946–1964), I, 615–654, based in large measure on J. G. van Dillen, "Effectenkoersen aan de Amsterdamsche beurs, 1723–1794," *Economisch-historisch jaarboek*, XVII (1931), 19–39. Posthumus printed the midmonth quotation, that is, the one that appeared "as closely as possible to the 15th of each month." *Prices in Holland*, lx, n. 3. For 1693–1694 see also Jacques Le Moine de l'Espine, *Den koophandel van Amsterdam* (Amsterdam, 1694), 2.

1660, 1663: Company of Royal Adventurers Trading into Africa, Waste Book, 1660–1663, T. 70/1221, Public Record Office.

1675–1707, 1718: Royal African Company, Copybook of Invoices Homeward, 1673–1743, T. 70/936–961.

1691: Mr. Abraham van Rincon, at Amsterdam, to Charles Peers and Edward Tooke, at London, 31 July 1691, Correspondence, Business Papers of Thomas Brailsford, 1687–1698, C. 110/152: *Brailsford v. Peers*, P.R.O.

1693: [Jacques] Le Moine de l'Espine, *Den koophandel van Amsterdam*, 2d ed., ed. I[saac] Le Long (Amsterdam, 1715), 58.

1696: *Proctor's Price-Courant: The Prices of Merchandise in London* (London), 28 Feb. 1695/96, 3 Apr., 30 Apr., and 11 June. For these London price currents see Appendix 2, below.

1696–1697: *Cours van koopmanschappen tot Amsterdam* (Amsterdam), 28 Apr., 11 Aug. 1696, 4 May, 31 Aug., 5 Oct., and 14 Dec. 1697, copies in Matthias Giesque and Co. Papers, bundle no. 68, in C. 104/128, pt. 2, Unknown Cause.

1700–1701: Royal African Co., Copybook of Bills of Exchange Received, 1701–1705, T. 70/278.

1740–1775: "Notitie van diverse Koopmanschappen uyt de Prijs-Courant Begonnen in Amsteldam," 1708–1788, Kress Library of Business and Economics in the Baker Library, Graduate School of Business Administration, Harvard University, Boston. These manuscript volumes are contemporary extracts from the source used by Posthumus and Van Dillen. The quotations of the agio in them were employed here to check, correct, and supplement Posthumus's series.

TABLE 2.7. **Rate of Exchange: Amsterdam on London, 1609–1699**

(Schellingen Banco per £1 Sterling)

Year	Jan.	Feb.	Mar.	Apr.	May	June	July	Aug.	Sept.	Oct.	Nov.	Dec.	Average
1609											34.67		34.67
1610													
1611													
1612													
1613													
1614													
1615													
1616													
1617													
1618								35.00					35.00
1619													
1620													
1621													
1622													
1623													
1624		36.17			36.17	36.33		35.38	35.77	35.75		35.50	35.90
1625		35.62	35.67			35.83	35.83	35.92	37.00	36.08		36.08	35.95
1626	36.00	35.88	35.88				35.75	35.83		35.92	35.67	35.50	35.80
1627													
1628									35.10				35.10
1629													
1630	35.88				36.33						36.58		36.26
1631	36.33			35.71	35.50	35.79	35.88	36.54				36.54	36.19
1632		36.50		36.50		36.67	36.54						36.54
1633		36.67	36.75	36.71	36.88								36.75
1634		37.12											37.12

TABLE 2.7 (Continued): **Amsterdam on London** (Schellingen Banco per £1 Sterling)

Year	Jan.	Feb.	Mar.	Apr.	May	June	July	Aug.	Sept.	Oct.	Nov.	Dec.	Average
1635					36.48	35.71	35.58						35.84
1636			34.75	34.96	35.00							36.42	35.38
1637			36.38		36.62								36.50
1638						35.62						35.46	35.54
1639													
1640									37.29				37.29
1641					39.04						38.66		38.85
1642					38.12		38.46	38.04	38.38				38.21
1643						39.96		38.25	38.00				39.04
1644													
1645	39.33	39.21					38.08	38.08		38.08			38.48
1646	37.71	37.75		37.67	37.50		37.12	37.17	36.54	36.38	36.29	36.08	37.13
1647													
1648								34.00	33.08	34.00	34.08		33.79
1649					32.12	31.96	32.92	32.75	32.92	33.25	32.75	33.33	32.67
1650	33.83	33.67	33.83	34.08	32.17								33.45
1651											36.92		36.92
1652								33.67		35.75			34.71
1653											35.67	35.79	35.73
1654	35.33	36.17	36.25	36.17	36.17								36.04
1655													
1656													
1657													
1658													
1659													
1660										37.33			37.33
1661													
1662													

TABLE 2.7 (Continued): **Amsterdam on London** (Schellingen Banco per £1 Sterling)

Year	Jan.	Feb.	Mar.	Apr.	May	June	July	Aug.	Sept.	Oct.	Nov.	Dec.	Average
1663													
1664												35.04	35.04
1665											33.54		33.54
1666													
1667													
1668													
1669		35.50	35.58	35.40		35.73			35.50	35.38	35.25		35.48
1670													
1671				35.92	35.21								35.56
1672		35.62	35.58		33.67								34.64
1673													
1674						33.88	33.83	34.12	34.46	34.29	34.46		34.13
1675										35.25			35.25
1676				35.88						36.50			36.19
1677	36.29	36.17	36.21	36.38			36.08						36.23
1678	35.54												35.54
1679		35.29										36.00	35.64
1680				36.00	35.83								35.92
1681											35.60		35.60
1682	35.46			35.25									35.36
1683											36.17		36.17
1684													
1685							35.10			35.90	35.92	35.96	35.51
1686	36.14	36.19	36.23	36.17	36.08	35.96	35.85	35.67	35.50	35.38	35.29	*35.69*	35.85
1687	*36.10*	36.50			36.00	35.96	35.51	35.71					35.96
1688	35.58				35.17	35.04	35.00	35.08	34.56	34.25			34.95
1689													

TABLE 2.7 (Continued): **Amsterdam on London** (Schellingen Banco per £1 Sterling)

Year	Jan.	Feb.	Mar.	Apr.	May	June	July	Aug.	Sept.	Oct.	Nov.	Dec.	Average
1690													
1691				33.67	33.71	33.75	34.00	33.25			34.67	33.75	33.84
1692		34.62				34.42							34.52
1693		33.54		33.65	33.62		33.44	33.31	32.88				33.46
1694	32.38	32.40					32.68	32.35	32.31		32.15	32.15	32.33
1695	32.15	31.94	31.75	30.54	30.62	28.59	28.62	29.78	28.12	28.00	27.00		29.55
1696		29.27	29.71	29.96	29.92			32.75					30.63
1697				35.29				35.33		35.00		35.23	35.24
1698													
1699		32.00	31.21										31.60

Notes and Sources: **TABLE 2.7**

1609–1699: N. W. Posthumus, *Inquiry into the History of Prices in Holland* (Leiden, 1946–1964), I, 590–595. Posthumus discussed his sources, the price currents published at Amsterdam, *ibid.*, xix–xxx, 587–588. Simon Hart has found and extracted quotations of the London-Amsterdam exchange rate from the protests of bills of exchange in the Amsterdam notarial records and has compiled these into five-year averages. For 1594–1600 the average was 34.50 schellingen banco per £1 sterling; for 1601–1605, 36.43; 1606–1610, 35.17; 1611–1615, 35.37; 1616–1620, 35.13; 1621–1625, 35.93; 1626–1630, 36.60; 1631–1635, 37.27; 1636–1640, 37.20; 1641–1645, 39.30; and for 1651, 37.63, and 1652, 36.33. See his "Amsterdam Shipping and Trade to Northern Russia in the Seventeenth Century," *Mededelingen van de Nederlandse Vereniging voor Zeegeschiedenis*, XXVI (1973), 8, 107; and Notarieel Archief, Gemeentelijke Archiefdienst, Amsterdam.

1631–1633: *Corso in Amsterd[am] di piusorte mercanti* ([Amsterdam]), 22 Dec. 1631, 26 Apr. 1632, and 18 Apr. 1633, copies in the Kress Library of Business and Economics in the Baker Library, Graduate School of Business Administration, Harvard University, Boston. These were the Italian-language versions of the Amsterdam price currents. See H. W. Aeckerle, "Amsterdamer Börsenpreislister 1624–1626," *Economisch-historisch jaarboek*, XIII (1927), 86–209.

1660: Company of Royal Adventurers Trading into Africa, Waste Book, 1660–1663, T. 70/1221, Public Record Office.

1679, 1685—1695: Royal African Company, Copybooks of Bills and Exchange Received, 1686, 1688, 1693–1694, Copybooks of Invoices Homeward, 1678–1680, 1691–1692, 1694–1696, T. 70/272, 274, 277, 938, 945, 947.

1691–1692, 1695: Mrs. Abraham van Rincon, at Amsterdam, to Charles Peers and Edmund Tooke, at London, 13 Apr. and 31 July 1691, 12 Feb. 1692, and 15 Nov. 1695, Correspondence, Business Papers of Thomas Brailsford, 1687–1698, C. 110/152: *Brailsford* v. *Peers*, P.R.O.

1696: *Proctor's Price-Courant: The Prices of Merchandise in London* (London), 28 Feb., 3 Apr., 30 Apr., 21 May, and 11 June 1696. For this London price current see Appendix 2, below.

1696–1697: *Cours van koopmanschappen tot Amsterdam* (Amsterdam), 28 Apr., 11 Aug. 1696, 4 May, 31 Aug., 5 Oct., and 14 Dec. 1697, copies in Matthias Giesque and Co. Papers, bundle no. 68, C. 104/128, pt. 2, Unknown Cause.

TABLE 2.8. Rate of Exchange: London on Amsterdam, 1660–1697

(Schellingen Banco per £1 Sterling)

Year	Jan.	Feb.	Mar.	Apr.	May	June	July	Aug.	Sept.	Oct.	Nov.	Dec.	Average
1660												38.33	38.33
1661													
1662					35.04								35.04
1663		35.83	36.67		35.46								35.86
1664													
1665													
1666													
1667							34.92						34.92
1668			35.25							35.88	36.15	36.00	35.63
1669	36.00	36.00	36.00	35.96	35.90	35.75	35.73	35.81	36.05	35.92	35.88	35.54	35.88
1670													
1671											36.29		36.29
1672	36.58	36.69	34.83		34.33				34.92		35.42	34.54	35.07
1673		34.42						33.98			33.92	33.98	34.12
1674	34.00		34.75			34.17	34.25					35.00	34.45
1675	35.08	35.33	35.50	35.58				35.83			35.81	37.25	35.81
1676													
1677								36.17	36.21				36.19
1678													
1679	35.75												35.75
1680		36.42						35.83	35.83			36.17	36.14
1681					36.29		36.25				36.17		36.24
1682			36.17			35.62		35.50	35.50	35.52			35.70
1683	36.67	36.08			36.58			36.42			36.58		36.49
1684	36.33											35.75	36.04
1685									36.42		36.29	36.42	36.39

TABLE 2.8 (Continued): **London on Amsterdam** (Schellingen Banco per £1 Sterling)

Year	Jan.	Feb.	Mar.	Apr.	May	June	July	Aug.	Sept.	Oct.	Nov.	Dec.	Average
1686					36.00								36.00
1687					35.75								35.75
1688						35.08		34.62					34.85
1689			34.71			35.88							35.30
1690													
1691	34.17					34.00	34.17			35.75			34.52
1692	35.75				34.21								34.98
1693			34.00					33.25					33.62
1694									32.75		32.83		32.79
1695	32.58	32.50	31.83	31.17	31.21	29.33	29.17	27.00	28.25	28.33	27.42	29.00	29.82
1696	30.00	29.50	29.75	29.67	30.50	30.17	29.25	32.50	35.17	36.67	37.00	37.67	32.32
1697	36.00	36.58	36.67	36.42	36.25	35.58	35.17	35.75	35.67	35.42	35.75	35.58	35.90

Notes and Sources: **TABLE 2.8**

Figures inserted in square brackets are assigned to that month arbitrarily; figures printed in italics are straight-line interpolations based on the two neighboring quotations.

1660–1663: Company of Royal Adventurers Trading into Africa, Waste Book, 1660–1663, T. 70/1221, Public Record Office.

1667–1697: London price currents as listed in Appendix 2, below.

1675–1693: Royal African Company, Copybooks of Invoices Homeward, 1673–1694, T. 70/936–946.

1684, 1687: Henry Ashurst, at London, to Conrad Calekberner, at Amsterdam, 4 Jan. 1683/84, 31 May 1687, Letter Book and Account Book of Henry Ashurst, 1674–1701, fols. 26v, 53v, Deposited Deeds, Ashurst, c: 1, Bodleian Library, Oxford.

1695–1697: *A Collection for Improvement of Husbandry and Trade* (London), 18 Jan. 1694/95–31 Dec. 1697 (the figure nearest the middle of the month).

TABLE 2.9. Rate of Exchange: London on Amsterdam, 1698–1775
(Schellingen Banco per £1 Sterling)

Year	Jan.	Feb.	Mar.	Apr.	May	June	July	Aug.	Sept.	Oct.	Nov.	Dec.	Average
1698	35.79	35.75	35.83	35.71	35.21	35.38	35.38	35.25	34.46	35.38	35.46	35.42	35.42
1699	35.25	35.33	35.29	35.25	35.17	35.12	35.42	35.42	35.50	35.42	35.46	35.67	35.36
1700	35.62	35.54	35.67	35.58	35.67	35.50	35.58	35.58	35.42	35.46	35.50	35.67	35.57
1701	35.46	37.00	36.62	36.12	36.46	36.25	36.38	36.42	36.83	36.58	36.58	36.58	36.44
1702	36.42	35.92	35.67	35.88	35.75	35.42	35.29	35.17	35.21	35.00	34.75	34.79	35.44
1703	34.54	34.58	34.25	34.25	34.33	34.38	34.25	34.17	34.29	34.00	34.38	34.46	34.32
1704	34.25	34.33	34.21	34.21	34.17	34.00	33.96	33.92	34.46	34.62	35.38	34.46	34.33
1705	34.00	34.46	34.96	34.42	34.42	34.42	34.50	34.46	34.50	34.58	34.88	34.92	34.54
1706	34.75	35.00	34.46	34.42	34.38	34.21	34.25	34.58	34.54	34.96	34.79	35.17	34.63
1707	34.50	34.92	34.67	34.58	34.71	34.58	34.62	34.62	34.58	34.67	34.71	34.67	34.65
1708	34.29	34.21	35.08	34.67	34.62	34.54	34.38	34.25	34.29	34.71	34.54	34.54	34.51
1709	34.33	34.38	34.25	34.17	33.62	33.58	33.54	33.54	33.67	33.62	33.88	33.58	33.85
1710	34.00	33.92	33.92	33.92	33.67	33.38	33.54	33.83	33.67	35.42	35.08	35.29	34.14
1711	34.71	34.38	34.33	34.50	34.17	33.88	33.83	33.88	34.58	34.62	34.79	35.00	34.39
1712	34.12	34.08	34.21	33.46	33.33	33.38	33.17	33.58	34.58	34.96	34.96	35.17	34.08
1713	35.50	35.71	35.79	36.21	35.54	35.67	35.62	35.62	36.00	36.04	35.88	36.29	35.82
1714	36.00	36.58	36.29	36.00	35.75	35.75	35.62	36.04	36.54	36.50	36.79	36.71	36.21
1715	36.62	36.62	36.54	36.46	36.38	36.12	35.58	35.96	36.17	36.29	36.92	36.38	36.34
1716	36.08	35.71	35.62	35.42	35.54	35.42	35.42	35.21	35.33	35.38	35.17	35.08	35.45
1717	34.75	35.04	35.08	34.96	34.92	34.67	34.75	34.67	34.46	34.50	34.00	34.17	34.66
1718	34.21	33.83	34.04	34.71	34.67	34.67	34.67	34.75	34.75	34.88	34.92	34.83	34.58
1719	34.71	34.79	36.04	35.96	35.50	35.54	35.00	35.42	35.62	35.67	35.33	35.33	35.41
1720	35.75	35.42	35.83	36.12	35.33	34.42	34.75	34.17	34.04	35.29	34.00	33.88	34.92
1721	33.50	34.08	34.29	34.21	34.38	34.92	34.79	34.79	35.12	35.46	35.38	35.29	34.68
1722	35.25	35.33	35.62	35.46	35.62	35.71	35.58	35.67	35.79	35.67	35.54	35.58	35.57

TABLE 2.9 (Continued): **London on Amsterdam** (Schellingen Banco per £1 Sterling)

Year	Jan.	Feb.	Mar.	Apr.	May	June	July	Aug.	Sept.	Oct.	Nov.	Dec.	Average
1723	35.12	35.25	35.17	35.00	35.17	35.08	35.50	35.17	35.21	35.17	35.00	35.39	35.19
1724	35.08	35.25	35.33	35.25	35.08	35.17	35.17	35.17	35.25	35.08	35.08	34.96	35.16
1725	35.00	35.00	35.17	34.96	34.96	35.17	35.25	35.08	35.08	35.08	34.96	35.00	35.06
1726	34.79	35.08	35.38	35.50	35.92	36.08	35.38	35.50	35.62	35.33	35.42	35.33	35.44
1727	35.21	35.38	35.12	35.08	35.00	35.00	34.83	34.79	34.92	34.83	34.67	34.75	34.96
1728	34.75	34.54	34.50	34.25	34.38	34.42	34.33	34.25	34.46	34.29	34.38	34.42	34.41
1729	34.33	34.33	34.42	34.58	34.33	34.42	34.42	34.29	34.50	34.42	34.42	34.33	34.40
1730	34.33	34.25	34.33	34.50	34.50	34.50	34.75	34.38	34.67	34.67	34.71	34.92	34.54
1731	34.79	34.88	34.92	34.96	34.79	34.92	34.92	34.92	35.00	35.00	35.08	34.96	34.93
1732	34.92	34.92	35.00	34.83	35.00	34.96	34.92	35.00	34.92	34.79	34.79	34.83	34.91
1733	34.83	34.72	34.92	34.81	34.83	34.88	34.88	34.92	35.00	35.06	35.46	35.79	35.01
1734	35.88	35.96	35.71	35.75	35.88	35.75	35.92	35.75	35.88	35.67	35.83	35.79	35.81
1735	35.79	35.83	35.75	35.83	35.96	36.00	35.92	35.96	36.00	35.96	35.88	35.83	35.89
1736	35.83	35.33	35.46	35.42	35.42	35.50	35.42	35.21	35.25	35.17	35.38	35.33	35.39
1737	35.25	35.17	35.25	35.08	35.00	34.83	34.83	34.75	34.92	34.83	34.92	34.92	34.98
1738	35.08	35.00	35.00	34.92	35.08	35.17	35.17	35.25	35.33	35.25	35.33	35.50	35.17
1739	35.42	35.42	35.42	35.33	35.50	35.50	35.67	35.75	35.75	35.67	35.58	35.67	35.56
1740	35.83	35.58	35.50	35.25	35.25	35.33	35.25	35.00	35.00	34.75	34.88	34.96	35.22
1741	34.92	34.79	34.67	34.58	34.50	34.50	34.75	34.67	34.75	34.67	34.67	34.92	34.70
1742	35.00	35.08	35.04	34.83	34.96	35.08	35.17	34.92	34.92	34.83	35.17	34.92	34.99
1743	34.92	34.83	34.75	34.58	34.58	34.83	34.92	34.83	34.83	34.75	34.83	35.00	34.80
1744	34.92	34.83	34.75	34.75	34.83	34.75	34.75	34.75	34.67	34.67	34.67	34.58	34.74
1745	34.92	34.83	34.75	34.75	34.67	34.83	34.83	35.00	35.17	35.62	35.83	37.42	35.22
1746	36.92	37.29	36.92	36.79	35.75	35.92	35.67	35.75	35.92	35.50	35.88	35.96	36.19
1747	35.92	35.58	35.58	35.21	35.25	35.25	35.33	35.42	35.50	35.50	35.42	35.50	35.46
1748	35.58	35.50	35.58	35.42	35.58	35.67	36.00	35.83	36.00	36.08	36.17	36.33	35.81
1749	36.25	36.17	36.08	36.00	35.58	35.83	35.75	35.58	35.58	35.50	35.42	35.50	35.77

TABLE 2.9 (Continued): London on Amsterdam (Schellingen Banco per £1 Sterling)

Year	Jan.	Feb.	Mar.	Apr.	May	June	July	Aug.	Sept.	Oct.	Nov.	Dec.	Average
1750	35.33	35.08	34.83	34.75	34.92	35.00	35.25	35.17	35.25	35.17	35.25	35.25	35.10
1751	35.33	35.33	35.08	35.38	35.50	35.58	35.58	35.58	35.58	35.58	35.58	35.50	35.47
1752	35.50	35.58	35.33	35.25	35.17	35.33	35.33	35.17	35.25	35.17	35.08	35.00	35.26
1753	35.08	35.00	35.08	35.08	35.08	35.08	35.17	35.17	35.25	35.33	35.33	35.33	35.16
1754	35.42	35.50	35.50	35.50	35.67	35.75	35.83	35.92	35.92	35.83	35.92	35.92	35.72
1755	36.00	36.17	36.33	36.25	36.50	36.42	36.50	36.54	36.58	36.25	36.08	36.08	36.31
1756	36.00	36.17	36.25	36.17	36.08	36.17	36.25	36.25	36.33	36.33	36.42	36.58	36.25
1757	36.58	36.42	36.50	36.50	35.92	34.92	35.08	35.33	35.33	35.08	35.17	35.25	35.67
1758	35.17	35.08	34.92	34.83	34.67	34.67	34.17	34.92	34.92	34.75	34.67	34.67	34.79
1759	34.83	35.08	35.33	35.33	35.67	35.50	35.83	35.92	36.25	36.25	36.25	36.25	35.71
1760	35.92	35.83	35.75	35.67	35.50	35.33	35.17	34.58	34.75	34.50	34.58	34.92	35.21
1761	34.58	34.42	34.33	34.33	33.92	33.75	33.92	34.00	34.17	34.58	35.75	35.00	34.40
1762	34.75	35.25	35.33	35.83	35.38	35.33	35.33	35.42	35.42	35.58	35.75	35.33	35.39
1763	35.00	35.00	34.92	34.75	34.58	35.25	35.00	34.75	34.11	35.42	35.83	36.17	35.06
1764	36.08	36.33	36.58	36.25	36.50	36.83	36.83	36.75	36.75	36.75	36.75	36.83	36.60
1765	36.58	36.67	36.50	36.33	36.50	36.33	35.83	36.00	35.67	35.50	35.33	35.42	36.06
1766	35.25	35.00	34.92	35.00	34.83	34.83	34.92	35.17	34.92	35.00	35.00	34.92	34.98
1767	34.83	35.08	34.83	34.92	34.75	34.75	34.75	34.92	34.92	34.92	35.00	35.00	34.89
1768	35.08	35.08	35.08	34.92	34.92	35.08	35.00	35.00	34.92	34.75	34.83	34.83	34.96
1769	34.75	34.75	34.67	34.67	34.58	34.58	34.75	34.50	34.25	34.25	34.33	34.25	34.53
1770	34.17	34.25	34.17	34.17	34.42	34.33	34.50	34.50	34.50	34.58	35.08	35.00	34.47
1771	35.00	34.83	34.92	35.00	34.75	34.75	34.33	34.33	34.42	34.33	34.33	34.33	34.61
1772	33.92	34.50	34.75	34.67	34.75	35.17	34.83	35.50	35.42	36.17	36.00	35.83	35.13
1773	36.08	35.33	35.75	35.83	35.92	35.92	35.92	36.00	36.00	36.00	36.25	36.33	35.94
1774	36.25	36.33	36.25	36.17	36.25	36.25	36.25	36.25	36.00	35.50	35.92	35.67	36.09
1775	35.58	35.75	35.75	35.58	35.58	35.58	35.67	35.75	35.67	35.58	35.58	35.50	35.63

Notes and Sources: **TABLE 2.9**

1698–1775: *The Course of the Exchange* (London), 1698–1775. See the discussion above in the initial section of this chapter and in n. 10.

TABLE 2.10. **The Course of the Exchange at Amsterdam**

On Cadiz	for grooten banco,	1 ducado de cambio of 375 maravedies
Copenhagen	100 rijksdaalders current,	for rigsdalers kurant
Hamburg	for stuivers banco,	1 thaler banco of 32 schilling-lubs
Lisbon	for grooten banco,	1 cruzado of 400 réis
London	for schellingen banco,	£1 sterling
Paris	for stuivers banco,	1 ecu of 60 sous tournois
Stockholm	100 rijksdaalders current,	for riksdalern

Hamburg

The course of the exchange between London and Hamburg is of more importance for this study in an indirect fashion than it is directly, since neither Hamburg nor any of the German states had colonies in the Western Hemisphere. Still, Hamburg was a major buyer of sugar from those countries that did own West Indian colonies, sugar that the city processed in one of the largest sugar-refining centers of Europe and that it exported northward and eastward to supply the needs of the Baltic Sea region. But Hamburg deserves inclusion here more because it was the center for exchange in the same Baltic area, a role in which it drew, of course, on its ancient Hanseatic connections. Hamburg occupied a place in European finance similar to that of Amsterdam, in that merchants and brokers in the city served as the intermediaries in exchange transactions between the Mediterranean, the Atlantic, and the Baltic.[54]

The analogy with Amsterdam extends further, for like Amsterdam and other European commercial centers, Hamburg's mercantile community was served by a bank (founded in 1619). "The Bank of Hamburg is reckon'd one of the best and richest, as well as one of the securest in Europe," commented an English writer early in the eighteenth century.[55] Just as at Amsterdam, Hamburg bank money (banco) was of somewhat greater value than current money, and for many

54. In this regard see Max[imilian] Neumann, *Geschichte des Wechsels im Hansagebiet bis zum 17. Jahrhundert*, in *Beilage heft zur Zeitschrift für das Gasammte Handelsrecht*, VII (Erlangen, 1863). See also K[arl] W. Pauli, "Über die frühere Bedeutung Lübecks als Wechselplatz des Norden," in Pauli's *Lübeckische Zustände im Mittelalter*, II (Lübeck, 1872), 98–171; Wilhelm Jesse, "Münzgeschichte der Hansestadte," *Hansische Geschichtsblätter*, XXXIII (1928), 78–109; and Jesse, "Hamburg Anteil am der deutschen Münz- und Geldgeschichte," *Zeitschrift des Vereins für Hamburgische Geschichte*, XXXVIII (1939), 117–144. For the record, one Baltic principality did try to establish a New World colony; the dukes of Courland expended considerable effort to settle the island of Tobago in the 17th century. See Edgar Anderson's definitive study *Senie kurzemnieki Amerikā un Tobāgo kolonizācija* ([Stockholm], 1970).

55. Hayes, *Negociator's Magazine*, 150. A useful introduction is J[ohann] G. Büsch, *La Banque de Hambourg rendue facile aux négocians de l'étranger* (Paris, [1801]). See also Heinrich Sieveking, "Die Hamburger Bank," in Van Dillen, ed., *Principal Public Banks*, 125–160. Important also is J[ohann] G. Büsch, *Ein*

of the same reasons. All foreign exchange was negotiated through the bank, and all exchange rates were quoted in bank money.[56] At the same time, business was carried on largely in current money, and the customary quotation of prices for many commodities was in current money.[57] The difference between the two, the agio, varied considerably during the eighteenth century, more so than at Amsterdam. At Hamburg, just as at Amsterdam, the rate quoted for the agio was the percentage of a sum in bank money by which it had to be increased to equal current money. An agio of 25 per-

cent indicated that 80 reichsthaler banco equaled 100 reichsthaler *courant*.[58]

Hamburg had two moneys of account, partly real, partly imaginary; both have to be understood, since exchange with some places used one money and with other places, the other money.[59] Hamburg shared one money of account with its near neighbor, the city of Lübeck; they both used marks-, schilling-, and pfennigen-Lübeck (abbreviated "lubs"). There were 12 pfennigen-lubs to one schilling-lubs and 16 schilling-lubs to one mark-lubs. The reichsthaler equaled three marks and was the unit in which accounts were kept. The second money of account owed its origin to the influence of the once all-important commercial center of Antwerp. Hamburg in the late eighteenth century still conducted much of its exchange in terms of the pfund-, schilling-, and grot-Flemish, or *vlamische* (abbreviated "vls."). There were 12 grote-vls. to one schilling-vls. and 20 schilling-vls. to one pfund-vls. Six schilling-lubs equaled one schilling-vls. Table 2.11 specifies some of the resulting interrelationships in a format typical of that found in eighteenth-century handbooks.[60] One must be sure to keep in mind that each of these moneys had both a bank value and a current value,[61] the difference between

---

Wort zu seiner Zeit über die Hamburgische Bank (Hamburg, [1790]), *passim*. This work was later reprinted in Büsch and C[hristoph] D. Ebeling, eds., *Handlungsbibliothek* (Hamburg, 1785–1797), III, 450–494, and in Büsch, *Sämtliche Schriften über Banken und Münzwesen*, [ed. Ebeling], 251–298.

56. "Those who deal only in exchange keep their accompts in bank money, and those that deal in any other commerce keep them in current money." [Justice], *General Treatise of Monies*, 2d pagination, 238. Ricard, *Traité général du commerce*, [ed. Marien], II, 131, seems to be saying that exchange with Leipzig was in current money, but that is a mistake. Cf. Kruse, *Hamburgischer Contorist*, 3d ed. (1766), I, 180.

57. One private Hamburg price current included this key to abbreviations used: "Prys van all Goederen is Courant-Gelt. B beduyt Banco." *Prys-Courant*, Hamburg, 18 Sept. 1696 (copy in Matthias Giesque and Co. Papers, bundle no. 68, C. 104/128, pt. 2, Unknown Cause, P.R.O.). This is one of the several subjects discussed in the detailed contemporary analysis of the Hamburg price currents by P[aul] J. M[arperger], *Erlaüterung der Hamburger und Amsterdamer warren-preiss-couranten* ([Dresden], ca. 1725), 4–20. For this work see Lehman, "Paul Jacob Marperger," *Jahrbuch für Wirtschaftsgeschichte*, [XI] (1971), 153–157 (no. 85). Ernest Baasch, "Geschichte des hamburgischen Waren-Preiskourant," in Baasch, *Forschungen zur hamburgischen Handelsgeschichte*, III (Hamburg, 1902), 141, made this distinction: "Die meisten und wichtigsten Waren wurden in Banko notiert; in Kourant notiert wurden von wichtigeren Artikeln z.B. Tabak und Thee." See also *ibid.*, 141–147, where he discusses the adoption, as of 20 Feb. 1787, of a uniform quotation of all prices in bank money.

58. Hayes, *Negociator's Magazine*, 155; Leman Thomas Rede, *The Laws of Hamburg respecting Bills of Exchange Translated into English with Notes Shewing the Laws of England upon the Same Subject* (Hamburg, 1805), 74. See also [Justice], *General Treatise of Monies*, 238; M[arperger], *Erlaüterung der Hamburger preiss-couranten*, 2, 27; Büsch, *La Banque de Hambourg*, 51, 54.

59. See note 56 above.

60. See, e.g., Ricard, *Traité général du commerce*, [ed. Marien], II, 126. See also Joachim Rademann, *Joachim Rademanns Hamburgisches wechselbaum* (Hamburg, 1717); Büsch, *La Banque de Hambourg*, 91.

61. "Toutes ces monnoies ont dans le commerce deux valeurs, dont l'une se nomme argent de banque; l'autre est l'argent courant." Ricard, *Traité général du commerce*, [ed. Marien], II, 126.

TABLE 2.11. **Moneys of Account of Hamburg: Their Denominations and Their Relationships**

Pfund	Reichs-thaler	Thaler	Mark	Schilling-vls.	Schilling-lubs	Grot	Pfennig
1	2½	3¾	7½	20	120	240	1,440
	1	1½	3	8	48	96	576
		1	2	5⅓	32	64	384
			1	2⅔	16	32	192
				1	6	12	72
					1	2	12
						1	6

them being the agio. Table 2.12 gives monthly figures for the agio at Hamburg, their source being the *Geld-Cours in Hamburg* published there from the beginning of 1687.[62]

62. This twice-weekly publication and its companion, the *Wechsel-Cours in Hamburg*, are the earliest surviving financial journals. Kruse, *Hamburgischer Contorist*, 3d ed. (1766), I, 467, states that the *Wechsel-Cours* first appeared in 1659 and the *Geld-Cours* in 1687. If so, then the set of the latter in the library of the Staatsarchiv, Hamburg, is virtually complete, since it begins with the number for 14 Jan. 1687 and lacks only the years 1726 and 1769–1770. Its original publisher, Herman Hermanssen, is also the publisher of the earliest copies I have seen of the *Wechsel-Cours* in the set for 1710 to 1724 in the Commerzbibliothek, Handelskammer, Hamburg. (There is a stray volume for 1726 in the Staatsarchiv.) Successive members of the de Vlieger family first collaborated with and later took over from Hermanssen. Both journals were distributed as printed forms in which the date and the figures were inserted by hand in pen and ink, although by the 1790s some, at least, were completely printed. See the three dozen numbers of each for May–July 1798 in Map Drawer 2⁴, John Carter Brown Library, Brown University, Providence, R.I. The titles of both changed over time. The *Wechsel-Cours in Hamburg* was called the *Wexsel-Cours zu Hamburg* at least until 1724; the *Geld-Cours in Hamburg* began as the *Preis folgen der Gelder*, changed to the *Cours der Gelder in Hamburg* in 1713, and became the *Geld-Cours* in 1760. Both continued to be published into the 19th century. Astrid Friis and Kristof Glamann, *A History of Prices and Wages in Denmark, 1660–1800* (London, 1958), 30, locate a series of both for 1692 to 1698 in Rentekammert, Rev. Rgsk., Hamborgske Faktorregnskaber, 1692–1698, Rigsarkivet, Copenhagen, and another series of the *Cours der Gelder in Hamburg*, for 1732 to 1754, in Kurantbanken, Tabeller over Kursnoteringen, 1727–1781, Rigsarkivet.

The eight members of the *Prys-Courant, Hamburg*, for 1696–1698 in the Giesque Papers (see n. 57, above) do not seem explicitly to have relied on Hermanssen for either their money or exchange data (nor do they quote the agio) but the later, official price current simply reprinted every Friday the latest figures from the *Geld-Cours* and the *Wechsel-Cours*. See the run of the *Preis Courant der Wahren in Partheijen* (Hamburg) in the Commerzbibliothek. It is said to have begun publication on 24 Feb. 1736, the date of the first dated number in that set. Baasch, "Geschichte des hamburgischen Waren-Preiskourant," in Baasch, *Forschungen zur hamburgischen Handelsgeschichte*, III, 131. (Baasch was the librarian of the Commerzbibliothek.) But that number is preceded in the set by another, undated one, and there is still an earlier copy for 10 Feb. 1736 in Akten Senat, Cl. VII, Lit. Ka., Nr. 8, Vol. 1, Fasc. 2, nr. 10, Staatsarchiv. Kruse, *Hamburgischer Contorist*, 3d ed. (1766), I, 175–179, reprinted and explained the issue for 31 Jan. 1766. I am indebted to Jacob M.

The exchange between London and Hamburg was quoted at a varying number of schilling- and grote-vls. banco per £1 sterling. The par of exchange during most of our period was 35 schilling and 6²/₃ grote per £1 sterling, and the exchange, as tables 2.13, 2.14, 2.15, and 2.16 indicate, regularly ran below par. Richard Hayes again provides us with an example of the calculation of an exchange transaction. For Hamburg he postulates a London remittance of £742.92 to Hamburg at 33 schilling- and 4 grote-vls. banco and finds that London must purchase 9,286 marks- and 9 schilling-lubs banco.[63]

Recall once again the meaning of banco; 9,286 marks bank money, at an agio of, say, 16 percent, would be the equivalent of roughly 11,000 marks current money. The exchange between other mercantile cities worked on different bases, for which see table 2.17.[64] Finally, for the more important silver and gold coins of Hamburg, the reader should consult tables 1.1 and 1.2.

Price for the loan of his microfilm of the *Preis Courant*. For Hamburg price currents in general, see Marperger, *Erlaüterung der Hamburger und Amsterdamer warren-preiss-couranten*; Richard Ehrenberg, "Ein Hamburgischer Waren- und Wechsel-Preiscourant aus dem XVI. Jahrhundert," *Hansische Geschichtsblätter*, XIII (1883), 165–170; and the Baasch essay cited above. The three price currents (for 10 Nov. 1693, 9 Mar. 1702, and 16 Dec. 1712) that Baasch (*ibid.*, 124) located in the Commerzbibliothek are there no longer. Finally, there are two copies of what appears to have been an English translation of selected parts of the official price current entitled *State of the Hamburg Market for Importations from America* ([Hamburg?]), dated 5 July 1793 and 6 June 1797, in MD 2⁴, John Carter Brown Library.

63. Hayes, *Negociator's Magazine*, 56–57. Computation: £742.925 times 33¹/₃ equals 24,764.2 schilling-vls.; with 1 schilling-vls. equal to 6 schilling-lubs, this is the equivalent of 148,585 schillings-lubs, or 9,286 marks and 9 schillings-lubs. And 9,286 marks banco multiplied by 1.16 equals 10,772 marks current money.

64. See also Guillaume Du Hamel, *Hamburger Wechsel-Cours oder Ausrechnung derr Wechsell auf Frankreich, Holland, Engelland, Spanien, Portugal, Venedig* . . . (Hamburg, 1685).

The information in table 2.17, the exchange rates in tables 2.13, 2.14, 2.15, and 2.16, and a reference or series of references to the exchange on Hamburg for any of the ports in this table will allow someone to compute the exchange on London with that port. As an example, see the Hamburg-Stockholm exchange rate series (1668–1815) in Heckscher, "Bank of Sweden," in Van Dillen, ed., *Principal Public Banks*, 194–199; and (1740–1803) in Karl Åmark, *Spannmålshandel och spannmålspolitik i Sverige, 1719–1830* (Stockholm, 1915), 364. Åmark's series is reprinted in Lennart Jörberg, *A History of Prices in Sweden, 1732–1914* (Lund, 1972), I, 84. See also [Johann Georg Canzler], *Mémoires pour servir à la connoissance des affaires politiques et économiques du Royaume de Suède, jusqu'à la fin de la 1775me année* (London, 1776), II, table XLII (A). Posthumus, *Prices in Holland*, I, 592–593, has Amsterdam-Stockholm exchange rate quotations for 1664 to 1672.

TABLE 2.12. **Agio on Hamburg Bank Money, 1672–1775**

(Percentage Premium on Bank Money for Current Money)

Year	Jan.	Feb.	Mar.	Apr.	May	June	July	Aug.	Sept.	Oct.	Nov.	Dec.	Average
1672											7.12		7.12
1687	10.25	10.69	*10.75*	10.75	*10.62*	10.56	10.50	10.12	9.75	9.50	9.00	10.00	10.21
1688	10.00	10.12	10.19	*10.16*	10.25	10.19	10.00	9.75	9.50	9.00	9.44	10.00	9.88
1689	10.00	10.62	10.75	10.75	10.69	10.12	9.50	9.50	9.62	9.69	9.50	10.75	10.12
1690	10.62	11.00	10.75	11.00	11.00	11.00	11.12	11.12	10.94	10.56	10.56	11.00	10.89
1691	11.00	11.31	11.06	11.00	11.00	11.00	11.00	10.75	10.06	10.00	9.94	10.62	10.73
1692	10.12	10.00	10.25	10.42	*10.25*	10.25	10.25	9.88	9.81	9.12	9.75	9.71	9.98
1693	9.50	9.58	9.50	9.62	9.62	9.56	9.88	9.62	9.21	8.94	9.38	10.75	9.60
1694	10.69	10.69	10.81	10.81	10.88	11.25	11.38	11.00	11.00	11.19	11.75	11.62	11.09
1695	11.88	12.25	12.00	12.44	12.31	12.44	12.44	12.50	12.44	12.56	14.12	14.62	12.67
1696	14.81	14.12	13.94	14.00	14.12	13.88	13.62	13.75	13.81	14.69	14.94	15.81	14.29
1697	14.81	15.00	14.00	13.81	13.00	*13.31*	13.62	13.75	13.19	14.04	14.19	15.06	13.98
1698	14.19	13.88	13.50	13.56	14.06	13.75	13.12	13.62	13.44	13.62	13.88	14.25	13.74
1699	13.62	13.50	13.62	13.54	13.62	13.50	13.62	13.12	13.25	12.96	14.06	14.44	13.57
1700	14.38	14.38	14.38	14.06	14.06	14.38	14.50	14.21	14.06	14.12	14.25	14.62	14.28
1701	14.56	14.38	14.38	14.06	*13.97*	12.94	12.25	12.69	12.44	12.44	12.62	14.00	13.39
1702	13.75	13.12	13.00	12.75	13.50	12.71	13.00	13.00	13.00	13.88	13.96	14.38	13.34
1703	14.38	14.12	14.12	14.12	14.62	14.88	15.50	15.12	15.04	16.38	16.25	16.71	15.10
1704	16.50	16.21	16.06	16.00	16.25	16.88	17.04	17.38	17.88	18.12	18.38	19.38	17.17
1705	19.19	17.69	17.56	17.62	19.12	18.88	19.00	19.19	19.12	19.31	19.31	19.62	18.80
1706	19.19	18.38	18.38	18.44	18.12	17.62	17.88	18.12	18.12	18.12	17.79	18.69	18.24
1707	17.69	17.62	17.38	17.12	17.54	17.75	17.62	17.38	17.29	17.67	17.75	17.88	17.56
1708	17.81	17.62	17.38	17.38	*16.99*	16.62	16.69	17.25	16.62	16.00	16.12	16.88	16.95
1709	16.69	16.88	16.88	16.88	16.88	16.88	16.94	17.19	17.19	15.88	16.38	16.75	16.78

TABLE 2.12 (Continued): Hamburg Agio (Percentage Premium for Current Money)

Year	Jan.	Feb.	Mar.	Apr.	May	June	July	Aug.	Sept.	Oct.	Nov.	Dec.	Average
1710	16.88	16.88	16.88	16.12	16.79	16.69	16.62	17.00	16.75	16.62	16.62	16.88	16.73
1711	16.75	16.75	17.00	16.62	16.75	16.62	16.62	16.69	16.88	16.62	16.62	16.62	16.71
1712	16.62	16.75	16.62	16.62	*16.62*	16.75	16.88	16.88	16.62	15.19	16.00	16.88	16.54
1713	16.88	16.81	16.75	16.75	17.06	17.25	17.44	18.00	17.38	17.44	17.81	17.75	17.28
1714	17.81	18.00	18.06	18.06	18.19	18.12	18.38	18.38	18.56	18.62	18.31	18.81	18.28
1715	18.81	18.69	18.88	18.88	19.09	19.25	19.88	19.92	20.71	20.69	20.75	20.81	19.70
1716	20.46	20.54	20.88	20.88	21.38	21.56	21.54	21.50	20.06	20.50	20.44	21.00	20.90
1717	21.50	21.88	23.25	23.69	24.00	25.38	26.12	26.25	26.12	26.12	26.00	26.31	24.72
1718	26.19	26.50	26.31	26.44	26.56	27.56	28.56	28.69	28.94	28.94	28.88	29.25	27.74
1719	29.19	29.31	29.31	29.12	29.81	30.50	30.62	30.75	29.50	29.75	28.81	29.75	29.70
1720	29.38	29.12	29.25	29.44	28.12	28.25	28.69	27.69	27.81	26.56	27.56	28.06	28.33
1721	27.94	27.50	28.00	28.12	28.31	29.44	29.50	29.44	29.44	29.31	29.50	29.62	28.84
1722	29.56	29.19	29.56	29.38	29.25	29.69	29.69	29.75	29.44	29.62	29.44	29.81	29.53
1723	29.62	30.50	30.50	30.12	30.38	30.31	30.31	30.44	30.44	30.31	30.44	30.88	30.35
1724	30.88	31.25	31.44	31.25	31.88	32.12	30.00	31.25	31.38	31.75	31.31	*31.66*	31.35
1725	*32.00*	32.50	*33.50*	*33.88*	33.75								33.24
1726												[16.00]	16.00
1727	16.00	16.00	16.00	16.00	16.00	16.00	16.00	16.00	16.00	16.00	16.00	16.00	16.00
1728	16.00	16.00	16.00	16.00	16.00	16.00	16.00	16.00	16.00	16.00	16.00	16.00	16.00
1729	16.00	16.00	16.00	16.00	16.00	16.00	16.00	16.00	16.00	16.00	16.00	16.00	16.00
1730	16.00	16.00	16.00	16.00	16.00	16.00	16.00	16.00	16.00	16.00	16.00	16.00	16.00
1731	16.00	16.00	16.00	16.00	16.00	16.00	16.00	16.00	16.00	16.00	16.00	16.00	16.00
1732	16.00	16.00	16.00	16.00	16.00	16.00	16.00	16.00	16.00	16.00	16.00	16.00	16.00
1733	16.00	16.00	16.00	16.00	16.00	16.00	16.00	16.00	16.00	16.00	16.00	16.00	16.00
1734	16.00	16.00	16.00	16.00	16.00	16.00	16.00	16.00	16.00	16.00	16.00	16.00	16.00
1735	16.00	16.00	16.00	16.00	16.00	16.00	16.00	16.00	16.00	16.00	16.00	16.00	16.00
1736	16.00	16.00	16.00	16.00	16.00	16.00	16.00	16.00	16.00	16.00	16.00	16.00	16.00
1737	16.00	16.00	16.00	16.00	16.00	16.00	16.00	16.00	16.00	16.00	16.00	16.00	16.00

TABLE 2.12 (Continued): Hamburg Agio (Percentage Premium for Current Money)

Year	Jan.	Feb.	Mar.	Apr.	May	June	July	Aug.	Sept.	Oct.	Nov.	Dec.	Average
1738	16.00	16.12	16.19	16.25	16.25	16.50	16.29	16.38	16.50	16.31	16.31	16.62	16.31
1739	16.75	17.00	17.00	17.75	17.75	17.50	17.50	17.75	17.75	17.75	17.50	17.75	17.48
1740	17.75	18.00	18.00	18.00	18.00	18.00	18.00	18.25	18.50	18.50	17.62	17.75	18.03
1741	17.75	18.00	17.88	17.88	17.50	17.88	17.88	17.62	17.12	17.00	16.50	16.88	17.49
1742	16.75	17.50	17.50	17.75	17.75	18.00	18.00	18.00	18.00	18.00	18.00	18.25	17.79
1743	18.50	18.50	18.50	18.75	18.62	18.75	19.25	19.12	19.12	19.00	19.00	19.12	18.85
1744	19.00	19.25	19.25	19.25	19.38	19.50	19.50	19.50	19.50	19.44	19.12	19.75	19.37
1745	19.75	20.00	20.25	20.25	20.25	20.50	20.75	20.75	20.25	18.50	18.81	20.00	20.00
1746	20.25	19.75	20.25	20.00	19.25	19.00	18.75	18.00	17.38	17.00	16.50	17.88	18.67
1747	17.00	17.12	17.00	17.25	16.50	16.75	16.75	15.75	15.75	15.50	15.75	16.88	16.50
1748	16.00	16.88	16.62	16.62	16.00	15.88	16.25	16.00	15.50	15.75	15.75	16.75	16.17
1749	16.62	17.38	17.38	17.38	17.12	17.38	17.00	17.00	17.00	16.00	16.38	18.00	17.05
1750	17.50	17.75	17.88	17.38	17.38	17.50	17.25	17.25	17.38	17.12	17.50	18.25	17.51
1751	17.88	18.50	18.00	18.00	17.50	17.62	18.12	17.62	17.62	17.88	16.62	16.75	17.68
1752	15.88	16.50	16.38	16.00	16.12	16.62	16.62	16.62	16.50	16.25	16.38	17.38	16.44
1753	17.25	17.62	17.50	17.62	17.38	17.25	17.38	17.50	17.00	17.00	17.25	17.38	17.34
1754	17.12	17.50	17.50	17.50	17.12	17.00	17.38	17.25	17.25	17.00	17.12	17.12	17.24
1755	17.25	17.50	17.50	17.50	17.38	17.62	17.75	17.69	17.62	17.38	17.50	18.00	17.56
1756	18.00	18.25	18.00	*18.00*	18.00	17.75	17.75	17.62	17.25	16.50	16.00	15.88	17.42
1757	15.25	15.75	15.00	13.88	12.12	9.88	12.38	10.88	10.62	8.00	8.75	7.88	11.70
1758	7.75	7.56	6.56	7.62	6.88	7.75	7.50	7.88	8.00	8.00	8.12	8.50	7.68
1759	8.38	8.69	8.62	*8.06*	6.88	6.25	6.50	8.00	9.00	7.94	8.12	9.75	8.02
1760	9.12	9.75	11.62	12.38	15.00	18.00	20.50	26.25	24.00	24.94	26.00	25.38	18.58
1761	25.12	24.00	23.75	24.25	24.75	25.50	25.12	25.00	25.00	24.50	25.75	25.25	24.83
1762	24.81	25.00	25.00	23.50	22.00	22.75	22.50	21.50	21.25	19.38	19.00	22.00	22.39
1763	22.00	22.75	23.12	23.00	22.88	23.25	23.50	24.50	25.00	25.25	25.38	25.62	23.85
1764	25.56	26.38	26.38	26.62	26.25	26.38	26.50	26.19	26.12	25.62	26.06	26.50	26.21

TABLE 2.12 (Continued): Hamburg Agio (Percentage Premium for Current Money)

Year	Jan.	Feb.	Mar.	Apr.	May	June	July	Aug.	Sept.	Oct.	Nov.	Dec.	Average
1765	25.88	*21.88*	*21.25*	22.12	20.25	21.12	20.62	21.00	21.00	19.81	20.56	21.75	21.44
1766	20.88	21.00	20.88	20.75	19.50	20.38	19.88	19.88	19.31	18.88	19.00	18.25	19.88
1767	18.25	18.50	18.50	18.12	17.25	17.00	*16.90*	*16.83*	16.75	17.00	*17.96*	*19.57*	17.72
1768	*20.86*	21.50	21.50	21.50	20.75	21.50	21.50	22.00	22.50	22.50	25.88	26.25	22.35
1769	26.50	27.25	25.00	24.50	23.75	24.75	25.00	24.00	23.75	22.75	23.50	24.50	24.60
1770	24.25	24.50	24.50	24.25	23.50	24.50	24.50	24.50	24.12	24.25	24.12	24.12	24.26
1771	24.25	24.88	24.88	24.62	24.00	24.62	24.50	24.75	25.12	24.62	24.50	25.00	24.64
1772	25.25	25.50	25.50	25.75	25.25	25.50	25.50	25.25	24.75	24.25	24.25	24.25	25.08
1773	24.25	25.50	25.50	25.50	25.50	24.75	24.75	24.50	24.88	23.88	23.25	24.25	24.71
1774	24.50	25.00	25.00	24.25	24.25	24.25	24.00	24.00	24.00	23.00	22.75	21.50	23.88
1775	23.25	23.00	23.50	22.62	22.00	20.75	20.75	21.25	21.50	21.00	21.50	21.50	21.88

Notes and Sources: **TABLE 2.12**

Figures inserted in square brackets are assigned to that month arbitrarily; figures printed in italics are straight-line interpolations based on the two neighboring quotations.

1672: Heinrich Sieveking, "Die Hamburger Bank," in J. G. van Dillen, ed., *History of the Principal Public Banks* (The Hague, 1934), 129.

1687–1775: *Geld-Cours in Hamburg*, 1687–1775. Title varies; see chap. 2, n. 62. I used the set in the library of the Staatsarchiv, Hamburg, which lacks the volumes for 1726, 1769, and 1770. There is a set for the years 1710 to 1724 in the Commerzbibliothek, Handelskammer, Hamburg. From 1736 on the most recent quotation of the agio in the *Geld-Cours* was reprinted every Friday in the *Preis Courant der Wahren in Partheijen* (Hamburg), which also survives in the Commerzbibliothek. See as well the mid-June and mid-December rates in J[ulius W.] Wilcke, *Kurantmønten, 1726–1781* (Copenhagen, 1927), [354–357], printed from Kurlister bilagte Plønske Kammerkasseregenskaber, 1732–1755, and Kurantbanken, Tabeller over Kursnoteringen, 1727–1781, Rigsarkivet, Copenhagen. Given here is the agio for the date closest to the 15th of each month. The gap in the series for 1725 and 1726 is largely the result of the monetary crisis in Hamburg which was resolved by the edict of 15 August 1726 that set the agio by law at 16 percent. See Joh[ann] Christoph Öhlers, *Cambio-Commune oder gantz accurate Müntz-Vergleich und Agio-Rechnung aller in dem Hamburgischen Münz-Edict vom 15ten Aug. Anno 1726 benannten . . .* (Hamburg, 1728), *passim*. The figure here supplied for December 1726 is based upon the expectation that the effect of that edict—so noticeable for the years 1727 and after—had actually begun by December 1726.

TABLE 2.13. **Rate of Exchange: London on Hamburg (via Amsterdam), 1609–1694**
(Schilling-vls. Banco per £1 Sterling)

Year	Jan.	Feb.	Mar.	Apr.	May	June	July	Aug.	Sept.	Oct.	Nov.	Dec.	Average
1609											26.73		26.73
1610													
1611													
1612													
1613													
1614													
1615													
1616													
1617													
1618													
1619								30.27					30.27
1620													
1621													
1622													
1623													
1624		35.47			35.87	35.84		34.83	35.22	34.93		35.22	35.36
1625		35.35	35.53			35.42	35.42	35.30	36.29	35.19		35.32	35.45
1626	35.18	35.05	35.12				34.41	34.47		34.57	34.33	34.42	34.67
1627													
1628									34.56				34.56
1629													
1630	35.29				35.77						35.68		35.58
1631	35.03			34.43	34.42	34.71	34.40	35.04				35.23	34.88
1632		35.46		34.42		35.86	35.70						35.43
1633		35.49	35.77	35.76	35.86								35.72
1634		36.08											36.08

TABLE 2.13 (Continued): London on Hamburg (Schilling-vls. Banco per £1 Sterling)

Year	Jan.	Feb.	Mar.	Apr.	May	June	July	Aug.	Sept.	Oct.	Nov.	Dec.	Average
1635					36.13	34.76	34.77						35.11
1636			34.15	34.79	32.64							35.07	34.31
1637			35.34		35.52								35.43
1638						34.38						34.51	34.44
1639													
1640									35.98				35.98
1641					37.64						36.80		37.22
1642					36.69		37.22	36.89	37.14				36.89
1643						38.10		36.54	36.43				37.29
1644													
1645	37.71	37.73					36.93	36.93		37.39			37.35
1646	37.02	36.88	*36.96*	37.05	36.89	*36.70*	36.52	36.56	36.15	36.06	36.01	35.56	36.53
1647													
1648								32.48	31.31	32.18	32.56		32.13
1649					30.69	30.53	31.60	31.52	31.18	32.12	31.40	31.26	31.21
1650	31.73	31.92	32.08	32.38	30.96								31.79
1651											35.87		35.87
1652								32.63		35.06			33.84
1653											35.02	34.97	35.00
1654	34.39	35.14	35.22	35.14	34.94								34.98
1655													
1656													
1657													
1658													
1659													
1660													
1661													

TABLE 2.13 (Continued): **London on Hamburg** (Schilling-vls. Banco per £1 Sterling)

Year	Jan.	Feb.	Mar.	Apr.	May	June	July	Aug.	Sept.	Oct.	Nov.	Dec.	Average
1662													
1663													
1664												34.01	34.01
1665										32.62			32.62
1666													
1667													
1668													
1669		35.23	35.28	34.88					34.92	35.07	35.01		35.02
1670													
1671				34.86	35.00								34.93
1672		34.63	35.17		33.28								34.09
1673													
1674						31.19	31.30	31.77	32.55	32.21	31.73		31.68
1675										32.76			32.76
1676				33.52						34.80			34.16
1677	34.80	34.61	34.65	34.88			34.99						34.85
1678	34.29												34.29
1679		34.09										34.71	34.40
1680				34.78	34.62								34.70
1681											34.61		34.61
1682	34.65			34.58									34.62
1683											33.70		33.70
1684													
1685							34.34						34.34
1686	34.17	34.89											34.53
1687		34.67											34.67
1688	34.15												34.15
1689													

TABLE 2.13 (Continued): London on Hamburg (Schilling-vls. Banco per £1 Sterling)

Year	Jan.	Feb.	Mar.	Apr.	May	June	July	Aug.	Sept.	Oct.	Nov.	Dec.	Average
1690													
1691											32.63		32.63
1692						32.51							32.51
1693		32.01		31.55	31.79		31.33	31.58	31.06				31.67
1694	30.30	30.60					30.91	30.70	30.66		30.65	30.65	30.62

Notes and Sources: **TABLE 2.13**

Figures printed in italics are straight-line interpolations based on the two neighboring quotations.

1609–1694: N. W. Posthumus, *Inquiry into the History of Prices in Holland* (Leiden, 1946–1964), I, 593–595.

1631–1633: *Corso in Amsterd[am] di piusorte mercanti* ([Amsterdam]), 22 Dec. 1631, 26 Apr. 1632, and 18 Apr. 1633 (see notes to table 2.7, above).

The computation involved converting the London-Amsterdam exchange rate from schellingen and grooten banco per £1 sterling into stuivers banco and then establishing the ratio between that figure and the figure for the same date for the Hamburg-Amsterdam rate expressed in stuivers banco per thaler banco of 32 schilling-lubs. The ratio of thaler per £1 sterling was then converted to schilling-vls. banco by multiplying it by $5^{1}/_{3}$. As an example, on 23 Nov. 1609, the London-Amsterdam rate was 34 schellingen and 8 grooten per £1 sterling, or 208 stuivers; the Hamburg-Amsterdam rate was 41.5 stuivers per thaler; the former divided by the latter indicated that 5.012 thaler, or 26.7304 schilling-vls., equaled £1 sterling. A shortcut to this procedure involves expressing the London rate in schellingen as a decimal (34.667), multiplying it by 32, and dividing the product by the Hamburg rate similarly decimalized (41.5). The London-Hamburg rate for Nov. 1609 is given above as 26.73 schilling-vls. per £1 sterling.

TABLE 2.14. Rate of Exchange: Hamburg on London, 1657–1698

(Schilling-vls. Banco per £1 Sterling)

Year	Jan.	Feb.	Mar.	Apr.	May	June	July	Aug.	Sept.	Oct.	Nov.	Dec.	Average
1657											32.50		32.50
1658											32.50	32.83	32.66
1659	*32.83*	32.83	33.08	33.04	33.08	33.44	34.08	34.17	34.86	35.14	35.38	35.81	33.98
1660	35.77	36.25	36.44	36.50	36.65	36.66	36.87						36.54
1661					36.75								36.75
1662													
1663							35.69	35.70	35.79	35.75	35.79	35.50	35.70
1664	35.21	*35.34*	35.46	35.21	34.92	34.62	*34.69*	34.76	34.83	34.67	34.75	34.08	34.88
1665	33.29	33.61	33.46	33.25	33.42						33.75		33.51
1666		32.50	32.72	32.79	32.36	31.29	31.54	31.83			31.67		32.03
1667		33.58		33.83		33.00	34.44	34.79	34.71				33.88
1668			34.12	33.71	33.82	34.03			34.50	34.62			34.27
1669	34.71	34.71	34.67			34.67		34.54			34.88	34.38	34.63
1670		34.83											34.83
1671					34.29								34.29
1672													
1673													
1674	31.00	31.00		31.58			30.83						31.14
1675								32.42	33.25	32.50		33.63	32.95
1676	33.17	*33.21*	33.25	33.33	33.81	33.88	*34.10*	34.33	34.27	34.25	*34.75*	35.25	33.97
1677	34.33	34.67											34.50
1678	34.92												34.92
1679													
1680													
1681													
1682													

TABLE 2.14 (Continued): Hamburg on London (Schilling-vls. Banco per £1 Sterling)

Year	Jan.	Feb.	Mar.	Apr.	May	June	July	Aug.	Sept.	Oct.	Nov.	Dec.	Average
1683													
1684													
1685													
1686													
1687													
1688													
1689	33.50			33.14			32.75		32.92	32.67	32.50		33.02
1690				32.58							32.42		32.50
1691		32.33	32.46	32.62									32.51
1692													
1693													
1694			32.29										32.29
1695													
1696		28.12			28.62	28.12		31.50	33.54				29.67
1697		34.62							34.21				34.42
1698					33.96								33.96

Notes and Sources: **TABLE 2.14**

Figures printed in italics are straight-line interpolations based on the two neighboring quotations.

1657–1678: William Atwood Papers, C. 109/23–24: *Atwood* v. *Hare*, Public Record Office.

1689–1694: Correspondence and Business Papers of Thomas Brailsford, 1687–1698, C. 110/152: *Brailsford* v. *Peers*.

1696–1698: *Prys-Courant, Hamburg*, 28 Feb., 15 May, 5 June, 14 Aug., and 18 Sept. 1696, 5 Mar. and 22 Oct. 1697, and 6 May 1698, copies in Matthias Giesque and Co. Papers, bundle no. 68, in C. 104/128, pt. 2, Unknown Cause.

TABLE 2.15. **Rate of Exchange: London on Hamburg, 1667–1697**
(Schilling-vls. Banco per £1 Sterling)

Year	Jan.	Feb.	Mar.	Apr.	May	June	July	Aug.	Sept.	Oct.	Nov.	Dec.	Average
1667							34.00						34.00
1668			35.42							35.50	35.50	35.25	35.42
1669			35.33	35.33	35.50	35.33	35.17	35.25	35.58	35.25	35.58	35.50	35.37
1670													
1671											35.33		35.33
1672	35.33	35.46	34.83		34.33				34.17		34.33	34.38	34.52
1673		34.08						32.92			32.50	32.42	33.15
1674	32.00		32.75			32.83	31.75					32.67	32.41
1675	32.29	32.42	32.88	33.08				33.08			33.75	34.75	33.24
1676													
1677													
1678													
1679			32.75										32.75
1680		35.00										35.17	35.08
1681					35.58		35.25			35.42	35.08		35.36
1682			35.21			34.96				34.50			34.89
1683	34.71	34.58			34.83			34.29		34.42			34.55
1684												34.42	34.42
1685									35.00		34.88	34.92	34.95
1686													
1687.													
1688													
1689						33.50							33.50

TABLE 2.15 (Continued): London on Hamburg (Schilling-vls. Banco per £1 Sterling)

Year	Jan.	Feb.	Mar.	Apr.	May	June	July	Aug.	Sept.	Oct.	Nov.	Dec.	Average
1690													
1691	32.75									33.00			32.88
1692	33.33												33.33
1693			32.00										32.00
1694									31.08		31.08		31.08
1695	32.00	30.67	30.42	30.08	29.92	28.33	28.08	25.83	27.33	27.17	26.33	29.17	28.78
1696	29.75	28.62	28.00	28.33	29.08	28.83	28.12	27.50	34.00	35.67	36.67	36.67	30.94
1697	35.17	35.33	35.83	35.92	35.75	37.17	34.83	35.25	35.17	34.92	35.42	35.17	35.49

Notes and Sources: **TABLE 2.15**

1667–1697: London price currents as listed in Appendix 2, below.

1681: Marion Balderston, ed., *James Claypoole's Letter Book, London and Philadelphia, 1681–1684* (San Marino, Calif., 1967), 65.

1695–1697: *A Collection for Improvement of Husbandry and Trade*, 18 Jan. 1694/95–31 Dec. 1697 (the figure nearest the middle of the month).

TABLE 2.16. **Rate of Exchange: London on Hamburg, 1698–1775**

(Schilling-vls. Banco per £1 Sterling)

Year	Jan.	Feb.	Mar.	Apr.	May	June	July	Aug.	Sept.	Oct.	Nov.	Dec.	Average
1698	35.04	34.83	34.83	34.71	34.25	34.33	34.17	34.04	34.21	34.21	34.25	34.04	34.41
1699	33.96	33.96	33.92	33.96	34.00	33.92	34.04	34.12	34.00	33.92	33.83	34.08	33.98
1700	34.08	34.04	34.17	34.42	34.67	34.50	34.46	34.46	34.33	34.46	34.46	34.50	34.38
1701	34.38	35.50	35.62	35.46	35.50	35.17	35.33	35.33	35.54	35.29	35.12	35.38	35.30
1702	35.21	34.58	34.46	34.62	34.67	34.25	34.00	33.71	33.58	33.42	33.25	33.25	34.08
1703	32.83	32.71	32.50	32.50	32.58	32.58	32.42	32.29	32.42	32.42	32.58	32.75	32.55
1704	32.50	32.58	32.62	32.62	32.58	32.62	32.33	32.33	32.88	32.96	32.62	32.79	32.62
1705	32.96	32.42	32.96	32.50	32.50	32.58	32.62	32.62	32.71	32.92	33.12	33.25	32.76
1706	33.08	33.54	33.12	32.88	33.21	33.12	33.33	33.58	33.58	33.96	34.17	34.46	33.50
1707	33.75	34.00	33.83	33.75	33.92	33.58	33.67	33.62	33.33	33.46	33.58	33.58	33.67
1708	33.21	33.08	34.00	33.67	33.67	33.50	33.38	33.17	33.29	33.67	33.54	33.54	33.48
1709	33.33	33.38	33.25	33.12	32.67	32.58	32.42	32.38	32.50	32.50	32.62	32.38	32.76
1710	32.71	32.50	32.58	32.50	32.50	32.12	32.21	32.21	32.12	32.62	34.08	34.21	32.70
1711	33.62	33.17	33.25	33.38	33.08	32.83	32.75	32.83	33.62	33.58	33.67	33.92	33.31
1712	33.12	33.00	33.25	32.50	32.88	32.96	32.67	32.96	33.50	33.83	33.96	34.08	33.23
1713	34.25	34.08	34.21	34.71	34.46	34.54	34.33	34.21	34.46	34.50	34.54	34.67	34.41
1714	34.58	35.08	34.96	35.00	34.75	34.62	34.33	34.50	34.79	35.04	35.12	35.17	34.83
1715	35.04	35.08	35.04	34.96	35.17	34.88	34.46	34.75	34.96	35.21	35.88	35.92	35.11
1716	34.67	34.42	34.46	34.50	34.62	34.50	34.50	34.38	34.50	34.58	34.33	34.08	34.46
1717	33.75	34.04	34.08	34.04	33.96	33.83	33.83	33.83	33.75	33.75	33.42	33.42	33.81
1718	33.50	33.29	33.42	33.67	33.62	33.67	33.71	34.00	34.17	34.29	34.50	34.00	33.82
1719	33.75	33.75	35.17	35.08	34.58	34.79	34.25	34.50	34.88	34.71	34.58	34.33	34.53
1720	34.50	34.38	34.50	35.04	34.62	34.25	34.42	33.33	33.17	34.29	34.08	33.33	34.16
1721	32.38	33.71	33.29	33.79	34.12	34.67	33.96	34.67	34.83	35.17	34.92	34.71	34.18
1722	34.79	34.79	35.08	35.00	35.08	35.12	35.04	35.00	35.21	35.17	35.21	35.04	35.04

TABLE 2.16 (Continued): London on Hamburg (Schilling-vls. Banco per £1 Sterling)

Year	Jan.	Feb.	Mar.	Apr.	May	June	July	Aug.	Sept.	Oct.	Nov.	Dec.	Average
1723	34.67	34.75	34.67	34.58	34.58	34.33	34.75	34.75	34.62	34.46	34.17	34.17	34.54
1724	33.71	34.25	34.33	34.25	34.00	33.88	33.96	34.00	34.25	33.88	33.92	33.75	34.02
1725	33.75	33.83	34.00	33.83	33.83	33.88	34.12	33.92	34.08	34.08	34.04	33.96	33.94
1726	33.83	34.08	34.42	34.58	34.96	35.08	34.46	34.75	35.00	35.00	35.17	35.17	34.71
1727	35.25	35.25	35.08	35.08	35.08	34.83	34.71	34.58	34.71	34.58	34.42	34.33	34.82
1728	34.29	34.04	32.12	34.96	34.04	33.83	34.62	33.50	33.88	33.62	33.67	33.67	33.85
1729	33.42	33.42	33.67	33.50	33.42	33.42	33.42	33.42	33.50	33.42	33.33	33.17	33.43
1730	33.00	33.08	33.08	33.17	33.17	33.08	33.21	33.17	33.33	33.25	33.33	33.50	33.20
1731	33.42	33.54	33.50	33.75	33.83	33.79	34.92	34.00	34.00	34.17	34.46	34.25	33.97
1732	34.12	34.12	34.25	34.17	34.33	34.33	34.12	34.25	34.17	34.04	34.12	34.17	34.18
1733	34.12	34.00	33.96	34.04	34.00	34.08	34.25	34.22	34.33	34.62	35.33	35.33	34.36
1734	35.46	35.67	35.54	35.58	35.75	35.67	35.83	35.79	35.83	35.38	35.54	35.25	35.61
1735	35.25	35.25	35.17	35.08	35.46	35.50	35.29	35.33	35.42	35.50	35.33	35.42	35.33
1736	35.25	35.00	34.88	34.92	34.92	34.92	34.62	34.33	34.33	34.21	34.33	34.08	34.65
1737	34.08	34.08	34.17	34.08	34.00	33.67	33.83	33.67	34.00	33.83	33.92	33.92	33.94
1738	34.00	33.92	33.83	33.83	33.92	33.83	33.83	33.92	34.08	33.92	34.17	34.25	33.96
1739	34.25	34.25	34.25	34.25	34.25	34.25	34.42	34.50	34.42	34.33	34.33	34.33	34.32
1740	34.50	34.42	34.33	34.04	34.17	34.17	34.17	33.92	34.00	33.79	33.96	34.00	34.12
1741	33.92	33.83	33.67	33.67	33.38	33.50	33.50	33.50	33.42	33.25	33.42	33.50	33.55
1742	33.58	33.58	33.54	33.58	33.67	33.67	33.75	33.75	33.54	33.50	33.62	33.75	33.63
1743	33.67	33.58	33.50	33.33	33.54	33.58	33.67	33.75	33.75	33.71	33.83	33.83	33.64
1744	33.75	33.58	33.58	33.58	33.58	33.67	33.50	33.58	33.50	33.50	33.42	33.50	33.56
1745	33.71	33.75	33.75	33.83	33.58	33.83	33.92	34.00	34.25	34.67	35.00	36.17	34.20
1746	35.96	36.42	36.12	36.12	35.04	35.46	35.17	35.33	35.33	35.25	35.67	35.58	35.62
1747	35.58	35.25	35.21	34.88	34.75	34.75	34.92	35.00	35.17	35.00	34.92	35.00	35.04
1748	35.00	34.92	35.00	35.00	34.75	34.75	34.88	34.67	34.42	34.58	34.67	34.75	34.78
1749	34.50	34.42	34.58	34.67	34.42	34.67	34.50	34.42	34.17	33.92	33.92	34.08	34.36

TABLE 2.16 (Continued): London on Hamburg (Schilling-vls. Banco per £1 Sterling)

Year	Jan.	Feb.	Mar.	Apr.	May	June	July	Aug.	Sept.	Oct.	Nov.	Dec.	Average
1750	33.75	33.42	33.42	33.50	33.58	33.58	33.75	33.67	33.67	33.42	33.50	33.42	33.56
1751	33.42	33.33	33.58	33.42	33.67	33.58	33.75	33.67	33.67	33.50	33.75	33.67	33.58
1752	33.58	33.58	33.42	33.33	33.42	33.42	33.42	33.33	33.33	33.25	33.42	33.25	33.40
1753	33.25	33.17	33.17	33.25	33.33	33.33	33.33	33.25	33.33	33.33	33.42	33.42	33.30
1754	33.33	33.33	33.42	33.50	33.50	33.58	33.58	33.75	33.58	33.50	33.50	33.75	33.53
1755	33.75	33.75	34.00	34.25	34.67	34.50	34.58	35.04	34.67	34.83	34.83	34.83	34.48
1756	34.83	35.08	35.33	35.25	35.42	35.75	35.83	36.00	36.17	36.33	36.42	36.67	35.76
1757	36.58	36.58	36.75	36.83	36.67	35.92	36.17	36.17	35.83	35.58	35.42	35.67	36.18
1758	35.58	35.50	35.42	35.58	35.50	35.58	36.17	35.83	35.92	35.75	35.75	35.75	35.69
1759	35.75	36.25	36.67	36.96	37.83	37.67	38.25	37.88	36.67	37.08	37.00	36.58	37.05
1760	36.50	36.08	35.83	35.83	35.17	33.83	33.50	32.75	32.17	32.00	31.83	32.25	33.98
1761	31.92	32.00	32.00	32.08	32.33	31.83	32.00	32.00	32.42	32.67	33.50	33.29	32.34
1762	33.08	33.92	33.00	34.46	34.17	34.42	34.92	34.92	34.92	35.00	35.17	34.12	34.34
1763	34.12	33.92	33.83	33.67	34.00	34.17	34.33	34.38	34.58	34.75	35.00	35.00	34.31
1764	34.83	34.92	35.08	34.75	34.83	35.17	35.25	35.17	35.00	35.08	35.17	35.25	35.04
1765	35.00	34.92	34.75	34.67	34.92	34.67	34.67	34.67	34.42	34.42	34.33	34.50	34.66
1766	34.50	34.58	34.50	34.67	34.83	35.08	35.08	35.33	35.33	35.42	35.67	35.50	35.04
1767	35.50	35.75	35.75	35.92	35.83	35.42	35.58	35.83	35.92	35.67	34.58	34.83	35.55
1768	34.67	34.33	34.58	34.50	34.58	34.58	34.67	34.42	34.17	33.67	33.33	32.67	34.18
1769	33.42	33.08	33.25	33.67	33.75	33.67	33.67	33.58	33.42	33.17	33.17	33.08	33.41
1770	33.25	33.17	33.17	33.25	33.25	33.08	33.33	33.33	33.25	33.17	33.42	33.50	33.26
1771	33.75	33.67	33.58	33.58	33.42	33.17	33.00	33.00	33.00	32.83	32.83	32.58	33.20
1772	32.67	32.83	32.92	33.00	32.92	33.17	33.17	33.42	33.33	33.83	33.83	33.83	33.24
1773	34.00	34.75	34.92	34.83	34.92	34.92	34.83	34.67	34.67	34.75	34.67	34.75	34.72
1774	34.75	34.75	34.75	34.58	34.67	34.75	34.75	34.58	34.42	34.17	34.25	34.25	34.56
1775	34.25	34.25	34.42	34.42	34.25	34.33	34.42	34.33	34.25	34.25	34.17	34.08	34.28

Notes and Sources: **TABLE 2.16**
   1698–1775: *The Course of the Exchange* (London), 1698–1775. See the discussion above in the initial section of this chapter and in n. 10.

TABLE 2.17. The Course of the Exchange at Hamburg

On Amsterdam	1 thaler banco of 32 schilling-lubs,	for stuivers banco
Cadiz	for grote-vls. banco,	1 ducado de cambio of 375 maravedies
Copenhagen	100 reichsthaler banco,	for rigsdalers kurant
Lisbon	for grote-vls. banco,	1 cruzado of 400 réis
London	for schilling-vls. banco,	£ sterling
Paris	for schilling-lubs banco,	1 ecu of 60 sous tournois
Stockholm	100 reichsthaler banco,	for riksdalern

Copenhagen

The exchange on Copenhagen finds a place in this handbook because Denmark owned the West Indian islands of St. Croix, St. Thomas, and St. John. Copenhagen was one of the more remote commercial centers; although the standard handbooks do indicate that some Danish bills were transacted on the London Exchange, bills from London were usually negotiated indirectly via Amsterdam. The London-Copenhagen bill rate therefore was not quoted by Castaing in *The Course of the Exchange*, but, luckily for us, London was more important in Copenhagen than Copenhagen was in London. The Danish commercial newspapers regularly listed the bill rates on London, and the bulk of the quotations that follow are from this source. The papers also listed the bill rates on Amsterdam and Hamburg, so that when there was no direct quotation of the London-Copenhagen rate, the rate has been computed indirectly, via Amsterdam.

Real money at Copenhagen was largely silver money, that is, the Danish rigsdaler and krone and the usual assort-ment of foreign coins. Between 1660 and 1800 "the amount of gold coins issued was so restricted that gold coins were medals rather than money."[65] No matter, the basic Danish coins in both gold and silver are listed in tables 1.1 and 1.2 (pp. 9–13). The rigsdaler was also a key unit in the Danish money of account and was equal to 6 marks and 96 skillinger (see table 2.18). As at Amsterdam and Hamburg, Copenhagen had in effect two moneys of account, the more valuable *specie* money and the less valuable *kurantmønt*, or current money. The difference between them, or, more precisely, the percentage increase in specie money necessary to equal kurantmønt, was the *opgelt*, or the agio. Fortunately for our purposes commodity prices and the course of the exchange were all quoted in kurantmønt; so we need not concern ourselves any further with the agio at Copenhagen.[66]

65. Friis and Glamann, *Prices and Wages in Denmark*, 14. See also Ricard, *Traité général du commerce*, [ed. Marien], II, 77–80; Hayes, *Negociator's Magazine*, 201–202.

66. Conversion tables were compiled for Friis and Glamann, *Prices and Wages in Denmark*, 15–28. There is an early (1784) and quite useful essay, "Von

TABLE 2.18. Moneys of Account of Denmark: Their Denominations and Their Relationships

Rigsdaler	Mark	Stiver	Skilling	Penning
1	6	48	96	1,152
	1	8	16	192
		1	2	24
			1	12

The par of exchange between London and Copenhagen in 1759 was 4s 6d (22.5p) sterling per rigsdaler at London, according to Thomas Slack.[67] At this rate £1 sterling equaled 4 rigsdalers and 43 skillinger, or 427 skillinger. If a merchant in Copenhagen had wished to purchase a bill on London for the equivalent of £120 sterling on, say, 14 February 1727, when the rate was 5 rigsdalers and 30 skillinger per £1 sterling, he would have had to pay 637 rigsdalers and 48 skillinger for it. If, however, our merchant were in London and wished to reverse the procedure, he would have run into some difficulty, for there were few or no bills for sale on Copenhagen. His option would have been to go through Amsterdam. On 14 February 1727 his £120 sterling would have purchased

him a bill on Amsterdam for 1,274 gulden banco at an exchange of 35 schellingen and 4.5 grooten. The agio in February 1727 was about 5.2 percent, making this the equivalent of 536 rijksdaalders.[68] The Amsterdam-Copenhagen exchange rate in February 1727 indicated that 100 Dutch rijksdaalders equaled 122.25 Danish rigsdalers,[69] yielding our London merchant 655 rigsdalers in Copenhagen for his £120 sterling. The difference between this and the sum purchased from Copenhagen, about 2.7 percent, most likely reflects both the usual difference in the rate between the two cities and some imprecision in the data.[70]

This rather elaborate explanation of the negotiation of a London-Amsterdam-Copenhagen bill is also an example of how table 2.19 was calculated. This is the first of the two tables giving the London-Copenhagen bill rate from 1696 to 1775, both of which are based essentially on Danish data. See also table 2.20. Table 2.21 completes the usual set by specifying the manner of exchange between Copenhagen and the other cities that concern us here. It is again noteworthy that we have information for so few cities. As the compilers of these series, Friis and Glamann, put it, their sources quoted "rates on Lübeck, Paris, Danzig, Königsberg, and Stockholm . . . for a few short periods" only, and such information was "too sporadic" for them even to present.[71]

der Copenhagener Bank," by Büsch in his *Sämtliche Schriften über Banken und Münzwesen*, [ed. Ebeling], 437–560. See also Axel Nielsen, *Specier, kroner, ant: En studie over den faldende Rigsdalerværdi i Danmark i tiden 1671–1726* (Copenhagen, 1907); Wilcke, *Kurantmønten*; and Knud Erik Svendsen et al., *Dansk pengehistorie, 1700–1960*, ed. Erik Hoffmeyer (Copenhagen, 1968), I, *passim*.

67. [Slack], *British Negociator*, 218. See also William Gordon, *The Universal Accountant and Complete Merchant*, 3d ed. (Edinburgh, 1770), I, 378.

68. See tables 2.6 and 2.9 above. The £120 sterling times 35.38 equals 4,245.6 schellingen divided by 3$\frac{1}{3}$ schellingen per gulden equals 1,273.7 gulden banco. The 4,245.6 schellingen banco times 1.0516 equals 4,464.7 schellingen current. There were 50 stuivers per rijksdaalder, so the 4,464.7 schellingen times 6 equals 26,788.2 stuivers, which divided by 50 equals 535.8 rijksdaalders.

69. Friis and Glamann, *Prices and Wages in Denmark*, 71. See also Hayes, *Negociator's Magazine*, 45.

70. See n. 31 in chap. 1, above.

71. Friis and Glamann, *Prices and Wages in Denmark*, 61.

TABLE 2.19. **Rate of Exchange: Copenhagen on London (via Amsterdam), 1696–1730**

(Skillinger per £1 Sterling)

Year	Jan.	Feb.	Mar.	Apr.	May	June	July	Aug.	Sept.	Oct.	Nov.	Dec.	Average
1696				377.8			372.5	414.8	448.9				394.9
1697											478.0		478.0
1698				471.1	464.5	462.5	456.1	452.8	441.6	450.2		449.1	455.3
1699		450.2			446.0		448.2	447.1	447.8	447.1	445.4	454.5	448.2
1700	454.0			460.0			466.4	467.5	455.8	456.3	456.1	461.1	458.8
1701						472.4	474.1	472.4	473.3				472.8
1702								449.4					449.4
1703			438.1				446.8						442.4
1704							444.5		452.4	454.5	464.4	452.4	452.8
1705	445.1	454.7					458.2	455.0					453.2
1706	465.6					456.7	464.4	467.8		474.3		477.5	466.1
1707	466.1								460.9				463.5
1708	460.7	454.5	469.2					450.9	451.4	457.1			456.6
1709													
1710	451.9	451.3											451.6
1711			455.5		453.4								454.4
1712	452.4					458.7			471.0	478.3	480.4		465.4
1713				492.9	483.7		483.8			460.2		476.5	480.2
1714						465.3	470.6						468.0
1715												521.3	521.3
1716											482.8	492.2	487.5
1717		485.9							514.7	519.4		477.4	499.7
1718								518.7					518.7
1719	529.8	531.1		544.6	535.5							530.1	533.5

TABLE 2.19 (Continued): Copenhagen on London (Skillinger per £1 Sterling)

Year	Jan.	Feb.	Mar.	Apr.	May	June	July	Aug.	Sept.	Oct.	Nov.	Dec.	Average
1720	544.4										513.7		529.0
1721									541.0		539.6	540.4	540.5
1722			552.8	550.3			545.7	544.9			540.8	543.6	547.6
1723	540.6	549.0		542.8	536.8		546.0		539.0	537.4	528.9	547.5	541.3
1724				540.9		533.8	538.0		537.3	528.7	525.8	525.5	533.9
1725			547.7	543.7	540.6	541.7	548.9	546.6	545.5	537.9	529.4		542.6
1726				552.9		551.0		490.6			495.4	494.8	512.6
1727	510.0	524.0		521.0			517.3			497.4	499.6	495.4	513.2
1728	495.4					483.9	492.4				481.8		488.4
1729	480.6	485.4		488.5	484.0			479.1				480.6	482.2
1730								473.5			486.3	479.2	478.1

Notes and Sources: **TABLE 2.19**

1696–1730: Astrid Friis and Kristof Glamann, *A History of Prices and Wages in Denmark, 1660–1800* (London, 1958), 69–71; and tables 2.6, 2.8, and 2.9, above. For computation, see text.

TABLE 2.20. **Rate of Exchange: Copenhagen on London, 1714–1775**

(Skillinger per £1 Sterling)

Year	Jan.	Feb.	Mar.	Apr.	May	June	July	Aug.	Sept.	Oct.	Nov.	Dec.	Average
1714						456.0							456.0
1715													
1716											483.0		483.0
1717						480.0						480.0	480.0
1718		480.0										480.0	480.0
1719													
1720													
1721													
1722												538.0	538.0
1723							528.0		524.0	531.5	520.0		525.9
1724		480.0		532.5		528.0	528.0	528.0		530.0	528.0		516.8
1725			536.0	540.0		533.7	536.0	540.0	570.0	529.0	522.0		536.8
1726						534.0		482.0			491.3	492.0	502.6
1727	492.0	510.0		512.0			510.0			490.0	486.0	488.0	502.8
1728	490.0												490.0
1729													
1730											468.0		468.0
1731	469.0	470.0	472.0	475.0	476.0	471.3	474.0	473.5	470.0	473.0	472.0	472.7	472.4
1732	476.0	478.0		479.0		478.0	479.0	476.0		476.0		472.5	476.8
1733	476.0		474.5	475.0	473.0	475.0		479.0		479.0	479.0	479.0	476.5
1734	479.0		489.0	501.0	499.0	497.0		499.0	501.0	501.0	497.0		495.5
1735			501.0	495.0	497.0	497.0	499.0	499.0		499.5	500.8		499.1
1736	500.0		497.0		495.0		489.0		483.0				493.2
1737										461.0			461.0
1738			468.0			471.5				472.0	472.0		470.5
1739		479.5					482.0	480.0	479.0	481.0			480.3

TABLE 2.20 (Continued): **Copenhagen on London** (Skillinger per £1 Sterling)

Year	Jan.	Feb.	Mar.	Apr.	May	June	July	Aug.	Sept.	Oct.	Nov.	Dec.	Average
1740							479.5	482.0		480.0		477.5	479.8
1741	480.0	477.5			476.0								477.4
1742	459.0		472.0								472.0		468.8
1743	480.0	483.5	484.0		484.0								483.2
1744						486.0				492.0			489.0
1745	492.0				488.0					492.0			490.7
1746			504.0			496.0							500.0
1747			488.0										488.0
1748	477.0	477.5	478.5	479.5	479.0	478.0	476.0	477.3	476.5	474.0	478.0	477.0	477.4
1749	481.0	482.0	485.0	485.0	485.0	479.0	479.0	473.0	470.0	472.0	472.2	472.5	478.0
1750	473.0	470.0	465.0	463.0	463.7	461.0	463.0	464.0	463.3	465.0	463.0	463.0	464.8
1751	467.0	467.0	467.0	467.0	469.0	471.0	469.0	468.0	467.0	467.0	467.0	467.0	467.8
1752	465.7	465.0	465.0	464.3	465.0	463.0	462.0	463.0	461.0	465.5	468.8	468.0	464.7
1753	467.0	469.0	467.5	466.8	467.5	461.0	462.5	466.0	464.0	465.5	468.8	465.5	465.9
1754	469.0	471.0	469.2	468.8	472.8	473.5	469.5	472.0	471.3	470.5	472.0	472.5	471.0
1755	474.5	479.0	477.3	481.0	487.0	479.5	484.5	491.0	481.8	484.7	484.5	484.5	482.4
1756	490.8	492.5	496.0	495.5	502.2	502.0	503.5	506.5	506.2	510.2	512.8	508.8	502.2
1757	508.2	507.2	501.5	496.8	490.0	475.0	481.0	486.5	482.0	474.0	478.0	472.8	487.8
1758	472.0	479.5	477.5	472.0	463.2	463.5	466.2	464.5	467.2	468.8	469.5	472.0	469.7
1759	477.0	478.0	481.0	480.8	471.0	472.5	480.5	480.5	481.5	486.0	485.3	478.0	479.3
1760	480.0	480.0	483.8	483.0	485.5	469.7	477.0	482.2	471.0	475.7	481.5	481.7	479.3
1761	482.5	486.0	485.7	489.0	500.0	504.3	495.0	485.2	492.5	494.0	506.2	510.0	494.2
1762	510.0	511.5	520.0	517.7	516.5	528.7	544.5	544.0	550.0	542.0	506.5	496.0	524.0
1763	497.2	496.0	499.0	500.0	499.5	495.5	499.0	499.0	510.5	524.0	536.0	528.0	507.0
1764	524.0	538.7	540.0	539.3	540.0	535.3	536.0	535.5	536.0	540.0	539.0	539.5	536.9
1765	535.0	508.0	496.0	496.7	497.0	496.0	498.5	493.0	490.3	492.0	490.0	491.0	498.6
1766	494.2	497.0	497.0	497.5	500.5	497.7	497.0	504.7	505.0	506.0	508.8	506.0	501.0
1767	508.5	511.5	513.5	516.5	514.5	506.0	506.0	507.0	513.2	510.0	508.3	500.5	509.6

TABLE 2.20 (Continued): Copenhagen on London (Skillinger per £1 Sterling)

Year	Jan.	Feb.	Mar.	Apr.	May	June	July	Aug.	Sept.	Oct.	Nov.	Dec.	Average
1768	504.0	504.0	498.0	499.5	499.8	501.0	504.0	502.5	496.7	502.0	508.0	505.5	502.1
1769	519.5	514.0	500.2	496.5	500.5	496.7	504.8	505.0	497.3	497.8	496.5	496.7	502.1
1770	496.0	494.0	495.0	491.5	491.0	491.7	492.5	498.5	499.5	502.8	501.7	501.2	496.3
1771	505.0	507.5	503.5	502.0	499.3	497.5	496.7	498.5	499.5	500.2	504.0	495.2	500.7
1772	500.2	498.5	501.0	503.5	500.5	498.0	501.8	509.5	505.0	516.0	515.0	517.8	505.6
1773	528.5	534.8	538.0	535.2	542.5	539.5	546.6	542.5	544.2	536.0	535.5	536.8	538.3
1774	538.5	540.5	536.2	531.5	526.2	524.8	526.0	522.0	516.3	504.0	502.8	503.7	522.7
1775	503.0	502.5	504.5	503.5	496.0	497.3	501.0	500.0	500.0	498.0	499.5	497.0	500.2

Notes and Sources: **TABLE 2.20**

1714–1775: Astrid Friis and Kristof Glamann, *A History of Prices and Wages in Denmark, 1660–1800* (London, 1958), 66–68, 78–92.

1770: *Royal Danish American Gazette* (Christiansted, St. Croix), 9 Jan. and 16 Feb. 1771, quoting the course of the exchange at Copenhagen on 12 Oct. and 9 Dec. 1770 (copy in Københavns Universitets-bibliotek, Fiolstræde, Copenhagen).

TABLE 2.21. The Course of the Exchange at Copenhagen

On	Amsterdam	rigsdalers kurant,	for 100 rijksdaalders current
	Hamburg	rigsdalers kurant,	for 100 reichsthaler banco
	London	rigsdalers kurant,	for £1 sterling
	Paris	skillinger kurant,	for 1 ecu of 60 sous tournois

Paris

After the complications of Amsterdam, Hamburg, and Copenhagen, the comparative simplicity of the mode of exchange between London and Paris is a pleasant contrast. Yet this is offset in some measure by the considerable confusion induced by the monetary chaos of the seventeenth and early eighteenth centuries, especially the years 1681 to 1725. In the face of imminent national bankruptcy, the legacy of Louis XIV's palaces and wars, the French government debased its coin. Recoinage after recoinage so altered the value of the real money of France that it caused strenuous economic difficulties at home and abroad and contributed to the havoc wrought by John Law. Only with "the great monetary reform and consolidations" of 1726 did this era end and one of stability lasting over fifty years begin for France.[72]

Happily for our purposes, however, the money of account in France, established in 1602, remained the same throughout the period. The value of the real money of France, some of which is specified in tables 1.1 and 1.2 (pp. 9–13), fluctuated much more than these tables can show.[73] One can turn to Frank C. Spooner's superb study for further information on this subject. But the system of accounting in livres tournois (see table 2.22) persisted throughout the ancien régime. And since foreign exchange used the money of account, more specifically the ecu, or crown, of 60 sous tournois, the difficulties of the French monetary system do not impinge directly on this study—even if they are reflected in sometimes wildly fluctuating quotations in the commercial rate of exchange.

The par of exchange between London and Paris reflected this same decline in the comparative value of the livre tournois and sterling. The ecu was worth at par 72d (30p) sterling in 1628, 54d (22.5p) from the 1640s, 36.5d (15.2p) as a result of the recoinage of 1709, and 29.2d (12.2p) after 15 June 1726.[74] The commercial rate of exchange fluctuated as usual in relationship to par (see tables 2.23, 2.24, and 2.25). Richard Hayes's example of an exchange transaction for Paris presumes a London remittance of £482.80 at 54.5d (22.7p) sterling per ecu. The yield at Paris is 6,378 livres, 5 sous, and 6 deniers.[75] French exchange upon other European countries was similarly uncomplicated. Table 2.26 shows the usual mode of such transactions.[76]

72. Frank C. Spooner, *The International Economy and Monetary Movements in France, 1493–1725*, Harvard Economic Studies, CXXXVIII (Cambridge, Mass., 1972). He calls this his second edition (*ibid.*, 208); the "first" is his *L'économie mondiale et les frappes monétaires en France, 1493–1680* (Paris, 1956). For the declining value of French coin, see Natalis de Wailly, *Mémoire sur les variations de la livre tournois depuis le règne de Saint Louis jusqu'à l'établissement de la monnaie décimale* (Institut Impérial de France, Académie des Inscriptions et Belles-Lettres, *Mémoires*, XXI, pt. ii [Paris, 1857]), 177–427. See also Henri Lévy-Bruhl, *Histoire de la lettre de change en France aux XVIIe et XVIIIe siècles* (Paris, 1933); and René Sédillot, *Le franc: Histoire d'une monnaie des origine à nos jours* (Paris, 1953).

73. Note that "les especes étrangers ne peuvent pas avoir cours en France en qualité de monnaies." Ricard, *Traité général du commerce*, [ed. Marien], II, 106. See also [Justice], *General Treatise of Monies*, 98.

74. N[icholas] H[unt], *The Merchants Jewell: or, a New Invention Arithmeticall* (London, 1628); "Considerations of the Value or Parr of the Coynes of France . . . ," [18 Nov. 1651], S.P. 18/16, fols. 224–227, P.R.O., and in Shaw, ed., *English Monetary History*, 91–97; Ricard, *Traité général du commerce*, 380; Isaac Newton to the Treasury, [Oct. 1712], T. 1/152, fol. 182r, and in Shaw, ed., *English Monetary History*, 162; [Slack], *British Negociator*, 104; Gordon, *Universal Accountant*, I, 365; "Intrinsic Par of Exchange . . . ," in "Report from the Select Committee on Gold Bullion," Great Britain, House of Commons, *Sess. Papers*, 1810, III (*Reports*), no. 349, p. 207.

75. Hayes, *Negociator's Magazine*, 58–59. Computation: £482 16s 0d times 240d per £1 equals 115,872d, which, divided by 54.5d to the ecu, equals 2,126.0917 ecus, or 6,378.275 livres tournois.

76. Ricard, *Traité général du commerce*, [ed. Marien], II, 111. See also Bléville, *Banquier et negociant universel*, I, 7–14, and *passim*.

TABLE 2.22. **Money of Account of France:
Its Denominations and
Their Relationships**

Ecu de Change	Livre Tournois	Sou Tournois	Denier Tournois
1	3	60	720
	1	20	240
		1	12

TABLE 2.23. **Rate of Exchange: London on Paris (via Amsterdam), 1619–1715**

(Pence Sterling per Ecu, or Crown, of Three Livres Tournois)

Year	Jan.	Feb.	Mar.	Apr.	May	June	July	Aug.	Sept.	Oct.	Nov.	Dec.	Average
1619								71.43					71.43
1620													
1621													
1622													
1623													
1624		68.99			69.12	68.26		70.53	69.47	70.07		69.72	69.39
1625		69.76	69.39			69.07	69.21	68.77	66.89	68.18		68.04	68.76
1626	68.06	67.18	67.46				67.06	67.82		67.87	67.85	69.16	67.77
1627													
1628									69.51				69.51
1629													

TABLE 2.23 (Continued): **London on Paris** (Pence Sterling per Ecu)

Year	Jan.	Feb.	Mar.	Apr.	May	June	July	Aug.	Sept.	Oct.	Nov.	Dec.	Average
1630	69.69				67.09						64.51		67.10
1631	64.68			64.76	63.52	63.70	63.35	63.49					64.03
1632		63.70				62.86	63.22						63.26
1633		64.30	63.40	63.27	63.05								63.50
1634		63.77											63.77
1635					62.23	62.94	63.09						62.84
1636			63.89	57.78								57.12	59.60
1637			57.04		55.84								56.44
1638						53.96						54.50	54.23
1639													
1640									51.82				51.82
1641					52.00							51.98	51.99
1642					52.26		52.26	54.54	52.51				52.68
1643						50.24		53.46	52.90				51.71
1644													
1645	49.96	49.99					52.25	52.65		52.32			51.58
1646	51.71	51.66	*51.66*	51.67	51.87	*52.54*	53.20	53.48	54.39	54.64	54.87	55.36	53.09
1647													
1648									61.17	61.25	61.47		61.26
1649													
1650	61.48	62.82	61.48		64.66								63.29
1651											53.09		53.09
1652								58.52		53.78			56.15
1653											53.97	48.34	51.16
1654	49.25	51.01	52.62	51.98	52.67								51.64
1655													
1656													
1657													

TABLE 2.23 (Continued): London on Paris (Pence Sterling per Ecu)

Year	Jan.	Feb.	Mar.	Apr.	May	June	July	Aug.	Sept.	Oct.	Nov.	Dec.	Average
1658													
1659													
1660													
1661													
1662													
1663													
1664												56.22	56.22
1665										55.45			55.45
1666													
1667													
1668													
1669		56.76	56.35	56.50					55.35	55.69	54.90		55.92
1670													
1671				55.06	54.68								54.87
1672		54.32	53.40		57.33								55.60
1673													
1674						56.53	57.19	57.14	57.32	57.96	56.30		56.96
1675									57.02				57.02
1676				55.19					54.66				54.92
1677	54.87	54.75	54.89	54.71			55.08						54.88
1678	53.60												53.60
1679		53.98										54.51	54.24
1680				55.10	55.40								55.25
1681											55.20		55.20
1682	55.28			55.43									55.36
1683											54.33		54.33
1684													

TABLE 2.23 (Continued): **London on Paris** (Pence Sterling per Ecu)

Year	Jan.	Feb.	Mar.	Apr.	May	June	July	Aug.	Sept.	Oct.	Nov.	Dec.	Average
1685							55.65						55.65
1686	54.06	53.97											54.02
1687			53.70										53.70
1688	52.98												52.98
1689													
1690													
1691											52.64		52.64
1692						52.37							52.37
1693		52.88		53.24	53.20		53.57	52.68	54.91				53.27
1694	55.52		54.95				57.12	58.26	57.49		57.51	56.97	56.70
1695	57.39	57.61	57.84	59.10	57.63	61.75	62.18	63.13	62.40	61.88			60.39
1696			58.78	58.03	57.25	58.00		53.74					56.76
1697					48.38			48.12		49.49		47.76	48.38
1698													
1699		57.81	58.49										58.15
1700					46.56								46.56
1701	45.38												45.38
1702													
1703													
1704													
1705				44.63						43.66			44.14
1706							37.61	37.29		45.93	46.16		41.75
1707													
1708										47.15		47.42	47.28
1709		48.49		48.70	44.52	46.15	50.82	50.15	50.12			47.76	48.27
1710	47.08	47.34	47.35	47.31	47.95	48.11	48.37						47.81
1711													
1712													

TABLE 2.23 (Continued): **London on Paris** (Pence Sterling per Ecu)

Year	Jan.	Feb.	Mar.	Apr.	May	June	July	Aug.	Sept.	Oct.	Nov.	Dec.	Average
1713													
1714								41.94					41.94
1715													

Notes and Sources: **TABLE 2.23**

1619–1715: N. W. Posthumus, *Inquiry into the History of Prices in Holland* (Leiden, 1946–1964), I, 590–596.

1631–1633: *Corso in Amsterd[am] di piusorte mercanti* ([Amsterdam]), 22 Dec. 1631, 26 Apr. 1632, and 18 Apr. 1633 (see notes to table 2.7, above).

1696–1697: *Cours van koopmanschappen tot Amsterdam* (Amsterdam), 28 Apr. and 11 Aug. 1696, 4 May, 31 Aug., 5 Oct., and 14 Dec. 1697, copies in Matthias Giesque and Co. Papers, bundle no. 68, C. 104/128, pt. 2, Unknown Cause, Public Record Office.

The computation involved converting the London-Amsterdam exchange rate from schellingen and grooten banco per £1 sterling into grooten and then establishing the ratio between that figure and the figure for the same date for the Paris-Amsterdam rate expressed in grooten banco per ecu. The ratio of ecus for £1 sterling had then to be reduced to pence per ecu. As an example, on 19 Aug. 1619 the London-Amsterdam rate was 35 schellingen per £1 sterling, or, at 12 grooten per schelling, 420 grooten; the Paris-Amsterdam rate was 125 grooten per ecu; the former divided by the latter indicated that 3.36 ecus equaled £1 sterling, or 1 ecu equaled 71.429 pence. The London-Paris rate for that date is given above as 71.43d per ecu. See also [Alexander Justice], *A General Treatise of Monies and Exchanges* (London, 1707), 116–117.

TABLE 2.24. **Rate of Exchange: London on Paris, 1663–1697**
(Pence Sterling per Ecu, or Crown, of Three Livres Tournois)

Year	Jan.	Feb.	Mar.	Apr.	May	June	July	Aug.	Sept.	Oct.	Nov.	Dec.	Average
1663	55.38												55.38
1664													
1665													
1666													
1667							57.25						57.25
1668		57.94								56.42	56.09	56.08	57.07
1669			56.75	56.69	56.75	56.75	56.75	56.81	56.75	54.62	54.50	54.84	56.23
1670													
1671											52.38		52.38
1672	52.00	52.50	55.75		55.53				54.50		54.88	54.75	54.56
1673	54.84	54.94	54.97	55.00	55.50	55.75	56.25	56.75	55.00	55.00	54.44	54.40	55.24
1674	54.94	55.00	55.00	55.25	56.50	56.62	56.81	57.12	57.12	57.50	57.50	57.72	56.42
1675	58.44	58.03	57.92	57.91	57.75	58.50	57.75	57.32	57.25	56.25	55.72	54.00	57.24
1676	54.75	55.00	54.50	55.00	55.50	55.25	55.39	55.50	54.75	54.88	54.56	54.50	54.96
1677	55.00	55.00	54.50										54.83
1678													
1679	53.62												53.62
1680		54.25										54.62	54.44
1681				54.62	54.62	55.25	55.29	55.29	54.88	55.00	55.00	55.00	54.99
1682	55.00	55.75	54.94	55.00	55.62	55.25	55.50	55.50	55.12	55.00	55.00	54.75	55.20
1683	54.75	54.53	54.62	54.75	54.50	54.62	54.62	54.31	54.00	54.19	54.00	54.00	54.41
1684	54.62	54.62	54.56	55.12	55.75	55.75	55.38	55.12	54.88	54.00	54.00	54.50	54.86
1685	54.75	54.38	54.38	54.75	54.50	54.50	54.75	54.75	54.00	54.62	54.06	54.06	54.46
1686	54.12	54.00	54.00	54.00	54.75	54.75	54.62	54.50	54.62	54.62	54.12	54.12	54.35
1687	54.25	54.25	54.25							53.38	53.25	53.25	53.77
1688	52.88	52.75	52.75	53.00	53.00	53.50	53.50	53.88	53.88	53.88			53.40
1689						55.94							55.94

TABLE 2.24 (Continued): London on Paris (Pence Sterling per Ecu)

Year	Jan.	Feb.	Mar.	Apr.	May	June	July	Aug.	Sept.	Oct.	Nov.	Dec.	Average
1690													
1691													
1692													
1693													
1694													
1695	56.75									62.50	63.25	57.00	58.83
1696	55.50	57.25	58.00	58.00	57.00	57.00	57.00	57.00					57.08
1697		48.00	46.50	47.00	47.25								47.19

Notes and Sources: **TABLE 2.24**

Figures printed in italics are straight-line interpolations based on the two neighboring quotations.

1663: Company of Royal Adventurers Trading into Africa, Wastebook, 1660–1663, T. 70/1221, Public Record Office. This is the rate used to convert to sterling the value of four bills drawn at Rouen.

1667–1697: London price currents as listed in Appendix 2, below.

1673–1676, 1681–1688: *The Course of the Exchange between London and Paris before the Revolution; or, a Demonstration That Our Bullion Was Then Exported upon the Balance of Our Trade with France* (London, 1713). Jacob M. Price told me of this source, and I am grateful to him.

1695–1697: *A Collection for Improvement of Husbandry and Trade* (London), 18 Jan. 1694/95–31 Dec. 1697 (the figure nearest the middle of the month).

TABLE 2.25. **Rate of Exchange: London on Paris, 1698–1775**

(Pence Sterling per Ecu, or Crown, of Three Livres Tournois)

Year	Jan.	Feb.	Mar.	Apr.	May	June	July	Aug.	Sept.	Oct.	Nov.	Dec.	Average
1698	47.00	47.00	46.44	45.74	46.56	45.75	45.56	45.25	44.62	44.31	44.56	45.69	45.71
1699	45.69	46.00	45.62	45.69	45.50	45.75	45.75	46.62	47.06	48.00	48.06	47.75	46.46
1700	47.00	47.62	46.56	46.50	45.69	46.19	46.12	45.81	46.00	45.50	45.12	45.00	46.09
1701	45.00	42.00	43.31	45.00	46.00	47.94	46.75	46.44	44.50	41.50	42.75	42.25	44.45
1702	43.38	43.75	44.00	44.38									44.04
1703													
1704													
1705													
1706													
1707													
1708													
1709													
1710													
1711													
1712													
1713					38.50	37.00	37.25	37.12	37.12	37.25	36.56	35.50	37.12
1714	35.50	35.75	36.12	36.31	36.81	38.75	40.75	42.38	43.62	43.25	42.88	42.88	39.58
1715	43.50	42.81	43.75	44.75	47.50	46.88	47.88	47.25	49.75	54.00	50.50	52.06	47.55
1716	40.00	43.38	44.25	46.00	46.00	46.44	45.24	46.25	46.81	46.62	46.56	46.81	45.36
1717	47.56	47.62	47.31	46.62	47.00	47.25	47.69	47.44	47.75	47.62	46.75	47.50	47.34
1718	47.50	45.38	44.12	42.75	40.25	32.56	32.06	31.94	31.75	31.38	30.25	30.19	36.68
1719	29.88	30.25	28.75	28.88	29.50	29.00	29.00	29.12	28.44	28.25	25.50	24.00	28.38
1720	22.89	19.25	19.25	18.25	19.75	14.12	12.12	7.50	15.12				16.47
1721	25.75	25.12	24.50	24.25	24.50	24.50	23.50	24.00	23.81	23.88	24.38	23.56	24.31
1722	23.72	24.00	23.56	23.12	23.38	23.31	22.69	22.81	22.88	22.81	22.94	21.50	23.06

TABLE 2.25 (Continued): **London on Paris** (Pence Sterling per Ecu)

Year	Jan.	Feb.	Mar.	Apr.	May	June	July	Aug.	Sept.	Oct.	Nov.	Dec.	Average
1723	22.62	23.00	22.94	22.56	22.46	22.62	22.12	23.00	22.44	22.00	22.44	22.25	22.54
1724	22.44	25.50	25.38	30.00	30.06	30.06	30.50	30.19	30.00	37.25	36.62	36.62	30.38
1725	36.44	36.88	37.50	38.31	38.38	38.81	38.75	38.56	38.12	38.25	38.38	37.81	38.02
1726	41.50	40.50	40.00	41.88	41.38	32.25	32.75	32.69	32.62	32.75	32.50	32.56	36.12
1727	33.00	33.00	33.06	33.12	33.00	33.00	33.00	33.25	33.00	32.75	32.75	32.69	32.97
1728	32.65	32.88	33.00	33.06	33.00	33.00	33.00	33.06	32.88	32.75	32.62	32.38	32.86
1729	32.38	32.62	32.50	32.50	32.50	32.69	32.88	32.75	32.75	32.88	32.88	32.88	32.68
1730	32.75	32.75	32.62	32.50	32.88	32.62	32.38	32.25	32.56	32.31	32.12	32.00	32.48
1731	31.62	31.94	31.81	31.50	31.62	31.69	31.69	31.62	31.74	31.62	31.62	31.62	31.67
1732	31.75	31.88	32.00	32.12	32.38	32.50	32.75	32.62	32.56	32.12	32.50	31.25	32.20
1733	32.12	32.25	32.06	32.12	32.12	32.00	32.06	31.75	31.88	30.75	30.56	30.38	31.67
1734	30.38	30.38	30.75	31.19	31.00	31.50	31.75	31.75	32.00	31.88	31.75	31.62	31.33
1735	31.56	31.50	31.50	31.38	31.44	31.09	31.19	31.25	31.19	30.88	30.62	30.88	31.21
1736	30.88	31.00	31.00	31.06	30.94	31.38	31.31	31.69	31.72	31.75	31.75	31.81	31.36
1737	32.00	32.44	32.12	32.31	32.50	32.31	32.38	32.75	32.34	32.38	32.38	32.22	32.34
1738	32.25	32.28	32.22	32.25	32.03	31.88	31.97	31.88	31.88	31.72	31.94	31.41	31.98
1739	31.09	31.38	31.25	31.25	31.00	30.94	30.94	31.00	31.12	31.94	31.28	31.50	31.22
1740	31.88	31.81	31.88	32.38	32.19	32.22	32.19	32.56	32.88	32.38	32.53	32.81	32.31
1741	32.72	32.50	32.81	32.75	32.69	33.00	32.69	33.38	31.72	32.06	32.19	31.94	32.54
1742	31.44	31.38	31.75	31.31	31.25	31.06	31.75	31.75	31.69	31.66	31.72	31.50	31.52
1743	31.50	31.75	31.81	31.75	32.12	32.75	32.50	33.03	32.69	32.81	32.75	32.94	32.37
1744	32.75	32.81	32.69	32.75	33.00	32.50	32.75	33.00	32.62	32.00	32.12	32.25	32.60
1745	31.88	32.06	32.25	32.25	32.19	32.12	32.12	32.00	31.94	31.25	31.25	30.38	31.81
1746	30.69	30.31	30.12	30.50	30.88	30.75	31.19	31.00	30.75	30.88	30.50	30.56	30.68
1747	30.75	31.12	31.31	31.88	32.00	32.12	32.12	31.94	31.75	31.75	31.56	30.88	31.60
1748	30.50	30.75	30.81	30.88	31.25	31.00	30.44	30.88	31.00	30.62	30.50	30.38	30.75
1749	30.56	30.75	31.25	30.75	31.12	31.12	31.81	31.75	31.69	31.69	31.56	31.50	31.30

TABLE 2.25 (Continued): London on Paris (Pence Sterling per Ecu)

Year	Jan.	Feb.	Mar.	Apr.	May	June	July	Aug.	Sept.	Oct.	Nov.	Dec.	Average
1750	31.62	31.81	31.91	31.62	31.75	31.50	31.44	31.44	31.28	31.44	31.25	31.19	31.52
1751	31.12	31.00	31.00	31.00	30.88	30.94	31.12	31.00	31.31	31.25	31.38	31.50	31.12
1752	31.31	31.38	31.38	31.50	31.25	31.44	31.56	32.00	31.81	32.00	32.25	32.31	31.68
1753	32.03	32.31	32.38	32.38	32.38	32.34	32.06	32.06	31.94	32.00	31.88	31.38	32.10
1754	31.75	31.50	31.56	31.50	31.41	31.44	31.31	31.38	31.38	31.50	31.25	31.22	31.43
1755	31.19	31.00	31.00	31.00	30.88	30.97	30.94	30.75	31.00	31.06	30.88	30.88	30.96
1756	30.00	30.59	30.62	30.62	30.38	30.12	30.38	30.31	30.31	30.19	30.12	30.00	30.30
1757	29.88	30.00	30.00	29.94	30.00	30.25	30.50	30.75	30.69	30.72	30.62	30.22	30.30
1758	30.75	30.81	30.84	31.31	31.38	31.38	31.38	31.31	31.25	31.31	31.31	31.38	31.20
1759	31.31	31.31	31.00	30.88	30.50	30.75	30.44	30.50	30.25	30.00	30.12	30.00	30.59
1760	30.12	30.25	30.25	30.44	30.38	30.56	30.50	31.00	31.00	31.12	31.25	30.62	30.62
1761	30.88	30.88	31.00	31.38	31.75	31.75	32.00	31.88	31.69	31.75	30.25	30.25	31.29
1762	30.62	30.50	30.50	30.75	30.31	30.62	30.62	30.62	30.12	30.25	30.75	31.50	30.60
1763	31.62	31.84	32.00	32.50	32.38	31.81	32.00	31.62	31.53	31.38	30.75	30.38	31.65
1764	30.62	30.50	30.38	30.31	30.56	30.38	30.38	30.75	30.50	30.62	30.75	30.50	30.52
1765	30.66	30.62	30.75	31.00	31.69	31.00	31.25	31.19	31.50	31.62	31.50	31.50	31.19
1766	31.75	31.69	31.88	31.94	31.88	31.75	31.84	31.69	31.88	31.88	31.75	31.75	31.81
1767	31.69	31.69	31.62	31.62	31.59	31.75	31.62	31.56	31.50	31.62	31.38	31.16	31.57
1768	31.13	31.25	31.19	31.25	31.31	31.38	31.56	31.56	31.38	31.50	31.56	31.50	31.38
1769	31.56	31.62	31.62	32.00	31.62	31.56	31.62	31.62	31.88	31.69	31.75	31.88	31.70
1770	31.88	32.00	32.12	32.00	31.50	31.50	31.38	31.38	31.50	31.56	31.25	31.12	31.60
1771	31.12	31.31	31.25	31.25	31.38	31.75	31.81	32.00	31.88	31.94	32.00	32.00	31.64
1772	32.12	32.31	32.00	31.88	32.06	31.88	31.75	31.31	31.25	30.75	30.44	30.62	31.53
1773	30.12	30.12	30.25	30.25	30.12	29.88	29.88	29.69	29.81	29.69	29.56	29.25	29.88
1774	29.50	29.66	29.75	29.81	29.81	30.00	30.25	30.56	30.69	31.12	30.62	30.75	30.21
1775	30.88	31.00	30.88	30.88	30.88	30.75	30.75	30.62	30.56	30.56	30.50	30.19	30.70

Notes and Sources: **TABLE 2.25**

   1698–1775: *The Course of the Exchange* (London), 1698–1775. See the discussion above in the initial section of this chapter and in n. 10.

TABLE 2.26. **The Course of the Exchange at Paris**

On Amsterdam	for 1 ecu of 60 sous tournois,	groots banco
Cadiz	livres tournois,	for 1 peso de cambio
Hamburg	ecus,	for 100 thaler banco
Copenhagen	for 1 ecu of 60 sous tournois,	skillinger kurant
Lisbon	for 1 ecu of 60 sous tournois,	réis
London	for 1 ecu of 60 sous tournois,	pence sterling

Cadiz

Cadiz must stand as our surrogate for Spain in this discussion. There is sufficient justification for the choice, in that Cadiz was the first and for a long time the only Spanish city quoted on the London Exchange. Moreover, most contemporary writers chose to talk of the Cadiz-London exchange even though Bilbao and Madrid also exchanged with London and at somewhat different rates. So did other Spanish cities. But they all shared the same monetary system, and they all transacted exchange in the same ways. Cadiz suffices.

Spain fits within the scope of this handbook not only because of her possession of one-half the New World and her claim to the other half but also because her mints there produced the "universal money" of the Atlantic world, the peso of eight reales, called variously the piastra, the cob, the dollar, and the piece of eight. This and other gold and silver coins minted in Spain and Spanish America made up the real money of the mother country and her empire. Spain had no need for foreign coins and in fact forbade their use: "Las monedas extrangeras no tienen curso en España, sino como

pasta."[77] For the real money of Spain see tables 1.1 and 1.2 (pp. 9–13).

In 1686, after a period of some difficulty with its money, Spain altered its monetary system, debased its coinage, and, in effect, established two moneys of account much as existed in Amsterdam and Hamburg.[78] The older moneda de plata antigua, continued in use as a more valuable money and a point of reference for the newer moneda de vellon. Alexander Justice put it quite succinctly in 1707:

The money of Spain is of two sorts: to wit, of plate and of bullion.
The money of plate is real and effective, and all of silver, and never changes its price.
But the money of bullion is partly imaginary, and partly a

77. Marien y Arróspide, *Tratado general de monedas*, 4. For another treatise on Spanish coinage, see Pedro de Cantos Benitez, *Escrutino de maravedises, y monedas de oro antiquas, su valor, reducción y cambio a las monedas corrientes* (Madrid, 1763). Very useful also is Humberto F. Burzio, *Diccionario de la moneda hispanoamericana*, 3 vols. (Santiago, Chile, 1956–1958).
78. Marien y Arróspide, *Tratado general de monedas*, xxxiii–xlvii, 2–4, is the best treatment of all of these developments and the source of much that follows. The *pragmática* of 14 Oct. 1686 implemented provisions of an earlier law of 23 Dec. 1642. See Chalmers, *History of Currency*, 392.

mixture of silver and brass, and is variable and changing in its price.[79]

People bought and sold goods by the moneda de vellon, and as Justice said, the government minted coins in that metal. But everyone's accounts were eventually settled in the old money, the plata antigua. The difference between the two changed over the years. Originally in 1686 moneda de vellon was worth two-thirds moneda de plata antigua; later, in 1730, new regulations reduced the proportion to one-half.[80] Exchange transactions continued to use the plata antigua.

Both the moneda de plata antigua and the moneda de vellon used the same notation of the Spanish money of account. The basic unit of the money of account was the maravedi; everything was equal to some compound of this basic unit. Some merchants tallied their accounts in maravedies and thousands of maravedies, similar to the Portuguese use of the réis and milréis. Others kept their books in maravedies and reales. As table 2.27 specifies, from 1536 on there were 34 maravedies to one real.

The piece of eight as a silver coin retained its intrinsic value throughout our period, a point noted above in chapter 1. And as a money of account it continued to be equated with 8 reales, called bits by the English. (In our current age of nostalgia, we are all reminded that a shave and a haircut once cost "two bits," a quarter of a dollar.) But the Spanish government debased the value of the real as a coin during the seventeenth and eighteenth centuries with the result that it took

greater numbers of reales as coins to equal the piece of eight, the coin. Before 1642, 8 reales plata antigua were the equivalent of one piece of eight; the law of 1642 (effective only in 1686) increased this to 10 reales; and in 1772 another law raised it to 11 reales. The piece of eight as a coin held its value; the real as a coin decreased in value. Thus it took more reales to equal one piece of eight.

Spaniards negotiated exchange transactions using the imaginary piece of eight, the piece of eight as a money of account, which was eight times the value of the real as a coin, moneda de plata antigua. Thus the piece of eight used for exchange purposes, the peso de cambio, was *not* the coin, and the peso de cambio declined in value relative to the coin as the real declined in value. (The peso de cambio was the equivalent of 272 maravedies; Spaniards also conducted exchange transactions using an imaginary ducado de cambio, the ducat, equivalent to 375 maravedies.) The piece of eight as a coin continued to be worth at par about 54d (22.5p) sterling throughout the period. That was also its value as the peso de cambio in the early seventeenth century. But the par value of the peso de cambio in 1770 was only about 40d (16.7p) sterling.

These relationships might well be summarized as they stood in about 1770. The peso de plata antigua, or the peso de cambio, was, as always, the equivalent of 8 reales de plata antigua. At London in 1769 and 1770 this was equal to about 39.5d (16.46p) sterling; at Cadiz it was equal to about 40.5d (16.88p) sterling in the same years.[81] All mercantile trans-

79. [Justice], *General Treatise of Monies*, 168.

80. Marien y Arróspide, *Tratado general de monedas*, xxxvii, xl. See also Thomas Snelling, *A View of the Coins at This Time Current Throughout Europe* (London, 1766), 12.

81. The following quotations of the rate at Cadiz on London appear in letters from Jesson, Welsh, and Co.; Bewickes, Timerman, and Romero; and Robert Herreis and Co. to Neil Jamieson of Norfolk, Va., in Neil Jamieson Papers, 1757–1789, IX, 2053, 2064, X, 2224, 2273, XI, 2503, XII, 2663, Library

TABLE 2.27. **Moneys of Account of Spain: Their Denominations and Their Relationships**

Doblon	Peso	Real	Maravedi
1	4	32	1,088
	1	8	272
		1	34

actions were conducted in moneda de vellon,[82] which was worth about half the moneda de plata. Thus the peso de cambio, the equivalent of 8 reales de plata, equaled 15 reales de vellon. The coin, the hard money piece of eight, equal to 54d (22.5p) sterling, was worth between 10 and 11 reales de plata and 20 reales de vellon. At a value of 10 reales de plata, the ratio between the coin and the peso de cambio was 1 to 1.25; at 11 reales de plata the ratio was 1 to 1.375. In fact, "l'agio [était] . . . de 33⅓ pout cent, plus ou moins; c'est-à-dire qu'on donne 100 piastres fortes pour 133⅓ piastres de change, plus ou moin."[83]

Richard Hayes supplies us with another example of the workings of the exchange. In this instance London remits £678.33 sterling at 56d (23.3p) per piastra, or piece of eight. The yield is 2,907 pesos and 1 real de plata antigua.[84] In 1770 this would have been the equivalent of 43,607 reales de vellon or 2,180 hard money pieces of eight. Tables 2.28, 2.29, and 2.30 indicate the rate of exchange at London on Cadiz between 1609 and 1775. Table 2.31 shows the course of the exchange on the other major European commercial centers.

between this place and England. The ryal of plate is composed of 16 quarts. 15 ryals vellon to a small fraction go to our current dollar." Brown Papers, L 74 M, John Carter Brown Library. See also Marien y Arróspide, *Tratado general de monedas*, xxxlx–xl, and *passim*. For the use of the piece of eight as a money of account in the Dutch, Danish, and French West Indies, see chap. 4, below. See also W. G. Sumner, "The Spanish Dollar and the Colonial Shilling," *American Historical Review*, III (1897–1898), 607–619.

84. Hayes, *Negociator's Magazine*, 60. Computation: £678.33 at 240d per £1 equals 162,799d, which, divided by 56d per peso, equals 2,907.125 pesos, or 2,907 pesos and 1 real. See also *Compleat Compting-House Companion*, 39.

of Congress. On 15 Jan. 1769, 40d; 27 Feb., 40d; 24 May, 40.5d; 25 July, 40.75d; 24 Mar. 1770, 41d; 2 Aug., 40.25d.

82. See, e.g., the prices current of Jesson, Welsh, and Co. of Cadiz, March and Tilebein of Barcelona, and Philip Roche of Sanlucar sent to Jamieson in the late 1760s and early 1770s. Jamieson Papers, IX, 2053, 2064, XV, 3524, XX, 4562.

83. Ricard, *Traité général du commerce*, [ed. Marien], II, 66, 288, 296. Bewickes, Timerman, and Romero of Cadiz expressed much of this in a letter to Nicholas Brown and Co. of Providence, R.I., 31 May 1774: "Our current dollar of 8 ryals plate is equal to 40 pence sterling on a par of exchange

TABLE 2.28. **Rate of Exchange: London on Cadiz (via Amsterdam), 1680–1714**

(Pence Sterling per Peso de Cambio)

Year	Jan.	Feb.	Mar.	Apr.	May	June	July	Aug.	Sept.	Oct.	Nov.	Dec.	Average
1680				49.26	49.49								49.38
1681												49.97	49.97
1682	49.09			50.10									49.60
1683											50.61		50.61
1684													
1685							51.07						51.07
1686	50.35	50.22											50.28
1687		49.88											49.88
1688	50.60												50.60
1689													
1690													
1691											51.44		51.44
1692						51.63							51.63
1693		53.01		52.49	52.63		52.12	52.26	53.06				52.68
1694	52.99		53.34				53.72	54.17	55.16		54.75	54.77	54.09
1695	54.96	55.22	55.34	57.59	59.45	61.98	61.83	63.30	62.35	63.34			60.17
1696			62.86	60.10				53.54					58.83
1697					47.99			48.17		50.67		51.26	49.04
1698													
1699		55.14	56.36										55.75
1700					51.51								51.51
1701	52.24												52.24
1702													
1703													
1704													
1705					50.45					49.84			50.14
1706								49.77		50.87	50.04		50.11

TABLE 2.28 (Continued): London on Cadiz (Pence Sterling per Peso de Cambio)

Year	Jan.	Feb.	Mar.	Apr.	May	June	July	Aug.	Sept.	Oct.	Nov.	Dec.	Average
1707													
1708										53.69		52.30	53.00
1709		52.14		51.34	48.33	50.26	54.02	53.14	53.37			53.82	52.36
1710	54.32	53.33	52.53	51.64	52.18	52.09	53.39						52.92
1711													
1712													
1713													
1714								51.49					51.49

Notes and Sources: **TABLE 2.28**

1680–1714: N. W. Posthumus, *Inquiry into the History of Prices in Holland* (Leiden, 1946–1964), I, 593–596.

1696–1697: *Cours van koopmanschappen tot Amsterdam* (Amsterdam), 28 Apr. and 11 Aug. 1696, 4 May, 31 Aug., 5 Oct., and 14 Dec. 1697, copies in Matthias Giesque and Co. Papers, bundle no. 68, C. 104/128, pt. 2, Unknown Cause, Public Record Office.

The computation involved first converting the London-Amsterdam exchange rate from schellingen and grooten banco per £1 sterling into grooten and then establishing the ratio between that figure and the figure for the same date for the Cadiz-Amsterdam rate expressed in grooten banco per ducado de cambio of 375 maravedies. Then it was necessary to convert this ratio from ducados to pesos de cambio of 272 maravedies, an operation accomplished by multiplying the ratio by 375 and dividing the product by 272. The quotient represents the number of pesos per £1 sterling; this was then converted to the number of pence per peso by dividing 240 by the quotient. As an example, on 17 May 1680 the London-Amsterdam rate was 35 schellingen and 10 grooten, or 430 grooten, per £1 sterling; the Cadiz-Amsterdam rate was 122.25 grooten per ducado; the former divided by the latter indicated that 3.5173 ducados, or 4.8492 pesos, equaled £1 and 49.492d equaled one peso. One can shorten this procedure by expressing the London rate as a decimal (35.8333), multiplying it by 16.5444, and dividing the product by the Cadiz-Amsterdam rate in grooten per ducado. The result is the number of pesos per £1, which is converted to pence per peso in the same way as above. The London-Cadiz rate for May 1680 is given above as 49.49d per peso de cambio.

TABLE 2.29. **Rate of Exchange: London on Cadiz, 1680–1697**

(Pence Sterling per Peso de Cambio)

Year	Jan.	Feb.	Mar.	Apr.	May	June	July	Aug.	Sept.	Oct.	Nov.	Dec.	Average
1680		49.25											49.25
1681					49.12		49.38				49.25		49.25
1682			50.25			50.50				51.38			50.71
1683	52.00	51.75			50.25			50.75		51.00			50.97
1684												50.12	50.12
1685									50.00		50.75	49.75	50.12
1686													
1687													
1688													
1689						49.50							49.50
1690													
1691	49.38									48.75			49.06
1692	48.25												48.25
1693													
1694										54.50	54.00		54.25
1695	54.75	54.75	55.50	56.25	57.00	60.25	60.50	65.50	62.00	63.50	67.50	58.00	59.62
1696	60.00	62.38	62.00	61.00	58.50	56.00	60.25	60.00	51.50	48.00	46.50	46.50	56.05
1697	47.75	47.00	46.00	48.25	47.00	47.25	48.50	48.00	49.25	51.00	50.23	51.25	48.46

Notes and Sources: **TABLE 2.29**

1680–1697: London price currents as listed in Appendix 2, below.

1695–1697: *A Collection for Improvement of Husbandry and Trade* (London), 18 Jan. 1694/95–31 Dec. 1697 (the figure nearest the middle of the month).

TABLE 2.30. **Rate of Exchange: London on Cadiz, 1698–1775**

(Pence Sterling per Peso de Cambio)

Year	Jan.	Feb.	Mar.	Apr.	May	June	July	Aug.	Sept.	Oct.	Nov.	Dec.	Average
1698	51.75	51.75	51.00	50.25	50.25	50.50	50.25	50.50	50.50	52.62	53.88	52.50	51.31
1699	53.50	53.75	52.75	53.50	53.50	53.75	52.75	53.75	53.00	54.00	53.56	53.25	53.42
1700	53.69	53.25	52.00	51.62	51.25	52.00	51.75	52.75	53.00	52.00	52.62	51.50	52.29
1701	52.00	50.00	49.00	49.50	50.00	50.00	49.25	49.50	50.12	49.75	49.75	50.25	49.93
1702	50.00	50.50	51.00	49.75									50.12
1703													
1704													
1705													
1706													
1707													
1708													
1709													
1710													
1711													
1712													
1713					*48.75*	48.75	48.50	49.50	49.25	48.75	48.75	48.62	48.85
1714	48.25	47.50	49.00	49.62	51.25	52.00	51.44	51.00	50.50	50.00	50.44	50.50	50.12
1715	49.50	48.50	49.38	48.62	48.75	48.50	48.50	48.25	49.75	49.62	47.75	48.25	48.78
1716	48.75	48.75	48.25	48.12	48.62	48.88	49.38	50.75	50.25	50.75	52.88	51.75	49.76
1717	51.50	51.50	51.00	50.50	51.25	51.62	51.62	51.88	52.12	52.06	52.50	52.62	51.68
1718	52.50	52.62	52.50	50.50	50.50	49.75	50.38	49.75	49.75	50.00	49.50	50.00	50.65
1719	49.00	48.88	48.38	47.25	47.88	47.88	48.44	47.62	47.75	48.25	48.25	48.00	48.13
1720	48.00	48.00	49.00	46.88	47.62	48.50	49.62	50.12	50.38	47.25	46.50	47.00	48.24
1721	49.38	49.00	48.00	47.50	47.25	47.62	48.12	47.88	47.50	49.25	49.00	48.75	48.27
1722	48.00	47.88	47.62	47.62	47.25	47.81	47.25	47.50	47.56	47.81	49.06	48.00	47.78

TABLE 2.30 (Continued): London on Cadiz (Pence Sterling per Peso de Cambio)

Year	Jan.	Feb.	Mar.	Apr.	May	June	July	Aug.	Sept.	Oct.	Nov.	Dec.	Average
1723	48.75	49.12	48.75	48.69	49.00	49.50	49.06	49.75	49.75	49.88	50.31	49.38	49.33
1724	50.00	49.88	49.94	49.94	50.00	50.25	50.38	50.75	50.06	50.00	49.94	50.00	50.10
1725	50.25	50.12	50.25	49.81	49.81	49.56	49.88	49.56	48.75	48.62	48.88	48.69	49.52
1726	48.00	46.25	41.50	43.25	42.00	44.00	43.44	42.62	42.88	43.06	43.00	43.00	43.58
1727	43.06	43.12	43.25	43.19	43.25	43.44	44.00	44.44	44.19	43.62	43.50	43.69	43.56
1728	43.75	44.00	44.00	44.12	44.50	44.94	44.50	45.12	44.88	43.19	43.38	43.62	44.17
1729	44.00	43.25	43.25	42.88	43.81	42.88	42.69	43.00	42.69	42.88	43.12	42.88	43.11
1730	42.94	42.94	42.75	42.50	42.38	42.50	42.25	42.25	42.69	42.69	42.25	42.38	42.54
1731	42.00	42.00	42.00	41.62	41.56	41.44	41.25	41.62	42.00	42.50	42.00	41.75	41.81
1732	41.75	41.94	41.94	42.06	42.31	42.56	42.69	42.62	42.38	42.50	42.62	42.25	42.30
1733	42.38	42.25	42.19	41.88	41.75	41.88	42.06	42.12	42.25	42.00	40.31	40.75	41.82
1734	41.00	40.31	40.31	39.88	39.50	39.75	40.44	40.25	40.31	40.25	40.50	40.75	40.27
1735	40.94	40.62	40.50	40.38	40.50	39.94	40.00	40.31	40.31	40.19	40.25	40.12	40.34
1736	40.71	40.81	40.81	40.81	40.75	40.88	41.00	41.06	41.25	41.75	41.25	41.25	41.03
1737	41.62	42.50	41.81	41.56	40.94	39.75	39.50	39.75	39.38	39.56	39.75	39.25	40.45
1738	39.50	39.38	39.44	39.25	39.50	39.62	39.62	39.81	39.69	40.00	40.31	39.62	39.64
1739	39.56	39.69	39.62	39.88	40.94	39.81	39.50	40.19	39.56	39.38	39.62	39.88	39.80
1740	40.19	40.44	40.88	41.12	41.50	42.00	42.06	42.50	42.50	42.25	42.62	42.50	41.71
1741	42.50	42.12	42.50	42.50	42.50	41.56	41.00	40.44	40.38	40.12	40.12	40.25	41.33
1742	40.12	39.75	39.25	39.06	39.12	39.25	39.25	39.62	39.75	39.88	39.62	39.62	39.52
1743	39.62	39.69	40.00	40.00	40.38	41.00	40.94	40.50	41.00	41.06	41.25	41.31	40.56
1744	41.50	41.94	41.00	41.25	41.38	41.75	41.88	42.00	41.12	41.12	40.62	40.81	41.36
1745	40.88	40.75	39.88	39.50	39.56	39.44	39.00	38.75	38.50	*38.19*	38.12	*36.00*	39.05
1746	*36.50*	*37.00*	37.00	37.00	37.00	37.12	38.00	38.00	39.00	38.19	38.50	38.25	37.63
1747	38.75	39.50	40.00	40.38	40.00	40.56	40.50	40.12	39.69	39.25	39.50	39.25	39.79
1748	*38.75*	38.12	*38.00*	38.25	39.00	38.75	39.25	39.75	39.12	39.25	39.62	39.62	38.96
1749	39.38	39.25	39.75	38.50	39.25	38.12	38.56	38.75	39.06	39.25	39.00	39.25	39.01

TABLE 2.30 (Continued): **London on Cadiz** (Pence Sterling per Peso de Cambio)

Year	Jan.	Feb.	Mar.	Apr.	May	June	July	Aug.	Sept.	Oct.	Nov.	Dec.	Average
1750	39.25	39.25	39.19	39.25	39.12	38.62	38.44	38.75	39.19	39.12	39.12	39.12	39.04
1751	39.00	39.25	39.25	39.12	38.56	38.75	39.00	39.12	39.25	39.75	39.69	39.75	39.21
1752	39.62	39.69	39.62	40.12	40.12	39.75	39.88	40.25	40.00	40.00	40.50	40.62	40.01
1753	40.50	40.19	40.50	40.19	40.00	40.38	40.38	40.00	40.00	40.12	40.12	40.00	40.20
1754	39.62	39.19	39.50	39.50	39.69	39.81	39.69	40.38	40.12	40.00	40.00	40.00	39.79
1755	39.62	38.88	39.00	39.00	38.88	39.06	38.56	38.31	*38.53*	38.19	38.50	38.00	38.71
1756	38.00	37.62	37.88	37.81	37.69	37.50	37.94	38.00	37.88	38.00	38.00	37.88	37.85
1757	37.62	38.00	38.12	38.31	38.12	38.12	38.12	38.56	38.50	38.81	38.75	39.00	38.34
1758	39.00	38.88	39.16	39.38	39.50	40.00	39.50	39.94	39.75	39.94	40.38	40.50	39.66
1759	40.62	40.25	40.25	40.00	39.38	39.88	39.69	39.75	39.06	39.00	38.38	38.50	39.56
1760	38.44	38.12	38.12	38.88	38.38	39.50	39.12	39.75	39.75	40.06	39.75	39.50	39.11
1761	39.25	39.50	39.62	39.62	39.88	40.00	39.81	40.00	40.00	39.50	39.00	38.88	39.59
1762	38.62	38.38	39.06	38.88	39.00	39.88	39.38	39.50	39.75	39.62	39.38	39.88	39.28
1763	40.25	40.25	40.12	40.50	40.12	39.62	39.50	38.75	37.75	38.38	38.00	38.00	39.27
1764	38.25	38.44	37.75	38.12	38.00	37.75	37.75	37.88	38.12	38.25	38.62	38.88	38.15
1765	38.88	38.88	38.50	38.88	38.88	38.75	39.00	38.75	39.62	39.50	40.00	39.88	39.13
1766	39.75	39.62	39.94	39.88	40.00	39.88	39.75	39.50	39.62	40.00	39.62	39.75	39.78
1767	39.31	39.00	39.12	39.25	39.62	39.88	39.75	39.81	39.75	39.75	39.62	39.50	39.53
1768	39.25	39.62	39.50	39.50	39.38	39.25	39.19	39.12	39.06	39.00	39.00	39.12	39.25
1769	39.25	39.38	39.31	39.38	39.38	39.38	39.50	39.50	39.88	40.00	39.75	39.81	39.54
1770	39.50	39.62	39.56	39.50	39.50	39.50	39.50	39.50	39.50	39.75	39.38	39.06	39.49
1771	39.00	39.00	39.25	39.38	39.62	39.62	39.88	39.88	39.62	39.81	39.88	39.94	39.57
1772	40.00	39.88	39.88	39.50	39.62	39.62	39.00	39.44	39.56	38.62	39.00	38.50	39.38
1773	38.25	37.62	37.75	38.00	38.00	38.00	37.50	37.38	37.38	37.38	37.25	36.88	37.62
1774	36.62	37.00	36.88	37.00	37.00	36.94	37.50	37.50	37.88	38.62	38.12	38.38	37.45
1775	38.00	38.00	37.94	38.25	38.25	38.25	38.12	38.25	38.00	38.12	38.12	38.00	38.11

Notes and Sources: **TABLE 2.30**

1698–1775: *The Course of the Exchange* (London), 1698–1775. See the discussion above in the initial section of this chapter and in n. 10.

TABLE 2.31. **The Course of the Exchange at Cadiz**

On Amsterdam	1 ducado de cambio of 375 maravedies,	for grooten banco
Hamburg	1 ducado de cambio of 375 maravedies,	for grote-vls. banco
Lisbon	1 peso de cambio,	for réis
London	1 peso de cambio,	for pence sterling
Paris	1 peso de cambio,	for livres tournois

Lisbon

Portugal had within its empire not only Brazil but also several oceanic islands—Madeira, the Azores, and the Cape Verdes. All of them had a place in the commerce of the Atlantic world, especially in the trade of Great Britain and its colonies. The importation of Madeira wine into the West Indies and the continental colonies was an early and continuing trade of some importance. Lisbon as the capital and major commercial city of Portugal and its empire was the locus of most English-Portuguese exchange transactions.

"La maniere de compter en Portugal est très-simple et facile"; the real (plural: réis) was the basic unit of the Portuguese money of account and its real money too.[85] One spoke and kept books in terms of réis and milréis (a thousand réis). It is conventional to use the dollar sign ($) to reproduce the Portuguese symbol (called the *cifrão*) indicating milréis; thus one hundred réis is written $100, and a thousand réis, or one

milréis, 1$000. Ten thousand milréis is denoted 10:000$000.[86] Yet again, the relative simplicity of the money of account is offset by a confusion of real money. The Portuguese government minted a bewildering variety of coins for its real money, a diversity made all the more bewildering when it devalued and reorganized its coinage in 1722. The largest of these, the dobrão, had a pre-1722 value of 24$000; all other coins were denominated proportionately.[87]

Portuguese foreign exchange was also based on the milréis. The par of exchange between Lisbon and London was 150d (62.5p) per 1$000 in 1628 and declined after that to 90d (37.5p) by 1700, and 67.5d (28.1p) in 1759 and after.[88] We can

85. Ricard, *Traité général du commerce*, [ed. Marien], II, 149. In general, on Portuguese money, see Frédéric Mauro, *Le Portugal et l'Atlantique au XVIIe siècle (1570–1670): Étude économique* (Paris, 1960), 395–432.

86. See also [Justice], *General Treatise of Monies*, 175; Philip M. Hamer *et al.*, eds., *The Papers of Henry Laurens* (Columbia, S.C., 1968–), I, xxxii.

87. One can trace this much more precisely in A[ugusto] C. Teixeira de Aragão, *Descripção geral e historica das moedas cunhadas em nome dos reis, regentes e governadores de Portugal* (Lisbon, 1874–1880). See, especially, *ibid.*, II, 237–239. See also J[oaquin] Ferraro Vaz, *Catálogo das moedas portuguesas: Portugal continental, 1640–1948* (Lisbon, 1948).

88. H[unt], *Merchants Jewell*; Ricard, *Traité général du commerce*, 380; [Desaguliers], *General Treatise of the Reduction of the Exchanges*, trans. J[ustice], table 24; [Slack], *British Negociator*, 133; "Intrinsic Par of Exchange," in "Reports from the Select Committee on Gold Bullion," Great Britain, House of

call up the usual example from Richard Hayes, but the procedure seems so straightforward as hardly to warrant it. If one in London wished to remit £826.80 to Portugal and the exchange rate were 53.5d (22.3p) per milréis, he would expect a yield of 3:709$009.[89] Tables 2.32, 2.33, 2.34, and 2.35 present the available quotations of the London-Lisbon exchange rate from 1619 to 1775.[90] Table 2.35 shows the exchange format with the other European cities with which Lisbon negotiated regularly. Transactions with them were as uncomplicated as they were with London.

Commons, *Sess. Papers*, 1810, III (*Reports*), no. 349, p. 207. See also Fisher, *Portugal Trade*, passim

89. Hayes, *Negociator's Magazine*, 68. Computation: £826.80 times 240d per £1 equals 198,432d, which, divided by 53.5d per milréis, equals 3,709.009 milréis. See also *Compleat Compting-House Companion*, 41.

90. We can compute an earlier rate via the Antwerp exchange. In 1564 the London-Lisbon exchange averaged 165d per milréis according to these quotations and in 1566, 156d. Vázquez de Prada, *Lettres marchandes d'Anvers*, I, 270–271.

TABLE 2.32. Rate of Exchange: London on Lisbon (via Amsterdam), 1619–1697

(Pence Sterling per Milréis)

Year	Jan.	Feb.	Mar.	Apr.	May	June	July	Aug.	Sept.	Oct.	Nov.	Dec.	Average
1619								155.71					155.71
1642					135.08								135.08
1643													
1644													
1645	102.97	103.29											103.13
1676										81.85			81.85
1677	82.32	81.22	81.82				82.45						82.12
1678	81.42												81.42
1679													
1680													
1681													
1682													
1683													

TABLE 2.32 (Continued): **London on Lisbon** (Pence Sterling per Milréis)

Year	Jan.	Feb.	Mar.	Apr.	May	June	July	Aug.	Sept.	Oct.	Nov.	Dec.	Average
1684													
1685													
1686	75.35	74.48											74.92
1687		72.26											72.26
1688	77.99												77.99
1689													
1690													
1691											71.39		71.39
1692						72.64							72.64
1693		76.02		76.16	76.77		76.54	77.67	78.52				76.69
1694	80.50		81.20				77.83	77.37	80.45		80.01	79.33	79.69
1695	78.46	78.38	77.95	78.58	78.78	80.90	80.57	81.60	85.33	83.93			81.03
1696		81.32	81.10			82.73		76.53					79.92
1697					71.55			68.64		69.20		67.15	69.46

Notes and Sources: **TABLE 2.32**

1619–1696: N. W. Posthumus, *Inquiry into the History of Prices in Holland* (Leiden, 1946–1964), I, 590–595.

1696: *Proctor's Price-Courant: The Prices of Merchandise in London* (London), 28 Feb., 3 Apr., 30 Apr., 21 May, and 11 June 1696. For these London price currents see Appendix 2, below.

1696–1697: *Cours van koopmanschappen tot Amsterdam* (Amsterdam), 28 Apr. and 11 Aug. 1696, 4 May, 31 Aug., 5 Oct., and 14 Dec. 1697, copies in Matthias Giesque and Co. Papers, bundle no. 68, C. 104/128, pt. 2, Unknown Cause, Public Record Office.

The computation involved converting the Lisbon-Amsterdam rate from grooten banco for 1 cruzado of 400 réis into grooten per milréis and then establishing the ratio between that figure and the figure for the same date for the London-Amsterdam rate converted from schellingen and grooten banco to grooten per £1 sterling. The ratio of milréis per £1 had then to be reduced to pence per milréis. As an example, on 19 Aug. 1619 the Lisbon-Amsterdam rate was 109 grooten banco per cruzado, or 272.5 grooten per milréis; the London-Amsterdam rate was 35 schellingen banco, or 420 grooten per £1 sterling; the former divided by the latter indicates that £0.6488, or 155.714d, equaled one milréis. A shortcut to this procedure involves multiplying the Lisbon rate in grooten by 50 and dividing the product by the London rate in schellingen decimalized (109 × 50 = 5,450 ÷ 35 = 155.714). The London-Lisbon rate for Aug. 1619 is given above as 155.71 pence sterling per milréis.

TABLE 2.33. **Rate of Exchange: London on Lisbon, 1680–1697**

(Pence Sterling per Milréis)

Year	Jan.	Feb.	Mar.	Apr.	May	June	July	Aug.	Sept.	Oct.	Nov.	Dec.	Average
1680		82.25											82.25
1681					78.75		77.25				78.50		78.17
1682			78.50			79.00				78.50			78.67
1683	79.25	79.00			76.00			77.00		77.00			77.28
1684												76.38	76.38
1685									74.75		75.00	75.50	75.00
1686													
1687													
1688													
1689						74.46							74.46
1690													
1691	73.00									72.00			72.50
1692	71.00												71.00
1693			76.00										76.00
1694										84.00		78.50		81.25
1695	78.25	77.12	77.25	76.50	77.50	78.75	79.25	87.00	74.00	89.00	87.00	78.00	79.97
1696	79.00	82.00	82.00	81.00	79.00	82.00	82.00	75.00	75.00	68.00	67.50	68.00	76.71
1697	72.00	70.00	69.00	69.00	68.00	67.25	67.00	68.00	68.50	68.75	66.50	67.00	68.42

Notes and Sources: **TABLE 2.33**

1680–1697: London price currents as listed in Appendix 2, below.

1695–1697: *A Collection for Improvement of Husbandry and Trade* (London), 18 Jan. 1694/95–31 Dec. 1697 (the figure nearest the middle of the month).

TABLE 2.34. Rate of Exchange: London on Lisbon, 1698–1775

(Pence Sterling per Milréis)

Year	Jan.	Feb.	Mar.	Apr.	May	June	July	Aug.	Sept.	Oct.	Nov.	Dec.	Average
1698	67.75	66.75	66.75	66.38	66.50	65.25	65.25	67.25	66.62	67.25	68.00	69.00	66.90
1699	71.00	69.25	71.00	70.25	71.25	71.88	70.75	72.75	73.00	74.25	75.00	75.12	72.12
1700	73.50	73.25	73.50	73.50	72.00	71.25	72.50	72.12	73.50	73.00	74.00	72.50	72.88
1701	72.50	69.00	69.00	70.00	70.25	71.25	70.00	70.25	69.75	69.50	69.50	69.75	70.06
1702	70.00	71.50	70.75	69.50	67.50	67.50	69.50	69.75	71.00	69.88	68.75	68.50	69.51
1703	68.75	68.00	70.00	68.50	67.50	69.25	69.00	71.25	70.50	72.50	72.75	71.00	69.92
1704	72.00	71.88	72.31	75.38	75.00	74.50	74.00	73.25	71.00	70.75	69.19	70.75	72.50
1705	69.62	70.25	69.00	69.62	68.25	69.00	68.88	69.25	70.50	69.75	68.75	69.25	69.34
1706	70.25	70.00	70.62	70.25	70.50	69.75	69.38	69.25	69.00	69.50	69.00	69.00	69.71
1707	69.62	68.75	69.00	69.12	68.25	67.75	67.25	66.00	66.50	65.75	65.00	63.50	67.21
1708	63.25	63.00	62.50	61.00	61.00	60.50	62.75	62.75	63.25	61.00	63.50	64.00	62.38
1709	65.38	64.00	63.00	62.38	62.50	64.50	64.00	65.50	65.25	67.25	68.25	67.88	64.99
1710	67.25	68.25	68.25	68.00	67.62	66.62	67.00	66.38	66.25	61.50	61.25	61.25	65.80
1711	61.50	62.00	62.50	61.75	61.62	61.25	62.62	61.88	60.62	61.00	61.12	60.00	61.49
1712	61.00	62.50	62.25	63.00	63.38	63.50	64.12	64.75	63.75	64.00	64.38	62.88	63.29
1713	63.25	63.12	62.50	62.62	63.00	64.25	64.12	64.50	64.25	64.00	64.81	64.75	63.76
1714	65.00	64.00	64.88	65.81	65.12	65.25	65.25	65.38	65.00	65.25	66.25	65.88	65.26
1715	65.75	65.12	65.31	65.00	65.38	65.38	65.31	64.75	65.25	65.00	63.62	64.88	65.06
1716	65.81	65.50	65.75	65.75	65.75	65.75	66.00	66.25	66.44	66.75	66.00	66.75	66.04
1717	66.88	66.38	66.38	66.25	66.25	66.25	66.25	66.25	66.50	66.75	66.69	67.00	66.49
1718	65.88	66.00	66.50	64.75	65.25	65.00	65.25	65.75	65.88	65.06	64.50	65.25	65.42
1719	64.94	65.50	63.75	63.50	64.00	63.75	64.25	64.31	64.75	65.00	64.25	65.00	64.42
1720	64.50	63.75	63.25	63.00	63.56	64.75	64.62	75.00	66.00	61.00	62.62	62.62	64.56
1721	63.00	64.00	65.12	64.88	64.56	64.00	64.25	65.12	64.88	63.88	63.81	62.62	64.18
1722	64.00	64.25	63.88	63.88	63.31	64.62	64.50	64.50	64.67	64.62	64.50	64.31	64.25

TABLE 2.34 (Continued): London on Lisbon (Pence Sterling per Milréis)

Year	Jan.	Feb.	Mar.	Apr.	May	June	July	Aug.	Sept.	Oct.	Nov.	Dec.	Average
1723	64.38	64.56	64.56	64.94	65.19	65.50	65.06	65.19	65.06	65.19	65.00	64.44	64.92
1724	64.50	64.31	65.00	65.19	65.56	65.62	66.06	65.62	65.88	65.50	65.44	65.62	65.36
1725	65.44	65.19	65.25	66.00	65.75	65.94	65.88	65.56	65.75	65.69	65.19	65.12	65.56
1726	65.06	64.44	64.19	64.69	63.25	63.69	64.25	64.56	64.56	64.06	64.31	64.44	64.29
1727	64.69	64.94	64.94	64.94	65.00	64.69	64.81	65.06	65.69	65.69	65.06	65.19	65.06
1728	65.56	65.50	65.88	66.00	66.06	65.75	66.25	66.38	66.12	66.31	66.50	66.31	66.05
1729	65.69	65.75	66.19	66.06	65.94	66.00	66.06	66.38	66.00	66.31	66.44	66.56	66.12
1730	66.50	66.44	66.44	66.44	66.25	66.44	65.81	66.06	65.94	66.00	65.69	65.62	66.14
1731	65.69	65.50	65.69	65.44	65.75	65.56	65.75	65.94	66.12	66.00	65.56	65.50	65.71
1732	65.69	65.69	65.44	66.00	65.69	65.88	66.00	66.00	65.94	65.81	65.69	65.50	65.78
1733	65.50	65.12	65.25	65.44	65.69	65.81	65.75	65.69	65.56	64.88	64.25	64.56	65.29
1734	64.31	64.44	64.62	64.25	64.81	65.46	65.19	65.44	65.75	65.69	65.88	65.81	65.14
1735	65.69	65.81	65.81	66.25	66.06	66.12	66.38	65.94	65.94	66.00	65.94	66.00	66.00
1736	66.00	66.12	66.12	65.98	66.00	65.69	65.69	65.91	65.88	65.81	65.44	65.12	65.81
1737	65.44	65.81	65.56	65.94	66.00	66.06	65.94	65.69	65.56	65.62	65.44	65.56	65.72
1738	65.50	65.08	65.28	65.38	65.50	65.44	65.50	65.56	65.56	65.62	65.56	65.66	65.47
1739	65.75	65.62	65.69	65.62	65.69	65.69	65.12	65.19	64.69	64.56	64.94	65.06	65.30
1740	65.03	64.69	65.19	65.50	65.19	65.31	64.44	64.21	63.85	64.12	65.06	64.75	64.78
1741	64.81	65.25	64.88	65.44	65.38	65.56	65.31	65.31	64.19	65.00	65.00	65.25	65.12
1742	65.19	65.06	65.00	65.38	65.38	65.50	65.38	65.69	65.44	65.88	65.50	65.69	65.42
1743	65.81	65.75	66.06	66.00	66.31	66.38	66.25	66.38	66.38	66.31	66.00	66.25	66.16
1744	66.25	66.44	66.31	65.12	64.00	64.19	64.00	64.19	64.12	65.06	64.94	65.00	64.97
1745	64.50	64.06	64.31	64.75	65.00	65.00	65.06	65.25	65.06	64.50	64.44	62.25	64.52
1746	62.44	62.75	62.44	64.00	64.62	64.50	65.06	65.31	65.38	65.38	65.25	64.62	64.31
1747	64.62	65.06	65.00	65.06	65.50	65.75	65.62	64.94	64.94	64.94	64.88	64.81	65.09
1748	64.06	63.69	63.69	64.38	65.62	65.25	65.19	65.38	65.56	65.44	65.06	65.06	64.86
1749	65.44	65.94	65.44	65.25	65.56	65.31	65.00	65.75	65.94	66.00	65.75	66.12	65.62

TABLE 2.34 (Continued): **London on Lisbon** (Pence Sterling per Milréis)

Year	Jan.	Feb.	Mar.	Apr.	May	June	July	Aug.	Sept.	Oct.	Nov.	Dec.	Average
1750	66.12	65.69	66.00	65.81	65.50	65.44	65.12	65.44	65.38	65.56	65.62	65.69	65.61
1751	65.56	65.31	65.38	65.50	65.69	65.44	65.38	65.50	65.61	66.00	66.00	65.75	65.59
1752	65.69	65.44	65.69	65.88	65.81	66.06	65.94	66.06	66.12	66.25	66.25	66.06	65.94
1753	66.00	65.88	66.06	65.06	65.94	65.88	65.69	66.00	65.94	66.00	65.62	65.75	65.82
1754	65.56	65.31	65.50	65.75	65.56	65.62	65.62	65.81	65.62	66.00	65.75	65.62	65.64
1755	65.62	65.31	65.25	65.25	65.00	65.31	64.88	64.56	64.50	64.50	64.69	64.37	64.94
1756	64.25	64.38	64.62	64.75	64.50	64.56	64.69	64.75	65.12	65.12	65.12	64.88	64.73
1757	64.75	65.12	65.25	65.00	64.25	64.00	64.12	64.00	64.19	64.62	64.56	64.62	64.54
1758	64.75	64.75	65.00	65.38	65.31	65.38	65.25	65.38	65.38	66.00	66.25	66.00	65.40
1759	65.62	65.75	65.88	65.75	65.56	65.75	65.50	65.44	65.56	65.56	65.38	65.12	65.57
1760	65.12	65.38	65.50	65.56	65.75	65.88	66.00	66.19	65.75	66.31	66.25	65.50	65.77
1761	65.25	65.56	65.50	65.25	65.94	66.00	66.00	66.00	67.25	66.19	66.00	65.81	65.90
1762	65.00	65.12	65.38	66.06	66.75	66.00	67.00	67.50	67.50	67.00	65.88	66.00	66.27
1763	66.00	66.25	66.75	67.00	67.50	66.75	67.12	66.31	66.06	66.69	66.88	65.50	66.57
1764	65.12	65.00	65.00	65.31	65.75	65.75	65.50	65.50	65.12	65.44	65.75	65.75	65.42
1765	65.62	65.75	65.75	65.88	65.81	66.00	66.06	66.06	66.00	66.00	66.00	66.00	65.91
1766	66.12	65.75	65.75	66.50	67.00	67.00	67.00	67.00	67.19	66.50	66.25	66.25	66.53
1767	66.38	66.62	66.50	66.75	66.69	67.00	67.19	66.88	66.88	66.75	66.50	66.50	66.72
1768	66.75	66.75	66.50	66.44	66.50	66.50	66.50	66.38	66.50	66.50	66.62	66.50	66.54
1769	66.31	66.38	66.62	66.62	67.50	67.50	67.12	67.25	67.62	67.12	67.00	66.88	66.99
1770	66.31	66.75	66.69	66.94	66.94	66.75	66.75	67.00	67.12	66.62	66.50	66.62	66.75
1771	66.25	66.12	66.62	66.50	67.00	67.75	67.75	67.75	67.75	68.00	68.25	67.94	67.31
1772	67.25	67.69	67.19	67.50	67.81	67.75	66.44	67.25	66.50	65.50	66.00	65.50	66.86
1773	65.12	65.50	65.75	65.81	65.75	65.75	65.25	65.44	65.75	65.75	65.75	66.00	65.64
1774	66.25	66.00	65.56	66.00	65.88	65.50	65.69	65.31	65.12	65.62	65.62	65.62	65.68
1775	65.69	65.00	65.00	64.62	65.12	65.12	65.00	65.12	65.25	65.25	65.12	65.06	65.11

Notes and Sources: **TABLE 2.34**

1698–1775: *The Course of the Exchange* (London), 1698–1775. See the discussion above in the initial section of this chapter and in n. 10.

[114] Lisbon

TABLE 2.35. Rate of Exchange: Lisbon on London, 1760–1775
(Pence Sterling per Milréis)

Year	Jan.	Feb.	Mar.	Apr.	May	June	July	Aug.	Sept.	Oct.	Nov.	Dec.	Average
1760	66.62												66.62
1761													
1762	66.75		66.44		67.75								67.17
1763													
1764							66.75	66.75					66.75
1765								67.00					67.00
1766	67.00	67.00											67.00
1767		67.25											67.25
1768							67.25			67.25			67.25
1769						68.00	68.25	68.00	68.00				68.04
1770	68.00			68.25	68.00								68.06
1771													
1772						68.75				67.50			68.12
1773													
1774	66.75	66.75		66.62				66.00	65.88				66.44
1775		66.00			65.75								65.88

Notes and Sources: **TABLE 2.35**

1760–1768: Mayne, Burns, and Mayne (later Mayne and Co.), at Lisbon, to Samuel Galloway, at Annapolis, Md., 23 Jan. 1760, 21 Jan. and 19 May 1762, 5 July 1764, 5 Aug. 1765, 11 Mar. 1766, 26 Oct. 1768, Galloway Correspondence, III, no. 8397, IV, no. 8685, V, no. 8748, VII, nos. 9121, 9123, VIII, nos. 9277, 9360, IX, no. 9543, Galloway-Maxey-Markoe Family Papers, 1654-1888, Library of Congress.

1762–1767: Mayne, Burns, and Mayne to Galloway and Stephen Steward, at Annapolis, Md., 8 Mar. and 19 May 1762, 1 Aug. 1764, 18 Jan. 1766, 21 Feb. 1767, Correspondence, 1739–1769, Galloway Papers, New York Public Library, New York City.

1768, 1774: Raymond Dea and Co., at Lisbon, to Coxe and Furman, at Philadelphia, 19 July 1768, and Parr, Bulkeley, and Co., at Lisbon, to Coxe and Furman, 18 May 1774, Correspondence, 1672–1775, Coxe Papers, Historical Society of Pennsylvania, Philadelphia.

1768–1772: Mayne and Co. to Neil Jamieson, at Norfolk, Va., 5 Aug. 1768, 17 June, 25 July, 8 Aug., and 22 Sept. 1769, 18 Jan., 20 Apr., and 7 June 1770, 10 Oct. 1772, and Pasleys and Co., at Lisbon, to Jamieson, 3 June 1772, Neil Jamieson Papers, 1757–1789, IX, no. 1967, X, nos. 2241, 2270, 2281, XI, nos. 2327, 2437, XII, nos. 2533, 2613, XV, no. 3417, XVI, no. 3595, Lib. Cong.

1774–1775: Parr, Bulkeley, and Co. to Christopher Champlin, at Newport, R.I., 25 Jan., 5 Feb., 9 Aug., 25 Aug., and 24 Sept. 1774, 1 Feb. and 14 June 1775, [Worthington C. Ford, ed.], *Commerce of Rhode Island, 1726–1800* (Massachusetts Historical Society, *Collections*, 7th Ser., IX–X [Boston, 1914–1915]), I, 479, 480, 504, 510, 515, II, 7, 23.

TABLE 2.36. **The Course of the Exchange at Lisbon**

On Amsterdam	1 cruzado of 400 réis,	for grooten banco
Cadiz	for réis,	1 peso de cambio
Hamburg	1 cruzado of 400 réis,	for grote-vls. banco
London	1 milréis,	for pence sterling
Paris	for réis,	1 ecu of 60 sous tournois

I have tried to assemble sufficient information in this chapter to enable a researcher to convert a value in one European currency into its equivalent in another currency. In order to make the use of the present data even easier, summary tables are presented in chapter 5 for comparison with similar tables from chapters 3 and 4. These tables indicate the annual average amount in each currency equivalent to £100 sterling, using figures that come directly from the tables in each chapter; therefore, for those years when data are lacking, no figures are recorded. However, the exchange rate can be estimated, as I have noted. I would first counsel the use of a value interpolated on a straight-line basis from the data already available. When the gap is too large, one can always revert to the par of exchange as a somewhat less satisfactory surrogate. Better than both of these attempts to "paper over" the gaps in the data presented here would be further research and the discovery of actual quotations.

Chapter 3

British Colonial Exchange on London:
The North American Colonies

"The colonies on the continent
very much differ in [the] proportion
[that] their currency beares to stirling,
and each collony dayly alters."[1]

An introduction to the subject of colonial exchange must touch on a variety of topics: the moneys in use, real and imaginary; the mechanical aspects of negotiating bills of exchange; and the nature of the sources used in compiling series of exchange rate quotations. As the general observations that follow on these topics are relevant to all the New World colonies, they will apply to the next chapter as well as to this one.

In Europe, as we have seen, the exchange rate varied around par in response to changes in the supply of and demand for bills of exchange. These changes themselves reflected both short- and long-term economic pressures, the most important of which was the shifting balance of payments situation of each country. The same was true in the

colonies. And the same mechanisms were available to relieve undue pressure on the rate of exchange induced by an increasing demand for and/or a decreasing supply of bills. Colonial trade was largely involved in multilateral arrangements designed indirectly to establish credits in London upon which to draw bills. Moreover, the colonists were well aware from the first of the "specie export point" and their option to export coin when the bill rate moved too high—when, to put it another way, the cost of a bill in terms of coin was so high as to yield a smaller return than what one could get by shipping the coin itself.

So limited was the supply of bills in some colonies in the seventeenth century that the bill rate rather regularly exceeded the specie export point. In consequence, the colonists frequently resorted to shipping gold and silver to pay their accounts in the mother country. Yet, without an indigenous source of gold or silver, the local supply of coin sometimes

---

1. Gov. Lewis Morris to Lt. Gov. Alexander Spotswood, at Virginia, 5 May 1740, [William A. Whitehead, ed.], *The Papers of Lewis Morris, Governor of the Province of New Jersey from 1738 to 1746* (New Jersey Historical Society, *Collections*, IV [New York, 1852]), 89, hereafter cited as *Papers of Lewis Morris*.

proved less than adequate both to service international trade and to provide a money for the colony's own internal trade. All of the English continental colonies, the West Indies islands of almost every European power, and even Brazil, had serious difficulty in maintaining an adequate supply of money within the confines of the local economy. How to repair this loss was a perplexing problem, the solutions to which were intimately tied to the market for colonial bills of exchange.

The colonists tried four successive modes of dealing with the perennial insufficiency of the circulating medium of exchange in their societies. And the adoption of a later, perhaps more sophisticated device did not necessarily mean the abandonment of an earlier one. By the time of the American Revolution, the colonists exchanged with one another using all four: barter, commodity money, overvalued coin, and paper currency.

Barter in the colonies quickly developed beyond the rather crude immediate trade of one commodity for another. What W. T. Baxter called "bookkeeping barter," in which two individuals kept running accounts of the money value of goods traded—in terms of the money of account—appears in the earliest mercantile records we have for the colonies.[2] Moreover, this "bookkeeping barter" not only involved commodities and two individuals but could and did extend to three-sided transfers of both goods and credit.[3] If A owed B a sum of money and C owed A similarly, the accounts of all three were frequently balanced by the transfer of something of value or a book credit from C to B. Bookkeeping devices

such as this were a significant addition to the medium of exchange.

So was commodity money. Sugar and tobacco early served as money in the West Indies and the Chesapeake. Fees, taxes, personal debts—all could be settled in pounds of these commodities. In other colonies with a diversity of locally produced crops, many of them were given an official value for the payment of taxes and would then "circulate" at that rate. In these instances the colonial legislature established the legal value of sugar, tobacco, or whatever. Elsewhere commodities with a consistent demand, notably molasses and rum, tended to take on the character of a commodity money without the benefit of law. In the eighteenth-century Chesapeake receipts for tobacco that had been delivered to official warehouses began to circulate as tobacco notes, and Baxter ascribes a similar currency to orders on distillers for rum to be produced out of deposited molasses.[4]

These measures were less than satisfactory for a number of reasons. As a medium of exchange, commodity money

2. W. T. Baxter, *The House of Hancock: Business in Boston, 1724–1775*, Harvard Studies in Business History, X (Cambridge, Mass., 1945), 17–21.

3. Much of what follows is derived from Baxter, *House of Hancock*, 24–26, 29–32. See also W. T. Baxter, "Credit, Bills, and Bookkeeping in a Simple Economy," *Accounting Review*, XXI (1946), 154–166.

4. Baxter, *House of Hancock*, 28. See also Providence distiller Daniel Tillinghast to Aaron Lopez, of Newport, R.I., 20 Mar. 1771, mentioning "the order you drew in favor of Mr. Eddy for 100 gallons" of rum, in [Worthington C. Ford, ed.], *Commerce of Rhode Island, 1726–1800* (Massachusetts Historical Society, *Collections*, 7th Ser., IX–X [Boston, 1914–1915]), I, 361, hereafter cited as *Commerce of Rhode Island*.

For commodity money see Curtis P. Nettels, *The Money Supply of the American Colonies before 1720*, University of Wisconsin Studies in the Social Sciences and History, No. 20 (Madison, Wis., 1934), 202–228. See also Clarence P. Gould, *Money and Transportation in Maryland, 1720–1765*, Johns Hopkins University Studies in Historical and Political Science, Ser. XXXIII, no. 1 (Baltimore, 1915), 48–73; Donald B. Scheick, "The Regulation of Commodity Money in Colonial Virginia" (Ph.D. diss., Indiana University, 1954). Tobacco warehouse certificates were in use in Antigua in the 1660s and 1670s. C. S. S. Higham, *The Development of the Leeward Islands under the Restoration, 1660–1688: A Study of the Foundations of the Old Colonial System* (Cambridge, 1921), 193–194.

had several defects related to the variable quality and perishable nature of the goods involved. No one paid much heed to these defects in public transactions—and government tax men regularly received the worst grain, tobacco, and sugar. Private transactions were another matter, however, and "country pay," a variation of commodity money, grew up as a way to overcome such difficulties.

Basically country pay involved the tendering and receiving of commodities at a regular discount from their official value, to compensate for the costs of storage, shipping, losses due to deterioration, and so forth. Prices of goods, which varied depending on the form of payment, were regularly higher, usually by a standard ratio, for purchases made with country pay. Such a system was at work in seventeenth-century New England and New York, in eighteenth-century North Carolina, and probably at other times and places too.[5] As bills of exchange were not usually purchased with country pay, it is of less significance for this handbook than the other devices to increase the local circulating medium of exchange.

Overvalued coin, the third such device, had as its object simply to attract to the colony and keep there more of the available gold and silver coin. Some colonists hoped to do so by giving that coin a higher value in their local money of account than the coin could command elsewhere. English, Dutch, Danish, and Brazilian colonial statute books are littered with legislation increasing the price per ounce of gold and silver coin to something above that paid in the mother country. Thus the piece of eight worth 4s 6d (22.5p) sterling in England passed for 5s (25p) in some colonies, 6s (30p) in others, and 9s 6d (47.5p) in still others. Although such laws appeared to have the desired effect, one could argue that the resulting influx of coin into the marketplace came not from outside the colony but from the strongboxes of colonists who, upon hearing that the legislature was considering such a bill, had withheld their coin from circulation until the bill's passage called it out to circulate at the new, higher value.[6] Moreover, prices of goods and services soon rose to reflect the increased value of gold and silver, thus reestablishing the old equilibrium.[7] Finally, neighboring colonies regularly retaliated by passing similar laws, which tended to draw to them the newly liberated coin from the colony that started it all.[8] About the only colonists who were uniformly successful in increasing their circulating medium of exchange by overvaluing coin were the French in the West Indies, who gave

5. [Sarah Kemble Knight], *The Journal of Madam Knight* (1704), ed. Theodore Dwight (New York, 1825), 40–41. Cf. Roger W. Weiss, "The Colonial Monetary Standard of Massachusetts," *Econ. Hist. Rev.*, 2d Ser., XXVII (1974), 583–584.

6. As was the case in 1698 with Jonathan Dickinson, at Philadelphia, who wrote his brother Caleb in Jamaica on 14 May 1698 of the £100 "in cash" that Caleb had "by me" and that "layes expecting an advance by raiseing of the money." The Pennsylvania legislature passed the law within the month. Dickinson/Logan Letter Book, 1698–1742, Logan Papers, 1664–1871, Historical Society of Pennsylvania, Philadelphia.

7. Nettels, *Money Supply, passim*. This "crying-up of money" was nothing more than what we know today as "devaluation." See Fernand P. Braudel and Frank C. Spooner's chapter, "Prices in Europe from 1450 to 1750," in E. E. Rich and C. H. Wilson, eds., *The Cambridge Economic History of Europe*, IV: *The Economy of Expanding Europe in the Sixteenth and Seventeenth Centuries* (Cambridge, 1967), 382–386; and E. James Ferguson, "Colonial Finance: An Interpretation of Colonial Monetary Practices," *William and Mary Quarterly*, 3d Ser., X (1953), 168.

8. The "inhancing the vallew of all foran quoine," as the freeholders of Accomack County, Va., understood in Oct. 1697, had the great disadvantage that "neighbouring provinces and governments" could do the same thing "to our impouvershment." William P. Palmer *et al.*, eds., *Calendar of Virginia State Papers and Other Manuscripts . . .* (Richmond, Va., 1875–1893), I, 53.

all coins currency by tale, not by weight as was common elsewhere. In this way the French West Indies became the dumping ground of all the underweight coin in the Western Hemisphere.[9] But they, at least, had a local money.

By the turn of the century most of these devices had been pretty much tried and found wanting. Then came the era of paper money, initiated when in the 1660s the *Wexelbank* (bank of exchange) in Stockholm issued paper notes to circulate in lieu of Swedish copper money, the largest "coin" of which weighed a staggering forty-three pounds.[10] The colonists' need, however, was to replace not a cumbersome currency but a disappearing one. French Canada became the first colony to turn to paper, in the 1680s, and Massachusetts was the next, a decade later. By the middle of the eighteenth century almost all of the English continental colonies had some form of paper money; following the example of the French and the English, much of the Atlantic world tried a paper currency before the end of the century that Johann Georg Büsch called "das papierene jahrhundert."[11]

In most colonies paper money took the form of bills of credit redeemable by the colonial government; in most places, too, these bills of credit eventually had in law the status of legal tender and were worth silver at the legal rate of its

value. The colonists thus united their money of account and their real money in paper money and helped, in part, to solve their problems with their circulating medium of exchange.[12] Governor Lewis Morris spoke for more than just the people of New Jersey when he wrote that "the generality" preferred "bills of credit currant amongst them, whose vallue they know, to silver and gold, [the value of] which they do not [know]."[13] It was not fortuitous that the issuance of paper money and a period of significant economic development accompanied each other; nor were Parliament's attempts to limit British colonial paper money and the American Revolution unrelated.

12. Nettels, *Money Supply*, 180n, 249, 250–277; Leslie Van Horn Brock, *The Currency of the American Colonies, 1700–1764: A Study in Colonial Finance and Imperial Relations* (Ph.D. diss., University of Michigan, 1941; reprinted New York, 1975), *passim*; Joseph Albert Ernst, *Money and Politics in America, 1755–1775: A Study in the Currency Act of 1764 and the Political Economy of Revolution* (Chapel Hill, N.C., 1973), *passim*.

13. Morris to Board of Trade, 16 Aug. 1741, C.O. 5/973, fol. 164v, P.R.O., and in *Papers of Lewis Morris*, 135. See also Morris to Gov. William Shirley of Mass., 9 Sept. 1743, *ibid.*, 167; and the news item, dateline London, 25 July, in the *Scots Magazine*, XXXVI (1774), 389. Numbers of the documents relating to the British colonies that are in the Public Record Office are also available in other forms. Many state and national historical agencies, for instance, have obtained transcripts and copies of documents that relate to their own history, mostly from the Colonial Office series; some have published such papers. The best known of these publication projects, done under the auspices of the P.R.O. itself, is the continuing W. Noel Sainsbury *et al.*, eds., *Calendar of State Papers, Colonial Series* (London, 1860–). Economic historians need to be cautious in using almost all of these calendars and collections, for two reasons. (1) Economic materials in the original documents are rarely included in the published versions; for example, the enclosures in official correspondence are seldom reproduced, and it is typically there that one finds the reports of the colonial treasurer, the results of colonial censuses, and so forth. (2) Even when economic materials are reproduced, they are frequently misinterpreted and distorted—for example, the Virginia petition that I used in preparing this handbook (C.O. 1/47, fol. 83r) discusses the need to inflate

9. See the discussion below in chap. 4 in the section on "The French Colonies and the Exchange on Paris." See also [Fayrer Hall], *Remarks upon a Book, Entituled, The Present State of the Sugar Colonies Consider'd* . . . (London, 1731), 17; "Extract of a letter from a gentleman at New York dated the 4th of March, 1772, to his friend in Quebec," *Quebec Gazette*, 28 May 1772.

10. Eli F. Heckscher, "The Bank of Sweden in Its Connection with the Bank of Amsterdam," in J. G. van Dillen, ed., *History of the Principal Public Banks* (The Hague, 1934), 169–171.

11. Johann Georg Büsch, *Sämtliche Schriften über Banken und Münzwesen*, [ed. Christoph D. Ebeling] (Hamburg, 1801), 221–230.

The colonists, then, used their real money expressed in terms of their money of account to purchase bills of exchange on their respective mother countries. These colonial moneys of account invariably employed the notation of the motherland, but their value, with some exceptions, was less than that of the metropolis. Colonial pounds were worth less than pounds sterling, colonial livres worth less than livres tournois, and so on. The par of exchange and the commercial rate of exchange were expressions of those differences.

The par of exchange was based on the legal value of the Spanish piece of eight as set down in the statute books of mother country and colony. A New York or Massachusetts law valuing the piece of eight at 6s (30p) local currency contrasted with British regulations that valued it as 4s 6d (22.5p) sterling; the resulting ratio, 1.33⅓ to 1, was the par of exchange between the particular colonial currency and sterling. Depending on the time and place, some colonists expressed this in terms of the percent over the British value ("the par of exchange is 33⅓"), and other colonists expressed par in terms of the percentage increase over the British value ("the par of exchange is 133⅓").

The expression of the commercial rate of exchange followed similar patterns. Sometimes one spoke of the sum necessary to buy a hundred units of the motherland's money. Henry Laurens of Charleston once wrote that exchange was "at 721 per cent"; he meant that he had to pay £721 South

Carolina currency to buy a bill for £100 sterling.[14] But sometimes, using the same phrases, the colonists spoke in terms of the percentage increase in local currency necessary to buy a bill on the metropolis. When Thomas Hancock of Boston spoke of bills that "go off at 800 per cent," he meant that it took £900 Massachusetts currency to buy a bill worth £100 sterling.[15] Hancock's was, in fact, the more usual style, but in several English colonies both were occasionally used interchangeably. In the French colonies the percentage difference indicated by the exchange rate specified the discount from livres tournois necessary to establish the equivalent to colonial livres.[16] The tables in these next two chapters regularly follow Laurens, however, and express the exchange rate as the total cost in colonial currency necessary to buy one hundred units of the currency of the mother country.

It is distinctly misleading, therefore, to refer to any colo-

14. Laurens to Joseph and Jonathan Brooks, of Liverpool, 17 Aug. 1763, Philip M. Hamer *et al.*, eds., *The Papers of Henry Laurens* (Columbia, S.C., 1968–), III, 530, hereafter cited as *Papers of Henry Laurens*. We can verify this by checking his arithmetic. He tells us that £497.35 sterling "at 721 per cent" amounted to £3,585.85 (i.e., 497.35 x 7.21 = 3,585.89). This is a good occasion to remind readers that calculations herein are not always in agreement, sometimes because of rounding, sometimes because of mistakes made by contemporaries. See also Laurens to Thomas Mears, of Liverpool, 15 July 1763, *ibid.*, 495.

15. Hancock to Capt. Bastide, at Halifax, 26 Jan. 1747/48, in Baxter, *House of Hancock*, 110. See also *ibid.*, 99n. [William Douglass], *An Essay, concerning Silver and Paper Currencies, More Especially with Regard to the British Colonies in New-England* (Boston, [1738]), 4, quoted the rate for New England as "400 per Cent" (meaning £500 Massachusetts currency for £100 sterling) and the rate for South Carolina as "700 per Cent" (meaning £700 South Carolina currency for £100 sterling). See [William Douglass], *A Discourse concerning the Currencies of the British Plantations in America* (Boston, 1740), 10, 18, 19–20; Board of Trade to Treasury, 28 Feb. 1749/50, C.O. 324/13, pp. 1–233 *passim*.

16. See the discussion below in chap. 4 in the section on "The French Colonies and the Exchange on Paris."

———

the currency value of *coin*, while the text as reproduced in Sainsbury *et al.*, eds., *Calendar of State Papers*, XI (*America and West Indies, 1681–1685*), 94, is a call "to enhance twenty-five per cent. upon your Majesty's and all foreign *corn*" (emphasis added). Whenever possible citations in this handbook are to the original documents.

nial currency as if it had the same local value as that of the mother country—even if the colonists themselves called their money "sterling" or whatever. They meant, of course, "sterling" in notation only, since everyone appreciated two facts: first, that little or no English coinage circulated in the colonies —it was a money of account only—and, second, that no sum in the colonial money of account could ever buy precisely the same sum in sterling. Any exchange transaction would always entail some costs, even if the two moneys of account were on par at parity (compare the case of Scotland, above in chapter 2). These costs would most regularly mean that to buy a sum in London one would need more than that sum in colonial money. Thus, even when the par of Massachusetts or Maryland currency and sterling was at parity (£100 Maryland currency equaled £100 sterling), the bill rate would have been something higher, maybe 3 or 4 percent even at the best of times. We are far better off referring to Maryland currency in Maryland, and so forth, no matter what par was, since this implies a difference and forces us to discover its extent. It also prevents the mistaken supposition that two colonies had currencies of the same value when they merely used sterling notation for their moneys of account.

In negotiating bills on the mother country, colonists followed the forms and procedures common to European exchange. Bills were drawn, presented, and protested in much the same way between Philadelphia and London as between Amsterdam—or, better, Dublin—and London.[17] One paid

for these bills in any medium acceptable to the seller, most usually in "currency," a word definable as the local money of account, to which all real moneys in the colony were reduced.[18] The preference was always for bills payable soon after sight and payable in the capital;[19] those drawn at longer

---

17. The colonists were well acquainted with mercantile law and could and did quote the standard tomes to their benefit. See, e.g., the knowledgeable citations to Gerard de Malynes, *Consuetudo, vel Lex Mercatoria, or, the Ancient Law-Merchant*, 2d ed. (London, 1658) in the case of *Mead and Ingram v. Turner*, session of 30 Jan. 1671/72, *Records of the Suffolk County Court,*

1671–1680 (Colonial Society of Massachusetts, *Publications*, XXIX–XXX [Boston, 1933]), I, 36–43. See also Herbert Alan Johnson, *The Law Merchant and Negotiable Instruments in Colonial New York, 1664 to 1730* (Chicago, 1963); Francis and Refle, of Philadelphia, to Obadiah Brown and Co., of Providence, R.I., 2 May 1767, Brown Papers, L 57–67 FR, John Carter Brown Library, Brown University, Providence, R.I.

18. Only with Maryland is any confusion possible over terms. There, as we shall see, two versions of the money of account existed between 1733 and 1765, much as was the case in Amsterdam, Hamburg, and elsewhere in Europe. For Maryland during these years one must refer to paper currency and to hard currency. See below, pp. 189–194. "Lawful Money" (or, less regularly, "Proclamation Money") meant colonial currency valued at the official par of £133.33 colonial currency per £100 sterling. See [Hugh Vance], *An Inquiry into the Nature and Uses of Money; More Especially of the Bills of Publick Credit, Old Tenor* (Boston, 1740), 47; Thomas Mortimer, *A New and Complete Dictionary of Trade and Commerce* (London, 1766–1767), I, s.v. "currency"; Franklin B. Dexter, ed., "A Selection from the Correspondence and Miscellaneous Papers of Jared Ingersoll," New Haven Colony Historical Society, *Papers*, IX (1918), 239–242; Charles M. Andrews, "Current Lawful Money in New England," *American Historical Review*, XXIV (1918–1919), 73–77; Lawrence H. Gipson, "Connecticut Taxation and Parliamentary Aid Preceding the Revolutionary War," *ibid.*, XXXVI (1930–1931), 727n; and Nettels, *Money Supply*, 180n.

19. The "usance"—the customary period after sight when bills were due to be paid—on London bills was 30 to 40 days at Philadelphia and Charleston; Virginia bills were drawn at 60 days. William Pollard, of Philadelphia, to Peter Holme, of Liverpool, 16 May 1772, William Pollard Letter Book, 1772–1774, p. 26, Hist. Soc. Pa. Anne Bezanson, Robert D. Gray, and Miriam Hussey, *Prices in Colonial Pennsylvania* (Philadelphia, 1935), 320; Henry Laurens to William Penn, at St. Augustine, 24 Dec. 1767, *Papers of Henry Laurens*, V, 528; James H. Soltow, *The Economic Role of Williamsburg* (Williamsburg, Va., 1965), 158–159. For the usance on 17th-century bills from the West Indies, see K. G. Davies, "The Origin of the Commission System in the West India

than the usual time and on other cities were less expensive.[20] Bills sold by the more reliable colonial firms and drawn on the better-known metropolitan establishments were also preferred. One could sell a questionable bill more readily if he could induce a local merchant to countersign or endorse it and thereby guarantee, if not its payment overseas, at least the repayment at home of the original sum plus penalty charges (called "damages") and interest (see fig. 10, pp. 236–237).[21] One Philadelphian, Reese Meredith, was charged with making quite a bit of money speculating in "doubtful bills with good endorsers." His accuser, Jacob Mordecai, was the son of Moses Mordecai, whom Jacob described as the first exchange broker in Philadelphia. Obviously echoing his father, Jacob suggested that Meredith was competing for the senior Mordecai's business and was therefore something of an exchange broker too. There were probably more exchange brokers in the colonies, in Philadelphia and elsewhere, but we do not yet know their names.[22]

In negotiating intercolonial exchange, colonists drew bills in one of two ways. Where there was an established trade in bills of exchange and consequently regular and reliable information on the bill rate, neighboring colonists bought and sold bills at that rate. Regional grouping evolved in this way. New England knew of and depended upon the rate of exchange at Boston; so did Nova Scotia. The rate at New York City had an influence not only in the lower Hudson River Valley but farther up the river at Albany and into the Mohawk River Valley, eastern New Jersey, Long Island Sound, and, after 1760, Montreal. Philadelphia influenced both the Delaware River Valley and the entire Chesapeake Bay region down

---

Trade [1650–1700]," Royal Historical Society, *Transactions*, 5th Ser., II (1952), 98. For this whole paragraph see also Soltow, *Economic Role of Williamsburg*, 156–176.

20. For example: "Merchants here [New York City] makes two and half [percentage points] difference between thirty and sixty days sight." John van Cortlandt to James Gibson, 30 Oct. 1766, John van Cortlandt Letter Book, 1762–1769, fol. 158r, Van Cortlandt Account Books, 1700–1875, New York Public Library, New York City. See also the Pollard letter cited in n. 19 and quoted above in chap. 2 at n. 18; Arthur S. Williamson, "Credit Relations between Colonial and English Merchants in the Eighteenth Century" (Ph.D. diss., University of Iowa, 1927), 29–30; and Soltow, *Economic Role of Williamsburg*, 162–163, 165n.

21. Soltow, *Economic Role of Williamsburg*, 160.

22. Whitfield J. Bell, Jr., "Addenda to Watson's Annals of Philadelphia: Notes by Jacob Mordecai, 1836," *Pennsylvania Magazine of History and Biography*, XCVIII (1974), 131, 138, 169. In the Philadelphia tax list for 1774, Moses

---

Mordecai had his occupation listed as "broker." William Henry Egle, ed., *Proprietary, Supply, and State Tax Lists of the City and County of Philadelphia for the Years 1769, 1774 and 1779* (*Pennsylvania Archives*, 3d Ser., XIV [Harrisburg, Pa., 1897]), 290. Meredith, who ranked as the fifth largest investor in ships registered at Philadelphia from 1726 to 1776, was of great importance to Baltimore merchant William Lux as the broker of Maryland bills of exchange. John J. McCusker, "The Philadelphia Shipping Industry in the Eighteenth Century" (unpublished MS, 1972), 229–232, Hist. Soc. Pa.; William Lux Letter Book, 1763–1768, New-York Historical Society, New York City. For indications of the existence of other brokers see the advertisements of Stephen Bordley, *Maryland Gazette* (Annapolis), 4 Oct. 1759, and of John Stevenson, *ibid.*, 1 Jan. 1761. See also John Watts on the "lowering" of the rate of exchange by "the money agents," who "have such a strong digestion that they govern the exchange." To John Erving, at Boston, 1 July 1762, and to Gedney Clarke, at Barbados, 15 July 1762, [Dorothy C. Barck, ed.], *Letter Book of John Watts, Merchant and Councillor of New York, January 1, 1762–December 22, 1765* (New-York Historical Society, *Collections*, LXI [New York, 1928]), 65, 68, hereafter cited as *Letter Book of John Watts*. See also Philip Cuyler, at New York, to Devonshire, Reeve, and Lloyd, at Bristol, 2 May 1759, Philip Cuyler Letter Book, 1755–1760, Philip Cuyler Papers, N.Y. Pub. Lib.; and Phyn, Ellice, and Co. to James Phyn, at London, 5 Sept. 1774, Phyn and Ellice Letter Books, Buffalo and Erie County Historical Society, Buffalo, N.Y., as quoted in R. H. Fleming, "Phyn, Ellice and Company of Schenectady," *Contributions to Canadian Economics*, IV (1932), 30.

through Tidewater Virginia.[23] But other than within these regions, intercolonial exchange negotiations were originally based not on the bill rate but on par, equal in the colonies to the comparative value given the piece of eight—"dollars being allways the standard" of exchange, as John Watts of New York put it.[24] Occasionally, however, especially later in the colonial period or when a transaction at par meant a considerable difference, merchants made the effort to discover the bill rate and used that instead of par.[25] Eventually colonial newspapers began to publish the London bill rate at the major cities.[26]

The increased sophistication of the colonial money market, a development implied in the advent of exchange brokers and the publication of the commercial rate of exchange, reflected a characteristic of the colonial economy not widely appreciated. However real the tight money situation might have been in the colonies in the 1670s and 1680s, however denuded of coin they were then, such conditions did not

23. Indications of these sometimes overlapping functional economic units abound hereinafter. After 1700 the intercolonial exchange regions became areas in which member colonies' paper money tended to circulate as well as areas that shared the same par of exchange. See Nettels, *Money Supply*, 105–107; William S. Sachs, "The Business Outlook in the Northern Colonies, 1750–1775" (Ph.D. diss., Columbia University, 1957), 201, 236; Gould, *Money in Maryland*, 14–15; and Soltow, *Economic Role of Williamsburg*, 170–175. South Carolina and Georgia constituted another such region. See Lilla Mills Hawes, ed., *The Letterbook of Thomas Rasberry, 1758–1761* (Georgia Historical Society, *Collections*, XIII [Savannah, Ga., 1959]), *passim*.

24. Watts to Gedney Clarke, Sr., of Barbados, 25 July 1763, *Letter Book of John Watts*, 160. See also: "The value of dollars . . . which governs all our settlements and draughts," in Watts to John Smith and Joseph Nutt, of Charleston, S.C., 31 Aug. 1763, *ibid.*, 180, and "pass'd to your credit at the par of exchange for dollars," in Laurens to Robert Waln, of Philadelphia, 6 Dec. 1762, *Papers of Henry Laurens*, III, 185. An earlier Watts-Clarke transaction shows the effect of this second mode of exchange. In a letter of 5 Nov. 1762 Watts credited Clarke's account with £130 7s 1d (£130.35) Barbados currency "at 25 per cent" (the percentage based on dollars), or £162 18s 10d (£162.94) New York currency. *Letter Book of John Watts*, 95. Watts's ratio, however, was off a bit (although he used it consistently—see *ibid.*, 2–3, 361). In 1762 New York valued pieces of eight, or dollars, at 8s (40p) and Barbados did so at 6s 3d (31.2p), making the ratio actually 1.28 and the corresponding amount with which Clarke should have been credited £166.85 New York currency, or £3.91 more. But had Watts used the bill rate rather than par, the difference would have been even greater. In Nov. 1762 the bill rate at Barbados was £130 and at New York £193.75 (see tables 3.5 and 4.1), a ratio of 1 to 1.49. At the bill rates £130.35 Barbados currency was worth £194.26 New York currency, a difference of about £31.32 New York currency, or about £16.16 sterling. Watts was correct in his use of par, but at considerable cost to Clarke, who, as one of the largest planters in Barbados and collector of customs there, and the owner of several plantations in Essequibo and Demerara, must surely have known what was involved in such transactions.

(On Clarke see *Papers of Henry Laurens*, I, 316n; Richard B. Sheridan, *Sugar and Slavery: An Economic History of the British West Indies, 1623–1775* [St. Lawrence, Barbados, 1974], 443–444.)

Some merchants complained of exchange based on par rather than on the bill rates. "I find also that instead of dollars being reckoned at 6/8d, the sterling should be brot into currency which makes an odds on the £157.10/ or £17.6.6 in my favour, dollars being at 6/8d from the policy of this island, not from the par of exchange or intrinsic value." Thomas Dolbeare, of Kingston, Jamaica, to Aaron Lopez, of Newport, R.I., 24 Jan. 1776, *Commerce of Rhode Island*, II, 37. Understandably, interregional exchange tended more and more to be based not on par but on the bill rate.

25. See, e.g., Laurens to Augustus and John Boyd, at London, 30 Aug. 1763, *Papers of Henry Laurens*, III, 554.

26. From 1773 on the appropriately named *Rivington's New-York Gazetteer; or, The Connecticut, New-Jersey, Hudson's River, and Quebec Weekly Advertiser* printed the London bill rate at New York, Philadelphia, and Boston and even supplied information for arbitrage transactions. On 22 Apr. 1773, for instance, readers were told that the rate at Philadelphia, £164, was equal to £173 at New York. During 1774 and 1775 the Schenectady-based firm of Phyn and Ellice engaged in quite complex and profitable exchange arbitrage transactions. Selling bills of exchange on London at New York, where the bill rate was high, they shipped the money they received to Quebec, where they bought bills on London at a considerably lower cost. Fleming, "Phyn, Ellice and Company," *Contrib. to Canadian Econ.*, IV (1932), 30–31.

continue unabated into the 1770s. The very development of alternate forms of real money indicates this. So too does the increased availability of gold and silver coin in the eighteenth century, as expanded colonial trade with the West Indies increased its supply and expanded colonial trade with the rest of the world decreased the occasions to export it in lieu of bills of exchange.[27] Moreover, intercolonial exchange provided a rather highly developed exchange arbitrage when the bill rate in one colony rose or fell too greatly. As early as the 1680s and 1690s Maryland and Virginia planters had the option of selling bills locally or disposing of them in Philadelphia.[28] By 1770 a Norfolk merchant could propose "going even so far as Boston" to find a satisfactory market for his bills.[29] Complaints about the "dearth of available coin" in the colonies should always be read with the added phrase supplied by the reader: "at a 'reasonable' price."

Complaints about the dearth of data for this and the subsequent chapter deserve more credence. We have nowhere near the number of quotations of the bill rate that we have for Europe; further, the materials are more difficult to use and are subject to some misinterpretation. Quotations of the colonial rate of exchange largely come not from price currents but from manuscript sources, particularly merchants' papers. Those used herein are mostly from actual exchange transactions, first- or secondhand: the record of a bill bought or sold or the simple statement that the current rate is at such-and-such a figure.[30] Occasionally quotations have been taken from internal accounting notations, when a merchant reduced a sum to sterling in his books;[31] but these figures are suspect,

27. Gould, *Money in Maryland*, 13–14, 20–21. Cf. Roger W. Weiss, "The Issue of Paper Money in the American Colonies, 1720–1774," *Journal of Economic History*, XXX (1970), 783. See also [Stephen Hopkins], *An Essay on the Trade of the Northern Colonies of Great Britain in North America* (Philadelphia and London, 1764), 7–8. In 1768 Gov. Francis Bernard of Massachusetts wrote that a colonist "well acquainted with money" told him that "greater inconveniences arose to the trade here from abundance of specie than from the want of it." To secretary of state, 16 July 1768, William Petty, Earl of Shelburne, Papers, LXXXV, fols. 201–204, William L. Clements Library, University of Michigan, Ann Arbor, quoted in Lawrence Henry Gipson, *The British Empire before the American Revolution* (Caldwell, Idaho, and New York, 1936–1969), X, 62.

28. Gary B. Nash, "Maryland's Economic War with Pennsylvania," *Maryland Historical Magazine*, LX (1965), 231–244; Soltow, *Economic Role of Williamsburg*, 170–174. For an example of a calculation of the arbitrage potential between New York and London, see John Austin Stevens, Jr., ed., *Colonial Records of the New York Chamber of Commerce, 1768–1784, with Historical and Biographical Sketches* (New York, 1867), 308n, apparently published originally in *Hugh Gaine's Pocket Almanac* for 1771.

29. William Aitchison to Charles Steuart, in London, 15 Mar. 1770, Correspondence and Papers of Charles Steuart, 1742–1784, fol. 91, Steuart Papers, MS 5040, National Library of Scotland, Edinburgh. See also Andrew

Black, of Boston, to Messrs. James Glassford and Co., at Norfolk, Va., 2 Apr. 1770, Neil Jamieson Papers, 1757–1789, XI, no. 2521, Library of Congress.

30. Normally the bill itself did not mention the rate of exchange, but one should be able to discover it on bills drawn in Virginia after 1 Oct. 1755. See William Waller Hening, ed., *The Statutes at Large; Being a Collection of All the Laws of Virginia, from the First Session of the Legislature, in the Year 1619* (Richmond, Va., New York, and Philadelphia, 1809–1823), VI, 479. Virginians were not consistent in following this regulation, however. See, e.g., the bill drawn on 27 Apr. 1771, in Galloway Correspondence, XI, no. 9807, Galloway-Maxey-Markoe Family Papers, 1654–1888, Lib. Cong. Barbados had no such law, but practice there apparently dictated the inclusion of the rate of exchange in the bill (see, e.g., fig. 11). A major source for table 4.1 was well over a hundred duplicate copies of bills of exchange strung together on a printed board labeled "Second or Third Bills of Exchange" in a packet marked "Useless Bills of Exchange" in the Mercantile Papers of Thomas Newson, bundle no. 88, C. 104/78, *Re Newson's Estate*, P.R.O.

31. Students of the rate of exchange must take care to distinguish it from the "advance" over the original cost of imported English goods. Expressed as a percentage, the advance incorporated the markup over purchase cost ("prime cost") and, on a unit basis, determined the selling price in colonial

as merchants sometimes used par for this kind of accounting entry.[32] This is even truer of the references to the conversion of local currency to sterling in official documents such as the records of a colonial bureaucracy or legislature, church records, estate inventories, probate proceedings, and so forth, for these have a tendency to give the official rate of exchange (par) and should be so recognized.[33] Compilation of the bill rate in the tables in this chapter follows the procedures set out in chapter 1.

The progress in this and the next chapter is from north to south, beginning with the English colonies and proceeding through the colonies of France, Holland, Denmark, Spain, and Portugal. The rest of this chapter is devoted mostly to the English continental colonies that later became the United States of America and Canada. Chapter 4 treats everything outside of English-speaking North America. The organization depends heavily upon the available data—thus, again, the lesson that much work remains to be done with this subject.

The Continental Colonies

Any discussion of money, bills of exchange, and the rate of exchange in the English continental colonies owes a substantial debt to the work of five others: Curtis P. Nettels, Leslie V. Brock, John M. Hemphill, E. James Ferguson, and Joseph A. Ernst.[34] Their combined attempts to tell the basic economic and political stories behind the colonists' attempts to solve the problem of their circulating medium leave us with little more to say in the matter. Some few tasks do remain—we still need to know for New England for the years after 1760 what Professor Ernst has told us about the rest of the continental colonies—but the history of colonial money has been fairly well written.

Basically it is the story of confrontation deferred. The colonists attempted for over 150 years to repair the defects in their money supply. Endowed with their own legislatures, they resorted to statute law to give force to their establishment of commodity money, overvalued coin, and paper currency. In the process they were not always careful to offer full protection to the rights of English merchants and the crown. Debts due in sterling could sometimes be lawfully paid in the colonies with a sum notationally equivalent to but really less than what was owed.[35] While such abuses were infrequent,

currency. It was expected to be sufficient to cover all shipping and handling charges *and* the costs of the bill of exchange. Thus the advance also was not the equivalent of net profit, although some historians still interpret it as such. A good explanation is in Stuart Weems Bruchey, *Robert Oliver, Merchant of Baltimore, 1783–1819*, Johns Hopkins University Studies in Historical and Political Science, Ser. LXXIV, no. 1 (Baltimore, 1956), 49. See also Philip L. White, *The Beekmans of New York in Politics and Commerce* (New York, 1956), 416n.

32. See, e.g., the entries for 1 Nov. 1772 in John Galloway's Journal, 1772–1786, p. 60, Galloway Daybook and Journals, 1765–1786, Box 76, Galloway-Maxey-Markoe Papers. On the same day that he purchased a bill of exchange at £150, he used the par rate, £166.67, as a conversion factor for an accounting entry. Occasionally merchants used par to settle an account that stretched over several years. See Samuel Galloway's account with Alexander and Andrew Symmer in Galloway Correspondence, VI, no. 8891, *ibid*.

33. See, e.g., the discussion below in the section in this chapter on Maryland.

34. Nettels, *Money Supply*; Brock, *Currency of the American Colonies*; John M. Hemphill II, "Virginia and the English Commercial System, 1689–1733: Studies in the Development and Fluctuations of a Colonial Economy under Imperial Control" (Ph.D. diss., Princeton University, 1964); Ferguson, "Colonial Finance," *WMQ*, 3d Ser., X (1953), 153–180; Ernst, *Money and Politics*. I am especially indebted to Joseph Ernst for sharing with me some of the results of his own research.

35. The laws establishing some imperial duties collected in the colonies failed to specify sterling, and the colonists naturally preferred to pay in the progressively depreciating colonial currencies. Notably this was the case

they pandered to the fears of the merchants of London and Bristol, men who found a ready ally in the Board of Trade. That body consistently worked to strike down every attempt in the colonies to inflate local money, and its efforts were fought vigorously by the colonial legislatures as part of a larger struggle over who should rule.[36]

Sometimes the Board of Trade won a battle—if not the war. The advent of Proclamation Money in the years before 1710, the Currency Act of 1751, and the Currency Act of 1764 were its notable successes. The first of these grew out of a fifty-year-old reaction to the colonists' attempts to inflate the value of their coin. In 1704 Queen Anne issued a proclamation announcing that the colonists were forbidden to inflate the value of their money by any more than one-third of its sterling equivalent. The par of exchange could be no more than £133.33 colonial currency to £100 sterling. Adverse reactions to both the message and the medium elicited a response from learned counsel that the proclamation could not bind the colonies, and Parliament, in 1708, had to give it

the force of law.[37] Proclamation Money, or "Lawful Money," in an effort to be quite precise, left the colonists numerous loopholes, for it defined the maximum inflation in terms of specific silver coins. The next thirty years found the colonists who were unhappy with that maximum turning to gold as their coinage where they could, especially in the West Indies, and to paper elsewhere. By the time of the great parliamentary inquiry into colonial money in 1739, 1740, and 1741, Proclamation Money was scarcely used anywhere.[38]

The spread of paper money through the continental colonies after 1700 was accompanied in some of those colonies by a rampant inflation. This was especially true in New England, the paper money of which was deemed a particular affront to Parliament and its Lawful Money. Inflation, of course, squeezed everyone—colonists as well as London merchants who had debts owed to them in colonial currency. While the colonists could and did learn to live with it, albeit uncom-

---

with the "Plantation Duties." Act of 25 Charles II, c. 7; Robert Quary, at Philadelphia, to commissioners of customs, 6 Mar. 1699/1700, C.O. 323/3, fol. 127v. See the accounts of the Plantation Duty collected on sugar at Jamaica, 1744–1751, in T. 38/363, P.R.O. Later acts repaired this fault and specified sterling or silver at sterling value. See, e.g., Acts of 6 George II, c. 7, and 7 George III, c. 46. See also *A Letter to a Noble Peer, Relating to the Bill in Favour of the Sugar-Planters* ([London?], 1733), 4. All references in this book to British laws enacted after 1713 are to [T. E. Tomlins and John Raithby, eds.], *The Statutes at Large, of England and of Great Britain* (London, 1811); for laws before 1714 see chap. 2, n. 26, above.

36. British governmental objections to colonial "altering and debasing" of the coinage can be traced back at least as far as a Treasury memorandum of 1662 quoted in Curtis P. Nettels, *The Roots of American Civilization: A History of American Colonial Life*, 2d ed. (New York, 1963), 271.

37. For much of this see Nettels, *Money Supply*, 242–249; Brock, *Currency of the American Colonies*, 130–167. The proclamation was published: *By the Queen: A Proclamation, for Settling and Ascertaining the Current Rates of Foreign Coins in Her Majesty's Colonies and Plantations in America* (London, 1704). It is reprinted in Clarence S. Brigham, ed., *British Royal Proclamations Relating to America, 1603–1783* (American Antiquarian Society, *Transactions and Collections*, XII [Worcester, Mass., 1911]), 161–163. The opinion referred to is in Edward Northey to Board of Trade, 19 Oct. 1705, C.O. 323/5, fol. 267r, and as printed in George Chalmers, ed., *Opinions of Eminent Lawyers on Various Points of English Jurisprudence, Chiefly concerning the Colonies, Fisheries, and Commerce, of Great Britain* (London, 1814). The law is Act of 6 Anne, c. 57.

38. For the investigation see Brock, *Currency of the American Colonies*, 187–195; Ernst, *Money and Politics*, 32–34. The Board of Trade collected and compiled a considerable body of information that survives today in "State of the Paper Currency in the British Plantations in America, . . . April 1740," C.O. 323/10, fols. 161–172, and in House of Lords, Main Papers, 28 Mar. 1740, 5 Mar. 1740/41, House of Lords Record Office, London. It remains for someone to sort through all the aspects of this subject.

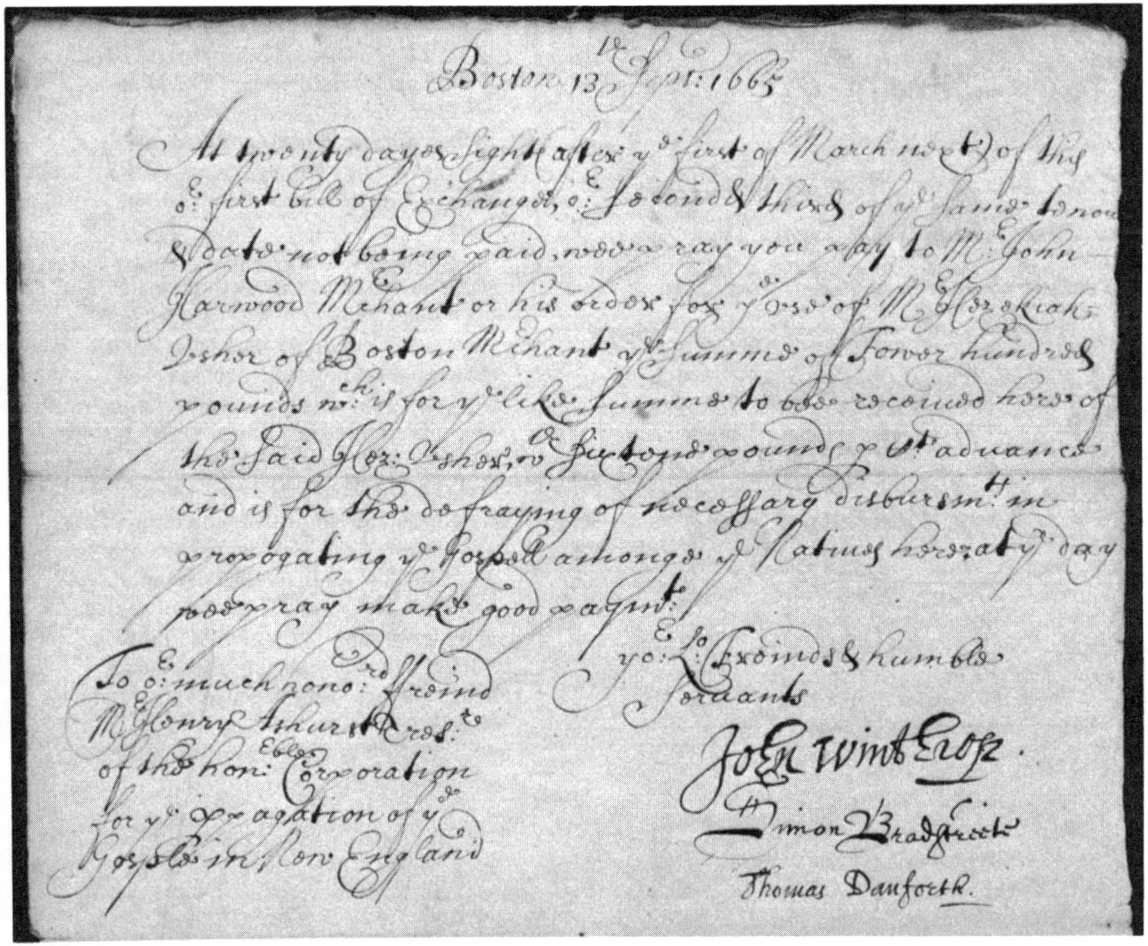

Boston 13 Sept: 1665

At twenty dayes sight after ye first of March next of this
our first bill of Exchange, our second & third of ye same tenor
& date not being paid, wee pray you pay to Mr John
Harwood Merchant or his order for ye use of Mr Hezekiah
Usher of Boston Merchant ye summe of Fower hundred
pounds wch is for ye like summe to bee received here of
the said Hez: Usher, wth sixtene pounds p Ct advance
and is for the defraying of necessary disbursemts in
propagating ye Gospell amonge ye Natives here at ye day
wee pray make good payment:

yor Lo: Friends & humble
Servants

John Winthrop.
Simon Bradstreet
Thomas Danforth.

To our much honord ffreind
Mr Henry Ashurst Tres:
of the hon: Corporation
for ye propagation of ye
Gospel in New England

Figures 3–7. Five North American Bills of Exchange. (Figure 3 is from the New England Company Archives, Guildhall Library, London; courtesy of the library. Figures 4–7 are from the John Reynell Papers; courtesy of the Historical Society of Pennsylvania, Philadelphia.)

3. Massachusetts, 13 September 1665. The interest of this bill is threefold. First, it is an exceptionally early example of a bill of exchange drawn in the colonies. Second, it was drawn and signed by three of the Massachusetts Bay Colony's leaders in the 1660s, in their capacity as resident commissioners of the oldest of the Protestant missionary societies, the "Corporation for the Propagation of the Gospel in New England." The commissioners sold the bill in Boston for "the summe of fower hundred pounds . . . with sixtene pounds per cent advance," that is, for £464 Massachusetts currency. This is the third notable element in the bill: the rate of exchange is expressed on the face, much as on the Jamaica and Barbados bills of the next century illustrated in figures 10 and 11.

Exchange for £345.13.4 Pha. currency Boston, April 15, 1763

At Ten days sight of this my first Bill of Exchange — Second of the same Tenor and Date not paid; pay unto Capt. Joseph Richardson or order Three hundred forty five pounds Thirteen Shillings and four pence Currency, being for Value Received of Mr. Patrick Tracy and Charge the Same to Acco.t, as p.r Advice from

Your Very humble Serv.t
Nat Wheelwright

To Mr. John Reynell,
Merchant
In Philadelphia

4. Massachusetts, 15 April 1763. Drawn by Nathaniel Wheelwright of Boston on John Reynell of Philadelphia in favor of Captain Joseph Richardson (or his payee), this intercolonial bill of exchange represents a type that became popular in the late colonial period. The sum to be paid is designated in Pennsylvania currency (not sterling), but Patrick Tracy paid for the bill in Boston in Massachusetts currency. How buyer and seller determined the rate of exchange between the two currencies is not known. One way would have been to compare the sterling exchange rate for both colonies in April 1763. On that basis (see tables 3.1 and 3.7), Richardson would have paid about £272 Massachusetts currency for the £345.67 Pennsylvania currency. The phrase "second of the same tenor and date not paid" (and similar phrases in each of the other bills) was necessary because bills were issued in multiple copies ("sets"); only the first one presented was paid, of course (see p. 20).

Exch^a for £19..6 - - - - Maryland, Augt 5..1747 —

AT thirty Days Sight, pay this my Fourth of Exchange (First, Second, nor Third paid) to Mr John Reynell — or Order Nineteen Pounds six shillings Sterling, Value received, per Advice from Gent^a Y^r hum: Servt —

To Messrs Tower & Philpot
Merch^ts in London   Darby Lux

Printed for G. Dawson and W. Baker, Stationers, in Lombard-street.

5. New York, 16 June 1741. This typical colonial bill of exchange drawn in sterling on London is interesting for two reasons. First, it involves three branches of the important Jewish merchant family, the Franks. Jacob and Moses Franks of New York here draw £100 sterling on Aaron Franks of London in favor of David Franks in Philadelphia. Second, the bill illustrates a solution to the problem of how to transfer funds from New York to Philadelphia (discussed on pp. 169–171). According to the endorsement on the reverse (not illustrated), David Franks sold the bill to John Reynell, who presumably then sent it to his payee in London.

6. Maryland, 5 August 1747. This bill of exchange shows a fairly early use of a printed form for a bill drawn in the colonies (note that the form was printed in London). It is also an example of bills drawn in the Chesapeake region for sale in Philadelphia. Darby Lux of Baltimore instructed Messrs. Tower and Philpot, merchants of London, to pay to John Reynell of Philadelphia, or to his order, the sum indicated.

7. Virginia, 10 April 1742. Showing still another instance in which a colonial bill of exchange was drawn for sale in Philadelphia, this bill has the added interest of originating at Accokeek Furnace, the ironworks built in 1726 by the Principio Company of Maryland on the plantation of Augustine Washington, George Washington's father. Nathaniel Chapman ordered Osgood Gee and Company of London to pay £50 sterling to Israel Pemberton, Jr., of Philadelphia. Presumably Gee and Company managed some of the iron company's assets.

fortably, the London merchants saw no need to. Their complaints initiated the inquiry of 1739 to 1741 and its ultimate result, the British Currency Act of 1751, which struck down the paper money of Massachusetts, Rhode Island, Connecticut, and New Hampshire by depriving it of its validity as legal tender in private payments.[39] The act was well timed, coming just after a large payment in silver to the New England colonies for their efforts in the War of the Austrian Succession. Massachusetts, and later, Connecticut took the opportunity to reorganize their whole currency systems, as we shall see below.[40] But the Board of Trade and Parliament had solved their problem in two colonies only.

The Currency Act of 1764 did to the colonies outside New England much of what the 1751 act had done to Massachusetts and Connecticut, but the timing was poorer. In the midst of the post–Seven Years' War depression and a growing struggle over the colonial prerogative, Parliament continued with its currency reform of the colonies by outlawing all paper money as legal tender in private debts. The Virginia attempt to manipulate the exchange rate for repayment of sterling debts owed British merchants provided the occasion.[41] But the act of 1764 was less a retaliation for that abuse than it was part of the now hundred-year-old concern of the crown and Parliament to second-guess colonial solutions of their monetary difficulties. Although the Board of Trade and later Parliament never offered any help, they were quite ready to regulate and restrict. The lesson was not lost on the continental colonists, and the dissatisfaction so engendered helped bring on the American Revolution.

New England

Massachusetts, Rhode Island, New Hampshire, and Connecticut, the four basic colonies that made up New England, had such an integrated economy, especially in regard to currency, that with minor exceptions we are able to treat them as a unit. Even from the earliest years they shared not only real money and money of account but also currency, par of exchange, and even paper money. Although Massachusetts tended to set the norm for the region—which ran from the Bay of Fundy to the Connecticut River Valley—each colony maintained full legal control over its own currency. The others could choose to follow the action of Massachusetts, but at their own pace. They could also choose to take advantage of the de facto acceptance throughout the area of their own paper currency. When Rhode Island took untoward advantage in the 1730s and 1740s, its action led to the suspension of regional monetary cooperation after 1750. The disintegration of the New England economic community in the years subsequent to the Currency Act of 1751 is a subject not yet fully explored. What all this means for the work at hand is that we must first deal with each of the parts of New England before we can understand the whole.

---

39. Brock, *Currency of the American Colonies*, 187–195. The law is Act of 24 George II, c. 53.

40. Brock, *Currency of the American Colonies*, 244–334.

41. For the antecedents and consequences of the statute see Ernst, *Money and Politics*, 43–88, and *passim*. The law is Act of 4 George III, c. 34. In a fashion similar to that of the Virginia House of Burgesses, Archibald Ingram, the receiver of quitrents and fines of the island of St. Vincent, attempted in 1776 to set artificially high the exchange rate at which he accepted payment

---

of fees. In this instance the colonists reacted strenuously. Gov. Valentine Morris of St. Vincent to secretary of state, 19 Sept. 1776, with enclosures, C.O. 260/4, fols. 40, 50–54. See also Ingram's petitions to the Treasury in 1774 asking direction in the matter. C.O. 5/146, fols. 3–6.

All of these colonies shared the same real money common to the Western Hemisphere. They relied heavily on Spanish silver, especially the piece of eight; in fact, the variations between their currencies were determined by the different legal valuation each colony gave to that coin. In the English colonies these currencies were all expressed in terms of the same, shared money of account: pounds, shillings, and pence. Massachusetts pounds and New York pounds were not the same, because the piece of eight in the one was legally valued at 6s (30p) and in the other at 5s (25p). They were in the ratio of 1.2 to 1, or, as it was more usually written, £120 to £100. Massachusetts pounds differed from English pounds sterling in the same way and for the same reason. But during most of our period all of New England agreed on the value of the piece of eight—"Boston money" was New England's currency.

In the seventeenth and eighteenth centuries, unlike the exchanges between European centers like Amsterdam and London, few of the relationships among the colonies or, more important, between the colonies and the mother country remained stable for very long. Between 1630 and 1750 the Boston-London rate fluctuated from parity to over £1,000 Massachusetts per £100 sterling; different terminology for paper currency was introduced; and the exchange was influenced to a considerably greater degree than was common in Europe by extraneous factors, especially by government intervention, both local and imperial. Although all of these topics deserve extensive treatment, requirements of space must limit our attention to them here. For more enlightenment, readers should turn to the works of Nettels, Brock, and Ernst.

Initially there was a state of near parity in the exchange between the Massachusetts Bay colony and England, because arriving immigrants brought with them sufficient coin and credits to meet all demands.[42] They bought their sterling bills with sterling. The end of immigration in the late 1630s stopped such imports and plunged Massachusetts into a balance-of-payments crisis and a depression beginning in 1640.[43] One response to depression was devaluation. In 1642 the colonial legislature devalued the currency not once but twice by increasing the local value of the piece of eight from its sterling worth, 4s 6d (22.5p), to first 4s 8d (23.3p) and then 5s (25p).[44] The par of exchange, based on the piece of eight, went from parity (£100 Massachusetts currency per £100 sterling) to £103.70 per £100 sterling and then to £111.11. Similar laws in later periods of economic difficulty devalued Massachusetts currency still further: to £133.33 in 1672, £136.60 in 1692, and £154.85 in 1705.[45] This was the limit to monetary inflation

42. See, e.g., Edward Trelawney's letter from Boston to his brother Robert in Plymouth, Eng., 10 Jan. 1635/36, in which he discussed bills of exchange, their value in sterling and their sight, but neither mentioned nor implied an exchange rate. James Phinney Baxter, ed., *Documentary History of the State of Maine*, III: *The Trelawney Papers* (Maine Historical Society, *Collections*, 2d Ser., III [Portland, Me., 1884]), 81–82. I am indebted to Everett Emerson for a reference to this correspondence. Cf. Weiss, "Monetary Standard," *Econ. Hist. Rev.*, 2d Ser., XXVII (1974), 577–592.

43. Marion H. Gottfried, "The First Depression in Massachusetts," *New England Quarterly*, IX (1936), 655–678.

44. Nathaniel B. Shurtleff, ed., *Records of the Governor and Company of the Massachusetts Bay in New England* (Boston, 1853–1854), II, 20, 29. The laws are dated 14 June and 27 Sept. 1642. See also Charles J. Hoadly, ed., *Records of the Colony and Plantation of New Haven, from 1638 to 1649* (Hartford, Conn., 1857), 86; J. Hammond Trumbull and Charles J. Hoadly, eds., *The Public Records of the Colony of Connecticut* (Hartford, Conn., 1850–1890), I, 86; and William G. Sumner, "The Coin Shilling of Massachusetts Bay," *Yale Review*, VI (1898–1899), 247–264, 405–420.

45. Shurtleff, ed., *Records of Massachusetts Bay*, III, 261–262, IV, pt. ii, 533–534; *The Acts and Resolves, Public and Private, of the Province of Massachusetts Bay* (Boston, 1869–1922), I, 70–71, 296; Nettels, *Money Supply*, 236n,

through the devaluation of the piece of eight, but it was just the beginning for Massachusetts.

The failure of the Phips expedition to conquer Quebec in 1690 was the occasion for Massachusetts to issue its first paper bills of credit.[46] Denominated in terms of the money of account (pounds, shillings, and pence), this paper currency was the real money of the colony for the next sixty years. It was designated as legal tender and was valid payment for all obligations, including the purchase of bills of exchange. The value of Massachusetts currency—later to be referred to as "Old Tenor"—remained stable for about a decade and then began an inflationary climb that did not end until the crown intervened and the colony redeemed its grossly inflated paper money in 1750.

As of 31 March 1750, Massachusetts returned to silver as the basis of its circulating medium and to the piece of eight as the measure of the value of its money.[47] There followed twenty-five years of marked stability in the course of the exchange in Massachusetts. Par was set once again at £133.33, a rate called Lawful Money (because it bore the legal ratio to sterling set out in Queen Anne's proclamation and subsequent law of 1708). The law redeeming the old paper money set its ratio at £7.50 Old Tenor to £1.00 Lawful Money, a ratio of some importance, since many people continued to keep accounts in Old Tenor.[48] The par of Massachusetts Old Tenor to sterling after 1750 was therefore £1,000 Old Tenor to £100 sterling.[49] Expressions of the rate of exchange in Old Tenor quoted the price; expressions in terms of Lawful Money frequently spoke of the percentage above or below par.[50]

Massachusetts transacted exchange negotiations with London in terms of its money of account, pounds Massachusetts currency (whether Old Tenor or Lawful Money). Bills of exchange were in use from the early days of settlement and were drawn on London in the same fashion as they were drawn in Europe and in the other colonies for the entire

---

243n. A Rhode Island law of 1670 implied a rate of £133.33. John Russell Bartlett, ed., *Records of the Colony of Rhode Island and Providence Plantations, in New England* (Providence, R.I., 1856–1865), II, 359–360. Nettels's suggestion that the 6s (30p) rate (and therefore the £133.33 par) was used as early as 1652 seems to be countered by a letter he himself once quoted. In a letter to England of 19 Sept. 1660, John Winthrop, Jr., advised prospective immigrants to New England that pieces of eight passed for 5s (25p) and that bills of exchange sold for "10 or 12 or 15 li [pounds] advantage." Curtis P. Nettels, "The Beginnings of Money in Connecticut," Wisconsin Academy of Science, Arts, and Letters, *Transactions*, XXIII (1928), 2, 26; *The Winthrop Papers* (Mass. Hist. Soc., *Colls.*, 5th Ser., VIII [Boston, 1882]), 66. See also commissioners of the Mint to Treasury, 15 Jan. 1684/85, C.O. 1/60, fols. 262–263, where they imply a par, based on the silver content of the Massachusetts "Pine Tree" shilling, of £130.

46. For the history of Massachusetts paper currency, see Brock, *Currency of the American Colonies*, 21–35, 244–291. See also Joseph B. Felt, *Historical Account of Massachusetts Currency* (Boston, 1839); Herman Belz, "Paper Money in Colonial Massachusetts," Essex Institute, *Historical Collections*, CI (1969), 149–163.

47. *Acts and Resolves of Massachusetts*, III, 430–441.

48. New Tenor and Middle Tenor, other pre-1750 issues of paper bills of credit, were redeemed at a ratio of £4 Old Tenor to £1 New or Middle Tenor. *Ibid.*, 430. See also *An Exact Table to Bring Old Tenor into Lawful Money . . .* (Boston, 1750), 1–5. This was first printed as a broadside dated 1 Jan. 1750 (i.e., 1749/50). Connecticut's New Tenor of 1740 bore a rate of only £3.50 Old Tenor to £1 New Tenor. Brock, *Currency of the American Colonies*, 45–46.

49. "Exchange at par which is 10 for one in O[ld] Tenor," Letter of 25 July 1766, Henry Lloyd Letter Book, 1765–1767, p. 422, Manuscript and Archives Division, Baker Library, Graduate School of Business Administration, Harvard University, Boston.

50. For instance, in a letter of 9 July 1770, Nathaniel Coffin, the assistant cashier of the Board of Customs in Boston, informed John Swift, the collector of customs at Philadelphia, that the rate of exchange was 7.5% under par, or 123.33. He indicated that £133.33 less 7.5%, or £10, was the bill rate at that time. Custom House Papers, 1704–1929, X, fol. 1261, Hist. Soc. Pa.

period under discussion.[51] Damages on protested bills, for instance, were 10 percent.[52] Tables 3.1 and 3.2 present the quotations collected to date.[53] Table 3.3 compares the market price in Old Tenor of one ounce troy of sterling silver at Boston with the official English mint price of 62d (25.8p) and with the market price at London from tables 1.3 and 1.4. This last ratio (column 3) might be called the metallic rate of exchange and, at some discount to allow for the costs of freight, insurance, and sale commissions, indicates the specie export point for silver.[54] That was the price at which it became more profitable to export silver from Massachusetts to London than to use it to buy a bill of exchange. On the average for the 1740s, the metallic rate of exchange was 3.2 percent higher than the bill rate in table 3.1, although the range was a great one, from +20.2 percent to −8.5 percent.[55] This calculation will have some additional use just below.

We have considerably less information about Massachusetts's intercolonial exchange. Except for the period from 1750 to about 1765, there was no need for exchange transactions between Massachusetts and the rest of New England, including, from 1710 to 1750, those parts of Nova Scotia in English control.[56] After 1750 Boston seems to have negotiated with Halifax using the bill rate.[57] For the rest of the colonies, exchange seems to have been transacted after 1750 using the cruder constant ratio system based on the comparative values given the piece of eight. The reason seems most likely to have been a lack of current information about the bill rate on London in each of the other colonies (see the epigraph for this chapter). Henry Lloyd regularly increased Lawful Money by one-third when converting to New York currency, and he exchanged with both Pennsylvania and Maryland at a ratio of £6 Old Tenor to £1 of those currencies. John Hancock used the same rate as Lloyd in his trade to Philadelphia. Nathaniel Shaw of New London, Connecticut, who maintained extensive connections with New York and whom we might expect to have relied on the bill rate, used the same ratio as Lloyd in that trade.[58] In his trade to Philadelphia, Shaw used a ratio of

51. See nn. 42 and 45 above. See also Adam Winthrop, [at Boston], to John Winthrop, Jr., 27 Nov. and 8 Dec. 1649, *Winthrop Papers* (Boston, 1929–1947), V, 378, 382.

52. This, at least, is the rate referred to in [James Hudson?], at Newbury, Mass., to [William Rathbone, at Liverpool], 27 July 1761, James Hudson and Benjamin Rolfe Account and Letter Book, 1747–1783, Hudson Family Papers, 1659–1862, I, N.Y. Pub. Lib.

53. Many of the sources consulted for table 3.2 were suggested by Weiss, "Monetary Standard," *Econ. Hist. Rev.*, 2d Ser., XXVII (1974), 577–592. He and I disagree over the reading of some of these figures, and I have distinguished between the London price for bills on Massachusetts and vice versa.

54. J[ohn] Wright, *The American Negotiator: or, The Various Currencies of the British Colonies in America . . . Reduced into English Money*, 3d ed., repr. (London, 1767), lxiv–lxv, prepared a similar table.

55. The years 1741, 1742, and 1745, when this comparison suggests a bill rate in excess of the specie export point, came in the midst of the War of the Austrian Succession, a period during which the value of silver relative to bills of exchange could be expected to decline somewhat because of the wartime difficulty in shipping silver. In 1744 Benjamin Tasker, the president of the Maryland Council, complained of the effect in the middle colonies:

"The great plentie of Spanish gold and silver brought into New York, Pennsylvania and Virginia, and the high insurance has made a great demand for bills of excha[nge]" and caused the price of silver to decline. Tasker to Charles Calvert, Lord Baltimore, 3 Dec. 1744, [William Hand Browne *et al.*, eds.], *The Calvert Papers* (Maryland Historical Society, *Fund Publications*, Nos. 28, 34, 35 [Baltimore, 1889–1899]), II, 117.

56. For Nova Scotia see Gustave Lanctot *et al.*, eds., *Documents Relating to Currency, Exchange and Finance in Nova Scotia, with Prefatory Documents, 1675–1758* (Ottawa, 1933), *passim*. See also [Douglass], *Discourse concerning Currencies*, 8.

57. See, e.g., John Hancock Waste Book, 1764–1767, Hancock Family Papers, 1712–1854, New England Historic and Genealogical Society, Boston.

58. See Shaw's Letter Book, 1765–1783, *passim*, as printed in Ernest E. Rogers, *Connecticut's Naval Office at New London during the War of the American*

£125 Pennsylvania currency to £100 Lawful Money, which is, of course, the same as £6 Old Tenor to £1 Pennsylvania currency (recall that Massachusetts and Connecticut shared the post-1750 ratio of £7.50 Old Tenor to £1 Lawful Money). Earlier John Erving's use of a 25 percent advance upon "Boston money" to equal South Carolina currency could only have been a temporary expedient.[59] Much more intriguing are both his and Henry Lloyd's fairly regular references to Dutch bills on Amsterdam.[60]

New Hampshire, Rhode Island, and Connecticut followed the monetary example of Massachusetts in almost every particular, with one key exception.[61] When Massachusetts redeemed its paper bills of credit and went back to a silver standard as of 31 March 1750, the other three chose for the first time not to do as Massachusetts did. As a result, after 31 March 1751, when the bills of credit of Rhode Island, New Hampshire, and Connecticut could no longer circulate in

Massachusetts, the century-old existence of a New England currency came to an end.[62] Originally Connecticut had chosen to go along with Massachusetts, but a series of amendments to Connecticut's enabling act delayed the conversion date until 1 November 1756.[63] Rhode Island and New Hampshire persisted in their use of inflated paper currencies until 1763,[64] and these currencies continued to inflate during the intervening period. When New Hampshire and Rhode Island estab-

---

Revolution (New London County Historical Society, *Collections*, II [New London, Conn., 1933]), 169–336.

59. John Erving Journal, 1733–1745, Baker Lib.

60. Equally interesting is the Jan. 1676 settlement of a suit in Boston that equated the livre tournois with 2s (10p) Massachusetts currency. *Records of the Suffolk County Court*, II, 661–669. It provides a neat check on the tables in this handbook, which yield, for 1676, almost precisely that figure. Table 5.1 for 1676 shows that £100 sterling equaled 1,310.04 livres tournois; table 5.2 indicates that £100 sterling equaled £129.17 or 12,917p, Massachusetts currency. The latter divided by the former gives a quotient of 9.86p Massachusetts currency per livre tournois.

61. For instance, they were usually quick to adopt the currency value of the piece of eight enacted by Massachusetts. Nettels, *Money Supply*, 107, 240n, 246n. For the history of their paper currencies, see Brock, *Currency of the American Colonies*, 37–50, 291–333. See also Charles J. Bullock, *Essays on the Monetary History of the United States* (New York, 1900), 207–259; John Blanchard MacInnes, "Rhode Island Bills of Public Credit, 1710–1755" (Ph.D. diss., Brown University, 1952).

62. *Acts and Resolves of Massachusetts*, III, 436. This caused many difficulties and at least one important lawsuit when Thomas Packer tried to repay part of an old debt using New Hampshire and Connecticut money. See Andrews, "Current Lawful Money," *Am. Hist. Rev.*, XXIV (1918–1919), 73–77, and the sources cited there, especially the two printed cases in the dispute of *Dering* v. *Packer* in Appealed Cases before the Privy Council, 1722–1769, III, fols. 44–48, Hardwicke Papers, DCCCLXX, Additional Manuscript 36218, British Library. Gaspare John Saladino has called the Massachusetts law that effected this change "the basic cause for Boston's decline in the Connecticut trade. . . . Hampered by this restriction, Connecticut businessmen traded with New York City whose merchants quickly seized the opportunity . . . and willingly accepted Connecticut currency." Saladino, "The Economic Revolution in Late Eighteenth-Century Connecticut" (Ph.D. diss., University of Wisconsin, 1964), 12. John Adams, in Connecticut on a visit in 1771, reported that "the people here all trade to N. York, and have very little connection with Boston. . . . Boston lost the trade of this colony by the severe laws vs. their old tenor." Lyman H. Butterfield *et al.*, eds., *Diary and Autobiography of John Adams* (Cambridge, Mass., 1961), II, 32.

63. Brock, *Currency of the American Colonies*, 306–324. For the laws involved see Trumbull and Hoadly, eds., *Public Records of Connecticut*, IX, 447–449, 474–475, 510–511. See also the sometimes inaccurate study by Henry Bronson, *A Historical Account of Connecticut Currency, Continental Money, and the Finances of the Revolution* (New Haven Colony Historical Society, *Papers*, I [New Haven, Conn., 1865]). By 1761 Connecticut paper money once again circulated in Massachusetts at par with Massachusetts currency. Brock, *Currency of the American Colonies*, 290, 320n.

64. Brock, *Currency of the American Colonies*, 291–306, 325–333. For the laws involved see Bartlett, ed., *Records of Rhode Island*, VI, 358–363; Nathaniel Bouton *et al.*, eds., *Documents and Papers Relating to the Province of New-Hampshire* (Concord, N.H., 1867–1943), VII, 77–78.

lished Lawful Money in 1763, the former set the par of its former currency at £20 Old Tenor to £1 Lawful Money (£2,675 New Hampshire to £100 sterling), and the latter at £23.33 Old Tenor to £1 Lawful Money (£3,111 Rhode Island to £100 sterling).[65] In 1769 Rhode Island's rate was reset at £26.67 Old Tenor to £1 Lawful Money (£3,560 Rhode Island to £100 sterling).[66] Table 3.4 constructs an exchange rate for each of these three colonies based on the commercial price of silver there and in London for the years after 1750. Such figures, in effect more the specie export point than the commercial rate of exchange, are probably, at an average, from 3 to 5 percent higher than the commercial or bill rate.[67] For the years 1750 and earlier the series in table 3.1 will do for all of New England.

What evidence we have for the period after 1764 suggests that New England once again had a common currency in Lawful Money. Quotations of the exchange rate that survive for the other New England colonies are almost always the same as those for Massachusetts set down in table 3.1. The only exceptions seem to be from those times when the Revolution overtook Boston with special fury. In the midst of the nonimportation movement, for example, the diminished demand for bills at Boston caused a decline in the rate of exchange, while at Portsmouth, New Hampshire, the rate stayed at par.[68] But that is said on the strength of one quotation only; until a great deal more work is done, we must use caution in extending the series in table 3.1 to all of New England for the ten years prior to the Revolution.

With the information in tables 3.1 through 3.4 at hand, however, we should have much less difficulty understanding the complexities of New England money. Consider, for instance, the following passage, which Worthington C. Ford once singled out as a particularly good example of "the confusion in the currency of Rhode Island": "Since I came up have spoke with my brother about the bills [of exchange] but your terms will not answer, [because] we can gett more for them than you offered. I will let you have fifty pounds sterling at par and about one hundred dollars in treasurers notes and take malasses to the amount at 36/ old tenor per gallon, if

65. "New Hampshire Old Tenor Exchange 26¾ for 1 Sterling," memorandum in "Invoices of the Costs and Outfits of the Ship Mary Harriott . . . ," Portsmouth, N.H., 25 Mar. 1765, in Business Papers of James Lynde, C. 110/163, *Fleming* v. *Lynde*; *Rhode Island Sessional Laws*, *At the General Assembly of the Governor and Company of the English Colony of Rhode-Island and Providence-Plantations, in New-England, in America* . . . ([Providence, R.I., 1908–1925; orig. publ. Newport, R.I., 1747–1800]), 1762–1764 [VII], 1764–1767 [VIII]. The Rhode Island ratio was inherent in the valuation of the piece of eight at 6s (30p) Lawful Money and £7 Old Tenor. See, e.g., the notation on a promissory note, dated 11 Nov. 1763: "NB. Lawful money at 23¹/₃ is equil to O[ld] Tenor." Brown Papers, zU-C. See also Wright, *American Negotiator*, lxi–lxii; Elisha Potter and Sidney S. Rider, *Some Account of the Bills of Credit or Paper Money of Rhode Island from the First Issue in 1710, to the Final Issue, 1786*, Rhode Island Historical Tracts, No. 8 (Providence, R.I., 1880), 95–100.

66. *At the General Assembly of Rhode-Island*, 1767–1770 [IX]; *Acts and Laws of the English Colony of Rhode-Island and Providence-Plantations, in New-England, in America: Made and Passed since the Revision in June, 1767* (Newport, R.I., 1772), 31–32. This was the effect of accepting £8 Old Tenor as the equivalent of 6s (30p) Lawful Money in payment of colonial taxes.

67. This is based on the discussion of table 3.3 above. But see Edward Channing, *A History of the United States* (New York, 1905–1925), II, 503, quoting a bill rate of £2,600 Rhode Island currency to £100 sterling for Oct.

1760 and one at £3,200 in 1762; and Bouton *et al.*, eds., *Documents Relating to New-Hampshire*, VI, 349, 376, 513, 744, 878, giving rates of £1,000 for Oct. 1751, £1,300 for Apr. 1755, £1,460–£1,500 for Apr. 1756, £2,500–£2,666.67 for Feb. 1760, and £2,500 for June 1763.

68. Cf. these quotations of the exchange at Portsmouth, N.H., with table 3.1; exchange is at par, £133.33 per £100 sterling, in all of the following months: Aug. 1766; Jan. 1767; Mar., Apr., and Aug. 1768; and Feb. 1770. Only in the last month is there a difference. From the journal, 1766–1774,

you'll take both bills and notes."[69] We might pose this as a puzzle by asking how many gallons of molasses the writer, Daniel Tillinghast, distiller of Providence, expected to buy from his correspondent, whom Ford does not identify but who was probably Aaron Lopez, merchant of Newport.[70] It is clear enough that Tillinghast and Lopez have been negotiating over this point and that Tillinghast is here making a counterproposal. What does not appear in the letter but what table 3.1 suggests is that, given the time—October 1770—Lopez probably expected to have any bills at a discount from par, perhaps as much as 7.5 percent (or £123.33 Rhode Island currency per £100 sterling). Tillinghast here replies that Lopez can have his bill of exchange for £50 sterling but only at par, equal to £66.67, and only if Lopez will take another hundred dollars in Rhode Island paper money—worth, at 6s (30p) per dollar, another £30 currency. In return Tillinghast would pay Lopez for the molasses at the sum of 36s, or £1.80, Old Tenor per gallon, which, at £26.67 Rhode Island Old Tenor to £1 Lawful Money, was the equivalent of 16.2d (6.75p) currency per gallon.[71] Tillinghast expected to buy something more than fourteen hundred gallons of molasses for just over a shilling (5p) sterling each.

---

and the daybook, or waste book, 1767–1775, of William Barrell, William Barrell's Journals, 1766–1775, Stephen Collins and Son Papers, 1749–1857, Library of Congress. But see the discussion below suggesting that bills were at par in Rhode Island in early Oct. 1770 when they were at a discount at Boston.

69. *Commerce of Rhode Island*, I, 348n.

70. See Tillinghast to Lopez, 21 June 1770, and 22 Mar. 1771, *ibid.*, 334–335, 361.

71. The £66.67 plus £30 equaled £96.67 Rhode Island currency, which, divided by 6.75p (£0.0675) per gallon, equals, 1,432 gallons of molasses.

TABLE 3.1. **Rate of Exchange: Massachusetts on London, 1649–1775**

(Pounds Massachusetts Currency per £100 Sterling)

Year	Jan.	Feb.	Mar.	Apr.	May	June	July	Aug.	Sept.	Oct.	Nov.	Dec.	Average
1649												[112.00]	112.00
1650													
1651													
1652													
1653													
1654													
1655													
1656													
1657													
1658													
1659													
1660									112.00				112.00
1661													
1662													
1663									112.00				112.00
1664									113.33				113.33
1665									115.33				115.33
1666													
1667									116.00				116.00
1668									115.75				115.75
1669									116.00				116.00
1670													
1671									125.00				125.00
1672													
1673												125.00	125.00
1674													

TABLE 3.1 (Continued): **Massachusetts on London** (Pounds Massachusetts Currency per £100 Sterling)

Year	Jan.	Feb.	Mar.	Apr.	May	June	July	Aug.	Sept.	Oct.	Nov.	Dec.	Average
1675							123.89						123.89
1676												[129.17]	129.17
1677													
1678													
1679							125.00					[119.00]	122.00
1680										122.50		[118.00]	120.25
1681													
1682													
1683													
1684											130.00		130.00
1685	130.00									125.00			127.50
1686							125.00			125.00		[125.00]	125.00
1687			122.83			120.00	120.00						120.94
1688			140.00										140.00
1689													
1690													
1691		130.00						130.00	135.00				131.25
1692							130.00			131.00			130.50
1693												[130.00]	130.00
1694						134.00						[133.33]	133.66
1695										139.86			139.86
1696												[129.17]	129.17
1697												[136.00]	136.00
1698													
1699			142.86							142.86		[133.33]	140.48
1700						142.86						[136.00]	139.43
1701			138.00						135.00				136.50

TABLE 3.1 (Continued): Massachusetts on London (Pounds Massachusetts Currency per £100 Sterling)

Year	Jan.	Feb.	Mar.	Apr.	May	June	July	Aug.	Sept.	Oct.	Nov.	Dec.	Average
1702	130.00												130.00
1703							140.00						140.00
1704													
1705												[135.00]	135.00
1706												[150.00]	150.00
1707													
1708													
1709	160.00					142.11							151.06
1710											160.00	[150.00]	155.00
1711			140.00						150.00		150.00		146.67
1712							150.00		150.00				150.00
1713											[150.00]	[150.00]	150.00
1714			150.00				150.00				160.00	[160.00]	153.33
1715					160.00		160.00	162.00				[160.00]	160.33
1716		160.00				160.00			170.00			[160.00]	162.50
1717									180.00			[160.00]	170.00
1718							200.00		200.00			[200.00]	200.00
1719	[212.50]					[220.00]			210.00		225.00	[225.00]	216.88
1720	223.12	221.25	214.17	207.08	200.00	200.00	235.00	222.50	230.00	230.00	225.00	225.00	219.43
1721	223.83	222.67	221.50	200.00	230.00	230.00	230.00	230.00	230.00	235.00	231.25	227.50	225.98
1722	220.00		223.75				235.00			220.00	237.50	240.00	229.79
1723	240.00	237.50	235.00	235.17	235.33	230.00	250.00	240.00	245.00	250.00	258.33	245.42	241.81
1724	250.00	260.00	250.00	255.00	260.00	270.00	280.00	280.00	275.00	276.67	278.33	280.00	267.92
1725	290.00	283.33	285.83	288.33	294.17	300.00	290.00	288.33	280.00	285.00	290.00	294.38	289.11
1726	290.00	290.00	292.50	295.00	295.00	290.00	290.00	287.50	288.75	281.00	288.33	294.17	290.19
1727	300.00	290.00	295.00	300.00	285.00	286.67	290.00	284.00	293.75	291.88	290.00	297.50	291.98
1728	286.67	300.00	295.00	290.00	280.00	300.00	296.67	300.00	303.75	307.50	311.25	315.00	298.82
1729	310.00	305.00	300.00	295.00	320.00	307.50	300.00	320.00	322.50	325.00	326.67	328.33	313.33

TABLE 3.1 (Continued): Massachusetts on London (Pounds Massachusetts Currency per £100 Sterling)

Year	Jan.	Feb.	Mar.	Apr.	May	June	July	Aug.	Sept.	Oct.	Nov.	Dec.	Average
1730	330.00	*340.00*	350.00	*350.00*	*350.00*	350.00	335.00	347.50	335.00	313.34	*321.67*	330.00	337.71
1731	330.00			330.00			335.00		330.00		342.50	347.00	334.31
1732	322.50	311.67	350.00		350.00	350.00	322.50		337.50			350.00	339.51
1733						350.00					350.00		350.00
1734				350.00	360.00								355.00
1735									360.00				360.00
1736					350.00		510.00						430.00
1737	525.00				525.00						500.00		516.67
1738				500.00									500.00
1739	500.00		500.00				500.00						500.00
1740	[500.00]	550.00										[525.00]	525.00
1741			550.00		550.00	550.00		550.00		550.00	531.25	550.00	548.44
1742		550.00	550.00	550.00			550.00	550.50	553.33		550.00	550.00	550.28
1743	550.00	560.00	560.00	550.00	550.00	560.00	556.67	*547.78*	*538.89*	530.00	*545.00*	560.00	550.70
1744	563.75	595.00	561.25			600.00					600.00	585.00	588.61
1745	600.00	550.00	550.00	700.00	700.00	570.00	700.00	*700.00*	*700.00*	700.00	650.00	*617.50*	644.79
1746	585.00								700.00				642.50
1747						950.00			875.00			950.00	925.00
1748			950.00				875.00						912.50
1749	1,000.00			975.00								[1,125.0]	1,033.33
1750	[150.00]			150.00		135.33			126.67	126.67	133.33		137.33
1751					133.33								133.33
1752													
1753			126.67		133.33								130.00
1754		133.33											133.33
1755						133.33	133.33	133.33	133.33	133.33	133.33	133.33	133.33
1756	*133.33*	133.33	133.33	133.33	133.33	133.33	133.33	133.33	133.33	133.33	133.33	133.33	133.33
1757				133.33	133.33							133.33	133.33

TABLE 3.1 (Continued): Massachusetts on London (Pounds Massachusetts Currency per £100 Sterling)

Year	Jan.	Feb.	Mar.	Apr.	May	June	July	Aug.	Sept.	Oct.	Nov.	Dec.	Average
1758		130.00			126.67	130.00				126.67			128.34
1759													
1760			126.33	127.50	127.08							135.00	129.54
1761		140.00		145.00		136.00		139.33	138.00	141.25			140.10
1762	142.75	142.75		145.08	142.67	138.00							142.33
1763				140.00	140.00	136.00	136.00			133.33		133.33	136.00
1764	133.33					135.00			133.33	133.33	133.33	133.33	133.75
1765	133.33	133.33	133.39	133.50	134.17	134.38	133.33	133.33	133.33	133.33	133.78	133.33	133.54
1766	133.33	129.78	133.33	133.33	133.33	133.33	133.33	133.33	133.33	133.33	133.33	133.33	133.03
1767			133.33	133.33	133.33					133.33	133.33	133.33	133.33
1768			133.33	133.33	133.33	133.33					133.33		133.33
1769	133.33		132.20	133.33					126.67			126.67	129.86
1770	126.67	130.00	127.78	130.00	125.83	123.33	123.33	125.00	123.33	123.33	128.33	128.75	126.31
1771	133.33		133.33										133.33
1772	133.33							128.33		133.49	128.89	131.67	131.00
1773	132.50	133.33	131.67	130.00	130.00	133.33	130.00	132.22	132.08	132.72	133.78	134.67	132.19
1774	136.46	136.07	136.67	136.67	135.33	136.67	136.67	134.33	136.67	135.00	133.33	129.79	135.30
1775	126.25	125.00			120.00			113.33		110.83			117.45

Notes and Sources: **TABLE 3.1**

Figures inserted in square brackets are assigned to that month arbitrarily; figures in italics are straight-line interpolations based on the two neighboring quotations.

1649–1744: New England Company Archives, MSS 7936, 7938, 7946, 7950, 7955, Guildhall Library, London. The first of these volumes has been printed as *Some Correspondence between the Governors and Treasurers of the New England Company in London and the Commissioners of the United Colonies in America, and the Missionaries of the Company and Others between the Years 1657 and 1712* (London, 1896); see pp. 6, 11, 24, 45–46. The second of these volumes is a transcript of MS Rawlinson C. 934, Bodleian Library, Oxford; the letter in it used here is that of Thomas Weld, at Gateshead, Co. Durham, to the New England Company in London, 2 Jan. 1649/50, which has been printed in G. D. Scull, ed., "Rev. Thomas Welde's 'Innocency Cleared,'" *New England Historical and Genealogical Register*, XXXVI (1882), 62–64.

Notes and Sources: **TABLE 3.1 (Continued)**

1660: John Winthrop, Jr., at Hartford, Conn., to [New England Company in London?], 19 Sept. 1660, *The Winthrop Papers* (Massachusetts Historical Society, *Collections*, 5th Ser., VIII [Boston, 1882]), 66.

1663–1667: David Pulsifer, ed., *Acts of the Commissioners of the United Colonies of New England*, Vols. IX and X of Nathaniel B. Shurtleff and David Pulsifer, eds., *Records of the Colony of New Plymouth in New England* (Boston, 1859), II, 293, 313, 330.

1673: George Parker Winship, ed., *The New England Company of 1649 and John Eliot* (Prince Society Publications, XXXVI [Boston, 1920]), 160. Winship printed the New England Company treasurer's ledger, 1650–1660, in the Bureau of Archives and History, State House, Trenton, N.J., and the Minutes of the New England Company, 1656–1686, now in the Massachusetts Historical Society, Boston. There is a photostatic copy of the latter volume in the New England Company Archives, MS 8011.

1675, 1679: *Records of the Suffolk County Court, 1671–1680* (Colonial Society of Massachusetts, *Publications*, XXIX–XXX [Boston, 1933]), II, 608–609.

1676–1719: Gloria Lund Main, "Personal Wealth in Colonial America: Explorations in the Use of Probate Records from Maryland to Massachusetts, 1650–1720" (Ph.D. diss., Columbia University, 1972), 20, table 1–2.

1680: James Hammond Trumbull and Charles James Hoadly, eds., *The Public Records of the Colony of Connecticut*, III (Hartford, Conn., 1859), 68–69.

1685, 1688: Henry Ashurst, at London, to Joseph Dudley and Daniel Allen, at Boston, 27 Jan. 1684/85, and to William Stoughton, at Boston, 19 Mar. 1684/85 and 8 June 1688, Letter Book and Account Book of Henry Ashurst, 1674–1701, fols. 40v, 41r, 66r, Deposited Deeds, Ashurst, c. 1, Bodleian Lib.

1685–1713: Harvard College Records, College Books I, III–V, Harvard University Archives, Widener Library, Harvard University, Cambridge, Mass. College Books I, III, and IV have been printed. See [Albert Matthews, ed.], *Harvard College Records* (Col. Soc. of Mass., *Pubs.*, XV–XVI [Boston, 1925]), I, 81, II, 426. College Book V is the Journal of Thomas Brattle, 1693–1713, the college treasurer; see pp. 50, 64, 71, 77. See also Margery Somers Foster, "*Out of Smalle Beginnings . . .*": An Economic History of Harvard College in the Puritan Period (1636 to 1712) (Cambridge, Mass., 1962), 45, 116–117, for these references and their context.

1686–1749: [Dorothy C. Barck, ed.], *Papers of the Lloyd Family of the Manor of Queens Village, Lloyd's Neck, Long Island, New York, 1654–1826* (New-York Historical Society, *Collections*, LIX–LX [New York, 1927]), I, 98, 111–113, 144, 148, 380, 421.

1689–1695: *Letter-Book of Samuel Sewall* [1686–1734] (Mass. Hist. Soc., *Colls.*, 6th Ser., I–II [Boston, 1886–1888]), I, 43, 119, 132, 133, 143, 150, 157.

1699–1700: Gov. Richard Coote, earl of Bellomont, to Board of Trade, from New York, 17 Apr. 1699, and from Boston, 24 Oct. 1699, 22 June 1700, C.O. 5/1042, fol. 11r, C.O. 5/860, fol. 378r, and C.O. 5/1044, fol. 88r, Public Record Office.

1701: Minutes of the Council, Boston, 19 Apr. 1701, C.O. 5/788, fol. 23v.

1705–1706, 1762: Roger W. Weiss, "The Colonial Monetary Standard of Massachusetts," *Economic History Review*, 2d Ser., XXVII (1974), 579, 586, 591.

1709: Memorandum dated 15 Jan. 1708/09, *Lilie v. Waterhouse*, C. 104/16, P.R.O.

1709: Isaac Norris Journal, 1709–1716, p. 10, Norris Papers, 1742–1860, Historical Society of Pennsylvania, Philadelphia.

1710: Joseph Cruttenden, at London, to Thomas Barton, at Salem, Mass., 3 Mar. 1710/11, Letter Book of Joseph Cruttenden, 1710–1717, p. 52, Rawlinson Letters 66, Bodleian Lib.

1710–1750: Gustave Lanctot *et al.*, eds., *Documents Relating to Currency, Exchange and Finance in Nova Scotia, with Prefatory Documents, 1675–1758* (Ottawa, 1933), xxxii, 25, 65, 80, 104, 118–120, 122–124, 127–130, 139, 154, 165, 170, 199, 221, 263, 278–279, 296.

1713–1744: *An Enquiry into the State of the Bills of Credit of the Province of the Massachusetts-Bay in New-England: in a Letter from a Gentleman in Boston to a Merchant in London* (n.p., 1743 [1743/44]), 7, 42.

1715–1716: Thomas Moffatt Letter Book, 1715–1716, New York Public Library, New York City.

1719–1728: Thomas Amory Letter Books, 1723–1725, 1726–1728, Amory Family Papers, 1697–1823, Library of Congress.

Notes and Sources: **TABLE 3.1 (Continued)**

1719–1758: Records of the International Scientific Committee on Price History (1928–1939), Case 5: Work Sheets, Boston, file: Exchange, 1719–1759, Manuscript and Archives Division, Baker Library, Graduate School of Business Administration, Harvard Univ., Boston. The bulk of this material is identified only as coming from "Fitch Acct. of Exchange." Presumably this is a reference to the Account Books, 1719–1753, Thomas Fitch Papers, Mass. Hist. Soc.

1720: Gov. Samuel Shute, at Boston, to Board of Trade, 17 Feb. 1719/20, C.O. 5/867, pt. ii, fol. 313v.

1720: John Colman, *The Distressed State of the Town of Boston Once More Considered* (Boston, [1720]), 6.

1726, 1737, 1739: Peter Jay Journal, 1724–1748, pp. 13, 181, 202, 203, 211, Peter Jay Papers, 1724–1770, New-York Historical Society, New York City.

1730–1732: Peter Faneuil Daybook, ca. 1726–1732, Hancock Family Papers, 1712–1854, New England Historic Genealogical Society, Boston.

1732: Gov. Jonathan Belcher, at Boston, to Board of Trade, 23 Dec. 1732, C.O. 5/875, fols. 121–124.

1734: Lt. Gov. Col. Lawrence Armstrong, at Annapolis Royal, N.S., to Board of Trade, 10 May 1734, C.O. 217/7, fol. 51v. See also Andrew Hill Clark, *Acadia: The Geography of Early Nova Scotia to 1760* (Madison, Wis., 1968), 197–198.

1736: Francis Wilks, at Austin Friars, [London], to Board of Trade, 30 July 1736, C.O. 5/1268, pt. ii, fol. 253r. Wilks was the London agent for the colony.

1738: [William Douglass], *An Essay concerning Silver and Paper Currencies, More Especially with Regard to the British Colonies in New-England* (Boston, [1738]), 4, 6.

1739: Samuel Wentworth, at Boston, to John Tomlinson, at London, 3 Mar. 1738/39, Samuel Wentworth Letters and Papers, 1738–1742, Ayer Manuscripts, Newberry Library, Chicago.

1740: [William Douglass], *A Discourse concerning the Currencies of the British Plantations in America* (Boston, 1740), 10, 19.

1741–1745: John Erving Journal, 1733–1745, Baker Lib.

1741–1746: *Journal of the House of Representatives of Massachusetts* (Boston, 1919–), XIX, 66, XX, 206–207, 374, XXI, 150, XXII, 54, 145–146.

1745–1746: John Barrell, at London, to Nathaniel Barrell, at Portsmouth, N.H., 15 Oct. 1765, Correspondence, 1749–1803, V, no. 10420, Stephen Collins and Son Papers, 1749–1857, Lib. Cong.

1747–1753: Bills of exchange drawn by Rev. Matthias Plant, Newbury, Mass., Archives of the Society for the Propagation of the Gospel in Foreign Parts, Class II, Ser. IV, United Society for the Propagation of the Gospel, London.

1750: William Douglass, *A Summary, Historical and Political, of the First Planting, Progressive Improvements, and Present State of the British Settlements in North America* (Boston, 1749–1751), II, 87n. See also Henry J. Phillips, *Historical Sketches of the Paper Currency of the American Colonies, Prior to the Adoption of the Federal Constitution* (New York, 1865–1866), 110.

1750: Letter dated 1 Oct. 1750, *Boston Weekly News-Letter*, 20 Dec. 1750.

1757: Samuel Hughes, at Boston, to Samuel Galloway, at Annapolis, Md., 13 Dec. 1757, Galloway Correspondence, II, no. 8271, Galloway-Maxey-Markoe Family Papers, 1654–1888, Lib. Cong.

1758: R. A. Apthorpe and Son, at Boston, to Tomlinson, Hanbury, Colebrook and Nesbitt, at London, 1 Nov. 1758, T. 1/380, no. 53, P.R.O.

1758–1761: James Hudson, at Newbury, Mass., to William Rathbone, at Liverpool, 17 Mar. and 26 May 1758, and to unspecified correspondent, at Portsmouth, N.H., 22 Dec. 1761, James Hudson and Benjamin Rolfe Account and Letter Book, 1747–1783, Hudson Family Papers, 1659–1862, N.Y. Pub. Lib.

1760, 1763: Papers of the ship *Oliver*, *Williamson v. Wallaby*, bundles D and E, C. 110/186, pt. ii.

1760–1761: Henry Lloyd, at Boston, to Thomas Clifford, at Philadelphia, 28 Apr., 5 May, 26 May, and 26 Dec. 1760, 28 Apr. 1761, Clifford Correspondence, III, 47, 53, 65, 156, 199, Pemberton Papers, Hist. Soc. Pa.

1761–1762: Lloyd to James Beekman, at New York City, 7 Aug. 1761, 11 Jan., 4 Feb., and 5 Apr. 1762, Philip L. White, ed., *The Beekman Mercantile Papers, 1746–1799* (New York, 1956), II, 673, 676–677.

Notes and Sources: **TABLE 3.1 (Continued)**

1761–1765: *The Acts and Resolves, Public and Private, of the Province of Massachusetts Bay* (Boston, 1869–1922), IV, 458, 581, 662, 720, 805.

1761–1772: Neil Jamieson Papers, 1757–1789, I, nos. 48, 113, 129, XI, nos. 2379, 2521, XIII, nos. 2814, 2835, 2877, XVI, nos. 3641, 3643, Lib. Cong.

1762: *Boston News-Letter and New-England Chronicle*, 17 June and 23 July 1762.

1763–1775: Henry Lloyd Letters, Brown Papers, P–L5, L 62–64 HL, L 63–66 HL, L 64–67 HL, L 67–69 HL, L 67–72 HL, L 71–75 HL, John Carter Brown Library, Brown University, Providence, R.I.

1764–1775: Letters of Boston Merchants, 1732–1790, I, II, Baker Lib.

1764–1775: John Hancock Waste Book, 1764–1767, and Journal, 1764–1782, Hancock Family Papers.

1765–1766: Henry Lloyd Letter Book, 1765–1767, Baker Lib.

1768: Amory Waste Book, 1768, presumably in Amory Family MSS, Mass. Hist. Soc., as cited in Elizabeth Donnan, ed., *Documents Illustrative of the History of the Slave Trade to America* (Washington, D.C., 1930–1935), III, 75n.

1769–1770: Nathaniel Coffin, at Boston, to John Swift, 12 Feb., 12 Mar., 28 Mar., 14 May, 21 June, 9 July, and 17 Dec. 1770, Custom House Papers, 1704–1929, X–XI, Hist. Soc. Pa.

1770–1774: Correspondence and Papers of Charles Steuart, Steuart Papers, MSS 5025, 5027–5028, National Library of Scotland, Edinburgh.

1772: "Charges of entring the schooner [*Lark*]," Newburyport, Mass., Aug. 1772, Shipping Papers, 1746–1772, James Hudson Accounts and Papers, 1742–1788, Hudson Family Papers.

1773–1774: *Rivington's New-York Gazetteer; or, The Connecticut, New-Jersey, Hudson's-River, and Quebec Weekly Advertiser*, 1773–1774.

1775: William B. Weeden, *Economic and Social History of New England, 1620–1789* (Boston and New York, 1891), II, 797n, citing "Amory Letter in MS.," dated 9 Oct. 1775, presumably in the Amory Family MSS.

1775: Pinkney's *Virginia Gazette* (Williamsburg), 2 Nov. 1775.

TABLE 3.2. **Rate of Exchange: London on Massachusetts, 1660–1775**
(Pounds Massachusetts Currency per £100 Sterling)

Year	Jan.	Feb.	Mar.	Apr.	May	June	July	Aug.	Sept.	Oct.	Nov.	Dec.	Average
1660				125.00									125.00
1661													
1662													
1663				117.50									117.50
1664			120.00										120.00
1665			120.00										120.00
1666													
1667													
1668													
1669				125.00	125.00	125.00							125.00
1670	125.00				125.00								125.00
1671			125.00	125.00	125.00		125.00		125.00				125.00
1672			125.00		125.00								125.00
1673				125.00		125.00							125.00
1674					125.00								125.00
1675			125.00		125.00								125.00
1676			125.00			125.00	125.00						125.00
1677			128.00										128.00
1678			128.00	128.00									128.00
1679	128.00				125.00		125.00						126.00
1680					125.00								125.00
1681									125.00	124.75			124.88
1682										128.00	128.00		128.00
1683						128.00							128.00
1684								130.00	130.00				130.00
1685									132.00	132.00			132.00
1686													

TABLE 3.2 (Continued): London on Massachusetts (Pounds Massachusetts Currency per £100 Sterling)

Year	Jan.	Feb.	Mar.	Apr.	May	June	July	Aug.	Sept.	Oct.	Nov.	Dec.	Average
1687				128.00						128.00			128.00
1688				128.00				128.00					128.00
1689													
1690				128.00	128.00		128.00			128.00	130.00		128.33
1691			130.00							128.00			129.00
1692		130.00	130.00	130.00						128.00	130.50		129.75
1693													
1694				128.33	130.00								129.16
1695						130.00		130.00			130.00	130.00	130.00
1696		130.00					130.00						130.00
1697					135.00	135.00	135.00		135.00			135.00	135.00
1698													
1699		133.00	133.00										133.00
1700						135.00		135.00					135.00
1701		135.00									134.30		134.65
1702		135.00											135.00
1703		135.00			135.00	135.83							135.21
1704		140.00						140.00					140.00
1705					145.00		145.00						145.00
1706													
1707				147.00									147.00
1708													
1709													
1710												140.00	140.00
1711							140.00	140.00					140.00
1712								125.00					125.00
1713													

TABLE 3.2 (Continued): **London on Massachusetts** (Pounds Massachusetts Currency per £100 Sterling)

Year	Jan.	Feb.	Mar.	Apr.	May	June	July	Aug.	Sept.	Oct.	Nov.	Dec.	Average
1714													
1715													
1716													
1717													
1718													
1719						210.00							210.00
1720													
1721													
1722		250.00											250.00
1723		260.00											260.00
1724													
1725								300.00					300.00
1726		310.00								310.00			310.00
1727							310.00	310.00					310.00
1728					300.00								300.00
1729						310.00							310.00
1730				340.00									340.00
1731				350.00			350.00						350.00
1732	350.00												350.00
1733		350.00		350.00									350.00
1734		380.00											380.00
1735			425.00										425.00
1736		500.00		500.00									500.00
1737		525.00			525.00				525.00				525.00
1738			500.00										500.00
1739			500.00										500.00
1740					525.00								525.00
1741							525.00						525.00

TABLE 3.2 (Continued): London on Massachusetts (Pounds Massachusetts Currency per £100 Sterling)

Year	Jan.	Feb.	Mar.	Apr.	May	June	July	Aug.	Sept.	Oct.	Nov.	Dec.	Average
1742			550.00										550.00
1743			550.00										550.00
1744				560.00									560.00
1745					600.00								600.00
1746							750.00						750.00
1747							1,000.00						1,000.00
1748							1,050.00						1,050.00
1749							1,050.00						1,050.00
1750													
1751				125.00		126.67							125.84
1752			126.67										126.67
1753				133.33									133.33
1754	133.33												133.33
1755	130.00										130.00		130.00
1756		130.00											130.00
1757			133.33										133.33
1758				133.33	133.33								133.33
1759				129.00	129.00								129.00
1760			129.00										129.00
1761					129.00	129.00							129.00
1762				133.33		133.33							133.33
1763			135.00			135.00							135.00
1764				135.00									135.00
1765			135.00			135.00							135.00
1766			135.00										135.00
1767				135.00									135.00
1768			135.00										135.00
1769			135.00										135.00

TABLE 3.2 (Continued): London on Massachusetts (Pounds Massachusetts Currency per £100 Sterling)

Year	Jan.	Feb.	Mar.	Apr.	May	June	July	Aug.	Sept.	Oct.	Nov.	Dec.	Average
1770				125.00									125.00
1771				133.33									133.33
1772				130.00									130.00
1773				130.00									130.00
1774			133.33					132.00					132.66
1775													

Notes and Sources: **TABLE 3.2**

1660–1664: David Pulsifer, ed., *Acts of the Commissioners of the United Colonies of New England*, Vols. IX and X of Nathaniel B. Shurtleff and David Pulsifer, eds., *Records of the Colony of New Plymouth in New England* (Boston, 1859), II, 240, 291, 313.

1665–1774: New England Company Archives, MSS 7911–7913, 7936, 7946, 7948, 7955, Guildhall Library, London. MS 7936 in this series has been printed as *Some Correspondence between the Governors and Treasurers of the New England Company in London and the Commissioners of the United Colonies in America, and the Missionaries of the Company and Others between the Years 1657 and 1712* (London, 1896); see pp. 6, 23, 71, 77–78.

1669–1685: George Parker Winship, ed., *The New England Company of 1649 and John Eliot* (Prince Society Publications, XXXVI [Boston, 1920]), 127, 131, 139, 146, 153, 161, 167, 169, 172, 182, 188–189, 194, 195–196, 197–198, 201, 204–205, 206–207. Winship printed the New England Company treasurer's ledger, 1650–1660, in the Bureau of Archives and History, State House, Trenton, N.J., and the Minutes of the New England Company, 1656–1686, now in the Massachusetts Historical Society, Boston. There is a photostatic copy of the latter volume in the New England Company Archives, MS 8011.

1685, 1692–1697: Henry Ashurst, at London, to William Stoughton, at Boston, 3 Oct., 12 Oct. 1685, 25 Mar., 22 Oct., 15 Nov. 1692, 20 July 1697, to James Taylor, at Boston, 7 Apr. 1694, and to Jackson and Co., at Boston, 6 July 1696, Letter Book and Account Book of Henry Ashurst, 1674–1701, fols. 43r, 44r, 83r, 84r, 85r, 96v, 119v, 136r, Deposited Deeds, Ashurst, c.1, Bodleian Library, Oxford.

1688–1761: New England Company, Copybook of Letters and Bills of Exchange Sent to New England, 1688–1761, Tracy W. McGregor Library, Alderman Library, University of Virginia, Charlottesville.

1710–1711: [Navy] Victualling Office to Treasury, 27 Nov. 1711, T. 1/139, fols. 166–170, Public Record Office. See also Ordnance Office to Treasury, 30 Oct. 1711, T. 1/139, fol. 36.

1712: Treasurer of the Navy to Treasury, 13 Aug. 1712, T. 1/151, fols. 7, 9–12; and Office for Sick and Wounded [Seamen] to Treasury, 16 Oct. 1712, T. 1/153, fol. 35.

TABLE 3.3. Price of Silver and Computed Metallic Rate of Exchange, at the Standard Price and at the Current Market Price of Silver in England—Boston, 1700–1753

(Prices—Shillings Currency per Ounce Troy; Rates—Pounds Massachusetts Currency per £100 Sterling)

Year	Price of Silver	Rate of Exchange		Year	Price of Silver	Rate of Exchange	
		At Standard Price	At Current Market Price			At Standard Price	At Current Market Price
	1	2	3		1	2	3
1700	7.00s	£135.48		1720	12.33s	£238.64	£226.62
1701	7.00	135.48	£126.32	1721	12.94	250.54	238.97
1702	7.00	135.48		1722	14.25	275.81	266.69
1703	7.00	135.48		1723	15.00	290.32	282.00
1704	7.00	135.48		1724	16.25	314.52	307.18
1705	8.00	154.84		1725	15.50	300.00	291.95
1706	8.00	154.84		1726	16.00	309.68	299.02
1707	8.00	154.84		1727	16.00	309.68	301.79
1708	8.00	154.84		1728	17.17	332.32	318.70
1709	8.00	154.84		1729	20.30	392.90	371.91
1710	8.00	154.84		1730	20.00	387.10	368.55
1711	8.33	161.23		1731	18.75	362.90	348.94
1712	8.50	164.52		1732	20.00	387.10	373.77
1713	8.50	164.52	154.54	1733	22.00	425.81	410.26
1714	9.00	174.19		1734	25.70	497.42	490.30
1715	9.00	174.19		1735	27.50	532.26	523.73
1716	10.00	193.55	181.82	1736	26.75	517.74	504.32
1717	10.00	193.55		1737	26.75	517.74	496.90
1718	11.00	212.90	201.59	1738	27.75	537.10	517.08
1719	12.00	232.26	222.84	1739	29.17	564.58	537.87

TABLE 3.3 (Continued): **Price of Silver and Computed Metallic Rate of Exchange at Boston**

Year	Price of Silver	Rate of Exchange		Year	Price of Silver	Rate of Exchange	
		At Standard Price	At Current Market Price			At Standard Price	At Current Market Price
	1	2	3		1	2	3
1740	28.62s	£553.94	£516.61	1747	56.80s	£1,099.36	£1,043.32
1741	28.25	546.77	502.07	1748	56.38	1,091.23	1,052.36
1742	28.25	546.77	507.33	1749	58.00	1,122.58	1,078.07
1743	31.00	600.00	558.56				
1744	33.00	638.71	589.55	1750	53.75	1,040.32	993.68
1745	36.00	696.77	649.62	1751	50.00	967.74	922.37
1746	43.00	832.26	805.50	1752	50.00	967.74	906.62
				1753	50.00	967.74	896.19

Notes and Sources: **TABLE 3.3**

Col. 1: Copy made 28 Oct. 1753 by Ezra Stiles from the original in the books of Jacob Hurd and Thomas Edward, goldsmiths, as printed in Franklin Bowditch Dexter, ed., *Extracts from the Itineraries and Other Miscellanies of Ezra Stiles, D.D., LL.D., 1755–1794, with a Selection from His Correspondence* (New Haven, Conn., 1916), 7–8. A less complete and slightly variant two-part account, taken from "a book kept by Edward Winslow, who was sheriff of Suffolk county," can be found in Suffolk Files 40289 and 46659 in the office of the Clerk of the Supreme Judicial Court of the Commonwealth, New Suffolk County Courthouse, Boston. It has been printed in Andrew McFarland Davis, *Currency and Banking in the Province of the Massachusetts-Bay* (American Economic Association, *Publications*, 3d Ser., I, no. 4, II, no. 2 [New York, 1900–1901]), I, 368. I owe thanks to James M. O'Toole for help with this source. See also *An Enquiry into the State of the Bills of Credit of the Province of the Massachusetts-Bay in New-England: in a Letter from a Gentleman in Boston to a Merchant in London* (n.p., 1743 [1743/44]); Reply No. 4, Massachusetts Bay, Account of Bills of Credit, 1701–1738, in Board of Trade to House of Lords, 27 Mar. 1740, House of Lords, Main Papers, 28 Mar. 1740, House of Lords Record Office, London; William Douglass, *A Summary, Historical and Political, of the First Planting, Progressive Improvements, and Present State of the British Settlements in North America* (Boston, 1749–1751), I, 494; J[ohn] Wright, *The American Negotiator: or, The Various Currencies of the British Colonies in America . . . Reduced into English Money,* 3d ed., repr. (London, 1767), lxi; Joseph B. Felt, *Historical Account of Massachusetts Currency* (Boston, 1839), 83, 135 (his source for the first table, 1710–1727, came from a table in a proposed act of 1 Dec. 1727); Frank Fenwick McLeod, "The History of Fiat Money and Currency Inflation in New England from 1620 to 1789," *Annals of the American Academy of Political and Social Science*, XII (1898), 241.

Col. 2: Col. 1 converted to pence and divided by 62d sterling.

Col. 3: Col. 1 converted to pence and divided by annual average figures for the same year in tables 1.3 and 1.4.

TABLE 3.4. **Price of Silver and Computed Metallic Rate of Exchange, at the Standard Price and at the Current Market Price of Silver in England—New Hampshire, Rhode Island, and Connecticut, after 1740**

(Prices—Shillings Currency per Ounce Troy; Rates—Pounds New Hampshire, Rhode Island, and Connecticut Currencies per £100 Sterling)

Year	New Hampshire			Rhode Island			Connecticut		
	Price of Silver	Rate of Exchange		Price of Silver	Rate of Exchange		Price of Silver	Rate of Exchange	
		At Standard Price	At Current Market Price		At Standard Price	At Current Market Price		At Standard Price	At Current Market Price
	1	2	3	4	5	6	7	8	9
1740	28.62s	£553.94	£516.61	27.50s	£532.26	£496.39	28.50s	£551.61	£514.44
1741	28.25	546.77	502.07	28.00	541.94	497.63	28.88	558.97	513.27
1742	28.25	546.77	507.33				28.00	541.94	502.84
1743	31.00	600.00	558.56				31.00	600.00	558.56
1744	33.00	638.71	589.55						
1745	36.00	696.77	649.62						
1746	43.00	832.26	805.50				42.33	819.29	792.94
1747	56.80	1,099.36	1,043.32				56.50	1,093.55	1,037.81
1748	56.38	1,091.23	1,052.36				57.00	1,103.23	1,063.93
1749	58.00	1,122.58	1,078.07	60.00	1,161.29	1,115.24	57.00	1,103.23	1,059.48
1750	51.83	1,003.16	958.19	64.30	1,244.52	1,188.72	53.00	1,025.81	979.82
1751	58.56	1,133.42	1,080.28	64.30	1,244.52	1,186.16			
1752	63.15	1,222.26	1,145.06	68.89	1,333.36	1,249.14	74.10	1434.19	1343.61
1753	65.45	1,266.77	1,173.11	80.37	1,555.55	1,440.54	74.63	1444.51	1337.72
1754	68.89	1,333.36	1,249.33	86.12	1,666.84	1,561.80	79.20	1532.90	1436.30
1755	80.37	1,555.55	1,494.10	97.60	1,889.03	1,814.41	85.00	1645.16	1580.17
1756	103.34	2,000.13	1,931.29	120.56	2,333.42	2,253.11	(6.89)	(133.33)	

TABLE 3.4 (Continued): **Price of Silver and Computed Metallic Rate of Exchange**

	New Hampshire			Rhode Island			Connecticut		
	Price of Silver	Rate of Exchange		Price of Silver	Rate of Exchange		Price of Silver	Rate of Exchange	
		At Standard Price	At Current Market Price		At Standard Price	At Current Market Price		At Standard Price	At Current Market Price
Year	1	2	3	4	5	6	7	8	9
1757	120.56s	£2,333.42	£2,249.95	132.04s	£2,555.61	£2,464.20			
1758	137.78	2,666.71	2,466.60	137.78	2,666.71	2,466.60			
1759	137.78	2,666.71	2,461.46	137.78	2,666.71	2,461.46			
1760	137.78	2,666.71	2,466.60	137.78	2,666.71	2,466.60			
1761	137.78	2,666.71	2,424.28	149.27	2,889.10	2,626.45			
1762	149.27	2,889.10	2,703.76	160.75	3,111.29	2,911.70			
1763	160.75	3,111.29	2,919.63	160.75	3,111.29	2,919.63			
1764	137.78	2,666.71	2,598.80	(6.89)	(133.33)				
1765	6.89	133.33							

Notes and Sources: **TABLE 3.4**

 Col. 1: Jeremy Belknap, *The History of New Hampshire*, III (Boston, 1792), 225. The figures for the years before 1750 are from a source common to those used in col. 1, table 3.3. Belknap wrote down a "58" for a "53" for 1747, however, an obvious mistake. See the same series in W[illiam] Winterbotham, *An Historical, Geographical, Commercial, and Philosophical View of the American United States, and of the European Settlements in America and the West Indies* (London, 1795), II, 111–112. Leslie Van Horn Brock, *The Currency of the American Colonies, 1700–1764: A Study in Colonial Finance and Imperial Relations* (New York, 1975; reprint of Ph.D. diss., University of Michigan, 1941), fig. IX, after p. 318, erroneously calls Belknap's data the price of the silver per ounce; they are the prices of the piece of eight and are here converted to the price per ounce by incrementing the given figures by 14.82% (the ratio between the official sterling prices of the full-weight piece of eight, 54d, and the official sterling price of the ounce troy of silver, 62d). Not all figures agree because of rounding. See also the currency values of the piece of eight as set down in the report of the New Hampshire treasurer, George Jaffery, to Gov. Benning Wentworth, 22 Sept. 1764, C.O. 323/19, fol. 15, Public Record Office; and Walter A. Ryal, "A Note on the Value of Currency in Provincial New Hampshire," *Historical New Hampshire*, XXVIII (1973), 196–205.

 Col. 4, 1740: Report of Gov. Richard Ward, at Newport, R.I., to Board of Trade, 9 Jan. 1740/41, John Russell Bartlett, ed., *Records of the Colony of Rhode Island and Providence Plantation in New England* (Providence, R.I., 1856–1865), V, 12–13.

Notes and Sources: **TABLE 3.4 (Continued)**

Col. 4, 1740–1749: Brock, *Currency of the American Colonies,* fig. III, after p. 29.

Col. 4, 1741–1749: Elisha R. Potter, *A Brief Account of the Emission of Paper Money Made by the Colony of Rhode Island* (Providence, R.I., 1837), as reprinted in Henry Phillips, Jr., *Historical Sketches of the Paper Currency of the American Colonies, Prior to the Adoption of the Federal Constitution* (New York, 1865–1866), I, 154.

Col. 4, 1750: William Douglass, *A Summary, Historical and Political, of the First Planting, Progressive Improvements, and Present State of the British Settlements in North America* (Boston, 1749–1751), II, 87n.

Col. 4, 1751–1763: "An Act Declaring What Is, and Shall Be, Lawful Money of the Colony," 13 June 1763, Bartlett, ed., *Records of Rhode Island,* VI, 361.

Col. 7, 1740–1750: Henry Bronson, *A Historical Account of Connecticut Currency, Continental Money, and the Finances of the Revolution* (New Haven Colony Historical Society, *Papers,* I [New Haven, Conn., 1865]), 52, 74.

Col. 7, 1752–1755: Franklin Bowditch Dexter, ed., *Extracts from the Itineraries and Other Miscellanies of Ezra Stiles, D.D., LL.D., 1755–1794, with a Selection from His Correspondence* (New Haven, Conn., 1916), 7–8.

Cols. 2, 5, and 8: Cols. 1, 4, and 7 converted to pence and divided by 62d sterling.

Cols. 3, 6, and 9: Cols. 1, 4, and 7 converted to pence and divided by annual average figures for the same year in table 1.4.

New York

The currency of New York also had a regional character. Before 1664, of course, New York was New Netherland and shared its real money and its money of account with Holland and with the other Dutch colonies in the New World.[72] Some of that international character lingered in New York's trade and in its currency too. By 1770 New York currency appertained not only in the Hudson River Valley but east to Connecticut and Rhode Island,[73] west to New Jersey,[74] and north into Canada, "at Quebec and Montreal," where "the New York traders, which supply the places with provisions, deal with the inhabitants in New York currency."[75] All of these areas shared the same real money, the gold and silver coin that we have come by now to recognize as a truly universal money during the seventeenth and eighteenth centuries.

Fortunately for historians, the records of the New York Chamber of Commerce set down in formal and binding resolutions what in other cities and other times passed as common knowledge or businessmen's understandings;[76] one of the first matters that the organization considered after its founding in 1768 was the real money in the colony. The Chamber of Commerce appointed a committee to establish the value in New York currency of the major coins in circulation; it accepted the report, ordered it published, and bound its members to "pay and receive all gold and silver in future at the above rates."[77] The result should have been a considerable increase in the ease with which such coin circulated—and anything that enhanced the circulating medium of exchange was a longstanding desideratum of the colonies.

The currency value of one coin, the piece of eight, had a particular importance in New York's monetary history, since it established the par of exchange there as elsewhere in the colonies. Under the Dutch regime, sometime in the 1640s or early 1650s, the director-general of the colony of New Netherland raised the legal value of the piece of eight to three florijns, or gulden, an increase of 20 percent over its value in Holland.[78] The action could well have been a response to the

---

72. In Sept. 1642 the Massachusetts General Court gave as one of its reasons for increasing the currency value of its coin a concern to enhance trade with New Netherland. Shurtleff, ed., *Records of Massachusetts Bay*, II, 29.

73. Nathaniel Shaw's letter book of the 1760s and 1770s is full of quotations of local prices in "York Currency." Rogers, *Connecticut's Naval Office*, *passim*. See also the advertisements in the *Connecticut Courant* (Hartford), such as that of Patrick and Andrew Thomson on 6 May 1765 offering to buy empty snuff bottles at "four shillings, N. York money, per dozen." Cf. Sachs, "Business Outlook in the Northern Colonies," 201.

74. Gov. Francis Bernard, at Perth Amboy, to Board of Trade, 31 Aug. 1758, C.O. 5/977, fols. 184v–185r. See also Donald L. Kemmerer, "A History of Paper Money in Colonial New Jersey, 1668–1775," New Jersey Historical Society, *Proceedings*, LXXIV (1956), 107–144.

75. Wright, *American Negotiator*, lxii.

76. Published as Stevens, ed., *Colonial Records of the New York Chamber of Commerce*. See Virginia D. Harrington, *The New York Merchants on the Eve of the Revolution*, Columbia University Studies in History, Economics, and Public Law, No. 404 (New York, 1935), 74–76. The merchants of Charleston founded a Chamber of Commerce in 1773. Leila Sellers, *Charleston Business on the Eve of the American Revolution* (Chapel Hill, N.C., 1934), 73. A useful work for early New York is Johnson, *Law Merchant*.

77. For all of this see Stevens, ed., *Colonial Records of the New York Chamber of Commerce*, 52, 56, 316–317n.

78. On 21 Jan. 1642/43 the 12 selectmen of New Netherland petitioned Director-General Kieft that "the value of money be raised in order that it be retained here and not exported hence by foreign nations." Kieft replied that the currency would be raised and that edicts ordering this had already been prepared. E. B. O'Callaghan and Berthold Fernow, eds., *Documents Relative to the Colonial History of the State of New York* (Albany, N.Y., 1853–1887), I, 203. The rate of 3 gulden is referred to in a resolution of the Kamer Amsterdam of the West-Indische Compagnie enclosed in a letter from the company to Director-General Pieter Stuijvesant, 10 May 1652. E. B. O'Callaghan, ed.,

Massachusetts law of September 1642, the stated purpose of which was to get an advantage in "the oft occasions wee have of trading with the Hollanders" at New Amsterdam.[79] If the same valuation remained in effect until the English conquered the province in 1664, then the par of exchange from perhaps as early as 1643 was 120 gulden New Netherland silver currency to 100 gulden current money of Amsterdam.

The Dutch at New Amsterdam supplemented their silver currency with two forms of country pay. Prices of goods were quoted regularly not only in silver but also in beaver and in wampum. In the fall of 1658 the three moneys were at a ratio of 10 to 15 to 21; that is, 21 gulden wampum value equaled 15 gulden beaver value or 10 gulden silver value New Netherland currency.[80] Neither of the two commodity moneys held their value particularly well. Wampum had depreciated about 60 percent between 1641 and 1658 and was to become much worse in the next four years. Beaver fared about as badly.[81] Although one can find references to "wampum value" into the 1670s, it quite possibly had already become only a money of account by then.[82] And by the 1670s New Netherland had itself become New York.

"The new rulers [of New York] made at first no alterations in the currency," we are told.[83] Thus the same par of exchange was in force, and £120 New York currency equaled £100 sterling at par up to 1672. In October of that year the Court of Assizes of New York, "acting then in a quasi-legislative capacity," revalued the piece of eight upward still higher to 6s (30p), effectively raising par to £133.33.[84] Twelve years later, in 1684, a pressure common to all of the colonies caused the piece of eight to be valued at 6s 9d (33.8p), with par therefore

Calendar of Historical Manuscripts in the Office of the Secretary of State, Albany, N.Y., I (Albany, N.Y., 1865), 277. See also Berthold Fernow, "Coins and Currency of New-York," in James Grant Wilson, ed., _The Memorial History of the City of New-York from Its Settlement to the Year 1892_, IV (New York, 1893), 298.

79. Shurtleff, ed., _Records of Massachusetts Bay_, II, 29.

80. See the lengthy list of commodity prices in all three currencies in the act of 11 Nov. 1658, E. B. O'Callaghan, ed., _Laws and Ordinances of New Netherlands, 1638–1674_ (Albany, N.Y., 1868), 359–360. For "country pay," see the discussion above in the initial section of this chapter.

81. O'Callaghan, ed., _Laws and Ordinances of New Netherlands_, 26, 115–116, 289–290, 317–320, 357–360, 433–434. See n. 82 below.

82. In two suits before the Suffolk (Mass.) County Court in the middle to

late 1670s, the decisions incorporated conversions from New York gulden "wampum value" to "Boston money." See _Sharp v. Rider etc._, 27 Jan. 1673/74, and _Dafforne v. Keen_, 29 July 1679, _Records of Suffolk County Court_, I, 359–363, II, 1052, 1123. The equation settled upon was 6d Massachusetts currency per gulden "wampum value" New York currency. (The original entry of the first suit had used the higher, pre-1672 value for the gulden and equated it to 6²/₃d, or 6.67d, Massachusetts currency.) In the 1670s the gulden current money of Amsterdam was worth about 21.7d sterling (tables 5.1 and 2.8); 6d Massachusetts currency was worth 4.8d sterling (table 5.2); New York currency and wampum value were thus in a ratio of 1 to 4.5. New York currency wampum value had depreciated considerably from the level of the 1650s. In 1658, 100 gulden current money of Amsterdam equaled 120 gulden silver currency of New Netherland and 250 gulden wampum value; in the 1670s (after 1672) £100 sterling equaled £133.33 New York currency and £600 wampum value.

83. Fernow, "Coins and Currency of New-York," in Wilson, ed., _Memorial History_, IV, 298.

84. "Orders made and confirmed at the Generall Court of Assizes," 2–7 Oct. 1672, "East-Hampton Book of Laws. June the 24th 1665," N.-Y. Hist. Soc., _Colls._, I (New York, 1811), 424. See also _The Colonial Laws of New York from the Year 1664 to the Revolution_ (Albany, N.Y., 1894–1896), I, 96–97. Quote from Fernow, "Coins and Currency of New-York," in Wilson, ed., _Memorial History_, IV, 300. The contention that the par of exchange was at £120 until the date of this order is supported by the differences in the valuation given to New York currency in New England before and after the change. See n. 82 above. Just as 120 and 133.33 are in the ratio of 1 to 1.11, so also are 6d and 6.67d.

at £150.[85] This was the rate that the governors of New York, Pennsylvania, and Virginia reported in effect in New York in 1700.[86] It was, of course, incompatible with the proclamation of 1704 and the subsequent act of 1708.

In the face of imperial pressures restricting the colonists' ability to manipulate the value of their silver coin, New Yorkers chose to adopt a supplementary circulating medium. The introduction of paper bills of credit in 1709 opened a new era in New York's monetary history.[87] A year earlier, in October 1708, the New York legislature effectively raised the par of exchange to £155 (precisely £154.83) when it rated the ounce of silver at 8s (40p). The Board of Trade had the law disallowed, but the rating continued in effect and reappeared as customary in subsequent legislation dealing with an issue of paper money.[88] Over the next thirty years the currency of New York inflated in value, just as did that of New England, but to nowhere near the same extent. By the 1740s the piece of eight had increased in market value from 6s 9d (33.8p) to 8s

(40p), where it stayed during the rest of the colonial period.[89] At 8s per piece of eight, the par of exchange was £177.77 New York currency to £100 sterling.[90] The commercial rate of exchange is the subject of table 3.5.[91]

Bills of exchange—purchased in coin, bills of credit, beaverskins, or whatever—were expressed in terms of the New York money of account: pounds, shillings, and pence New York currency. Bills on London were drawn in the usual way. They came in all denominations. Philip Cuyler told one correspondent in 1756 that rarely were bills negotiated for less than £100, but later that same year he sent another correspondent four £25 bills and three £50 bills in one letter.[92] Most bills were drawn at thirty to forty days sight; John van Cortlandt in 1766 indicated that "merchants here make two and half difference between thirty and sixty days sight." In 1762 Gerald S. Beekman had sent one of his correspondents a bill "at 85 per cent at 60 days sight," explaining that "those drawn at 30 days sell for 87½" (that is, bills payable sixty days after presentation cost £185 New York currency per £100 sterling, and those payable in half that time, £187.50).[93]

85. William Zebina Ripley, *The Financial History of Virginia, 1609–1776*, Columbia University Studies in History, Economics, and Public Law, IV, no. 1 (New York, 1893), 115. See also Fernow, "Coins and Currency of New-York," in Wilson, ed., *Memorial History*, IV, 301.

86. Enclosure in Gov. Richard Coote, earl of Bellomont, to Board of Trade, 17 Oct. 1700, C.O. 5/1045, fol. 87r. See also Fernow, "Coins and Currency of New-York," in Wilson, ed., *Memorial History*, IV, 301–302, citing "Council Minutes, IX, 182, 183." Cf. Nettels, *Money Supply*, 240n, 241, 243–244n, 246n, who argues that par was really at £155, because the law applied that value to lightweight coin.

87. For the history of New York paper currency to 1764, see Brock, *Currency of the American Colonies*, 66–74, 336–353. After 1764 see Ernst, *Money and Politics*, 251–260, 264–281.

88. Fernow, "Coins and Currency of New-York," in Wilson, ed., *Memorial History*, IV, 305–306, 316; Nettels, *Money Supply*, 246–247n. See also Gov. Robert Hunter to Board of Trade, 7 July 1718, C.O. 5/1051, fol. 353r.

89. See Board of Trade to House of Lords, 27 Mar. 1740, enclosure no. 2, House of Lords, Main Papers, 28 Mar. 1740; collected silver prices at New York in Frank Ashmore Pearson Papers, Vol. 1-P, Albert R. Mann Library, Cornell University, Ithaca, N.Y.; and Brock, *Currency of the American Colonies*, 73n.

90. See Bullock, *Monetary History of the United States*, 21–22.

91. There is one quotation of the rate at London on New York—£130 in June 1711. Enclosure in Ordnance Office to Treasury, 30 Oct. 1711, T. 1/139, fol. 36.

92. Philip Cuyler to Isaack Clockener & Son, of Amsterdam, 18 Feb. 1756, and to Dirk van der Heyden, of London, 17 July 1756, Cuyler Letter Book, Cuyler Papers. See also Harrington, *New York Merchants*, 111.

93. John van Cortlandt to James Gibson, 30 Oct. 1766, John van Cortlandt Letter Book, 1762–1769, fol. 158r, Van Cortlandt Account Books; Gerald G. Beekman to Adam Schoals, of Londonderry, 5 Feb. 1762, Philip L. White,

The rate for damages for bills that were returned "protested" for nonpayment was 25 percent in 1670, "according to Custome," but this had been lowered to 20 percent by the beginning of the eighteenth century.[94] In 1768 the Chamber of Commerce established a scale of rates for the collection of damages and interest for these bills: the members agreed to continue collecting the usual 20 percent on European bills (that is, bills drawn on merchants resident in Europe) and set a 5 percent rate on "inland," or North American, bills and a 10 percent rate on West Indian bills.[95] Interest due was charged at 7 percent.[96] One could gain partial protection from the problems of protested bills by getting someone to endorse, or guarantee, any particular bill. For this service Philip Cuyler once received 2.5 percent of the value of the bill, the same rate as was later set by the Chamber of Commerce.[97]

Intercolonial exchange at New York appears to have been negotiated, as John Watts has been quoted above as saying,

"dollars being allways the standard." What he meant was that intercolonial exchange was effected at par based on the comparative values of the piece of eight of the two colonies involved rather than on the comparative commercial rates of exchange on London at the time of the transaction. Our evidence comes, again, mostly from the period after 1750, but it clearly shows the existence of customary rates of intercolonial exchange. We have already seen that the accepted ratio between New York currency and the Lawful Money of New England was £133.33 to £100.[98] New Jersey, Pennsylvania, presumably Delaware, and Maryland were all lumped together at "6²⁄₃ per cent exchange as dollars regulate."[99] In other words, £100 Maryland or Pennsylvania currency cost £106.67 New York currency, at least from 1762 on. Earlier it seems to have varied somewhat,[100] but in 1768 the Chamber of Commerce officially adopted the £106.67 rate.[101] New Jersey and Pennsylvania paper money circulated in New York, unofficially of course,[102] and the Chamber of Commerce be-

ed., *The Beekman Mercantile Papers, 1746–1799* (New York, 1956), I, 403. See also Beekman to John McConnell, of Londonderry, 25 Jan. 1762, *ibid.*, 402.

94. Berthold Fernow, ed., *The Records of New Amsterdam from 1653 to 1674* (New York, 1897), VI, 246–247; Richard B. Morris, ed., *Select Cases of the Mayor's Court of New York City, 1674–1784* (New York, 1935), 539, 541. See Johnson, *Law Merchant*, 72, n. 9. See also the award of interest only (at 8%) in the 1648 case of two protested bills in Arnold J. F. Van Laer, ed. and trans., *New York Historical Manuscripts: Dutch* (Baltimore, 1974), IV, 557.

95. Stevens, ed., *Colonial Records of the New York Chamber of Commerce*, 19–20, 25, 84, 310n. See also John Watts's letters to Thomas Astin, at Essequibo, 30 Jan. 1762, to Charles Baird, comptroller of customs of Canada, 7 Nov. 1763, and to Moses Franks, at London, 9 June 1764, *Letter Book of John Watts*, 15, 191–192, 264–265.

96. Watts to Baird, 7 Nov. 1763, and to Franks, 9 June 1764, *ibid.*, 192, 265.

97. Cuyler to Cornelius Cuyler, at Albany, 28 May 1757, Cuyler Letter Book, Cuyler Papers; Stevens, ed., *Colonial Records of the New York Chamber of Commerce*, 50, 85.

98. See Cuyler Letter Book, *passim* (e.g., on 16 Oct. 1755, £31.56 Lawful Connecticut Money equaled £42.08 New York currency), Cuyler Papers; Beekman to Joseph Bull, at Rhode Island, 13 May 1750, White, ed., *Beekman Mercantile Papers*, I, 107.

99. Watts to Ezekiel Forman, 1 Feb. 1762, *Letter Book of John Watts*, 20. See also *ibid.*, 31, 78, 160, 272; John van Cortlandt, Journal C, 1764–1772, *passim* (e.g., 29 May 1769, 12 July 1770, etc.), Van Cortlandt Account Books; and Stephen and John Van Cortlandt Letter Book, 1771–1792, fol. 23, *ibid*.

100. An effective rate of 8.69% applied in 1694, of 6.25% in 1755, of 7.58% in 1759, and of 7.63% in 1761. Minutes of 26 May 1694, *Minutes of the Provincial Council of Pennsylvania, . . . from March 10, 1683, to November 27, 1700 (Colonial Records of Pennsylvania*, I [Philadelphia, 1852]), 462; Philip Cuyler Letter Book, 4 Aug. 1755, Cuyler Papers; John van Cortlandt Daybook, 1757–1762, 30 Nov. 1759, 28 Nov. 1761, Van Cortlandt Account Books.

101. Stevens, ed., *Colonial Records of the New York Chamber of Commerce*, 10, 18, 84.

102. "Jersey money passes here as current as N.Y." Philip Cuyler to Cornelius Cuyler, 26 Aug. 1756, Cuyler Letter Book, Cuyler Papers.

came involved in a dispute over the rate at which especially New Jersey bills should have currency. Most merchants, in a move to protect and enhance New York's own medium of exchange, accepted New Jersey bills of credit at something more than its legal value in New Jersey.[103] Shades of overvalued coin! John van Cortlandt regularly increased Virginia currency by one-third to equate currency values there with New York values.[104] And there is evidence in Van Cortlandt's journal and in the letters of Charleston merchant Levinus Clarkson that they considered it satisfactory to negotiate bills between the two cities by equating New York currency with one-quarter the value in South Carolina currency.[105]

The practice of negotiating exchange using customary rates based on par apparently was even more prevalent for New Yorkers in their business dealings beyond the neighboring colonies. Peter Jay in the middle 1720s compared the local and the Jamaica value given the piece of eight and found he could increase Jamaica currency by 20 percent to equate it with New York currency.[106] In 1728 Jay used the same rate for

Barbados, but by 1731 he had switched to a 25 percent increment (£125 New York to £100 Barbados), a rate John Watts was still employing thirty years later—although it was a bit low, a more accurate calculation yielding 28 percent.[107] Watts also calculated the exchange with Nova Scotia using the piece of eight, at £160 New York to £100 Halifax, but his contemporary John van Cortlandt seems to have negotiated bills on Quebec at the current bill rates there and in New York.[108] This might well confirm Quebec's position well within New York's trading orbit.

New Yorkers never quite severed their ties with Amsterdam and the Dutch colonies in the New World, and we therefore find some instances of exchange negotiations with Amsterdam. In the 1750s James Beekman worked indirectly, buying sterling bills on London that he mailed to Amsterdam and that his correspondents sold on the exchange there. His debts in Amsterdam were, of course, payable in current money, and the sales of sterling bills yielded bank money (banco), which had then to be converted to currency.[109] That he understood all of this and was able to take account of

103. Stevens, ed., *Colonial Records of the New York Chamber of Commerce*, 10, 11, 15–16, 84, 143, 152–153, 186–187, 308–309n, 334n, 335n, 384–385. See also Ernst, *Money and Politics*, 255–256. For the impact of this on New Jersey, see *ibid.*, 248–249. See also Kemmerer, "Paper Money in Colonial New Jersey," N.J. Hist. Soc., *Procs.*, LXXIV (1956), 107–144. This welcome did not extend to the grossly inflated paper money of Rhode Island, however. Philip Cuyler wrote Joseph Wanton, Jr., of Newport, R.I., 1 Dec. 1755: "As for old tenor [it] is of no use to me here and [I] beg you not to send me" any. Cuyler Letter Book, Cuyler Papers.

104. John van Cortlandt, Journal C, 1764–1772, *passim*, Van Cortlandt Account Books.

105. *Ibid.*, 23 Apr. 1772; Clarkson to David van Horne, of New York, 20 Mar. 1773, Levinus Clarkson Papers, 1772–1793, Lib. Cong.

106. Peter Jay Journal, 1724–1748, pp. 1, 4, 9, 14, and *passim*, Peter Jay Papers, 1724–1770, N.-Y. Hist. Soc. On occasion, however, he used 10% or 15%. *Ibid.*, 12, 20, 21.

107. Peter Jay Journal, p. 31, 66, *ibid.*; *Letter Book of John Watts*, 2–3, 95, 361. See n. 24 above.

108. *Letter Book of John Watts*, 40, 384, 394; John van Cortlandt Daybook, 11 Nov. 1761, Van Cortlandt Account Book.

109. White, ed., *Beekman Mercantile Papers*, II, 685–694. For an example of such a negotiation, see above, chap. 2, n. 53. See also a similar calculation, dated 8 Nov. 1743, in the Peter Jay Journal, p. 313, Jay Papers, which permits us to compare the London-Amsterdam figures using the standard New York ratio of 3s 3d (16.25p) per gulden and the results using the then current bill rate (£175). On the former basis, £45.81 sterling yielded £80.51 New York; on the latter basis, £80.17, or almost precisely the same amount (a difference of less than 0.5%). In 1708 the Account Book of a New York Merchant, 1706–1714, fol. 47, Lib. Cong., credited one account in Amsterdam with pieces of eight incremented by an agio of 6%. Another account was kept in "Banco geldt." *Ibid.*, fol. 159.

variables such as the Amsterdam rate on London and the agio between bank money and current money indicates a certain sophistication. Philip Cuyler, his contemporary, seems to have transacted his affairs in the same indirect way; however, his comment in September 1755 that "no bills on Amsterdam are to be had" could be seen to imply that they were once available.[110] Nevertheless, despite these indications of exchange at the bill rate, the ubiquitous standard ratio seems to have had a certain use even in New York–Amsterdam exchange negotiations. Jacobus van Cortlandt, over the thirteen years from 1700 through 1712, invariably converted from Dutch gulden to New York currency at the rate of 2s 6d (12.5p) per gulden.[111] Peter Jay in 1736 employed a rate of 3s (15p) per gulden, but during the war years 1743 and 1744 he used 3s 3d (16.25p) per gulden.[112] George Patterson in 1752 also used 3s per gulden.[113] Even James Beekman, in 1764, used such a standard ratio, this time 3s 4d (16.7p).[114] This was no mere bookkeeping figure, since some accounts were rendered and settled at these rates. Again, there is no record of any complaint. We must presume that both parties found it satisfactory.

110. Cuyler Letter Book, 13 Sept. 1755, 13 Sept. 1756, Cuyler Papers.

111. Jacobus van Cortlandt Ledger, 1700–1714, *passim*, Van Cortlandt Account Books. See, e.g., the entry for 15 June 1712: "Hollants [gelt] zynde gereduceert tot New York gelt at 2/6 per gul[den]." See also the Account Book of a New York Merchant, 1706–1714, fols. 53, 66, 97, Lib. Cong., which used a figure of 2s 10.5d (14.4p) in May and Oct. 1708 and June 1709 and 2s 9d (13.8p) in Dec. 1711 and Apr. 1713.

112. Peter Jay Journal, pp. 146, 313, 341, Jay Papers.

113. George Patterson Ledger B, 1751–1755, fol. 23r, Van Cortlandt Account Books.

114. Journal B, 1758–1767, p. 411, James Beekman Papers, Beekman Family Papers, N.-Y. Hist. Soc.

TABLE 3.5. **Rate of Exchange: New York on London, 1680–1775**

(Pounds New York Currency per £100 Sterling)

Year	Jan.	Feb.	Mar.	Apr.	May	June	July	Aug.	Sept.	Oct.	Nov.	Dec.	Average
1680			125.00										125.00
1681													
1682													
1683													
1684													
1685													
1686													
1687													
1688				130.06									130.06
1689													
1690													
1691													
1692													
1693													
1694				133.33	125.00								129.16
1695											[130.00]		130.00
1696					130.00				130.00				130.00
1697													
1698									130.00				130.00
1699													
1700						131.43				137.00	140.00		134.96
1701					135.00				130.00				132.50
1702												133.33	133.33
1703				140.00									140.00
1704													
1705													
1706													

TABLE 3.5 (Continued): **New York on London** (Pounds New York Currency per £100 Sterling)

Year	Jan.	Feb.	Mar.	Apr.	May	June	July	Aug.	Sept.	Oct.	Nov.	Dec.	Average
1707													
1708													
1709	150.00											[150.00]	150.00
1710					140.00					150.19		[150.00]	145.05
1711					152.25							[150.00]	151.12
1712						153.75				157.50			155.62
1713						153.75							153.75
1714				150.00		150.00	155.56	151.88	156.70			[160.00]	154.90
1715	150.00		150.00	150.00	150.00		155.56	150.00				[160.00]	153.20
1716	[160.00]										155.55		157.78
1717												[160.00]	160.00
1718													
1719					155.00					150.00	150.00	160.00	154.17
1720				162.50	165.00			165.00			165.00	155.00	162.92
1721	160.00				165.00							165.00	163.33
1722													
1723						165.00						165.45	165.22
1724					165.00					165.00	165.00		165.00
1725				165.00								165.00	165.00
1726				165.00	165.00			165.00	165.00			165.00	165.00
1727				165.00	165.00						165.00	165.00	165.00
1728						165.00		165.00					165.00
1729	165.00		165.00				165.00	165.00					165.00
1730	165.00				165.00			165.00			170.00	175.00	166.88
1731					165.00					165.00			165.00
1732				165.00				165.00	165.00				165.00

TABLE 3.5 (Continued): **New York on London** (Pounds New York Currency per £100 Sterling)

Year	Jan.	Feb.	Mar.	Apr.	May	June	July	Aug.	Sept.	Oct.	Nov.	Dec.	Average
1733			165.00			165.00				165.00		165.00	165.00
1734						165.00		165.00				165.00	165.00
1735			165.00		165.00	165.00				165.00	165.00	165.00	165.00
1736					165.00			165.00		165.00		165.00	165.00
1737			165.00	165.00	165.00		165.00	165.00			165.00		165.00
1738			165.00	165.00	165.00	165.00					165.00		165.00
1739	[170.00]		165.00	165.00	170.00							165.00	166.67
1740							170.00	165.00		165.00	165.00		166.25
1741				160.00	150.00	150.00		160.00				165.00	159.44
1742				170.00	167.50	170.00			170.00		172.50	175.00	170.97
1743						174.00	175.00				175.00	175.00	174.67
1744	175.00			175.00		175.00					175.00	177.50	175.42
1745		190.00					175.00			185.00			183.33
1746	[192.50]					190.00						175.00	185.83
1747					195.00	193.75	190.00					190.00	191.46
1748	[190.00]								185.00	175.00	175.00	175.50	183.39
1749			175.00	175.00							183.75	175.00	176.46
1750		175.00	175.00	182.50	180.00				182.12		177.88	180.00	179.33
1751		182.50	180.00	179.00						182.50	185.00	180.00	181.50
1752			172.50							179.25	180.00	178.75	175.92
1753	180.00					178.67	177.77			180.00	180.00	180.00	179.39
1754				179.40	180.00					180.00	178.91	180.00	179.72
1755	*180.68*	181.25	180.00	*180.42*	180.83	177.50	*178.75*	180.00	179.37	178.50	*180.92*	183.33	180.13
1756	185.00	*183.12*	181.25	181.67	180.00	180.00	182.50	185.00	185.00	181.91	184.50	181.88	182.65
1757	182.50	*181.88*	181.25	180.83	177.50	177.50	176.90	175.00	180.00	178.67	175.00	173.75	178.40
1758	*173.12*	172.50	174.02	175.00	*175.00*	175.00	175.00	170.67	*170.81*	*170.96*	171.10	168.00	172.60
1759	171.25	170.50	169.50	*169.40*	*169.29*	169.19	168.30	170.00	168.50	163.75	166.12	164.72	168.39

TABLE 3.5 (Continued): New York on London (Pounds New York Currency per £100 Sterling)

Year	Jan.	Feb.	Mar.	Apr.	May	June	July	Aug.	Sept.	Oct.	Nov.	Dec.	Average
1760	163.01	167.25	168.50	166.50	166.50	166.17	*167.17*	*168.17*	169.16	164.00	*168.00*	*172.00*	167.20
1761	176.00	*177.33*	*178.67*	180.00	*181.20*	182.39	185.00	183.75	182.50	183.75	182.86	183.50	181.41
1762	185.83	187.12	*187.60*	188.07	190.75	187.54	189.64	190.50	194.38	187.50	193.75	194.38	189.76
1763	183.75	*185.83*	*187.92*	190.00	185.00	185.00	187.50	190.00	190.00	187.30	181.00	187.50	186.73
1764	187.50	186.00	*185.50*	185.00	182.57	184.38	185.00	185.00	184.67	182.60	185.00	185.00	184.85
1765	181.50	180.33	*182.66*	185.00	183.75	183.12	183.75	181.88	185.00	183.75	182.50	180.30	182.80
1766	175.00	177.50	180.00	179.92	176.87	177.50	177.60	179.64	180.00	178.50	177.42	166.25	177.18
1767	174.06	175.00	177.50	177.77	180.00	178.75	180.00	182.50	180.00	180.83	180.00	*181.12*	178.96
1768	182.25	180.00	185.00	180.00	180.00	180.50	180.00	180.00	179.60	176.75	179.33	175.00	179.87
1769	176.25	175.00	173.29	170.00	*173.57*	177.14	179.00	172.50	170.00	163.00	171.43	*168.42*	172.47
1770	165.42	165.00	162.50	164.50	162.54	*161.90*	161.25	170.00	168.50	*168.92*	169.35	170.91	165.90
1771	174.41	178.95	177.50	179.38	180.00	178.67	179.78	179.50	180.00	180.31	*177.66*	175.00	178.43
1772	174.32	176.67	174.00	175.00	171.80	172.08	172.50	*172.50*	172.50	172.50	172.50	*172.92*	173.27
1773	173.33	*174.16*	175.00	177.50	175.83	177.77	180.00	180.00	180.00	179.38	180.00	179.58	177.71
1774	180.00	180.00	180.00	180.00	180.00	180.00	180.67	181.75	185.00	181.88	180.44	177.67	180.62
1775	170.62	170.00	169.71	171.60	166.29	165.83	167.12	167.50	170.62	176.43	183.12		171.55

Notes and Sources: TABLE 3.5

Figures inserted in square brackets are assigned to that month arbitrarily; figures in italics are straight-line interpolations based on the two neighboring quotations.

1680: Papers presented in the appeal to the Privy Council of *Ward v. Palmer*, London, 2 and 4 Mar. 1679/80, C.O. 1/44, fols. 87, 88, Public Record Office.

1688: "The Case of the Pet[itione]r Robert Livingston," 22 Aug. 1695, C.O. 5/1039, fol. 75r.

1694: Gov. Benjamin Fletcher, at London, to Board of Trade, 24 Dec. 1698, C.O. 5/1041, fols. 398r–v.

1694: *Minutes of the Provincial Council of Pennsylvania . . . from March 10, 1683, to November 27, 1700* (*Colonial Records of Pennsylvania*, I [Philadelphia, 1852]), 462.

1695: Treasury to the King in Council, 2 Jan. 1695/96, C.O. 5/1039, fols. 141r-v.

1696: Fletcher, at New York, to Board of Trade, 30 May and 9 Nov. 1696, C.O. 5/1039, fols. 159r-v, 285r.

1698, 1700: Gov. Richard Coote, earl of Bellomont, at New York, to Board of Trade, 21 Sept. 1698, 15 Oct. and 28 Nov. 1700, C.O. 5/1041, fol. 46r, C.O. 5/1045, fols. 86r, 142v, 150r; Bellomont to Admiralty, 23 Nov. 1700, C.O. 5/1045, fol. 231r; Bellomont to Treasury, 23 Nov. 1700, C.O. 5/1045, fol. 222v.

1701: Robert Livingston, at New York, to Board of Trade, 13 May 1701, C.O. 5/1046, fol. 190v.

Notes and Sources: **TABLE 3.5 (Continued)**

1701: Jacobus van Cortlandt Ledger, New York, 1700–1714, 9 May and 23 Sept. 1701, Van Cortlandt Account Books, 1700–1875, New York Public Library, New York City.

1702: Gov. Edward Hyde, Lord Cornbury, at New York, to Board of Trade, 12 Dec. 1702, C.O. 5/1048A, fol. 22v.

1703: Robert Quary, at Philadelphia, to secretary of state, Apr. 1703, C.O. 5/1233, nos. 85–86. See also Quary, to the agent of the Victualling Office at Jamaica, Apr. 1703, *ibid.*, nos. 83–84.

1709–1714: Account Book of New York Merchant, 1706–1714, Library of Congress.

1709–1740: Lt. Gov. George Clarke, at New York, to Board of Trade, 2 June 1738, 3 Dec. 1739, 4 Aug. 1740, C.O. 5/1059, pt. i, fols. 49r, 120r–121v, pt. ii, fol. 151v.

1710: Gov. Robert Hunter, [at New York], to Board of Trade, [3 Oct. 1710], C.O. 5/1050, fol. 14v.

1710–1721: Nathan Simson Papers, *Isaac* v. *Defriez*, C. 104/13–14, P.R.O.

1714–1715: Accounts of the Treasurer of New York, signed Thomas Byerley, 1 July 1714 and 1 July 1715, C.O. 5/1222, fols. 13r, 19r.

1716: James Logan Account Book, 1712–1720, p. 196, Logan Papers, 1664–1871, Historical Society of Pennsylvania, Philadelphia.

1721: Logan, at Philadelphia, to William Aubrey, 10 May 1721, Parchment Logan Letter Book, 1717–1731, p. 185, Logan Papers.

1723: Thomas Amory, at Boston, to Messrs. Francis Holmes, Sr. and Jr., at Charleston, S.C., 11 June 1723, Thomas Amory Letter Book, 1723–1725, Amory Family Papers, 1697–1823, Lib. Cong.

1723: Alexander Wooddrup Account Books, 1720–1739, I, 16 Dec. 1723, *ibid.*

1723–1730: De Peyster Daybook, 1723–1733, Frederick Ashton De Peyster Manuscripts, Box 2, De Peyster Family Papers, 1677–1881, New-York Historical Society, New York City.

1726–1763: Peter Jay Journal, 1724–1748, and Account Book, 1724–1770, Peter Jay Papers, 1724–1770, N.-Y. Hist. Soc.

1742–1743: John and Robert Sanders Letter Book, Albany, N.Y., 1742–1743, Sanders Papers, *ibid.*

1742–1747: John and Robert Sanders Voyage Book, 1739–1748, Merchant Shipping Papers, Item 1, Glen-Sanders Papers, 1674–1957, *ibid.*

1746: Board of Trade to Treasury, 27 Feb. 1749/50, C.O. 324/13, p. 205.

1747–1771: Philip L. White, ed., *The Beekman Mercantile Papers, 1746–1799* (New York, 1956), I and II, *passim.*

1748: Virginia D. Harrington, *The New York Merchants on the Eve of the Revolution*, Columbia University Studies in History, Economics, and Public Law, No. 404 (New York, 1935), 108.

1750–1751: Agreement between William Alexander and James Parker, 14 Apr. 1750, and letter from Alexander, at New York, to James Stevenson, 7 May 1751, William Alexander Correspondence, 1744–1782, nos. 87, 130, Alexander Papers, N.-Y. Hist. Soc.

1751: Board of Trade to Treasury, 5 Feb. 1752, Gustave Lanctot *et al.*, eds., *Documents Relating to Currency, Exchange and Finance in Nova Scotia, with Prefatory Documents, 1675–1758* (Ottawa, 1933), 363.

1752–1775: James Beekman Ledger A, 1752–1767, Ledger B, 1769–1799, and Journal B, 1758–1767, James Beekman Papers, Beekman Family Papers, N.-Y. Hist. Soc.

1755–1757: Robert Sanders Letter Book, 1752–1758, Sanders Papers.

1755–1757: William Alexander Manuscripts, I-II, N.-Y. Hist. Soc.

1755–1760: Philip Cuyler Letter Book, 1755–1760, Cuyler Papers, N.Y. Pub. Lib.

1755–1764: Account of the Treasurer of New York, signed H. De Peyster, 20 July 1764, C.O. 323/19, fol. 73r.

1756: Gov. Charles Hardy, at Fort George, N.Y., to Board of Trade, 13 Oct. 1756, C.O. 5/1067, fol. 197r.

Notes and Sources: **TABLE 3.5 (Continued)**

1759: *New-York Mercury*, 5 Nov. 1759.

1760: John van Cortlandt Daybook, 1757–1762, 10 Jan. and 19 Mar. 1760, Van Cortlandt Account Books.

1762: Chief Justice Benjamin Pratt, at Milton, N.Y., to Board of Trade, 24 May 1762, C.O. 5/1070, p. 71.

1762: Beverly Robinson, at New York, to James Glassford, at Quebec, 27 June 1762, and James McEver, at New York, to Glassford, 12 July 1762, Neil Jamieson Papers, II, nos. 256, 264, Lib. Cong.

1762–1765: [Dorothy C. Barck, ed.], *Letter Book of John Watts, Merchant and Councillor of New York, January 1, 1762-December 22, 1765* (N.-Y. Hist. Soc., *Colls.*, LXI [New York, 1928]), *passim*.

1764–1772: John van Cortlandt, Journal C, 1764–1772, Van Cortlandt Account Books.

1765–1767: "Abstract of Cash paid by General [Thomas] Gage . . . on Account of the publick Service . . . ," 1764–1767, T. 1/465, fols. 331–346, P.R.O. For evidence of a similar earlier list, see Gage, at New York, to Treasury, 20 Dec. 1765, T. 1/450, as printed in Clarence Edwin Carter, ed., *The Correspondence of General Thomas Gage, 1763–1775* (New Haven, Conn., 1931–1933), II, 327–328.

1765–1768: Walter and Robert Livingston Daybook or Waste Book, 1765–1769, N.-Y. Hist. Soc.

1766: Gage, at New York, to Treasury, 22 Dec. 1766, Gage Manuscripts, William L. Clements Library, University of Michigan, Ann Arbor, as printed in Carter, ed., *Correspondence of Gage*, 402.

1766: Gov. Sir Henry Moore, at Ft. George, N.Y., to secretary of state, 30 Apr. and ca. Dec. 1766, C.O. 5/1072, pt. ii, fol. 51v, and in Reports of the Governors of the North American Colonies, 1766–1767, pp. 122–123, King's Manuscript 206, British Library.

1766–1767: John van Cortlandt Letter Book, 1762–1769, *passim*, Van Cortlandt Account Books.

1771–1772: Stephen and John van Cortlandt Letter Book, 1771–1792, *ibid*.

1773–1775: *Rivington's New-York Gazetteer; or, The Connecticut, New-Jersey, Hudson's-River, and Quebec Weekly Advertiser*, 22 Apr. 1773–23 Nov. 1775.

New Jersey

New Jersey suffered from monetary schizophrenia. In the eighteenth century, just as today, Philadelphia dominated western New Jersey, and New York dominated eastern New Jersey. Not only did New Jersey's neighbors draw off its paper money for their own use, but they controlled its foreign exchange. The best authorities tell us that eastern New Jersey negotiated bills at the going rate in New York and that western New Jersey's bill rate was the same as Philadelphia's. But there is a problem in accepting this. After the mid-1730s New Jersey's paper money circulated in New York at a premium, which reduced the cost of bills there for New Jerseyites. New Jersey's paper circulated in Philadelphia at par—western New Jersey might have shared the Pennsylvania bill rate. A lack of data for the New Jersey bill rate compounds the problem by inhibiting our ability to answer the questions posed. New Jersey stood on the border between two significant economic regions in the colonial period, but we have still to sort out how this influenced her economic history.

New Jersey shared with its neighbors the dual real moneys we by now have come to expect—coin and paper. And its monetary history contains no real surprises. Before 1710 the colonists of New Jersey "cryed up" the currency value of their coin in an attempt to retain what they had and, they hoped, to attract more. By 1676 the piece of eight already had attained a value of 7s 8d (38.3p), equivalent to a par of exchange of £170 New Jersey currency to £100 sterling.[115] That same year the colony split in two, and East New Jersey and West New Jersey remained separate until 1702. Later, in 1693, West New Jersey raised its value still higher when its

assembly officially adopted the rate that Pennsylvania had enacted that year, £181.00. Meanwhile, in East New Jersey the assembly had passed an act in 1685 that valued an underweight piece of eight at 7s 6d (37.5p) for an effective par of about £165. The assembly repealed the act the same year, perhaps because it had overshot New York's valuation, which had been something of a guide for East New Jersey. "After the union of the two Jerseys, the official rate of the province was that of New York, although in West New Jersey foreign coin continued to circulate at the higher Pennsylvania level."[116] At the New York rate the par of exchange for New Jersey at the turn of the century was £150 New Jersey currency per £100 sterling.[117]

Initially New Jersey reacted to the proclamation of 1704 and the act of 1708 in much the same way as did its neighbors. Resistance quickly followed panic, and in 1709 the assembly passed an act that valued silver at 8s (40p) per ounce, just as New York had done, setting par at £155.[118] Then the colony turned to paper.[119] New Jersey's first issue of paper money appeared in 1711. Subsequent issues followed at regular intervals in response to the demands to supplement coin and thereby to increase the circulating medium of exchange. New Jersey's currency, paper, and coin experienced the same moderate inflation over the next thirty years that was com-

115. Ripley, *Financial History of Virginia*, 115.

116. Nettels, *Money Supply*, 122, 241n.

117. See table 3.5. But cf. the report enclosed in the letter of Gov. Bellomont to Board of Trade, 17 Oct. 1700, C.O. 5/1045, fol. 87r, that grouped New Jersey with Pennsylvania and said that the value of the piece of eight in both colonies was 7s 8d (38.3p) for a par of £170.

118. Nettels, *Money Supply*, 247n.

119. For the history of New Jersey's paper money to 1764, see Brock, *Currency of the American Colonies*, 84–93, 393–409. For the years after 1764, see Ernst, *Money and Politics*, 246–251, 260–264, 285–293, 316–318.

mon to New York and Pennsylvania. Measured in the increased value of silver, New Jersey currency by 1740 had a par of exchange of £178, the same as that of New York.[120] Later issues of paper money were tied to the slightly lower value for the piece of eight in Pennsylvania, 7s 6d (37.5p) rather than 8s (40p), for a par of £167. This is the source of the standard ratio between both Pennsylvania and New Jersey currencies and that of New York, 6⅔ percent.[121]

While New Jersey's real money consisted of the usual assortment of coin and the colony's own paper bills of credit, its imaginary money can be less easily specified. Much like "wampum value" in New York, "country pay" in several other colonies, and "Maryland money" in that colony in the years after 1764, New Jerseyites had a shadow money. Most important business dealings, including the buying and selling of bills of exchange, used New Jersey "pounds proclamation" (often abbreviated "proc") as the money of account. A second, less valuable currency, "Jersey light," seems from the few references available to have been one-sixth worse than "proc." In other words, £100 New Jersey proc appears to have been the equivalent of £116.67 Jersey light.[122] Since

New York's currency was worth not quite as much less than proc as was Jersey light, the three ranked in order of descending value: New Jersey pounds proclamation (proc), New York currency, and Jersey light. This means that, given the same sum of money in all three currencies, the New York money would buy more sterling than Jersey light and less sterling than pounds proclamation. Finally, if the ratio between proc and Jersey light indeed did not vary, then New Jersey's shadow money resembled the post-1764 Maryland money more than New York's continually deteriorating "wampum."

New Jersey's paper money bills of credit were denominated in pounds proclamation. Their history is exceptional only in the demand for them in the neighboring colonies of New York and Pennsylvania. One estimate suggests that up to two-thirds of 'the paper money of New Jersey circulated outside the colony.[123] There were two reasons for this phenomenon. In the years before 1750, when intercolonial exchange was more difficult because of continuing and disparate currency inflation, using New Jersey paper money served New York and Pennsylvania merchants as a convenient alternative to negotiating bills of exchange on each other. Perhaps William Douglass exaggerated a bit, but his point was well taken when he wrote in 1740 that "New York bills [of credit] not being current in Pennsylvania, and Pennsylvania bills not current in New-York, but Jersey bills current in both, all

120. "Report from the Committee of the Council," signed John Hamilton, 4 Dec. 1739, enclosure no. 3 in Board of Trade to House of Lords, 27 Mar. 1740, House of Lords, Main Papers, 28 Mar. 1740; Gov. Lewis Morris of New Jersey to Board of Trade, 26 May 1739, C.O. 5/973, fol. 126–132.

121. For example, in 1758 Gov. Bernard of New Jersey reported that pieces of eight "cost 7–6 proc." To Board of Trade, 31 Aug. 1758, C.O. 5/977, fol. 185r. At par the £6 bill New Jersey currency passed in New York for £6.40 New York currency, the £3 bill at £3.20, and so forth. *New York Gazette and Weekly Mercury*, 2 May 1774, as cited in Stevens, ed., *Colonial Records of the New York Chamber of Commerce*, 334n. See also *ibid.*, 384–386, 388; Board of Trade to Treasury, 28 Feb. 1749/50, C.O. 324/13, pp. 204–205.

122. See, e.g., entry for 2 Jan. 1730/31 in Daybook, 1723–1728, 1730–1733, p. 133, Frederick Ashton De Peyster MSS, Box 2, item 4, De Peyster

Family Papers, 1677–1881, N.-Y. Hist. Soc.; account of sale of John Stevens's slave, 14 July 1750, and "Mr. Pinneirs account, 1769," in Box 11: Bills and Receipts, 1749–1783, Alexander Papers, *ibid*.

123. Kemmerer, "Paper Money in Colonial New Jersey," N.J. Hist. Soc., *Procs.*, LXXIV (1956), 115, citing "N.J. Archives, V, 289." See also Morris to Col. William Blakeney, 28 Aug. 1740, *Papers of Lewis Morris*, 107; and Edward A. Fuhlbruegge, "New Jersey Finances during the American Revolution," N.J. Hist. Soc., *Procs.*, LV (1937), 170.

payment between New-York and Pennsylvania are made in Jersey bills."[124] After about 1750 intercolonial exchange became somewhat easier with the stabilization of the ratios between currencies, and in the 1760s Pennsylvania bills began to circulate, unofficially of course, in New York.[125] But the popularity there of New Jersey paper money continued, now as a vital supplement to New York's own paper. So important was it to New York's commerce that it passed at a premium over the legal ratio, "dollars being allways the standard."[126]

124. [Douglass], *Discourse concerning Currencies*, 16. He gave another reason for their popularity: "In the Jersies failure of the loan payments at the days appointed, is equivalent to judgment, and therefore only 30 days redemption of mortgages is allowed." See also Morris to Blakeney, 28 Aug. 1740, and to Gov. William Shirley, of Massachusetts, 9 Sept. 1743, *Papers of Lewis Morris*, 107, 167; Bernard to Board of Trade, 31 Aug. 1758, C.O. 5/977, fol. 184v–185r. Bernard stated that New Jersey bills were current in New York and Pennsylvania and New York and Pennsylvania bills current in New Jersey. See also Andrew Burnaby, *Travels through the Middle Settlements in North-America, in the Years 1759 and 1760*, 2d ed. (London, 1775), 60. For examples of the use of New Jersey bills in payments between Pennsylvania and New York see Elizabeth Hill, at Philadelphia, to Cadwallader Colden, 23 Apr. 1725, and Colden, at New York, to John Armitt, at Philadelphia, Oct. 1743(?), *The Letters and Papers of Cadwallader Colden* (N.-Y. Hist. Soc., *Colls.*, L–LVI, LXVII–LXVIII [New York, 1918–1937]), VII, 179, 302. In 1743 Jacob Franks of New York sent to his son David in Philadelphia bills for £300 sterling, which "I desire you to dispose of out of hand for the highest exchange for Jersey money." He could not do so profitably in New York. Letter of 9 Mar. 1742/43 as quoted in David Franks to Haphtali Franks, 14 Mar. 1742/43, Leo Hershkowitz and Isidore S. Meyer, *The Lee Max Friedman Collection of American Jewish Colonial Correspondence: Letters of the Franks Family, 1733–1748*, Studies in American Jewish History, No. 5 (Waltham, Mass., 1968), 112. See fig. 5.

125. Stevens, ed., *Colonial Records of the New York Chamber of Commerce*, 18, 84.

126. Quotations of this premium are few and not always easy to interpret, in part because of the changing relationship at par of New Jersey currency and New York currency. While after midcentury it took £106.67 proclamation in New Jersey currency to equal £100 New York currency,

before that time the two currencies were supposedly of equal value at par. But it seems that until about 1750 the residents of New Jersey spoke of this relationship in terms of New Jersey "light money" as their currency; of this, one had to have £116.67 to equal £100 New York currency at par (or £100 New Jersey proclamation currency, for that matter). Thus Gov. Morris wrote in June 1743 that the 20s note in New Jersey currency had a "nominal" value of 23s 4d in New York currency (telling us, among other things, that New Jersey paper money was denominated in "light money"). In the same sentence he announced that the current value of that bill was only 22s 9d. While this in fact represented a 2.2% discount from the par, or "nominal," value, it was, as he pointed out, a premium over the face value of 13.75%. He elsewhere congratulated himself that during his administration this premium had advanced from 2.5% in July 1740 to 5% in that August before reaching in a very few months the 12% to 13% level of 1743. But it is quite clear that this "premium" over the face value was also a discount, albeit a decreasing one, from the par value.

It likewise appears that earlier writers who spoke of the ratio between New York and New Jersey currencies were also talking about percentage variations around a par of £116.67 New Jersey "light money" per £100 New York currency. Thus in 1724 and 1725 when, we are told, there was a 3% to 4% discount on New Jersey money, this meant that £100 New York currency equaled £120 to £121 New Jersey currency. This discount is supposed to have ended about Feb. or Mar. 1726, after which both currencies were at par for a short while. But by Dec. 1726, New Jersey currency, according to the merchants of New York, was at a premium of from 2.5% to 5% over New York currency ("now there is 6d., 9d. and 12d. given at New York to get payment in New Jersey money"). In other words, one had to pay £102.50 to £105 New York currency to get £116.67 New Jersey currency, or, to turn it around, £100 New York currency equaled £111 to £114 New Jersey currency. By 1733 the two currencies were back again at par, a condition, according to William Douglass, that lasted to 1738, when there was again a premium of 2.5% on New Jersey money.

The change at midcentury from a par of £116.67 New Jersey light currency (or £100 New Jersey proclamation money) to £106.67 New Jersey proclamation money for £100 New York currency did nothing to alter the continuing preference at New York for New Jersey bills of credit. But we have no further reference to any premium until a passing mention in a mercantile correspondence in the spring of 1766, which might be an indication of what the "usual" rate was during these years. Samuel and Jonathan Smith, of Philadelphia, wrote to Jacob Rodriquez Rivera, of Newport, R.I., explaining that "it is difficult procuring drafts [i.e., bills of exchange] from

The members of the New York Chamber of Commerce almost came to blows over a demand by some of them that the practice be stopped. Finally the New York assembly had to intervene and legislate its end. As of 1 May 1774, New Jersey paper money could no longer pass for any more than the "legal" 6⅔ percent advance.[127] We are entitled to some doubts about the effectiveness of this law.

The colonists of New Jersey benefited from the popularity of their paper money when they bought bills of exchange. We could specify this much more had we more data, but the

outline is clear enough. First, of course, they had a choice of markets in which to purchase bills. In practice merchants in western New Jersey could buy bills at home or in Philadelphia, while merchants in eastern New Jersey could choose between whatever local bills were available and what could be had in New York. This meant both a certain convenience and an opportunity to bargain a bit for a lower price. The price paid in New Jersey currency—which, recall, before about 1750 shared a par with New York (£177) and after that time with Philadelphia (£167)—we would expect, then, to tend to be somewhat below the average price for bills in either of these cities. But the colonists of New Jersey paid less for their bills of exchange on London not only because of the benefits of "comparison shopping." The premium for New Jersey paper money in New York provided New Jerseyites who purchased bills of exchange there with a still further advantage. A bill of exchange at New York on London for £100 sterling that was priced at £177 New York currency and that at par would cost £167 New Jersey currency could be purchased for something less by using New Jersey paper money —perhaps at £163 or £165 New Jersey currency, the equivalent of £174 or £176 New York currency. This "discount for New Jersey paper money" was no doubt of some advantage for New Jersey merchants. Table 3.6 offers the only rates of exchange for New Jersey bills of exchange that have been found to date, and it tends to confirm the suggestion of a lower cost for New Jersey bills when compared with the rates for New York (table 3.5) and Pennsylvania (table 3.7). We need more information not only about New Jersey's bill rate but also about the premium rate for New Jersey paper money at New York.

N.Y. on this place exchange being in our favor almost continually. We have for a long time had money laying there and must at last order it here in N.J. money which is 1¼ per cent less than dollars." Evidently Rivera followed the Smiths' implied advice; they later acknowledged receipt of £360 New York currency, which they credited to his account as equal to £332.31 Pennsylvania currency. At the par of exchange ("dollars") £332.31 Pennsylvania currency was the equivalent of only £354.48 New York currency, a difference of £5.52, or 1.6%. From all of this it is fair to conclude that New Jersey paper money cost from 1.25% to 1.6% over its par value at New York in the spring of 1766. The £6 New Jersey currency note that at par equaled £6.40 New York currency would then have cost £6.48 or £6.50 New York currency.

See the two memorials, one of New York merchants dated 1 Dec. 1726 and one of Perth Amboy merchants dated 15 Dec. 1726, C.O. 5/972, fols. 129r and 131r; Isaac Norris, of Philadelphia, to Ann Coaksley, 23 Sept. 1723, Norris Letter Book, 1716–1730, p. 337, Norris Papers, 1742–1860, Hist. Soc. Pa.; [Douglass], *Discourse concerning Currencies*, 15–16; Morris to Blakeney, 10 July and 9 Aug. 1740, to Board of Trade, 16 Aug. 1741, 15 Dec. 1742, and 1 June 1743, and to Shirley, 9 Sept. 1743, *Papers of Lewis Morris*, 94, 103, 134–135, 156, 167, and C.O. 5/973, fol. 164v, C.O. 5/974, fol. 15v; Colden to Armitt, Oct. 1743(?), *Letters and Papers of Cadwallader Colden*, VIII, 302; Smith and Smith to Rivera, 21 Apr. and 28 June 1766, Samuel and Jonathan Smith Letter Book, 1765–1770, Peter Force Papers, Ser. VIII D, Lib. Cong. (See also their letter to Gabriel Ludlow, 21 Apr. 1766, *ibid.*) Note too that [Douglass], *Discourse concerning Currencies*, 16, says that in 1738 New Jersey currency also was at a 10% premium over Pennsylvania currency.

127. See n. 121 above.

TABLE 3.6. Rate of Exchange: New Jersey on London, 1703–1775

(Pounds New Jersey Currency per £100 Sterling)

Year	Jan.	Feb.	Mar.	Apr.	May	June	July	Aug.	Sept.	Oct.	Nov.	Dec.	Average
1703												166.67	166.67
1716					142.86								142.86
1717													
1718													
1719								155.18					155.18
1720													
1721				155.55									155.55
1737		170.00											170.00
1738													
1739					170.00				165.00		170.00	170.00	168.33
1740	160.00							161.25					160.62
1741	150.00			150.00		125.00		140.00					142.50
1742												150.00	150.00
1743						160.00							160.00
1744													
1745													
1746												[182.50]	182.50
1747													
1748													
1749	170.00			170.00									170.00
1750	173.75												173.75
1751	172.50												172.50
1752	166.25												166.25

TABLE 3.6 (Continued): **New Jersey on London** (Pounds New Jersey Currency per £100 Sterling)

Year	Jan.	Feb.	Mar.	Apr.	May	June	July	Aug.	Sept.	Oct.	Nov.	Dec.	Average
1753	167.50												167.50
1754	168.17												168.17
1755				168.00				169.50				172.50	170.00
1756						171.83						160.00	165.92
1757			167.17			167.50				163.62			166.10
1758				161.25				161.25					161.25
1759			156.25										156.25
1760			153.30										153.30
1761			171.25										171.25
1762			176.25						177.50				176.88
1763												169.83	169.83
1764		172.88							171.17				172.02
1765													
1766												160.00	160.00
1767													
1768													
1769													
1770													
1771													
1772													
1773													
1774			169.50										169.50
1775													

Notes and Sources: **TABLE 3.6**
  Figures inserted in square brackets are assigned to that month arbitrarily.

Notes and Sources: **TABLE 3.6 (Continued)**

1703: Robert Quary, at Perth Amboy, N.J., to Board of Trade, 20 Dec. 1703, C.O. 5/970, fols. 29r–v, Public Record Office.

1716: Charles Dunster and James Ormston, at London, to James Alexander, Apr. [*sic*, for late May] 1716, William A. Whitehead *et al.*, eds., *Documents Relating to the Colonial History of the State of New Jersey (Archives of the State of New Jersey*, 1st Ser., I–XXXIII [Newark, Paterson, Trenton, etc., N.J., 1880–1928]), IV, 241.

1719: *Ibid.*, XIV, 125–126.

1737: Enclosure dated 20 Oct. 1749 in Gov. Jonathan Belcher, at Perth Amboy, N.J., to Board of Trade, 24 Oct. 1749, *ibid.*, VII, 357.

1739–1740: Annis Josephine Keyes, "New Jersey Paper Currency, 1709–1775" (M.A. thesis, Yale University, 1927), 34. See also enclosure no. 3 in Board of Trade to House of Lords, 27 Mar. 1740, House of Lords, Main Papers, 28 Mar. 1740, House of Lords Record Office.

1739–1742: [William A. Whitehead, ed.], *The Papers of Lewis Morris, Governor of the Province of New Jersey, from 1738 to 1746* (New Jersey Historical Society, *Collections*, IV [New York, 1852]), 49, 103, 104, 133, 157.

1740–1743: Morris, at Trenton, N.J., to Board of Trade, 16 Aug. 1741, and 10 June 1743, C.O. 5/973, fol. 163v, C.O. 5/974, fols. 11r, 17v.

1746: Report of Lords of the Treasury, 28 Feb. 1749/50, C.O. 324/13, p. 204.

1749: Belcher, at Burlington, N.J., to Board of Trade, 21 Apr. 1749, C.O. 5/975, no. 74r.

1749–1764: "State of the Bills of Credit in New Jersey," 10 Sept. 1764, C.O. 323/19, fol. 38r. This is said to be the "rate of exchange at Philadelphia currency." See also "An Account of Bills of Credit created and Issued in the Colony of New Jersey . . . and rate of Exchange . . . at the time Issued," in "Letters of Joseph Sherwood, Agent for the Province of New Jersey in Great Britain, from 1761 to 1766," N.J. Hist. Soc., *Proceedings*, 1st Ser., V (1850–1851), 147; Donald L. Kemmerer, "A History of Paper Money in Colonial New Jersey, 1688–1775," *ibid.*, LXXIV (1956), 131.

1762: Account dated 9 Sept. 1762, William Alexander Accounts, Bills and Receipts, Alexander Papers, New-York Historical Society, New York City.

1766: Enclosure dated 28 Dec. 1766 in Gov. William Franklin, at Burlington, N.J., to secretary of state, 21 Feb. 1767, C.O. 5/112, fols. 53–54; Reports of the Governors of the North American Colonies, 1766–1767, p. 125, King's Manuscript 206, British Library.

1774: Franklin, at Burlington, N.J., to secretary of state, 28 Mar. 1774, C.O. 5/992, fol. 53r.

Pennsylvania and Delaware

By the late 1760s Pennsylvania's currency circulated in a region about as extensive as that of New York and that of New England. The merchants of Philadelphia had early moved to a position of some prominence not only in the Delaware River Valley but also throughout the Chesapeake. Their role in the commerce of the region inevitably developed into a financial role as well. Well-mixed cargoes in the holds of Philadelphia trading vessels found a ready market at the river wharves of the lower Delaware and the Chesapeake. In return the bills of exchange drawn by the tobacco lords of the Chesapeake found an equally ready market in Philadelphia both directly and, late in the colonial period, indirectly by way of Philadelphia's satellite city, Baltimore. By then the quid pro quo was cash as frequently as it was English or West Indian commodities, for the Philadelphians had become the near-bankers of their corner of the world.[128] The names of Reese Meredith and Willing and Morris sprinkle the pages of the letter books and account books of the Chesapeake. With them came Pennsylvania currency.[129]

The real money and the money of account of Philadelphia and its hinterland were the same as those of all the English colonies. Pennsylvanians counted up the money in their purses and treasure chests in terms of pounds, shillings, and pence. (An exception, Delaware, the three lower counties of Pennsylvania, had its own currency—called "New Castle Money"—but it never varied in its nominal value from Pennsylvania currency.[130]) But Pennsylvania pounds differed in value from those of other colonies, just as they all differed from one another. From the beginning Penn's Quaker colony strove to retain its own supply of coin by establishing a premium for silver. The value of the piece of eight rose steadily from 6s (30p) in 1683 to 6s 2d (30.8p) in 1693 and to 7s 10d (39.2p) in 1700. The par of exchange therefore rose from £133.33 Pennsylvania currency per £100 sterling to £137.00 and then, in 1700, to £174.00. Confusion characterized the next decade, as laws raising the currency value of silver still higher were passed, disallowed, and passed again.[131] Finally, in compliance with the act of 1708, the Pennsylvania legisla-

---

128. For all of this see such studies as Gould, *Money in Maryland*, 13–15, 41–42, and *passim*; and Soltow, *Economic Role of Williamsburg*, 86–88, 97. See also Nash, "Maryland's Economic War with Pennsylvania," *Md. Hist. Mag.*, LX (1965), 231–244. The involvement of Philadelphia merchants in the development of the upper Chesapeake in the period after 1740 can be traced in their letter books but has yet to be fully researched and analyzed. See, e.g., Hugh Davey and Samuel Carson, of Philadelphia, to Robert Travers, of Cork, Ireland, 5 June 1746, Davey and Carson Letter Book, 1745–1750, fol. 35, Lib. Cong. The view from Maryland is well described in Ronald Hoffman, *A Spirit of Dissension: Economics, Politics, and the Revolution in Maryland* (Baltimore, 1973), 60–80.

129. Not only as a money of account but, later in the 18th century, the paper money too. The inventory of the estate of Philip Thomas of Worcester Co. on the Eastern Shore of Maryland, dated 13 Mar. 1763, listed, among other things, various kinds of money: 8s sterling, presumably in coin; 32s 5d in Maryland paper money; 38s 6d in Virginia paper; and 37s 6d in Pennsylvania paper money. Prerogative Court Records, Inventories, Vol. 84, p. 83, Maryland Hall of Records, Annapolis.

130. See the discussion below at the end of this section.

131. Staughton George *et al.*, eds., *Charter to William Penn, and Laws of the Province of Pennsylvania, Passed between the Years 1682 and 1700, Preceded by Duke of York's Laws in Force from the Year 1676 to the Year 1682* (Harrisburg, Pa., 1879), 74, 145, 146, 238, 275; James T. Mitchell and Henry Flanders, eds., *The Statutes at Large of Pennsylvania from 1682 to 1801*, II (Harrisburg, Pa., 1896), 87–88, 276–278; Nettels, *Money Supply*, 240n, 244n. See also James Claypoole, of Philadelphia, to Edward Claypoole, of Barbados, 2 Dec. 1683, and to Thomas Cooke, of Cork, Ireland, 1 Mar. 1683/84, Marion Balderston, ed., *James Claypoole's Letter Book, London and Philadelphia, 1681–1684* (San Marino, Calif., 1967), 224, 231.

ture voted in 1709 to adopt Proclamation Money—what the New Englanders called Lawful Money. As of 1 May 1709 it revalued Pennsylvania currency by one-quarter, returning the piece of eight to 6s (30p) and changing the par of exchange down from £177.77 to £133.33 Pennsylvania currency per £100 sterling.[132]

The next dozen years were troubled ones for the colony's economy, but Pennsylvanians were slower than their northern neighbors to adopt paper currency as a solution to their problems. Finally, in 1723, in an effort to expand the circulating medium of exchange and thereby to revive agriculture, commerce, and industry, the Pennsylvania legislature introduced the colony to paper money.[133] At the same time, it left Proclamation Money and the par of exchange intact—at least theoretically. Devaluation occurred, nevertheless, as was probably expected, and the next several years witnessed an interesting anomaly. Silver at 6s (30p) per piece of eight remained the accounting medium for the purchase of bills of exchange, but one soon learned to pay a premium in Pennsylvania currency in order to purchase bills at the silver value.

The "silver exchange" fluctuated from 10 to 30 percent, which meant that at 10 percent one paid £146.67 (£133.33 plus 10 percent) Pennsylvania currency to buy £100 sterling and at 30 percent, £173.33.[134] References to this mere device had disappeared by the end of the 1720s and with it all pretense of Proclamation Money.

This left the colony without an official, legal value for silver or for coin. As in the other colonies, however, the market value itself began to stabilize and acquire the force of custom. But the lack of any legal value for their coin proved a difficulty for Pennsylvanians, as for other colonists, since it tended to leave coin in the category of a commodity rather than a currency, thereby unnecessarily constricting the circulating medium. In 1721 a group of merchants had tried to alleviate this situation by publishing their agreement to accept coin at set rates, but their effort seems to have gotten lost in the difficult years that followed.[135] A similar agreement in 1742,

132. Nettels, *Money Supply*, 247n; Mitchell and Flanders, eds., *Statutes of Pennsylvania*, II, 294–297. Isaac Norris began a new journal as of 1 May 1709, the better to keep his accounts in "new money." Isaac Norris Journal, 1709–1716, Norris Papers. Neither Pennsylvania currency nor the exchange really dropped in value, since everything was reduced in the same proportion. In order to compare prices, rates of exchange, or whatever before and after 1 May 1709, one must convert at the ratio of 4 to 3, just as contemporaries did. Thus, in comparison with the exchange rate the previous November, £155, that for May 1709, £125 "new money" or £166 "old money," is higher, not lower.

133. For the history of Pennsylvania's paper money before 1764, see Brock, *Currency of the American Colonies*, 74–84, 353–393. For its later history, see Ernst, *Money and Politics*, 207–215, 304–308, 313–315.

134. This can be seen clearly in the extended computations of, for example, James Logan, of Philadelphia, to William Aubrey, of Newcastle, 8 Oct. 1725, Parchment Logan Letter Book, 1717–1731, p. 394, Logan Papers, 1664–1871, Hist. Soc. Pa. Logan sent Aubrey three bills of exchange worth a total of £121.89 sterling. Their total cost in Pennsylvania currency was £189.16, for an effective rate of exchange of £155. In the breakdown of their cost, two of them are specified as having been purchased at "55£ per cent in paper." He purchased the other one "at 35£ per cent in gold" with a further "exchange for the gold" of "15£ per cent," for a total of £155.20 Pennsylvania currency for a bill for £100 sterling. Most such references are not extended, and numerous instances quote just the silver or gold exchange over the £133.33 Proclamation Money rate. The analogy between this and the bank money/current money of Amsterdam is not as close as was the case with Maryland, to be discussed below. Still the "silver exchange" rate bore a distinct similarity to the agio on bank money. See the discussion above in chap. 2 in the section on "Amsterdam."

135. *American Weekly Mercury* (Philadelphia), 31 Jan. 1720/21.

subscribed to by seventy-five merchants and widely broadcast, apparently worked to better effect. "Whereas gold and silver since the emission of paper money has not been current among us at any fixed or certain rate, which has been of great disadvantage to the trade and commerce of this province . . . we will receive in all payment . . . pieces of eight at seven shillings and sixpence [37.5p]. . . ."[136] The par of exchange, set here at £166.67, had in fact applied somewhat before 1742; it was to continue at that rate till the Revolution.[137] Not only was this action by the merchants noted outside the colony,[138] but within a decade both New Jersey and Maryland had adopted the same currency value for the piece of eight and therefore the same par.[139]

136. *Pennsylvania Gazette* (Philadelphia), 16 Sept. 1742.

137. Bezanson, Gray, and Hussey, *Prices in Colonial Pennsylvania*, 323. According to the submission made to the Board of Trade at the time of the inquiry into colonial paper money, the value per ounce troy of silver in Pennsylvania currency (and the computed metallic par of exchange at the standard price for silver in sterling, 5s 2d) varied as follows: 1700–1709, 9s 2d (45.8p), 177; 1709–1720, 6s 10.5d (34.4p), 133; 1720–1723, 7s 5d (37.1p), 144; 1723–1726, 8s 7d (41.2p), 160; 1726–1730, 8s 5d (40.4p), 156; 1730–1738, 8s 9d (43.8p), 169; 1739, 8s 6d (42.5p), 164. Enclosure no. 7 in Board of Trade to House of Lords, 27 Mar. 1740, House of Lords, Main Papers, 28 Mar. 1740. This is evidently a contemporary copy of the report to the Pennsylvania legislature dated 23 Nov. 1739, in [Gertrude MacKinney and Charles F. Hoban, eds.], *Votes and Proceedings of the House of Representatives of the Province of Pennsylvania, Dec. 4, 1682–Sept. 26, 1776* (Samuel Hazard et al., eds., *Pennsylvania Archives*, 8th Ser., I–VIII [Harrisburg, Pa., 1931–1935; orig. publ. Philadelphia, 1752–1776]), III, 2523.

138. Morris to Shirley, 9 Sept. 1743, *Papers of Lewis Morris*, 168. Morris believed that the merchants regularly accepted coin at an inflated value: "They have allways done the same thing since the existence of a paper currency."

139. See the discussion of each of these colonies, above and below, in this chapter.

Bills of exchange were bought and sold at Pennsylvania in much the same way as elsewhere, with the significant difference that the source of supply was wider. So far-reaching were his contacts that Reese Meredith could and did draw to Philadelphia bills "from Lisbon, the Streights, Virginia and Maryland, and some from the West Indies."[140] The best of these were local bills drawn on London at thirty and forty days sight.[141] In 1769 Willing and Morris sold their own bills at £164 and somewhat less reliable bills from the West Indies at £163.50. Both were on London and for the same sight. As was usual, bills on the outports and those drawn at longer sight commanded a still lower price, although in 1755 Thomas Willing quoted the same rate, £170, for "exchange on London or Bristol."[142] Samuel and Jonathan Smith once wrote that "bills are now sold at 62½ to 63½ 30 days on London[;] outport bills and [ones] of longer sight few incline to purchase at near that exc[hang]e even when bills on London are scarce but when plenty its not easy to negotiate them."[143] Irish bills in the 1740s sold for a full ten points less than bills on London, reflecting in part, of course, the lower value of Irish currency.[144] Damages for protested bills were assessed

140. Meredith to Samuel Galloway, of Annapolis, Md., 27 Mar. 1769, Galloway Correspondence, X, no. 9597, Galloway-Maxey-Markoe Papers.

141. Thomas Clifford to Walter Franklin, 11 Mar. 1769, Clifford Letter Books, Pemberton Papers, Hist. Soc. Pa.

142. Willing to John Noble, 5 Mar. 1755, Willing and Morris Letter Book, p. 74, Hist. Soc. Pa. A month earlier he had told Whately, Meyler, and Hall of Jamaica that bills drawn at 60 days sight sold for 2.5 points less than those drawn at 30 days. Letter of 1 Feb. 1755, *ibid.*, p. 69.

143. Smith and Smith to John Soley, [Mar. 1769], Smith and Smith Letter Book, Force Papers. See also their letter to Jonathan Williams, of Boston, 16 Nov. 1768.

144. Letters of 24 May 1742 and 15 Aug. 1744, Letter Books of the two Isaac Norrises, 1699–1766, Norris Papers.

Figures 8 and 9. Two Philadelphia Bills of Exchange.
(From the John Reynell Papers; courtesy of the Historical Society of Pennsylvania, Philadelphia.)

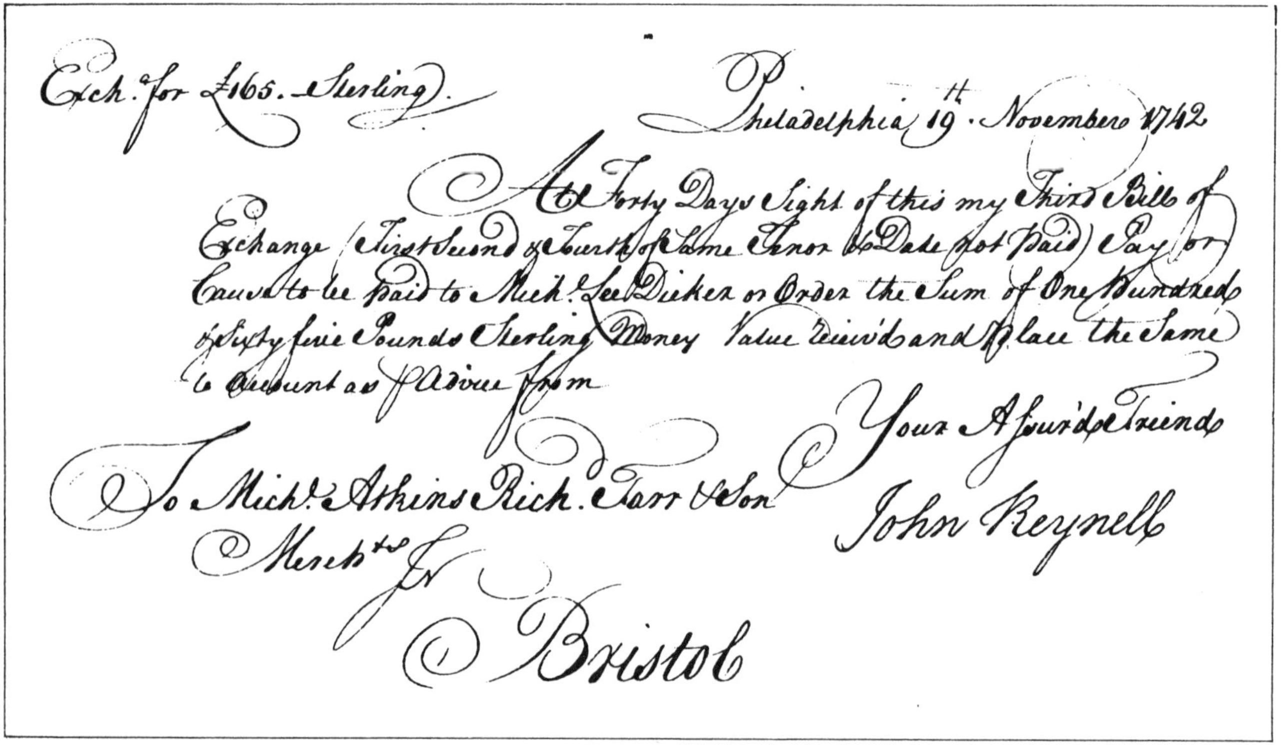
Exch.a for £165. Sterling
Philadelphia 19th November 1742
At Forty Days Sight of this my Third Bill of Exchange (First Second & Fourth of same Tenor & Date not Paid) Pay or Cause to be Paid to Mich.l Lee Dicker or Order the Sum of One Hundred & Sixty five Pounds Sterling Money Value Receiv'd and Place the Same to Account as p Advice from
Your Assur'd Friend
John Reynell
To Mich.l Atkins Rich.d Farr & Son
Merch.ts &c
Bristol

8. Philadelphia, 19 November 1742. This is the third copy of a typical bill of exchange, drawn by John Reynell of Philadelphia on the Bristol merchant house of Michael Atkins, Richard Farr, and Son for payment to Michael Lee Dicker.

Exchange for £300 Sterling.   [No. 96]   Philadelphia, *October* 20th 1761.

AT Thirty Days Sight of this our *Third per* Exchange (our Firſt, Second and Fourth, of the ſame Tenor and Date, unpaid) pay unto *John Reynell*   or Order, *Three hundred Pounds Sterling*, for Value received, and charge it to the Province of *Pennſylvania* ; but if it is not paid at ſaid Thirty Days Sight, then pay INTEREST on that Sum, from the Expiration of the ſaid Thirty Days, until paid, at the Rate of *Six Pounds per Centum per Annum* ; and if this *Bill* and *Intereſt* is not paid in one Year from the Date hereof, we do hereby oblige ourſelves, our Heirs, Executors, and Adminiſtrators, to pay the ſaid *Bill* with *Intereſt* from the Date thereof, at the above Rate, until paid, when it ſhall be returned with a *Proteſt* to us, but no other Damages ; *on this Condition*, *neverthelefs*, that if Payment be not demanded within *Six Months* after the Date of the ſaid *Proteſt*, the *Intereſt* from that Time ſhall determine and ceaſe.

To *Benjamin Franklin Eſqr.*
    in London

Chs. Norris
Thos. Leech
Mahlon Kirkbride

9. Philadelphia, 20 October 1761. An example of the more elaborate printed form for bills of exchange that came into use late in the colonial period, this bill was drawn by officers of the Pennsylvania government on their London account in the control of their agent, Benjamin Franklin. John Reynell, who bought the bill, sold it in turn to Hillary and Scott of Philadelphia, to whom he endorsed it on the other side (not illustrated). This bill was indented (not illustrated) and numbered to hinder counterfeiters in the same way as were some issues of colonial paper money.

at 20 percent, but the evidence suggests that this was the rate for European bills only.[145] Perhaps a sliding scale existed here as at New York for bills on the West Indies and nearby colonies. Jacob Mordecai's accusation that Reese Meredith was getting rich by dealing in questionable bills with good endorsers was possibly true, because the endorser not only guaranteed to reimburse the face value of the bill but also paid the damages and the interest.[146]

Meredith and others could have prospered in such a fashion only in a rather stable money market. Otherwise, in a place such as pre-1750 Boston where the exchange rate fluctuated greatly, 20 percent damages would not have begun to cover the cost of a new bill. But the exchange rate at Philadelphia was remarkably stable after the mid-1730s. Except for certain understandable periods of disruption, the London bill rate stayed within a few points of par. The reasons for this are the same as those for the similar stability in Europe. Philadelphia's rapidly expanding trade provided the man who wished to remit to London with a range of real options. With "no bills nor anything else worth remitting direct to be had," Samuel Powel, Jr., recognized his choice of remitting "to the West Indies in order to get money in England."[147] Three months later, with bills still in short supply, Powel simply shipped gold bullion.[148] And when in the 1760s the bill rate moved beyond par to £170, "every one that can pick up dollars" exported them instead of buying bills with them, rightly "expecting to make a remittance in them at 65 to 66 per cent."[149] In other words, Pennsylvanians had the coin, and they had a choice. They could sell the coin locally and buy bills at £170, or they could ship the coin and, even paying freight and insurance, expect to settle their debts at an effective rate of £165 or £166. With the demand for bills lessened and all other things being the same, the bill rate would fall. Reciprocally, when the bill rate fell at Philadelphia, it was not too long before such news brought orders for bills from elsewhere.[150] Arbitrage transactions such as these had the effect of stabilizing Pennsylvania's rate of exchange. For that exchange, see table 3.7.[151]

145. George et al., eds., Charter to Penn and Laws of Pennsylvania, 146, 211; Mitchell and Flanders, eds., Statutes of Pennsylvania, II, 86. See also William Fishbourne, of Philadelphia, to Daniel Richardson, of Talbot Co., Md., 19 May 1715, 22 May 1718, Mercantile Papers of William Fishbourne and David Richardson, 1711–1729, John Leeds Bozman Papers, Lib. Cong.; James Logan, of Philadelphia, to Timothy Forbes, 13 Nov. 1722, Parchment Logan Letter Book, 1717–1731, p. 294, Logan Papers.

146. See the discussion above in the initial section of this chapter. See also John Reynell, of Philadelphia, to Michael Lee Dicker, of Exeter, 5 July 1737, John Reynell Letter Book, 1734–1737, Coates and Reynell Papers, Hist. Soc. Pa. ("There's profit enough on protested bills where the drawer or indorser is substantial and I generally take pretty good care as to that.")

147. Samuel Powel, Jr., to David Barclay, of London, 28 Dec. 1730, Samuel Powel, Jr., Letter Books, 1727–1747, I, Hist. Soc. Pa.

148. Powel to Thomas Hyam, of London, 24 Mar. 1730/31, Powel Letter Books.

149. Letter of 26 Sept. 1767, Smith and Smith Letter Book, Force Papers.

150. Daniel Roberdeau, of Philadelphia, to Breese and Hoffman, of New York, 16 Dec. 1766, Daniel Roberdeau Letter Book, 1764–1771, Roberdeau Papers, 1761–1831, Hist. Soc. Pa.

151. The compilation of quotations in this table, while unusually dependent on what others have already done, represents a considerable amount of fresh information as well. Bezanson, Gray, and Hussey, Prices in Colonial Pennsylvania, 431–432, published monthly and annual figures for the years 1720 to 1775 based on some of the same sources used for table 3.7 as well as on the figures in Victor S. Clark, History of Manufactures in the United States, rev. ed. (Washington, D.C., 1929), III, 361–362. The annual averages from the series in Prices in Colonial Pennsylvania are reproduced in United States, Department of Commerce, Bureau of the Census, Historical Statistics of the United States, Colonial Times to 1970: Bicentennial Edition (Washington, D.C.,

The impression of commercial and financial importance attached to Philadelphia is strengthened when we look through a mass of records for evidence of intercolonial exchange. There is little such evidence. It would almost seem that one did not negotiate colonial bills at Philadelphia. One dealt there in commodities, sterling bills, and currency. By the early 1750s New Jersey, Delaware, and Maryland all had the same par of exchange and therefore the same value for their currency. New Yorkers, as we have seen, bought New Jersey paper currency to settle debts at Philadelphia. And even New Englanders negotiated with Pennsylvania by way of New York. In his dealings with Thomas Clifford, Henry Lloyd of Boston did, however, convert from Old Tenor to Pennsylvania (and Maryland) currency using a standard ratio, 6 to 1. But that is only one of two such ratios based on the par of exchange. New Yorkers after the mid-1760s used the 6⅔ ratio that their Chamber of Commerce institutionalized in 1768; before that the rate of exchange at New York on Philadelphia was varied. When Philadelphians equated other colonial currencies with their own, they tended to fall back to the comparative value of coins as their guide. In 1723 Peter Baynton equated "Carolina Money" with Pennsylvania cur-

rency using the comparative values of silver per ounce troy in each currency.[152] Samuel Powel, Jr., once converted Bermuda currency to Pennsylvania currency using the comparative value of the gold guinea as his guide.[153] It is symptomatic of the commercial and financial strength of Philadelphia that Powel and the others could and did have such a range of resources and options.

Delaware currency was always valued the same as Pennsylvania currency. Dominated by its larger neighbor politically as well as economically, Delaware paralleled the history of Pennsylvania with regard to the changing nominal values for the piece of eight, alterations in the par of exchange, and emissions of paper currency.[154] The paper money of each of these two colonies had currency and circulated in the other, but Pennsylvania's economic strength was so much greater that its paper money maintained its real value slightly better than did Delaware's. Although "New Castle Money" was legally at par with Pennsylvania currency, in the marketplace it passed at a discount, the size of which we have only scant indication. In June 1729 the discount was 10 percent, meaning

1976), II, 1198, ser. Z 585. Both Clark's and Bezanson's original manuscript notes have been consulted to avoid duplication; their basic data and what is new here have been integrated; and new monthly and annual averages have been calculated. See Box 3, "Currency-Exchange," Victor S. Clark Collection, 1607–1928, Baker Lib.; Box 16, Exchange Rates, "(Industrial Research Department), Wholesale Prices" Collection, Wharton School of Finance and Commerce, University of Pennsylvania, Philadelphia. This last collection had yet to find a permanent home when I used it in May 1971; it was then in the care of Dorothy S. Brady of the Department of Economics, University of Pennsylvania, to whom I am extremely grateful for permission to make use of parts of it.

152. For a good example of a New Englander dealing with Philadelphia by way of New York City, see John Collins, of Newport, R.I., to Thomas Clifford, 6 Dec. 1757, Clifford Correspondence, II, fol. 18, Pemberton Papers, Hist. Soc. Pa. Lloyd wrote Clifford on 26 May 1760, *ibid.*, III, fol. 65. The Baynton reference is to his "Ledger A," May 1723, Hist. Soc. Pa.

153. Powel to Col. Francis Jones, 10 Mar. 1744/45, Powel Letter Books.

154. Richard S. Rodney, *Colonial Finances in Delaware* (Wilmington, Del., 1928), *passim*. Delaware's record of the currency price of silver submitted in 1739 duplicated that of Pennsylvania. Enclosure no. 8, 15 Dec. 1739, in Board of Trade to House of Lords, 27 Mar. 1740, House of Lords, Main Papers, 28 Mar. 1740. For Delaware paper money see Brock, *Currency of the American Colonies*, 95–99, 391–393.

that it took £110 Delaware currency to buy £100 Pennsylvania currency.[155] Thus, as reference to table 3.7 will show, the Delaware exchange rate on London in that month was about £165 Delaware currency to £100 sterling. In the years 1758 through 1760 the Delaware bill rate averaged about £172.50, while the Pennsylvania rate was closer to £161.60, a difference of 6.7 percent.[156] We have little other information about the Delaware exchange rate, but all that we do have argues for the constancy of this difference, which the above data suggest regularly ranged between 5 and 10 percent.[157]

155. Entry for June 1729, Alexander Wooddrup Account Book, 1720–1734, II, Lib. Cong. The next spring the merchants of Philadelphia advertised their willingness to work "towards abolishing all distinction" between Pennsylvania currency and Delaware currency. *American Weekly Mercury* (Philadelphia), 2 Apr. 1730. See also Rodney, *Colonial Finances in Delaware*, 23.

156. Rodney, *Colonial Finances in Delaware*, 37–39.

157. Thomas Harris of Philadelphia advertised in 1774 to exchange "Maryland and New-Castle ragged Money . . . at a very moderate rate." *Pennsylvania Journal; and the Weekly Advertiser* (Philadelphia), 31 Aug. 1774.

TABLE 3.7. **Rate of Exchange: Pennsylvania on London, 1683–1775**

(Pounds Pennsylvania Currency per £100 Sterling)

Year	Jan.	Feb.	Mar.	Apr.	May	June	July	Aug.	Sept.	Oct.	Nov.	Dec.	Average
1683												125.00	125.00
1684			125.00										125.00
1685													
1686													
1687													
1688													
1689						130.00							130.00
1690													
1691													
1692													
1693													
1694					135.86								135.86
1695													
1696								150.00					150.00
1697													
1698											150.00		150.00
1699													
1700			155.00										155.00
1701					150.00			145.00			150.00	147.50	147.92
1702	148.75				151.50	150.00	150.00	150.00	152.69	150.00		155.00	150.72
1703	150.00	164.28	148.75	150.00	150.00	150.00	150.00	150.00	150.00	146.43	150.62	150.00	150.84
1704	150.00	150.00	150.00	*150.00*	150.00	150.00	150.00	150.00	150.00	150.00	150.00	*150.00*	150.00
1705	150.00	*150.00*	150.00	150.00	150.00	150.00	151.67	150.00	150.00	150.00	150.00	150.00	150.14
1706	*150.00*	150.00	148.50	*149.25*	150.00	150.00	151.67	155.00	152.50	150.00	150.00	150.00	150.58
1707	150.00	*150.17*	*150.33*	150.50	155.00	150.00	165.00	150.00	150.00	*151.67*	*153.33*	155.00	152.58
1708	150.00	150.00	150.00	150.00	150.00	157.50	*158.75*	160.00	155.00	155.00	155.00	*156.25*	153.96
1709	*118.13*	*119.06*	120.00	112.50	124.67	120.60		116.25	123.75	123.75	120.00		120.05

TABLE 3.7 (Continued): Pennsylvania on London (Pounds Pennsylvania Currency per £100 Sterling)

Year	Jan.	Feb.	Mar.	Apr.	May	June	July	Aug.	Sept.	Oct.	Nov.	Dec.	Average
1710			135.47			122.56		132.57	120.00		125.00	133.33	128.16
1711													
1712			133.33			119.90	135.00		131.66		125.00	133.33	128.93
1713		140.00	129.16		125.00	133.33	130.00	125.00	130.55	125.00	133.33		130.36
1714			135.42	137.50	129.17		125.00	133.33	131.66	135.00		127.50	132.50
1715	125.00			131.25		133.33		134.17		130.00			130.36
1716				137.50		133.61		131.66		133.33	133.33		133.52
1717		133.33			146.66	135.00	130.00		130.00				134.72
1718					133.33			130.00			133.33		132.22
1719								137.50		133.33	133.33		135.42
1720						138.75			140.00		137.50		138.75
1721											137.50		137.50
1722							133.33		133.33	136.66	135.93	137.50	135.01
1723							137.50		147.33			138.33	140.37
1724	133.33						143.00		145.92	151.55			143.11
1725							133.55		145.12				139.34
1726													
1727							146.67				155.00	150.00	149.58
1728					150.00	152.50				150.00			150.62
1729			148.34	150.00	150.00						145.00	150.00	148.61
1730						150.00			151.75	155.00	155.50	152.50	152.03
1731			150.75	152.50		152.50	150.00	161.67		150.00	158.06		153.28
1732		162.50	162.50			161.88	160.00	156.67					160.90
1733			162.50			173.33				165.00			166.94
1734						170.00							170.00
1735				166.67				166.67				165.00	166.11
1736	[175.00]					168.00			165.00	160.00	160.00		167.00
1737			170.50								170.00		170.25

TABLE 3.7 (Continued): **Pennsylvania on London** (Pounds Pennsylvania Currency per £100 Sterling)

Year	Jan.	Feb.	Mar.	Apr.	May	June	July	Aug.	Sept.	Oct.	Nov.	Dec.	Average
1738				165.00				166.25			150.00		160.42
1739	170.00			170.00			170.00	170.00	170.00		170.00	167.50	169.69
1740	*170.00*	172.50	170.00	170.00	170.00	170.00	167.50	161.25	170.00	160.44	153.75	150.00	165.45
1741	150.00	147.50	151.25	143.33	134.30	128.75	142.50	150.00	147.50	149.25	*152.83*	*156.41*	146.14
1742	160.00	162.50	*162.92*	*163.33*	163.75	162.50	*161.25*	160.00	*155.42*	150.83	155.00	*155.00*	159.38
1743	*155.00*	*155.00*	155.00	*157.50*	160.00	162.50	162.50	*161.25*	160.00	*161.25*	162.50	165.00	159.79
1744	168.75	160.00	*162.50*	165.00	*166.25*	167.50	167.50	170.00	170.00	170.00	*167.50*	165.00	166.67
1745	*168.33*	*171.67*	175.00	175.00	175.00	*175.00*	*175.00*	175.00	*175.31*	175.62	176.33	180.00	174.77
1746	182.50	181.25	180.00	180.94	181.95	180.94	179.83	175.00	175.00	177.50	180.36	183.00	179.86
1747	179.38	190.00	186.25	180.62	183.12	181.25	185.00	185.00	183.54	183.75	183.12	184.38	183.78
1748	181.25	185.00	181.25	180.00	180.00	174.50	173.12	170.00	165.62	167.00	166.67	165.00	174.12
1749	168.75	170.00	*171.25*	172.50	171.25	172.50	170.00	170.42	170.00	175.00	172.50	172.50	171.39
1750	170.50	*171.50*	172.50	172.50	172.50	172.70	175.00	171.25	168.75	165.00	167.08	167.92	170.60
1751	*169.58*	171.25	170.00	172.00	172.50	170.00	170.62	*169.68*	168.75	165.00	165.83	173.12	169.86
1752	168.00	168.75	170.00	167.50	*167.50*	167.50	166.75	167.50	167.50	167.50	161.25	162.50	166.85
1753	170.00	167.50	167.50	168.25	168.50	166.50	167.67	167.50	167.50	162.50	167.50	169.00	167.49
1754	167.50	170.00	170.00	170.00	169.50	168.50	168.30	167.00	168.00	166.60	166.50	168.25	168.35
1755	167.50	168.75	168.75	167.50	170.00	*169.12*	168.25	168.75	167.75	168.47	168.75	171.88	168.79
1756	173.75	*174.25*	174.75	174.00	172.00	171.25	171.50	172.75	172.62	171.50	172.50	170.00	172.57
1757	170.50	170.50	167.00	165.00	165.00	166.88	167.50	166.25	166.25	164.69	161.88	161.42	166.07
1758	163.00	163.75	162.25	161.50	159.58	160.00	157.42	155.33	158.12	155.00	156.00	156.00	159.00
1759	156.00	156.41	155.00	156.67	153.06	150.00	150.00	153.33	152.50	154.05	151.25	154.00	153.52
1760	155.00	154.47	155.00	153.48	153.29	155.50	156.36	157.21	159.75	164.38	169.41	169.50	158.61
1761	170.00	172.50	167.96	*170.36*	172.75	175.00	171.33	177.50	174.67	172.79	172.71	175.00	172.71
1762	174.38	174.69	176.75	175.25	175.00	180.00	175.00	178.13	*178.07*	178.00	175.00	174.88	176.26
1763	175.00	170.00	173.75	172.50	*172.50*	172.50	171.67	173.12	175.00	175.00	172.50	172.50	173.00
1764	172.12	172.50	174.38	173.10	172.19	173.00	173.33	172.50	172.75	173.25	172.75	172.50	172.86

TABLE 3.7 (Continued): **Pennsylvania on London** (Pounds Pennsylvania Currency per £100 Sterling)

Year	Jan.	Feb.	Mar.	Apr.	May	June	July	Aug.	Sept.	Oct.	Nov.	Dec.	Average
1765	172.50	172.50	172.00	172.50	172.50	172.50	172.50	*171.25*	170.00	166.83	164.29	159.58	169.90
1766	160.00	*162.50*	165.00	165.00	165.50	168.75	170.50	167.50	160.06	167.00	153.13	150.57	162.96
1767	155.00	160.00	162.50	161.00	168.75	170.00	172.50	171.25	170.00	167.75	166.00	167.50	166.02
1768	170.00	168.75	163.75	166.88	167.59	167.38	168.75	164.33	167.92	*166.71*	165.50	161.94	166.62
1769	165.25	164.75	160.60	163.75	159.17	157.50	160.00	156.50	154.17	150.00	149.00	150.00	157.56
1770	152.50	150.50	151.06	150.33	150.00	150.00	151.25	155.00	158.77	159.50	158.12	160.00	153.92
1771	166.00	166.25	166.92	167.58	167.50	167.50	167.56	167.50	165.00	164.00	162.50	160.00	165.69
1772	164.50	165.00	163.33	162.50	162.50	159.75	159.50	159.17	157.50	157.40	159.00	159.85	160.83
1773	162.50	165.00	164.16	164.50	165.75	167.06	167.92	167.62	166.65	167.35	168.96	167.78	166.27
1774	169.30	164.86	168.44	167.78	169.33	169.92	170.97	172.70	173.09	171.07	168.12	167.88	169.46
1775	163.50	162.50	162.08	157.50	156.25	157.50	153.33	154.29	153.21	167.50	171.33	174.50	161.12

Notes and Sources: **TABLE 3.7**

Figures inserted in square brackets are assigned to that month arbitrarily; figures in italics are straight-line interpolations based on the two neighboring quotations.

All manuscript collections cited below are in the Historical Society of Pennsylvania, Philadelphia, unless otherwise indicated. Note the shift to "new money" as of 1 May 1709 at a ratio of 4 to 3 (see n. 132 in this chapter). In order to compute a proper mean for the year, the figures for the months Jan. through Apr. have been converted to "new money"; they can be converted back by incrementing them by one-third.

1683–1684: James Claypoole, at Philadelphia, to Edward Claypoole, at Barbados, 2 Dec. 1683, and to Thomas Cooke, at Cork, Ireland, 1 Mar. 1683/84, Marion Balderston, ed., *James Claypoole's Letter Book, London and Philadelphia, 1681–1684* (San Marino, Calif., 1967), 224–231. See also [William Penn], *A Further Account of the Province of Pennsylvania and Its Improvements* (London, 1685), 17; and Robert Quary, at Philadelphia, to Commissioners of the Customs, 6 Mar. 1699/1700, C.O. 323/3, fol. 127v, Public Record Office.

1689: Letter, 22 June 1689, "Old Letter Book," p. 58, Ridgway Branch, Library Company of Philadelphia, as noted in Richard Pares Transcripts, Box I, Rhodes House Library, Oxford. The reference has proven impossible to trace in the manuscript collections of the Library Company, all of which are now on deposit in the Hist. Soc. Pa.

1694, 1739: *Minutes of the Provincial Council of Pennsylvania . . . from March 10, 1683 to November 27, 1700* (*Colonial Records of Pennsylvania*, I [Philadelphia, 1852]), 462; *Minutes of the Provincial Council of Pennsylvania . . . from February 7th, 1735–6, to October 15th, 1745* (*Col. Recs. of Pa.*, IV [Harrisburg, 1851]), 320.

1696: Unidentified Philadelphia Merchant Account Book, 1694–1698, Am. 905.

1698–1706: Deborah Logan and Edward Armstrong, eds., *Correspondence between William Penn and James Logan, Secretary of the Province of Pennsylvania, and Others, 1700–[1711]* (Historical Society of Pennsylvania, Memoirs, IX–X [Philadelphia, 1870–1872]), I, 34, 138, 316, II, 43, 161.

1700: Quary to Customs, 6 Mar. 1699/1700, C.O. 323/3, fol. 127v.

1701: Jonathan Dickinson, at Philadelphia, to Isaac Gale, at Jamaica, 20 May 1701, Dickinson-Logan Letter Book, 1698–1742, Logan Papers, 1664–1871.

1701–1709: William Trent Ledgers "B" and "C," 1701–1703, 1703–1709, the former in the Stephen Collins and Son Papers, Library of Congress, the latter in Hist. Soc. Pa.

1703: Quary, at New York, to Board of Trade, 16 June 1703, Harleian Manuscript 6273, fol. 3v, British Library.

1703–1732: James Logan Letter Books, I–IV (1701–1708, 1702–1726,1721–1731,1717–1743), Parchment Logan Letter Book, 1717–1731, Letter Book, 1712, 1714, Logan Account Book, 1712–1719, Logan Ledger, 1720–1729, Logan Daybook, 1722–1723, all in Logan Papers.

1709–1765: Letter Books of Isaac Norris, Sr., and Isaac Norris, Jr., 1699–1766, Norris Journal, 1709–1716, Norris Daybook, 1722–1764, Norris Ledgers, 1724–1764, Norris Transcript to Journal, 1762–1765, all in Norris Papers, 1742–1860.

1723: Lt. Gov. Sir William Keith, at Philadelphia, to Board of Trade, 12 Dec. 1723, C.O. 5/1266, fol. 142r.

1723–1734: Alexander Wooddrup Account Books, 1720–1734, Lib. Cong.

1727–1747: Samuel Powel, Jr., Letter Books, 1727–1747.

1733–1767: John Reynell Correspondence, 1729–1773, John Reynell Letter Books, 1729–1784, Coates and Reynell Papers.

1738: [William Douglass], *An Essay concerning Silver and Paper Currencies, More Especially with Regard to the British Colonies in New-England* (Boston, [1738]), 4.

1740: [William Douglass], *A Discourse concerning the Currencies of the British Plantations in America* (Boston, 1740), 17, 20.

1745: Charles Carroll of Carrollton Papers, 1684–1771, fol. 615, Carroll Family Papers, 1684–1832, Lib. Cong.

1745–1750: Davey and Carson Letter Book, 1745–1750, *ibid*.

1745–1755: Pemberton Papers, in Pemberton Papers, 1641–1800.

1746: John Armitt, at Philadelphia, to Cadwallader Colden, 3 Apr. and 21 May 1745, *The Letters and Papers of Cadwallader Colden* (New-York Historical Society, *Collections*, L–LVI, LXVII–LXVIII [New York, 1918–1937]), VIII, 338, 339.

1747–1751: John Swift Letter Books, 1747–1813.

1747–1757: Joseph Richardson Letter Book, 1732–1757.

1748, 1773–1775: Letters, all written at Philadelphia, of John Reynell to Abraham Redwood, of Newport, R.I., 2 Sept. 1748, Stocker and Wharton to Christopher Champlin, at Newport, R.I., 18 June, 6 Aug. 1773, 8 Sept. and 5 Dec. 1774, Thomas Charles Williams and Co. to Champlin, 1 Nov. 1773, and Josiah Hewes to Champlin, 6 Apr. 1775, all in [Worthington C. Ford, ed.], *Commerce of Rhode Island, 1726–1800* (Massachusetts Historical Society, *Collections*, 7th Ser., IX–X [Boston, 1914–1915]), I, 58, 441, 449, 513, 523, II, 19n.

1748–1749: Account with Robert Greenway, at Philadelphia, in Robert Morris Ledger B, 1747–1750, the reverse of the Clerk's Fee Book, 1762–1763, Dorchester County, Md., Circuit Court, Maryland Hall of Records, Annapolis.

1749–1751: William Griffith Letter Book, 1748–1752, Norris Papers.

1749–1756: John Kidd Letter Book, 1749–1763.

1749–1774: Galloway Correspondence, Galloway Business Papers, 1654–1819, Galloway-Maxey-Markoe Family Papers, 1654–1888, Lib. Cong.

1751–1752, 1760: Henry Callister Letter Books, 1741–1766, fols. 179, 187, 188, 196, 202, 363, 385, 386, Callister Family Papers, 1741–1788, Maryland Diocesan Archives of the Protestant Episcopal Church, Maryland Historical Society, Baltimore.

1751–1769: Letter Book, 1750–1792, Journal B, 1757–1761, Thomas Riché Papers, 1749–1792.

1755–1758: Thomas Wharton Letter Book, 1752–1759, Wharton Papers, 1679–1834.

1755–1758: Willing and Morris Letter Book, 1754–1761.

1755–1764: "An Account of . . . the Bills of Credit . . . of Pennsylvania," 20 July 1764, enclosure in Gov. John Penn to Board of Trade, 11 Aug. 1764, C.O. 323/19, fol. 42r.

Notes and Sources: **TABLE 3.7 (Continued)**

1757: Allen and Turner, at Philadelphia, to Austin and Laurens, at Charleston, S.C., 24 Dec. 1757, Philip M. Hamer *et al.*, eds., *The Papers of Henry Laurens* (Columbia, S.C., 1968–), II, 541.

1757–1767: Tench Francis and John Relfe Letters, Brown Papers, John Carter Brown Library, Brown University, Providence, R.I.

1757–1775: John and Peter Chevalier Journal, 1757–1761, "Day Book 1770[–1783]," and Daybook 1757–1766, John and Peter Chevalier Papers, 1757–1783.

1759–1762: Solomon Fussell Account Book, 1758–1762, Collins Papers.

1759–1774: Abel James and Henry Drinker Letter Books, 1756–1809, Henry Drinker Papers, 1756–1869.

1759–1774: Clifford Letter Books, Pemberton Papers.

1761–1763: Daniel Clark Letter Book and Invoice Book, 1759–1763.

1761–1770: Neil Jamieson Papers, 1757–1789, II, no. 375, III, no. 518, IV, no. 708, IX, nos. 1879, 1909, 1915, 1960, XI, nos. 2380, 2385, XII, no. 2607, XIII, no. 2976, Lib. Cong.

1762: Mifflin and Massey Ledger, 1760–1763, Logan Papers.

1762: [Dorothy C. Barck, ed.], *Letter Book of John Watts, Merchant and Councillor of New York, January 1, 1762–December 22, 1765* (N.-Y. Hist. Soc., *Colls.*, LXI [New York, 1928]), 78, 79.

1764–1765: Joel and Nathan Zane Receipt Book, 1761–1764.

1764–1772: Galloway Correspondence, 1739–1812, Papers of Samuel and John Galloway, 1739–1812, New York Public Library, New York City.

1765–1766: Daniel Roberdeau Letter Book, 1764–1771, Receipt Book, 1761–1767, Roberdeau Papers, 1761–1831.

1765–1767: William Lux Letter Book, 1763–1768, New-York Historical Society, New York City.

1765–1770: Samuel and Jonathan Smith Letter Book, 1765–1770, Peter Force Papers, Ser. VIII D, Lib. Cong.

1766: Simson, Baird, and Co., Piscataway Store Journal, 1766–1767, fol. 124, John Glassford and Co. Records, 1753–1844, Lib. Cong.

1767–1768: Orr, Dunlope, and Glenholme Letter Book, 1767–1769.

1768: Joshua Fisher and Sons, at Philadelphia, to Charles Ridgely, at Baltimore, 13 Apr. 1768, Ridgely Papers, 1733–1858, MS 692.1, Md. Hist. Soc.

1768: Bill of exchange, Philadelphia, 10 May 1768, Correspondence, 1672–1775, Coxe Papers.

1768–1769: Samuel Meredith Letters, 1771–1799, Clymer-Meredith-Read Papers, Box I, N.Y. Pub. Lib.

1768–1771: Levi Hollingsworth Invoice Book, 1767–1770, Hollingsworth Correspondence, 1770–1771, Hollingsworth Collection, 1748–1887.

1769–1774: Clement Biddle and Co. Letters, Brown Papers.

1770: [Amos?] Strettell to James Robinson, at Falmouth, Va., 31 Jan. 1770 (as referred to in Robinson to William Henderson, 12 Feb. 1770), Robinson to Henderson, 20 Mar. and 9 Apr. 1770, and Willing and Morris, at Philadelphia, to Robinson, 16 July 1770 (as referred to in Robinson to John Nielson, 25 July 1770), all in James Robinson Letter Book, 1767–1773, Bundle 0, Letter Books and Correspondence of William Cuninghame and Co., Glasgow, 1761–1789, Box 58, Collection Deposited by Messrs. John C. Brodie, W.S., Gift and Deposit No. 247, Scottish Record Office, Edinburgh.

1770–1773: William Pollard Letter Book, 1772–1774.

1771–1772: William Barrell Journal B, 1767–1775, William Barrell Journals, 1766–1775, Item No. 154, Collins Papers.

1771–1775: William Smith Letter Book, 1771–1775.

1773–1775: *Rivington's New-York Gazetteer; or, The Connecticut, New-Jersey, Hudson's-River and Quebec Weekly Advertiser*, 1773–1775.

1774: Levi Hollingsworth, at Philadelphia, to Mark Alexander, at Baltimore, 7 Apr. 1774, Mark Alexander Correspondence, 1757–1794, Corner Collection, Box II, MS 1242, Md. Hist. Soc.

1774: Thomas and Isaac Wharton, at Philadelphia, to Nathaniel Shaw, 9 Dec. 1774 (as referred to in Shaw's reply, at New London, Conn., 15 Dec. 1774), Ernest E. Rogers, ed., *Connecticut's Naval Office at New London during the War of the American Revolution, Including the Mercantile Letter Book of Nathaniel Shaw, Jr.* (New London County Historical Society, *Collections*, II [New London, Conn., 1933]), 263.

Maryland

The history of Maryland's money, the course of its exchange, and its economic development were greatly influenced by events in Pennsylvania on the one hand and Virginia on the other. Maryland belonged in fact to two separate but overlapping economic regions, the Delaware River Valley and the Chesapeake, a circumstance that explains much of what happened in the colony. Until the first decades of the eighteenth century Maryland's monetary history paralleled much of that of Virginia; later it copied first the paper money and then the par of exchange of Pennsylvania, joining that circle of colonies from New Jersey to the Potomac River within which the piece of eight had the same legal value. But the story of Maryland's money is no mere echo. In a unique way for the colonies, Maryland existed for thirty years with a dual currency, the closest parallels for which were the bank money–current money systems of Amsterdam, Hamburg, and Venice.

For real money Marylanders shared the usual gold and silver coin of the Atlantic world (see tables 1.1 and 1.2, pp. 9–13), and their money of account was that common to all Englishmen: pounds, shillings, and pence. Like the other colonies, Maryland had difficulty maintaining an adequate circulating medium of exchange. And, like the rest, it went the route from barter to commodity money to overvalued coin to paper money. Tobacco served as commodity money from the earliest days of the colony until 1812, and in the eighteenth century a good deal of care was expended perfecting the system.[158] To keep what coin the province had and to

attract more, Maryland joined the other colonies in passing legislation to inflate the value of coin in terms of Maryland currency; although three such laws were enacted, in 1671, 1686, and 1692, none was allowed to stand, and all were repealed within a few years. Until 1708, therefore, the piece of eight circulated in Maryland at its sterling value, 4s 6d (22.5p), except for the months April 1671 through June 1676, November 1686 through November 1689, and June 1692 through June 1694. In each of these periods it passed at 6s (30p) Maryland currency, or at an effective par of £133.33 Maryland currency per £100 sterling.[159] From 1634 until

158. Gould, *Money in Maryland*, 48–73, devotes a chapter to "Tobacco Currency." See also "The Provincial Currency of Maryland," *Fisher's National Magazine and Industrial Record*, II (1846), 693; Nettels, *Money Supply*, 202–228.

159. For the various statutes see "An Act for the Advancement of Forreigne Coynes," 1671, chap. XII, "An Act for Repeale of Certain Lawes," 1676, chap. II, "An Act for the Advancement of Coines," 1692, chap. XLIV, "An Act for Repealing Certain Laws of this Province," 1694, chap. XVII, in William Hand Browne *et al.*, eds., *Archives of Maryland* (Baltimore, 1883–1972), II, 286–287, 542–551, XIII, 142–144, 493, 495, XIX, 88; also the report enclosed in Bellomont to Board of Trade, 17 Oct. 1700, C.O. 5/1045, fol. 87r. See as well "An account of the present state and government of Virginia," enclosed in Henry Hartwell, James Blair, and Edward Chilton to Board of Trade, 20 Oct. 1697, C.O. 5/1309, fol. 91r, and printed as Henry Hartwell, James Blair, and Edward Chilton, *The Present State of Virginia and the College* (London, 1727); also Nettels, *Money Supply*, 238–239. The most complete printing of the laws of colonial Maryland appears in the *Proceedings and Acts of the General Assembly* (1638–1774), which, in 32 volumes, were published as part of Browne *et al.*, eds., *Archives of Maryland*. This does not fully supersede two earlier editions: Thomas Bacon, ed., *Laws of Maryland at Large, with Proper Indexes* (1638–1763) (Annapolis, Md., 1765), and [Alexander C. Hanson, ed.], *Laws of Maryland, Made Since M,DCC,LXIII* (Annapolis, Md., 1787). Hereafter references to Maryland laws will include title, year of passage, chapter number from Bacon's and Hanson's editions, and location in the *Archives of Maryland*.

It is probably not insignificant that the years 1680 to 1683 witnessed the replacement of tobacco as a commodity money by Maryland currency (not sterling—see the discussion above in the initial section of this chapter). Russell R. Menard, "Farm Prices of Maryland Tobacco, 1659–1710," *Maryland Historical Magazine*, LXVIII (1973), 80–85; *Historical Statistics of the United States*, II, 1198, ser. Z 583–584.

1708, with those exceptions, Maryland currency was on par at parity with sterling (£100 Maryland currency per £100 sterling). What the commercial rate of exchange during those years was we have yet to determine.

In 1708, when Parliament decreed that the colonies could value silver coin at no more than a one-third advance over sterling, Marylanders were in a position quite different from most other colonists. They hurried to conform with the act of 1708 not by lowering the currency value of the piece of eight but by raising its legal value once again, secure this time in the knowledge that the Board of Trade would not seek the disallowance of their act.[160] There is reason to suspect that Maryland currency had already in practice inflated to the level set by Queen Anne's proclamation of 1704.[161] With the piece of eight at 6s (30p), the legal par of exchange in Maryland from the spring of 1709 through the fall of 1753 was at the level of "Proclamation Money," £133.33 Maryland currency to £100 sterling. As usual, the commercial rate of exchange fluctuated around par; table 3.8 has a few quotations of the bill rate for these years.

Just as Maryland came to overvalued coin relatively late, so too was it slow to issue paper money. Only in 1733 did its legislature authorize the issuance of a form of paper currency,

some £90,000 Maryland currency in bills of credit.[162] Because of two features of that currency which affected its value in opposite directions over the next generation, it behaved in ways atypical of colonial paper money.[163] On the one hand, the legal status of Maryland bills of credit was unusually restricted—they were not constituted legal tender for private debts, and, moreover, their public function was hedged about with some limitations. These restrictions tended to undermine the value of Maryland paper money. On the other hand, in an attempt to insure that its bills of credit would retain their value, the Maryland legislature provided in the original law for the eventual redemption of the bills. For this purpose the law established a "sinking fund" based upon a tax of 15d (6.2p) currency per hogshead of tobacco exported from the colony, the proceeds of which were regularly sent to England, where commissioners in charge of the fund invested them in Bank of England stock. The success of this plan and the redemption of the bills in two stages (29 September 1748 through 29 March 1749 and 29 September 1764 through 29 March 1765) created a precedent for future issues of paper currency. This second factor tended, obviously, to reinforce and enhance the value of Maryland paper money.

160. "An Act for Setling the Rates of Foreigne Silver Coyns within this Province," 1708, chap. IV, Browne *et al.*, eds., *Archives of Maryland*, XXVII, 350–352. Gould, *Money in Maryland*, 29, speculated that Maryland's attempts to alter its coin might even have been a remote cause of the Proclamation of 1704 and the act of 1708.

161. Thus one researcher found no discontinuity in inventory price levels in the period around 1708. Gloria Lund Main, "Personal Wealth in Colonial America: Explorations in the Use of Probate Records from Maryland to Massachusetts, 1650–1720" (Ph.D. diss., Columbia University, 1972), 14. Any apparent increase in prices over the decade 1700 to 1710 could have reflected the depreciation of the value of Maryland currency.

162. For the statute see "An Act for Emitting and Making Current, Ninety Thousand Pounds, Current Money of Maryland, in Bills of Credit," 1733, chap. VI, Browne *et al.*, eds., *Archives of Maryland*, XXXIX, 92–113. Beginning in June 1734 the colony distributed over £40,000 of the paper money free at the rate of £1.50 to every taxable. Report of a committee of the upper house, 14 Apr. 1735, *ibid.*, 204; Gould, *Money in Maryland*, 85–86.

163. For the other, fuller accounts of the history of Maryland paper money, see Gould, *Money in Maryland*, 78–111; Kathryn L. Behrens, *Paper Money in Maryland, 1727–1789*, Johns Hopkins University Studies in Historical and Political Science, Ser. XLI, no. 1 (Baltimore, 1923); Brock, *Currency of the American Colonies*, 96–106, 412–428; and Ernst, *Money and Politics*, 153–168, 318–329.

Such opposing pressures on Maryland paper currency had several effects over the years 1733 through 1765. Its restricted use caused an almost immediate depreciation in the value of Maryland paper money,[164] which in turn had the further effect of severing its relationship to the currency value of coin in the colony. We have seen a similar development in Pennsylvania in the 1720s, but there it had more the appearance of a bookkeeping device. In the 1730s in Maryland one quickly learned the real need to distinguish between hard currency prices and paper currency prices. Phrases such as "Maryland current silver" and "Maryland current gold" started to appear in account books and correspondence, denoting hard money at the old value in Maryland with par at £133.33.[165] But coin soon began to serve a supplementary,

even secondary role. From the 1730s to the mid-1750s "the current money of Maryland" meant paper money. In order to keep their coin and their paper, however, Marylanders learned to live with both. The years 1733 through 1765 witnessed a dual currency in use in the colony. Contracts and prices could be quoted in either—and in sterling too, for that matter—but these quotations always stipulated either "currency," meaning paper money (hereafter called paper currency), or "Maryland gold," meaning coin (hereafter called hard currency).[166]

Among the things that the colonists purchased with their currency were, of course, bills of exchange on London. Tables 3.8 and 3.9 record the prices paid for sterling bills, the former in terms of hard currency (1702 to 1775) and the latter in terms of paper currency (1734 to 1765).[167] The early lack of

164. See Stephen Bordley, at London, to Charles Hynson, at Chestertown, Md., 23 Dec. 1734, Stephen Bordley Letter Books, I, 132–133, MS 81, Maryland Historical Society, Baltimore; Lord Baltimore to Benjamin Tasker, 25 Mar. 1735, Orders and Instructions of Charles, Lord Baltimore, 1729–1750, p. 66, Calvert Papers, 1621–1775, MS 174, *ibid*.

165. See the Account Book of a Charlestown (Port Tobacco) Merchant, 1740–1741, Box 10, bundle 4, Collections Deposited by Messrs. Tods, Murray, and Jamieson, W. S., Gift and Deposit No. 237, Scottish Record Office, Edinburgh; Robert Morris Ledger B, 1747–1750, the reverse of the Clerk's Fee Book, 1762–1763, Dorchester County, Md., Circuit Court, 1762–1763, Maryland Hall of Records, Annapolis. My tentative identification of the first of these manuscripts as originating at Charlestown (later Port Tobacco), Charles County, Md., and belonging to Samuel Hyde is surely confirmed in the former by its numerous reductions from sterling into Maryland currency and "Maryland current gold" and its references to Charlestown and the Potomac River. (E.g., Hyde's ship *Charles*, mentioned repeatedly in the account book, entered and cleared the port of South Potomac in 1737. C.O. 5/1445, fols. 7–8. The matching records for the port of North Potomac have not survived.) The attribution to Hyde seems less certain if he was Samuel Hyde, the London agent of the Baltimore Company. See Keach Johnson, "The Baltimore Company Seeks English Markets: A Study of the Anglo-American Iron Trade, 1731–1755,"

WMQ, 3d Ser., XVI (1959), 37–60. For the second account book see James S. Shepherd, "Ledger B: Story of Robert Morris, 'Factor' in Provincial Maryland, and of His Son, Robert Morris, Patriot and Financier of the Revolution," Maryland Original Research Society, *Bulletin*, III (1913), 120–125.

166. See Gould, *Money in Maryland*, 31–32. Examples of this are almost too numerous to cite. Some can be consulted conveniently in the published papers of Dr. Charles Carroll of Annapolis; see, e.g., his letter to Michael Macnemara, 23 Jan. 1746/47, "Extracts from Account and Letter Books of Dr. Charles Carroll, of Annapolis," *Md. Hist. Mag.*, XXII (June 1927), 195.

167. Some of the exchange quotations come from Baltimore, some from Annapolis, and a few from elsewhere in the colony. We would expect them all to be rather similar for the same time period, regardless of place, but perhaps less so at the beginning of the colony's history. In the instances where we have figures for the same date, the rates are the same. See rates of exchange in Letter Book of John Smith & Sons, 1774–1786, Vol. I of Smith Letter Books, MS 1152, I, Md. Hist. Soc.; in Richard K. MacMaster and David C. Skaggs, eds., "The Letterbooks of Alexander Hamilton, Piscataway Factor [1774–1776]," *Md. Hist. Mag.*, LXI (1966), 146–166, 305–328, LXII (1967), 135–169; and in James Dick and Stewart Company Letter Book, Duke University Library, Durham, N.C. I am grateful for this last reference, and for much else, to Ronald Hoffman.

trust in the value of the paper bills of credit that is reflected in these tables resulted not only in a sharp, initial depreciation of the value of paper currency but also in an increasing divergence in the cost of bills of exchange—and of everything else—that were purchased with paper currency from those paid for with hard currency. The decline in the value of paper currency seems to have reached its nadir in the late 1740s.

An important effect of this dual currency was the extralegal creation of a new par of exchange for hard currency. In June 1752 the county court of Frederick County, Virginia, recognized this par as a fait accompli when it "ordered that Maryland money be rated at the same value as Pennsylvania money," that is, at £166.67 Maryland currency to £100 sterling.[168] A year later the Maryland legislature showed official cognizance of the same fact when it raised the value of coin to the same level.[169] After as early as mid-1752 Maryland and

Pennsylvania had the same par of exchange,[170] used a common currency, and had bill rates that were almost always related in their fluctuations.

The redemption of one-third of the bills of credit during the six months from 29 September 1748 through 29 March 1749 had only a limited and temporary influence on the value of the bills of credit. Although the exchange rate dropped in the fall of 1748 to as low as £170 Maryland paper currency per £100 sterling, by early 1749 it had returned to £180 and £190; in these months it never did decline to the redemption value, £133.33.[171] But the successful redemption and the knowledge that in 1749 the London fund against which the moneys were drawn already had in it about half the sum needed by 1764 to redeem the remainder of the bills did influence their value. Doubts about the worth of the bills disappeared in the face of the certainty that on and after 29 September 1764, £133.33 Maryland currency would buy what £180 bought in May 1750. Maryland paper currency over those intervening fifteen years increased in value to reflect this appreciation.

168. This was done in connection with judgments rendered in a series of suits brought by George Mason and the Ohio Company against various defendants. Frederick County Court, Order Book, No. 4, 1751–1753, pp. 181–182, Frederick County Courthouse, Winchester, Va.

169. "An Act for Amending the Staple of Tobacco, for Preventing Fraud in His Majesty's Customs, and for the Limitation of Officers Fees," 1753, chap. XXII, Browne et al., eds., Archives of Maryland, L, 303–367. The rates at which coins were valued in Maryland currency are specified, ibid., 362. Thus Gov. Horatio Sharpe explained the impact of this "Inspection Law" as follows: "There is now gold and silver enough in the province for every one to discharge his publick debts. . . . Before this law took place . . . £152 or a little more [paper] currency would purchase £100 sterling. Now from £155 to 160 currency is required to purchase a bill of that value; but notwithstanding this law you cannot procure such a bill of exchange for less than from £162.10 to 165 and sometimes more gold or silver valued according to the Inspection Law, so that the difference at least between paper and gold or silver currency is 4 or 5 per cent." Letter to Cecilius Calvert, 8 Aug. 1754, ibid., VI, 85–86. Note that in specifying "the difference," Sharpe was in fact quoting the agio.

170. The par of exchange, pieces of eight being always the measure, was £166 13s 4d (£166.67), but in common practice this was sometimes rounded to the nearest convenient number, £165. Gould, Money in Maryland, 46n. As an example see the 1753 comment from the ledger of the Bladensburg, Md., store of John Glassford and Co. (Glasgow), in which par is said to be "65 per cent currency as appears from pieces of 8 passing at 7/6 currency and pistoles at 27/." Ledger, fol. 104, John Glassford and Company Records, 1753–1844, Lib. Cong. See also ibid., fol. 128; Clark, History of Manufactures, III, 361n.

171. Moreover, the effect of the redemption on the exchange rate was not foreseen and came as something of a shock. See Henry Callister's letters to Charles Craven and to Foster Cunliffe and Sons, both of Liverpool, 1 Aug. 1748, Henry Callister Letter Books, 1741–1766, fols. 126–127, Callister Family Papers, 1741–1788, Maryland Diocesan Archives of the Protestant Episcopal Church, Md. Hist. Soc. Callister began a career in Maryland in 1740 as a

Awareness of the implications of the eventual redemption of the paper bills of credit seems to have struck forcefully early in the 1750s when prices began to go down as paper currency rose in value.[172] Except for a short period in the midst of the Seven Years' War, prices in terms of paper currency continued to decline. But, as had happened in the 1730s, the "good" money tended to be driven from circulation by the "bad," and paper currency ceased to circulate.[173] From about 1752 on colonists obviously preferred to spend the currency of less secure value and to keep that of more certain worth—especially so in this case, since Marylanders were certain not only of the value of their paper currency but also that it would increase in value. More and more in the 1750s we find the return of hard currency to circulation in Maryland, largely in the form of Pennsylvania money. We get some sense of the changes that had taken place from a letter written in January 1762 by Henry Callister, the Eastern Shore tobacco merchant and planter, in which he admonished his correspondent: "I said currency, which does not imply Maryland [paper] money, of which there is hardly any current—I think I was yet more particular, for I spoke of money and exchange as current in Pennsylvania which is our current money at present."[174]

The parallels between the dual currency of Maryland from 1733 to 1764 and the dual currencies of Holland or Hamburg cannot be extended too far, but they do exist. The common money in both instances was coin; the official money, paper. In the Dutch instance the official money was the issue of the Amsterdam exchange bank; in Maryland the legislature issued the paper currency partly to establish a mortgage bank while leaving the control of the fund backing it to London-based commissioners. Maryland paper currency began its life at a value lower than the current hard currency; Amsterdam's bank money ended its life in a similar condition. When both were at a premium over coin, the difference was talked of in terms of the percentage increase over hard currency necessary to equal paper. Although no one in Maryland ever used the term "agio" to designate the difference, it was certainly applicable.[175] Perhaps the most important distinction for present purposes was that, in Amsterdam, bank money was nearly always used for exchange transactions, whereas in Maryland the colonists bought bills on London using tobacco, bills of

factor of the Cunliffe firm; he later became an important Eastern Shore merchant and planter in his own right with sizable holdings at Townside, his estate on the Chester River some dozen miles above Chestertown, and elsewhere in the vicinity. See also Lawrence C. Wroth, "A Maryland Merchant and His Friends in 1750," *Md. Hist. Mag.*, VI (Sept. 1911), 213–240. In the early 1930s the Diocesan Archives photostated the letter book and sold bound copies that are available in several repositories, including the Newberry Library in Chicago and the New York Public Library.

172. Gould, *Money in Maryland*, 99–100. Gov. Sharpe spoke of the option that people had "to value the several sorts of money as they think proper and require different prices for their commodities in proportion," in his letter to Calvert, 8 Aug. 1754, Browne *et al.*, eds., *Archives of Maryland*, VI, 85.

173. See Jerman Baker to Duncan Rose, 15 Feb. 1764, in *WMQ*, 1st Ser., XII (1904), 239; Calvert to Sharpe, 29 Feb. 1764, Browne *et al.*, eds., *Archives of Maryland*, XIV, 141. See also Gould, *Money in Maryland*, 105–107; Behrens, *Paper Money in Maryland*, 46–47.

174. "Mr. [Nathan] Wright's Query's answer'd by H[enry] C[allister]," [Jan. 1762], Callister Letter Books, fol. 491. See also William Fitzhugh Ledger "H," fols. 57, 78, Fitzhugh Account Books, 1761–1774, MS 1831, Md. Hist. Soc.

175. See Callister to Foster Cunliffe and Sons, 4 May and 21 Aug. 1746, 23 Feb. 1746/47, 28 Dec. 1747, Callister Letter Books, fols. 58, 69, 79, 115; Sharpe to Calvert, 8 Aug. 1754, Browne *et al.*, eds., *Archives of Maryland*, VI, 86; and William Lux to Reese Meredith, 10 Dec. 1765, Lux Letter Book.

credit, hard currency, and anything else the seller would accept.

The second redemption of Maryland paper currency during the months from September 1764 through March 1765 withdrew it from circulation and ended its history as a real money.[176] Yet after March 1765, Marylanders continued to use it as a form of imaginary money of account in much the same way as New Englanders continued to use Old Tenor. Mercantile records from the 1760s and 1770s occasionally refer to "Maryland currency" or "Maryland money," meaning money at the old paper currency rate.[177] (This situation might have caused confusion when the colony issued a new paper money in 1766, but the Maryland assembly avoided any problems by valuing the new paper money as hard currency and denominating it in "dollars."[178]) The most persistent use of the old paper currency rate occurred in the valuation of estate inventories, because the law required it, despite attendant difficulties.[179] Still, these difficulties were rather easily over-

come, since as an imaginary money of account, Maryland currency, or "Maryland money," bore a regular, set ratio to hard currency after 1764. Just as the post-1750 ratio of Massachusetts Old Tenor to Massachusetts Lawful Money never varied from the 7.5 to 1 rate set by law, so also the old paper currency rate in Maryland stayed at the fixed ratio to hard currency of 1.25 to 1. At this ratio £100 Maryland currency equaled £125 Maryland hard currency from September 1764 on. (Before that date, when the old paper currency had existed as a real, separate currency, the ratio between it and hard currency varied considerably and altered radically over time, a condition that tables 3.8 and 3.9 indicate clearly.) After 1764 business dealings in the colony were settled in hard currency even if one chose to state the sum in the more traditional "Maryland money." This included the purchase of bills of exchange.

The mechanics of buying and selling bills of exchange varied little if at all in Maryland from the practice in other colonies. One distinction to keep in mind, however, was the ancient alternate market for Maryland bills of exchange at Philadelphia. Even as late as 1769 William Lux of Baltimore could comment on the comparative inactivity of the exchange market in Maryland, and his point of comparison was even then not Philadelphia but Virginia.[180] Still, with the rise of

---

176. Gould, *Money in Maryland*, 104–105.

177. For examples of this usage see William Fitzhugh Ledger "H," fols. 84, 234, Fitzhugh Account Books; James Hollyday Ledger, "Lib[er] A," 1746–1784, fols. 67, 97, MS 454.1, Md. Hist. Soc.; and Account Book of Charles Carroll of Annapolis, 1754–1784, fols. 53, 54, MS 211, *ibid.*

178. "An Act for the payment of the Publick Claims for Emitting Bills of Credit," 1766, chap. XXVI, Browne *et al.*, eds., *Archives of Maryland*, LXI, 264–275. See also the acts for emitting bills of credit, 1769, chap. XIV, and 1773, chap. XXVI, *ibid.*, LXII, 131–151, LXIV, 242–253. Concerning this money, and especially the first of these three issues, see Behrens, *Paper Money in Maryland*, 49–56; Hoffman, *Spirit of Dissension*, 58–59; and Ernst, *Money and Politics*, 153–168, 318–329. Sharpe wrote to Frederick Calvert, Lord Baltimore, 7 Dec. 1766: "I am told that one of the principal merchants in Philadelphia who knows on what foundation the bills are to be emitted has declared that he will make no difference between those bills and the number of dollars to be therein mentioned." Browne *et al.*, eds., *Archives of Maryland*, XIV, 352.

179. Elie Vallette, *The Deputy Commissary's Guide within the Province of Maryland* (Annapolis, Md., 1774), 20–21. See also *ibid.*, 52–53, 239–245. Vallette was the register of the Prerogative Court from 1764 to 1777. He distinguished between "current money," what is herein called money at the old paper currency rate, and "common money," or hard currency. These 18th-century ambiguities continue to plague the modern researcher. See, e.g., *Historical Statistics of the United States*, II, 1175, 1197, ser. Z 169–191, Z 578–582.

180. Lux to Joseph Watkins, of Rappahannock River, Va., 13 Dec. 1765, Lux Letter Book.

Baltimore, the market for bills of exchange in the province did increase and at least on occasion was attractive enough to call bills down from Philadelphia.[181] In Maryland, as we might expect, most bills were drawn on London. "They are a very strange sett of people here," wrote one commentator from Baltimore. "They will not look at a Glasgow bill."[182] The usual sight for bills they did "look at" was thirty to sixty days,[183] with the standard preference for bills at short sight and drawn on London meaning a difference in price; the preferred bills sold for something more.[184]

Bills of exchange protested in Great Britain and returned were subject to an assessment for damages and interest from the date of protest. Provinces in which more sellers of bills than buyers had power in the assembly tended to be more sympathetic to the seller of a protested bill than to the buyer. Early in the eighteenth century Maryland witnessed a partially

successful attempt to lower the rate of damages payable from 20 to 10 percent, no doubt an outgrowth of such pressures. The new, compromise statute of 1715 put a premium on the speedy return of protested bills and lowered the rate a bit. "The laws of our province," wrote Dr. Charles Carroll of Annapolis in 1759, "allows 15 per cent under 18 months on protests and 20 after."[185]

The limited references that we have to intercolonial exchange at Maryland suggest a far greater reliance on the bill rate than elsewhere. This was certainly the case with exchange between Maryland and its near neighbors Pennsylvania and Virginia. William Lux once found himself in the middle of a dispute involving just this. In 1764 he wrote James Campbell of Yorktown that he had credited Campbell's account with the equivalent in Maryland currency of £130 Virginia currency paid to Lux on Campbell's behalf by Thomas Harrison. Lux gave Harrison credit on Campbell's account for the money "at 15 per cent, tho he [Harrison] grumbles about it, and indeed the difference in bills is not so much as 12½."[186] In

181. Capt. Taylor, of Baltimore, to Neil Jamieson and Co., of Norfolk, 24 Nov. 1765, Jamieson Papers, VI, no. 1252.

182. *Ibid.*

183. See, e.g., the bills drawn between Oct. 1774 and Jan. 1776 by the Baltimore house of Woolsey and Salmon, in George Woolsey and George Salmon Letter Book, 1774–1784, Ser. VIII D, Force Papers. See also Callister to George Maxwell, at Wye River, Md., 15 May 1759, and the list of bills of exchange sent by Callister to Ellis Cunliffe and Co., 1759, in Callister Letter Books, fols. 305, 345, and the "Schedule of Bills drawn by William Lux on William Molleson in 1766 and 1767," Exhibit E, in *William Molleson v. Daniel Bowley*, Baltimore County, 1800, Chancery Papers 3643, Md. Hall of Recs. There was some dispute over the sight of these last bills; see Lux to Godhard Hagan and Co., of London, 12 Nov. and 8 Dec. 1766, and to Molleson, of London, 21 Nov. 1766 and 26 Jan. 1767, Lux Letter Book.

184. Woolsey and Salmon, on 25 Feb. 1775, bought a 60-day bill on Ireland payable in London at one point less than the London rate. Woolsey and Salmon Letter Book, Force Papers. In Apr. 1775, 90-day bills were available at from 5 to 7.5 points less than the usual rate. *Ibid.* See also Lux to Molleson, 9 Nov. 1766, 26 Jan. 1767, Lux Letter Book.

185. Letter to Messrs. John and William Ballandine, of Occoquan, Va., 4 Apr. 1755, "Letter Books of Dr. Charles Carroll," *Md. Hist. Mag.*, XXVII (1932), 329. See also Darby Lux, at Baltimore, to John Reynell, 2 July 1746, Coates-Reynell Correspondence, 1729–1863, Box 1 (1729–1764), Coates-Reynell Papers, Hist. Soc. Pa.; Wm. Lux to Molleson, 9 Nov. 1766, Lux Letter Book; and deposition of Daniel Bowley, 9 Dec. 1800, p. 24, in *Molleson v. Bowley*, Chancery Papers. See the three acts "Ascertaining What Damages Shall be Allowed upon Protested Bills of Exchange," for 1699, chap. V, 1704, chap. LXXIII, and 1715, chap. VII, and a "Supplementary Act" to another such act for 1765, chap. III, all in Browne *et al.*, eds., *Archives of Maryland*, XXII, 464–465, XXVI, 356–357, XXX, 243, LIX, 264. The last of these four acts extended the rate for damages on foreign bills to inland bills. See also Nettels, *Money Supply*, 57–58.

186. Lux to Campbell, 14 May 1764, Lux Letter Book.

other words, the exchange cost Harrison £150 Maryland currency but he thought that it should have been only about £146 Maryland currency, if Lux had used the proper bill rate. The point here is that Lux used the bill rate, incorrectly or not, rather than use a ratio based on the comparative par values of the piece of eight.

Exchange on the West Indies seems also to have been at the bill rate or at least at a close approximation of the two bill rates. This was true of Robert Morris's transactions in the 1740s. In contrast to John Watts of New York, for whom pieces of eight were always the guide, Morris first reduced his Barbados accounts into sterling, quoting the Barbados rate on London, and then, where necessary, equated the sterling with Maryland paper currency values. He did the same for Antigua accounts.[187] Fifteen years later William Lux did much the same thing.[188] One is hard put to explain why Watts did it one way and Morris and Lux the other.

In concluding this section on Maryland a word about the sources for tables 3.8 and 3.9 might be in order, given the great potential for confusion in interpreting the data assembled in them. One obviously has to be extremely careful not to confuse prices in hard currency and prices in paper currency. Thus I have relied almost exclusively on commercial accounts, mercantile correspondence, and similar records where the references to transactions tend to be explicit. Moreover, I have omitted all debatable quotations for the period 1733 through 1764. In following these guidelines I have therefore not tapped the particularly rich Maryland probate records, especially the extensive estate inventories and accounts. With few exceptions, rates of exchange quoted in these records were not the commercial rate but an official rate ordered by the commissary general and administered by the other probate officers, more immediately by the deputy commissaries in the several counties.[189] The official rate tended to be set at par and remained unaltered over long periods. The par of exchange is an imperfect surrogate for the commercial rate of exchange, especially in times of extreme fluctuation. For example, to use par, £133.33, to estimate the commercial rate for paper currency in the late 1730s is to be wrong by 50 percent.

187. Morris, Ledger B, *passim*, Clerk's Fee Book, Dorchester Co. Circuit Court.

188. Lux to Daniel Rundle, of Philadelphia, 13 May 1764, and to Darby Lux, at Bridgetown, Barbados, 13 Sept. 1765, Lux Letter Book.

189. Vallette, *Deputy Commissary's Guide*, 20–21, 52–53. See the statement in the probate records that the rate of exchange used there was "allowed by order of the Commissary General." Account of William Barnes, St. Mary's County, 3 Dec. 1744, Prerogative Court Records, Accounts, Vol. 21 (Liber DD No. 9), p. 141. I am indebted to Lois Green Carr of the St. Mary's City Commission of Maryland for considerable help with these records. See also Gould, *Money in Maryland*, 46–47, 87–88. Obviously, too, all official dealings concerned with the London sinking fund converted from sterling to currency at £133.33, the official rate. See, e.g., Browne *et al.*, eds., *Archives of Maryland*, XIV, 170, XLVI, 529.

TABLE 3.8. **Rate of Exchange: Maryland on London, Hard Currency, 1702–1775**

(Pounds Maryland Hard Currency per £100 Sterling)

Year	Jan.	Feb.	Mar.	Apr.	May	June	July	Aug.	Sept.	Oct.	Nov.	Dec.	Average
1702												[111.11]	111.11
1703													
1704													
1705													
1706													
1707													
1708													
1709													
1710													
1711													
1712													
1713													
1714													
1715													
1716													
1717													
1718													
1719										113.33			113.33
1720					133.33								133.33
1721											114.36		114.36
1722							127.50						127.50
1723				133.33			125.00			128.00			128.78
1724													
1725										128.00			128.00
1726													
1727													
1728						137.50				135.00			136.25
1729							133.33						133.33

TABLE 3.8 (Continued): **Maryland on London, Hard Currency** (Pounds Maryland Hard Currency per £100 Sterling)

Year	Jan.	Feb.	Mar.	Apr.	May	June	July	Aug.	Sept.	Oct.	Nov.	Dec.	Average
1730					133.33								133.33
1731			133.33	133.33					133.45				133.37
1732			133.33	133.33					133.33		133.33	133.33	133.33
1733													
1734			133.33			133.33			133.33	133.33			133.33
1735										133.33			133.33
1736	133.33				133.33					133.90		[133.33]	133.42
1737							140.00		140.00				140.00
1738						133.33	137.50						135.42
1739													
1740								136.67	140.00	140.00	140.00		139.17
1741	140.00			140.00	140.00	129.17	140.00			136.67	140.00	140.00	138.82
1742	140.00	137.78	140.00	140.00	140.00	140.00	140.00		133.33				138.64
1743	140.00	140.00	140.00	140.00	140.00					133.33			137.78
1744			133.33		140.00							145.00	139.44
1745	140.00												140.00
1746	133.33				140.00	140.00		140.00					137.78
1747		140.00										145.00	142.50
1748				141.94						140.00			140.97
1749													
1750	130.00								133.33				131.66
1751										140.00			140.00
1752													
1753						150.00			150.00			150.00	150.00
1754	150.00							163.75				165.00	159.58
1755								165.00					165.00
1756			162.50					165.00		167.50	167.50		165.00
1757		163.75	165.00		162.50			166.25			165.00		164.53

TABLE 3.8 (Continued): **Maryland on London, Hard Currency** (Pounds Maryland Hard Currency per £100 Sterling)

Year	Jan.	Feb.	Mar.	Apr.	May	June	July	Aug.	Sept.	Oct.	Nov.	Dec.	Average
1758	166.67	163.33	160.00	162.50	161.25	160.00	150.00	153.75	150.00	152.19	154.38	150.00	157.01
1759			165.00	150.00	150.00	150.00			150.00	150.00			153.75
1760	150.00	[155.00]	152.50	150.00	150.00	152.50	155.00	155.00	155.00	157.50	160.00	162.50	154.58
1761	150.00	157.50	166.25	175.00	171.25	160.00	165.00	173.75	174.17	175.00	176.67	178.33	168.58
1762	180.00	172.50	169.03	170.00	170.00	168.33	167.50	173.47	176.88	169.58	165.56	165.00	170.65
1763	165.00	164.90	164.79	164.68	164.58	167.92	170.00	170.25	170.81	168.33	165.56	170.00	167.24
1764	166.67	168.33	174.29	165.54	164.44	166.25	166.25	160.97	165.67	169.47	166.67	166.67	166.77
1765	166.67	166.67	167.62	168.40	168.89	167.78	165.93	166.20	166.67	167.04	166.75	161.11	166.65
1766	166.67	166.46	166.67	166.67	167.50	167.50	166.53	162.50	164.79	162.92	160.64	149.00	163.99
1767	166.67	160.00	163.54	163.86	164.17	164.44	166.67	165.54	166.67	166.67	162.92	163.89	164.59
1768	166.67	168.33	165.00	161.36	166.67	166.67	165.87	165.08	166.88	162.50	163.98	160.00	164.92
1769	166.25	162.50	166.67	166.67	166.67	166.67	165.84	165.00	156.88	148.75	147.75	148.50	160.68
1770	149.25	150.00	150.62	151.25	150.00	150.00	150.00	150.00	150.00	150.00	157.50	153.75	151.03
1771	158.33	160.55	162.78	165.00	165.00	165.00	150.00	156.25	162.50	166.67	165.55	164.44	161.84
1772	163.33	161.67	160.00	159.17	157.50	160.00	157.50	158.12	156.25	157.50	155.00	157.50	158.63
1773	160.00	163.75	163.33	162.92	162.50	163.33	166.67	170.21	168.02	165.83	168.75	166.25	165.13
1774	166.38	166.53	166.67	166.67	166.67	166.67	167.50	168.33	169.72	167.80	166.72	165.56	167.10
1775	162.00	160.28	157.82	155.08	155.28	153.36	148.75	145.62	147.50	162.11	165.75	166.67	156.68

Notes and Sources: **TABLE 3.8**

Figures inserted in square brackets are assigned to that month arbitrarily; figures in italics are straight-line interpolations based on the two neighboring quotations.

All manuscript collections cited below are in the Maryland Historical Society, Baltimore, unless otherwise indicated.

1702–1772: Clement Hill Papers, 1670–1805, MS 446.

1706: Presentment of the Commissioners for Prizes to the Lord High Treasurer, London, 20 Den. 1706, T. 1/100, no. 53, Public Record Office.

1719, 1731: Charles Carroll of Annapolis, Letter Books and Business Accounts, 1716–1755, I, fols. 7, 14, MS 208.

1720: Account of Richard Harrison, Calvert Co., 17 May 1720, Prerogative Court Records, Accounts, Vol. 3 (Liber TB No. 6), pp. 11–14, Maryland Hall of Records, Annapolis.

Notes and Sources: **TABLE 3.8 (Continued)**

1721–1746: John Digges Account Book, 1720–1749, Library of Congress.

1723–1728: *Proceedings and Acts of the General Assembly*, in William Hand Browne *et al.*, eds., *Archives of Maryland* (Baltimore, 1883–1972), XXIV, 688, XXV, 327, XXVI, 230.

1728: James Logan, at Philadelphia, to William Aubrey, at London, 26 June 1728, Parchment Logan Letter Book, 1717–1731, p. 526, Logan Papers, 1664–1871, Historical Society of Pennsylvania, Philadelphia.

1731: Entry of Apr. 1731, Alexander Wooddrup Account Books, 1720–1734, II, Lib. Cong.

1732, 1740–1743: Collector of Customs, Port of Oxford, Maryland, Account Book, 1731 1743, MS 638.

1734–1757: Charles Carroll of Carrollton Account Book, 1734–1825, Carroll Family Papers, 1684–1832, Lib. Cong. This is duplicated, in part, by a volume cataloged as Account Book of Charles Carroll of Annapolis, 1730–1757, MS 211.1.

1736: Ledger, 1734–1738, p. 40, Ridgely Account Books, MS 691.

1737–1775: Correspondence, Business Papers, and Accounts of John and Samuel Galloway and Thomas Ringgold, Galloway-Maxey-Markoe Family Papers, 1654–1888, Lib. Cong.

1738: Order Book, 1738–1749, p. 14, Spotsylvania County Courthouse, Spotsylvania, Va.

1740–1741: Account Book of a Charlestown (Port Tobacco) Merchant, 1740–1741, fols. 1, 21, 27, Box 10, bundle 4, Collections Deposited by Messrs. Tods, Murray, and Jamieson, W.S., Gift and Deposit No. 237, Scottish Record Office, Edinburgh.

1742–1748: Robert Morris Ledger B, 1747–1750, the reverse of the Clerk's Fee Book, 1762–1763, Dorchester County, Md., Circuit Court, Md. Hall of Recs.

1744: Benjamin Tasker, at Annapolis, Md., to Charles Calvert, Lord Baltimore, 3 Dec. 1744, [William Hand Browne *et al.*, eds.], *The Calvert Papers* (Maryland Historical Society, *Fund Publications*, Nos. 28, 34–35 [Baltimore, 1889–1899]), II, 117.

1746–1747, 1756–1766: Henry Callister Letter Books, 1741–1766, Callister Family Papers, 1741–1788, Maryland Diocesan Archives of the Protestant Episcopal Church.

1748: Charles Carroll of Annapolis to Ashbury Sutton, 18 Apr. 1748, "Extracts from Account and Letter Books of Dr. Charles Carroll, of Annapolis," *Maryland Historical Magazine*, XXII (1927), 370.

1752: Dr. Walter Tullideph, at Antigua, to Henry Lowes, of Somerset Co., Md., 12 May 1753, Letter Books of Dr. Walter Tullideph, 1734–1767, Tullideph Papers, in the possession of Sir David J. W. Ogilvy, Winton House, Pencaitland, East Lothian, Scotland (II, 122, of the typescript extracts from the letter books made by Richard B. Sheridan, to whom I am grateful for the loan of a microfilm copy of his transcript).

1753: Ledger of John Glassford and Co. Store, Bladensburg, Md., 1753, fol. 104r, John Glassford and Co. Records, 1753–1844, Lib. Cong.

1753–1761: Correspondence of Gov. Horatio Sharpe, Browne *et al.*, eds., *Archives of Maryland*, VI, 45, 85, 138, IX, 157, 195–196, 208, 246, 448, 538–539.

1754: Cecilius Calvert, at London, to Rev. Thomas Bacon, at Maryland, 5 Jan. 1754, [Browne *et al.*, eds.], *Calvert Papers*, II, 176.

1757–1760: Samuel Massey's account with Daniel Wolstenholme, 1757–1769, Corner Collection, Box I, MS 1242.

1758–1766, 1775: Galloway Correspondence, 1739–1812, Thomas Ringgold Correspondence, 1760–1770, Papers of Samuel and John Galloway, 1739–1812, New York Public Library, New York City.

1758–1774: Ridgely Papers, 1733–1858, MS 692.1.

1758–1775: Account Book of Charles Carroll of Annapolis, 1754–1784, MS 211.

1760: Agreement of 28 July 1760, *William Buchanan* v. *Thomas Ringgold and Samuel Galloway*, 8 Oct. 1762, Chancery Records, Vol. 10 (Liber DD No. 1), 1761–1764, p. 255, Md. Hall of Recs.

1761: Correspondence, I, nos. 9713, 9720, Stephen Collins and Son Papers, 1749–1857, Lib. Cong.

1761–1769: William Fitzhugh Ledgers "H" and "I," 1761–1769, Fitzhugh Account Books, 1761–1774, MS 1831.

Notes and Sources: **TABLE 3.8 (Continued)**

1761–1773: James Hollyday Ledger, "Lib[er] A," 1746–1784, MS 454.1.

1762: Dulany Papers, 1659–1799, Box IV, MS 1265.

1762–1765: Col. Charles Ridgely Ledger A, 1763–1765, Ridgely Account Books.

1763–1765: Charles Ridgely Journal, 1762–1765, *ibid*.

1763–1768: William Lux Letter Book, Baltimore, 1763–1768, New-York Historical Society, New York City.

1765–1772: Neil Jamieson Papers, 1757–1789, IX–XV, *passim*, Lib. Cong.

1766: Simson, Baird, and Co., Piscataway Store Journal, 1766–1767, fol. 63r, Glassford Records.

1770: James Robinson, at Falmouth, Va., to William Henderson, at Cabin Point, James River, Va., 12 Feb. 1770, and to David Walker, at Port Tobacco, Charles Co., Md., 17 Apr. and 11 July 1770, James Robinson Letter Book, 1767–1773, Bundle O, Letter Books and Correspondence of William Cuninghame and Co., Glasgow, 1761–1789, Box 58, Collections Deposited by Messrs. John C. Brodie, W.S., Gift and Deposit No. 247, Scot. Rec. Office.

1770: Edward Sprigg and Co., at Upper Marlboro, Md., to Hollingsworth and Rudulph, at Philadelphia, 15 June 1770, Hollingsworth Correspondence, 1769–1770, Hollingsworth Collection, 1748–1887, Hist. Soc. Pa.

1770–1773: Invoices dated Alexandria, Va., 15 June 1770, 20 Oct. 1773, Hooe, Stone, and Co. Invoice Book, 1770–1784, Robert T. Hooe Papers, N.Y. Pub. Lib.

1770–1774: Thomas C. Williams Letters, Brown Papers, L 68–71 M, Miscellaneous Correspondence, John Carter Brown Library, Brown University, Providence, R.I.

1772–1774: Henry Hollyday Account Book, 1745–1790, MS 454.

1773: *Maryland Journal and Baltimore Advertiser* (Baltimore), 20 Aug. 1773.

1773: Thomas Charles Williams and Co., at Philadelphia, to Christopher Champlin, at Newport, R.I., 1 Nov. 1773, [Worthington C. Ford, ed.], *Commerce of Rhode Island, 1726–1800* (Massachusetts Historical Society, *Collections*, 7th Ser., IX–X [Boston, 1914–1915]), I, 459.

1774–1775: Richard K. MacMaster and David C. Skaggs, eds., "The Letterbooks of Alexander Hamilton, Piscataway Factor [1774–1776]," *Maryland Historical Magazine*, LXI (1966), 310, 325, LXII (1967), 145, 148, 152.

1774–1775: Letter Book of John Smith and Sons, 1774–1786, I of Smith Letter Books, MS 1152.

1774–1775: George Woolsey and George Salmon Letter Book, 1774–1784, Peter Force Papers, Ser. VIII D, Lib. Cong.

TABLE 3.9. **Rate of Exchange: Maryland on London, Paper Currency, 1734–1765**

(Pounds Maryland Paper Currency per £100 Sterling)

Year	Jan.	Feb.	Mar.	Apr.	May	June	July	Aug.	Sept.	Oct.	Nov.	Dec.	Average
1734									160.00				160.00
1735		140.00											140.00
1736										230.00			230.00
1737									250.00				250.00
1738				200.00			250.00						225.00
1739	[200.00]									229.38		[220.00]	212.34
1740	[220.00]	200.00	220.00	250.00				214.00		280.00	[200.00]	215.00	228.08
1741	225.00			280.00		[188.00]				280.00		231.00	238.17
1742		240.00	280.00	240.00	280.00				300.00		280.00		275.00
1743	210.52		280.00	325.00									285.13
1744				166.67									166.67
1745											200.00		200.00
1746					200.00			220.00					210.00
1747		222.50			200.00	289.10	220.00	221.50	200.00			220.00	225.22
1748				212.90	248.56	215.00		187.50		176.50	190.00	[200.00]	200.61
1749		192.49	192.49			180.00	190.00	180.00		182.50	180.00	[180.00]	184.58
1750	177.50				180.00					177.50		175.00	177.92
1751		175.00	164.36				162.50		162.50			165.47	166.83
1752			161.25			157.50			150.00	155.00		155.00	155.62
1753									150.00	152.00		[155.00]	151.75
1754								157.50		150.00			153.75
1755													
1756												[170.00]	170.00
1757		140.00										150.00	145.00
1758	150.00												150.00
1759							150.00						150.00

TABLE 3.9 (Continued): **Maryland on London, Paper Currency** (Pounds Maryland Paper Currency per £100 Sterling)

Year	Jan.	Feb.	Mar.	Apr.	May	June	July	Aug.	Sept.	Oct.	Nov.	Dec.	Average
1760	145.00						145.00		150.00				146.25
1761						150.00			150.00	150.00	140.85		148.48
1762			144.45										144.45
1763			140.00										140.00
1764						140.00		140.00	133.33	133.33	133.33	133.33	136.67
1765	133.33	133.33	133.33										133.33

Notes and Sources: **TABLE 3.9**

Figures inserted in square brackets are assigned to that month arbitrarily.

All manuscript collections cited below are in the Maryland Historical Society, Baltimore, unless otherwise indicated.

1734, 1739: Stephen Bordley, at London, to Charles Hynson, at Chestertown, Md., 23 Dec. 1734, and to John Bordley, at Annapolis, Md., 31 Oct. 1749, Stephen Bordley Letter Books, 1727–1759, I, 131–133, IV, 3, MS 81.

1735: "Further Instructions to . . . Benjamin Tasker," 25 Mar. 1735, in Orders and Instructions of Charles, Lord Baltimore, 1729–1750, Calvert Papers, 1621–1775, MS 174. See also [William Douglass], *A Discourse concerning the Currencies of the British Plantations in America* (Boston, 1740), 17.

1736–1738: John Digges Account Book, 1720–1749, Library of Congress.

1738: [William Douglass], *An Essay concerning Silver and Paper Currencies, More Especially with Regard to the British Colonies in New-England* (Boston, [1738]), 6.

1739: Enclosure no. 12 in Board of Trade to House of Lords, 27 Mar. 1740, House of Lords, Main Papers, 28 Mar. 1740, House of Lords Record Office.

1739: "State of the Paper Currency in the British Plantation in America," Apr. 1740, C.O. 323/10, fol. 165, Public Record Office.

1739–1760: Galloway Correspondence, Galloway Business Papers, 1654–1819, Galloway-Maxey-Markoe Family Papers, 1654–1888, Lib. Cong.

1740: [Douglass], *Discourse concerning Currencies*, 20.

1740: [Hugh Vance], *An Inquiry into the Nature and Uses of Money; More Especially of the Bills of Publick Credit, Old Tenor* (Boston, 1740), 49. See also [Wavel Smith], *Observations Occasion'd by Reading a Pamphlet, Intitled, A Discourse concerning the Currencies of the British Plantations in America* (London, 1741), 1.

1740: "Account of Paper Money in the Province of Maryland," received from J[ohn] Sharpe, 14 Mar. 1739/40, C.O. 5/1269, fol. 176v.

1740: Deputy Gov. Samuel Ogle to Board of Trade, Dec. 1740, C.O. 5/1270, fol. 160v.

1740–1741: Account Book of a Charlestown (Port Tobacco) Merchant, 1740–1741, fols. 11, 13, 24, 41, Box 10, bundle 4, Collections Deposited by Messrs. Tods, Murray, and Jamieson, W.S., Gift and Deposit No. 237, Scottish Record Office, Edinburgh.

1740–1743: Collector of Customs, Port of Oxford, Maryland, Account Book, 1731–1743, MS 638.

1742–1743: Daybook, 1741–1742, Daybook, 1742–1743, Ridgely Account Books, MS 691.

1742–1749: Accounts of Thomas and Margaret Litton, 30 Sept. 1742, and of John Yoston Gostwietz, 29 May 1750, Baltimore County, Administration Accounts, Liber C, No. 3, p. 295, Maryland Hall of Records, Annapolis.

1742–1750: Robert Morris Ledger B, 1747–1750, the reverse of the Clerk's Fee Book, 1762–1763, Dorchester County, Md., Circuit Court, *ibid*.

Notes and Sources: **TABLE 3.9 (Continued)**

1744, 1751–1752, 1757: Charles Carroll of Carrollton Account Book, 1734–1825, Carroll Family Papers, 1684–1832, Lib. Cong. See the comment on this volume in the notes to table 3.8, above.

1745–1752: Henry Callister Letter Books, 1741–1766, Callister Family Papers, 1741–1788, Maryland Diocesan Archives of the Protestant Episcopal Church, Maryland Historical Society, Baltimore.

1748–1751: Dr. Charles Carroll of Annapolis to Ashbury Sutton, 18 Apr. 1748, and to Reese Meredith, at Philadelphia, 1 Mar. 1750/51, "Extracts from Account and Letter Books of Dr. Charles Carroll, of Annapolis," *Maryland Historical Magazine*, XXII (1927), 370, XXIV (1929), 183.

1749–1764: "An Account of the Paper Currency . . . in the Province of Maryland," 1749–1764, enclosure in Gov. Horatio Sharpe, at Annapolis, Md., to Board of Trade, 1 Aug. 1764, C.O. 323/19, fols. 46r–47v.

1751: Promissory note, 31 Dec. 1751, *John Nutter* v. *George Parris*, Princess Anne, [17] Mar. 1752, Somerset County, Md., Court Records, 1751–1752, fol. 162 [bis], Md. Hall of Recs.

1752: James Hollyday Ledger, "Lib[er] A," 1746–1784, fols. 36, 39, MS 454.1.

1752: Account dated 19 Aug. 1752, *William Norris* v. *William Shirley*, 21 Nov. 1753, Frederick County, Md., Court Records, Liber H, 1753–1757, p. 189, Md. Hall of Recs.

1753: Cecilius Calvert, at London, to Rev. Thomas Bacon, 5 Jan. 1754, [William Hand Browne *et al.*, eds.], *The Calvert Papers* (Maryland Historical Society, *Fund Publications*, Nos. 28, 34, 35 [Baltimore, 1889–1899]), II, 176.

1753–1754: Sharpe, at Annapolis, Md., to Cecilius Calvert, 8 Aug. 1754, William Hand Browne *et al.*, eds., *Archives of Maryland* (Baltimore, 1883–1972), VI, 85.

1757–1758: Samuel Massey's account with Daniel Wolstenholme, 1757–1769, Corner Collection, Box I, MS 1242.

1760: Agreement of 28 July 1760, *William Buchanan* v. *Thomas Ringgold and Samuel Galloway*, 8 Oct. 1762, Chancery Records, Vol. 10 (Liber DD No. 1), 1761–1764, p. 255, Md. Hall of Recs.

1760: Receipts dated 15 Sept. 1760, Accounts of Henry Damall, 1759–1761, *ibid.*, 166.

1761: Clement Hill Papers, 1670–1805, MS 446.

1761: Advertisement of Alexander and Andrew Symmer, *Maryland Gazette* (Annapolis), 4, 11, 18 June 1761.

1761: John Pagan and Co., St. Mary's Store Ledger, 1761–1762, entry for 20 Oct. 1761, John Glassford and Co. Records, 1755–1844, Lib. Cong.

1761: William Fitzhugh Ledger "H," 1761–1764, fol. 9, Fitzhugh Account Books, 1761–1774, MS 1831.

1763–1764: Inventory, Estate of Philip Thomas, 13 Mar. 1763, 29 June 1764, Prerogative Court Records, Inventories, Vol. 84 (Liber SB No. 8), pp. 78, 83, Md. Hall of Recs.

Virginia

Virginia, as the first continental colony founded, was the first to experience problems with its circulating medium of exchange. It was also the first to try to alleviate them by increasing the currency value of its real money. Yet Virginia was the last major colony on the continent to issue paper money to supplement its circulating medium. By the time it did so in 1755, English patience with colonial paper money schemes had reached an end. Complaints that Virginians were manipulating the rate of exchange for the repayment of sterling debts and forcing debtors to accept a sharply depreciated paper currency were crucial in the debate over the Currency Act. The story of Virginia's currency is an interesting one indeed.[190]

As early as March 1631/32, in an action taken as a sign of its "developing . . . independent consciousness," the Virginia House of Burgesses petitioned the Privy Council for, among other things, "a current coyne debased to 25 per centum."[191] We know little of the economy of Virginia during this period, but it is clear from the petition that the colonists felt a need to increase the medium of exchange that served their local markets. By depreciating their currency they probably hoped not

only to retain what coinage did circulate but also to attract a bit more from outside the colony. Whatever their hopes, nothing much seems to have happened for another dozen years. In the meantime Virginians continued to keep their accounts in terms of pounds, shillings, and pence and used as their real money what coin they had and, of course, tobacco as a commodity money.[192]

The House of Burgesses waited until 1645 for a reply to its petition; then, with all England in turmoil, it acted on its own and in so doing began a century-long period during which inflating the currency value of foreign coin served as its only device for dealing with defects in the colony's circulating medium of exchange. The act of 1645 decreed that the piece of eight would pass at 6s (30p) currency; the par of exchange so established was £133.33 Virginia currency per £100 sterling. Ten years later, in 1655, a second act reduced the inflated value of the piece of eight to 5s (25p), with par thus at £111.11, but since this valuation came by custom to be applied to coins of less than full weight the new par of exchange was effectively £121.55 Virginia currency to £100 sterling. The law of 1655, reaffirmed in 1662, remained on the statute books until after the proclamation of 1704 and the act of 1708. In spite of several attempts to raise the currency value of the piece of eight, it stayed at 5s from 1655 through 1710.[193]

190. These and subsequent comments about Virginia and its paper money are dependent upon, and will be greatly elucidated by reference to, both Hemphill, "Virginia and the English Commercial System," 98–148, and Joseph Albert Ernst, "Genesis of the Currency Act of 1764: Virginia Paper Money and the Protection of British Investments," *WMQ*, 3d Ser., XXII (1965), 33–74, which he developed further in his monograph, *Money and Politics*, 43–88, and *passim*.

191. H. R. McIlwaine, ed., *Journals of the House of Burgesses of Virginia, 1619–1659* (Richmond, Va., 1905), xxxiii, 55–56. See also *ibid.*, 124–125, and Thomas Jefferson, *Notes on the State of Virginia* (1787), ed. William Peden (Chapel Hill, N.C., 1955), 170.

192. Ripley, *Financial History of Virginia*, 110–111; Philip Alexander Bruce, *Economic History of Virginia in the Seventeenth Century: An Inquiry into the Material Condition of the People* (New York, 1896), II, 495–500. See also Gov. Sir John Harvey *et al.* to Privy Council, 18 Jan. 1638/39, C.O. 1/10, fols. 8–11.

193. For the laws mentioned see Hening, ed., *Statutes at Large*, I, 308, 397, 410–411, 493, II, 125. See also Hemphill, "Virginia and the English Commercial System," 105–126. A currency value of 5s (25p) for a full-weight piece of eight of 17.5 dwt. would yield a ratio of 1.11 to 1 (3.43d [1.43p] ÷ 3.1d [1.29p] sterling per dwt.). For the customary value of the piece of eight

By custom, again, the par of exchange seems to have been at £115 Virginia currency to £100 sterling over much of that same period.[194]

Despite the provisions of the act of 1708, Virginia was not permitted immediately to alter the currency value of the piece of eight to conform to the limits established in the act. Only in 1710 did the Board of Trade and the Privy Council allow a new Virginia currency act to stand, and then it was one that merely confirmed the existing situation in which by valuing underweight pieces of eight at 5s (25p) the colony effectively valued full-weight coins at 5s 5.5d (27.3p). The

effective par was still £121.55 Virginia currency to £100 sterling, and the force of custom retained par at £115.[195] While table 3.10 shows the commercial rate of exchange "to have been consistently below par until the end of the decade after 1710," it rose to par in the late 1710s and stayed there into the 1720s. Then, during a period of some economic difficulty in the 1720s—a period common to most of the colonies—the commercial or bill rate rose, creating in Virginia the usual effect. With the bill rate above the specie export point, it became more profitable to settle debts by exporting coin rather than by using the coin in the colony to buy bills. The further result was pressure to raise the currency value of coin, which was done in 1728.[196] Silver coin was now to pass at 4d (1.7p) per pennyweight or 6s 8d (33.3p) per ounce. The new par of exchange, £125 Virginia currency per £100 sterling, remained in effect until the American Revolution.[197]

Virginians never again officially resorted to inflating the

---

see, e.g., "the present state of Virginia," enclosed in Hartwell, Blair, and Chilton to Board of Trade, 20 Oct. 1697, C.O. 5/1309, fol. 91r; the report enclosed in Gov. Bellomont to Board of Trade, 17 Oct. 1700, C.O. 5/1045, fol. 87r; Gov. Nathaniel Blakiston, at Maryland, to Board of Trade, 25 May 1701, C.O. 5/715, fol. 189r; and Robert Beverley, *The History and Present State of Virginia* (1705), ed. Louis B. Wright (Chapel Hill, N.C., 1947), 285. See also Nettels, *Money Supply*, 237; Hemphill, "Virginia and the English Commercial System," 108.

194. This was certainly the case after the passage of the Virginia act of 1710, which "merely confirmed and extended to other foreign silver coins the long-existing customary value of five shillings for a piece of eight of good metal weighing sixteen pennyweight," as Hemphill clearly demonstrated, in "Virginia and the English Commercial System," 136–140. See also Hugh Jones, *The Present State of Virginia, from Whence is Inferred a Short View of Maryland and North Carolina* (1724), ed. Richard L. Morton (Chapel Hill, N.C., 1956), 81–82. An earlier disallowed act of 1703, by attempting to set the currency value of all silver per dwt. at 3.5d (1.46p), recognized a par of about £113. Hemphill, "Virginia and the English Commercial System," 118, and his citation to C.O. 5/1314, pt. i, fol. 12r. Although par on the basis of 5s currency for the piece of eight should have been as high as £122 and seems by custom to have been the somewhat lower £115, Hemphill, on the basis of the Council's certainly confusing argument against a money bill, assumed that in 1706 par was at £100 Virginia currency to £100 sterling. *Ibid.*, 127. For the Council's statement, 20 June 1706, see H. R. McIlwaine and W. L. Hall, ed., *Executive Journals of the Council of Colonial Virginia, 1680–1754* (Richmond, Va.. 1925–1945), III, 110.

195. Hening, ed., *Statutes at Large*, III, 502–504; Hemphill, "Virginia and the English Commercial System," 136–139. The mechanisms at work in pegging customary par at Virginia at some 5% to 6% below par as usually computed after the turn of the century might have hinged on the distinction between the official English value of silver at 62d (25.8p) sterling per oz.t. and the market price for silver, which in 1710 was closer to 65d or 66d (27.1p or 27.5p) sterling per oz. The law of 1710 set the value of silver in Virginia at 3.75d (1.56p) per dwt., or 75d (31.2p) per oz. At 65d sterling per oz., the par for Virginia currency would have been £115.38. This same distinction seems to have operated later in the 18th century too.

196. Hening, ed., *Statutes at Large*, IV, 218–220; Hemphill, "Virginia and the English Commercial System," 145–147.

197. Again, at the standard rate for silver, 62d (25.8p) sterling per oz.t., par should have been £129. At the commercial price for silver, which table 1.4 shows to have averaged 64.14d (26.7p) per oz.t. during 1727–1728, par was £125. That the latter figure was accepted as par can be seen from numerous sources (e.g., Wright, *American Negotiator*, lxii). See also Hening, ed., *Statutes at Large*, V, 540.

value of their coin as a device for devaluing their currency. In this way the act of 1708 appeared to succeed in Virginia as elsewhere. Despite appearances, however, just as in all the other colonies, when economic difficulties created a demand to expand the circulating medium of exchange, Virginia resorted to paper money. It did not take such a step until 1755, when the pressures of the French and Indian War began to work on the colony's supply of money. Afterwards paper money rapidly depreciated, as the bill rate in Virginia currency recorded in table 3.10 starkly shows. When the Currency Act of 1764 forced the withdrawal of the old paper currency, Virginians returned to their earlier currency valuation. The par of exchange, as has been said, remained at £125 throughout.

Virginians bought and sold bills of exchange against extensive sterling balances in Great Britain. These balances were, in general, either the product of the sale of tobacco by Virginia planters or, alternately, the resources of the Scottish tobacco merchants. Both the planters and the Scottish tobacco firms had the usual options for transferring their moneys to Virginia. They could ship goods; they could ship coin; or they could sell bills of exchange in the colonies and receive goods or coins there in return. We have usually viewed the market for bills of exchange in the colonies through the eyes of buyers, who naturally hoped to find the bill rate low—close to par or even below it. Sellers of bills of exchange had just the opposite interest. They hoped to maximize the return in local currency for any bill sold.

The existence in Virginia of both buyers and sellers created an exchange market in bills of exchange that resembled nothing so much as the fairs of late medieval and early modern France and Spain. Without a major urban center to service the colony's financial needs, Virginians early agreed to do business at Williamsburg during the four annual periods when the courts were in session. Buyers and sellers of bills of exchange assembled there, bickered for days over the price, and finally settled on a rate satisfactory to most. Down to the time of the American Revolution, the rate of exchange in Virginia depended significantly on the transactions at Williamsburg effected during "Public Times."[198]

Bills of exchange on Great Britain negotiated in Virginia, either during court days or not, were drawn in the usual ways. The preference for good bills drawn at short sight on London increased their value. Bills on less obviously secure balances, at longer sight, or drawn on the outports—including Glasgow—sold for somewhat less.[199] But both buyers and

198. Soltow, *Economic Role of Williamsburg*, 6–8, 10–14. In 1767 William Lux of Baltimore traveled south to Williamsburg to buy a bill of exchange with Virginia paper money he had accumulated. Lux to Molleson, 2 May 1767, Lux Letter Book.

199. See, e.g., William Lee, in London, to Robert Carter Nicholas, of Williamsburg, 25 Oct. 1770: "I must again beg leave to mention that bills on Glasgow, though payable here at 30 days, and bills on Glasgow payable there at 2-1/2 per cent. less exchange, are just equal to bills on London at 60 days." William Lee Letter Books, 1769–1795, I (1769–1771), Robert E. Lee Memorial Association, Stratford Hall Plantation, Stratford, Va. See also, Wm. Lee to Francis Lightfoot Lee, 24 Apr. 1772, Arthur Lee Letter Book, 1763–1774, Houghton Library, Harvard University, Cambridge, Mass. The same 2.5 point spread was mentioned in 1727, 1770, and 1773. See Robert Carter to John Stork, of Glasgow, 19 May 1727, Robert Carter Letter Books, Alderman Library, University of Virginia, Charlottesville, as cited in Hemphill, "Virginia and the English Commercial System," 144n; Andrew Black, of Boston, to Messrs. James Glassford and Co., of Norfolk, 2 Apr. 1770, Jamieson Papers, XI, no. 2521; Charles Yates to Samuel Martin, 10 Dec. 1773, cited in Soltow, *Economic Role of Williamsburg*, 165n, from the Letter Book of Charles Yates, 1773–1783, Alderman Library; Francis Jerdone, of New Kent Co., Va., to Messrs. Alexander Speirs and Hugh Brown, of Glasgow, 15 May 1756, Letter Book of Francis Jerdone, 1756–1763, Jerdone Papers, College of William and Mary, Williamsburg, Va.

sellers could resort to other alternatives if they did not like the price for their bills locally. Sellers of bills found the markets of Maryland, Pennsylvania, and even Boston sometimes more attractive. The Scottish factors especially seem to have played the market to find the best return for the Glasgow bills on London (that is, bills drawn on Glasgow merchants but payable in London); they would sell their bills in Philadelphia and the upper Chesapeake and ship the proceeds—in gold, silver, and even paper currency—southward by coastwise trading vessels.[200] Before the middle of the eighteenth century London bills returned protested to Virginia drew the customary assessment for damages, although at a somewhat lower rate than usual, 15 percent of the value of the bill, and interest at 10 percent from the date of protest.[201] But in October 1748 a new law effectively repealed earlier statutes and eliminated all charges for damages, leaving only interest payable on protested bills.[202] While I have not yet seen evidence of bills drawn at Virginia on places in Europe other than Great Britain, any shipments of tobacco to Amsterdam or Bordeaux would have allowed for this possibility. Such bills would have been negotiated in ways similar to what was done at Boston, New York, and Philadelphia.

As for intercolonial bills of exchange negotiated at Virginia, we have less than adequate information, which probably means that they were used only infrequently—a conclusion that is supported by the fact that Virginians usually paid with tobacco, other agricultural products, and sterling bills on London when trading for commodities with their neighbors. John van Cortlandt of New York, who traded extensively with Virginia, used a ratio of 1 to 1.33 after 1764 to equate Virginia currency with New York currency. While accounts were certainly settled on this basis, no bills of exchange were negotiated. Virginians seemed well aware of the rate of exchange in Pennsylvania, and negotiations between the two colonies were no doubt based on the rates of exchange in each of them. William Lux of Baltimore settled his accounts with Virginia correspondents using the two bill rates, although, as we have seen, not without some complaint.[203]

One wonders how Virginians and North Carolinians handled their exchange, given the considerable differences in their two rates of exchange. The suspicion is that Virginia–North Carolina negotiations were based on the two bill rates. If so, the use of the commercial rate of exchange for settling accounts with Virginia extended from Pennsylvania through North Carolina and thereby defines for us the region of Virginia's closest colonial trading partners.

200. Soltow, *Economic Role of Williamsburg*, 165–176. For more of this, see Letter Books of James Robinson, 1767–1773, 1772–1774, Bundle 0, Letter Books and Correspondence of William Cuninghame and Co., Glasgow, 1761–1789, Box 58, Collections Deposited by Messrs. John C. Brodie, W.S., Gift and Deposit No. 247, Scottish Record Office, Edinburgh.

201. Before 1666 the rate had been 30%. Hening, ed., *Statutes at Large*, II, 171, 243. See also William Fitzhugh to Cornelius Serjaant, of Bristol, 23 July 1693, in Richard Beale Davis, ed., *William Fitzhugh and His Chesapeake World, 1676–1701: The Fitzhugh Letters and Other Documents*, Virginia Historical Society Documents, No. 3 (Chapel Hill, N.C., 1963), 316.

202. Hening, ed., *Statutes at Large*, VI, 85–87.

203. For these examples, see the discussion above at the end of the section on Maryland in this chapter. Because of the difference in par values, Maryland paper money did not circulate all that easily in Virginia and vice versa. Lux to Molleson, 20 Jan. 1767, and to Col. Francis Willis, of Gloucester Co., Va., 21 Jan. 1767, Lux Letter Book.

TABLE 3.10. Rate of Exchange: Virginia on London, 1691–1775

(Pounds Virginia Currency per £100 Sterling)

Year	Jan.	Feb.	Mar.	Apr.	May	June	July	Aug.	Sept.	Oct.	Nov.	Dec.	Average
1691		110.00	110.00										110.00
1692													
1693													
1694													
1695													
1696													
1697													
1698													
1699													
1700													
1701													
1702													
1703													
1704													
1705													
1706						115.00							115.00
1707													
1708													
1709				105.25						110.00			107.62
1710													
1711							110.00		112.00			106.00	108.50
1712		110.00											110.00
1713													
1714											110.00		110.00
1715													
1716													

TABLE 3.10 (Continued): Virginia on London (Pounds Virginia Currency per £100 Sterling)

Year	Jan.	Feb.	Mar.	Apr.	May	June	July	Aug.	Sept.	Oct.	Nov.	Dec.	Average
1717											105.50		105.50
1718													
1719	[110.00]											111.00	110.50
1720	115.00						115.00						115.00
1721										115.00			115.00
1722					115.00	115.00							115.00
1723		115.00			115.00								115.00
1724				115.00	115.00	116.33					115.00	[119.88]	116.44
1725		120.00		115.00	115.00								117.50
1726			115.00	115.00							113.02		114.34
1727							117.50					115.00	116.25
1728					115.00	125.00							120.00
1729						117.50			120.00				118.75
1730				122.33	117.50								119.92
1731				122.33									122.33
1732				122.33	120.00								121.16
1733								120.00					120.00
1734								120.00					120.00
1735								120.00					120.00
1736					125.00			120.41					122.70
1737								121.63					121.63
1738				125.00				122.50					123.75
1739								122.50					122.50
1740											119.17		119.17
1741											120.53		120.53
1742					120.00						120.00		120.00

TABLE 3.10 (Continued): Virginia on London (Pounds Virginia Currency per £100 Sterling)

Year	Jan.	Feb.	Mar.	Apr.	May	June	July	Aug.	Sept.	Oct.	Nov.	Dec.	Average
1743											120.00		120.00
1744						120.00		122.50	125.00				121.88
1745			130.00						122.79		130.00		127.60
1746	125.00		133.33			133.33	130.00	133.33		145.00	130.00		131.87
1747			136.69					133.33		135.00			135.01
1748			135.00	135.42		133.33				130.00	125.00		132.29
1749				122.50		122.50				125.00	122.50	[127.50]	123.75
1750	[127.50]		125.00		125.00		125.00				127.50		125.94
1751	[130.00]			125.00						130.00	130.50		128.42
1752	[130.00]						127.50		130.00	132.00	[130.00]		129.92
1753	[130.00]			128.00					130.00		[130.00]		129.50
1754	[127.50]						130.00		120.28		[130.00]		127.55
1755				130.00		130.00					[127.50]	130.00	129.38
1756				127.50	130.00	125.00		125.00		132.50	[130.00]	136.00	128.44
1757				138.25		140.00	135.00		140.00	140.00	[142.50]	145.00	139.71
1758			140.00	140.00		140.00			135.00	135.00	[135.00]	140.00	137.92
1759	140.00	140.00	134.33	135.31	135.00	140.00	140.00	145.00	145.00	145.00	[135.00]	145.00	139.97
1760	143.75	142.50	141.25	140.83	140.83	141.04	141.25	143.00	142.75	142.50	135.00	[142.50]	141.43
1761	141.25	140.00	140.00	140.00	142.92	145.83	140.00	142.50	155.00	145.00	145.83	146.25	143.72
1762	145.83	145.42	145.00	149.67	148.33	157.50	150.00	155.00	155.00	160.42	155.00	161.67	152.40
1763	158.34	155.00	157.50	160.00	160.00	160.00	160.62	160.94	161.25	163.02	161.88	[160.00]	159.88
1764	160.00	160.00	160.00	160.00	160.00	160.00	160.00	160.00	161.25	162.50	162.50	162.50	160.73
1765	162.50	162.50	165.00	160.00	164.17	163.44	163.12	162.81	162.50	162.50	155.83	140.00	160.36
1766	140.00	140.00	123.75	130.00	123.75	125.56	126.10	130.00	125.00	125.60	126.21	125.83	128.48
1767	125.00	124.69	125.00	126.25	125.00	125.56	130.00	125.00	125.00	125.00	125.00	125.00	125.54
1768	123.12	125.00	126.25	125.00	125.00	125.62	125.00	125.00	125.00	125.00	124.84	125.00	124.99
1769	124.17	122.08	120.00	124.17	122.27	122.50	122.50	122.50	125.00	120.50	121.25	116.67	121.97

TABLE 3.10 (Continued): Virginia on London (Pounds Virginia Currency per £100 Sterling)

Year	Jan.	Feb.	Mar.	Apr.	May	June	July	Aug.	Sept.	Oct.	Nov.	Dec.	Average
1770	121.29	111.25	116.25	117.50	115.00	115.95	115.83	120.34	120.00	123.86	120.00	118.75	118.00
1771	120.00	*130.00*	140.00	*130.00*	120.00	120.00	120.00	*120.00*	120.00	121.25	122.00	120.00	123.60
1772	*120.00*	120.00	128.00	*124.00*	120.00	126.00	120.00	125.00	*125.00*	125.00	125.00	125.13	123.59
1773			125.00	127.00	130.00	138.75			130.00	132.13		132.07	129.75
1774	132.50		127.50	129.17	132.50		128.75		135.00		131.66	133.33	130.30
1775			115.00	115.00	115.00							125.00	120.00

Notes and Sources: **TABLE 3.10**

Figures inserted in square brackets are assigned to that month arbitrarily; figures in italics are straight-line interpolations based on the two neighboring quotations.

1691, 1721: Royal African Co., Copybook of Letters Received, 1720–1746, p. 21, Copybook of Bills of Exchange Received, 1691–1693, T. 70/4, 276, Public Record Office.

1706–1749: H. R. McIlwaine and W. L. Hall, eds., *Executive Journals of the Council of Colonial Virginia, 1680–1754* (Richmond, Va., 1925–1945), III, 110, 457, 536, IV, 14, 35, 68, 82, 99, 215, 239, 274, 279, 369, V, 86, 157, 172, 209, 2 9–220, 233, 243, 248, 292, 303. I have been directed to this, as to much else below, by the work of John M. Hemphill II, especially his "Virginia and the English Commercial System, 1689–1733: Studies in the Development and Fluctuations of a Colonial Economy under Imperial Control" (Ph.D. diss., Princeton University, 1964).

1709–1711: Louis B. Wright and Marion Tinling, eds., *The Secret Diary of William Byrd of Westover, 1709–1712* (Richmond, Va., 1941), 27, 100, 374, 404, 457.

1711: H. R. McIlwaine, ed., *Legislative Journals of the Council of Colonial Virginia, 1619–1776* (Richmond, Va., 1918–1919), I, 515–516, 529.

1711: H. R. McIlwaine, ed., *Journals of the House of Burgesses of Virginia, 1703–1712* (Richmond, Va., 1905–1915), 326.

1712–1729: Inventories of various decedents' estates, York County Court, "Orders, Wills & Ca.," No. 14 (1709–1716), pt. i, 135, pt. ii, 373, No. 16 (1721–1729), pt. i, 235, 310, pt. ii, 341, 473, 525, 613, York County Courthouse, Yorktown, Va.

1719–1720: Robert Bristow, at London, to Thomas Booth, at Va., 30 Dec. 1719, 28 Jan. 1719/20, Robert Bristow Letter Book, Virginia State Library, Richmond, as quoted by Hemphill, "Virginia and the English Commercial System," 142n.

1722–1725: Annual accounts of the receiver of the quitrents, 1722–1725, enclosed in Lt. Gov. Alexander Spotswood, at Virginia, to Board of Trade, 11 June 1722, and Lt. Gov. Hugh Drysdale, at Virginia, to Board of Trade, 29 June 1723, 10 July 1724, and 30 May 1725, C.O. 5/1319, fols. 73r, 123r, 204r, 228r, P.R.O.

1724: Inventories, No. 1, 1723–1746, fol. 29r, Westmoreland County Courthouse, Montross, Va.

1724: Answers to Queries from the Society for the Propagation of the Gospel in Foreign Parts by Rev. John Brunskill, Rev. Alexander Forbes, and Rev. John Bagg, General Correspondence, XII, nos. 41–44, 51, 60–72, Fulham Papers, Lambeth Palace Library, London.

1725–1726: Diary of Robert "King" Carter, 13 Feb. 1725, 22 Mar. 1726, Carter Family Papers, Alderman Library, University of Virginia, Charlottesville, as quoted by Hemphill, "Virginia and the English Commercial System," 309.

Notes and Sources: **TABLE 3.10 (Continued)**

1727–1729: Letters of Robert Carter, 26 July and 28 July 1727, 21 May 1728, and 15 Sept. 1729, Robert Carter Letter Books, Carter Papers, 1705–1785, Virginia Historical Society, Richmond, as quoted by Hemphill, *ibid*.

1727–1732: Letters of Robert Carter, 12 Dec. 1727, 29 May 1732, Robert Carter Letter Books, Carter Papers, as quoted by Hemphill, *ibid*.

1728: Lt. Gov. William Gooch, at Williamsburg, Va., to secretary of state, 9 June 1728, C.O. 5/1337, pt. i, fol. 125r.

1729–1730: Edmund Bagge Account Book, 1726–1733, pp. 93, 125, Manuscript Collections, Research Department, Colonial Williamsburg Foundation, Williamsburg, Va., as quoted by Hemphill, "Virginia and the English Commercial System," 309.

1733–1749: Annual Statements of Account of Blair-Prentis-Cary Partnership, Papers of William Prentis, 1733–1780, Univ. Va. After midcentury the quoted rate in these accounts remained at par, £125. See Edward M. Riley, "William Prentis & Co.: Business Success in Eighteenth-Century Williamsburg," *Financial Executive*, XXXVI (1968), 37–38, 41.

1738: [William Douglass], *An Essay concerning Silver and Paper Currencies, More Especially with Regard to British Colonies in New-England* (Boston, [1738]), 4.

1743–1775: Edward Dixon Records, 1743–1796, Library of Congress.

1745–1746: *Virginia Gazette* (Williamsburg), 21 Nov. 1745, 9 Jan. 1745/46.

1746, 1761: Isaac Greenleaf, at Williamsburg, Va., to John Reynell, at Philadelphia, 30 Oct. 1746, and bill of exchange, 28 Feb. 1761, John Reynell Correspondence, 1729–1773, Coates and Reynell Papers, Historical Society of Pennsylvania, Philadelphia.

1749: Francis Jerdone, at Yorktown, Va., to William Montgomery, 12 May 1749, "Letter Book of Francis Jerdone," *William and Mary Quarterly*, 1st Ser., XI (1903), 155.

1750–1755: "Average Annual Exchange Rates, Virginia Currency on Sterling, 1740–1775," prepared by John M. Hemphill, as published in James H. Soltow, *The Economic Role of Williamsburg* (Williamsburg, Va., 1965), table XV, after p. 166. These are annual average figures, the components of which are not indicated. I have used them here only for those five years for which I have little or no other data. They are assigned arbitrarily to Jan. of each year and are averaged with any other data for the same year.

1752–1773: Robert Carter Nicholas to Purdie and Dixon, editors of *Virginia Gazette* (Williamsburg), 30 Sept. 1773, as reprinted, "Paper Money in Colonial Virginia," *WMQ*, 1st Ser., XX (1912), 255.

1755–1764: Joseph Albert Ernst, "Genesis of the Currency Act of 1764: Virginia Paper Money and the Protection of British Investments," *ibid.*, 3d Ser., XXII (1965), table II, 45. As there appears to be no overlap between the sources used in Ernst's table and those used here, they are all averaged to obtain the several annual mean figures.

1755–1773: Victor S. Clark, *History of Manufactures in the United States*, [rev. ed.] (Washington, D.C., 1929), III, 362.

1756: Francis Jerdone, [at New Kent Co., Va.], to Messrs. Alexander Speirs and Hugh Brown, at Glasgow, 15 May 1756, Letter Book of Francis Jerdone, 1756–1763, Jerdone Papers, College of William and Mary, Williamsburg, Va. See also "Proceedings of the Virginia Committee of Correspondence," *Virginia Magazine of History and Biography*, XI (1904), 347, XII (1904), 1–4.

1757–1764: Extract from Judgments and Decrees of the General Court of Virginia, Benjamin Waller, clerk of General Court, 29 Aug. 1764, enclosure in Lt. Gov. Francis Fauquier, at Williamsburg, Va., to Board of Trade, 30 Aug. 1764, C.O. 323/19, fol. 51r.

1759: Henry Callister, at Oxford, Md., to Ellis Cunliffe and Co., at Liverpool, 18 and 30 Apr. 1759, Henry Callister Letter Books, 1741–1766, fol. 301, Callister Family Papers, 1741–1788, Maryland Diocesan Archives of the Protestant Episcopal Church, Maryland Historical Society, Baltimore.

1760–1761: Bills of exchange dated Virginia, 3 Nov. 1760, 17 Mar. 1761, in papers concerning the condemnation of the ship *Indian Trader*, 1761, H.C.A. 32/202, P.R.O.

1760–1762: Correspondence, Papers of Samuel and John Galloway, 1739–1812, New York Public Library, New York City.

Notes and Sources: **TABLE 3.10 (Continued)**

1760–1764: Galloway Correspondence, Galloway Business Papers, 1654–1819, Galloway-Maxey-Markoe Family Papers, 1654–1888, Lib. Cong.

1761–1768: William Fitzhugh Ledgers "H" and "I," 1761–1769, Fitzhugh Account Books, 1761–1774, MS 1831, Maryland Historical Society, Baltimore.

1761–1775: Neil Jamieson Papers, 1757–1789, *passim*, Lib. Cong.

1763–1770: Samuel and William Vernon Papers, 1750–1775, Box VII, "Slavery MSS.," New-York Historical Society, New York City.

1763–1771: Virginia Letters, Brown Papers, Miscellaneous Correspondence, John Carter Brown Library, Brown University, Providence, R.I.

1770–1772: Letters to Charles Steuart, at London, from William Aitcheson, at Norfolk, Va., 2 Jan. 1770, James Parker, at Norfolk, Va., 31 Dec. 1771, and Thomas Rudoach, at Port Royal, Va., 30 May 1772, Charles Steuart Correspondence, Steuart Papers, 1758–1798, MS 5026, fols. 1–3, MS 5027, fols. 82–83, 160–167, National Library of Scotland, Edinburgh.

1770–1773: Letters of James Robinson, Robinson Letter Books, 1767–1773, 1772–1774, Bundle O, Letter Books and Correspondence of William Cuninghame and Co., Glasgow, 1761–1789, Box 58, Collections Deposited by Messrs. John C. Brodie, W.S., Gift and Deposit No. 247, Scottish Record Office, Edinburgh.

1771–1774: Invoice Book, Alexandria, Va., 1770–1784, Robert T. Hooe Papers, N.Y. Pub. Lib.

1773: Charles Yates to Samuel Martin, 10 Dec. 1773, Letter Book of Charles Yates, 1773–1783, Univ. Va., as cited in James H. Soltow, *The Economic Role of Williamsburg* (Williamsburg, Va., 1965), 165n.

North Carolina

North and South Carolina were one colony until 1712. They therefore shared much of their early monetary history. As with all the other colonies, Carolina's attempts to expand its circulating medium of exchange progressed through several stages in the seventeenth century. Commodity money in the Carolinas suffered from the lack of a dominant staple commodity. Instead, it was necessary to set official values for several agricultural products, with considerable confusion as the result. Carolinians "cryed up" their coin too. Until 1683 the piece of eight had a currency value of 5s (25p), for an effective par of £111.11 Carolina currency. In 1683 a new law increased the currency value of the piece of eight to 6s (30p), for a par of £133.33; in 1691 it was raised once again to a par of £150; and in November 1701 to something more.[204] The last law was repealed almost immediately, and the customary par at the introduction of paper money into the Carolinas in 1703 was £150 Carolina currency to £100 sterling, a level it retained through 1712, when North Carolina and South Carolina were split into two separate colonies.[205] Later, in 1715,

North Carolina explicitly decreed that its own paper currency was to pass at £150 currency to £100 sterling.[206]

Between 1712 and 1748 North Carolina's paper money experienced an enormous depreciation, on the order of that of Massachusetts. Finally in 1748 an attempt was made to establish Proclamation Money as the value of North Carolina currency. Old Tenor, the pre-1748 valuation of North Carolina currency, was reduced to New Tenor at a ratio of 7.5 to 1; the par of exchange was lowered from £1,000 to £133.33 North Carolina currency per £100 sterling.[207] Again, however, the commercial rate of exchange rose in North Carolina as a result of continuing economic difficulties. By the time of the Seven Years' War the commercial value of the piece of eight was 8s (40p), and the par of exchange £177.77. This continued to be the case until after the beginning of the Revolution.[208]

204. The rate quoted is based on the comparative value per dwt. of the full-weight piece of eight in sterling, 4.62d, and of the 13 dwt. coin in Carolina currency, 3.09d per dwt. Ripley, *Financial History of Virginia*, 115, citing John H. Hickcox, *History of the Bills of Credit; or, Paper Money Issued by New York, from 1709 to 1789* (New York, 1866), 10, and B. R. Carroll, ed., *Historical Collections of South Carolina (1492–1776)* (New York, 1836), II, 137; Thomas Cooper and David J. McCord, eds., *The Statutes at Large of South Carolina* (Columbia, S.C., 1836–1841), II, 72–73, 77, 94–95, 130, 156–157, 163–164, 178, 214–215, 299, 332–333. The text of the Mar. 1701 law is not in this collection, but see William L. Saunders and Walter Clark, eds., *The State Records of North Carolina* (Winston and Goldsboro, N.C., 1886–1907), XXV, 142. See also Nettels, *Money Supply*, 241n.

205. For the rate of exchange in the Carolinas prior to 1712, see table 3.12 below.

206. Saunders and Clark, eds., *State Records of North Carolina*, III, 178, IV, 418. For this and all other remarks about North Carolina's paper money, see Bullock, *Monetary History of the United States*, 125–183; Brock, *Currency of the American Colonies*, 106–113, 428–446; and Ernst, *Money and Politics*, 199–207, 220–230, 293–300.

207. *A Collection of All of the Public Acts of Assembly, of the Province of North-Carolina: Now in Force and Use* (New Bern, N.C., 1752), 266–270; Saunders and Clark, eds., *State Records of North Carolina*, XXIII, 292–296. See also *ibid.*, IV, 345, XXIII, 392–393. "The old currency of North Carolina, know as 'Old Proc.,' was superseded by the issue of 1748, which was henceforth known as 'Proc.'" Bullock, *Monetary History of the United States*, 156. See also Hugh Williamson, *The History of North Carolina* (Philadelphia, 1812), II, 114–115.

208. For 8s (40p) as the customary value of the piece of eight "by long usage" in North Carolina, see John Rutherford to Board of Trade, 19 June 1756, C.O. 5/297, fol. 366v; Saunders and Clark, eds., *State Records of North Carolina*, XXIV, 23, 185, 256, 321; Sec. of Finance Robert Morris to president of Congress, 15 Jan. 1782, Jared Sparks, ed., *The Diplomatic Correspondence of the American Revolution*, XII (Boston, 1830), 91; Williamson, *History of North Carolina*, II, 115; Bullock, *Monetary History of the United States*, 191–192n.

Information about the negotiation of bills of exchange in North Carolina is very scanty. Even quotations of the rate of exchange are very few, as table 3.11 gives evidence. We are forced regularly to fall back upon the price of silver and the par of exchange as surrogate values for the bill rate. As for the mechanical aspects of drawing bills, we can only presume that they were much the same in North Carolina as they were elsewhere, especially in South Carolina and Virginia. The law governing damages upon protested bills of exchange was copied directly from Virginia's early law and set the rate at 15 percent.[209] At a guess, North Carolinians probably exchanged with their near neighbors, South Carolina and Virginia, on the basis of a comparison of their respective commercial rates of exchange and with all other colonies using ratios based on par. Our ability to answer these questions more completely is restricted by a lack of commercial records for North Carolina.[210]

209. *Collection of Public Acts of North-Carolina*, 147–148; Saunders and Clark, eds., *State Records of North Carolina*, II, 167, III, 188, XXIII, 81, 177–178.
210. H. Roy Merrens, *Colonial North Carolina in the Eighteenth Century: A Study in Historical Geography* (Chapel Hill, N.C., 1964), *passim*.

TABLE 3.11. **Rate of Exchange: North Carolina on London, 1712–1775**
(Pounds North Carolina Currency per £100 Sterling)

Year	Jan.	Feb.	Mar.	Apr.	May	June	July	Aug.	Sept.	Oct.	Nov.	Dec.	Average
1712													
1713													
1714													
1715											150.00	[150.00]	150.00
1716													
1717													
1718													
1719													
1720													
1721													
1722												[500.00]	500.00
1723													
1724	500.00												500.00
1725													
1726													
1727													
1728													
1729												[500.00]	500.00
1730													
1731					650.00								650.00
1732													
1733													
1734													
1735												720.00	720.00
1736										700.00			700.00
1737			1,000.00						700.00	900.00			866.67
1738													
1739			1,000.00										1,000.00

TABLE 3.11 (Continued): **North Carolina on London** (Pounds North Carolina Currency per £100 Sterling)

Year	Jan.	Feb.	Mar.	Apr.	May	June	July	Aug.	Sept.	Oct.	Nov.	Dec.	Average
1740		1,000.00	1,000.00					933.33					966.66
1741	1,000.00												1,000.00
1742													
1743													
1744													
1745			1,000.00										1,000.00
1746						1,000.00							1,000.00
1747													
1748	[1,000.00]			133.33							146.67		1,033.33
1749													
1750									133.33				133.33
1751													
1752													
1753													
1754												[166.67]	166.67
1755	160.00												160.00
1756						179.80							179.80
1757													
1758													
1759	190.00		190.00								180.00		185.00
1760					190.00			190.00					190.00
1761												200.00	200.00
1762			200.00										200.00
1763					200.00								200.00
1764	[188.00]					190.00					200.00	200.00	192.67
1765						200.00							200.00
1766													
1767						179.25						[166.67]	172.96
1768					180.00								180.00
1769													

TABLE 3.11 (Continued): North Carolina on London (Pounds North Carolina Currency per £100 Sterling)

Year	Jan.	Feb.	Mar.	Apr.	May	June	July	Aug.	Sept.	Oct.	Nov.	Dec.	Average
1770													
1771													
1772							160.00						160.00
1773													
1774												[175.00]	175.00
1775													

Notes and Sources: **TABLE 3.11**

Figures inserted in square brackets are assigned to that month arbitrarily.

Note that in computing the average for 1748, the values of the Apr. and Nov. figures are increased by a factor of 7.5 in order to make the average comparable with earlier years. The average could be reduced by the same ratio in order to compare it with later years.

1715: "Mem[orandum] Concerning the Endowment of the Church in North Carolina," [Apr. 1723?], General Correspondence, VI, no. 214, Fulham Papers, Lambeth Palace Library, London. See also Nicholas Trott, ed., *The Laws of the British Plantations in America, Relating to the Church and the Clergy, Religion and Learning* (London, 1721), 88.

1715–1767: William L. Saunders and Walter Clark, eds., *The State Records of North Carolina* (Winston and Goldsboro, N.C., 1886–1907), III, 178, 283, IV, 24, 225, 246, 266, 282–283, 345, 418, 419, 529, 558, 574, 576, 588, 754, 808, 878, 1073, V, 318, VI, 4, 17, 134, 249, 305, 598–599, 612, 621, 712, 988, 1046, 1047, 1048, 1057, 1245, 1304, VII, 491, 493. See also "State of the Paper Currency in the British Plantations in America," C.O. 323/10, fol. 164, Public Record Office.

1724: Bill of exchange drawn on Col. Edward Moseley, of N.C., by James Moore, at Charleston, S.C., 24 Jan. 1723/24, as recorded in Thomas Amory Letter Book, 1723–1725, and in Francis Holmes account with Thomas Amory in Amory Estate Papers, 1697–1724, Amory Family Papers, Library of Congress.

1740: [William Douglass], *A Discourse concerning the Currencies of the British Plantations in America* (Boston, 1740), 18, 20.

1748: William Douglass, *A Summary, Historical and Political, of the First Planting, Progressive Improvements, and Present State of the British Settlements in North America* (Boston, 1749–1751), I, 494n.

1764: Hugh Williamson, *The History of North Carolina* (Philadelphia, 1812), II, 115.

1765: James Reed, at New Bern, N.C., to the secretary of the Society for the Propagation of the Gospel in Foreign Parts, 10 July 1765, General Correspondence, VI, no. 302–303, Fulham Papers.

1768: Account of Messrs. John Jamieson and Son, 21 May 1768, Neil Jamieson Papers, 1757–1789, XII, no. 2768, Lib. Cong.

1772: James Iredell, at Edenton, N.C., to Francis Iredell, at Bristol, 20 July 1772, in Griffith J. McRee, *Life and Correspondence of James Iredell* (New York, 1857–1858), I, 115.

1774: [Hugh Gaine], *Gaine's Universal Register, or, American and British Kalendar, for the Year 1775* (New York, [1774]), 79.

South Carolina

Since North and South Carolina existed under one government until 1712, what is said above about the early period of North Carolina's monetary history applies for South Carolina too. South Carolina's issue of paper currency in 1703 sufficed for the entire colony for the next ten years and served as a model for its northern sibling when the two separated.[211] South Carolinians experienced similar if only slightly less steep inflation of their paper money, which compared with that of North Carolina. The major difference in the monetary history of the two colonies was that South Carolina did not deflate the value of its paper money in the late 1740s. This decision stemmed more from strength than from weakness, since by that decade South Carolina's paper money had attained a security and stability rare in the colonies. The par of exchange between London and South Carolina remained at £700 South Carolina currency to £100 sterling from the 1730s through the 1770s.[212] As usual, the commercial rate of exchange fluctuated around par (see table 3.12).

South Carolina is thus typical of the majority of the English colonies on the North American continent with regard to its real money. The colonists there used a combination similar to that used in Massachusetts, Pennsylvania, and everywhere else: commodity money, overvalued coin, and paper. They denominated all of these by the same terms as the moneys of account of Great Britain and the other colonies: pounds, shillings, and pence. But, despite these several points of coincidence, the key fact to appreciate is that the value of South Carolina currency was not the same as currencies used elsewhere.

For just that reason, South Carolinians maintained foreign exchange relationships as much with their near neighbors as they did with merchants in London and Portugal. They negotiated bills of exchange in the usual way, whether overseas bills or intercolonial bills. South Carolinians shared in the advantages common to the Chesapeake colonies when they drew bills on London. Exports of the colony's agricultural products, especially rice and indigo, created balances in England against which bills of exchange could be drawn. Bills drawn by reputable planters on an established mercantile house payable in London at short sight were always preferred and therefore sold at a higher price. As Henry Laurens wrote in 1767: "The method of doing business here is to . . . ship

---

211. For the history of South Carolina's paper money see Brock, *Currency of the American Colonies*, 114–127, 446–462; Ernst, *Money and Politics*, 30–33, 215–220, 334–350. See also Richard M. Jellison's articles, "Antecedents of the South Carolina Currency Acts of 1736 and 1746," *WMQ*, 3d Ser., XVI (1959), 556–567, and "Paper Currency in Colonial South Carolina: A Reappraisal," *South Carolina Historical Magazine*, LXII (1969), 134–147, which were derived from his "Paper Currency in Colonial South Carolina, 1703–1764" (Ph.D. diss., Indiana University, 1952).

212. The piece of eight should have been worth 31s 6d (157.5p) South Carolina currency at this rate. In fact, over much of the period the official piece of eight maintained a value of 31s (155p), and in 1752 the legislature raised the rate from 31s to 31s 10d (159.2p). See, e.g., Brock, *Currency of the American Colonies*, 446–447, 456. See also "An Account of the Rise and Progress of the Paper Bills of Credit in South Carolina," 1700–1739, in Cooper and McCord, eds., *Statutes of South Carolina*, IX, 780. There the

market price of silver is given as 7s 6d (37.5p) currency per oz.t. in 1700, 8s (40p) in 1710, £1 7s 6d (137.5p) in 1720, £1 16s 3d (181.2p) in 1730, and £2 3s 0d (215p) in 1739. The authorship of the "account" is usually ascribed to Lt. Gov. William Bull, Sr.; see M. Eugene Sirmans, *Colonial South Carolina: A Political History, 1663–1763* (Chapel Hill, N.C., 1966), 368. Then, in Mar. 1771, "The principal merchants, land-holders [and] mechanics" of Charleston agreed to take the piece of eight at 32s 6d (162.5p), or at a rate of £722. *The South-Carolina Gazette; and Country Journal* (Charleston), 5 Mar. 1771.

goods and . . . to draw as soon as the bills of loading are signed upon some person in England at 30 to 40 days payable in London."[213] Bills with less attractive pedigrees tended to sell at lower prices. Bills not accepted and returned protested were subject to a penalty payment of 15 percent for damages and interest at 8 percent from the date of protest.[214] The 15 percent rate for damages, the lower of the two rates common to the continental colonies, was characteristic of colonies in which the legislature was more heavily influenced by those selling bills than by those buying them.

Early in the eighteenth century intercolonial exchange transactions that involved South Carolina relied more on the comparative bill rates of the two places than was usual elsewhere. This condition might have been caused by the rapid inflation of the 1720s and 1730s, the effect of which would certainly have influenced such negotiations well into the next ten years. It was true even with exchange between South Carolina and Boston in the 1740s, as the letter book of Charlestonian Robert Pringle gives evidence.[215] Later in the 1750s and 1760s there seems to have been a more frequent reference to "the par of exchange for dollars," as Henry Laurens wrote a correspondent in Philadelphia.[216] In the same decades South Carolinians exchanged with both Barbados and Jamaica at a ratio of 5 to 1 and, in 1773, at 4 to 1 with New York. These too were based on the comparative pars of exchange.[217]

213. Laurens to Penn, 24 Dec. 1767, *Papers of Henry Laurens*, V, 528. See also Laurens to Richard Oswald and Co., at London, 23 Aug. 1756, *ibid.*, II, 295.

214. Sellers, *Charleston Business*, 78. See also Pringle to John Erving, at Boston, 13 Mar. 1743/44, Walter B. Edgar, ed., *The Letterbook of Robert Pringle, 1737–1745* (Columbia, S.C., 1972), II, 665 ("re-exchange is 15 per cent here on bills"); Laurens to Nathaniel and George Bethune, at Boston, 25 July 1764, *Papers of Henry Laurens*, IV, 356; *Well's Register; Together with an Almanack for 1775* (Charleston, S.C., [1774]). This last is a publication of the rates adopted by the Charleston Chamber of Commerce.

215. Pringle to Peter Faneuil, at Boston, 12 Apr. 1742, and to Erving, 11 Feb. 1742/43, Edgar, ed., *Letterbook of Robert Pringle*, I, 362–363, II, 503.

216. Laurens to Robert Waln, at Philadelphia, 6 Dec. 1762, *Papers of Henry Laurens*, III, 185.

217. *Ibid.*, II, *passim*; Levinus Clarkson, at Charleston, to David van Horne, at New York, 9 Mar. 1773, Clarkson Papers.

TABLE 3.12. **Rate of Exchange: South Carolina on London, 1699–1775**

(Pounds South Carolina Currency per £100 Sterling)

Year	Jan.	Feb.	Mar.	Apr.	May	June	July	Aug.	Sept.	Oct.	Nov.	Dec.	Average
1699						111.75							111.75
1700						146.00							146.00
1701													
1702													
1703		150.00											150.00
1704													
1705													
1706													
1707							150.00						150.00
1708			150.00										150.00
1709													
1710												[150.00]	150.00
1711			150.00								150.00		150.00
1712						150.00							150.00
1713												[150.00]	150.00
1714												[200.00]	200.00
1715								200.00				[400.00]	300.00
1716													
1717												[575.00]	575.00
1718					500.00								500.00
1719													
1720												[400.00]	400.00
1721												[533.33]	533.33
1722	[520.00]	600.00										[600.00]	580.00
1723					650.00							[700.00]	675.00
1724		600.00										[700.00]	650.00
1725		656.48					650.00					[710.00]	672.16

TABLE 3.12 (Continued): **South Carolina on London** (Pounds South Carolina Currency per £100 Sterling)

Year	Jan.	Feb.	Mar.	Apr.	May	June	July	Aug.	Sept.	Oct.	Nov.	Dec.	Average
1726												[700.00]	700.00
1727				700.00		700.00						[700.00]	700.00
1728												[700.00]	700.00
1729												[700.00]	700.00
1730	[600.00]											[687.50]	643.75
1731								700.00				[700.00]	700.00
1732												[700.00]	700.00
1733												[700.00]	700.00
1734												[700.00]	700.00
1735												[700.00]	700.00
1736	[750.00]								740.00		740.00	[740.00]	743.33
1737	800.00	750.00	747.01	701.75				750.00			850.00	[740.00]	753.10
1738							750.00		800.00				775.00
1739			750.00		830.00	800.00	800.00	800.00			805.30	800.00	791.91
1740				800.00	800.00		800.00	800.00	800.00	813.56	800.00	750.00	795.95
1741	720.00	700.00	685.00	680.00									690.83
1742	700.00	700.00	700.00	700.00	700.00	700.00	700.00	695.84	691.67	700.00	700.00	700.00	698.96
1743	700.00	700.00	700.00		700.00	700.00	700.00			700.00	700.00	700.00	700.00
1744	700.00	700.00		700.00	700.00	700.00	700.00		700.00	700.00	700.00	700.00	700.00
1745	700.00	700.00		700.00									700.00
1746													
1747						762.50	750.00	741.67	750.00	770.00	775.00		760.74
1748	775.00	775.00	775.00					750.00				762.50	762.50
1749	740.62	718.75	727.50	727.50	727.50	718.75	707.50	730.85	741.25	715.83	728.33	720.00	725.36
1750	714.17	706.88	701.25	703.75	701.25	700.00	700.00	700.00	700.00	700.00	700.00	700.00	702.28
1751	700.00	700.00	700.00	700.00	700.00	700.00	700.00	700.00			700.00		700.00
1752				700.00								[700.00]	700.00

TABLE 3.12 (Continued): **South Carolina on London** (Pounds South Carolina Currency per £100 Sterling)

Year	Jan.	Feb.	Mar.	Apr.	May	June	July	Aug.	Sept.	Oct.	Nov.	Dec.	Average
1753												[700.00]	700.00
1754												[700.00]	700.00
1755				700.00	700.00	700.00	700.00	700.00	700.00		700.00	700.00	700.00
1756	700.00	700.00	700.00	710.42	712.50	712.50	708.56	712.50	712.50	712.50	731.25	[750.00]	713.56
1757	700.00	701.67	700.00	700.00			700.00			700.00			700.19
1758		700.00											700.00
1759			700.00									700.00	700.00
1760							700.00		700.00				700.00
1761		700.00											700.00
1762							700.00	700.00			700.00	700.00	700.00
1763	714.00	715.75	714.00	714.39	714.00	716.62	721.00	721.00	717.50	710.06	721.00	719.25	716.55
1764	717.50	717.33	707.58	714.00	721.00		717.50		721.00		721.00		717.97
1765				700.00	700.00	721.00	721.00	721.00				700.00	709.33
1766		714.00									700.00		707.00
1767	700.00			700.00				700.00			700.00	700.00	700.00
1768	700.00	700.00	700.00	700.00	700.00	700.00	700.00						700.00
1769													
1770							672.00					[762.00]	717.00
1771												[762.00]	762.00
1772	679.00	679.00											679.00
1773											728.00		728.00
1774					700.00								700.00
1775	735.00						800.00	777.00	770.00				758.67

Notes and Sources: **TABLE 3.12**

Figures inserted in square brackets are assigned to that month arbitrarily; figures in italics are straight-line interpolations based on the two neighboring quotations.

1699: Jonathan Dickinson, at Philadelphia, to Alexander Parris, at Charleston, S.C., 29 Apr. 1699, Dickinson/Logan Letter Book, 1698–1742, Logan Papers, 1664–1871, Historical Society of Pennsylvania, Philadelphia.

Notes and Sources: **TABLE 3.12 (Continued)**

1700: Gov. Richard Coote, earl of Bellomont, at Boston, to Board of Trade, 22 June 1700, C.O. 5/1044, fol. 85r, Public Record Office.

1700–1739: [Lt. Gov. William Bull, Sr.], "An Account of the Rise and Progress of the Paper Bills of Credit in South Carolina," 1700–1739, in Thomas Cooper and David J. McCord, eds., *The Statutes at Large of South Carolina* (Columbia, S.C., 1836–1841), IX, 766–780. For 1700 see also Curtis P. Nettels, *The Money Supply of the American Colonies before 1720*, University of Wisconsin Studies in the Social Sciences and History, No. 20 (Madison, Wis., 1934), 241, 248.

1710–1773: David Duncan Wallace, *The Life of Henry Laurens, with a Sketch of the Life of Lieutenant-Colonel John Laurens* (New York, 1915), 53; and Wallace, *The History of South Carolina* (New York, 1934), I, 315.

1713–1737: *The Report of the Committee of the Commons House of Assembly of the Province of South-Carolina, on the State of the Paper-Currency of the Said Province* (London, 1737), *passim*.

1718: William Tredwell Bull, at St. Paul's Parsonage, S.C., to Bishop John Robinson, 15 May 1718, General Correspondence, IX, no. 75–76, Fulham Papers, Lambeth Palace Library, London.

1721: Cooper and McCord, eds., *Statutes of South Carolina*, III, 174; Martin Bladen and Richard Plumer, at Whitehall, to Bishop Edmund Gipson, 20 Aug. 1724, General Correspondence, IX, no. 152–153, Fulham Papers.

1723: Peter Baynton Ledger and Letter Book, 1721–1726, Hist. Soc. Pa.

1725: Francis Holmes account with Thomas Amory, Amory Estate Papers, 1697–1724, Amory Family Papers, Library of Congress.

1725: Royal African Company, Copybook of Invoices Homeward, 1725–1729, pp. 9–10, T. 70/959, P.R.O.

1727: Alexander Nisbett Journal, 1727–1730, Box 10, bundle 4, Collections Deposited by Messrs. Tods, Murray, and Jamieson, W.S., Gift and Deposit No. 237, Scottish Record Office, Edinburgh.

1736: Account enclosed in Harman Verelst, at London, to Thomas Jenys, at Charleston, S.C., 4 Aug. 1738, C.O. 5/667, pp. 150, 154.

1736–1737: John Wesley, at Savannah, Ga., to the Trustees of Georgia, 1 Mar. 1737, C.O. 5/639, fol. 207r.

1737: Samuel Eveleigh, at Charleston, S.C., to James Oglethorpe, 3 Jan. 1736/37, and Thomas Causton, at Savannah, Ga., to Trustees of Georgia, 24 Feb. 1736/37, C.O. 5/639, fols. 106r, 136v; Minutes of the Georgia Council, London, 10 Aug. 1737, C.O. 5/690, p. 98; Harman Verelst, at London, to Causton, 11 Aug. 1737, C.O. 5/667, p. 56.

1737–1745: Walter B. Edgar, ed., *The Letterbook of Robert Pringle, 1737–1745* (Columbia, S.C., 1972), *passim*.

1743–1752: Jonathan Scott, at Charleston, S.C., to John Reynell, at Philadelphia, 10 June, 2 Nov. 1743, 30 Apr. 1745, and John Sinclair, at Charleston, S.C., to Reynell, 20 Nov. 1751, 11 Apr. 1752, John Reynell Correspondence, 1729–1773, Coates and Reynell Papers, Hist. Soc. Pa.

1747–1768: Philip M. Hamer *et al.*, eds., *The Papers of Henry Laurens* (Columbia, S.C., 1968–), *passim*.

1749–1750: *South Carolina Gazette* (Charleston), Mar. 1749–Sept. 1750.

1749–1751: Austin and Laurens Waste Book, 1749–1751, Henry Laurens Papers, 1747–1882, South Carolina Historical Society, Charleston.

1755–1756: Accounts, Austin and Laurens, 17 July 1756, Gabriel Manigault, 12 Apr. 1755, Samuel and William Vernon Papers, 1750–1775, Box VII, "Slavery MSS.," New-York Historical Society, New York City.

1756–1758: Henry Bouquet Letter Book, 1757, fols. 22v, 27v, *ibid.*, 1757–1758, fols. 9r, 28r, 30r, Henry Bouquet Papers, 1757–1765, Additional Manuscripts 21631–21632, British Library.

1759, 1774: William Parker, at Charleston, S.C., to Obadiah Brown and Co., 29 Mar. 1759, and Levinus Clarkson, at Charleston, S.C., to Nicholas Brown and Co., May 1774, Brown Papers, L 57–59 M, John Carter Brown Library, Brown University, Providence, R.I.

1759–1761: Lilla Mills Hawes, ed., *The Letter Book of Thomas Rasberry, 1758–1761* (Georgia Historical Society, *Collections*, XIII [Savannah, Ga., 1959]), 90, 114, 118, 127.

Notes and Sources: **TABLE 3.12 (Continued)**

1762: Galloway Correspondence, V, no. 8790, Galloway-Maxey-Markoe Family Papers, 1654–1888, Lib. Cong.

1763: Bill of exchange, Charleston, S.C., 18 Oct. 1763, C.O. 5/377, pt. ii, fol. 296v.

1765: Robertson, Jamieson, and Co., at Charleston, S.C., to Neil Jamieson, at Norfolk, Va., 8 May, 31 Dec. 1765, Neil Jamieson Papers, 1757–1789, V, no. 1070, XIV, no. 3154, Lib. Cong.

1767: Account Book of James Laurens, 1767–1775, Laurens Papers.

1770: John Stuart, at Charleston, S.C., to Gov. Norborne Berkeley, Lord Botetourt, of Virginia, 12 July 1770, C.O. 5/1348, fol. 135.

1772–1775: Leila Sellers, *Charleston Business on the Eve of the American Revolution* (Chapel Hill, N.C., 1934), 76–77, 115.

1772–1775: Elizabeth Donnan, ed., *Documents Illustrative of the History of the Slave Trade to America* (Washington, D.C., 1930–1935), III, 375, IV, 443.

1775: Henry Laurens, at Charleston, S.C., to James Laurens, at London, 19 July and 22 Sept. 1775, Letters to James Laurens, Chiefly from Henry Laurens, 1773–1777, Laurens Papers.

Georgia

Where South Carolina was typical of colonial monetary history, Georgia was different. Georgia was founded very late in the colonial period, and for much of the time before 1755 when it was still a proprietary colony, a large part of its circulating medium of exchange consisted of endorsed bills of exchange drawn in the colony on the trustees in London.[218] Some South Carolina paper currency circulated there too, but there was little silver or gold coin. One reason for the lack of coin was the absence in Georgia's legal code of any provision for an inflated currency value for coin. Someone with pieces of eight would obviously have been wiser to use his silver to buy South Carolina paper currency in Charleston at £600 or £700 per £100 sterling and then use the paper money in Georgia. This is in fact what most men did. With no legal provision for inflating its coin and with its currency partly in sterling bills on London, Georgia's "currency" was effectively sterling during this era. Par was even at £100 Georgia money for £100 sterling.

We have little idea how the commercial rate of exchange varied from par until much later in Georgia's history. And the issue is confused in that quotations in the 1730s were sometimes made in terms of South Carolina currency. In 1735 the trustees of Georgia, in order to overcome some of the problems caused by the unauthorized drawing of bills of exchange, ordered the printing and distribution of a form of paper money—preprinted bills of exchange that were issued in single units rather than in sets and were thus called "sola" bills. Denominated in the money of account, these "sola" bills were worth their face value in pounds sterling in England, and the trustees of Georgia guaranteed to accept them as such.[219] But some doubt about their acceptance, as well as the time involved in sending them home for redemption, led initially to their passing only at a discount in Georgia and South Carolina. At a time when a bill of exchange for £100 sterling cost about £750 in South Carolina currency, the rate in sola bills was closer to £800, a discount of 6 to 7 percent.[220] Later in the 1730s Georgia currency passed at a premium of 5 percent, but in 1740 a dispute between Georgia and South Carolina reduced its value to par and below.[221] Thus between 1735 and 1740, with par at £100 Georgia currency per £100 sterling, the bill rate fluctuated from £107 to £95 and back again. Later in the 1740s and early 1750s sola bills seem again

218. William Estill Heath, "The Early Colonial Money System of Georgia," *Georgia Historical Quarterly*, XIX (1935), 145–160. See also Brock, *Currency of the American Colonies*, 127–128, 462–464a; Ernst, *Money and Politics*, 169–173, 304.

219. See also Charles C. Jones, Jr., *The History of Georgia* (Boston, 1883), I, 429; Trevor Richard Reese, *Colonial Georgia: A Study in British Imperial Policy in the Eighteenth Century* (Athens, Ga., 1963), 35–36. Bills of exchange were issued and mailed in sets to protect against loss in the post. The same object was obtained for sola bills by recording and mailing a "list of the dates, letters and numbers" of the bills as well as copies of the ship captain's receipt. In case of loss the "list and receipt will serve to recover the amount of the bills." Laurens to Stephen Perry, Jr., of Bristol, 28 Aug. 1747, *Papers of Henry Laurens*, I, 51.

220. Allen D. Candler and Lucian Lamar Knight, eds., *The Colonial Records of the State of Georgia* (Atlanta, 1904–1916), XXI, 299, as cited in Heath, "Money System of Georgia," *Ga. Hist. Qtly.*, XIX (1935), 151. See also James Oglethorpe, at Savannah, Ga., to the trustees, June 1736, Mills Lane, ed., *General Oglethorpe's Georgia: Colonial Letters, 1733–1743* (Savannah, Ga., 1975), I, 276; Robert G. McPherson, ed., *The Journal of the Earl of Egmont: Abstract of the Trustees for Establishing the Colony of Georgia, 1732–1738* (Athens, Ga., 1962), 158.

221. Candler and Knight, eds., *Colonial Records of Georgia*, V, 421, 464, 481, as cited in Heath, "Money System of Georgia," *Ga. Hist. Qtly.*, XIX (1935), 155. See also McPherson, ed., *Journal of Egmont*, 265.

to have passed at something of a premium, but again our information is very poor.[222]

In 1754 Georgia became a royal colony, and within a year it issued its own paper currency. This new Georgia paper money followed the example of the old sola bills in maintaining a par value at parity with sterling. While we know that the post-1754 paper money also circulated in South Carolina and East Florida,[223] we have only the thinnest evidence about its continuing relationship to sterling. Despite its local popularity, this new paper money did not circulate as far as London, as had the old sola bills, which would suggest some depreciation in value. Moreover, sometime after 1764 the currency value of the piece of eight rose to 5s (25p), increasing the par of exchange to £111.11 Georgia currency per £100 sterling.[224] The few quotations of the commercial rate of exchange uncovered to date are for the 1760s and 1770s (see table 3.13). They imply that the bill rate was usually something lower than par.

222. Heath, "Money System of Georgia," *Ga. Hist. Qtly.*, XIX (1935), 156–160. For references to the sola bills and an indication of their usefulness for the economies of both South Carolina and Georgia, see Edgar, ed., *Letterbook of Robert Pringle, passim,* and *Papers of Henry Laurens,* I and II, *passim.*

223. Thomas Rasberry to Josiah Smith, 6 Feb. 1761, Hawes, ed., *Letterbook of Thomas Rasberry,* 147; Georgia Committee of Correspondence to Charles Garth, 4 Sept. 1764, Robert W. Gibbes, ed., *Documentary History of the American Revolution* (New York, 1853–1857), I, 2.

224. See John Tobler, *The South-Carolina and Georgia Almanack, for the Year of Our Lord 1772* (Charleston, S.C., [1771]), last page; Morris to president of Congress, 15 Jan. 1782, Sparks, ed., *Diplomatic Correspondence,* XII, 91; Johann David Schöpf, *Travels in the Confederation* (1788), trans. Alfred J. Morrison (Philadelphia, 1911), I, 8–9; Sylvester S. Crosby, *The Early Coins of America and the Laws Governing Their Issue* (Boston, 1878), 308.

TABLE 3.13. **Rate of Exchange: Georgia on London, 1765–1775**

(Pounds Georgia Currency per £100 Sterling)

Year	Jan.	Feb.	Mar.	Apr.	May	June	July	Aug.	Sept.	Oct.	Nov.	Dec.	Average
1765					108.00			109.00					108.50
1766													
1767													
1768	108.69	109.02					109.00						108.93
1769													
1770													
1771													
1772							108.00	109.52					108.76
1773													
1774													
1775				108.00									108.00

Notes and Sources: **TABLE 3.13**

1765–1775: *The Letters of Hon. James Habersham, 1756–1775* (Georgia Historical Society, *Collections*, VI [Savannah, Ga., 1904]), 36, 43, 190, 203, 235.

1768: Philip M. Hamer *et al*., eds., *The Papers of Henry Laurens* (Columbia, S. C., 1968–), V, 547, 589, 752.

Beyond the Continental Colonies

The English founded or conquered other colonies in North America during the seventeenth and eighteenth centuries, some to the north and some to the south of the continental colonies. Limited information prohibits little more than a mention of their names. We look first to the south of Georgia.

Florida

Great Britain acquired East and West Florida in 1763 as a result of the Seven Years' War and the Treaty of Paris. Prior to 1763 Florida, as a Spanish colony, presumably conformed to the practices standard in other Spanish colonies, which are discussed below in chapter 4. After 1763 the government and merchants of Florida duplicated there the mechanisms common to the other English colonies—but with a certain mixture of Spanish traditions. In the 1760s several of the bills that Evan Jones of Mobile, West Florida, sent to John van Cortlandt of New York for payment there were drawn in terms of pieces of eight.[225] At about the same time Governor George Johnstone of West Florida complained of an "exchange which is 23 per cent against us," implying a rate of £123 West Florida currency per £100 sterling. He had recently drawn bills on the Treasury totaling £1,000 at sixty days sight. They were to be negotiated at New Orleans.[226] Further research should be able to provide more information about exchange in West Florida as well as tell us something about exchange in East Florida.

225. John van Cortlandt Letter Book, 1762–1769, *passim*, Van Cortlandt Account Books.

Newfoundland, Nova Scotia, and "Canada"

Newfoundland, the oldest of England's colonies, owed its existence to the fishing industry, and, as we might expect, fish were the basis of Newfoundland's currency. But the island maintained an extraordinarily close relationship with the mother country. The annual fishing fleets from England's west country ports brought out crews who were used to and preferred to think and do business in terms of sterling.[227] As a result the island had two parallel currencies; depending on whether one was prepared to pay for goods with sterling bills of exchange or with fish, the price was quoted in "bill pay" or "fish pay." The latter seems to have been the more regular form of quotation, but one finds the occasional reference to a sterling price. In August 1759, for instance, Robert Bulley wrote to Thomas Clifford and Company of Philadelphia that "the price of fish was broke yesterday at 16/9 per quntle, that is deducting 25 per cent 12/6 ¾ sterling."[228] In other words, at least in 1759, £133.33 "fish pay" (that is, Newfoundland cur-

226. Johnstone, at Mobile, to secretary of state, 19 Feb. 1765, C.O. 5/574, pt. i, fols. 118r, 120r. But cf. [Hugh Gaine], *Gaine's Universal Register, or, American and British Kalendar, For the Year 1775* (New York, [1774]), 61, 64.

227. "In Newfoundland, all large sums are transacted in sterling bills of exchange; small dealings in English coin sterling value, and in pieces of eight at 4s 6d. [22.5p] being the sterling value." [Douglass], *Discourse concerning Currencies*, 8. See also Board of Ordnance, "Inquiry into the Nature of the Contracts in America," 1750, Townshend Papers, Lib. Cong.

228. Bulley wrote from St. John's on 7 Aug. Clifford Correspondence, II, 205, Pemberton Papers, Hist. Soc. Pa. See also Bulley to Clifford and Co., 11 Sept., 8 Oct. 1759, and John Bulkeley, from Harbour Grace, Nfld., to Thomas Clifford, 8 Sept. and, from St. John's, 1 Nov. 1759, *ibid.*, 218, 232, 249, V, 122. See also the "Amount of Sails of the Sloop Four Brothers Cargoe in Newfound-land," 23 Oct. 1763, Brown Papers, V-F6; George Sears, of St. John's, to Aaron Lopez, of Newport, R.I., 11 July 1771, 17 July 1772, 8 July 1773, *Commerce of Rhode Island*, I, 372–373, 406, 444–445.

rency) equaled £100 sterling. Newfoundland currency thus conformed to the rate promulgated in the proclamation of 1704 and the law of 1708. With this as the par of exchange, we might well suspect that there were occasional variations around par in a commercial rate of exchange. There are no data.

While English interest in Nova Scotia was of long standing, the colony remained firmly French until 1711. In that year, with the definitive capture of Annapolis Royal, the parts of modern New Brunswick and Nova Scotia that front on the Bay of Fundy, and the Atlantic shore of Nova Scotia up to Cape Canso, fell into English hands.[229] The driving force behind English interest had come from the Yankees of New England who had considered the territory theirs all along. Thus it was only natural that New England currency ruled the area from 1711 through 1749.[230] The commercial rates quoted in table 3.1 applied as far north as Canso during this era.[231]

The year 1749 marks the terminus of this domination less because of the changes in New England currency at that time than because of the changes in Nova Scotia. England's decision to organize a buffer colony in the north against the French similar to the role played by Georgia in the south against the Spanish meant the establishment not only of a full colonial government but also of a colonial capital worthy of the name,

Halifax. As in Georgia, Nova Scotia's earliest currency was at a parity with sterling, but, again as was the case in Georgia, the colonists quickly discovered a real difference, probably caused by the function of time in making remittances in bills of exchange. By fall 1750 at the latest the piece of eight had a value of 5s (25p) Halifax currency, a rate set by law in 1758 and one that still pertained in the middle of the nineteenth century. The par of exchange in Nova Scotia was £111.11 Halifax currency to £100 sterling. And after 1 December 1752 bills of exchange returned from England protested for nonpayment paid damages at 15 percent; colonial bills paid only 10 percent. Prior to that date all such bills had paid 10 percent damages and 5 percent interest.[232]

In 1759 on the Plains of Abraham, England completed its conquest of French North America.[233] The early military government of the captured province, originally based at Halifax, simply extended the dominance of Halifax currency down

229. For a sense of the regions of Nova Scotia during the 18th century, see Andrew Hill Clark, *Acadia: The Geography of Early Nova Scotia to 1760* (Madison, Wis., 1968). For its history see W. S. MacNutt, *The Atlantic Provinces: The Emergence of Colonial Society, 1712–1857* (Toronto, 1965). See also John Bartlet Brebner, *New England's Outpost: Acadia before the Conquest of Canada* (New York, 1928).

230. Lanctot *et al.*, eds., *Documents Relating to Currency*, xviii–xxxiii, and *passim*. See also [Douglass], *Discourse concerning Currencies*, 8.

231. Local conditions are thought sometimes to have increased the price of Nova Scotia bills over that at Boston, but evidence for this has yet to be collected.

232. Lanctot *et al.*, eds., *Documents Relating to Currency*, 292, 296, 315, 383; Horace A. Fleming, "Halifax Currency," *Journal of the Canadian Bankers' Association*, XXX (1922–1923), 88–96, 199–209. In the spring of 1750 the rate of exchange was £106.67, the equivalent of pieces of eight at 4s 9.5d (24p). Lanctot *et al.*, eds., *Documents Relating to Currency*, 292, 293, 327. For the rates for damages and interest on protested bills, see *ibid.*, 385. As for the commercial rate of exchange, I have found only one quotation. On 20 June 1761 Slayter and Watson, of Halifax, wrote to Thomas Clifford that "exchange" was "8 per cent some ask 9 and 10." Clifford Correspondence, III, 212.

For a while after its fall in 1758, Louisbourg became an English trading community, and there was a "Louisbourg currency." In Feb., June, and Sept., 1759 the rate of exchange was said to be £105 Louisbourg currency per £100 sterling; in May 1760 it was at £107.50 "Accompt [of] disbursements for damages, 1759," in Papers of the Ship *Oliver*, C. 110/187, pt. ii: *Williamson v. Wallaby*; account of John Rockett, June–Sept. 1760, and Rockett to Clifford, 28 May 1760, Clifford Correspondence, II, 222, III, 67.

233. For exchange in French Canada, see below, pp. 284–285.

the Saint Lawrence River to Quebec City and Montreal.[234] Neither city proved comfortable under this imposition, however. Before a year had passed, Montreal and Three Rivers, already well within New York's trading circle, adopted 8s (40p) as the value of the piece of eight.[235] Quebec pressed for a similar increase, or so it seems. Finally in 1764 a new ordinance, effective 1 January 1765, tried for both legality and uniformity and set a colony-wide standard of 6s (30p) for the piece of eight, which was, of course, the highest rate authorized by the act of 1708.[236] Montreal conformed by lowering par to £133.33 and henceforward using "Lawful Money." Quebec, by that time more amenable to Halifax currency,

continued to use the par at Halifax, £111.11, as its own par. Both Lawful Money at Montreal and Halifax currency at Quebec survived down to the Revolution.[237]

It is only for Montreal that we have any idea of the relationship between the commercial rate of exchange and par. And our information is almost all from one source, the letters of Montreal merchant Lawrence Ermatinger.[238] The course of the exchange at Montreal in the period from 1765 to 1775 seems to have resembled nothing so much as that at Boston (see table 3.1). Through mid-1769 most exchanges seem to have been at par,[239] and Ermatinger drew some accounts even after that time in the same way. But in October 1770 he used a rate of £127.98, and four months later, in February 1771, he used a rate of £129.33. Still later, in September 1772, when good bills were hard to find, Ermatinger equated £875 "Lawful Money" with £618 19s 7d sterling, for an effective rate of £141.36. Canada awaits the collection of a bit more data before any table can be constructed. It is unfortunately not unique.

234. Proclamation dated 23 Nov. 1759, in "Ordinances and Proclamations of the Règne Militaire of Quebec, 1759–1764," 3–4, Appendix B of *Report of the Public Archives . . . 1918* (Ottawa, 1920). See also Fernand Ouellet, *Histoire économique et sociale du Québec, 1760–1850: Structures et conjoncture* (Montreal and Paris, [1966]), 59.

235. Ordinance dated Montreal, 8 Feb. 1760, and Quebec, 1 Oct. 1760, in "Ordinances and Proclamations," 39, 88, Appendix B of *Report of the Public Archives . . . 1918*. But, cf., *ibid.*, 134. See also Isabel Craig, "Economic Conditions in Canada, 1763–1783" (M.A. thesis, McGill Univ., 1937), 211; Ouellet, *Histoire économique du Québec*, 60.

236. *Ordinances Made for the Province of Quebec, by the Governor and Council of the Said Province/Ordonnances, faites pour la province de Québec, par le gouverneur et conseil de la dite province* (Quebec, 1767), 306; *Quebec Gazette*, 4 Oct. 1764. (This volume of laws was reprinted in Appendix E of the *Report of . . . the Public Archives . . . 1913* [Ottawa, 1914].) The ordinance passed the council on 14 Sept. 1764. Just two weeks earlier the council had recommended that the rate to be effective on 1 Jan. 1765 be that of New York, and it had indeed established the colony's fee schedule in New York currency for both "the districts of Quebec and Montreal." Quebec Legislative Council, Minute Book A (1764–1765), 27–30, Records of the Executive Council, RG 1, A2, Public Archives of Canada, Ottawa, Ontario. For the ordinance itself, see *ibid.*, 40–43. The same ordinance also established that the livre previously in use in the colony was, after 1 Jan. 1765, to be considered the equivalent of 1s (5p) Quebec currency; the piece of eight was thus worth 6s (30p) or 6 livres. See also pp. 283, 286 in chap. 4, below.

237. Craig, "Economic Conditions in Canada," 211–212. Ouellet, *Histoire économique du Québec*, 61, says that "Certains commerçants montrélais, en contact avec les New-Yorkais, continuent à utilises le cours d'York, ce qui simplifie leur comptabilité." In 1777 a new ordinance reintroduced Halifax currency throughout the colony. Dated 29 Mar. 1777, this can be found in "Ordinances Made for the Province of Quebec by the Governor and Council of the Said Province, from 1768 until 1791," Appendix C of the *Report of . . . the Public Archives . . . 1914 and 1915* (Ottawa, 1916), 73–74. See also Ouellet, *Histoire économique du Québec*, 61.

238. Letter Book of Lawrence Ermatinger, 1770–1778, Lawrence Ermatinger Papers, Ermatinger Estate Papers, 1755–1894, MG 19, A2, Pub. Arch. Canada.

239. See the various government accounts in T. 1/469, fols. 9, 139, 141, 191, 252, 256, 338. See also *Quebec Gazette*, 15 Mar. 1770.

The commercial rates of exchange in the several English colonies on the continent of North America maintained a diversity totally disruptive of any simple means of comprehension. Despite basic similarities in the mode of exchange and despite the occasional union of currencies, the colonies exhibited enough differences to require both contemporaries and later interested individuals to spend some time sorting it all through. This chapter has attempted just that task and, in sorting out the various colonial currencies, tries to provide the basic data to do what only a few colonists could do at any one time: reduce an amount in one colonial money to its equivalent in all others. The individual tables offer that capability and also supply the basic figures for the summary tables in chapter 5. The materials assembled there from this chapter, the previous chapter, and what follows give the reader a capacity for international monetary comparisons never before available.

Chapter 4

Colonial Exchange in the Caribbean and Latin America

"I caution you against all West India bills [of exchange],
particularly those from the late Ceded Islands
as not one in seventy of them
are regularly paid."[1]

The British Caribbean Colonies and the Exchange on London

Much that chapter 3 says about the North American colonies applied as well to the British colonies in the Caribbean. For instance, they all used the same real money—the gold and silver coins of Spanish and Portuguese America—and the same money of account—pounds, shillings, and pence. And the general ways of negotiating bills of exchange on London were the same. In fact, the similarities in form and substance between the North American and the Caribbean colonies far outweigh the differences. The first pages of the previous chapter, which discuss the moneys, real and imaginary, of the British colonies and the negotiation of bills of exchange,

1. William Neate, at London, to Levinus Clarkson, at Charleston, S.C., 18 Feb. 1773, Levinus Clarkson Papers, 1772–1793, Library of Congress.

serve also to introduce the material in this chapter. Yet it is the differences that attract our attention.

The British West Indies faced many of the same monetary problems that plagued the continental colonies, and the solutions they sought initially tended to be similar. Each Caribbean colony tried several devices to enhance its circulating medium of exchange. In the West Indies commodity money was largely sugar, of course, but Barbados used tobacco for a while in the 1630s. And all of the West Indian legislatures expended considerable effort during the sixty years prior to the act of 1708 in framing statutes to increase the currency value of the available silver coin. It was at just that juncture, in reaction to the act of 1708 and its stipulated upper limit for silver coin, that the West Indies broke step with the continental colonies.

The West Indians were as interested as the North Americans in evading the restrictions of the act of 1708. The various colonies on the continent turned one after another to paper currency both as a supplement to hard currency and as money free of the imperial restraints on silver. In the same way the Caribbean colonies turned to gold coin, which had been omitted from the limitations set in the act. The increased availability of gold, particularly in the form of coin minted from the newly discovered mines of Brazil, made this possible. From 1708 on the West Indian governments obeyed the limits set on silver but for practical purposes ceased using it as a money. Gold was their money, at steadily inflated rates; silver was a commodity.[2] The West Indians maintained this legal fiction well into the early 1740s, until the lack of interest in enforcing the spirit of the act of 1708 *in the West Indies* permitted them thereafter to do pretty much as they chose.

West Indian inflation was tolerated largely because it was innocuous. London merchants, for example, had little to complain about with regard to the Leeward Islands. A rate of exchange there in 1740 of £160 or £170 currency per £100 sterling was small when compared to New England or the Carolinas. Moreover, the rates of exchange in the West Indies were relatively stable, because of the islands' economic situation as exporters of major staple commodities, particularly

sugar. The supply of bills of exchange in the West Indies kept up better with demand and at times ran ahead of demand.

The West Indians had a ready market for any bills of exchange that could not be sold satisfactorily in the islands; they sold them in the continental colonies (see figs. 10 and 11, pp. 236–238). North American merchants who traded with the West Indies exported in return for goods they sold there not only commodities and coin but bills on London too. Yet— as the epigraph at the beginning of this chapter suggests— such bills had a mixed reception in North America because they were sometimes dishonored and returned protested for nonpayment. Still, the alternate market for their bills provided the West Indians with a valuable additional way to pay for the goods they purchased. Their bills of exchange helped to finance the mutually rewarding North America–West India trade of the seventeenth and eighteenth centuries.

2. Joseph Estridge (president of the Council of St. Christopher and Montserrat), at St. Christopher, to Gov. William Mathew, at Antigua, 12 Dec. 1739, in Mathew to Board of Trade, 8 Jan. 1739/40, C.O. 152/33, fol. 256, Public Record Office; [Wavel Smith], *Two Letters to Mr. Wood, on the Coin and Currency in the Leeward Islands, &c.* (London, 1740), *passim*. Smith was the secretary of the Leeward Islands; William Wood was the secretary of the customs. The copy of Smith's work in the British Library (press mark: 1139.k.7) is bound with manuscript notes on the vote of the House of Commons on the plantation money bill (25 Apr. 1740). See also Joseph Albert Ernst, *Money and Politics in America, 1755–1775: A Study in the Currency Act of 1764 and the Political Economy of Revolution* (Chapel Hill, N.C., 1973), 32–33.

Figures 10 and 11. Two British West Indian Bills of Exchange Resold in North America.
These two bills, illustrated front and back, are good examples of bills of exchange drawn in the islands and then resold in the continental colonies. Both show the standard practice in Barbados (much rarer in Jamaica) of specifying the rate of exchange on the face of the bill.
(From the John Reynell Papers; courtesy of the Historical Society of Pennsylvania, Philadelphia.)

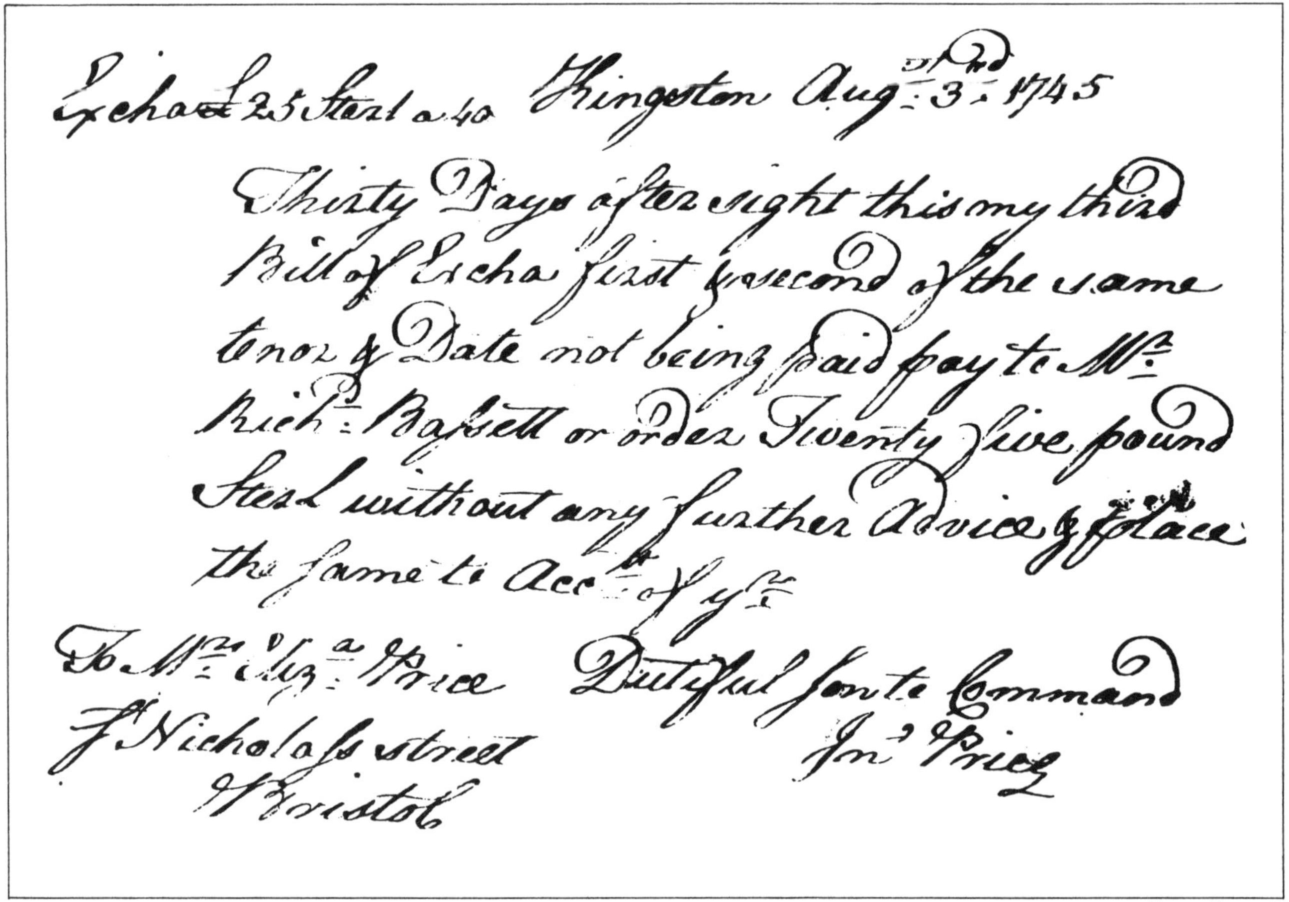
Excha £25 Sterl a 40 Kingston Augst 3rd 1745

Thirty Days after sight this my third Bill of Excha first & second of the same tenor & Date not being paid pay to Mr. Richd. Bassett or order Twenty five pounds Sterl without any further Advice & place the same to Acct. of yr

To Mrs. Eliza Price Dutiful son to Command
St Nicholass street Jno Price
Bristol

Front, figure 10

10. Jamaica, 3 August 1745 (front and reverse). In this bill John(?) Price at Kingston drew on Mrs. Elizabeth Price at Bristol (this is another outport bill) in favor of Richard Bassett. On the reverse Bassett ordered it paid to Daniel Flexney and Jacob Chitty for the account of John Reynell of Philadelphia, who bought it from Bassett. The bill was countersigned by John Bringhurst, Jr., presumably at Reynell's insistence, to guarantee its payment. Thus, if the bill were returned protested for nonpayment, Reynell would not have to find Bassett or Price but could have collected the principal, interest, and damages from Bringhurst.

Reverse, figure 10

11. Barbados, 21 July 1747 (front and reverse). There was less need to seek a guarantee for this bill than for that pictured in figure 10, since this one was drawn in favor of a major planter in Barbados, who was also the collector of the customs, against one of the largest London sugar houses of the era. James Carber here directed Lascelles and Maxwell to pay Gedney Clarke's payee the specified sum. As the endorsements on the reverse show, the bill passed through several hands before John Reynell purchased it at Philadelphia. Clarke paid Carber £87 Barbados currency for the bill (£60 sterling "at 45 per cent"); Reynell paid about £110 Pennsylvania currency for it (see table 3.7). (This illustration is about 70 percent of the size of the original bill.)

Front, figure 11

Reverse, figure 11

Barbados

Barbados, as one of the oldest of England's colonies in the New World, had to face the problem of an adequate money supply with little or no outside example to follow, other than perhaps Ireland and Virginia. The earliest currency on Barbados must have been close to sterling at its value in England. The Barbadians, perhaps in imitation of the Virginians, soon turned to tobacco as a commodity money to supplement whatever coin was available. Early in the 1640s they changed to sugar in response to the revolution in their agricultural sector.[3] At about the same time, the island's assembly passed the first of numerous measures to increase the local currency value of foreign coin.

The par of exchange for Barbados currency in the 1640s, 1650s, and 1660s is somewhat uncertain, because the texts of the numerous laws passed during these years do not survive. What appears to have been the second such piece of legislation, dated 12 September 1651, raised the value of gold and silver by one-third with the explicit purpose of "encouraging the importing of gold and silver into the island."[4] At this rate par was £133.33 Barbados currency to £100 sterling. The 1651 law seems to have had a limited term, for it was renewed in September 1661 and again in March 1661/62 and had lapsed sometime before April 1666, when a new law "for advancing and raising the value of pieces of eight" set their value at 5s (25p), for a par of £111.11. A later act of November 1668 repeated this valuation.[5] Par at that rate continued in effect until 1740, when the currency value of the piece of eight was raised to 6s 3d (31.25p), equal to £138.89. There it remained for another hundred years.[6]

Needless to say, par valued on the piece of eight did not reflect the actual par of exchange at the commercial rate, especially during the years between 1700 and 1740.[7] In fact, as early as 1691 we have an indication that Barbadians, by accepting underweight pieces of eight as if they were full-weight coins, were operating with an effective par of exchange

3. J. Harry Bennett, "The English Caribbees in the Period of the Civil War, 1642–1646," *William and Mary Quarterly*, 3d Ser., XXIV (1967), 371. See "An Act for the appointing, or regulating of the Fees of the several Officers, and Courts of this Island," 17 Sept. 1652, as one example of many similar laws, in [John Jennings, ed.], *Acts and Statutes of the Island of Barbados* (London, [1654]), 92–101; and Robert Chalmers, *A History of Currency in the British Colonies* (London, [1893]), 46–47. Further research into Barbadian subjects will be greatly facilitated by Jerome S. Handler, *A Guide to Source Materials for the Study of Barbados History, 1627–1834* (Carbondale, Ill., 1971).

4. The titles of this and one or perhaps two earlier laws (one dated 13 May 1646) are in Richard Hall, Sr., and Richard Hall, Jr., eds., *Acts, Passed in the Island of Barbados. From 1643, to 1762, Inclusive* (London, 1764), 459, 460, 463. None of these is in [Jennings, ed.], *Acts and Statutes of Barbados*. Chalmers, *History of Currency*, 48, does not give a source for the text of the 1651 act.

5. Hall and Hall, eds., *Acts of Barbados*, 468, 472, 475. See also William Rawlin, ed., *The Laws of Barbados, Collected in One Volume* (London, 1699), 55, 88, 111. The limited term of the act of 12 Sept. 1651 is explained in part by its having been suspended in Mar. 1652 along with all other acts passed during the governorship of Francis, Lord Willoughby. [Jennings, ed.], *Acts and Statutes of Barbados*, 68–71, 131–132, 160–161. See also John Poyntz, *The Present Prospect of the Famous and Fertile Island of Tobago*, 1st ed. (London, 1683), 31, 43.

6. John Oldmixon, *The British Empire in America*, (London, 1708), II, 165; Ida Greaves, "Money and Currency in Barbados," *Journal of the Barbados Museum and Historical Society*, XX (1952), 8–9. See also F. Pridmore, "Notes on Colonial Coins: The Cut Money of Barbados," *ibid.*, XXX (1964), 169–181; and Chalmers, *History of Currency*, 53n.

7. *Barbados Gazette* (Bridgetown), 5 May 1733, as printed in [Samuel Keimer, ed.], *Caribbeana: Containing Letters and Dissertations . . . Chiefly Wrote by Several Hands in the West Indies* (London, 1741), 160–161; [John Ashley], *The Sugar Trade, with the Incumbrances Thereon, Laid Open* (London, 1734), table opp. p. 4; James Dottin, at Barbados, to Board of Trade, 9 Nov. 1739, C.O. 28/25, fols. 94–95; [William Douglass], *A Discourse concerning the Currencies of the British Plantations in America* (Boston, 1740), 19.

of £133.33.[8] Depending on how old this custom was, real par might have been £133.33 all the way back to 1651 and maybe even earlier. Still, there are some indications that, in the period of peace prior to King William's War, the commercial rate was closer to a par based on the piece of eight at 5s (25p), or £111.11.[9] Perhaps in summary we can point to an effective par of £133.33 from at least 1651 to the mid-1660s, £111.11 from 1666 to 1689, £133.33 from 1689 through 1740, and £138.89 from 1740 through 1838. The commercial rate of exchange fluctuated around par, as was usual.[10] In this regard see table 4.1.[11]

Residents of Barbados drew bills of exchange against their London correspondents in the same way as did residents of the continental colonies. The prime drawing seasons were the spring and fall, May and September.[12] Bills were drawn at longer sight than was customary in North America, nor-mally ninety days, to allow for the arrival and sale of the sugar cargoes in Great Britain.[13] Protested bills incurred a percentage fine for damages and paid interest from the date of protest until renegotiations were completed. The rate for damages was 20 percent of the value of the bill from some-time before 1668 until February 1669, when it was lowered to 10 percent for the damages and interest. The implication seems to be that the buyer received one lump sum, and no more, for both damages and interest combined. The legisla-tors repealed that law in 1728 but only to insert a still lower rate of 8 percent for the now combined charges for damages and interest. In 1754 they reduced the general legal rate of interest to 6 percent, but returned to 10 percent the rate allowed for damages and interest on protested bills.[14] There was a considerable business in Barbados bills in the North American colonies, as the discussion in chapter 3 showed. Most negotiations involving Barbados and a North American colony were based on the comparative pars of the two colo-nies calculated on the local values of the piece of eight.[15]

8. Gov. Christopher Codrington, at Antigua, to Board of Trade, 13 July 1691, C.O. 152/38, fol. 102. See also Chalmers, *History of Currency*, 9–10, 48–49.

9. See also invoice dated Barbados, 20 Apr. 1678, Royal African Company, Copybook of Invoices Homeward, 1676–1678. T. 70/937, P.R.O.; Gov. James Kendall, at Barbados, to Board of Trade, July 1689, C.O. 28/37, fol. 116v; Oldmixon, *British Empire in America*, II, 165.

10. The Barbadian experiment with paper currency that caused the dis-tortion in 1706–1707 is recounted in Curtis P. Nettels, *The Money Supply of the American Colonies before 1720*, University of Wisconsin Studies in the Social Sciences and History, No. 20 (Madison, Wis., 1934), 269–271.

11. There are a few references to the rate at London on Barbados. In July 1711 it was £125 Barbados currency per £100 sterling; in Aug. 1711, £120; and in Aug. 1712, £110. Enclosure in Ordnance Office to Treasury, 30 Oct. 1711, T. 1/139, fol. 36; treasurer of the Navy to Treasury, 13 Aug. 1712, T. 1/151, fol. 12; Office for Sick and Wounded [Seamen] to Treasury, 16 Oct. 1712, T. 1/153, fols. 35r–35v; report of the treasurer of the Navy, 24 Feb. 1712/13, T. 1/158, fol. 200r.

12. *Barbados Gazette* (Bridgetown), 5 May 1733, as printed in [Keimer, ed.], *Caribbeana*, 160–161.

13. "The difference [between par at £133.33 and the usual rate for bills of exchange, £130] being allowed for three or four months usance," accord-ing to [Smith], *Two Letters to Mr. Wood*, 38, 61. K. G. Davies, "The Origin of the Commission System in the West India Trade [1650–1700]," Royal Histori-cal Society, *Transactions*, 5th Ser., II (1952), 98, examined the records of some 1,500 bills of exchange sent to the Royal African Company between 1672 and 1694 (in T. 70/269–277, 282). He discovered that the sights of 30 or 40 days common in the 1670s lengthened to as much as 6 to 12 months later in the 1680s. See also Richard B. Sheridan, *Sugar and Slavery: An Economic History of the British West Indies, 1623–1775* (St. Lawrence, Barbados, 1974), 288, 290.

14. For these acts see Rawlin, ed., *Laws of Barbados*, 70, 83; *Acts of Assembly, Passed in the Island of Barbados, from 1648 . . .* (London, 1732), 363–364; Hall and Hall, eds., *Acts of Barbados*, 359–360.

15. This did not always result in completely equitable transactions, as is shown in the Watts-Clarke example above in chap. 3, n. 24.

TABLE 4.1. **Rate of Exchange: Barbados on London, 1687–1775**

(Pounds Barbados Currency per £100 Sterling)

Year	Jan.	Feb.	Mar.	Apr.	May	June	July	Aug.	Sept.	Oct.	Nov.	Dec.	Average
1687	110.00				110.00								110.00
1688				110.00		110.00	111.00	110.00				[111.00]	110.50
1689		110.00					110.00						110.00
1690	110.00		112.00	111.00		110.00	110.00	110.00		110.00	110.00		110.38
1691	110.00			110.00	112.00	110.00	110.93						110.53
1692			115.00				113.50	115.00			115.00	115.00	114.75
1693	115.00	113.38	115.00		114.00				115.00				114.49
1694	115.00		115.00	115.00	114.72	113.75		115.00					114.83
1695													
1696													
1697													
1698													
1699													
1700	110.00		110.00		110.00	117.50			110.00	114.67			112.10
1701													
1702						122.50	122.00			125.50	130.00		124.08
1703						120.00		120.00	126.50				121.62
1704				110.00		119.53	115.00	130.00			115.38	122.50	118.74
1705				140.00			142.50						141.25
1706						[160.00]		157.50	177.50				163.75
1707	177.50	177.50									182.50	182.50	180.00
1708												[135.00]	135.00
1709							135.00	135.00	135.00				135.00
1710					135.00		130.00	135.00					133.75
1711							125.00	125.00	127.50	130.00		120.00	125.42
1712								120.00				122.60	121.30

TABLE 4.1 (Continued): **Barbados on London** (Pounds Barbados Currency per £100 Sterling)

Year	Jan.	Feb.	Mar.	Apr.	May	June	July	Aug.	Sept.	Oct.	Nov.	Dec.	Average
1713									120.00	121.00			120.50
1714	125.00	122.00											123.50
1715													
1716	125.00							130.00					127.50
1717	130.00												130.00
1718		130.00									125.50	127.50	128.25
1719		128.00			128.00		130.00						128.67
1720	128.00					130.00	130.00	130.00					129.33
1721												130.00	130.00
1722							130.00						130.00
1723											128.00		128.00
1724				128.00					128.00	128.00	128.05		128.01
1725						127.94							127.94
1726				128.00									128.00
1727							130.00				130.00		130.00
1728	130.00			130.00	130.00	130.00							130.00
1729				130.00	130.00		130.00						130.00
1730				128.33	130.00		128.00			128.00	128.00	130.00	128.61
1731				128.00			130.00					128.00	128.67
1732		130.00		130.00		130.00	130.00		130.00				130.00
1733		132.00		133.00	132.00			132.00					132.17
1734			132.00	132.00	132.00	132.00							132.00
1735								130.00	130.00	130.00	130.00	136.84	131.71
1736						130.00							130.00
1737						130.00	130.00	130.00	130.00			130.00	130.00
1738						130.00	130.00	130.00	130.00			130.08	130.03
1739							130.00	130.00			130.00		130.00

TABLE 4.1 (Continued): Barbados on London (Pounds Barbados Currency per £100 Sterling)

Year	Jan.	Feb.	Mar.	Apr.	May	June	July	Aug.	Sept.	Oct.	Nov.	Dec.	Average
1740						130.00				130.00			130.00
1741	130.00			130.00	130.00					128.00	128.00	128.17	129.35
1742	130.00			128.00				128.00	128.00	128.00	128.00		128.50
1743			130.00							136.00			133.00
1744			138.00						145.00				141.50
1745	150.00												150.00
1746							143.75	140.00				150.00	145.94
1747						145.00	145.00	145.00		145.00			145.00
1748						137.50	135.00		135.00	135.00	135.00	140.00	136.39
1749	140.00	140.00				135.00	135.00		136.41		135.00	135.00	136.43
1750					135.00								135.00
1751													
1752													
1753													
1754													
1755													
1756	140.00	137.50					140.00			140.00	140.00	140.00	139.58
1757						140.00	140.00	140.00			140.00		140.00
1758					140.00		140.00				140.00		140.00
1759													
1760				135.00	135.00								135.00
1761											135.00		135.00
1762	130.00		135.00					135.00	130.00				132.50
1763											135.00		135.00
1764					135.00	135.00			135.00				135.00
1765								135.00		135.00	135.00		135.00
1766													
1767							135.00					135.00	135.00

TABLE 4.1 (Continued): **Barbados on London** (Pounds Barbados Currency per £100 Sterling)

Year	Jan.	Feb.	Mar.	Apr.	May	June	July	Aug.	Sept.	Oct.	Nov.	Dec.	Average
1768	[135.00]												135.00
1769		125.00							130.00				127.50
1770						130.00	130.00						130.00
1771			130.00									130.00	130.00
1772											130.00	[130.00]	130.00
1773	130.00	130.00	130.00				130.00			135.00		130.00	130.83
1774					130.00			135.00				[135.00]	133.33
1775						140.00						[140.00]	140.00

Notes and Sources: **TABLE 4.1**

Figures inserted between square brackets are assigned to that month arbitrarily.

1687–1714: Royal African Company, Copybooks of Letters Received, 1683–1715, Copybooks of Bills of Exchange Received, 1688–1718, T. 70/2, 8, 12–14, 16–18, 274–279, 283, Public Record Office.

1688, 1706, 1708: John Oldmixon, *The British Empire in America* (London, 1708), II, 165. See Pat Rogers, "An Early Colonial Historian: John Oldmixon and *The British Empire in America*," *Journal of American Studies*, VII (1973), 113–123.

1689: Col. James Kendall, at Barbados, to Board of Trade, July 1689, C.O. 28/37, fol. 116v, P.R.O.

1702–1704: William Trent Ledgers "B" and "C," 1701–1703, 1703–1709, the former in the Stephen Collins and Son Papers, Library of Congress, the latter in the Historical Society of Pennsylvania, Philadelphia.

1704: Account of ship *Samuel*, dated Barbados, 8 June 1704, C. 104/15, pt. i, *Lilie* v. *Waterhouse*, P.R.O.

1707: Presentment of Grand Jury of Barbados to Samuel Cox, chief justice of the Court of Pleas, 2 Jan. 1706/07, C.O. 28/9, fol. 344v.

1709–1711: Richard Poor, Jr., Journal, 1699–1713, Codex English 7, John Carter Brown Library, Brown University, Providence, R.I.

1716–1774: Letters and accounts from Barbados to Society for the Propagation of the Gospel, Archives of the S.P.G., Class II, Ser. C: Miscellaneous Unbound MSS, Group WI, and Ser. X: Miscellaneous, United Society for the Propagation of the Gospel, London.

1718–1719: Hugh Hall, Jr., Letter Book, 1716–1720, Houghton Library, Harvard College Library, Harvard University, Cambridge, Mass. See Samuel E. Morison, "The Letter-Book of Hugh Hall, Merchant of Barbados, 1716–1720," Colonial Society of Massachusetts, *Publications*, XXXII (*Transactions, 1933–1937*), 514–521.

1718: James Logan, at Philadelphia, to Robert Watts, at Bridgetown, Barbados, 1 Dec. 1718, Parchment Logan Letter Book, 1717–1731, p. 53, Logan Papers, 1664–1871, Hist. Soc. Pa.

1720: Entry for 17 May 1720, Alexander Wooddrup Account Books, 1720–1734, I (1720–1724), Lib. Cong.

1722: John Atkins, *A Voyage to Guinea, Brasil, and the West-Indies; in His Majesty's Ships, the Swallow and Weymouth* (London, 1735), 209.

Notes and Sources: **TABLE 4.1 (Continued)**

1724–1748: Mercantile Papers of Thomas Newson, C. 104/77–80, *Re Newson's Estate*. See chap. 3, n. 30, above.

1724–1775: Newton Plantation Accounts, Newton Papers, 1706–1920, MS 523, University of London Library.

1730: Gov. Henry Worsley, at Barbados, to Board of Trade, 23 Dec. 1730, C.O. 28/22, fol. 109v.

1734–1762: John Reynell Correspondence, 1729–1773, Coates and Reynell Papers, Hist. Soc. Pa.

1737–1740: Roberts Plantation Accounts, C. 108/25, *Re Roberts*.

1741: *Journals of the Assembly of Jamaica, from January 20th,1663–4* . . . (St. Jago de la Vega, Jamaica, 1795–1829), III, 574.

1744: Robert Dinwiddie, at Barbados, to Commissioners of the Customs, 30 Mar. 1744, T. 1/315, fol. 82v, P.R.O.

1744–1745: Samuel Powel, at Philadelphia, to Thomas Hothersall, at Barbados, 16 Oct. 1744, and to Thomas Plumsted, at London, 12 Feb. 1744/45, Samuel Powel, Jr., Letter Books, 1727–1747, II, Hist. Soc. Pa.

1746–1749: Robert Morris Ledger B, 1747–1750, reverse of Clerk's Fee Book, 1762–1763, Dorchester County, Md., Circuit Court, Maryland Hall of Records, Annapolis.

1748: Coates-Reynell Correspondence, 1729–1836, Box I (1729–1764), Coates-Reynell Papers, Hist. Soc. Pa.

1749–1750: Austin and Laurens Waste Book, 1749–1751, Henry Laurens Papers, 1747–1882, South Carolina Historical Society, Charleston.

1756–1758, 1765: Galloway Correspondence, Galloway Business Papers, 1654–1819, Galloway-Maxey-Markoe Family Papers, 1654–1888, Lib. Cong.

1757–1760: Clifford Correspondence, Vol. II, fol. 8, Vol. III, fols. 46, 55, Pemberton Papers, Hist. Soc. Pa.

1758: Hudson Letters, 1743–1785, Hudson Family Papers, 1659–1862, New York Public Library, New York City.

1761–1773: John Smith, at Barbados, to Samuel Munckley and Co., at Bristol, 4 Dec. 1761, 13 Jan. 1762, and Philip Lycott and Co., at Barbados, to Munckley, 2 Oct. 1773, Munckley Papers, Bristol Archives Office, Council House, Bristol, Eng.

1762: Ledger, 1762–1763, fol. 202, Edward Dixon Records, Lib. Cong.

1762: Correspondence, 1749–1803, II, no. 9858, Collins Papers.

1763: Account, Barbados, 10 Nov. 1763, Samuel and William Vernon Papers, 1750–1775, Box VII, "Slavery MSS.," New-York Historical Society, New York City.

1765–1770: Thomas Applethwaite, at Barbados, to Henry Tucker, at Norfolk, Va., 20 Oct. and 23 Nov. 1765, Cornelius Donovan, at Barbados, to Neil Jamieson, at Norfolk, Va., 18 July 1770, Neil Jamieson Papers, 1757–1789, VI, nos. 1201, 1248, XII, no. 2673, Lib. Cong.

1767: Henry and John Cruger "Copy Book of Letters," 1764–1768, memorandum of bill of exchange, inside front cover, Cruger Papers, N.-Y. Hist. Soc.

1768: [Henry Frere], *A Short History of Barbados from Its First Discovery and Settlement to the End of the Year 1767* (London, 1768), 75.

1769: Edward Grace Account Book, 1768–1769, Edward Grace and Company Papers, MS 12052, Guildhall Library, London.

1771–1775: William Senhouse Diary, 1750–1800, I, 268, 276, 281, 285, 295, 299, Rhodes House Library, Oxford, and "The Autobiographical Manuscript of William Senhouse," *Journal of Barbados Museum and Historical Society,* II (1935), 115, 119, 123, 125, 131, 134.

1773: Darby Lux, at Barbados, to Charles Ridgely, at Baltimore, 5 Dec. 1773, Ridgely Papers, 1733–1858, MS 692.1, Maryland Historical Society, Baltimore.

1773: Elizabeth Donnan, ed., *Documents Illustrative of the History of the Slave Trade to America* (Washington, D.C., 1930–1935), III, 267.

Jamaica

The conquest of Jamaica in 1655 as part of Oliver Cromwell's "Western Design" deprived Spain of her ancient colony but so disrupted the island that its conquerors could not begin to turn it to production for another decade and more. During these first years the influx of English soldiers and colonists provided enough English coinage to satisfy local demands for currency. As the money supply began to tighten, Jamaicans at first tried to import more coin. In January 1668/69 James Modyford wrote to Andrew King, merchant of London, advising him on what would make a good cargo for the Jamaica market. He encouraged him to send "good liquors," white indentured servants ("Highlanders . . . the best of white servants"), and "readie money." By this last he meant "English money," which was better than "Spanish" money because "a piece of ⁸/₈ goes butt att 4s [20p] per piece here and will cost you more att home, but 4s of English money is 4s current alsoe here."[16] In other words, in Jamaica in 1669 Jamaica currency at par was equal to sterling (£100 Jamaica currency equaled £100 sterling). The colonists preferred sterling coin over pieces of eight because the latter were frequently underweight.

Within three years of Modyford's letter the situation had

gotten even worse. Money had become much tighter. In order to "bring and keep plenty of money in this His Majesties island," the Jamaica assembly voted in February 1671/72 to give the piece of eight "a vallue . . . equall to what is practiced by His Majesties subjects in other settlements. . . ." Henceforth the piece of eight had a value of 5s (25p) Jamaica currency; at that rate the par of exchange was £111.11 Jamaica currency per £100 sterling. Renewed several times subsequently, the 1672 rating was still the legal value of the piece of eight in Jamaica 120 years later.[17]

Despite this apparent stability, Jamaica is a good example of the legal fiction maintained in the West Indies about the value of silver. As early as September 1683 the assembly moved to increase the currency value of the piece of eight. After a long fight an act of April 1688 succeeded in making the piece of eight of seventeen pennyweight worth 6s (30p). Imperial opposition voided the law in October 1689 but could not alter practice.[18] By the time of the proclamation of 1704 the seventeen-pennyweight piece of eight had passed at 6s for some while, most likely from 1688 on.[19] Later, probably

16. Modyford to King, 20 Jan. 1668/69, Muniment No. 11922, as printed in A. P. Thornton, ed., "The Modyfords and Morgan: Letters from Sir James Modyford on the Affairs of Jamaica, 1667–1672, in the Muniments of Westminster Abbey," *Jamaican Historical Review*, II (1952), 52. The quotation about the Highland Scots is from Modyford to King, 24 May 1669, Muniment No. 11925, *ibid.*, 53. For the 4s value for pieces of eight (because of the imperfect state of the coinage), see *Edwards v. Sheafe*, session of 30 Jan. 1671/72, *Records of the Suffolk County Court, 1671–1680* (Colonial Society of Massachusetts, *Publications*, XXIX–XXX [Boston, 1933]), I, 60–62; and Chalmers, *History of Currency*, 97–98.

17. The quoted rationale is from the first of these renewals, dated 14 Mar. 1673/74. For the act of 1672 see Gov. Thomas Lynch, at Jamaica, to Board of Trade, 10 Mar. 1671/72, C.O. 1/28, fol. 58r; and *Journals of the Assembly of Jamaica from January 20th, 1663–4 . . .* (St. Jago de la Vega, Jamaica, 1795–1829), I, 5. For the renewals of 1674, 15 May 1675, 23 June 1677, and 18 Mar. 1680/81, see *ibid.*, 7, 11, 14, 19, 57, and C.O. 139/3, pp. 447–448, C.O. 139/4, fol. 78, C.O. 139/7, pp. 42–43. That last version continued in force at least until 1792. See *The Laws of Jamaica. Comprehending All the Acts in Force, Passed between the Thirty-Second Year of the Reign of King Charles the Second, and the Thirty-Third Year of the Reign of King George the Third* (St. Jago de la Vega, Jamaica, 1792–1808), I, 25–27. See also Chalmers, *History of Currency*, 98–99.

18. *Journals of the Assembly of Jamaica*, I, 71, 106–118, 130. See also Nettels, *Money Supply*, 234–236, and his citations to C.O. 140/4, fols. 182–318 *passim*. For the disallowance see C.O. 138/6, pp. 273–278.

19. At a meeting of the Board of Trade on 21 Apr. 1703 the three agents

not until the troubled times of the early 1720s, mercantile custom oversaw another rise to 6s 3d (31.25p),[20] and in 1758 a new law, also disallowed, increased the value to 6s 8d

(33.3p).[21] At these rates the par of exchange at Jamaica by custom was £111.11 per £100 sterling from 1672 to the mid-1680s, £133.33 from then to the early 1720s, and £138.89 (in practice, £140) until 1758. The rate in the act of 1758 would have raised par to £148.15.

After 1758 Jamaicans seem to have used two different valuations for the piece of eight, one for domestic, internal trade and the other for foreign trade—except when they stood to lose thereby. There is no question that within the island the piece of eight continued to be rated at the old value, customary since the 1720s, of 6s 3d (31.25p).[22] Moreover, bills of exchange negotiated on the island maintained the old level of exchange, £140 Jamaica currency to £100 sterling, which argues further that the price of coin was

for Jamaica, Sir Gilbert Heathcote, Sir Bartholomew Gracedieu, and Benjamin Way, reported that the piece of eight of 16 dwt. passed for 5s 6d, equivalent to 6s for the full-weight coin of 17.5 dwt. C.O. 391/16, p. 85. See Lillian M. Penson, *The Colonial Agents of the British West Indies: A Study in Colonial Administration, Mainly in the Eighteenth Century* (London, 1924), *passim*. See also Heathcote to Richard Hill, [1700 or 1701], T. 1/71, fol. 328r.

20. See the petitions enclosed in John, Lord Carteret, to Gov. Henry Bentwick, duke of Portland, 22 Oct. 1722, C.O. 324/34, pp. 196–206 (Carteret was secretary of state for the Southern Department; Portland was the new governor of Jamaica); [Smith], *Two Letters to Mr. Wood*, 17–18; and letter from Jamaica, 22 Sept. 1725, reporting that "a practice hath prevailed so much of late years, that pieces of eight of an uncertain weight, now pass current in tale at ten ryals or 6s.3d. each," in [James Knight], *The State of the Island of Jamaica, Chiefly in Relation to Its Commerce, and the Conduct of the Spaniards in the West-Indies, Address'd to a Member of Parliament by a Person Who Resided Several Years at Jamaica* (London, 1726), 34. This was the equivalent of 7.5d per real, or bit, for the piece of eight of 10 reales. It is the value mentioned repeatedly for Jamaica in 1725 and 1726 in the Peter Jay Journal, 1724–1748, pp. 1, 4, and *passim*, Peter Jay Papers, 1724–1770, New-York Historical Society, New York City. See also Chalmers, *History of Currency*, 100–101; Edward Long's notebook extracts from the 1741 report of "Mr. Colebrook," paymaster of the Royal Army, on the "par of money between England and Jamaica," in his Miscellaneous Notes and Memoranda, I, fol. 27, Charles Edward Long Manuscripts, Additional Manuscript 12411, Brit. Lib.; Lt. Gov. Henry Moore, at Spanish Town, Jamaica, to Board of Trade, 25 Feb. 1759, C.O. 137/30, fol. 149; [Charles Leslie], *A New and Exact Account of Jamaica*, 3d ed. (Edinburgh, 1740), 40; and *The Importance of Jamaica to Great-Britain, Consider'd; with Some Account of That Island, from Its Discovery in 1492 to This Time . . . in a Letter to a Gentleman* (London, [1741]), 81. L. W. Hanson, *Contemporary Printed Sources for British and Irish Economic History, 1701–1750* (Cambridge, 1963), 367, is less than confident in attributing the *State of the Island of Jamaica* to Knight (citing A. Boyer, *Political State*, XXXVI, 240), but Knight claimed the book in his "Thoughts on the sugar trade and Jamaica," c. 1725–1727, Long MSS, Add. MS 22677, fol. 3. There are strong reasons for also attributing the authorship of the last-mentioned work, *The Importance of Jamaica*, to Knight.

21. For the text of the act see C.O. 139/19, no. 15. See also *Journals of the Assembly of Jamaica*, V, 61–103 *passim*. For the disallowance see Matthew Lamb to Board of Trade, 25 Jan. 1760, C.O. 137/31, fol. 9r–v; *Journal of the Commissioners for Trade and Plantations . . . Preserved in the Public Record Office . . .* (London, 1920–1938), XI (1759–1763), 138–140, 185; and *Laws of Jamaica*, I, 417. See also the later act of 1774 that rated gold coins, *ibid.*, II, 136–140; and *An Almanack, and Register, for the Year of Our Lord, 1775* (Kingston, Jamaica, [1774]).

22. E.g., see the account of the hire of slaves, dated 18 Dec. 1775, in Spring Plantation Account, 1775, Spring Plantation Papers, Ashton Court Papers, Woolnough Papers, AC/WO 16(27) 95(d), Bristol Archives Office, Council House, Bristol, Eng. At "3 bits per day," 1,709 man-days of labor is extended to equal £160 4s 4d; the piece of eight of 10 reales, or bits, here the equivalent of 6s 3d. A useful introduction to these records is Julian P. Marsh, "The Spring Plantation Estate: A Study of Some Aspects of a Jamaican Sugar Plantation, 1747–1801" (B.A. thesis, University of Nottingham, 1969). See also "A Table, for the more ready Casting up the Coins in Jamaica," in *An Almanack and Register, for Jamaica, for the Year of Our Lord, 1762* (Kingston, Jamaica, [1761]); and Sidney W. Mintz, "Currency Problems in Eighteenth Century Jamaica and Gresham's Law," in Robert A. Manners, ed., *Process and Pattern in Culture: Essays in Honor of Julian H. Steward* (Chicago, [1964]), 248–265.

unaltered on the island and that par remained at the level set by the piece of eight at 6s 3d (see table 4.2). It is equally clear that after 1758 Jamaicans persisted in telling correspondents that dollars were "passing here at 6/8" (33.3p), the rate specified in the disallowed act of 1758 and a rate at which Jamaicans billed merchants in North America.[23] Thomas Dolbeare quoted this as the cost of pieces of eight when calculating the dollar value of a credit balance of £2,276.62 in the favor of the Newport, Rhode Island, firm of Rivera and Lopez. At the foreign rate Dolbeare owed Rivera and Lopez 6,830 dollars; at the internal rate of 6s 3d, he would have owed them 7,285 dollars. The purpose of the deception obviously was to cut down on the export of pieces of eight.

Dolbeare—and Jamaica—remained quite happy with this deception until Rivera and Lopez once settled an account with Dolbeare by resolving the difference between Rhode Island and Jamaica currency in the same way: using a ratio based on the respective currency values of the piece of eight. This time the result was not in Dolbeare's favor, and, however inconsistently, he complained; he wanted Rivera and Lopez to use the comparative bill rates on sterling: "I find also that instead of dollars being reckoned at 6/8d [33.3p], the sterling should be brot into currency which makes an odds

. . . in my favour, dollars being at 6/8d from the policy of this island, not from the par of exchange or intrinsic value."[24] "The policy of this island" to cheat the merchants of the continental colonies stemmed from Jamaican unhappiness with the venerable North American practice of selling goods on the island for cash and then taking the cash to buy molasses and rum—not Jamaican molasses and rum but French molasses and rum.[25]

Jamaicans drew bills of exchange on credit balances in London at rates of exchange that remained incredibly stable over much of the century, at least insofar as we have data. After the mid-1730s the bill rate seems almost never to have varied from £140 Jamaica currency to £100 sterling (see table 4.2).[26] What did vary was the usance—the length of

23. Thomas Dolbeare, at Kingston, Jamaica, to Rivera and Lopez, at Newport, R.I., 7 Dec. 1773, [Worthington C. Ford, ed.], *Commerce of Rhode Island, 1726–1800* (Massachusetts Historical Society, *Collections*, 7th Ser., IX–X [Boston, 1914–1915]), I, 467, hereafter cited as *Commerce of Rhode Island*. Dolbeare's (and Jamaica's) deception is made evident in the same sentence when he effectively tells Rivera and Lopez that the bit is worth 7.5d Jamaica currency. At 10 bits to the dollar this, of course, makes the dollar worth 6s 3d, not 6s 8d. For other uses of this "North American rate," see the John and Peter Chevalier "Day Book 1770[–1783]," entries dated 24 June 1772, 15 May 1773, 2 May 1774, John and Peter Chevalier Papers, 1757–1783, Historical Society of Pennsylvania, Philadelphia.

24. Dolbeare to Aaron Lopez, 24 Jan. 1776, *Commerce of Rhode Island*, II, 37.

25. See the explanation for the act of 1758 offered by [Edward Long], *The History of Jamaica* (London, 1774), I, 535. Bryan Edwards, in his "Notes on Longs Jamaica" (1779), called this "a very foolish and fruitless expedient." Codex English 87, John Carter Brown Library, Brown University, Providence, R.I. Edwards's own copy of Long's *History* contains the original of these "Notes" as marginalia; it survives in the collections of the library of the University of the West Indies, Mona, Jamaica. Kenneth Everard Niven Ingram, "A Bibliographical Survey of Jamaica History, 1655–1838, with Particular Reference to Manuscript Sources" (M.Phil. thesis, University of London, 1970), I, 137, n. 57.

26. There are a few references to the rate at London on Jamaica. In July and August 1701 and in 1706 it was at £115 to £120; during the same period (1701–1706) Sir Gilbert Heathcote had a contract with the Victualling Office to supply the troops in Jamaica at the rate of £108 currency for every £100 sterling paid him in London; in Aug. 1711, the rate was £118. Letters, all dated at London, from: Laurence Galdy and Co. to Treasury, 25 July 1701, T. 1/75, fol. 135r; Sir Bartholomew Gracedieu to Treasury, 31 July 1701, T. 1/75, fol. 172r; memorandum on the rate of exchange, [Aug. 1701?], T. 1/71, fol. 330r; minutes of meeting of Lords of the Treasury, 5 Aug. 1701, T. 29/13, p. 34; [Navy] Victualling Office to Treasury, 27 Nov. 1711, T. 1/139, fols.

time after presentation that was allowed to intervene before the bill had to be paid. Like Barbados, Jamaica regularly drew bills payable well beyond the usual thirty- to forty-day period. Fifty, sixty, ninety days, and even longer, was not unknown.[27] And such bills sold at a disadvantage. Thomas Willing once told the firm of Whatley, Meyler, and Hall of Jamaica that their bills "at 60 days sight . . . being 30 days longer than usual" would only sell at Philadelphia at 2.5 points lower than the going rate, a discount of 1.5 percent.[28] Protested bills paid damages at a low 8 percent, and interest was 6 percent.[29] We know little else about the drawing of bills on Jamaica.

168v–169r; memorial of Heathcote to commissioners of the public accounts, 9 Feb. 1710/11, in Robert Harley, Earl of Oxford, Official Papers, Miscellaneous MSS, Vol. 48: "Victualling," Duke of Portland MSS, Vol. 292, Loan 29, Brit. Lib.

27. Spring Plantation Account, 1762, Spring Plantation Papers, AC/WO 16(27) 48(c); [Long], *History of Jamaica*, I, 568–569; and the statement by Beeston Long in "Report from the Select Committee, to Whom It Was Referred to Consider and Examine the Accounts of the Extraordinary Services Incurred and Paid, and Not Provided for by Parliament, Which Have Been Laid Before the House of Commons in the Years 1776, 1777, and 1778" (1778), Great Britain, House of Commons, *Sessional Papers, 1731–1800*, XXXV (Reports, V), No. 36, p. 39.

28. Willing, at Philadelphia, to Whatley, Meyler, and Hall, 1 Feb. 1755, Willing and Morris Letter Book, 1754–1761, p. 69, Hist. Soc. Pa.

29. Spring Plantation Account, 1762, Spring Plantation Papers, AC/WO 16(27) 48(c).

TABLE 4.2. **Rate of Exchange: Jamaica on London, 1675–1775**

(Pounds Jamaica Currency per £100 Sterling)

Year	Jan.	Feb.	Mar.	Apr.	May	June	July	Aug.	Sept.	Oct.	Nov.	Dec.	Average
1675					106.50								106.50
1676	115.00												115.00
1677													
1678													
1679		109.43	110.00										109.72
1680													
1681										108.00			108.00
1682													
1683				103.25	105.00				118.00			[120.00]	114.04
1684												120.00	120.00
1685													
1686							110.00		117.65	110.00			111.91
1687		117.65											117.65
1688						110.00							110.00
1689						120.00							120.00
1690							120.00	120.00	120.00				120.00
1691												125.00	125.00
1692	125.00												125.00
1693													
1694													
1695													
1696													
1697													
1698													
1699													

TABLE 4.2 (Continued): Jamaica on London (Pounds Jamaica Currency per £100 Sterling)

Year	Jan.	Feb.	Mar.	Apr.	May	June	July	Aug.	Sept.	Oct.	Nov.	Dec.	Average
1700													
1701													
1702													
1703													
1704												[125.00]	125.00
1705							130.00					[125.00]	127.50
1706	[125.00]							120.00	125.00	120.00	120.00	120.00	122.50
1707											116.00	120.00	118.00
1708	120.00						120.00						120.00
1709					116.00								116.00
1710												125.00	125.00
1711											135.00		135.00
1712													
1713												130.00	130.00
1714													
1715												135.00	135.00
1716						135.00							135.00
1717								135.00					135.00
1718													
1719													
1720						135.00		135.00					135.00
1721													
1722			130.00		130.00	125.00				130.00		135.00	130.00
1723	130.00		130.00		130.00	130.00							130.00
1724				130.00	135.00		135.00			135.00		135.00	134.17
1725	135.00					135.00		135.00	137.50				135.42
1726			135.00		135.00								135.00
1727													

TABLE 4.2 (Continued): Jamaica on London (Pounds Jamaica Currency per £100 Sterling)

Year	Jan.	Feb.	Mar.	Apr.	May	June	July	Aug.	Sept.	Oct.	Nov.	Dec.	Average
1728												[135.00]	135.00
1729		135.00											135.00
1730											135.00	[135.00]	135.00
1731													
1732	135.00												135.00
1733			135.00				140.00						137.50
1734					140.00								140.00
1735	137.50											[140.00]	138.75
1736					140.00								140.00
1737													
1738									140.00		140.00		140.00
1739								140.00			140.00		140.00
1740												[135.00]	135.00
1741				140.00							140.00		140.00
1742					137.50			140.00	140.00				138.75
1743			140.00										140.00
1744													
1745	[145.00]							140.00				[150.00]	145.00
1746													
1747													
1748													
1749													
1750													
1751				140.00									140.00
1752						140.00							140.00
1753			140.00	140.00			140.00	140.00					140.00
1754	140.00				140.00								140.00

TABLE 4.2 (Continued): Jamaica on London (Pounds Jamaica Currency per £100 Sterling)

Year	Jan.	Feb.	Mar.	Apr.	May	June	July	Aug.	Sept.	Oct.	Nov.	Dec.	Average
1755							140.00						140.00
1756		140.00											140.00
1757						140.00		140.00	140.00			140.00	140.00
1758											140.00	140.00	140.00
1759					140.00							140.00	140.00
1760	140.00				140.00	140.00							140.00
1761		140.00					140.00						140.00
1762						140.00					140.00		140.00
1763							140.00				140.00		140.00
1764													
1765													
1766											140.00		140.00
1767													
1768			140.00									140.00	140.00
1769													
1770		140.00			140.00							140.00	140.00
1771											140.00	140.00	140.00
1772	[140.00]						140.00						140.00
1773	[140.00]				141.25	140.00						140.00	140.21
1774	[140.00]												140.00
1775	[140.00]			140.00									140.00

Notes and Sources: **TABLE 4.2**

Figures inserted in square brackets are assigned to that month arbitrarily.

1675–1713: Letters and Accounts, Bybrook Plantation Records, Items 1089–1090, Helyar of Coker Court Documents and Muniments, Somerset Record Office, Taunton, Eng. J. H. Bennett based two very useful articles on these papers: "Cary Helyar, Merchant and Planter of Seventeenth-Century Jamaica," *William and Mary Quarterly*, 3d Ser., XXI (1964), 53–76, and "William Whaley, Planter of Seventeenth-Century Jamaica," *Agricultural History*, XL (1966), 113–123. In the former

Notes and Sources: **TABLE 4.2 (Continued)**

article he indicated (p. 55, n. 8) that all of the values found in these papers and reproduced in his article were in sterling. He either did not see or missed the significance of the several references in the letters and accounts to the rate of exchange between Jamaica currency and sterling. Helyar and Whaley, on the island, were talking in terms of local currency, said so, and expressed the difference between it and sterling.

1679–1726: Royal African Company, Copybooks of Letters Received, 1720–1746, p. 1, 1706–1718, pp. 19, 25, 53, 57, 89, 201, 1683–1698, pp. 61, 85, 1704–1706, fol. 93r, 1678–1681, fol. 8v, 1681–1684, fol. 52v, 1687–1693, fols. 12v, 49v, 1714–1719, fol. 19v, Copybooks of Bills of Exchange Received, 1689–1693, 1705–1718, 1720–1726, *passim*, Copybook of Invoices Homeward, 1678–1680, pp. 77, 83, 1680–1681, p. 192, 1686, pp. 169, 176, 1688, p. 54, 1716–1721, p. 96, T. 70/4, 8, 12, 14–17, 19, 275, 276, 279, 280, 938–939, 942–943, 957, Public Record Office.

1683: [Francis Hanson, ed.], *The Laws of Jamaica, Passed by the Assembly, and Confirmed by His Majesty in Council, Feb. 23, 1683* (London, 1683), "Preface."

1684: Jamaica, Account Current, Aug.–Dec. 1684, C.O. 140/4, fol. 64, P.R.O.

1704–1706: Account of Mrs. Rebecca Elbridge with Spring Plantation, 1717, Spring Plantation Papers, Ashton Court Papers, The Woolnough Papers, AC/WO 16(4)a, Bristol Archives Office, Council House, Bristol, Eng.

1711–1741: *Journals of the Assembly of Jamaica from January 20th 1663–4 . . .* (St. Jago de la Vega, Jamaica, 1795–1829), II, 58, 414, 677, III, 62, 180, 249, 573.

1722: John Atkins, *A Voyage to Guinea, Brasil, and the West-Indies; in His Majesty's Ships, the Swallow and Weymouth* (London, 1735), 244.

1725: Letter from Jamaica, 22 Sept. 1725, in [James Knight], *The State of the Island of Jamaica* (London, 1726), 33.

1728: Gov. Robert Hunter, at Jamaica, to Board of Trade, 24 Dec. 1730, C.O. 137/19, fol. 49r.

1730–1742: Clarke Plantation Accounts, Nos. 1, 2, and 4, C. 107/148, *Clarke v. Knight*, P.R.O.

1730–1745: Edward Long's Miscellaneous Notes and Memoranda, I, fols. 21v, 22v, 27r, 28r, Charles Edward Long Manuscripts, Additional Manuscript 12411, British Library.

1733: Entry dated Apr. 1733, Alexander Wooddrup Account Books, 1720–1734, II, Library of Congress.

1736–1756: John Reynell Correspondence, 1729–1773, Coates and Reynell Papers, Historical Society of Pennsylvania, Philadelphia.

1741: "State of Jamaica," in Gov. Edward Trelawney, at Jamaica, to Board of Trade, 21 Nov. 1741, William Petty, Earl of Shelburne, Papers, XLV, fol. 26, William L. Clements Library, University of Michigan, Ann Arbor. (I wish here to thank John C. Dann, curator of manuscripts of the Clements Library, for his help with this item.)

1751–1773: Spring Plantation Accounts, 1747–1776, Spring Plantation Papers, AC/WO 16(27), 1–97. See also (for 1752–1762) Gov. William Henry Lyttelton, at Jamaica, to Board of Trade, 9 July 1763, C.O. 137/33, fol. 57.

1753: Gov. Charles Knowles, at Jamaica, to Board of Trade, 12 Jan. 1754, C.O. 137/27, fol. 22.

1753: Invoice and account of Peter du Bois, Kingston, Jamaica, Aug. and Sept. 1753, Frederick Ashton De Peyster MSS, Box 7, De Peyster Family Papers, 1677–1881, New-York Historical Society, New York City.

1756–1772: Caleb Dickinson Journal B, 1756–1770, pp. 14–15, 16, 51, 62, and Barton Isles Estate and Appleton Estate Plantation Accounts, 1770–1772, Items 406, 469, Muniments of the Dickinson Family of Kingweston, Somerset Record Office.

1757: Account book of the snow *Venus*, 1756–1757, Samuel and William Vernon Papers, 1750–1775, Box VII, "Slavery MSS.," N.-Y. Hist. Soc.

1763: Lyttelton to Board of Trade, 9 July 1763, C.O. 137/33, fol. 57v.

1764: Account of William Boyd, at Kingston, Jamaica, with John Cole and Co., at Liverpool, 20 Sept. 1764, Running Letters, Records of the Society, Society of Merchant Venturers, Bristol, Eng., as quoted in Elizabeth Donnan, ed., *Documents Illustrative of the History of the Slave Trade to America* (Washington, D.C., 1930–1935), II, 525.

1768: Chancey Hill Plantation Account, 1768, Maynard Clark Papers, item no. 1, in C. 104/8, *Walter v. Evans*.

Notes and Sources: **TABLE 4.2 (Continued)**

1768: Account of snow *Honduras Packet*, Capt. John Orrock, 1768–1769, in bundle no. 5, *Ex parte Hill, a bankrupt*, C. 110/54.

1770: Account of Archibald Montgomerie, at Kingston, Jamaica, 11 May 1770, Neil Jamieson Papers, 1757–1789, XII, no. 2556, Lib. Cong.

1772–1775: *Proceedings of the Hon. House of Assembly of Jamaica, on the Sugar and Slave-Trade, in a Session Which Began the 23rd of October 1792* (St. Jago de la Vega, Jamaica, 1792), Appendix XIII.

1773: John and Peter Chevalier "Day Book 1770[–1783]," John and Peter Chevalier Papers, 1757–1783, Hist. Soc. Pa.

1773: Thomas Dolbeare, at Kingston, Jamaica, to Rivera and Lopez, at Newport, R.I., 7 Dec. 1773, in [Worthington C. Ford, ed.], *Commerce of Rhode Island, 1726–1800* (Massachusetts Historical Society, *Collections*, 7th Ser., IX–X [Boston, 1914–1915]), I, 467.

1775: Capt. Peleg Clarke, at "St. Lucea" [Lucea, Jamaica], to John Fletcher, at London, 21 Apr. 1775, Clarke Letter Books, I, no. 76, Newport Historical Society, as printed in Donnan, ed., *Documents Illustrative of the History of the Slave Trade*, III, 309.

Leeward Islands

The British Leeward Islands denoted both a geographical entity and an administrative unit. Geographically the group included Antigua, St. Christopher (otherwise St. Kitts), Nevis, Montserrat, and the British Virgin Islands, the major islands in which were Tortola and Anguilla. Administrative membership in the Leeward Islands government, established in 1671, changed during the next three centuries both because of French conquest and, less frequently, because of governmental reorganization. The major variation before 1775 concerned St. Christopher, which was half English and half French during most of the seventeenth century and wholly English only after 1702. The various Leeward Islands did not become separate colonies until 1956.

Variety more than uniformity was the rule in the history of the Leewards' currency. The islands did have a common real money and money of account, which they shared with all the English colonies. And during part of the period after 1671 they had a common legislature that could and did establish the same currency rate for pieces of eight, thereby setting for a time a common par of exchange. But this did not mean that there was a uniform commercial rate of exchange. Even the fragile unity that had existed broke down in the eighteenth century, probably around the time of the proclamation of 1704 and the act of 1708. A combination of diverse solutions to the new problem for their currency caused by the act of 1708 and growing differences in the economic conditions of the islands worked to establish real and sometimes considerable differences in the commercial rate of exchange of each

of them. The phrase "Leeward Islands currency" is more misleading than accurate.[30]

Before 1708 the Leeward Islands did what all the other English colonies did in the face of a less than adequate circulating medium of exchange. The islanders resorted first to commodity money and then to a legally overvalued coin. The early history of this latter effort is unknown for want of evidence. Between 1670 and 1672 Montserrat, Antigua, and Nevis all passed laws raising the value of the piece of eight to

30. For bookkeeping convenience West Indian merchants apparently agreed upon a set of conventional exchange ratios between their various currencies. There is little indication of this before the middle of the 18th century, but thereafter references to "British West Indian currency" and "French West Indian currency" occur regularly. (The convention might well have been adopted by English merchants who settled on Martinique and Guadeloupe after Great Britain captured the islands during the Seven Years' War. See the discussion of Cuba below.) The former, at an apparent par of £166.67 per £100 sterling, must have been based on the currency of the Leeward Islands; the latter was at the standard ratio of 150 livres per 100 livres tournois (see below). We can appreciate the reason for this convention when we see that, given an average rate of exchange between London and Paris for the period from 1765 to 1774 of about 31.25d (13p) per ecu, it was possible to equate any number of livres French West Indian currency with the same *number* of shillings British West Indian currency. Thus in Oct. 1771, at Môle St. Nicolas, 84 livres and 10 sous French West Indian currency was said to equal 84s 6d British West Indian currency. Account of Capt. John Forsyth with Neil Jamieson, Norfolk, Va., 30 Apr. 1773, Neil Jamieson Papers, 1757–1789, XVII, no. 3971, Lib. Cong. See also the articles of agreement of Charles d'Anmous as agent for Louis Mimerel of Basse-Terre, Guadeloupe, and Francis Rouvelet of St. Eustatius with James Campbell and Neil Jamieson of Norfolk, Va., 8 Dec. 1772, no. 3682, *ibid.* While the convention proved handy as an accounting device for small amounts, actual commercial transactions were settled by bills of exchange. E.g., see n. 90, below. Later in the 18th century, changing exchange rates destroyed the symmetry; yet the use of the terms continued. See Thomas Jefferson to George Washington, 23 Dec. 1791, Paul Leicester Ford, ed., *The Writings of Thomas Jefferson* (New York, 1892–1899), V, 413.

6s (30p), and the first of these acts, that of Montserrat in September 1670, refers to the earlier valuation of 5s (25p).[31] Since these islands had been settled largely from Barbados, it seems likely that the colonists had brought with them the valuation of 5s in force in Barbados from April 1666. In fact, given the dominance of Barbados during this formative period, the Leeward Islanders may have followed the example of Barbados from the beginning. If so, the par of exchange in the Leewards was at parity in the 1620s, 1630s, and 1640s; rose to £133.33 in the 1650s and early 1660s; fell to £111.11 from 1666 to 1670; and finally returned to £133.33 from the early 1670s. All but the last of this sequence is conjectural.

While the legal valuation of the piece of eight continued by law—or, in the case of St. Christopher, by custom—at 6s and was reenacted by the General Assembly of all the islands in 1694,[32] the colonists raised its effective value still higher. They used the popular device of simply accepting underweight coins at full value. In 1691 Christopher Codrington, the governor-general of the Leeward Islands, reported that such coins were worth on an average 3s 9d (18.8p) sterling.[33] Par at this valuation was about £160. The act of 1694 legiti-

mated this practice by setting the currency value of the full-weight coin at 7s 2.5d (36.1p), for a par of £160.50. Further acts of 1699 confirmed this.[34] While the commercial rate of exchange in the islands eventually rose to this level, this rate was not customarily recognized as the par of exchange. In establishing such a high figure, the Leeward Islanders did what other colonists had done before them—set an upward limit.

The proclamation of 1704 and the act of 1708 deprived the Leeward Islanders of the flexibility that was inherent in their former situation. They could no longer manipulate the value of their silver coin to alleviate their monetary problems. Fortunately the laws on their statute books seemed to conform to the level demanded by proclamation and act. Par could be said to be £133.33; yet they could raise it no higher. In the same situation the colonists in North America established paper money as their currency and inflated it to expand their supply of money. The Leeward Islanders turned to gold, which they accepted at rates similar to those for silver in the 1690s. It was said of the first decade of the eighteenth century that English and Portuguese gold coins passed at an effective par of £150; "French or Spanish gold did not yield above 100£ ster[ling] for 160£ this currency." "Pieces of 8 . . . were generally made a merchandize of . . . and were sold at 10 to 12 per cent advance," a practice similar to that employed in Pennsylvania in the 1720s and one that raised the currency value of silver to, again, £150 currency per £100 sterling. The situation continued over the next three decades

31. *Acts of Assembly, Passed in the Island of Montserrat, from 1668 to 1740, Inclusive* (London, 1740), 19–20; "Lawes, Regulations, and Orders in force at the Leeward Islands, From 1668; to 1672," C.O. 154/1, fols. 44, 100. Although the Nevis act is undated, internal evidence shows that it passed while Charles Wheeler was governor-general of the Leeward Islands, i.e., from early 1671 to early 1672. See also Chalmers, *History of Currency*, 64; C. S. S. Higham, "The Accounts of a Colonial Governor's Agent in the Seventeenth Century," *American Historical Review*, XXVIII (1923), 263–285.

32. *Acts of Assembly, Passed in the Charibbee Leeward Islands from 1690, to 1730* (London, 1734), 4.

33. "Our pieces of eight [even though] generally not being worth above 3s6d and 3s9d [and] some 4s . . . pass . . . in these Islands for 6s." Codrington, at Antigua, to Board of Trade, 13 July 1691, C.O. 152/38, fol. 102.

34. *Acts of Assembly, Passed in the Island of Nevis, from 1664, to 1739, Inclusive* (London, 1740), 19, 28; C.O. 185/3, fol. 8. See also the testimony of Richard Cary, agent for the Leeward Islands, before the Board of Trade, 21 Apr. 1703, C.O. 391/16, p. 85.

with one change only. In the 1720s "heavy silver advanced in the way of merchandize from 10 to 12 per cent to 15 and 20 per cent. . . ."[35] At the latter figure par even in silver ("in the way of merchandize") was £160 currency to £100 sterling. A bill of exchange purchased with full-weight silver coin, not as money but as a commodity valued at the proclamation level plus the 20 percent advance, cost the buyer £160 currency per £100 sterling.

Inflationary pressures continued into the 1730s and resulted in still further depreciation of the currency in the Leeward Islands. In the spring of 1736 the assembly of Antigua passed a law that raised the par of exchange to £175 Antigua currency per £100 sterling. Montserrat followed suit. Both laws contained the required clause suspending their execution until approved by London. The effect of the bill in Antigua was immediate, however, and was reinforced two years later when the lieutenant governor, his council, and the assembly met in Parham to agree amongst themselves that they would accept gold at the rate set out in the act. What happened in Montserrat is unknown, but neither law received the required approval. At the end of the decade the exchange for St. Christopher, Nevis, and Montserrat remained at the old level of £160 currency per £100 sterling while that of Antigua was at the higher rate of £175 currency.[36] Antigua

maintained par at that level well into the 1750s, but sometime between 1752 and 1765 it increased the currency value of the piece of eight from 7s 10.5d (39.4p) to 8s 3d (41.2p) and raised par, thereby, to £183.33. The same rate applied for the piece of eight at St. Christopher in 1773.[37] What happened on the other islands remains unclear, although the limited data available for the commercial rate of exchange (see tables 4.3, 4.4, and 4.5) suggest a certain coincidence in the commercial rate by the 1760s and 1770s.[38] Perhaps by 1775 par for all the Leeward Islands was £183.33. If so, we might be able to speak of a "Leeward Islands currency," at least during this period.

Letter Books of Walter Tullideph, 1734–1767, Tullideph Papers, in the possession of Sir David J. W. Ogilvy, Winton House, Pencaitland, East Lothian, Scotland (from microfilm of transcripts made by Richard B. Sheridan); Mathew, at Montserrat, to Board of Trade, 31 May 1736, C.O. 152/23, fol. 2.

37. For Antigua see John Jourdain, at Antigua, to John Reynell, at Philadelphia, 19 Jan. 1752, and bill of lading, signed Humphrey Chase, at Antigua, June 1752, John Reynell Correspondence, 1729–1773, Coates and Reynell Papers, Hist. Soc. Pa.; "Book Containing What the men have taken up on the Voyage on board the Brigantine Othello[,] Thos. Rogers Commander," 1764–1766, Samuel and William Vernon Papers, 1750–1775, Box VII, "Slavery MSS.," N.-Y. Hist. Soc.; Capt. Thomas James's account, 18 Oct. 1773, Jamieson Papers, XVIII, no. 4227. For St. Christopher see Moore Furman, at Philadelphia, to John Stevens, at N.J., 13 Aug. 1773, Calendars of Manuscript Collections in New Jersey: Calendar of the Stevens Family Papers, Stevens Institute of Technology Library, Lieb Memorial Room, Hoboken, New Jersey, 1664–1777, II (Newark, N.J., 1941), 131.

38. We have exchange rates for Montserrat for three months only. In Mar. 1722 it was £150 per £100 sterling; in July 1724 it was the same; and in May 1751 it was £175. Royal African Co., Copybook of Bills of Exchange Received, 1720–1726, fol. 14v, T. 70/280; Gov. John Hart, at St. Christopher, to Board of Trade, 12 July 1724, C.O. 152/14, fol. 326v; and Austin and Laurens Waste Book, 1749–1751, Henry Laurens Papers, 1747–1882, South Carolina Historical Society, Charleston. We have some later rates for these same islands. On 9 Apr. 1784, the exchange at Antigua was £180; in May

35. Charles Dunbar and Richard Oliver, at Antigua, to Gov. William Mathew, 2 Jan. 1739/40, in Mathew to Board of Trade, 8 Jan. 1739/40, C.O. 152/23, fols. 257–258. Dunbar and Oliver were members of the Council of Antigua. A copy of their letter is enclosure no. 9 in Board of Trade to House of Lords, 27 Mar. 1740, House of Lords, Main Papers, 28 Mar. 1740, House of Lords Record Office, London. The islands accomplished much the same objective (and raised their par to £155.56) by allowing the French crown to pass at 7s after 1715. [Smith], Two Letters to Mr. Wood, 23–24, 38.

36. [Smith], Two Letters to Mr. Wood, 31–34, 39–40, 52n, 55, 61. See also Walter Tullideph, at Antigua, to William Dunbar, at London, 1 Apr. 1735,

The mechanisms for drawing bills of exchange in the Leeward Islands are somewhat less a mystery than the bill rate, because the assumption seems safe that practices there were the same as elsewhere in the English colonies. Bills drawn at Antigua and later protested were subject to damages at 10 percent of their face value and interest at 10 percent per year from the date of protest. That was the interest rate in 1731, anyhow; it had been lowered to 6 percent by 1753.[39] London merchant Edward Grace, writing in 1767, stated that the same rates applied on all "our islands."[40] The West Indian proclivity for drawing bills at somewhat longer sight than was usual in North America applied in Antigua, at least in Walter Tullideph's case. His letter book shows him drawing bills at from thirty to ninety days sight. His letters also indicate a not unexpected interisland trade in bills. This trade included bills drawn at St. Eustatius on Amsterdam merchants but payable in London. So large was "the number of Dutch bills sent up" to Antigua in 1756 that Tullideph thought they were the reason that "hath kept exchange at 65 per cent" (see fig. 12, p. 294).[41]

1784, £185 at St. Christopher and Nevis; and in 1788, £175 at St. Christopher. William Reyner to George Chalmers, 8 July 1784, and [James?] Baillie to William Gemmell, 13 July 1784, both dated London, in West India and Antigua Papers, 1762–1825, fols. 24, 26, George Chalmers Collection, Peter Force Papers, Ser. VIII A, Lib. Cong.; Composite View of Prices Current, May and June 1784, Great Britain Trade Papers, 1640–1804, Chalmers Coll., *ibid.*; and Grenada and St. Christopher, Answers Nos. 8 and 29, in Pt. III of the "Report of the Lords Committee of [the Privy] Council [for] . . . Trade and Foreign Plantations . . . [on] the Trade to Africa" (1789), Great Britain, House of Commons, *Sess. Papers, 1731–1800*, LXXXIV (*Accounts and Papers*, XXVI), No. 646a, hereafter cited as "Report on the Trade to Africa" (1789). There are a few references to the earlier rate at London on the Leeward Islands. In Aug. 1701 the rate on Nevis stood at £125 currency per £100 sterling; in May and Aug. 1711 the rate on Antigua was £125; and in the latter month it was £145 on St. Christopher. Joseph Martyn, at London, to Treasury, 7 Aug. 1701, T. 1/75, fol. 225r; memorandum on the rate of exchange [Aug. 1701?], T. 1/71, fol. 330r; minutes of meeting of Lords of the Treasury, 7 Aug. 1701, T. 29/13, p. 36; and [Navy] Victualling Office to Treasury, 27 Nov. 1711, T. 1/139, fols. 166–170.

39. See Henry Bonnin to Rabley and Reynell, at Philadelphia, 15 Feb. 1730/31, the account in John Jourdain to John Reynell, 24 Jan. 1753, William Dunbar to Reynell, 7 June 1753, and the account in David Fogo to Reynell, 3 May 1757, all from Antigua and in John Reynell Correspondence.

40. Grace to Capt. Edward Williamson, 23 May 1767, in T. S. Ashton, ed., *Letters of a West African Trader: Edward Grace, 1767–70* ([London], 1950), 7, 8. See also John Wright, *The West-India Merchant, Factor and Supercargoes Daily Assistant, in the Disposal of a Cargoe of Merchandize* (London, 1765), 77, where he states that interest amounted to 6% throughout "British America."

41. Tullideph to Richard Oliver, at London, 16 Oct. 1756, Letter Books of Dr. Walter Tullideph, Tullideph Papers. On the sight of his bills and for evidence of the interisland bill trade see *ibid.*, *passim*.

TABLE 4.3. **Rate of Exchange: Antigua on London, 1704–1775**

(Pounds Antigua Currency per £100 Sterling)

Year	Jan.	Feb.	Mar.	Apr.	May	June	July	Aug.	Sept.	Oct.	Nov.	Dec.	Average
1704												[130.00]	130.00
1705													
1706													
1707		155.00											155.00
1708			137.21										137.21
1709													
1710												[142.50]	142.50
1711													
1712													
1713													
1714													
1715													
1716													
1717													
1718													
1719													
1720						150.00							150.00
1721									150.00				150.00
1722					150.00								150.00
1723			150.00										150.00
1724							150.00						150.00
1725													
1726													
1727						150.00							150.00
1728											150.00		150.00
1729													

TABLE 4.3 (Continued): **Antigua on London** (Pounds Antigua Currency per £100 Sterling)

Year	Jan.	Feb.	Mar.	Apr.	May	June	July	Aug.	Sept.	Oct.	Nov.	Dec.	Average
1730					155.00								155.00
1731		155.00			154.44		155.00						154.81
1732													
1733					170.00								170.00
1734													
1735	156.25		155.00	158.75			160.00						158.12
1736						160.00							160.00
1737						160.00		165.00					162.50
1738				165.00		170.00		175.00			170.00		170.83
1739							172.50						172.50
1740	[175.00]			170.00			170.00						171.67
1741													
1742							165.00	165.00	162.50		165.00		164.58
1743						165.00		165.00	165.00				165.00
1744	165.00					165.00		170.00					166.67
1745	170.00	170.00									170.00		170.00
1746		166.25	166.25	165.00									165.62
1747					165.00	165.00	165.00	165.00	165.00	165.00			165.00
1748			165.00			165.00						[180.00]	170.00
1749		170.00		170.00		172.50			173.75				171.67
1750		175.00		175.00	175.00	175.00	175.00		175.00				175.00
1751					178.75					176.88			177.82
1752	175.00	173.75	170.00	175.00	175.00	175.00	175.00	172.50	170.00	165.00	166.25	167.50	171.67
1753	165.00	168.75	170.00	165.00	161.88	160.62	161.56	162.50	163.75	165.00	165.00	165.00	164.50
1754	165.42	166.25	166.46	166.67	165.00	165.00	165.46	165.92	165.46	165.00	165.00	165.00	165.55
1755	165.00			165.00		165.00					165.00	165.00	165.00
1756	165.00					165.00				165.00	165.00		165.00
1757						160.00	160.00			160.00		160.00	160.00

TABLE 4.3 (Continued): **Antigua on London** (Pounds Antigua Currency per £100 Sterling)

Year	Jan.	Feb.	Mar.	Apr.	May	June	July	Aug.	Sept.	Oct.	Nov.	Dec.	Average
1758	160.00				152.50							165.00	159.17
1759											160.00		160.00
1760					150.00			155.00					152.50
1761	160.00				167.50	165.00	168.50	170.00	171.88		165.00		165.34
1762					160.00				165.00	180.00		170.00	166.67
1763	170.00						175.00			177.50		175.00	173.75
1764				171.25	172.50	172.50	175.00			175.00			174.03
1765	178.75	178.75	*176.88*	175.00	*175.00*	175.00	171.88	170.00	170.00	*170.00*	170.00	*170.00*	173.44
1766	*170.00*	*170.00*	170.00	170.00	170.00	170.00	170.00	172.50					170.42
1767													
1768													
1769	170.00							165.00	162.50			162.50	165.42
1770									168.75		170.00		169.38
1771													
1772				165.00	165.00						165.00		165.00
1773							165.00						165.00
1774													
1775				175.00			177.50		177.50				176.25

Notes and Sources: **TABLE 4.3**

Figures inserted in square brackets are assigned to that month arbitrarily; figures printed in italics are straight-line interpolations based on the two neighboring quotations.

1704, 1740: [Wavel Smith], *Two Letters to Mr. Wood, on the Coin and Currency in the Leeward Islands* . . . (London, 1740), 55, 61.

1707: James Parke to earl of Sunderland, 15 Feb. 1706/07, as quoted in Robert Chalmers, *A History of Currency in the British Colonies* (London, [1893]), 68n.

1708, 1720–1723: Royal African Company, Copybooks of Bills of Exchange Received, 1705–1718, fol. 35v, 1720–1726, fols. 15v, 28v, 29v, 30v, 1703–1718, p. 83, Copybooks of Invoices Homeward, 1715–1721, p. 143, 1723–1724, pp. 18, 101, 102, T. 70/279, 280, 283, 957–958, Public Record Office.

1710: "From the year 1700 to 1710 . . . most remittances that were then made were either in the produce of the country, or heavy money in pieces of 8, or in bills of exchange, from 40 to 45 per cent. . . ." Charles Dunbar and Richard Oliver, at Antigua, to Gov. William Mathew, 2 Jan. 1739/40, in Mathew to Board of Trade, 8 Jan. 1739/40, C.O. 152/23, fol. 257, P.R.O.

1724: Gov. John Hart, at St. Christopher, to Board of Trade, 12 July 1724, C.O. 152/14, fol. 326v.

1727: "Some Account of the Sale of the French Lands in the Island of St. Christopher, with the Consequences of it to that Island and England," dated June 1727, as quoted in [Robert Robertson], *A Detection of the State and Situation of the Present Sugar Planters of Barbados and the Leeward Islands* (London, 1732), 37–38.

1728: Representation of the Assembly of Antigua, 28 Feb. 1727/28, C.O. 152/17, fol. 93r. See also Vere Langford Oliver, *The History of the Island of Antigua, One of the Leeward Caribbees in the West Indies, from the First Settlement in 1635 to the Present Time* (London, 1894–1899), I, xcvii.

1728–1764: Parham Plantation Accounts, 1727–1766, Tudway-Wells Manuscripts, Somerset Record Office, Taunton, Eng.

1730: Josiah Martin, at Antigua, to Joshua Young, [in England?], 29 May 1730, Letter Book of Josiah Martin, 1730–1740, fol. 21, Martin Papers, VII, Additional Manuscript 41352, British Library.

1731: Edward Byam, at Antigua, to Abraham Redwood, at Newport, R.I., 22 May 1731, [Worthington C. Ford, ed.], *Commerce of Rhode Island, 1726–1800* (Massachusetts Historical Society, *Collections*, 7th Ser., IX–X [Boston, 1914–1915]), I, 21.

1731–1763: John Reynell Correspondence, 1729–1773, Coates and Reynell Papers, Historical Society of Pennsylvania, Philadelphia. For 1751–1762, see also Marc Matthew Egnal, "The Pennsylvania Economy, 1748–1762: An Analysis of Short-Run Fluctuations in the Context of Long-Run Changes in the Atlantic Trading Community" (Ph.D. diss., University of Wisconsin, 1974), 326–327.

1735: "Extract of the Objections made by the Planters, &c. in Antigua to the Additional Instructions given to the Officers for Collecting the 4-½% Duty," in John Ashley, *Memoirs and Considerations concerning the Trade and Revenues of the British Colonies in America* (London, 1740–1743), II, 115. Dated here to Jan. 1735. See also *ibid.*, 59–60.

1735–1764: Letter Books of Dr. Walter Tullideph, 1734–1767, Tullideph Papers, in the possession of Sir David J. W. Ogilvy, Winton House, Pencaitland, East Lothian, Scotland. See table 3.8, above.

1742–1744: Robert Morris Ledger B, 1747–1750, in the reverse of Clerk's Fee Book, 1762–1763, Dorchester County, Md., Circuit Court, Maryland Hall of Records, Annapolis.

1746: Mathew to Board of Trade, 15 Apr. 1746, C.O. 152/25, fol. 194v. See copies of this letter in William Petty, Earl of Shelburne, Papers, XLV, fol. 161, William L. Clements Library, University of Michigan, Ann Arbor, and in Report on the State of the British Colonies, 1721–1764, p. 867, King's Manuscript 205, Brit. Lib.

1748: William Douglass, *A Summary, Historical and Political, of the First Planting, Progressive Improvements, and Present State of the British Settlements in North America* (Boston, 1749–1751), I, 494n.

1748–1763: Coates-Reynell Correspondence, 1729–1836, Box I (1729–1764), Coates and Reynell Papers.

1749: Austin and Laurens Waste Book, 1749–1751, Henry Laurens Papers, 1747–1882, South Carolina Historical Society, Charleston.

1749–1750: Henry and William Livingston, at Antigua, to William Alexander, at New York, 21 Sept. 1749, 11 July 1750, William Alexander Correspondence, 1744–1782, nos. 57, 92, Alexander Papers, New-York Historical Society, New York City.

1754–1762: Galloway Correspondence, I, no. 8142, V, nos. 8826–8827, Galloway-Maxey-Markoe Family Papers, Library of Congress.

1756–1775: Letter Books of Samuel Martin, Sr., 1756–1776, Martin Papers, IV–VI, Add. MSS 41349–41351, Brit. Lib. For the period 1756–1775 (and after, to 1803), cf. Nathaniel Marchant, Thomas D. Harman, and Daniel Hill, Jr., *The Report of the Joint Committee of the Legislature of Antigua, Appointed to Take into Consideration the State of the Coin Current, and the Expediency of Procuring a Silver and Copper Coinage for the Internal Commerce of the Island* (Antigua, 1803), 3–5. There is a copy of this printed report in C.O. 152/85.

Notes and Sources: **TABLE 4.3 (Continued)**

1757–1766: Clifford Correspondence, Pemberton Papers, Hist. Soc. Pa.

1763–1773: Neil Jamieson Papers, 1757–1789, III, nos. 575, 696, 738, 783, V, no. 1116, VII, no. 1546, IX, no. 2062, XI, nos. 2314, 2412, XV, nos. 3371, 3401, XVI, no. 3634, XVIII, no. 4089, Lib. Cong.

1764: [William Young], *Some Observations Which May Contribute to Afford a Just Idea of the Nature, Importance, and Settlement, of Our New West-India Colonies* (London, 1764), 48 (a later version of his *Considerations Which May Tend to Promote the Settlement of Our New West-India Colonies, by Encouraging Individuals to Embark in the Undertaking* [London, 1764]).

1764: Account of sale of slaves, at Antigua, 23 Nov. 1765, Samuel and William Vernon Papers, 1750–1775, Box VII, "Slavery MSS.," N.-Y. Hist. Soc.

1769: Samuel Redwood, at Antigua, to William Codrington, c/o Messrs. Codrington and Miller, at London, 14 Aug. 1769, as quoted in Robson Lowe, *The Codrington Correspondence, 1743–1851* (London, 1951), 21.

1775: Deposition of William Goodrich, 31 Oct. 1775, C.O. 5/1353, pp. 707–709.

TABLE 4.4. **Rate of Exchange: St. Christopher on London, 1710–1775**

(Pounds St. Christopher Currency per £100 Sterling)

Year	Jan.	Feb.	Mar.	Apr.	May	June	July	Aug.	Sept.	Oct.	Nov.	Dec.	Average
1710				150.00									150.00
1711													
1712													
1713													
1714													
1715													
1716													
1717													
1718													
1719													
1720					150.00								150.00
1721					150.00	150.00							150.00
1722													
1723													
1724			150.00			150.00							150.00
1725			150.00										150.00
1726			150.00										150.00
1727						150.00							150.00
1728			150.00										150.00
1729			150.00										150.00
1730			150.00										150.00
1731													
1732													
1733													
1734													
1735													

TABLE 4.4 (Continued): St. Christopher on London (Pounds St. Christopher Currency per £100 Sterling)

Year	Jan.	Feb.	Mar.	Apr.	May	June	July	Aug.	Sept.	Oct.	Nov.	Dec.	Average
1736													
1737					160.00								160.00
1738													
1739													
1740	[160.00]												160.00
1741													
1742													
1743													
1744													
1745													
1746													
1747						160.00							160.00
1748												[160.00]	160.00
1749										165.00			165.00
1750		165.00											165.00
1751													
1752			175.00	175.00							165.00	165.00	171.67
1753		165.00			165.00		160.00	160.00			160.00		162.50
1754													
1755													
1756												160.00	160.00
1757													
1758													
1759						160.00		160.00					160.00
1760									155.00				155.00
1761									170.00				170.00

TABLE 4.4 (Continued): St. Christopher on London (Pounds St. Christopher Currency per £100 Sterling)

Year	Jan.	Feb.	Mar.	Apr.	May	June	July	Aug.	Sept.	Oct.	Nov.	Dec.	Average
1762										171.25			171.25
1763								175.00					175.00
1764							160.00						160.00
1765													
1766		175.00			170.00	175.00							173.75
1767							170.00						170.00
1768		175.00											175.00
1769					167.50								167.50
1770						165.00	165.00						165.00
1771													
1772													
1773													
1774													
1775													

Notes and Sources: **TABLE 4.4**

Figures inserted in square brackets are assigned to that month arbitrarily.

1710: Minutes of the General Council and Assembly of the Leeward Islands, St. Christopher, 1 Apr. 1710, as printed in George French, *The History of Col. Parke's Administration Whilst He Was Captain General and Chief Governor of the Leeward Islands; with an Account of the Rebellion in Antegoa* (London, 1717), 288.

1720: Entry for 17 May 1720, Alexander Wooddrup Account Books, 1720–1734, I, Library of Congress.

1721: Royal African Company, Copybook of Bills of Exchange Received, 1720–1726, fols. 1v, 2v, T. 70/280, Public Record Office.

1724: Gov. John Hart, at St. Christopher, to Board of Trade, 12 July 1724, C.O. 152/14, fol. 326v, P.R.O.

1724–1730: Mead Plantation Accounts, 1723–1729, Collections Deposited by Messrs. Tods, Murray, and Jamieson, W.S., Box No. 139, Gift and Deposit No. 237, Scottish Record Office, Edinburgh.

1737: Gov. William Mathew, at St. Christopher, to Board of Trade, 26 May 1737, C.O. 152/23, fol. 26v.

1740: [Wavel Smith], *Two Letters to Mr. Wood, on the Coin and Currency in the Leeward Islands . . .* (London, 1740), 61.

1747: Joseph Manesty, at Liverpool, to John Bannister, at Newport, R.I., 14 June 1747, John Bannister Letter Book, Newport Historical Society, as quoted in Elizabeth Donnan, ed., *Documents Illustrative of the History of the Slave Trade to America* (Washington, D.C., 1930–1935), III, 141.

1748: William Douglass, *A Summary, Historical and Political, of the First Planting, Progressive Improvements, and Present State of the British Settlements in North America* (Boston, 1747–1751), I, 494n.

Notes and Sources: **TABLE 4.4 (Continued)**

1749–1750: Austin and Laurens Waste Book, 1749–1751, Henry Laurens Papers, 1747–1882, South Carolina Historical Society, Charleston.

1752–1766: Letters of Thomas Mills, 1752–1767, Mills Papers, in the possession of Mr. E. P. English, Grove Bank, Bentham, near Lancaster, Eng. A transcript of these letter books forms an appendix to D. W. Thoms, "West India Merchants and Planters in the Mid-Eighteenth Century with Special Reference to St. Kitts" (M.A. thesis, University of Kent at Canterbury, 1967). See also Thoms, "The Mills Family: London Sugar Merchants of the Eighteenth Century," *Business History*, XI (1969), 3–10.

1756–1762: Clifford Correspondence, Vol. I, fol. 195, Vol. II, fol. 82, Vol. III, fol. 242, Vol. IV, fol. 33, Pemberton Papers, Historical Society of Pennsylvania, Philadelphia.

1759: Ship Daybook, 1756–1757, James Hudson Account Books, 1742–1788, Hudson Family Papers, 1659–1862, New York Public Library, New York City.

1760: Asher Mott, at St. Christopher, to John Reynell, at Philadelphia, 30 Sept. 1760, John Reynell Correspondence, 1729–1773, Coates and Reynell Papers, Hist. Soc. Pa.

1763: Henry Laurens, at Charleston, S.C., to Augustus and John Boyd, at London, 30 Aug. 1763, Philip Hamer *et al.*, eds., *The Papers of Henry Laurens* (Columbia, S.C., 1968–), III, 554.

1766–1770: Neil Jamieson Papers, 1757–1789, VIII, no. 1889, XII, nos. 2641, 2685, 2690, 3983, Lib. Cong.

1769: Hollingsworth and Rudulph, at Philadelphia, to Patterson, Scott, and Buckley, of St. Eustatius and St. Christopher, 3 June 1769, Levi Hollingsworth Invoice Book, 1767–1770, Hollingsworth Collection, 1748–1887, Hist. Soc. Pa.

TABLE 4.5. **Rate of Exchange: Nevis on London, 1706–1775**

(Pounds Nevis Currency per £100 Sterling)

Year	Jan.	Feb.	Mar.	Apr.	May	June	July	Aug.	Sept.	Oct.	Nov.	Dec.	Average
1706	125.00												125.00
1707													
1708													
1709										150.00			150.00
1710													
1711													
1712													
1713													
1714													
1715												135.00	135.00
1716													
1717								140.00					140.00
1718													
1719													
1720													
1721													
1722						140.00							140.00
1723													
1724							150.00						150.00
1725													
1726													
1727													
1728													
1729													
1730													
1731													

TABLE 4.5 (Continued): **Nevis on London** (Pounds Nevis Currency per £100 Sterling)

Year	Jan.	Feb.	Mar.	Apr.	May	June	July	Aug.	Sept.	Oct.	Nov.	Dec.	Average
1732				150.00									150.00
1733													
1734													
1735													
1736													
1737													
1738													
1739													
1740													
1741													
1742													
1743													
1744													
1745													
1746													
1747													
1748													
1749													
1750													
1751												[175.00]	175.00
1752													
1753													
1754							160.00						160.00
1755													
1756													
1757												[160.00]	160.00
1758							160.00						160.00
1759													

TABLE 4.5 (Continued): Nevis on London (Pounds Nevis Currency per £100 Sterling)

Year	Jan.	Feb.	Mar.	Apr.	May	June	July	Aug.	Sept.	Oct.	Nov.	Dec.	Average
1760													
1761													
1762													
1763													
1764													
1765	175.00					175.00	167.50				175.00	170.00	172.50
1766	170.00	170.00	175.00	175.00	170.00	171.67							171.94
1767		175.00		174.29	175.00		175.00		175.00		175.00	175.00	174.91
1768	175.00			175.00		171.50							173.83
1769	170.00		170.00	170.00	170.00	165.00	165.00	165.00	166.67			165.00	167.22
1770	166.00	*166.50*	165.00	165.00	165.00	165.00	165.00	165.00	165.00	*165.00*	165.00	165.00	165.21
1771		165.00	165.00	165.00	165.00	165.00	165.00	165.83				165.00	165.10
1772	165.00	165.00	165.00	165.00	165.00	165.00	165.83	167.50			165.00	165.00	165.42
1773				165.00		165.00	166.88	166.88	167.50		170.00		167.36
1774	165.00	167.50	166.25	170.00	170.00	170.00	170.00			165.00		175.00	169.06
1775		175.00	175.00	176.25	175.00	175.00	174.72			175.00		175.00	175.03

Notes and Sources: **TABLE 4.5**

Figures inserted in square brackets are assigned to that month arbitrarily; figures in italics are straight-line interpolations based on the two neighboring quotations.

1706–1775: West Indies Papers, Boxes B, C, D, and F, John Pinney Letter Book, and John Pinney Account Books, Pinney Papers, University Library, University of Bristol, Bristol, Eng. Cf. Richard Pares, *A West-India Fortune* (London, [1950]), 349n.

1724: Gov. John Hart, at St. Christopher, to Board of Trade, 12 July 1724, C.O. 152/14, fol. 326v, Public Record Office.

1732: [Robert Robertson], *A Supplement to the Detection of the State and Situation of the Present Sugar Planters of Barbados and the Leeward Islands* (London, 1733), 2–3.

1751: Treasurer's Account, Nevis, 1751, C.O. 152/28, no. Bb55.

Windward Islands

After the Seven Years' War a new source of bills of exchange opened in the Caribbean when the British Windward Islands were added to the growing empire, like Quebec on the North American continent. The sale of the land on Dominica, Grenada, St. Vincent, and Tobago, all formerly French colonies, attracted much money to the region. Also, when the planters of the islands began shipping produce home, they established balances against which to draw bills. These were, however, the "Ceded Islands" warned against in the epigraph to this chapter. Obviously, then, their monetary history over the twelve years covered by this handbook was not an entirely satisfactory one.

The money of account and the real money of the Windward Islands were the same as those of the Leeward Islands and the rest of the British colonies. The only indication we have about their currency suggests that it "was derived from, and identical with, that of the Leewards."[42] If so, par in the Windward Islands was £183 currency per £100 sterling, and the piece of eight had a currency value of about 8s 3d (41.2). But this figure is a customary rather than a statutory value, for no law has yet been found stipulating that rate for the Windward Islands. In fact, such speculations not only have little substantiation but seem to run counter to the few pieces of data found so far. Par seems more likely to have been at the £166.67 level (and the piece of eight worth 7s 6d [37.5p]). Consider Grenada, for instance. Bryan Edwards, even though writing after our period, did pronounce that the rate of exchange at Grenada "is commonly 65 per cent. worse than

sterling."[43] Moreover, the few quotations of the bill rate that are assembled in table 4.6 support him, especially so when we remember that rates were down in the early 1770s. For Grenada, then, the par of exchange before 1775 seems more likely to have been £166.67 than £183 Grenadian currency per £100 sterling.[44] Edwards's statement can be seen to apply to the entire period 1763 through 1775.

The picture is less clear for Dominica because we have fewer figures and because those figures that we do have come partly from the era after 7 September 1778, when the French captured the island during the American Revolution. During that fall the commercial rate of exchange was £185 Dominica currency per £100 sterling; the next August it was £182.50.[45] This rate was continued after the war. In the 1790s, when the colony was once again in English hands, the bill rate was £180.[46] But the three prewar figures support the general contention here. In April 1765 the commercial rate of

42. Chalmers, *History of Currency*, 82.

43. Bryan Edwards, *The History, Civil and Commercial, of the British Colonies in the West Indies* (Dublin, 1793), I, 371.
44. In the 1780s it did go up. A Grenada act of 21 Mar. 1787 recognized and reinforced a continuing currency value for the piece of eight of 8s 3d (41.25p) and for the bit, at one-eleventh of the piece of eight, of 9d (3.75p). C.O. 103/8, no. 41, and as printed in George Smith, ed., *The Laws of Grenada, from the Year 1763, to the Year 1805* (London, 1808), 172–173. At these rates par would have been £183.33. In 1789 the island's agent, Charles Spooner, presented figures that implied a rate of £171.43. Grenada and St. Christopher, Answer No. 8, Pt. III of the "Report on the Trade to Africa" (1789). A 1766 law set damages on protested bills at 10% and interest from the date of protest at 6%. C.O. 103/2, fols. 5–7, and in Smith, ed., *Laws of Grenada*, 3–4.
45. Thomas Atwood, *The History of the Island of Dominica* (London, 1791), 156; Charles Winstone, at Dominica, to Messrs. Langston and Dixon, at London, 6 July/12 Aug. 1779, Charles Winstone Letter Book, 1777–1786, William L. Clements Library, University of Michigan, Ann Arbor. See also Joseph A. Boromé, "Dominica during the French Occupation, 1778–1784," *English Historical Review*, LXXIV (1969), 48n.
46. Atwood, *History of Dominica*, 184.

exchange was £170; in June 1771 it was quoted at £165; and three years later it was the same.[47]

We have no quotations at all from Tobago, but our one reference to the situation on St. Vincent indicates that the "usual standard is 65."[48] This quotation is from a letter that arose out of a fight on the island over the receiver general's attempts to set the rate at £182.50. Another communication in the same dispute spoke of the higher rate as one that the inhabitants felt "takes about twelve and a half per cent out of their pockets."[49] One might reconcile this with the "usual standard" by suggesting that this second quotation was indicative of the commercial rate in the late summer of 1776—£170 St. Vincent currency to £100 sterling. Insofar as any pattern is discernible in all this, par in the dozen years before the American Revolution appears to have been at £165 for the Windward Islands.

Just as the inhabitants of the British Windward Islands derived their moneys and rates of exchange in part from their neighbors, so also can we assume that the practice of drawing bills there was similar to that elsewhere. The common usance was probably from sixty to ninety days, with most bills being drawn in the late spring and summer as sugar was shipped to market. On Tobago the rate for damages on protested bills of exchange was low, 8 percent, and the rate for interest from the date of protest was high, 8 percent, when compared with the Leeward Islands.[50] The greater demand for money on the newer, developing islands (and thus its higher cost) and the greater likelihood of bills not being properly paid explain both of these apparent anomalies.

47. "A List of Vessels Cleared in the Custom House, Roseau, Dominica, . . . between 14th December 1764 and 5th January 1765," C.O. 76/4, fol. 4; Elliston Perrot, at Dominica, to Hollingsworth and Rudulph, at Philadelphia, 21 June 1771, Correspondence, 1770–1771, Hollingsworth Collection, 1748–1887, Hist. Soc. Pa.; James Monsell, [at London], to Treasury, 12 June 1774, T. 1/505, fol. 299. But cf. Isaac Werden's statement, in the midst of a list of prices current, that the dollar was "worth 8/3" at Dominica. That was the equivalent of a par of £183.33. Werden, at Grenada, to Aaron Lopez, at Newport, R.I., 12 Sept. 1770, *Commerce of Rhode Island*, I, 346.

48. Charles P. Sharpe, at St. Vincent, to Archibald Ingram, 30 Aug. 1776, enclosed in Gov. Valentine Morris, at St. Vincent, to secretary of state, Nov. 1776, C.O. 260/4, fol. 52. (Sharpe was the acting attorney general of the island; Ingram was the receiver of quitrents and fines.) That rate is confirmed for Feb. and Mar. 1769 in the Edward Grace Account Book, 1768–1769, Edward Grace and Co. Papers, MS 12052, Guildhall Library, London.

49. Sharpe to Morris, 3 Sept. 1776, in Morris to secretary of state, Nov. 1776, C.O. 260/4, fol. 54.

50. *Acts of the Legislature of the Island of Tobago; from 1768, to 1775, Inclusive* (London, 1776), 1–3.

TABLE 4.6. **Rate of Exchange: Grenada on London, 1767–1775**

(Pounds Grenada Currency per £100 Sterling)

Year	Jan.	Feb.	Mar.	Apr.	May	June	July	Aug.	Sept.	Oct.	Nov.	Dec.	Average
1767				168.75									168.75
1768												165.00	165.00
1769													
1770												160.00	160.00
1771													
1772			160.00	160.00									160.00
1773													
1774													
1775													

Notes and Sources: **TABLE 4.6**

1767: Dominick Hanly, at Grenada, to Neil Jamieson, at Norfolk, Va., 26 Apr. 1767, Neil Jamieson Papers, 1757–1789, VIII, no. 1715, Library of Congress.

1768: Account of snow *Honduras Packet*, Capt. John Orrock, 1768–1769, in bundle no. 5, *Ex parte Hill, a bankrupt*, C. 110/54, Public Record Office.

1770: Inventory of Baccaye (later Westershall) Plantation of Lt. Col. Alexander Johnstone, Grenada, 1 Dec. 1770, West Indies Documents, 41/32, University Library, University of Bristol, Bristol, Eng. See also Douglass Hall, "Incalculability as a Feature of Sugar Production during the Eighteenth Century," *Social and Economic Studies*, X (1961), 341.

1772: Mount Nesbitt Plantation, Grenada, 6 Mar. 1772, as cited in Vere Langford Oliver, ed., *Caribbeana: Being Miscellaneous Papers Relating to . . . the British West Indies* (London, 1909–1919), IV, 332.

1772: Campbell and Blane, at Grenada, to James Glassford, at Norfolk, Va., 9 Apr. 1772, Jamieson Papers, XV, no. 3357.

Bermuda, the Bahamas, and Honduras

Great Britain had still other New World colonies, which had in common their location on the periphery of the Caribbean. They included two island groups, Bermuda and the Bahamas, and the settlements on the western littoral of the Caribbean along the Bay of Honduras in modern Belize and Honduras. For each of these colonies we have only a small bit of information.

The basic currency of the British settlements in Honduras was that of Jamaica. Numerous references in legal and commercial records indicate this explicitly.[51] From as early as 1766 until 1784 the inhabitants of the colony supplemented their use of Jamaica currency with "Bay currency," which they defined as four times the value of Jamaica currency.[52] Since the rate of exchange on Jamaica over this period was consistently £140 Jamaica currency per £100 sterling, the rate on St. George's Cay, the main dwelling place of the Bay colony, off modern Belize City, must have been at £560 Bay currency per £100 sterling. This explains the advance indicated in a November 1767 invoice of goods sent to Daniel Hill, the resident partner on St. George's Cay of the firm of Blake, Hollings, Smith, and Hill: "To sell at Bay Currency you must multiply the sterling cost by 8—and that will tell you the average Bay selling price—and less than that will not do."[53] In June 1784 the colony returned to the exclusive use of Jamaica currency.[54]

The Bahama Islands, in the words of William Douglass, were "scarce reckoned a colony" of Great Britain until after the 1740s.[55] Douglass did not offer any indication of the value of Bahama currency, but we can piece together some crude information. In 1700 one John Tyzack reported to the Board of Trade that the piece of eight cost 5s (25p) in the Bahamas.[56] Par at this rate would have been £111.11 Bahama currency per £100 sterling. Gold replaced silver as the coinage of the colony during the next several decades, as it did in the rest of the Caribbean islands. William Stewart, the colony's treasurer, indicated that in June 1734 the exchange rate was £150 currency to £100 sterling, equivalent to a valuation for the piece of eight of 6s 9d (33.8p).[57] This is essentially the same rate for the piece of eight that was quoted in 1774 for "Turks

51. The initial article of Burnaby's Laws (9 Apr. 1765), the first codification of law in the colony's history, collected a fine in Jamaica currency for cursing. John Alder Burdon, ed., *Archives of British Honduras* (London, 1931–1935), I, 102. As a codification of existing law and practice, it presumably included regulations of considerably older origin, among which the use of Jamaica currency was no doubt one. See Narda Dobson, *A History of Belize* ([Port of Spain, Trinidad and Tobago, 1973]), 87–88. Occasional entries in Jamaican records show this same usage. See, e.g., the Spring Plantation Account, 1766, Spring Plantation Papers, AC/WO 16(27) 64(c). So do references in the books of merchants in the continental colonies. See, e.g., Chevalier "Day Book 1770[–1783]," entries dated 18 July 1772, 29 Jan. 1773, 16 Aug. 1774. See also [Long], *History of Jamaica* (London, 1774), I, 327; Chalmers, *History of Currency*, 139–140; and Dobson, *History of Belize*, 275–276. All of this is explicitly extended to the settlements along the Mosquito Shore by entries in "Henry and John Crugers Waste Book," 1762–1768, Cruger Papers, N.-Y. Hist. Soc. See, e.g., entry dated 14 July 1762.
52. See laws of 15 May 1766 in Burdon, ed., *Archives of British Honduras*, I, 112.

53. "An Invoice of first Cost of Merchandize sent per our Brig *Defiance* Capt. John Orrock . . . ," London, Nov. 1767, in bundle no. 4, *Ex parte Hill, a bankrupt*, C. 110/54, P.R.O.
54. Burdon, ed., *Archives of British Honduras*, I, 145.
55. [Douglass], *Discourse concerning Currencies*, 18.
56. Memorial of John Tyzack, received 5 July 1700, C.O. 323/3, fol. 204r. See also Chalmers, *History of Currency*, 7, 12.
57. Treasurer's account in Gov. Richard Fitzwilliam, at New Providence, Bahamas, to Board of Trade, 11 Mar. 1734/35, C.O. 23/3, fols. 122–132.

Island money"; the Turks Islands were then part of the Bahamas.[58] It seems to have held through the end of our period, until another assembly act of 1788 rated the piece of eight at 8s (40p) and thereby raised par to £177.78.[59]

Bermuda's monetary history, given the ancient settlement of the islands in 1609, underwent many of the twists and turns that we have noted in Virginia, Barbados, and Massachusetts. Until midcentury the colony's currency was a mixture of sterling and tobacco as a commodity money.[60] As we have seen above with Jamaica, the piece of eight circulated at a value of 4s (20p), but with sterling at par, the exchange on England was even.[61] In June 1658 the colony's government "ordered that all peeces of eight which formerly passed currency for 4s. per peece should henceforward pass current betweene party and party at 5s. per peece."[62] Par was now set at £111.11 Bermuda currency per £100 sterling. By 1669 it was necessary to raise the currency value of the piece of eight

still higher, to 5s 4d (26.7p), for a par of £118.52.[63] Later in the seventeenth century the Bermudians began to accept underweight coins at full weight, raising par to an effective level of £140 by the turn of the century.[64] This is the rate for par for gold coins that the colony's government established in the act of 9 May 1707 to try to overcome the disabilities in the proclamation of 1704.[65] The Bermudas have the distinction of being the first to defeat the royal proclamation by legal weapons.[66]

In the eighteenth century, despite a somewhat higher rate for par, exchange quotations were made at the proclamation level of £133.33 Bermuda currency per £100 sterling. This is misleading, however, as Governor Alured Popple told the Board of Trade in 1739. Silver coins "being often scarce," he wrote, "the merchants do sometimes give a premium of 5, 6 or 8 per cent, in order to obtain silver to make remittance home."[67] At this last figure, Popple admitted to a rate of exchange of £144, a rate for which we have other indications in the 1730s.[68] In the next decade the commercial rate of

58. Account current of snow *Flora*, Capt. Thomas Forrester, 20 Dec. 1774, Aaron Lopez Account Book, 1774–1781, Aaron Lopez Papers, American Jewish Historical Society, Waltham, Mass. Early in 1745 the assembly set out the currency value of all gold coins, values that argue for a par of £166.67. Act of 21 Feb. 1744/45, reenacted 3 Mar. 1749/50, in C.O. 25/2, [nos. 5 and 15]. See also Chalmers, *History of Currency*, 162–163.

59. C.O. 25/6, no. 162. For the 1769 act that established damages on protested bills, see *Acts of Assembly of the Bahama Islands, from the Year 1764 to the Year 1799, Inclusive* (Nassau, 1801), 13–15.

60. Chalmers, *History of Currency*, 150–152. In 1615 the Bermuda Company sent out sixpence and shilling coins for the island; this was the famous "hog money," called so for the design on the coins. J. H. Lefroy, ed., *Memorials of the Discovery and Early Settlement of the Bermudas or Somers Islands, 1515–1685* (London, 1877–1879), I, 59, 96, 98, 101, 113, 114.

61. See the council minutes and the governor's proclamation of Apr. 1653 in Lefroy, ed., *Memorials of the Bermudas*, II, 40.

62. *Ibid.*, III, 113. See also the enactment of June 1662/63, *ibid.*, 191.

63. "Law for raissing the value of Spanish Coines," 10 Feb. 1669/70, *ibid.*, II, 307. See also Chalmers, *History of Currency*, 6, 152–154.

64. Chalmers, *History of Currency*, 154–155 and 155n. Note that he calls this a "conjectural history" based on an analogy with Jamaica and other British West Indian colonies.

65. *Acts of Assembly, Made and Enacted in the Bermuda or Summer-Islands, from 1690 to 1713–14* (London, 1719), 76. See also C.O. 40/2, sec. E, pp. 18, 20, 21, 22. This is the rate based on a comparison of the value for the pistole, £1 4s 0d (120p) in Bermuda currency and 17s 3d (86p) in sterling.

66. Chalmers, *History of Currency*, 154.

67. Popple, at Bermuda, to Board of Trade, 20 Dec. 1739, C.O. 37/13, fol. 138r, and copy as enclosure no. 14 in Board of Trade to House of Lords, 27 Mar. 1740, House of Lords, Main Papers, 28 Mar. 1740.

68. Lt. Gov. John Pitt to Board of Trade, 22 Mar. 1732/33, C.O. 37/12, fol. 130 (see also *ibid.*, fols. 172–173, 193–194); [Douglass], *Discourse concerning Currencies*, 18; Robert Dinwiddie, at Bermuda, to Popple, 17 Aug. 1738, C.O.

exchange rose to a par of £150 and stayed there well beyond the end of our period (see table 4.7). As Henry Tucker and Sons wrote Neil Jamieson of Norfolk in November of 1770, this meant that the piece of eight had a par value of 6s 8d (33.3p) Bermuda currency.[69] Thus this became the par value for Bermuda's paper money, issued first in the early 1760s,[70] the only paper money of importance in a British island colony.

37/13, fol. 63r; Samuel Powel, Jr., at Philadelphia, to Col. Francis Jones, at Bermuda, 10 Mar. 1744/45, Samuel Powel, Jr., Letter Books, 1727–1747, II, 330, Hist. Soc. Pa.

69. Letter of 2 Nov. 1770, Jamieson Papers, XII, no. 2762. See also entries for 4 Nov. and 17 Nov. 1765 and 10 June 1768, William Fitzhugh Ledger "I," fol. 128, Fitzhugh Account Books, 1761–1774, MS 1831, Maryland Historical Society, Baltimore.

70. Chalmers, *History of Currency*, 156–157, presumably from C.O. 39/8.

TABLE 4.7. **Rate of Exchange: Bermuda on London, 1738–1775**
(Pounds Currency per £100 Sterling)

Year	Jan.	Feb.	Mar.	Apr.	May	June	July	Aug.	Sept.	Oct.	Nov.	Dec.	Average
1738								140.00					140.00
1739												141.77	141.77
1740													
1741													
1742													
1743													
1744													
1745			147.00										147.00
1746													
1747													
1748													
1749							150.00						150.00
1764									150.65				150.65
1765											148.16		148.16
1766						150.00							150.00
1767													
1768													
1769													
1770											147.50		147.50
1771													
1772													

TABLE 4.7 (Continued): **Bermuda on London** (Pounds Bermuda Currency per £100 Sterling)

Year	Jan.	Feb.	Mar.	Apr.	May	June	July	Aug.	Sept.	Oct.	Nov.	Dec.	Average
1773													
1774													
1775													

Notes and Sources: **TABLE 4.7**

1738: Robert Dinwiddie, at Bermuda, to Gov. Alured Popple, 17 Aug. 1738, C.O. 37/13, fol. 63r, Public Record Office.

1739: Popple, at Bermuda, to Board of Trade, 20 Dec. 1739, copy as enclosure no. 14 in Board of Trade to House of Lords, 27 Mar. 1740, House of Lords, Main Papers, 28 Mar. 1740, House of Lords Record Office, London.

1745: Samuel Powel, Jr., at Philadelphia, to Col. Francis James, at Bermuda, 16 Mar. 1744/45, Samuel Powel, Jr., Letter Books, 1727–1747, II, 330, Historical Society of Pennsylvania, Philadelphia.

1749: Enclosure in Gov. William Popple, at Bermuda, to Board of Trade, 9 July 1749, C.O. 37/6. See also Report on the State of the British Colonies, 1721–1764, p. 801, King's Manuscript 205, British Library; and William Petty, Earl of Shelburne, Papers, XLIV, fol. 54, William L. Clements Library, University of Michigan, Ann Arbor.

1764: Gov. George James Bruere, at Bermuda, to Treasury, 10 Sept. 1764, C.O. 37/19, no. P79.

1765: William Fitzhugh Ledger "I," fol. 128, Fitzhugh Account Books, 1761–1774, MS 1831, Maryland Historical Society, Baltimore.

1766: Roger H. Elletson, at Jamaica, to Bruere, 13 June 1766, [Hedley P. Jacobs, ed.], "Roger Hope Elletson's Letter Book," *Jamaican Historical Review*, I (1946–1948), 197.

1770: Henry Tucker and Sons, at Bermuda, to Neil Jamieson, at Norfolk, Va., 2 Nov. 1770, Neil Jamieson Papers, 1757–1789, XII, no. 2762, Library of Congress.

The French Colonies and the Exchange on Paris

The history of money, bills of exchange, and the rate of exchange in the French colonies in the New World has much in common with that of the British colonies. And so we might expect, since the colonial experiences of both grew from a European system that the two mother countries shared. Moreover, each metropolis pursued similar national purposes for its empire, and thus the monetary and exchange practices within the two empires evoked many of the same responses and regulations. All of the same may be said as well for the Dutch and Danish colonies, discussed later in this chapter.

The French colonists in North America and the West Indies bought and sold bills of exchange for the usual reasons. The seller of a bill had assets in France that he sought to transfer to the New World; the buyer had assets in the colony that better served his purposes in Paris. The two worked an exchange. The price of that exchange, which in the English colonies was based on the cost in colonial currency of £100 sterling, expressed the rate of exchange. In the French colonies one spoke of the *monnaie du pays*, which was the colonial currency, and the *monnaie de France*. The *perte* was the percentage loss involved in negotiating the bills. A loss at a rate of 25 percent meant that 100 livres *monnaie du pays* yielded 75 livres tournois *monnaie de France*. Thus while a reference to a rate of "35 percent" in Massachusetts indicated that £100 sterling cost £135 Massachusetts currency, a rate of "35 *pour cent*" in St. Domingue indicated that 100 livres *monnaie* of St. Domingue equaled 65 livres tournois or, to turn it around, that 100 livres tournois cost 153.84 livres *monnaie* of St. Domingue.

Because of the potential for confusion in these two separate meanings for the same percentage rate, the quotation of French rates of exchange will henceforth regularly follow the English system. Reference will hereinafter be made to the numbers of livres French colonial currency needed to purchase 100 livres tournois, and each quotation or citation to a quotation in original materials will be accompanied by its equivalent in these terms. The tables for St. Domingue below are calculated in this fashion, and the transposition of this data to the tables in chapter 5 will use the same method. Thus sums of money can be converted from or into livres *monnaie du pays* using the rates in these tables in the same way as for the British colonies—and, as we shall see, for Danish and Dutch colonies too. To convert from livres St. Domingue currency into livres tournois, take the quoted rate as a percentage and divide by that rate (e.g., 10,000 livres St. Domingue currency divided by 1.5384 equals 6,500 livres tournois); to convert from livres tournois to colonial currency, take the quoted rate as a percentage and multiply (6,500 livres tournois times 1.5384 equals 10,000 livres St. Domingue currency). Note too that henceforth we will speak in terms of each given colony's currency and of livres tournois of France.

It should be apparent already that the French colonists used the money of account of the mother country, just as did the English colonies. Accounts in French America were kept in livres, sous, and deniers; there were twenty sous to one livre and twelve deniers to one sou. (This relationship can be converted to decimalized notation using the table in Appendix 1.) The real money in the French colonies was the same motley collection of coin used throughout the hemisphere. Although some French coin circulated in the New World, France's colonists were as dependent on Spanish silver and Portuguese gold as was everyone else. The piece of eight was, again, the measure of all money. Called the "piastre gourde," it was not only the universal coin but the basis for exchange quotations in the French Caribbean.[71] The comparative price of the piastre gourde in livres tournois and in French colonial livres established the percentage loss mentioned above. Rates of exchange quoted that loss.

The French colonists faced an inadequate supply of money similar to that which so concerned the British colonists, and they reacted in parallel fashion. One presumes that French colonists exchanged using book credits and bookkeeping barter in ways close to those described in chapter 3. The French employed tobacco as a form of commodity money, and they established an artificially high value for coin in order to attract and retain it.[72] They also allowed underweight coin to circulate at full value by tale (by count), rather than by weight, as an effective device for keeping coin within the islands.[73] And it was the French in Canada that introduced the use of paper

money into the New World. Thus, all four of the British modes of dealing with an endemic insufficiency in the circulating medium of exchange were also part of the French experience.

We find the first significant difference between the French and the British colonies in the matter of overvalued coin. The existence of different currencies in the British colonies was as much a function of different pars of exchange as it was of different variations around par. The legislatures of each of the British colonies set par themselves and also changed it through their laws establishing currency values for the piece of eight and other coins. But the French colonies had only limited local governments and a much stronger central administration.[74] The crown through the Ministry of Marine reserved the establishment of the value of the *monnaie du pays* to itself. It set par, and it set one par for all the French colonies. Colonial attempts to change this by establishing a local value for the piastre gourde were frowned on and reversed.[75] What variations existed among the French colonies stemmed only from the fluctuations in the commercial rate of exchange, and even these were unacceptable to the Ministry.[76] An official rate of exchange at a par rate set in Paris ruled the French colonies in the Western Hemisphere.

71. See M[édéric] L. E. Moreau de Saint-Méry, *Description topographique, physique, civile, politique et historique de la partie française de l'isle Saint-Domingue* (1797), ed. Blanche Maurel and Étienne Taillemite, new ed. (Paris, 1958), I, 14–15.

72. For the use of tobacco as a commodity money see Jacob M. Price, *France and the Chesapeake: A History of the French Tobacco Monopoly, 1674–1791, and Its Relationship to the British and American Tobacco Traders* (Ann Arbor, Mich., 1973), I, 76, 79, 84, 89. For high local values for coin see, e.g., the memorandum on this subject dated 12 Apr. 1717 in Archives Colonies, C^{11A} 37, p. 199, Archives Nationales, Paris, and as printed in Adam Shortt, ed., *Documents Relating to Canadian Currency, Exchange and Finance during the French Period* (Ottawa, 1925), I, 378–379.

73. See the discussion in the introductory section to chap. 3, above. See also the "Arrêt du Conseil du Cap, qui ordonne que le Monnaie d'Espagne continuera d'avoir cours, comme depuis l'établissement de la Colonie, à la piece et non au poids," St. Domingue, 10 Mar. 1758, in [Médéric L. E.] Moreau de Saint-Méry, ed., *Loix et constitutions des colonies françoises de l'Amérique sous le Vent* (Paris, [1784–1790]), IV, 221–222.

74. Pierre Henri Boulle, "The French Colonies and the Reform of Their Administration during and following the Seven Years' War" (Ph.D. diss., University of California at Berkeley, 1968), incorporates a most intelligent analysis of the intricacies of French colonial government.

75. See, e.g., the "Arrêt du Conseil de Leogane, touchant la Monnaie," St. Domingue, 5 Nov. 1708, and the response it generated in Moreau de Saint-Méry, ed., *Loix et constitutions des colonies françoises*, II, 136–142.

76. This was the cause of the difficulties in which the intendant and the commandant-général of Martinique found themselves in 1761. Paul-Pierre Le Mercier de la Rivière, the intendant and a celebrated economist, and Louis-Charles Le Vassor de la Touche found it impossible to explain the effect

The par of exchange for the French colonies was changed several times in the seventeenth and eighteenth centuries by imperial edicts. Because these changes pertained to all of the colonies together, we can discuss them now and reserve for subsequent sections the course of the commercial rate of exchange in the individual colonies. It is clear that already by 1650 a French colonial currency existed, since lightweight pieces of eight ("les reaux d'Espagne") were passing in the colonies for more than their intrinsic value.[77] Regulations, which apparently applied only to French Canada, rated coin above its value in France as early as October 1661.[78] This was the origin of the one-quarter discount or one-third advance, which was made law for all the French colonies by the arrêt of 18 November 1672 and was to stand until the 1720s.[79] The par

of exchange between France and her American colonies was 133$\frac{1}{3}$ livres colonial currency (*monnaie du pays*) per 100 livres tournois (*monnaie de France*) from perhaps as early as the 1640s to 1727.[80]

In the wake of the financial debacle wreaked by John Law, France undertook a complete reorganization of its monetary system. One part of the new order was the formal reestablishment of colonial currency. A royal edict of 5 July 1717 had abolished *monnaie du pays*, but the execution of the edict met delay after delay.[81] It seems never to have been implemented anywhere except in French Canada, where from 1717 to 1759 "the currency of Canada was identical with the currency of France."[82] Suffice it to say that a new edict of 1726 had the impact of reintroducing colonial currency—but at a new level. Previously the loss had been set at one-quarter; now it was to be one-third.[83] From 1727 till 1775, and well

of the declining bill rate to the minister of Marine, Nicolas René Berryer de Ravenoville, comte de la Ferrière, or to the secretary of state for foreign affairs, Étienne-François de Choiseul, duc de Choiseul et d'Amboise. See Le Vassor de la Touche, at Martinique, to Berryer, 6 June 1761, and Le Mercier de la Rivière to Choiseul, 24 Feb. and 7 June 1761, and to Berryer, 23 July and 22 Oct. 1761, all in Archives Colonies, C⁸ᴬ 63, fols. 2, 161–164, 193, 204–207, 211–215. See also Berryer, at Paris, to Le Mercier de la Rivière, 15 June 1761, Archives Colonies, B111, fol. 227; Louis-Philippe May, *Histoire économique de la Martinique (1635–1763)* (Paris, 1930), 187–190; and Boulle, "French Colonies," 123–191. For a similar situation on St. Domingue at the same time see minister of Marine to Jean-Étienne-Bernard de Clugny, in Moreau de Saint-Méry, ed., *Loix et constitutions des colonies françoises*, IV, 323–324. Clugny was the intendant of St. Domingue.

77. See also the "Déclaration du Roi touchant la Monnaie," dated 13 Dec. 1650, and the "Arrêt du Conseil de la Martinique touchant les Monnaies," of 9 May 1654, in Moreau de Saint-Méry, ed., *Loix et constitutions des colonies françoises*, I, 70, 73.

78. Ordinances of 7 Oct. 1661 and 20 Mar. 1662, Shortt, ed., *Documents Relating to Canadian Currency*, I, xli, 5.

79. Moreau de Saint-Méry, ed., *Loix et constitutions des colonies françoises*, I, 266–267. "Mémoire sur la valeur que doit l'argent dans les Isles de l'Amérique, et la Martinique et de St. Domingue," 20 May 1766, in A Collection of

Manuscript Copies of Papers Relating to French Colonies, 1702–1750, II, 259–266, Ayer Manuscripts, Newberry Library, Chicago; [Émilien] Petit, *Droit public, ou gouvernement des colonies françoises, d'après les loix faites pour ces pays* (Paris, 1771), II, 366–380.

80. See, e.g., the report on the finances of French Canada prepared by Jean Talon, the intendant of New France, in 1669, in Shortt, ed., *Documents Relating to Canadian Currency*, xli. See also *ibid.*, lix, 207.

81. *Ibid.*, 399ff. The government of the colony was still trying in 1727 to effect the edict when it condemned some colonists for failure to observe "la réduction du quart." Ordinance of 16 Nov. 1727, *Édits, ordonnances royaux, déclarations et arrêts du Conseil d'État du roi concernant le Canada*, rev. ed. (Quebec, 1854–1856), II, 486–494. See also Shortt, ed., *Documents Relating to Canadian Currency*, II, 733, 775; and Council of Marine to Louis de Courbon, comte de Blénac, and Jean-Jacques Mithon de Senneville, 12 Oct. 1715, in Moreau de Saint-Méry, ed., *Loix et constitutions des colonies françoises*, II, 473. Blénac was the first governor-general of St. Domingue, and Mithon de Senneville was the subdélégué of the intendant of the West Indies.

82. Chalmers, *History of Currency*, 177.

83. Ordinances of 11 June and 9 Sept. 1726, Moreau de Saint-Méry, ed.,

beyond that year, the par of exchange for the French colonies (other than Canada) was 150 livres colonial currency per 100 livres tournois.[84]

The intrinsic value of the piece of eight as a coin did not change during these two centuries, as the discussion in chapters 1 and 2 showed. But because of the considerable fluctuations in French currency, in France its value varied considerably, rising and falling sometimes by 100 percent in the space of a year, especially in the 1720s.[85] During the 1760s and 1770s the commercial price seems to have stayed fairly close to 5.25 livres tournois, although Malouet complained of an effective value of 6 livres tournois.[86] Fortunately, our purposes do not require that we pay attention to these differences. Given our knowledge of the commercial exchange rate between London and Paris and the information above about the par of exchange

Loix et constitutions des colonies françoises, III, 171–172. See also minister of Marine to de Clugny, *ibid.*, IV, 323–324.

84. Contemporary references to this level for par are ubiquitous. See, e.g., [William Douglass], *An Essay concerning Silver and Paper Currencies, More Especially with Regard to the British Colonies in New England* (Boston, [1738]), 4; Petit, *Droit public*, II, 366–380; *Mémoire des négocians de Nantes, sur la présence des vaisseaux anglais dans les ports de Saint-Domingue, & sur l'introduction des fausses monnaies* (Nantes, 1773), 3 (copy in Archives Colonies, F[2B] 3); R[ober-jot] L[artigue], *Comptes faits des monnoies d'or coupé et cordonné d'Espagne et de Portugal, qui ont cours dans la partie française de l'isle Saint-Domingue* (Paris, 1776), 170, with manuscript additions in copy in Kress Library of Business and Economics in the Baker Library of the Graduate School of Business Administration, Harvard University, Boston. See also [Michel-René Hilliard d'Auberteuil], *Considérations sur l'état présent de la colonie française de Saint-Domingue* (Paris, [1776–1777]), I, 256–257; Gov. Pierre-Victor de Malouet, at Cayenne, to Marine, 28 Oct. 1777, in Malouet, *Collection de mémoires et correspondances officielles sur l'administration des colonies, et notamment sur la Guiane française et hollandaise* (Paris, [1802]), II, 104; Samuel Ricard, *Traité général du commerce*, [ed. Tomás Antonio de Marien y Arróspide], new ed. (Amsterdam, 1781), II, 138; Bryan Edwards, *An Historical Survey of the French Colony in the Island of St. Domingo* (London, 1797), 198; E. Zay, *Histoire monétaire des colonies françaises d'après les documents officiels* (Paris, 1892); and Robert Lacombe, "Histoire monétaire de Saint-Domingue et de la République d'Haïti des origines à 1874," *Revue française d'histoire d'Outre-Mer*, XLIII (1956), 273–337. Moreover, official accounts invariably used the par of exchange. On St. Domingue: "Tableau du movement quie les productions de la Colonie de St. Domingue," 11 June and 21 July 1764, Archives Colonies, C[9A] 123; [Charles-François Pichot de] Kerdisien-Trémais, at Cap Français, to Marine, 11 Nov. and 14 Nov. 1765, *ibid.*, C[9A] 126; "Mémoire du Roy . . . sur les finances de St. Domingue," 18 Mar. 1766, *ibid.*, B123, fol. 70; [Jean-François Vincent, seigneur de] Montarcher, at Cap Français, to Marine, 28 Oct. 1771, *ibid.*, C[9A] 139, no. 55. Montarcher was the intendant of St. Domingue from 1771 to 1774; Kerdisien-Trémais was the subdélégué-général of the intendant. The city of Cap Français, or "Le Cap"—modern Cap Haïtien—on the northern coast of the island, was the colonial capital. On Guadeloupe: M. Montdenoix, at Basse-Terre, to Marine, 1 June 1770, *ibid.*, C[7A] 31, fol. 26. Montdenoix was

the ordonnateur of the colony. On Grenada: Gov. George Scott, at Fort Royal, to Lord Egremont, 19 Jan. 1763, C.O. 101/9, fol. 17. References such as these could be multiplied indefinitely.

85. Louis Dermigny, "Circuits de l'argent et milieux d'affaires au XVIIIe siècle," *Revue historique*, CCXII (1954), 239–278. See also Lacombe, "Histoire monétaire de Saint-Domingue," *Rev. fran. d'hist. d'Outre-Mer*, XLIII (1956), 284–285. For the changing value of the livre tournois see Natalis de Wailly, *Mémoire sur les variations de la livre tournois depuis le règne de Saint Louis jusqu'à l'établissement de la monnaie décimale* (Institut Impérial de France, Académie des Inscriptions et Belles-Lettres, *Mémoires*, XXI, pt. ii [Paris, 1857]), 177–427.

86. Malouet to Marine, 28 Oct. 1777, in Malouet, *Collection de mémoires et correspondances*, II, 87. Malouet's figure for the commercial price of 5 livres and 5 sous tournois is confirmed in numerous contemporary quotations of the price of the piastre gourde in France. See, e.g., Pierre Dardel, *Navires et marchandises dan les ports de Rouen et du Havre au XVIIIe siècle* (Paris, 1963), 190n, citing the "cours de la piastre à Marseille en 1746"; *Gazette de Saint-Domingue* (Cap Français), 7 Mar. 1764, referring to the price at Bordeaux on 7 Dec. 1763; "Extrait de l'État des d'Entrées et Marchandises," Rochelle, 1767, Archives Colonies, F[2B] 3; *Almanach de Saint-Domingue, historique, curieux et utile, pour l'année bissextile 1776* (Nantes, [1775?]), 60. See also Robert Richard, "A propos de Saint-Domingue: La monnaie dans l'economie coloniale (1674–1803)," *Rev. fran. d'hist. d'Outre-Mer*, XLI (1954), 22–46; and Dermigny, "Circuits de l'argent," *Rev. hist.*, CCXII (1954), 239–278.

between France and her colonies, we can convert prices in French Canada or in the French West Indies into sterling. We can thus quite easily sidestep the intricate and confused shifts in the value of the livre tournois. The need now is to discover the commercial rate of exchange between France and her colonies.

French North America

With the par of exchange controlled by royal edict, the residents of the French colonies had few local options when confronted with problems in their money supply. English colonists competed with one another for coin by raising its currency value. Only after this avenue was closed to them by the act of 1708 were they in a situation analogous to that of the French Canadians. In that condition they resorted to a device that had first been adopted by the colonists of Quebec: paper money.

In 1685, in order to supplement their money supply, the residents of French Canada had introduced a form of paper currency called "card money." The colony ran a perpetual deficit in its balance of payments, a deficit that was met in part by the exportation of the available coin. To alleviate this situation, simply to keep the colony alive, the French government annually allotted some moneys to the colonial government. (Parallels in the English settlements include Georgia and Nova Scotia; French Louisiana and Spanish Florida were run on a similar basis.) But these funds, in the form of credits on the colony's account in France, did little to increase the supply of coin available for its internal trade. Card money, a

paper money with currency only in French Canada, was the perfect solution to the problem.[87]

Card money worked because holders of this form of paper currency had first claim each year on the colonial government's drafts on its annual allocation. Thus, in theory, card money was fully backed and negotiable in the spring of each year for the purchase of bills of exchange at par on the French government. But it had two flaws: it maintained its value only if the French government accepted and paid the bills drawn on it and only if the annual allocation was equal to or exceeded the amount of card money in circulation. In practice the former consideration, given the periodic troubles of the French government, especially in wartime, proved the most damaging to the value of card money. Then it depreciated badly as the colonists either bid up the price of what bills were available, offering payment in hard currency, or shipped the coin instead. Either way, in terms of coin, the value of French Canadian paper money fell. These periods of depreciation, followed by periods of return to par, were reflected in quotations of the commercial rate of exchange—and could be traced in such quotations, if they were still available.

Not only do we lack quotations of the commercial rate of exchange in French Canada, but we have little information, beyond what has been said above, about the mechanisms for drawing or protesting bills of exchange. We can fill the latter gap by resorting to analogy and the presumption that prac-

87. For card money see Zay, *Histoire monétaire des colonies françaises*, 125–187; Adam Shortt, "Canadian Currency and Exchange under French Rule," *Journal of the Canadian Bankers Association*, V (1897–1898), 271–290, 285–401, VI (1898–1899), 1–21, 147–165, 233–247; Shortt, ed., *Documents Relating to Canadian Currency*, passim; and Richard A. Lester, *Monetary Experiments: Early American and Recent Scandinavian* (Princeton, N.J., 1939), 37–55.

tices must have been somewhat similar to those in Europe and in the English colonies. Again, there is considerable room for further work on this subject.

The other French colonies in North America (all of which together comprised New France) were somewhat better off than Quebec—or less unfortunate, anyhow. Acadia tended to rely on New England for its money. Cape Breton Island (Isle Royale), especially after the establishment of the entrepôt at Louisbourg, benefited from a more prosperous economy.[88] Louisiana, centered at New Orleans, had a situation similar to that of Quebec and made use of a paper currency.[89] All of them used the money of account of France, the real money common to the Western Hemisphere, and a colonial currency based on the piece of eight at the official par of exchange.

The French West Indies

The French colonies in the Caribbean, like the colonies of New France, used the money of account of the mother country, whatever real money was available in the Western Hemisphere, and a colonial currency based on the piece of eight at the official par of exchange. From the island of St. Domingue

88. [Douglass], *Discourse concerning Currencies*, 8; Gustave Lanctot *et al.*, eds., *Documents Relating to Currency, Exchange and Finance in Nova Scotia, with Prefatory Documents, 1675–1758* (Ottawa, 1933), 182, 221, 222, 273, 277, and *passim*. The par of exchange at Acadia was the same as for all of the other French colonies except Canada. Shortt, "Canadian Currency and Exchange," *Jour. Canadian Bankers Assoc.*, VI (1898–1899), 151.

89. John G. Clark, *New Orleans, 1718–1812: An Economic History* (Baton Rouge, La., [1970]), 35–36, 107–125, and *passim*. See also Zay, *Histoire monétaire des colonies françaises*, 125–187. In 1775 at least one merchant kept his accounts in pieces of eight and bits. See William Redwood, at New Orleans, to Oliver Pollock, 10 Oct. 1775, Oliver Pollock Papers, 1767–1788, I, fol. 133, Peter Force Papers, Ser. VIII D, Lib. Cong.

in the north, southward to the ill-fated Cayenne on the northeasterly coast of South America, there was no variation in form and little variation in practice from colony to colony. The only significant variation from New France was the use, especially in the export trade, of the piece of eight as a money of account as well as a coin. The piece of eight as coin was the equivalent of ten bits until 1773; thereafter it equaled eleven bits. While we have only slightly more information about the rate of exchange in the French West Indies than for French North America, the West Indies do provide us with the only series of quotations of the commercial rates of exchange for any of the French colonies in the New World.

The major French colony in the Caribbean—and in fact in the entire Atlantic world—was St. Domingue, modern Haiti, the western tip of the island of Hispaniola (the eastern portion was Spanish Santo Domingo, the modern Dominican Republic). By the 1770s St. Domingue produced more sugar than any other sugar colony, making it not only France's most valuable possession but probably the most valuable single colony in terms of output in the entire world. Trade with St. Domingue, besides occupying the interest of French merchants, also attracted considerable attention from English colonial merchants resident in both the continental colonies and the British West Indies. Despite the work of such superb scholars as Gabriel Debien, we are only just beginning to appreciate the central role of St. Domingue in the history of the economy of the Western Hemisphere in the second and third quarters of the eighteenth century.

The colonists of St. Domingue negotiated bills of exchange on Paris just as the colonists of Jamaica and Philadelphia did on London. Unfortunately, we know few of the details of these negotiations, such as the usual sight of bills or the procedures and penalties for those that were protested. We do know that the par of exchange after the mid-1720s was 150 livres St. Domingue currency per 100 livres tournois.[90] And we know the form of quotations of the commercial rate of exchange and the course of exchange from 1764 to 1775 and beyond.

The piece of eight, or piastre gourde, was not only the basic coin in circulation on St. Domingue but also the measure of exchange. An ordonnance of July 1774 spoke of the "prix variable attribue par le commerce aux piastres gourdes,

et connu sous le nom de prix du change."[91] Exchange was at par, in the terms used in the island, when the loss or discount from the value in livres for the piece of eight was one-third. A quotation indicating "les piastres gourdes 35 pour cent" specified a rate above par, equivalent, in the usual fashion for quoting exchange in this handbook, to stating that 153.85 livres St. Domingue currency equaled 100 livres tournois. A quotation giving the price of the piece of eight in livres St. Domingue currency occurred rarely in the pre-1775 era. When it did, it seemed to be in comparison to the commercial value of the piastre in France during the year—five livres and five sous—rather than the official value of six livres.[92]

The monthly quotations of the commercial rate of exchange on St. Domingue that are the basis of tables 4.8 and 4.9 are compiled from the weekly issues of St. Domingue's only newspaper, the *Gazette de Saint-Domingue*. The paper began publication in February 1764 and continued at least through 1791 with several changes in name; after 1766 and through most of its history it bore the title *Les affiches americaines*. Although it was published at first at Cap Français, the governor-general and the intendant insisted in early 1768 that it move to Port-au-Prince, the better to keep an eye on it. It stayed there, except for the period from June 1770 through

90. This is the legal par of exchange, as set out above, but the average commercial rate of exchange at Cap Français for the eleven years from 1764 through 1774 (from table 4.8) is closer to 155 livres. With the piastre gourde rated at 8 livres and 5 sous St. Domingue currency and 5 livres and 5 sous tournois, the par of exchange on this basis was 157.14 livres St. Domingue currency per 100 livres tournois. For that rating see, e.g., the printed price current of Wall and Tardy, Cap Français, dated 1 June 1786, Prices Current, Box I, Welcome-Arnold Papers, John Carter Brown Library; Moreau de Saint-Méry, *Description de l'isle Saint-Domingue*, ed. Maurel and Taillemite, I, 14. See also the commercial rate quoted for Aux Cayes during 1774 in *Les affiches americaines* (Cap Français), *passim*. That contemporaries considered the 155 livre figure as the usual rate is confirmed in the account sent by Musculus and Rondineau, at Môle St. Nicolas, to Neil Jamieson, at Norfolk, Va., 19 Oct. 1771, in which the rate "55%" is used without comment and a conversion "@5% lost" is calculated as 160.25 livres. See Jamieson Papers, XIV, no. 3172. In this account Musculus and Rondineau rendered the results of their sale of two bills of exchange totaling £600 sterling. Given the London-Paris rate for 1771 (see table 2.25) and the Paris-St. Domingue rates they quoted, rates verified in table 4.8, they should have credited Jamieson with roughly 20,900 livres St. Domingue currency. Instead they cheated him of almost 1,700 livres (roughly £73 sterling) by basing their calculations on the pretense that a pound sterling equaled 20 livres tournois, when at the current rate it equaled some 22.8 livres tournois. See also Clement Biddle, at Philadelphia, to Samuel Galloway, at Annapolis, Md., 25 May 1764, and Mesnier Frères, at Cap Français, to Galloway, 22 July 1765, Galloway Correspondence, 1739–1769, Papers of Samuel and John Galloway, 1739–1812, New York Public Library, New York City.

91. "Ordonnance de MM. les Général & Intendant des Isles Françaises de l'Amérique sous le Vent," dated Port-au-Prince, 8 July 1774, as printed in L[artigue], *Comptes faits des monnoies d'or*. See also *Les affiches americaines* (Cap Français), 13 July 1774.

92. See n. 86 above for this commercial value. The official value is referred to in Malouet, *Collection de mémoires et correspondances*, II, 87; in *Les affiches americaines* (Cap Français), 12 Feb. 1766; and in the Minutes notariales, M. Lascroisade and Marigot, 23 Apr. 1787, Archives Départementales de la Guadeloupe, Basse-Terre, as cited in Christian Schnakenbourg, "L'industrie sucrière dans la partie française de Saint-Martin au XVIIIe siècle," *Bulletin de la Société d'Histoire de la Guadeloupe*, VIII (1967), 22n.

March 1771, when it was again published "au Cap" because of the earthquake that had devastated Port-au-Prince on 3 June 1770. This shift was facilitated by the existence all along of a second press at Cap Français, which had continued to publish a supplement to the *Gazette*, entitled *Avis du Cap*.[93]

The *Gazette* published commodity prices from the beginning, taking "les plus grandes precautions pour donner les prix les plus justes."[94] The editors collected quotations from the several major markets of the island and were always careful to give the date of each quotation. Included were regular indications of the exchange rate. While in one year, 1765, there were exchange quotations from as many as the five major ports of the colony (Cap Français, Port-au-Prince, Cayes, Leogane, and St. Marc), these came mostly from Cap Français and Port-au-Prince. In the earlier years the quotations at Cap Français occurred with greater frequency and probably more reliability, but the removal of the editor to Port-au-Prince eventually brought a diminution of both the regularity and, one imagines, the quality of the reporting of quotations from Cap Français. The annual averages transferred to the next chapter (table 5.3) include an average for 1771 from both table 4.8 and table 4.9 comprising the figures for both cities, using

quotations from Cap Français for January through August and from Port-au-Prince from August through December.

Most of St. Domingue's trade with the English colonists centered in the northern coast of the island, where the exchange at Cap Français was presumably the prevailing rate. In Spanish Santo Domingo, just to the east of the border with St. Domingue, were the town and bay of Monte-Christi—the site of the extensive contraband trade between the French and merchants from the English colonies during the Seven Years' War. One of these merchants reported from there in 1759 that "prices do not differ greatly from those at the Cap."[95] And at the northwestern tip of the island was Môle Saint Nicolas, which was established after the war as a free port through which much of the colony's foreign trade was channeled. Prices there were quoted both in livres St. Domingue currency and in piastres gourdes, depending, apparently, on the commodity involved.[96] Exchange with the English colonial merchants seems usually to have been based on the piece of eight as a money of account.[97]

93. For all of this see Moreau de Saint-Méry, *Description de l'isle Saint-Domingue*, ed. Maurel and Taillemite, I, 493–496; M.-A. Ménier and G[abriel] Debien, "Journaux de Saint-Domingue," *Rev. fran. d'hist. d'Outre-Mer*, XXXVI (1949), 424–475; and the newspaper itself. What is apparently a unique run of the *Gazette* is in the collections of the Bibliothèque Nationale, Paris. (See also Moreau de Saint-Méry, *Description de l'isle Saint-Domingue*, ed. Maurel and Taillemite, I, 495.)

94. *Avis divers et petites affiches américaines* (Cap Français), 26 June 1765. Such quotations were sometimes copied in Paris commercial newspapers. See the *Gazette du commerce, de l'agriculture et des finances* (Paris), 1765 on, *passim*.

95. Daniel Wolstenholme, at Annapolis, Md., to Samuel Galloway, at West River, Md., 12 Jan. 1760, Galloway Correspondence, N.Y. Pub. Lib.

96. *Commerce of Rhode Island*, I, *passim*. Still another example both of how these tables may be used and of their accuracy is the statement by Isaac Eaton, formerly of Philadelphia, who had recently established himself in business at Môle St. Nicolas, St. Domingue, that "45 sous" there were "equall to 2s/3d New York money." Letter to Nicholas Brown and Co., at Providence, R.I., 21 Nov. 1769, Brown Papers, L 59–72 M, John Carter Brown Lib. Tables 5.1, 5.2, and 5.3 for 1769 show that 2s 3d (11.2p) New York currency equaled 6.5p sterling (11.2 ÷ 1.7247), 29.5 sous tournois (6.5 x 20 x .227129), and 45.8 sous St. Domingue currency (6.5 x 20 x .352686). This is a difference of only 1.8% in an era of sharply fluctuating exchange rates at New York.

97. In Mar. 1773 the island's government raised the value at which the piastre gourde would pass from 10 to 11 "escalins," or bits, a fact noted immediately in neighboring Jamaica, as it increased the purchasing power of

Comparable data for the other French West Indian islands do not exist or have yet to be discovered. At best we have an occasional reference to exchange transactions, but these, almost without exception, are official in nature and at the par of exchange. At the least, such references do confirm the universality of the one-third loss as par, equivalent to a rate of 150 livres colonial currency to 100 livres tournois. Because of the extent to which St. Domingue dominated the other islands, one might want to argue that the commercial rate there was duplicated elsewhere. If that was the case, the quotations in tables 4.8 and 4.9 applied to the entirety of the French West Indies. A more cautious and more justifiable method for the reduction of colonial currency values from the islands other than St. Domingue would require a recourse to par.[98]

the piece of eight there from 6s 8d to 6s 10.5d Jamaica currency. Moreau de Saint-Méry, ed., *Loix et constitutions des colonies françoises*, V, 445; Thomas Dolbeare, at Kingston, Jamaica, to Rivera and Lopez, at Newport, R.I., 7 Dec. 1773, *Commerce of Rhode Island*, I, 467. At least one shipowner warned his master: "You'll be careful that your freight is calculated in money of old France and not of the islands." Tristram Dalton, at Newburyport, Mass., to Edward Fettsplace, Jr., 4 Dec. 1782, E. Arnot Robertson, *The Spanish Town Papers: Some Sidelights on the American War of Independence* (London, 1959), 121.

98. In Sept. 1762 Abraham Whipple recorded a difference between "Martinico curancy" and Barbados currency in the ratio of 120 to 100, implying that the former had an exchange value of £162 Martinique currency per £100 sterling. "Sloop George Account Book," 1762, Abraham Whipple, master, Brown Papers, V-G45. Exchange between Martinique and Maryland in 1776 and 1777 was based on the comparative value of the piece of eight in each currency, 8 livres and 5 sous in Martinique currency and 6 shillings in Maryland currency. Invoice Book, 1770–1784, and Ledger, 1775–1777, Robert T. Hooe Papers, N.Y. Pub. Lib. See especially the "NB" on the invoice dated St. Pierre, Martinique, 31 Oct. 1776, Invoice Book. See also "Notes de numismatique martiniquaise," *Rev. fran. d'hist. d'Outre-Mer*, XI (1921), 313–316.

TABLE 4.8. **Rate of Exchange: St. Domingue (Cap Français) on Paris, 1764–1775**

(Livres St. Domingue Currency per 100 Livres Tournois of France)

Year	Jan.	Feb.	Mar.	Apr.	May	June	July	Aug.	Sept.	Oct.	Nov.	Dec.	Average
1764		148.81	150.65	150.94	153.14	153.07	152.39	153.85	153.85	153.61	152.67	153.26	152.16
1765	153.85	153.85	153.85	153.85	153.85	153.85	153.85	155.64	156.25	156.25	156.25	156.25	154.80
1766	156.25	156.25	156.25	156.25	156.25	*157.49*	158.73	158.73	158.73	158.73	159.69	160.00	157.78
1767	160.00	160.00	158.88	159.11	160.00	160.00	160.00	160.00	160.00	160.00	160.00	160.00	159.83
1768	159.52	155.64	154.08	154.04	156.10	156.25	156.25	156.10	154.13	152.53	151.01	151.24	154.74
1769	151.24	151.33	151.38	151.52	153.37	155.64	156.25	158.10	158.98	158.73	158.73	158.50	155.31
1770	158.73	157.48	151.74	150.65	151.79	156.67	153.85	153.61	156.54	157.48	157.48	157.48	155.29
1771	156.99	149.81	137.93	139.37	149.81	151.98	155.04	158.73	159.57	157.62			152.67
1772										150.38	150.38	150.38	150.38
1773	149.52	145.98										166.67	157.21
1774	161.29												161.29
1775													

Notes and Sources: **TABLE 4.8**

Figures printed in italics are straight-line interpolations based on the two neighboring quotations.

1764–1774: *Gazette de Saint-Domingue* ([title varies] Cap Français and Port-au-Prince), 1764–1774. See the text.

1771: Account from Musculus and Rondineau, at Môle St. Nicolas, 19 Oct. 1771, Neil Jamieson Papers, 1757–1789, XIV, no. 3172, Library of Congress.

TABLE 4.9. **Rate of Exchange: St. Domingue (Port-au-Prince) on Paris, 1765–1775**

(Livres St. Domingue Currency per 100 Livres Tournois of France)

Year	Jan.	Feb.	Mar.	Apr.	May	June	July	Aug.	Sept.	Oct.	Nov.	Dec.	Average
1765		150.38		153.85	153.85	151.52	151.52	151.52	150.38	153.85	155.45	155.04	152.34
1766	155.04	156.25	155.04	152.67		152.67							154.06
1767							158.73	158.73	156.27	155.64	156.67	158.73	157.46
1768	156.72	156.25	156.25										156.41
1769													
1770													
1771			158.73	158.98	158.73	158.73	158.73	158.73	158.73	158.73	158.73	158.73	158.75
1772	158.73	158.73	158.73	158.73	158.73	158.73	158.73	158.73	158.73	157.78	157.78	158.73	158.57
1773	158.73	158.73	158.73	158.73	158.73	158.73	158.73	158.73	158.73	158.73	158.73	159.36	158.78
1774	160.00	160.00	160.00	160.00	160.00	160.00	160.00	160.00	160.00	160.00	160.00	160.00	160.00
1775	160.00	160.00	160.00	160.00	160.00	160.00	160.00	160.00	160.00	160.00	160.00	160.00	160.00

Notes and Sources: **TABLE 4.9**

1765–1775: *Gazette de Saint-Domingue* ([title varies] Cap Français and Port-au-Prince), 1764–1775. See the text.

The Dutch Colonies and the Exchange on Amsterdam

The Dutch colonists brought to the New World their money of account, some of their own coins, and an understanding of the workings of the Amsterdam exchange. Their position in command of European trade in the first half of the seventeenth century accustomed them to dealing with the problems of different coinages. Their colonies were largely trading posts at first, and their colonists were merchants who were used to the vagaries of money. While it would be almost impossible to demonstrate conclusively, there is every reason to suppose that the Dutch had fewer problems with their colonial currency than did the English or the French.

Dutch colonial currency was a money of account established by raising the local value of coin. Much as the English colonies accepted the piece of eight at more colonial shillings and pence than it passed for in London, and the French colonists valued the same coin at more livres *monnaie du pays* than it passed for in Paris, so did the Dutch colonies simply value the piece of eight or the "Joe" at more gulden and stuivers in the colonies than they passed for in Amsterdam.[99] Thus they created the Surinam current money, the current money of their West Indian Islands, the current money of New Netherland, and presumably even a current money for the period of their control of part of Brazil. All contemporary sources talk about colonial *currency*. They therefore imply that any exchange negotiated between colony and mother country was between colonial current money and the current money of Holland, not on bank money.[100] In this way exchange on the Dutch colonies resembled exchange transactions between Amsterdam and Sweden or Denmark.

The earliest Dutch colonial currency of which we have record was that of New Netherland. In January of 1642/43, Director General William Kieft responded positively to a request from the colony's selectmen that he raise the value of coin by announcing to them that he had already prepared edicts effecting the increase. Early in the next decade complaints reached the governors of the West India Company that Director General Pieter Stuijvesant had raised the value of the piece of eight to three florijns, or gulden, New Netherland currency. This effectively created a par of exchange of 120 gulden New Netherland currency to 100 gulden current money of Amsterdam.[101]

William Douglass, writing in 1738, ascribed the same par of exchange to all of the Dutch colonies.[102] At that time the Dutch controlled several West Indian islands and a series of settlements on the northeast coast of South America. Since Stuijvesant had come to New Amsterdam from Curaçao, where he had been appointed director general in 1642, and since he continued to hold his older position after he assumed his newer one, it is possible either that his order was based on a similar edict in force in the West Indies or that his order

99. In the West Indies after 1686 the piece of eight was also used as a money of account compounded of 10 bits and 48 stuivers. After 1772 it was valued at 11 bits. See Ricard, *Traité général du commerce*, [ed. Marien], II, 232. See n. 97 above and the discussion in the section on Cadiz in chap. 2.

100. Thus prices in Surinam were quoted in "Surinam guilders," and bills were drawn in "Hollands courant gelt." See, e.g., Ambrose Page, at Paramaribo, Surinam, to Obadiah Brown and Co., at Providence, R.I., 8 Sept. 1760, Brown Papers, L 57–59 M, and the Surinam bills of exchange dated 10 Dec. 1770, 2 Feb. 1771, and 29 Mar. 1771, *ibid.*, U-C.

101. See the discussion in the section on New York and in n. 78 in chap. 2, above.

102. [Douglass], *Essay concerning Silver and Paper Currencies*, 4.

had concurrent effect there. It therefore seems likely that par at 120 gulden colonial currency per 100 gulden current money of Amsterdam applied to all the Dutch colonies from as early as Stuijvesant's era and perhaps as a result of his or Kieft's edicts. That same rate continued in effect in the Dutch South American colonies down through the end of our period, as we will see below. But this was not to be the case in the West Indies, where we have references to a different, higher figure from as early as 1753.[103] If the lower figure indeed ever applied to the island colonies, then a change must have occurred there, probably around 1740.[104]

On the Dutch islands of Curaçao, St. Eustatius, and Saba, and on the Dutch part of St. Martin, exchange transactions were influenced by some of the same factors that we will see at work in the Danish islands. Both were polyglot societies, governed by their respective mother countries but populated as numerously by Englishmen as they were by their own nationals. Interested in trading with the entire Caribbean, the inhabitants tended to vary their money with their trading partners.[105] While we would expect, then, to find merchants in the Dutch West Indies quoting prices in gulden and stuivers or even in pieces of eight, it is a bit surprising to see them using "English" pounds. All of these were moneys of account; real money, as always, consisted of the Spanish and Portuguese silver and gold. The piece of eight as a Dutch West Indian money of account equaled eight reals ("ryals" in the Dutch islands); each real equaled six stuivers. In the period after about 1740 this compared with a value in Amsterdam of 38 stuivers current money.[106] The

103. Nicholas Magens, *An Essay on Insurances*, [2d ed., enlrg.] (London, 1755), I, 21; John Weskett, *A Complete Digest of the Theory, Laws and Practice of Insurance* (London, 1781).

104. This, at least, was true when the New York merchants who traded to Curaçao lowered the book value of the piece of eight "Curaçao money." Peter Jay Journal, 1724–1748, Jay Papers; John and Robert Sanders Voyage Book, 1739–1748, Merchant Shipping Papers, Item 1, Glen-Sanders Papers, 1674–1957, N.-Y. Hist. Soc. Jay equated it with 7s (35p) New York currency in the 1720s and 1730s but used several lower values (6s [30p] to 6s 4.5d [31.88p]) in the 1740s. The Sanders used 6s 9d (33.75p) through May 1740 and 6s 6d (32.5p) thereafter.

105. Examples of much of this can be found in the correspondence of Patterson, Scott, and Buckley of St. Eustatius with Hollingsworth and Rudulph of Philadelphia. See the Levi Hollingsworth Invoice Book, 1767–1770, and Correspondence, 1761–1771, Hollingsworth Collection, 1748–1887, Hist.

Soc. Pa. Particularly useful are the letters of Patterson, Scott, and Buckley to Hollingsworth and Rudulph of 7 May 1769; of Hollingsworth and Rudulph to Patterson, Scott, and Buckley of 3 June 1769; and of Oliver Pollock, at St. Eustatius, to Hollingsworth and Rudulph, 18 Sept. 1769, with the statement of account of 16 Sept. 1769. The St. Eustatius firm maintained at least the figment of an office on St. Christopher. See Hollingsworth and Rudulph's letter to them of 14 Dec. 1768. See also the Curaçao account, Nov. 1732, in the Alexander Wooddrup Account Books, 1720–1734, II, Lib. Cong.

106. Ricard, *Traité général du commerce*, [ed. Marien], II, 82, 232, 288, 290. We have several indications in the records of New York merchants of the value of the Curaçao piece of eight as a money of account. See n. 104, above. In the 1760s the firm of Henry and John Cruger of New York City regularly reduced it to 6s (30p) New York currency. Waste Book, Cruger Papers. With the New York-London rate over the period 1762 to 1768 at an average of about £183, this suggests a value of about 3s 3d (16.4p) sterling. That value was probably exaggerated a bit because of the family nature of these transactions; the Cruger brothers seem to have been giving a somewhat preferential rate of exchange to the firm of Cruger and Gouverneur of Curaçao because the former partner was the son of Henry and the nephew of John. Father and uncle wrote on 28 Apr. 1767 to say that Nathaniel Marston, merchant of New York, "will pay your bill . . . but not at 6s per piece 8/8 because your pieces are really not worth more than about 5/6." Henry and John Cruger "Copy Book of Letters," 1764–1768, *ibid*. See also the Waste Book entries of 31 Jan. and 21 July 1767. At 5s 6d (27.5p) New York currency in Apr. 1767, the Curaçao piece of eight as a money of account equaled roughly 3s 1d (15.3p) sterling, a difference that is perhaps reflected in another way in these same papers. the piece of eight as a coin equaled about 1.34 pieces Curaçao money in Feb. 1763, but the money of account had depreciated

ratio of the two values shows par to have been at roughly 125 colonial gulden to 100 Amsterdam gulden, the same rate as that quoted for 1753. The "pound" at St. Eustatius appears to have been that of the island of St. Christopher, its nearest neighbor; at least this was the case in the 1760s and 1770s.[107]

This proliferation of currencies found a parallel in the equally diverse methods of drawing bills of exchange in the Dutch West Indies. Bills of exchange in payment of balances due North American or British merchants were drawn on Amsterdam merchants but made payable in London. At least some of them were valued in sterling. These were the Dutch bills about which Walter Tullideph of Antigua remarked in 1756 (see fig. 12, p. 294).[108] Returns from Curaçao to Amsterdam involved sending sealed bags of Spanish silver as frequently as bills of exchange.[109] Moreover, these bills apparently had a somewhat different character than elsewhere. Pieter Diedenhoven of Curaçao regularly settled his account with Robert Sanders of Albany by dispatching "bodemary briefs" (bottomry letters) to Amsterdam, where they were credited to Sanders's account at their face value, much as the £100 sterling bill of exchange would have been at London. Thus a bottomry letter for "200 pieces 8/8 @ 48" stuivers posted in mid-1746 yielded the expected 480 gulden in Amsterdam in October of that year. Diedenhoven credited his own account with the cost of the bills to him: "220 pieces 8/8 Caracoa Money," because, as it was said, "the agio" was "at 10 per cent."[110]

Not all of this is perfectly clear, but some things do emerge. These were not bottomry transactions of the usual sort, no matter what Diedenhoven called them. Bottomry was a method of obtaining a loan by using a vessel as collateral, much as one takes out a mortgage loan on a house. Interest rates were very high, making such loans relatively

such that the ratio was 1.43 in July 1767. See the Waste Book, 7 Feb. 1763, and the letter to Cruger and Gouverneur, 30 July 1767, in the letter book. Since the coin was worth 4s 6d (22.5p) sterling, the piece of eight Curaçao money was thus worth 3s 4d (16.8p) sterling in 1763 and 3s 2d (15.7p) sterling in 1767, figures close to those derived by way of New York currency.

107. Hollingsworth and Rudulph to Patterson, Scott, and Buckley, 3 June 1769, Hollingsworth Invoice Book, Hollingsworth Collection; John Galloway, at St. Eustatius, to Samuel Galloway, at Annapolis, Md., 24 Jan. 1770, Galloway Correspondence, X, no. 9669, Galloway-Maxey-Markoe Family Papers, 1654–1888, Lib. Cong. The first quotes the exchange rate; the second talks of a 10% difference between St. Eustatius "money" and Maryland currency at a time when the same difference existed between Maryland currency and that of St. Christopher. This indicated a rate on St. Eustatius of 165. In 1763 John Relfe wrote that "the exchange" at St. Eustatius "is only 65 per cent"; presumably he had this on the authority of a recent letter to him from a friend there, Jeremiah Peniston. Relfe, at Philadelphia, to Nicholas Brown and Co., 26 Sept. 1763, Brown Papers, L 58–67 FR. In the spring of 1775 it was reported that the "Joe" was worth £3.30 at St. Eustatius; on that basis par would have been £183.33 St. Eustatius currency. Entry dated 24 May 1775, Aaron Leaming Diaries, 1750–1777, III (1774–1775), Hist. Soc. Pa. Later that same year, in Sept., the commercial rate of exchange was at £175. Deposition of William Goodrich, 31 Oct. 1775, and the account of Goodrich with Isaac van Dam of St. Eustatius, 6 Dec. 1775, C.O. 5/1353, pp. 707–709, 723. For the context of the deposition see George M. Curtis III, "The Goodrich Family and the Revolution in Virginia, 1774–1776," *Virginia Magazine of History and Biography*, LXXXIV (1976), 49–74.

108. See the discussion in the section on the Windward Islands, above.

109. What follows is based largely on the records of the triangular trade of Robert Sanders in Albany, N.Y., with Pieter Diedenhoven of Curaçao and with Bernard (later Jan and Willem) van der Grift of Amsterdam as preserved in the Sanders Voyage Book, 1739–1748, Glen-Sanders Papers, and in the John and Robert Sanders Voyage Book, 1748–1764, and the Robert Sanders Letter Book, 1752–1758, Sanders Papers, N.-Y. Hist. Soc. Silver from Curaçao sold at Amsterdam for current money, according to these records; gold sold for bank money. Cf. N. W. Posthumus, *Inquiry into the History of Prices in Holland* (Leiden, 1946–1964), I, lvii–lx, 23*–27*, 394–397.

110. Sanders Voyage Book, fols. 74v–75r, Glen-Sanders Papers.

Figure 12. A Dutch West Indian Bill of Exchange.
(From the John Reynell Papers; courtesy of the Historical Society of Pennsylvania, Philadelphia.)

St. Eustatius, 19 June 1756. This bill is an example of the Dutch West Indian bills of exchange drawn at St. Eustatius on an Amsterdam merchant but payable in London pounds sterling. Jacobus von Doncken (probably in payment for British West Indian sugar or molasses) ordered Matthias Treher of Amsterdam to see to the delivery of £75 sterling to Robert Stevenson or his payee in London. Treher most likely accomplished this by himself drawing a bill in Amsterdam on his own London drawee for the required sum.

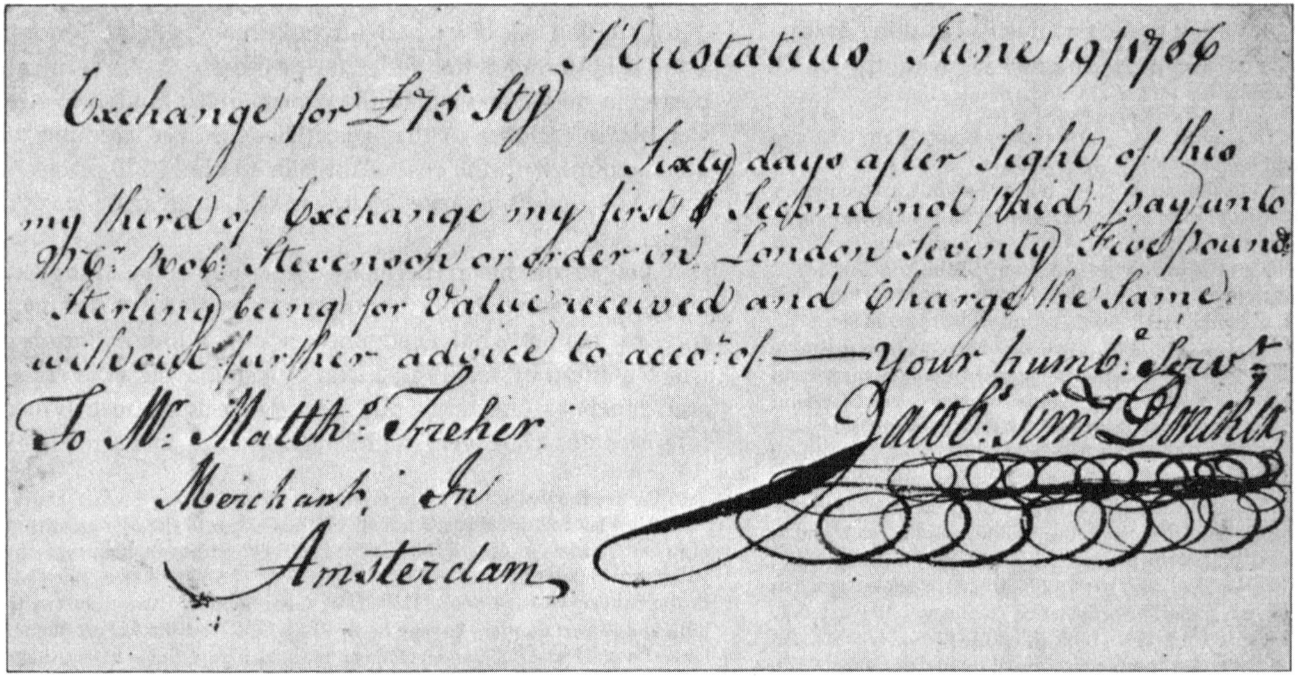
St Eustatius June 19/1756

Exchange for £75 Sty

Sixty days after Sight of this my third of Exchange my first & Second not Paid; pay unto Mr. Rob: Stevenson or order in London Seventy Five pounds Sterling being for Value received and Charge the same without further advice to acco.t of — Your humb.e Serv.t

Jacob: Von Doncken

To Mr. Matth.s Treher Merchant In Amsterdam

infrequent—matters only of "great necessitie," according to Gerard de Malynes.[111] We can no more than speculate on the reason for the terminology Diedenhoven employed, but it was possible to demand that the drawer of a bill of exchange issue a certificate of hypothecation that allowed the payer of a bill the right to take and to sell the vessel or cargo if the payee refused to accept the bill.[112]

Diedenhoven's use of the word "agio" does not refer to the difference between Amsterdam banco and Amsterdam current money. Instead he distinguished between Curaçao current money and Amsterdam current money. Apparently this was the form at Curaçao of the quotation of the commercial rate of exchange on Amsterdam. Other references to the agio at Curaçao indicate that it varied from 7 percent in November 1730 and February 1731 to 10 percent in mid-1746, 8 percent in January 1747, 9 percent in January 1750, 12 percent in September 1752, and 22 percent in November 1753.[113] Based on the same material, and working backwards using table 2.9 and table 5.1, we can determine that the piece of eight as a money of account on Curaçao had a value of 19.2p sterling in 1746, 20p in 1747, 19.9p in 1750, 19.4p in 1752, and 17.8p in 1753.[114]

On the South American continent the Dutch maintained three colonies: Surinam, Essequibo and Demerara, and Berbice. They acquired Surinam in 1667 from the English in exchange for giving up all claim to New Netherland. As an English colony it had been settled from and closely related to Barbados.[115] How far English Surinam followed the example of Barbados in its currency is conjectural. Our earliest indication of a Surinam currency is a potentially anachronistic reference to "f 747,330 Surinaamsch of f 622,800 Hollandsch courant" in 1712.[116] This is at a ratio of 120 gulden Surinam current to 100 gulden current money of Amsterdam,[117] a rate that continued to be quoted as par down into the 1780s and beyond.[118] It applied as well to Surinam as to the two neigh-

---

111. *Consuetudo, vel Lex Mercatoria, or, the Ancient Law-Merchant* (London, 1622), 171.

112. See also Robert Pringle, at Charleston, S.C., to Samuel Starke, at London, 18 May 1742, Walter B. Edgar, ed., *The Letterbook of Robert Pringle, 1737–1745* (Columbus, S.C., 1972), I, 375.

113. Peter Jay Journal, 1724–1748, pp. 63, 65, Jay Papers; Sanders Voyage Book, fols. 74v–75r, 83v–84r, Glen-Sanders Papers; Sanders Voyage Book, fols. 9v, 22v–23r, Sanders Papers; Robert Sanders to Diedenhoven, 13 Nov. 1753, Sanders Letter Book, Sanders Papers.

114. From 1740 to 1747 Robert Sanders equated the piece of eight "Curaçao money" with 6s 6d (32.5p) New York currency (see n. 104, above). Taking the average rate of exchange for the five years from 1740 through 1744 at

£170 New York per £100 sterling (table 3.5), this was the equivalent of 3s 10d (19.1p) sterling.

115. James A. Williamson, *English Colonies in Guiana and on the Amazon, 1640–1688* (Oxford, 1923), 151–177.

116. Jan Jacob Hartsinck, *Beschryving van Guiana, of de Wilde kust in Zuid-Amerika* (Amsterdam, 1770), II, 721 and n; M[arten] D. Teenstra, *De landbouw in de kolonie Suriname* (Groningen, 1835), II, 39. See also [J. D. Herlein], *Beschryvinge van de Volk-Plantinge Zuriname* (Leeuwarden, 1718), 62.

117. In an interesting confirmation of this rate during the 1720s, Peter Jay of New York valued the Surinam gulden at 2s 6d (12.5p) New York currency and the Amsterdam gulden at 3s (15p). Peter Jay Journal, 1724–1748, pp. 6, 13, 146, Jay Papers.

118. E.g., Aschenbrenner and Vossenberg, *Uitreekening van Surinams in Hollands geld* (Amsterdam, [c. 1768]), *passim*; "Account of Bills of Exchange etc. belonging to Nicholas, Joseph and Moses Brown now in Surinam," 5 Sept. 1775, Brown Papers, U-C; Ricard, *Traité général du commerce*, [ed. Marien], II, 253, 291, 295; Anthony Blom, *Verhandeling van den landbouw in de colonie Suriname* (Amsterdam, 1787), 85. What appears to be a unique copy of the Aschenbrenner and Vossenberg pamphlet exists as an enclosure in a letter from Laurens Storm van 's Gravesande, at Rio Essequibo, to Kamer Zeeland of the Westindische Compagnie, at Middelburg, 9 Feb. 1769, C.O. 116/36, no. 183. There is now a photocopy of this work in the Universiteits-Bibliotheek, Amsterdam. Storm, who had come out to the colony in 1738,

boring eighteenth-century Dutch settlements, on the coast, Essequibo-Demerara and Berbice.[119]

We have only one indication of a bill rate for Surinam different from par. In 1768 economic difficulties prompted the authorities in the colony to issue a form of paper money to supplement the diminished supply of coin. John Stedman, an Englishman in Surinam, wrote that the stamped cards "passed as cash at a discount of ten per cent" and that "the exchange premium for specie is often above ten per cent."[120] What he seems to have been saying is that bills of exchange for 100 gulden Amsterdam current money cost 130 gulden Surinam currency but could still be had for as little as 120 gulden currency in coin. But paper money was the colony's "cash" and therefore the measure of its currency.[121] In 1774 the "advance" on "this carency or money" was from 4 to 5 percent, suggesting a rate of 124.50 gulden Surinam currency per 100 gulden current money of Amsterdam.[122] The premium for coin was still in existence in 1790 at a level of 10 to 15 percent; bills of exchange on Holland were then "worth about 6 per. cent," indicating a bill rate of 126 gulden Surinam currency or close to the Dutch island rate for par.[123]

Numerous bills of exchange drawn against Amsterdam accounts in Surinam and the other Dutch colonies in South America traveled home by way of New England, sent there to pay for provisions and supplies exported southward from places like Boston and Newport, Rhode Island. Insofar as these bills were typical of all others drawn in the colony, Dutch colonial bills hardly differed from those drawn in the English colonies. Usance was expressed in weeks and ran frequently to six weeks, or practically the same length of time as the forty-day usance so often the rule in the continental colonies. Although usually written in Dutch, the bills were sometimes in English, presumably to facilitate their sale in Boston, where there was a regular market for Dutch bills in the 1760s and 1770s. Perhaps this market was also sustained by the high rate for damages against protested bills of exchange, 25 percent.[124]

---

was the director-general of Essequibo and Demerara from 1752 to 1772; his dispatches to the company survive in the P.R.O. Selected extracts were published in [Laurens] Storm van 's Gravesande, *The Rise of British Guiana, Compiled from His Despatches*, comp. C. A. Harris and J. A. J. de Villiers, Hakluyt Society Publications, 2d Ser., XXVI–XXVII (London, 1911). See also M. A. P. Meilink-Roelofsz, "Archivalia betreffende de voormalige Nederlandse koloniën Essequebo, Demerary en Berbice in het Public Record Office te London," *Nieuwe West-Indische gids*, LXI (1961–1962), 127–140.

119. Ricard, *Traité général du commerce*, [ed. Marien], II, 253, 291, 295. See also the list of the currency value of coins, dated, 3 Oct. 1768, in Storm van 's Gravesande, at Rio Essequibo, to Westindische Compagnie, 6 Jan. 1772, C.O. 116/38, no. 11, p. 16.

120. J[ohn] G. Stedman, *Narrative, of a Five Years' Expedition, against the Revolted Negroes of Surinam, in Guiana, on the Wild Coast of South America; from the Year 1772, to 1777* (London, 1796), I, 74, 290.

121. While Stedman implied that the situation persisted throughout the period he discussed (1772–1777), Storm van 's Gravesande suggested that the crisis of 1768 ended quickly. By 25 Mar. 1770 he could write to the Westindische Compagnie that things had returned to normal. C.O. 116/37, no. 18. Perhaps there were two separate crises, the second precipitated by the financial difficulties of Europe in 1772.

122. Capt. Simon Smith, at Paramaribo, Surinam, to Nicholas Brown and Co., 5 Nov. 1774, Brown Papers, L 74 M.

123. George Henry Apthorp, "A Topographical Description of the Dutch Colony of Surinam . . . in a Letter to His Father James Apthorp, Esq., of Braintree," [Nov. 1790], Massachusetts Historical Society, *Collections*, 1st Ser., I (1792), 66.

124. There are copies of such bills in the Brown Papers (e.g., one dated 21 Jan. 1772 in L 57–82 M). See also n. 100, above. Henry Lloyd of Boston frequently acted as the agent for the Browns in the sale of these bills. See his letters to the Browns in the Brown Papers, *passim*. For protested bills see the "Account of Bills of Exchange," 5 Sept. 1775, *ibid.*, U-C. See also J. Th. de

The Danish Colonies and the Exchange on Copenhagen

Denmark owned three West Indian islands in 1775: St. Thomas, St. John, and St. Croix. The first had been settled in 1671, and the second in 1717; the French sold the last island to Denmark in 1733. Three moneys of account were in use in the Danish West Indies. Some colonists settled their accounts in Danish rigsdalers and skillinger (see table 2.18); others used pieces of eight as a money of account at eight bits each;[125] and still others used the English system of pounds, shillings, and pence. The real money was even more diverse, being the usual mixture of gold and silver coins, with some Danish and Danish West Indian coins as well. St. Thomas even had a

short-lived paper currency. The Danish colonies, a polyglot society, had an equally cosmopolitan monetary system.

By law the par of exchange between the Danish West Indies and Copenhagen was at parity before 1770. But practice had established a difference between West Indies current money—*vestindisk courant* ("v.c.")—and Danish current money—*dansk courant* ("d.c.")—well before that date. The earliest mention we have of such a difference is in the 1720s, but it must even have preceded that era. One can presume in the usual fashion that a bill on Copenhagen for 100 rigsdalers d.c. cost from 105 to 110 rigsdalers v.c. on St. Thomas almost from its foundation. During the universally difficult period after the Treaty of Utrecht in 1713, the shortage of coin there brought on a familiar solution—paper currency. "In order to pay our militia and others of our servants," wrote Governor Erik Bredal in 1717, "our only resource lies in doing as is being done in Carolina and Canada: namely, to make use of paper bills with the [Danish West India] Company's seal." The paper money served the colony well, but by 1726 the exchange had risen to 125 rigsdalers v.c. per 100 rigsdalers d.c. In 1727 the company withdrew the paper money and returned the colony to hard currency.[126] We do not know what happened to the bill rate as a result.

We do know that thirteen years later the Danish West India Company caused a coinage to be issued for the particu-

---

Smidt and T. van der Lee, eds., *Plakaten, ordonnantiën en andere wetten, uitgevaardigd in Suriname, 1667–1816,* in J. A. Schiltkamp and J. Th. de Smidt, eds., West Indisch Plakaatboek, No. 1, Werken der Vereniging tot Uitgaaf der Bronnen van het Oud-Vaderlandse Rechts, 3d Ser., No. 24/1 (Amsterdam, 1973), I, 60–61, 443–444, II, 745–746. For some further discussion of Dutch colonial bills see Johannes Petrus van de Voort, *De Westindische plantages van 1720 tot 1795: Financiën en handel* (Eindhoven, [1973]), 114–117, 172–176, and *passim,* citing, among other items, the "wisselbriefboken" of the Middelburgse Commercie Compagnie, Middelburgse Commercie Compagnie Archiven, 1720–1889, nos. 1758–1760, Rijksarchief in Zeeland, Middelburg, The Netherlands.

125. Ricard, *Traité général du commerce,* [ed. Marien], II, 231–232. St. Croix's treasurer kept the colony's accounts in pieces of eight, bits, and stivers, with 6 stivers per bit and 8 bits per piece of eight. *Royal Danish American Gazette* (Christiansted, St. Croix), 10 Dec. 1774. See also Waldemar [C.] Westergaard, *The Danish West Indies under Company Rule (1671–1754), with a Supplementary Chapter, 1755–1917* (New York, 1917), 34n, 197. In trade the piece of eight had 10 bits. Ricard, *Traité général du commerce,* II, 231–232; J[ulius W.] Wilcke, *Kurantmønten, 1726–1788* (Copenhagen, 1927), 284. The *Royal Danish American Gazette* survives in a unique, if incomplete, copy in Københavns Universitets-bibliotek, Fiolstræde, Copenhagen.

126. For this whole episode see Westergaard, *Danish West Indies,* 196–197. The quotation (*ibid.,* 196) is from a letter from Gov. Erik Bredal, at St. Thomas, to the company, 27 Sept. 1717, Breve og Dokumenter indekomne til Vestindisk-Guineiske Kompagnies Direction fra Vestindien, 1717–1720, Rigsarkivet, Copenhagen. Despite the perhaps insignificant difference in dates, this is probably Breve og dokumenter fra Vestindien, 1715–1719, Vestindisk-guineisk Kompagniets Arkiv, Nr. 94, as cataloged in J. O. Bro-Jørgensen and Aa[ge] Rasch, *Asiatiske, vestindiske og guineske handelskompagnier,* Vejledende Arkivregistraturer XIV (Copenhagen, 1969), 176.

lar use of its island colonies.[127] The intrinsic value of these coins was two-thirds the intrinsic value of coins of the same denomination in Denmark. The effective par of exchange established thereby was 150 rigsdalers v.c. for 100 rigsdalers d.c. The purpose of the difference in values was to keep the coins in the colonies, and it seems to have been effective. At the same time, par based on the piece of eight appears to have been somewhat lower than this, and the bill rate higher.

We have some fascinating if not completely intelligible references to both the commercial rate of exchange and par during the first thirty years of the life of this coinage, 1740 to 1770. One modern source, speaking of the years 1757 to 1763, indicates a bill rate of from 125 to 133.33 rigsdalers v.c. to 100 rigsdalers d.c.[128] This seems somewhat low and either represents in fact the par of exchange (see below) or reflects dislocations caused by the coming of the Seven Years' War. Once for the 1750s and twice for the 1760s we have examples of a considerably higher rate, expressed in English notation. In May 1754 Thomas Riché wrote from St. Croix that he had "disposed of almost 40 or 50 £ sterling at 82½ per cent"; in March 1760 the sum of £1,680 sterling was said to equal £2,876.16 "Saint Croix currency," for a rate of 171.20; and in December 1767 the rate calculated in the same way was 187.25.[129] This form of expression, using the English money

of account, should not confuse the issue, since it was probably based on a percentage increase that would be the same for all currencies. Both of these last two accounts valued the piece of eight at 6s (30p) in the "currency of St. Croix," the equivalent of a par of £133.33 St. Croix currency per £100 sterling. At that figure for par, the commercial rate of exchange in the Danish West Indies was well above par by the end of the 1760s.

In 1770 the Danish West Indies underwent a currency reform similar to that which occurred in New England twenty years earlier. A royal edict reduced the par of exchange to 125 rigsdalers v.c. per 100 rigsdalers d.c., a rate that applied until 1813.[130] The currency value of the coinage in circulation was lowered equivalently; the real, or bit—one-eighth of the piece

---

127. For the coinage of the Danish West Indies see Wilcke, *Kurantmønten*, 271–284; and Lincoln W. Higgie, *The Colonial Coinage of the U.S. Virgin Islands* (Racine, Wis., 1962).

128. Jean Louise Willis, "The Trade between North America and the Danish West Indies, 1756–1807, with Special Reference to St. Croix" (Ph.D. diss., Columbia University, 1963), 64n.

129. Riché to Thomas Preston, 30 May 1754, Thomas Riché Letter Books, I, fol. 34v, Thomas Riché Papers, 1749–1792, Hist. Soc. Pa.; account of Thomas Teakle Taylor, at St. Croix, with Samuel and William Vernon, at

Newport, R.I., 22 Apr. 1760, and Cornelius Durant's account of sale of slaves from brigantine *Royal Charlotte*, Wilbur Pinnigin, master, dated St. Croix, 14 May 1768, Samuel and William Vernon Papers, 1750–1775, Box VII, "Slavery MSS.," N.-Y. Hist. Soc. See also Elizabeth Donnan, ed., *Documents Illustrative of the History of the Slave Trade to America* (Washington, D.C., 1930–1935), III, 181–183, 217–220. This use of pounds, shillings, and pence was not unique to the correspondents of Riché or the Vernons. See, e.g., the letters, from St. Croix, of Pieter Heyliger, Jr., to [Samuel Galloway, at Annapolis, Md.], 25 May 1764, Galloway Correspondence, VII, no. 900, Galloway-Maxey-Markoe Papers, and James Warden to Neil Jamieson, at Norfolk, Va., 15 Jan. and 16 June 1774, Jamieson Papers, XIX, nos. 4349, 4359, XX, no. 5420. During 1766 and 1767 Henry and John Cruger of New York City equated the piece of eight St. Croix money of account with 6s (30p) New York currency, making it worth roughly 3s 4d (16.7p) sterling. Compared with the sterling value of the coin, 4s 6d (22.5p), this suggests, again, a par of exchange of 133.33 St. Croix currency. See Cruger Waste Book, entries for 16 Sept. and 14 Oct. 1766, and 2 Feb., 27 Feb., 28 May, and 26 June 1767, Cruger Papers.

130. Wilcke, *Kurantmønten*, 280–282; Jens Vibæk, *Dansk Vestindien, 1755–1848: Vestindiens storhedstid*, II of *Vore Gamle Tropekolonier*, ed. Johannes Brøndsted, 2d ed. (Copenhagen, 1966), 54. See also Ricard, *Traité général du commerce*, [ed. Marien], II, 231–232; Daniel Thibou, *A Table of Money, from One*

of eight—dropped in value from 12 skillinger v.c. to 10 skillinger v.c. as a money of account.[131] No new coins were minted until 1782, but when they were, their intrinsic value was at the new par.[132] We can only imagine what happened to the commercial rate of exchange as a result of these changes. If the case of New England after 1749 is any example, the bill rate fell to par and stayed there—at least for a while.

It seems probable that the planters and merchants of the Danish West Indies drew bills on Copenhagen in much the same way as colonists elsewhere. An ordinance of 2 September 1769 dealt with bills drawn in the islands that were returned protested for nonacceptance. They were subject to a payment of 10 percent for damages and to another payment for interest from the due date assessed at 1 percent per month. That last was equal to an annual rate of 12.67 percent, but it applied for the first twelve months only; thereafter the rate was 0.5 percent per month, equivalent to 6.18 percent per year.[133] Presumably this was a change from some earlier regulation and most likely represented only an alteration in the percentage rates.

Ryal to One Thousand Pieces of Eight, Calculated according to the Late Ordinances; Shewing the Difference betwixt the Old and New, published at Christiansted in Aug. 1770 as advertised in the *Royal Danish American Gazette* (Christiansted), 11 Aug. 1770. Thibou was the publisher of the newspaper. I have failed to locate any copy of this publication. Despite this edict Charles Read, Jr., of St. Croix, wrote to James Pemberton, at Philadelphia, on 8 Mar. 1774 that "money is here at £3.15 [£3.75] for a ½ Johannes [equal to]12½ pieces of ⁸/₈ of this country." With the piece of eight thus said to be worth 72d (30p) St. Croix currency, the par of exchange was still £133.33 per £100 sterling. Pemberton Papers, XXVI, fol. 27, Pemberton Papers, Hist. Soc. Pa.

131. Wilcke, *Kurantmønten*, 282.

132. *Ibid.*, 284.

133. Georg [H.] Høst, *Efterretninger om Øen Sanct Thomas og dens gouverneurer optegnede der paa landet fra 1769 indtil 1776* (Copenhagen, 1791), 161.

The Spanish Colonies and the Exchange on Cadiz

Spanish America was the place where the "universal coin" of the Atlantic world was mined and minted. Mexico and Peru were the home of the piece of eight. Thus the currency of Spanish America was the currency of the world, including the mother country, Spain. By law the piece of eight had the same value in Spain as in Spanish America.[134] But given the costs of freight and insurance, we might expect the piece of eight to have been worth slightly less in Mexico and Peru than in Spain. In other words, with par at parity, we should not be surprised to find that a bill of exchange for 100 pesos at Cadiz would cost something more than 100 pesos in Lima or Buenos Aires. A discussion of the exchange in 1760 confirms this suspicion, showing an effective rate at Mexico City and Lima of 104.56 and at Buenos Aires of 105.96.[135] Similar rates

----

134. Ricard, *Traité général du commerce*, [ed. Marien], II, 66–67, 178–179. See also Tomás Antonio de Marien y Arróspide, *Tratado general de monedas, pesas, medidas y cambios de todas las naciones, reducidas á las que se usan en España* (Madrid, 1789), 157.

135. Thomas de Bléville, *Le Banquier et negociant universel, ou traité général de changes étrangers et des arbitrages, ou viremens de place en place* (Paris, 1760), I, 9, 12, 353–366. Thomás de Mercado, *Summa de tratos, y contratos* (Seville, 1571), Pt. 2, fol. 69v (or p. 399 of Madrid, 1975 edition, ed. Restituto Sierra), said that the following were the rates of exchange at Seville on the places indicated (he stated the rates in terms of the percentage loss; I have converted them to the format used in this handbook): Santo Domingo, 111; Mexico, 118; Panama, 118; Peru, 133; Chile, 154. See also André-É. Sayous, "Les changes de l'Espagne sur l'Amérique en 16ᵉ siècle," *Revue d'economie politique*, XLI (Nov.–Dec. 1927), 1417–1443. There is much useful information about the monetary system internal to Spanish America in Àdám Szászdi, "Spain and American Treasure: The Depreciation of Silver and Monetary Exchange in the Viceroyalty of Lima, 1550–1610," *Journal of European Economic History*, IV (1975), 429–458. See also Juan de Belveder, *Libro general de las reduciones de plata, y oro* (Lima,1597) and Philippe de Echagoyn, *Tablas de reduciones de monedas, y del valor de todo genero de plata y oro . . .* ([Mexico], 1603), 1–2.

no doubt applied throughout the colonial period from all of the Spanish colonies.

Just as English merchants and the English money of account penetrated the Caribbean colonies of other European nations, so also were they present in Spanish America. Our evidence is from Cuba. During the Seven Years' War the English captured Havana and held it for some time. That period was an important one for the beginnings of the growth, under English stimulus, of the Cuban economy.[136] While the English in Cuba at that time no doubt used an English style currency, we have no record of the practice until twenty years later. Printed price currents issued by the firm of Joseph and Joshua Grafton of Havana in 1781 and 1782 carry the *nota bene*: "8s. is a dollar."[137] At that rate the par of exchange was £177.78 "Cuban currency" per £100 sterling, the same par as applied at New York in the 1760s, the time when supporting forces for the invasion of Havana had sailed from that city.[138]

The Portuguese Colonies and the Exchange on Lisbon

In the same way that the mines of Mexico provided the silver for the piece of eight, so, after the 1690s, did the mines of Brazil yield gold for the "Joe," the universal gold coin of the Atlantic world, the dobra de quatro escudos. The money of account in Brazil was Portuguese and the basic unit of that money was the réis.[139] To supplement a limited supply of coin, sugar was early used as a commodity money, and the pressure to create an overvalued coinage as a special money for Brazil began at the start of the seventeenth century.[140] The law of 1694 that established a colonial mint at Bahia included a provision to continue the existence of a distinct Brazilian currency. To insure its circulation exclusively in Brazil, the value of this currency was set at 110 réis Brazilian currency per 100 réis Portuguese currency.[141] "The colonial 10 percent" continued to apply through the end of our period.[142] This

136. For the English conquest of Havana and its impact, see J. H. Parry, *The Spanish Seaborne Empire* (New York, 1966), 304. See also John Lynch, *Spanish Colonial Administration* (London, 1958), 18, 50–51.

137. Copies in Map Drawer 2⁹, John Carter Brown Lib.

138. This was, in fact, the valuation in New York currency given to the piece of eight as a money of account at Havana in an entry, dated 31 Jan. 1763, in the Henry and John Cruger Waste Book, Cruger Papers. For New York's role in the invasion see David Syrett, "American Provincials and the Havana Campaign of 1762," *New York History*, XLIX (Oct. 1968), 375–390. See also Syrett, ed., *The Siege and Capture of Havana, 1762*, Navy Records Society, Publications, CXIV (London, 1970), *passim*. There is a good deal about all of this in [Dorothy C. Barck, ed.], *Letter Book of John Watts, Merchant and Councillor of New York, January 1, 1762–December 22, 1765* (New-York Historical Society, *Collections*, LXI [New York, 1928]).

139. Ricard, *Traité général du commerce*, [ed. Marien], II, 58. See also Severino Sombra, *Historia monetária do Brasil colonial: Repertorio cronológico com introdução, notas e carta monetária* (Rio de Janeiro, 1938).

140. Frédéric Mauro, *Le Portugal et l'Atlantique au XVIIᵉ siècle (1570–1670): Étude économique* (Paris, 1960), 397–398, 426.

141. "Lei de 8 de Março de 1694," as quoted in Sombra, *Historia monetária do Brasil*, 103. See also André João Antonil [pseud. for Giovanni Antonio Andreoni], *Cultura e opulencia do Brazil por suas drogas e minas* (1711), ed. and trans. Andrée Mansuy (Paris, 1968), 272–273, 364–365, 374, n. 16; and Roberto C. Simonsen, *História econômica do Brasil (1500–1820)*, 5th ed. (São Paulo, [1967]), 222–225.

142. See Sombra, *Historia monetária do Brasil*, 182–184, 218; Julius Meili, *Das Brasilianische Geldwesen* (Zurich, 1897–1905), I, 23–30, 75, 119. See also Ricard, *Traité général du commerce*, [ed. Marien], II, 58, 150. By the end of our period we can trace the beginnings of a paper currency in Brazil. Meili, *Das Brasilianische Geldwesen*, III, *passim*.

was the par of Brazilian currency. Presumably it was also the par of exchange for bills of exchange. We can expect that the commercial rate of exchange varied somewhat around this par, as was invariably the case elsewhere.

The Portuguese islands in the Atlantic—Madeira, the Azores, and the Cape Verdes—used the Portuguese money of account and a mixture of Portuguese and Spanish coins.[143] Their par of exchange with Portugal seems to have been the same as that of Brazil, 110 colonial réis per 100 réis in Portuguese currency. That, at least, is the indication gotten from the correspondence between wine merchants resident on Madeira and their customers in the English colonies. Accounts from Madeira during the third quarter of the eighteenth century reduced sums in réis to "sterling" at a set rate of 5s 6d (27.5p) per milréis, a figure essentially the same as the London-Lisbon rate.[144] But the Madeira merchants accepted payment of these accounts in coin at an inflated value. "Pistreens always turn to account as 5 of them are equal to 5/6 [27.5p] sterling and our exchange never varies," Fergusson, Murdock, and Com-

pany informed Neil Jamieson of Norfolk, Virginia, in 1764.[145] Five pistareens had a sterling value of only 5s (25p), however, as table 1.1 shows. This meant, in effect, that while 5s sterling would buy only $909 in Lisbon, it would buy 1$000 on Madeira. Presuming this to have established the par of exchange between Madeira and Lisbon at 110 réis colonial currency per 100 réis Portuguese currency, we can suppose that the commercial rate for bills of exchange would have, as always, varied sometimes above, sometimes below, par.[146] Most likely the same par applied to all of the Portuguese islands in the Atlantic.

145. Letter dated Madeira, 8 Apr. 1764, item no. 701, Jamieson Papers. See also James Beekman's note on his letter from Chambers, Hiccox, and Chambers, at Madeira, 2 Sept. 1758, in Philip L. White, ed., *The Beekman Mercantile Papers, 1746–1799* (New York, 1956), II, 569. This explains, obviously, why colonial merchants such as Beekman "usually . . . paid in pistarines." Philip L. White, *The Beekmans of New York in Politics and Commerce, 1647–1877* (New York, 1956), 402. See also Gov. William Popple, at Bermuda, to Board of Trade, 9 July 1749, C.O. 37/6; and Henry and John Cruger, at New York, to Scott, Pringle, Cheap, and Co., at Madeira, 2 June 1767, Cruger Letter Book, Cruger Papers.

146. This was the same par as that suggested for still another Portuguese colony, the island of São Thomé off the coast of Africa. The piece of eight was said to be worth 5s (25p) there in 1677, equal to a ratio of 111 to 100. Royal African Company, Account Book of ship *Sarah Bonaventure*, 1676–1677, under date 4 Aug. 1677, T. 70/1212, [last folio], and as quoted in Donnan, ed., *Documents Illustrative of the History of the Slave Trade*, I, 221. Information about the market in the Azores for bills on Lisbon is a consistent theme in the letters of Thomas Amory, an English merchant resident in the city of Angra on the island of Terceira. See Thomas Amory Letter Books, 1711–1720, Amory Family Papers, 1697–1823, Box 1, Lib. Cong. On 19 July 1711 he wrote his London mentor Nicholas Oursel that he "could have gott a good quantity of good bills for Lisbon" recently.

143. T. Bentley Duncan, *Atlantic Islands: Madeira, the Azores and the Cape Verdes in Seventeenth-Century Commerce and Navigation* (Chicago, 1972), 263–266.

144. E.g., these letters and accounts, dated Madeira: Hill, Lamar, and Hill to Samuel Galloway, at West River, Md., 31 Dec. 1754, Galloway Correspondence, 1658–1875, II, no. 8183, and in Galloway Business Papers, 1654–1819, item 69, Galloway-Maxey-Markoe Papers; Lamar, Hill, and Bisset to Galloway and Stephen Steward, at Annapolis, Md., 18 Mar. 1769, Galloway Correspondence, X, no. 9584; John Searle to Galloway, at Annapolis, Md., 29 Aug. 1763, Correspondence, 1739–1769, Galloway Papers, 1739–1812, N.Y. Pub. Lib.; and Fergusson, Murdock, and Co. to Neil Jamieson, at Norfolk, Va., 2 Aug. 1771, Jamieson Papers, IV, no. 701, XIV, no. 3144. See also table 2.34, above.

Nothing strikes the researcher into this subject more than the similarities in the monetary systems and exchange practices of the New World colonies. Almost all of them dealt with shortages in their supply of hard currency by legislating a higher value for coin in local currency than it had in the mother country. Many of them, well aware of what the others were doing, went further and issued a paper currency. In the West Indies the French, Dutch, and Danish colonies all used the Spanish piece of eight as a money of account. And colonists everywhere recognized that same coin, the piece of eight, as a form of real money, whatever its currency value.

They all traded with one another basing much of their exchange on the piece of eight as the common denominator for their local currencies. And they were all aware of the exchange rate between themselves and their respective mother countries. Insofar as the last statement is valid and insofar as documents survive recording that rate of exchange, we have the basis for the data provided in the tables in this chapter. The annual averages from these tables and from those compiled in chapters 2 and 3 comprise the substance of the tables in chapter 5.

Chapter 5

Comparative Rates of Exchange in the Atlantic World

"Tis certain all currency, i.e. money,
should turn out sterling,
for no commerce can be held where it does not—
'tis central to all points."[1]

The function of this chapter is to summarize the data compiled into the tables in the preceding chapters and to provide an explanation for the reduction of a sum in one currency into its equivalent in another currency. Therefore much of this chapter is tabular and, by definition, repetitious. Its raison d'être is convenience and, perhaps, clarity.

The first table in this chapter, table 5.1, assembles the annual average figures from the several tables in chapter 2.[2] In one glance, as a result, we are able to see the approximate amounts required of the various European currencies to purchase £100 sterling. For those years for which there are no figures the gaps can be filled by using one of two devices.

Interpolated figures calculated as a straight-line average between the two neighboring figures will do for short gaps. Over longer periods it seems wiser to use the par of exchange. Obviously, in each instance we seek the best surrogate for the commercial rate of exchange.

Subsequent tables in this chapter (tables 5.2 and 5.3) collect and collate the annual average figures from the tables in chapters 3 and 4. Each of the original tables presented a series giving the cost in colonial currency of one hundred units of the currency of the mother country. As in the tables for the English colonies, when the colonies all shared the same metropolis, we have the capability not only of comparing the relative costs of exchange in each colony but also of establishing through sterling the relative values of each colonial currency. Where the colonies do not share the same metropolis, the same objective is possible but with an extra step; through the agency of table 5.1 it is first necessary to

1. Cecilius Calvert to Frederick, Lord Baltimore, 10 Jan. 1764, [William Hand Browne *et al.*, eds.], *The Calvert Papers* (Maryland Historical Society, *Fund Publications*, Nos. 28, 34, 35 [Baltimore, 1889–1899]), II, 218.

2. In those instances in which we have data for the same years from different sources, the preference is always for the rate at London.

establish the equivalency in the currencies of the respective mother countries of the sum in colonial currencies.

An example of the procedure might clarify matters. In November 1765 the subdélégué of the intendant of St. Domingue, Charles-François Pichot de Kerdisien-Trémais, indicated in a letter to the Ministry of Marine from Cap Français that the indemnity for the Turks Islands affair amounted to 192,882.48 livres "argent de St. Domingue." This was the sum agreed on in settlement of the claims arising out of the descent upon the island by a French fleet in 1764. The money was to be distributed amongst the Englishmen who lost property as a result of the raid. The conversion of the sum into Jamaica currency, for instance, concerned some of the people involved.[3] Reference to the appropriate tables allows us to determine that 192,882.48 livres St. Domingue currency (at Cap Français) in 1765 equaled about 124,600 livres tournois of France, £5,400 sterling in London, and £7,560 Jamaica currency.[4] One gets the same result somewhat more easily and

more directly by consulting table 5.3. Such examples can be multiplied endlessly.

Here, at the end of this handbook, the reader should be reminded of at least two of the several weaknesses inherent in such a study. While the blame for both must rest on the head of the author, the reader must be aware of them and can correct for them. Samuel Eliot Morison once wrote in comment upon a series of his calculations: "Tabulated by the author, accuracy not guaranteed."[5] A similar warning should be posted here, for, despite constant checking, mistakes undoubtedly have occurred. It behooves the careful scholar to recheck an average. The reader needs also to be rescued from the second defect of the present work. Much research needs to be done to fill the gaps in the data in this handbook. Individual students of particular places perhaps will find it much easier to uncover further quotations of the commercial rate of exchange for their own work. They should not rely solely on what they find here. Let this be only a start.

3. Letter of 14 Nov. 1765, Archives Colonies, C⁹ᴬ 126, Archives Nationales, Paris. For the Turks Islands affair see M[édéric] L. E. Moreau de Saint-Méry, *Description topographique, physique, civile, politique et historique de la partie française de l'isle Saint-Domingue* (1797), ed. Blanche Maurel and Étienne Taillemite, new ed. (Paris, 1958) III, 1411–1413; and Brigitte Poussin, "L'administration de Saint Domingue sous le gouvernement du Comte d'Estaing (27 décembre 1763–8 juillet 1766)" (thesis, École des Chartres, 1957), 299–311. I am indebted to the author, now Mme. Alexandre Labat, for permission to use her thesis. See also Roger Hope Elletson, at Jamaica, to Gov. George James Bruere, at Bermuda, 13 June 1766, [Hedley P. Jacobs, ed.], "Roger Hope Elletson's Letter Book," *Jamaican Historical Review*, I (1946), 197–198.
4. Computation (see tables 2.25, 4.2, and 4.8). The initial sum, 192,882.48, divided by the 1765 exchange rate for St. Domingue, 154.80, equaled 124,601.08 livres. That, at the London-Paris rate of 31.19d (13p) sterling per ecu, equaled £5,397.65 sterling, which, multiplied by the London-Jamaica rate of 140, equaled £7,556.72. The rates are always dealt with as percentages, of course.

5. Morison, "The Commerce of Boston on the Eve of the Revolution," American Antiquarian Society, *Proceedings*, N.S., XXXII (1922), 39n.

TABLE 5.1. **European Exchange Rates, 1600–1775**

(Approximate Equivalents in Local Currencies of £100 Sterling)

Year	Dublin (Pounds Irish Currency)	Amsterdam (Gulden, or Florijns, Banco)	Hamburg (Reichsthaler Banco)	Copenhagen (Rigsdaler)	Paris (Livres Tournois)	Cadiz (Pesos de Plata)	Lisbon (Milréis)
1600							
1601							
1602							
1603							
1604							
1605							
1606							
1607							
1608							
1609		1,040.10	334.12				
1610							
1611							
1612							
1613							
1614							
1615							
1616							
1617							
1618							
1619		1,050.00	378.38		1,007.98		154.13
1620							
1621							
1622							
1623							
1624		1,077.00	442.00		1,037.61		

TABLE 5.1 (Continued): European Exchange Rates (Equivalents of £100 Sterling)

Year	Dublin (Pounds Irish Currency)	Amsterdam (Gulden, or Florijns, Banco)	Hamburg (Reichsthaler Banco)	Copenhagen (Rigsdaler)	Paris (Livres Tournois)	Cadiz (Pesos de Plata)	Lisbon (Milréis)
1625		1,078.50	443.12		1,047.12		
1626		1,074.00	433.38		1,062.42		
1627							
1628		1,053.00	432.00		1,035.82		
1629							
1630		1,087.80	444.75		1,073.02		
1631		1,085.70	436.00		1,124.47		
1632		1,096.20	442.88		1,138.16		
1633		1,102.50	446.50		1,133.86		
1634		1,113.60	451.00		1,129.06		
1635		1,075.20	438.88		1,145.77		
1636		1,061.40	428.88		1,208.05		
1637		1,095.00	442.88		1,275.69		
1638		1,066.20	430.50		1,327.68		
1639							
1640		1,118.70	449.75		1,389.42		
1641		1,165.50	465.25		1,384.88		
1642		1,146.30	461.12		1,366.74		177.67
1643		1,171.20	466.12		1,392.38		
1644							
1645		1,154.40	466.88		1,395.89		232.72
1646		1,113.90	456.62		1,356.19		
1647							
1648		1,013.70	401.62		1,175.32		
1649		980.10	390.12				

TABLE 5.1 (Continued): **European Exchange Rates** (Equivalents of £100 Sterling)

Year	Dublin (Pounds Irish Currency)	Amsterdam (Gulden, or Florijns, Banco)	Hamburg (Reichsthaler Banco)	Copenhagen (Rigsdaler)	Paris (Livres Tournois)	Cadiz (Pesos de Plata)	Lisbon (Milréis)
1650		1,003.50	397.38		1,137.62		
1651		1,107.60	448.38		1,356.19		
1652		1,041.30	423.00		1,282.28		
1653		1,071.90	437.50		1,407.35		
1654		1,081.20	437.25		1,394.27		
1655							
1656							
1657			406.25				
1658			408.25				
1659			424.75				
1660		1,149.90	456.75				
1661			459.38				
1662	103.00	1,051.20					
1663		1,075.80	446.25		1,300.11		
1664		1,051.20	436.00		1,280.68		
1665		1,006.20	418.88		1,298.47		
1666	105.50		400.38				
1667		1,047.60	423.50		1,257.64		
1668		1,068.90	428.38		1,261.61		
1669		1,076.40	432.88		1,280.46		
1670			435.38				
1671	115.00	1,088.70	428.62		1,374.57		
1672	112.50	1,052.10	431.50		1,319.65		
1673		1,023.60	414.38		1,303.40		
1674		1,033.50	405.12		1,276.14		

TABLE 5.1 (Continued): European Exchange Rates (Equivalents of £100 Sterling)

Year	Dublin (Pounds Irish Currency)	Amsterdam (Gulden, or Florijns, Banco)	Hamburg (Reichsthaler Banco)	Copenhagen (Rigsdaler)	Paris (Livres Tournois)	Cadiz (Pesos de Plata)	Lisbon (Milréis)
1675		1,074.30	415.50		1,257.86		
1676		1,085.70	424.62		1,310.04		293.22
1677		1,086.90	431.25		1,313.15		292.26
1678		1,066.20	436.50		1,343.28		294.77
1679	103.00	1,069.20	409.38		1,342.78		
1680	108.25	1,084.20	438.50		1,322.56	487.31	291.79
1681	108.00	1,087.20	442.00		1,309.33	487.31	307.02
1682	107.75	1,071.00	436.12		1,304.35	473.28	305.07
1683	108.94	1,094.70	431.88		1,323.29	470.86	310.68
1684		1,081.20	430.25		1,312.43	478.85	314.22
1685	108.50	1,065.30	436.88		1,322.07	478.85	320.00
1686	107.00	1,075.50	431.62		1,324.75	477.33	320.34
1687	109.93	1,078.80	433.38		1,339.04	481.16	332.13
1688		1,048.50	426.88		1,348.32	474.31	307.73
1689		1,059.00	412.75		1,287.09	484.85	322.32
1690			406.25				
1691	106.25	1,015.20	406.38		1,367.78	489.20	331.03
1692	106.25	1,035.60	416.62		1,374.83	497.41	338.03
1693	109.50	1,003.80	400.00		1,351.60	455.58	312.95
1694	105.75	969.90	388.50		1,269.84	443.70	301.17
1695	104.67	894.60	359.75		1,223.86	402.55	300.11
1696	109.94	969.60	386.75	411.33	1,261.39	428.19	312.87
1697	117.38	1,077.00	443.62	497.88	1,525.75	495.25	350.78
1698	116.62	1,062.60	430.12	474.24	1,575.15	467.74	358.74
1699	119.06	1,060.80	424.75	466.84	1,549.72	449.27	332.78

TABLE 5.1 (Continued): European Exchange Rates (Equivalents of £100 Sterling)

Year	Dublin (Pounds Irish Currency)	Amsterdam (Gulden, or Florijns, Banco)	Hamburg (Reichsthaler Banco)	Copenhagen (Rigsdaler)	Paris (Livres Tournois)	Cadiz (Pesos de Plata)	Lisbon (Milréis)
1700	120.96	1,067.10	429.75	477.89	1,562.16	458.98	329.31
1701	114.65	1,093.20	441.25	492.47	1,619.80	480.67	342.56
1702	109.60	1,063.20	426.00	468.10	1,634.88	478.85	345.27
1703	107.67	1,029.60	406.88	460.80			343.25
1704	107.20	1,029.90	407.75	471.64			331.03
1705	108.22	1,036.20	409.50	472.05	1,631.17	478.66	346.12
1706	108.13	1,038.90	418.75	485.49	1,724.55	478.95	344.28
1707	107.56	1,039.50	420.88	482.78			357.09
1708	108.73	1,035.30	418.50	475.59	1,522.84	452.83	384.74
1709	109.99	1,015.50	409.50		1,491.61	458.36	369.29
1710	108.35	1,024.20	408.75	470.39	1,505.96	453.52	364.74
1711	107.97	1,031.70	416.38	473.30			390.31
1712	108.46	1,022.40	415.38	484.76			379.21
1713	107.06	1,074.60	430.12	500.18	1,939.66	491.30	376.41
1714	107.28	1,086.30	435.38	487.47	1,819.10	478.85	367.76
1715	109.40	1,090.20	438.88	542.99	1,514.20	492.00	368.89
1716	110.02	1,063.50	430.75	507.78	1,587.30	482.32	363.42
1717	110.22	1,039.80	422.62	520.49	1,520.91	464.40	360.96
1718	111.06	1,037.40	422.75	540.28	1,962.92	473.84	366.86
1719	111.77	1,062.30	431.62	555.69	2,537.00	498.65	372.56
1720	112.76	1,047.60	427.00	551.01	4,371.58	497.51	371.75
1721	110.98	1,040.40	427.25	562.98	2,961.74	497.20	373.95
1722	110.50	1,067.10	438.00	560.38	3,122.29	502.30	373.54
1723	110.84	1,055.70	431.75	547.78	3,194.32	486.52	369.69
1724	111.79	1,054.80	425.25	538.30	2,369.98	479.04	367.20

TABLE 5.1 (Continued): European Exchange Rates (Equivalents of £100 Sterling)

Year	Dublin (Pounds Irish Currency)	Amsterdam (Gulden, or Florijns, Banco)	Hamburg (Reichsthaler Banco)	Copenhagen (Rigsdaler)	Paris (Livres Tournois)	Cadiz (Pesos de Plata)	Lisbon (Milréis)
1725	110.27	1,051.80	424.25	559.13	1,893.74	484.65	366.08
1726	112.53	1,063.20	433.88	523.51	1,993.36	550.71	373.31
1727	112.30	1,048.80	435.25	523.72	2,183.80	550.96	368.89
1728	111.40	1,032.30	423.12	510.38	2,191.11	543.36	363.36
1729	111.26	1,032.00	417.88	502.26	2,203.18	556.72	362.98
1730	111.48	1,036.20	415.00	487.47	2,216.75	564.18	362.87
1731	111.06	1,047.90	424.62	492.05	2,273.44	574.02	365.24
1732	110.87	1,047.30	427.25	496.64	2,236.02	567.38	364.85
1733	111.52	1,050.30	429.50	496.32	2,273.44	573.89	367.59
1734	111.42	1,074.30	445.12	516.11	2,298.12	595.98	368.44
1735	111.77	1,076.70	441.62	519.86	2,306.95	594.94	363.64
1736	111.26	1,061.70	433.12	513.72	2,295.92	584.94	364.69
1737	109.77	1,049.40	424.25	480.18	2,226.34	593.32	365.19
1738	108.26	1,055.10	425.50	490.07	2,251.41	605.45	366.58
1739	108.95	1,066.80	429.00	500.28	2,306.21	603.02	367.53
1740	108.16	1,056.60	426.50	499.76	2,228.41	575.40	370.48
1741	109.25	1,041.00	419.38	497.26	2,212.66	580.69	368.55
1742	110.01	1,049.70	420.38	488.30	2,284.26	607.29	366.86
1743	108.55	1,044.00	420.50	503.30	2,224.28	591.72	362.76
1744	108.02	1,042.20	419.50	509.34	2,208.59	580.27	369.40
1745	109.86	1,056.60	427.50	511.11	2,263.44	614.60	371.98
1746	107.76	1,085.70	445.25	520.80	2,346.81	637.79	373.19
1747	107.84	1,063.80	438.00	508.30	2,278.48	603.17	368.72
1748	108.65	1,074.30	434.75	497.26	2,341.46	616.02	370.03
1749	108.27	1,073.10	429.50	497.88	2,300.32	615.23	365.74

TABLE 5.1 (Continued): European Exchange Rates (Equivalents of £100 Sterling)

Year	Dublin (Pounds Irish Currency)	Amsterdam (Gulden, or Florijns, Banco)	Hamburg (Reichsthaler Banco)	Copenhagen (Rigsdaler)	Paris (Livres Tournois)	Cadiz (Pesos de Plata)	Lisbon (Milréis)
1750	109.22	1,053.00	419.50	484.14	2,284.26	614.75	365.80
1751	108.91	1,064.10	419.75	487.26	2,313.62	612.09	365.91
1752	108.15	1,057.80	417.50	484.03	2,272.73	599.85	363.97
1753	109.79	1,054.80	416.25	485.28	2,242.99	597.02	364.63
1754	109.69	1,071.60	419.12	490.59	2,290.80	603.17	365.63
1755	108.45	1,089.30	431.00	502.47	2,325.58	620.00	369.57
1756	108.38	1,087.50	447.00	523.09	2,376.24	634.08	370.77
1757	107.64	1,070.10	452.25	508.09	2,376.24	625.98	371.86
1758	108.12	1,043.70	446.12	489.24	2,307.69	605.14	366.97
1759	109.52	1,071.30	463.12	499.24	2,353.71	606.67	366.02
1760	108.25	1,056.30	424.75	499.24	2,351.40	613.65	364.91
1761	107.67	1,032.00	404.25	514.76	2,301.06	606.21	364.19
1762	108.02	1,061.70	429.25	545.80	2,352.94	611.00	362.16
1763	108.27	1,051.80	428.88	528.09	2,274.88	611.15	360.52
1764	109.07	1,098.00	438.00	559.24	2,359.11	629.10	366.86
1765	108.88	1,081.80	433.25	519.34	2,308.43	613.34	364.13
1766	108.76	1,049.40	438.00	521.84	2,263.44	603.32	360.74
1767	109.37	1,046.70	444.38	530.80	2,280.65	607.13	359.71
1768	108.41	1,048.80	427.25	522.99	2,294.46	611.46	360.68
1769	109.14	1,035.90	417.62	522.99	2,271.29	606.98	358.26
1770	110.03	1,034.10	415.75	516.95	2,278.48	607.75	359.55
1771	108.91	1,038.30	415.00	521.53	2,275.60	606.52	356.56
1772	109.13	1,053.90	415.50	526.63	2,283.54	609.45	358.96
1773	109.73	1,078.20	434.00	560.69	2,409.64	637.96	365.63

TABLE 5.1 (Continued): European Exchange Rates (Equivalents of £100 Sterling)

Year	Dublin (Pounds Irish Currency)	Amsterdam (Gulden, or Florijns, Banco)	Hamburg (Reichsthaler Banco)	Copenhagen (Rigsdaler)	Paris (Livres Tournois)	Cadiz (Pesos de Plata)	Lisbon (Milréis)
1774	108.06	1,082.70	432.00	544.44	2,383.32	640.85	365.41
1775	108.06	1,068.90	428.50	521.01	2,345.28	629.76	368.61

Notes and Sources: TABLE 5.1

Dublin: Tables 2.3 and 2.4.

Amsterdam: Table 2.7 to 1654 and for 1664, 1665, 1676–1679, 1685–1688, and 1691–1694; table 2.8 for 1660–1663, 1667–1675, 1680–1684, 1689, and 1695–1697; and table 2.9 for 1698–1775. The annual average figure in this table equals the figure for the same year from those tables times a factor of 30.

Hamburg: Table 2.13 to 1654 and for 1686–1688; table 2.14 for 1657–1671, 1676–1678, and 1689–1691; table 2.15 for 1672–1675, 1679–1685, and 1692–1697; and table 2.16 for 1698–1775. The factor for Hamburg is 12.5.

Copenhagen: Table 2.19 for 1696–1721 and 1729, and table 2.20 for 1722–1775 (except for 1729). The factor for Copenhagen is 1.0416.

Paris: Table 2.23 for 1619–1654, 1664–1665, 1678, 1691–1694, and 1705–1710; table 2.24 for 1663 and 1667–1697 (except for 1678 and 1691–1694); and table 2.25 for 1698–1702 and for 1713–1775. The annual average figure in this table equals 72,000 divided by the figure for the same year from these tables.

Cadiz: Table 2.29 for 1680–1697 (except for 1686–1688 and 1693–1694); table 2.28 for 1686–1688, 1693–1694, and 1705, 1706, 1708–1710; and table 2.31 for 1698–1775. The dividend for Cadiz is 24,000.

Lisbon: Table 2.32 for 1619–1678, 1686–1688, and 1693–1694; table 2.33 for 1680–1697 (except for 1686–1688 and 1693–1694); and table 2.34 for 1698–1775. The dividend for Lisbon is also 24,000.

TABLE 5.2. **Colonial Exchange Rates: English Continental Colonies, 1649–1775**
(Approximate Equivalents in Pounds Local Currencies of £ 100 Sterling)

Year	Mass.	N.Y.	N.J.	Pa.	Md. (Hard Currency)	Md. (Paper Currency)	Va.	N.C.	S.C.	Ga.
1649	112.00									
1650										
1651										
1652										
1653										
1654										
1655										
1656										
1657										
1658										
1659										
1660	112.00									
1661										
1662										
1663	112.00									
1664	113.33									
1665	115.33									
1666										
1667	116.00									
1668	115.75									
1669	116.00									
1670	125.00									
1671	125.00									

TABLE 5.2 (Continued): Colonial Exchange Rates, Continental Colonies (Equivalents of £100 Sterling)

Year	Mass.	N.Y.	N.J.	Pa.	Md. (Hard Currency)	Md. (Paper Currency)	Va.	N.C.	S.C.	Ga.
1672	125.00									
1673	125.00									
1674	125.00									
1675	123.89									
1676	129.17									
1677	128.00									
1678	128.00									
1679	122.00									
1680	120.25	125.00								
1681	124.88									
1682	128.00			125.00						
1683	128.00			125.00						
1684	130.00									
1685	127.50									
1686	125.00									
1687	120.94									
1688	140.00	130.06								
1689				130.00						
1690	128.33									
1691	131.25						110.00			
1692	130.50									
1693	130.00									
1694	133.66	129.16		135.86						
1695	139.86	130.00								
1696	129.17	130.00		150.00						
1697	136.00									
1698		130.00		150.00						
1699	140.48								111.75	

TABLE 5.2 (Continued): Colonial Exchange Rates, Continental Colonies (Equivalents of £100 Sterling)

Year	Mass.	N.Y.	N.J.	Pa.	Md. (Hard Currency)	Md. (Paper Currency)	Va.	N.C.	S.C.	Ga.
1700	139.43	134.96		155.00					146.00	
1701	136.50	132.50		147.92						
1702	130.00	133.33		150.72	111.11					
1703	140.00	140.00	166.67	150.84					150.00	
1704	140.00			150.00						
1705	135.00			150.14						
1706	150.00			150.58			115.00			
1707				152.58					150.00	
1708				153.96					150.00	
1709	151.06	150.00		120.05			107.62			
1710	155.00	145.05		128.16					150.00	
1711	146.67	151.12					108.50		150.00	
1712	150.00	155.62		128.93			110.00		150.00	
1713	150.00	153.75		130.36					150.00	
1714	153.33	154.90		132.50			110.00		200.00	
1715	160.33	153.20		130.36				150.00	300.00	
1716	162.50	157.78	142.86	133.52						
1717	170.00	160.00		134.72			105.50		575.00	
1718	200.00			132.22					500.00	
1719	216.68	154.17	155.18	135.42	113.33		110.50			
1720	219.43	162.92		138.75	133.33		115.00		400.00	
1721	225.98	163.33	155.55	137.50	114.36		115.00		533.33	
1722	229.79			135.01	127.50		115.00	500.00	580.00	
1723	241.81	165.22		140.37	128.78		115.00		675.00	
1724	267.92	165.00		143.11			116.44	500.00	650.00	
1725	289.11	165.00		139.34	128.00		117.50		672.16	
1726	290.98	165.00					114.34		700.00	

TABLE 5.2 (Continued): Colonial Exchange Rates, Continental Colonies (Equivalents of £100 Sterling)

Year	Mass.	N.Y.	N.J.	Pa.	Md. (Hard Currency)	Md. (Paper Currency)	Va.	N.C.	S.C.	Ga.
1727	291.98	165.00		149.58			116.29		700.00	
1728	298.82	165.00		150.62	136.25		120.00		700.00	
1729	313.33	165.00		148.61	133.33		118.75	500.00	700.00	
1730	337.71	166.88		152.03	133.33		119.92		643.75	
1731	334.31	165.00		153.28	133.37		122.33	650.00	700.00	
1732	339.51	165.00		160.90	133.33		121.16		700.00	
1733	350.00	165.00		166.94			120.00		700.00	
1734	355.00	165.00		170.00	133.33	160.00	120.00		700.00	
1735	360.00	165.00		166.11	133.33	140.00	120.00	720.00	700.00	
1736	430.00	165.00		167.00	133.42	230.00	122.70	700.00	743.33	
1737	516.67	165.00	170.00	170.25	140.00	250.00	121.63	866.67	753.10	
1738	500.00	165.00		160.42	135.42	225.00	123.75		775.00	
1739	500.00	166.67	168.33	169.69		212.34	122.50	1,000.00	791.91	
1740	525.00	166.25	160.62	165.45	139.17	228.08	119.17	966.66	795.95	
1741	548.44	159.44	142.50	146.14	138.82	238.17	120.53	1,000.00	690.83	
1742	550.28	170.97	150.00	159.38	138.64	275.00	120.00		698.96	
1743	550.70	174.67	160.00	159.79	137.78	285.13	120.00		700.00	
1744	588.61	175.42		166.67	139.44	166.67	121.88		700.00	
1745	644.79	183.33		174.77	140.00	200.00	127.60	1,000.00	700.00	
1746	642.50	185.83	182.50	179.86	137.78	210.00	131.87	1,000.00		
1747	925.00	191.46		183.78	142.50	225.22	135.01		760.74	
1748	912.50	183.39		174.12	140.97	200.61	132.29	1,033.33	762.50	
1749	1,033.33	176.46	170.00	171.39		184.58	123.75		725.36	
1750	137.33	179.33	173.75	170.60	131.66	177.92	125.94	133.33	702.28	
1751	133.33	181.50	172.50	169.86	140.00	166.83	128.42		700.00	
1752		175.92	166.25	166.85		155.62	129.92		700.00	

TABLE 5.2 (Continued): Colonial Exchange Rates, Continental Colonies (Equivalents of £100 Sterling)

Year	Mass.	N.Y.	N.J.	Pa.	Md. (Hard Currency)	Md. (Paper Currency)	Va.	N.C.	S.C.	Ga.
1753	130.00	179.39	167.50	167.49	150.00	151.75	129.50		700.00	
1754	133.33	179.72	168.17	168.35	159.58	153.75	127.55	166.67	700.00	
1755	133.33	180.13	170.00	168.79	165.00		129.38	160.00	700.00	
1756	133.33	182.65	165.92	172.57	165.00	170.00	128.44	179.80	713.56	
1757	133.33	178.40	166.10	166.07	164.53	145.00	139.71		700.19	
1758	128.34	172.60	161.25	159.00	157.01	150.00	137.92		700.00	
1759		168.39	156.25	153.52	153.75	150.00	139.97	185.00	700.00	
1760	129.54	167.20	153.30	158.61	154.58	146.25	141.43	190.00	700.00	
1761	140.10	181.41	171.25	172.71	168.58	148.48	143.72	200.00	700.00	
1762	142.33	189.76	176.88	176.26	170.65	144.45	152.40	200.00	700.00	
1763	136.00	186.73	169.83	173.00	167.24	140.00	159.88	200.00	716.55	
1764	133.75	184.85	172.02	172.86	166.77	136.66	160.73	192.67	717.97	
1765	133.54	182.80		169.90	166.65	133.33	160.36	200.00	709.33	108.50
1766	133.03	177.18	160.00	162.96	163.99		128.48		707.00	
1767	133.33	178.96		166.02	164.59		125.54	172.96	700.00	
1768	133.33	179.87		166.62	164.92		124.99	180.00	700.00	108.93
1769	129.86	172.47		157.56	160.68		121.97			
1770	126.31	165.90		153.92	151.03		118.00		717.00	
1771	133.33	178.43		165.69	161.84		123.60		762.00	
1772	131.00	173.27		160.83	158.63		123.59	160.00	679.00	108.76
1773	132.19	177.71		166.27	165.13		129.75		728.00	
1774	135.30	180.62	169.50	169.46	167.10		130.30	175.00	700.00	
1775	117.45	171.55		161.12	156.68		120.00		758.67	108.00

Notes and Sources: TABLE 5.2

Massachusetts: Figures for 1670, 1672, 1674, 1677–1678, 1681–1683, 1690, and 1704 are from table 3.2; all other figures are from table 3.1.

The remaining figures come from the appropriate tables in chap. 3.

TABLE 5.3. **Colonial Exchange Rates: West Indies, 1675–1775**

(Approximate Equivalents in Local Currencies of £100 Sterling)

Year	Barbados (Pounds)	Jamaica (Pounds)	Antigua (Pounds)	St. Christopher (Pounds)	Nevis (Pounds)	Grenada (Pounds)	Bermuda (Pounds)	St. Domingue (Livres)
1675		106.50						
1676		115.00						
1677								
1678								
1679		109.92						
1680								
1681		108.00						
1682								
1683		114.04						
1684		120.00						
1685								
1686		111.91						
1687	110.00	117.65						
1688	110.50	110.00						
1689	110.10	120.00						
1690	110.38	120.00						
1691	110.53	125.00						
1692	114.75	125.00						
1693	114.49							
1694	114.83							
1695								
1696								
1697								
1698								
1699								

TABLE 5.3 (Continued): **Colonial Exchange Rates, West Indies** (Equivalents of £100 Sterling)

Year	Barbados (Pounds)	Jamaica (Pounds)	Antigua (Pounds)	St. Christopher (Pounds)	Nevis (Pounds)	Grenada (Pounds)	Bermuda (Pounds)	St. Domingue (Livres)
1700	112.10							
1701								
1702	124.08							
1703	121.62							
1704	118.74	125.00	130.00					
1705	141.25	127.50						
1706	163.75	122.50			125.00			
1707	180.00	118.00	155.00					
1708	135.00	120.00	137.21					
1709	135.00	116.00			150.00			
1710	133.75	125.00	142.50	150.00				
1711	125.42	135.00						
1712	121.30							
1713	120.50	130.00						
1714	123.50							
1715		135.00			135.00			
1716	127.50	135.00						
1717	130.00	135.00			140.00			
1718	128.25	135.00						
1719	128.67							
1720	129.33	135.00	150.00	150.00				
1721	130.00		150.00	150.00				
1722	130.00	130.00	150.00		140.00			
1723	128.00	130.00	150.00					
1724	128.01	134.17	150.00	150.00	150.00			
1725	127.94	135.42		150.00				

TABLE 5.3 (Continued): Colonial Exchange Rates, West Indies (Equivalents of £100 Sterling)

Year	Barbados (Pounds)	Jamaica (Pounds)	Antigua (Pounds)	St. Christopher (Pounds)	Nevis (Pounds)	Grenada (Pounds)	Bermuda (Pounds)	St. Domingue (Livres)
1726	128.00	135.00		150.00				
1727	130.00		150.00	150.00				
1728	130.00	135.00	150.00	150.00				
1729	130.00	135.00		150.00				
1730	128.61	135.00	155.00	150.00				
1731	128.67		154.81					
1732	130.00	135.00			150.00			
1733	132.17	137.50	170.00					
1734	132.00	140.00						
1735	131.71	138.75	158.12					
1736	130.00	140.00	160.00					
1737	130.00		162.50	160.00				
1738	130.03	140.00	170.83				140.00	
1739	130.00	140.00	172.50				141.77	
1740	130.00	135.00	171.67	160.00				
1741	129.35	140.00						
1742	128.50	138.75	164.58					
1743	133.00	140.00	165.00					
1744	141.50		166.67					
1745	150.00	145.00	170.00				147.00	
1746	145.94		165.62					
1747	145.00		165.00	160.00				
1748	136.39		170.00	160.00				
1749	136.43		171.67	165.00			150.00	
1750	135.00		175.00	165.00				
1751		140.00	177.82		175.00			
1752		140.00	171.67	171.67				

TABLE 5.3 (Continued): **Colonial Exchange Rates, West Indies** (Equivalents of £100 Sterling)

Year	Barbados (Pounds)	Jamaica (Pounds)	Antigua (Pounds)	St. Christopher (Pounds)	Nevis (Pounds)	Grenada (Pounds)	Bermuda (Pounds)	St. Domingue (Livres)
1753		140.00	164.50	162.50				
1754		140.00	165.55		160.00			
1755		140.00	165.00					
1756	139.58	140.00	165.00	160.00				
1757	140.00	140.00	160.00		160.00			
1758	140.00	140.00	159.17		160.00			
1759		140.00	160.00	160.00				
1760	135.00	140.00	152.50	155.00				
1761	135.00	140.00	165.34	170.00				
1762	132.50	140.00	166.67	171.25				
1763	135.00	140.00	173.75	175.00				
1764	135.00		174.03	160.00			150.69	3,589.62
1765	135.00		173.44		172.50		148.16	3,573.45
1766		140.00	170.42	173.75	171.94		150.00	3,571.26
1767	135.00			170.00	174.91	168.75		3,645.16
1768	135.00	140.00		175.00	173.83	165.00		3,550.45
1769	127.50		165.42	167.50	167.22			3,526.86
1770	130.00	140.00	169.38	165.00	165.21	160.00	147.50	3,538.25
1771	130.00	140.00			165.10			3,478.94
1772	130.00	140.00	165.00		165.42	160.00		3,621.01
1773	130.83	140.21	165.00		167.36			3,826.03
1774	133.33	140.00			169.06			3,813.31
1775	140.00	140.00	176.25		175.03			3,813.31

Notes and Sources: **TABLE 5.3**

    See the tables in chap. 4. For St. Domingue, the annual average figure for 1771 is based upon the combined data from Cap Français (through July 1771) and from Port-au-Prince (from Aug. 1771). The reduction to pounds sterling incorporates the rate of exchange with livres tournois from tables 4.8 and 4.9 and the rate in livres tournois for sterling from table 5.1.

Appendixes

1. Decimal Currency Converter for Pounds Sterling

Shillings and Old Pence to New Pence

s	d	new pence	s	d	new pence	s	d	new pence
	1	0.5p	2	1	10.5p	10	6	52.5p
	2	1 p	2	2	11 p	11	0	55 p
	3	1 p	2	3	11 p	11	6	57.5p
	4	1.5p	2	6	12.5p	12	0	60 p
	5	2 p	2	9	14 p	12	6	62.5p
	6	2.5p	3	0	15 p	13	0	65 p
	7	3 p	3	3	16 p	13	6	67.5p
	8	3.5p	3	6	17.5p	14	0	70 p
	9	4 p	3	9	19 p	14	6	72.5p
	10	4 p	4	0	20 p	15	0	75 p
	11	4.5p	4	3	21 p	15	6	77.5p
1	0	5 p	4	6	22.5p	16	0	80 p
1	1	5.5p	4	9	24 p	16	6	82.5p
1	2	6 p	5	0	25 p	17	0	85 p
1	3	6 p	5	6	27.5p	17	6	87.5p
1	4	6.5p	6	0	30 p	18	0	90 p
1	5	7 p	6	6	32.5p	18	6	92.5p
1	6	7.5p	7	0	35 p	19	0	95 p
1	7	8 p	7	6	37.5p	19	6	97.5p
1	8	8.5p	8	0	40 p	20	0	100 p
1	9	9 p	8	6	42.5p	30	0	150 p
1	10	9 p	9	0	45 p	40	0	200 p
1	11	9.5p	9	6	47.5p	100	0	500 p
2	0	10 p	10	0	50 p	500	0	2500 p

2. Survey of Extant Copies of London Price Currents

In an effort to encourage and stimulate a search for other copies of these important newspapers, I have presented in this list the dates of all copies that I have found and their locations.[1] The list also serves the bibliographic purpose of specifying the sources used for many of the tables in chapter 2.

1. This compilation is heavily dependent upon the work of Jacob M. Price, the author of "Notes on Some London Price-Currents, 1667–1715," *Economic History Review,* 2d Ser., VII (1954–1955), 240–250, and the scholar who has stimulated much interest in collecting these papers. See also [N. W. Posthumus], "Lijst van documenten [aansezig in de bibliotheek van het Nederlandsch Economisch-Historisch Archief]," *Economisch-historisch jaarboek,* XIII (1927), xliii–lx; and Price, "A Note on the Circulation of the London Press, 1704–1714," *Bulletin of the Institute of Historical Research,* XXXI (1958), 215–224. I have tried to look at each of the items that follow—for the purposes of this book—and in the process have corrected some small details in Price's listing and have added some things. A persistent difficulty arises from the problem that, prior to 1752, the first day of the new year for the English was 25 Mar. Thus contemporaries numbered the three months following Dec. 1680, for example, as Jan. 1680, Feb. 1680, and, through the 24th, Mar. 1680. The convention of double numbering these three months each year (e.g., Jan. 1680/81) did not become widespread until the 18th century. Thus confusion can arise (and has arisen) concerning the dating of some of these papers (see nn. 4, 5, and 9, below).

It is indeed possible that additional copies of these price currents might still be found. We know, for instance, that the Board of Trade subscribed to them from as early as 1676; that it continued to buy at least Whiston's, Proctor's, and something called the "Dutch and English Price Current"; and that there were five bound volumes of them (two volumes of "Bills of [Proctor's?] Price Current" and three volumes of "[Whiston's Merchants] Weekly Remembrance[r]") in its library in 1696. See the "Entries relating to the Establishment and Accompts of the Committee for Trade and Plantations," 1675–1696, Additional Manuscripts 9767–9768, British Library, and the continuation of these accounts in C.O. 388/75–84, Public Record Office, and the inventory of books and papers transferred in 1696 by the outgoing secretary of the Board, John Povey, to his successor, William Popple, C.O. 326/1, p. 150. See also Charles M. Andrews, *Guide to the Materials for American History, to 1783, in the Public Record Office of Great Britain,* I (Washington, D.C., 1912), 94; and C. S. S. Higham, *The Colonial Entry-Books: A*

1. *The Prices of Merchandise in London,* 1667–1669. Edited by Humphrey Brome and, later, by William Bannister. Printed in French, also, as *Prix courrant des merchandises à Londres* (specified by "Fr." below). Located in Yale University Library, New Haven, Conn., and Economisch-Historisch Archief, The Hague.[2] All except the first two are in the former location.

Brief Guide to the Colonial Records in the Public Record Office before 1696, Helps for Students of History, No. 45 (London, 1921), 43.

There now seems little doubt that at least one London price current continued to be published throughout the 18th century, even if there is no known run of the paper (or papers) available today. The existence of *Proctor's London Price-Courant Reviv'd* for the late 1720s and early 1730s is demonstrated below on the strength of one extant copy (item no. 8). Robert Willock's *West-India Monthly Packet of Intelligence* (London) published some prices throughout the years 1745 to 1762 that quite obviously were not his own compilation and that he once identified as being reprinted from "the Price Courant" (27 Dec. 1745). (A nearly complete run of Willock's paper can be found in the Library of Congress.) A firm of London sugar factors, Lascelles and Maxwell, sent their Barbados correspondent a copy of "the price current" in their letter of 5 Nov. 1757, although they describe it as "often very faulty." Lascelles and Maxwell Letter Book, 1756–1760, fol. 148, Wilkinson and Gaviller, Ltd., Papers, Vol. VII, as noted in Richard Pares Transcripts, Box IV, Rhodes House Library, University of Oxford. And we know that William Prince began the publication of *The London Price Current* in Jan. 1777, from scattered copies of the earliest numbers that survive in places such as the John Carter Brown Library, Brown University, Providence, R.I. Finding further copies of any of these awaits a comprehensive survey of extant English newspapers.

2. These locations are the ones given by Price, "Notes on Price-Currents," *Econ. Hist. Rev.,* 2d Ser., VII (1954–1955), 241, with the exception of those issues of which he was not aware. See also Margaret Canney and David Knott, comps., *Catalogue of the Goldsmiths' Library of Economic Literature* (Cambridge, 1970–1975). Photocopies of most of the price currents are available in the Goldsmiths' Library, University of London, and the Kress Library of Business and Economics in the Baker Library, Graduate School of Business Administration, Harvard University, Boston.

1667: 8 July

1668: 7 May (Fr.)
1 (Fr.), 8, 15, 22, 29 October
5, 12, 19, 26 November
3, 10, 17, 24 December

1669: 25 March
1, 8, 22 April
6, 13, 20, 27 May
10, 17, 24 June
1, 8, 15, 22, 29 July
5, 12, 19, 26 August
2, 9, 16, 23, 30 September
7, 14 (Fr.), 21, 28 October
4, 11, 18, 25 November
2, 9, 16, 23 December

1671: 22 November (Fr.)

1672: 31 January
14, 21 February (Fr.)
27 March (Fr.)
8, 22 May (Fr.)
25 September (Fr.)
6 November (Fr.)
31 December (Fr.)

1673: 19 February (Fr.)
6, 20 August (Fr.)
12 November
3, 10 December

1674: 7 January (Fr.)
25 March
17, 24 June (Fr.)
15 July (Fr.)
9, 23 December (Fr.)

1675: 27 January (Fr.)
24 February (Fr.)
17, 31 March (Fr.)
14 April (Fr.)
18 August (Fr.)
2 November (Fr.)
8 December (Fr.)

1679: 29 January (Fr.)

1680: 15 December (Fr.)

1682: 21 June
25 October (Fr.)[5]

1683: 3 January

1684: 30 December (Fr.)

1685: 30 December

1696: 12 February

2. *The Prices of Merchandise in London*, 1671–1696. Probably a continuation of price current no. 1, above. Edited by Robert Woolley, with a French edition also.[3] Located in British Library (formerly the British Museum), Public Record Office, and Economisch-Historisch Archief, The Hague.[4]

3. *Whiston's Merchants Weekly Remembrancer, of the Currant Present-Money-Prices of Their Goods Ashoar in London*, 1680–1707.[6] Originally titled *The Merchant's Remembrancer*. Edited by James Whiston.[7] Printed also in French as *Le memorial des marchands à Londres* (specified by "Fr." below). Located in Public Record Office; British Library; Economisch-Historisch Archief, The Hague; Arents Collection, New York Public Library, New York City; and Kress Library of Business and Economics in the Baker Library of the Graduate School of Business Administration, Harvard University, Boston.

3. One can find a bit more about Woolley (1638–1696), said to be worth £30,000 in 1682, in J. R. Woodhead, *The Rulers of London, 1660–1689: A Biographical Record of the Aldermen and Common Councilmen of the City of London* (London, 1965), 180. He was the purchaser of a variety of goods at East India Co. sales in the 1660s and 1670s and of sugar at the Royal African Co. sales in the 1670s and 1680s. India Office Records, General Records, Home Miscellaneous Series, VII, 39, 125, 133, VIII, 328, 345, 352, 377–378, 381, 383, 388, India Office Library, London; Royal African Co., Court of Assistants, Minute Books, III, fol. 153, IV, fol. 42, T. 70/77–78, P.R.O.

4. The references (here and below) to the P.R.O. are to the Matthias Giesque and Co. Papers, bundle no. 68, C. 104/128, pt. ii, Unknown Cause. This collection has the last issue of Woolley listed here, 12 Feb. 1696. Since Price stated ("Notes on Price-Currents," *Econ. Hist. Rev.*, 2d Ser., VII [1954–1955], 241) that two copies of Woolley are in the Brit. Lib., one could infer that all the remainder come from The Hague. The microfilm and photostatic copies of these in the Kress and the Goldsmiths' libraries are vague, at best, in their designation of the provenance of the originals (and the latter incorrect in mistaking Chancery Court Records for Colonial Office Papers in the P.R.O.). Any confusion over the dating of Woolley's price current for the months of Jan., Feb., and Mar. is compounded by the editor's own lack of consistency in dating the paper. Most problems can ultimately be resolved by comparing dates of publication against a calendar, since the paper was published every Wednesday. The question of which of two years is the right one can be answered by checking to see in which year the date fell on a Wednesday. Useful in this regard is C. R. Cheney, ed., *Handbook of Dates for Students of English History*, Royal Historical Society Guides and Handbooks, No. 4 (London, 1961).

5. This number is dated 1681 on the face but on the second side, more convincingly, 1682; 25 Oct. 1682 was a Wednesday, the regular day of publication (see n. 4 above).

6. See price current no. 6, below, for the probable continuation of this paper.

7. Like Woolley, Whiston frequented the auctions of the Royal African Co. in the 1670s and 1680s. See T. 70/77, fol. 42, or T. 70/78, fol. 127. He was the author of several tracts on trade published between 1681 and 1704.

1680: 16 February

1681: 23 May
4 July
14 November (Fr.)

1682: 20 March (Fr.)
8 June (Fr.)

1683: 12 February (Fr.)
14 May (Fr.)
20 August (Fr.)
8 October (Fr.)

1685: 28 September (Fr.)
9 November (Fr.)

1689: 17 June

1691: 26 January
26 October

1692: 25 January

1693: 3 April

1694: 10 September
19 November

1696: 23 March
20 April
13 July
31 August
12 November
7 December

1697: 1, 29 March
26 April
14 June
16 August

1698: 17 January
7 March
4, 18 July

1699: 9 January

1701: 17 November

1702: 16 November

1707: 7 July

1696: 28 February
3, 30 April
21 May
11 June
24 September
29 October (Fr.)
15, 26 November
17 December

1697: 21 January
19 February
18 March
29 April
5 August
7 October
18 November

1698: 24 February
3 March
4 August

1706: 17 January[9]

1717: 28 November

5. *Prix courant de marchandises à Londres*, 1698–1717.[10] Edited by Étienne Mahieu. Located in Economisch-Historisch Archief, The Hague, and Public Record Office.

1699: 22 June

1715: 10 February

1717: 5 December

4. *Proctor's Price-Courant: The Prices of Merchandise in London*, 1694–1717. The title in 1717 had changed to *Proctor's Price-Current Improv'd*.[8] Edited by Samuel Proctor. Printed also in French as *Prix courant de S. Proctor . . . Londres* (specified by "Fr." below). Located in Public Record Office; Arents Collection, New York Public Library; and Kress Library.

6. *Robinson's Merchants Weekly Remembrancer of the Present Money Prices of Their Goods Ashore in London*, 1708–1714.[11] Edited by Francis Robinson and probably a continuation of price current no. 3,

8. This (and the Dec. 1717 copy of Mahieu, below) are in the Papers of the Ship *Hartford*, bundle E, C. 106/132, *Hutchinson* v. *George*. It is included here, despite the variation in the title, because the serial numbering is continuous. John M. Hemphill told me about the location of these two price currents, and I am grateful to him for his help.

9. This is misdated to 1705 by L. W. Hanson, *Contemporary Printed Sources for British and Irish Economic History, 1701–1750* (Cambridge, 1963), no. 498, for the reasons mentioned in n. 1, above. See also Price, "Notes on Price-Currents," *Econ. Hist. Rev.*, 2d Ser., VII (1954–1955), 250. See price current no. 8, below.

10. Since the earliest extant copy is no. 66, the date of initial publication was, most likely, 24 Mar. 1697/98. Price, "Notes on Price-Currents," *Econ. Hist. Rev.*, 2d Ser., VII (1954–1955), 248.

11. Since the only issue that has been found is no. 264, no. 1 dated from the spring of 1708. Price, *ibid.*, has shown that the paper continued to be published into 1714.

above. Located in Constance Meade Memorial Collection, Commerce, Folder 1, Oxford University Press, Oxford.

1713: 23 March

7. *Great Britain's Weekly Pacquet: Containing the Prices of Goods*, 1716. Edited by Thomas Hartwell. Located in Edinburgh University Library and Bodleian Library, University of Oxford.

1716: 21 July
     13 October

8. *Proctor's London Price-Courant Reviv'd*, 1727–1731. Edited by Samuel Proctor. Located in British Library.

1731: 1 July

3. African Currency and the Exchange on London

The tentativeness of much that appears in the body of this handbook takes on the character of certitude when compared with the few, random things one can say about monetary systems in use on the west coast of Africa. European traders adopted and used for their own purposes older African moneys, and the result, at least for the English, was a minimum of three monetary systems. But about all of this we have only the sketchiest information. Africa is relegated to an appendix not because it fails to fit in the Atlantic world but because the state of our understanding is so imperfect.[1]

Along the coast of West Africa, the English operated a string of trading posts that we can divide into at least three sets based on their moneys of account. In the more southerly areas along the Gold Coast, the "ounce" was the fundamental unit of the money of account.[2] The "ounce," one-eighth of a mark, also equaled sixteen "accys" (spelled various ways, such as "acke" and "ackie"); an accy in turn was worth twelve "taccae." The "ounce" was nominally the ounce of gold valued at a conventional rate of £4; the accy was thus

worth 5s (25p). These valuations hold true for the entirety of the pre-1775 period for which we have evidence.[3]

In a 1966 article Marion Johnson determined that there was a considerable "devaluation" of the "trade ounce" between 1753 and 1777. The trade ounce as a money of account appears to have been worth in 1777 half of its value in 1753, or so the article concluded.[4] What is meant, in the words of a ship captain named Chalmers, is that in 1777 the real ounce of gold "reckoned two ounces of trade."[5] This was the same as saying that £4 sterling bought £8 in the West African money of account; £4 sterling equaled two "trade ounces," 32 accys, and so forth.

The only problem with Johnson's exposition is the date assigned to the beginning of this value for the trade ounce. The quotation dated 1753 and used as evidence of an older and different valuation in fact says exactly what is said above: the ounce used in trade on

---

1. This is not to deny the good work done to date; it is only to agree with those who have studied African economic history that much needs to be learned. See the excellent survey in A. G. Hopkins, *An Economic History of West Africa* (New York, 1973), 66–71, 111–112. Much information on currency and exchange in Africa has been assembled in Lars Sundström, *The Trade of Guinea*, Studia Ethnographica Upsaliensia XXIV (Lund, 1965), which has recently been reissued as *The Exchange Economy of Pre-Colonial Tropical Africa* (New York, 1975). See also Johannes Postma, "The Dutch Participation in the African Slave Trade: Slaving on the Guinea Coast, 1675–1795" (Ph.D. diss., Michigan State University, 1970), 194–195.

2. See Marion Johnson, "The Ounce in Eighteenth-Century West African Trade," *Journal of African History*, VII (1966), 197–214. For a broader perspective that incorporates a useful survey of some of the relevant literature, see B. Marie Perinbam, "Trade and Society in the Western Sahara and the Western Sudan: An Overview," *Bulletin de l'Institut Fondamental d'Afrique Noire*, Sér B, XXXIV (1972), 778–801.

3. The interrelationships of the money appear from bills, accounts, and the like; so do the conventional valuations. See, for instance, Elizabeth Donnan, ed., *Documents Illustrative of the History of the Slave Trade to America* (Washington, D.C., 1930–1935), II, 8n; W. E. Minchinton, ed., *Politics and the Port of Bristol in the Eighteenth Century: The Petitions of the Society of Merchant Venturers, 1698–1803* (Bristol Record Society, Publications, XXIII [Bristol, 1963]), 74. See also Royal African Company, List of Ships and Voyages, T. 70/1225, fols. 122–123, Public Record Office (a piece of blue blotting paper inserted there); K. G. Davies, *The Royal African Company* (London, [1957]), 238; Sammy Tenkorang, "British Slave-Trading Activities on the Gold and Slave Coasts in the Eighteenth Century and their Effects on African Society" (M.A. thesis, University of London, 1964), 38; Johnson, "Ounce in Eighteenth-Century West African Trade," *Jour. African Hist.*, VII (1966), 197–204.

4. Johnson, "Ounce in Eighteenth-Century West African Trade," *Jour. African Hist.*, VII (1966), 202–205.

5. *Journal of the Commissioners for Trade and Plantations . . . Preserved in the Public Record Office . . .* (London, 1920–1938), XIV (1776–1782), 142.

the African coast and valued there at a conventional £4 was worth only half that in European terms. Given the consistent tendency in all colonies to establish a colonial currency at something less than the value in the mother country, it seems likely that the trade ounce in Africa was always, at par, worth half its face value. Chalmers's statement that the ounce of gold "reckoned two ounces of trade" was probably as applicable in 1700 as in 1777. If this is true, then throughout the eighteenth century the par of exchange was 200 trade ounces Gold Coast currency per 100 ounces of gold in London.

Further north and west, along the Guinea Coast (Gambia, Sierra Leone, and Sherbro in the Royal African Company's experience), accounts "were kept in bars, shillings and pence [as] a currency of account."[6] Although nominally the value of a bar of iron, the bar of account was worth something less than the bar of iron. The former had a value of 4s (20p) sterling, the latter a value of 6s (30p) currency on the Guinea Coast.[7] These conventional values come largely from the records of the Royal African Company late in the seventeenth century; they imply a par of exchange of 150 bars of account per 100 bars of iron. In the eighteenth century the Gold Coast "ounce" currency seems to have spread north to the Guinea Coast and to have supplanted, at least in part, the bar of account.[8]

East of the Gold Coast at Whydah, cowries were used as a money of account. Of ancient origin, cowrie currency served the African trade well into the nineteenth century. The "ounce" seems also to have come to be used at Whydah, beginning perhaps as late as the third quarter of the eighteenth century.[9]

6. Davies, *Royal African Company*, 238.

7. J. M. Gray, *A History of the Gambia* (Cambridge, 1940), 91n, citing T. 70/78, 29; Davies, *Royal African Company*, 238, citing T. 70/108 and T. 70/546.

8. Johnson, "Ounce in Eighteenth-Century West African Trade," *Jour. African Hist.*, VII (1966), *passim*. The "trading book" of the schooner *Active*, 1769, has an entry for 8 bars at 3s 6d (17.5p) at Anomabu on the Gold Coast. Samuel and William Vernon Papers, 1750–1775, Box VII, "Slavery MSS.," New-York Historical Society, New York City.

9. Johnson, "Ounce in Eighteenth-Century West African Trade," *Jour. African Hist.*, VII (1966), 206–208. See also Marion Johnson, "Cowrie Currency in West Africa," *ibid.*, XI (1970), 17–49, 331–353; Perinbam, "Trade and Society in the Western Sahara," *Bulletin d'Inst. Fond. d'Afrique Noire*, Sér B, XXXIV (1972), 783–786.

Bibliography

The following listing of primary sources consulted for this study includes unpublished manuscripts only. Because most of the other sources are already commented upon in the footnotes and assembled there in the most useful arrangement for the reader, it was thought unnecessary to list them here also. Those who seek the full bibliographical information for any work cited can consult the index, which incorporates a reference to each use of every work cited in this handbook. The first reference will give complete bibliographical information.

The manuscripts have been grouped into two categories—Domestic Repositories and Foreign Repositories—each of which is arranged alphabetically by jurisdiction, repository, and collection.

1. DOMESTIC REPOSITORIES

District of Columbia

WASHINGTON

Library of Congress

Amory Family Papers, 1697–1823
    Thomas Amory Letter Books, 1711–1728
    Thomas Amory Estate Papers, 1697–1724
John Leeds Bozman Papers
    Mercantile Papers of William Fishbourne and Daniel Richardson, 1711–1729
Carroll Family Papers, 1684–1832
    Charles Carroll of Carrollton Papers, 1684–1771
    Charles Carroll of Carrollton Account Books, 1765–1829
    Charles Carroll of Carrollton Account Book ("Liber A"), 1734–1825

Levinus Clarkson Papers, 1772–1793
Stephen Collins and Son Papers, 1749–1857
    Correspondence, 1749–1803
    William Barrell's Journals, 1766–1775
    Solomon Fussell Account Book, 1758–1762
    William Trent "Ledger B," 1701–1703 (formerly identified as the Joseph Pidgeon Ledger)
Davey and Carson Letter Book, 1745–1750
John Digges Account Book, 1720–1749
Edward Dixon Records, 1743–1796
Peter Force Papers
    Series VIII A: George Chalmers Collection, 1641–1824
        Great Britain Trade Papers, 1640–1804
        Quebec Papers, 1781–1801
        West Indian and Antigua Papers, 1762–1825
    Series VIII D: Various
        Oliver Pollock Papers, 1767–1788
        Samuel and Jonathan Smith Letter Book, 1765–1770
        Woolsey and Salmon Letter Book, 1774–1784
Galloway-Maxey-Markoe Family Papers
    Galloway Correspondence
    John Galloway Letter Book, 1737–1738
    Samuel Galloway Letter Book, 1766–1772
    Galloway Business Papers, 1654–1819
    Galloway Daybook and Journals, 1765–1786
    Galloway Miscellaneous Accounts, 1754–1805
Edmund Charles Genêt Papers, 1750–1832
John Glassford and Company Records, 1753–1844

John Glassford and Company, Bladensburg Store Ledger, 1753

John Pagan and Company, St. Mary's County Store Ledger, 1761–1762

Simson, Baird and Company, Piscataway Store Journal, 1766–1767

Neil Jamieson Papers, 1757–1789

Account Book of New York Merchant, 1706–1714

Townshend Papers

Alexander Wooddrup Account Books, 1720–1734 (formerly identified as the Gibbons account books and, alternatively, as the account books of an unknown Philadelphia merchant)

Illinois
CHICAGO
Newberry Library

Ayer Manuscripts
Collection of Papers Relating to French Colonies (no. 293)
Samuel Wentworth Letters and Papers, 1738–1742 (nos. 972–973)

Maryland
ANNAPOLIS
Maryland Hall of Records

Baltimore County Administrative Accounts

Chancery Papers

Chancery Records

Dorchester County Circuit Court, Clerk's Fee Book, 1762–1763, incorporating Robert Morris Ledger B, 1747–1750

Frederick County Court Records

Prerogative Court Records
Accounts
Inventories

Somerset County Court Records

BALTIMORE
Maryland Historical Society

Maryland Diocesan Archives of the Protestant Episcopal Church
Callister Family Papers, 1741–1788
Henry Callister Letter Book, 1741–1766

Stephen Bordley Letter Book, 1727–1759 (MS 81)

Calvert Papers, 1621–1775 (MS 174)
Orders and Instructions of Charles, Lord Baltimore, 1729–1750

Charles Carroll of Annapolis, Letter Books and Business Accounts, 1716–1755 (MS 208)

Charles Carroll of Annapolis Account Book, 1730–1784 (MSS 211, 211.1)

Collector of the Customs, Port of Oxford, Maryland, Account Book, 1731–1743 (MS 638)

Corner Collection (MS 1242)

Dulany Papers, 1659–1799 (MS 1265)

Fitzhugh Account Books, 1761–1774 (MS 1831)

Clement Hill Papers, 1670–1805 (MS 446)

Henry Hollyday Account Book, 1745–1790 (MS 454)

James Hollyday Ledger, 1746–1784 (MS 454.1)

Ridgely Account Books (MS 691)
Ledger, 1734–1738
Daybook, 1741–1742, 1742–1743
Charles Ridgely Ledgers A–C, 1763–1775
Charles Ridgely Journal, 1762–1765

Ridgely Papers, 1733–1858 (MS 692.1)

Smith Letter Books, 1774–1821 (MS 1152)
Letter Book of John Smith and Sons, 1774–1786

Massachusetts
BOSTON
Baker Library, Graduate School of Business Administration, Harvard University

Kress Library of Business and Economics
"Notitie van diverse Koopmanschappen uyt de Prijs-Courant Begonnen in Amsteldam," 1708–1788
Manuscript and Archives Division
Letters of Boston Merchants, 1732–1790
Victor S. Clark Collection, 1607–1928
John Erving Journal, 1733–1745
Records of the International Scientific Committee on Price History, 1928–1939
Henry Lloyd Letter Book, 1765–1767
Massachusetts Historical Society
Amory Family Manuscripts
Thomas Fitch Papers, 1719–1753
New England Company Minutes, 1656–1686
New England Historic Genealogical Society
Hancock Family Papers, 1712–1854
Peter Faneuil Papers, 1725–1739
Daybook, c. 1726–1732
John Hancock Papers, 1755–1786
Waste Book, 1764–1767
Journal, 1764–1782
Office of the Clerk of the Supreme Judicial Court of the Commonwealth, New Suffolk County Courthouse
Suffolk Files

CAMBRIDGE
Harvard College Library, Harvard University
Houghton Library
Hugh Hall, Jr., Letter Book, 1716–1720
Arthur Lee Letters, 1763–1774
Widener Library
Harvard University Archives
Harvard College Records

WALTHAM
American Jewish Historical Society
Aaron Lopez Papers

Michigan
ANN ARBOR
William L. Clements Library, University of Michigan
Gage Manuscripts
William Petty, Earl of Shelburne, Papers
Charles Winstone Letter Book, 1777–1786

New Jersey
TRENTON
Bureau of Archives and History, State House
New England Company, Treasurer's Ledger, 1650–1660

New York
ALBANY
New York State Library
New York Colonial Manuscripts

BUFFALO
Buffalo and Erie County Historical Society
Phyn and Ellice Letter Books, 1767–1776

ITHACA
Albert R. Mann Library, Cornell University
Frank Ashmore Pearson Papers

NEW YORK CITY
New-York Historical Society
The Alexander Papers
William Alexander Accounts, Bills and Receipts
William Alexander Correspondence, 1744–1782
William Alexander Manuscripts, 1743–1782
Beekman Family Papers
James Beekman Papers
Ledgers A and B, 1752–1799
Journals B and C, 1758–1806
De Peyster Family Papers, 1677–1881
Frederick Ashton De Peyster Manuscripts

Glen-Sanders Papers, 1674–1957
  John and Robert Sanders Voyage Book, 1738–1748
  Sanders Correspondence
Peter Jay Papers, 1724–1770
William Lux Letter Book, 1763–1768
Sanders Papers
  John and Robert Sanders Letter Book, 1742–1743
  Robert Sanders Letter Book, 1752–1758
  John and Robert Sanders Voyage Book, 1748–1764
Samuel and William Vernon Papers, 1750–1777
  Slavery Manuscripts (Box VII)
New York Public Library
Clymer-Meredith-Read Papers
  Samuel Meredith Letters, 1771–1799
Philip Cuyler Papers
  Philip Cuyler Letter Book, 1755–1760
  Philip Cuyler Ledger, 1763–1794
Papers of Samuel and John Galloway, 1739–1812
  Galloway Correspondence, 1739–1812
  Thomas Ringgold Correspondence
Robert T. Hooe Papers
  Hooe, Stone, and Company Invoice Book, 1770–1784
Hudson Family Papers, 1659–1862
  James Hudson Accounts and Papers, 1742–1788
  James Hudson and Benjamin Rolfe Account and Letter Books, 1747–1783
Thomas Moffatt Letter Book, 1715–1716
Van Cortlandt Account Books, 1700–1875
  Jacobus van Cortlandt Ledger, 1700–1875
  George Petterson Ledger B, 1751–1755
  John van Cortlandt Daybook, Journals, and Ledgers, 1757–1772
  John van Cortlandt Letter Books, 1762–1769, 1771–1792

North Carolina
DURHAM
Duke University Library
  James Dick and Stewart Company Letter Book, 1773–1781

Pennsylvania
PHILADELPHIA
Historical Society of Pennsylvania
  Peter Baynton Ledger and Letter Book, 1721–1726
  John and Peter Chevalier Daybook and Journals, 1757–1783
  Daniel Clark Letter Book and Invoice Book, 1759–1763
  Coates and Reynell Papers, 1702–1843
    Coates-Reynell Correspondence, 1729–1836
    John Reynell Business Records
    John Reynell Correspondence, 1729–1773
    John Reynell Letter Books, 1729–1784
  Coxe Papers
    Correspondence, 1672–1775
  Custom House Papers, 1704–1929
  Henry Drinker Papers, 1756–1869
    Abel James and Henry Drinker Letter Books, 1756–1809
  Hollingsworth Collection, 1748–1887
    Levi Hollingsworth Invoice Book, 1767–1770
    Hollingsworth Correspondence, 1768–1771
  John Kidd Letter Book, 1749–1763
  Aaron Leaming Diaries, 1750–1776
  Library Company of Philadelphia Collection
    "Old Letter Book" [not found]
  Logan Papers, 1664–1871
    James Logan Letter Books, 1701–1743
    Parchment Logan Letter Book, 1717–1731
    Dickinson-Logan Letter Book, 1698–1701, 1731–1742
    James Logan Daybook, 1722–1723
    James Logan Account Book, 1712–1720
    Mifflin and Massey Ledger, 1760–1763

Norris Papers, 1742–1860
    Norris Letter Books, 1699–1766
    Norris Account Book, 1705–1761
    William Griffith Letter Book, 1748–1752
Orr, Dunlope, and Glenholme Letter Book, 1767–1769
Pemberton Papers, 1641–1800
    Clifford Correspondence
    Clifford Letter Books
    Pemberton Papers
William Pollard Letter Book, 1772–1774
Samuel Powel, Jr., Letter Books, 1727–1747
Thomas Riché Letter Books and Journal, 1751–1771
Roberdeau Papers, 1761–1831
    Daniel Roberdeau Letter Book, 1764–1771
    Daniel Roberdeau Receipt Book, 1761–1767
William Smith Letter Book, 1771–1775
John Swift Letter Books, 1747–1813
William Trent Ledger C, 1703–1709
Unidentified Philadelphia Merchant Account Book, 1694–1698 (Am. 905)
Wharton Papers, 1679–1834
    Thomas Wharton Letter Book, 1752–1759
Willing and Morris Letter Book, 1754–1761
Joel and Nathan Zane Receipt Book, 1761–1764
Wharton School of Finance and Commerce, University of Pennsylvania
    Papers of the Industrial Research Department
        Wholesale Prices

SWARTHMORE
Friends Historical Library, Swarthmore College
    Miscellaneous Manuscripts
        Micah Shields Account and Letter Book, 1759–1777

Rhode Island

NEWPORT
Newport Historical Society
    John Bannister Letter Book
    Clark Letter Books

PROVIDENCE
John Carter Brown Library, Brown University
    Brown Papers
    Codices English
        7 Richard Poor, Jr., Journal, 1699–1713
        87 Bryan Edwards, "Notes on [Edward] Long's [History of] Jamaica," 1789
    Map Drawers
    Welcome-Arnold Papers

South Carolina

CHARLESTON
South Carolina Historical Society
    Henry Laurens Papers, 1747–1882
        Account Book of James Laurens, 1767–1775
        Austin and Laurens Wastebook, 1749–1751
        Letters to James Laurens, Chiefly from Henry Laurens, 1773–1777

Virginia

CHARLOTTESVILLE
Alderman Library, University of Virginia
    Carter Family Papers
        Diary of Robert "King" Carter
        Robert Carter Letter Book
    Papers of William Prentis, 1733–1780
    Letter Book of Charles Yates, 1773–1783
Tracy W. McGregor Library, University of Virginia
    New England Company, Copybook of Letters and Bills of Exchange Sent to New England, 1688–1761

MONTROSS
Westmoreland County Courthouse
Inventories No. 1, 1723–1746

RICHMOND
Virginia Historical Society
Carter Papers, 1705–1785
Robert Carter Letter Books
Robert Bristow Letter Book

SPOTSYLVANIA
Spotsylvania County Courthouse
Order Book, 1738–1749

STRATFORD
Robert E. Lee Memorial Association, Stratford Hall Plantation
William Lee Letter Books, 1769–1795

WILLIAMSBURG
Colonial Williamsburg Foundation Research Department
Edmund Bagge Account Book, 1726–1733
College of William and Mary
Jerdone Papers
Letter Book of Francis Jerdone, 1756–1763

WINCHESTER
Frederick County Courthouse
Order Book, No. 4, 1751–1753

YORKTOWN
York County Courthouse
"Orders, Wills & Ca.," 1712–1729

2. FOREIGN REPOSITORIES

Canada
OTTAWA, ONTARIO
Public Archives of Canada
Ermatinger Estate Papers, 1755–1894 (MG 19, A2)
Lawrence Ermatinger Papers
Letter Book of Lawrence Ermatinger, 1770–1778
Records of the Executive Council (RG 1, E1)
Quebec Legislative Council Minute Books, 1764–1791

Denmark
COPENHAGEN
Rigsarkivet
Vestindisk-guineisk Kompagniets Arkiv
Københavnske arkivalier
Direktionens korrespondance
Breve og dokumenter fra Vestindien
Universitets-bibliotek (Fiolstræde)
Royal Danish-American Gazette (St. Croix)

France
PARIS
Archives Nationales
Archives des Colonies
Séries B. Correspondance envoyée, Ordres du Roi
Séries C. Correspondance générale, Lettres reçues
C⁷ Guadeloupe
C⁸ Martinique
C⁹ Saint-Domingue
C¹¹ Canada et colonies d'Amérique du Nord
Bibliothèque Nationale
Gazette de Saint-Domingue ([title varies] Cap Français and Port-au-Prince

Germany

HAMBURG

Commerzbibliothek, Handelskammer
   Preis Courant der Wahren in Partheijen (Hamburg)
   Geld-Cours in Hamburg
   Wechsel-Cours in Hamburg

Staatsarchiv
   Akten Senat
   Geld-Cours in Hamburg
   Wechsel-Cours in Hamburg

Great Britain

BENTHAM, NEAR LANCASTER

Personal Collection of Mr. E. P. English, Grove Bank
   Mills Papers

BRISTOL

Bristol Archives Office
   Ashton Court Papers, The Woolnough Papers
      Spring Plantation Papers
   Munckley Papers, 1741–1909
Society of Merchant Venturers
   Records of the Society
      Running Letters
University Library, University of Bristol
   Pinney Papers
      John Pinney Account Book
      John Pinney Letter Books
      West Indies Papers
   West Indian Documents

LONDON

British Library (formerly British Museum)
   Additional Manuscripts
      12411 Charles Edward Long Manuscripts: Edward Long's
      Notes and Memoranda, I

22677 Charles Edward Long Manuscripts: Letters of James Knight, Charles Long, and Others
36218 Hardwicke Papers, Vol. DCCCLXX: Appeal Cases before the Privy Council, 1722–1769
38342 Liverpool Papers, Vol. CLIII, 1772–1778
41349–41351 Martin Papers, Vols. IV–VI: Letter Books of Samuel Martin, Sr., 1756–1776
41352 Martin Papers, Vol. VII: Letter Book of Josiah Martin, 1729–1740
Harleian Manuscripts
   660 Tracts Relating to Bullion, Coinage, and Exchange
   6273 Papers Relating to Colonial Affairs
King's Manuscripts
   205 Report on the State of the British Colonies, 1721–1764
   206 State of Manufacture, Mode of Granting Land, Fees of Office, etc., in America
Loans
   29 Duke of Portland Manuscripts
      Vol. 292, Robert Harley, Earl of Oxford, Official Papers, Miscellaneous Manuscripts (Victualling)
Guildhall Library
   New England Company Archives, MSS 7908–8011
   Edward Grace and Company Papers, MSS 12048–12053
House of Lords Record Office, Westminster
   Main Papers
India Office Library
   General Records
      Home Miscellaneous Series
Lambeth Palace Library
   Fulham Papers
      General Correspondence
Public Record Office
   Chancery Court Records
      Chancery Masters' Exhibits
         C. 104/8 *Walter* v. *Evans*: Maynard Clark Papers
         C. 104/13–14 *Isaac* v. *Defriez*: Nathan Simson Papers

C. 104/15–16 *Lilie* v. *Waterhouse:* David Waterhouse Papers

C. 104/77–80 *Re Newson's Estate:* Mercantile Papers of Thomas Newson

C. 104/126–129 Unknown Cause: Matthias Giesque and Company Papers

C. 106/132 *Hutchinson* v. *George:* Papers of the ship *Hartford*

C. 107/148 *Clarke* v. *Knight:* Clarke Plantation Accounts

C. 108/25 *Re Roberts:* Roberts Plantation Accounts

C. 109/23–24 *Atwood* v. *Hare:* William Atwood Papers

C. 110/54 *Ex parte Hill, a bankrupt:* Business Papers of Daniel Hill

C. 110/152 *Brailsford* v. *Peers:* Correspondence and Business Papers of Thomas Brailsford, 1687–1698

C. 110/163 *Fleming* v. *Lynde:* Business Papers of James Lynde

C. 110/186–187 *Williamson* v. *Wallaby:* Papers of the Ship *Oliver*

Colonial Office Records

C.O. 1 Colonial Papers, General Series

C.O. 5 America and West Indies

C.O. 23 Bahamas, Original Correspondence

C.O. 25 Bahamas, Acts

C.O. 28 Barbados, Original Correspondence

C.O. 37 Bermuda, Original Correspondence

C.O. 39 Bermuda, Acts

C.O. 40 Bermuda, Sessional Papers

C.O. 76 Dominica, Shipping Returns

C.O. 101 Grenada, Original Correspondence

C.O. 103 Grenada, Acts

C.O. 116 British Guiana, Miscellaneous

C.O. 137 Jamaica, Original Correspondence

C.O. 138 Jamaica, Entry Books

C.O. 139 Jamaica, Acts

C.O. 140 Jamaica, Sessional Papers

C.O. 152 Leeward Islands, Original Correspondence

C.O. 154 Leeward Islands, Acts

C.O. 185 Nevis, Acts

C.O. 217 Nova Scotia, Original Correspondence

C.O. 260 St. Vincent, Original Correspondence

C.O. 323 Colonies, General, Original Correspondence

C.O. 324 Colonies, General, Entry Books

C.O. 326 Board of Trade, Registers and Indexes

C.O. 388 Board of Trade, Original Correspondence

C.O. 391 Board of Trade, Minutes

Records of the Exchequer, King's Remembrancer

E. 134 Depositions Taken by Commission

High Court of Admiralty Papers

H.C.A. 32 Prize Court Papers

State Paper Office Records

S.P. 18 State Papers Domestic, Interregnum

Treasury Office Papers

T. 1 Treasury Board, In-Letters

T. 29 Treasury Minute Books

T. 38 Accounts, Departmental

T. 70 Expired Commissions, African Companies

United Society for the Propagation of the Gospel

Archives of the Society for the Propagation of the Gospel in Foreign Parts

Class II. Closed Series

Series IV. Accounts, Bills of Exchange, Receipts, 1745–1785

Series X. Miscellaneous Bound Records

Vols. 34–41. Barbados Letters and Plantation Accounts

Series C. Miscellaneous Unbound Records

Group W.I. Codrington Donation Records

University of London Library, Senate House

The Newton Papers, 1706–1920 (no. 523)

Newton Plantation Accounts

Westminster Abbey, Muniment Room and Library

Muniments

Sir James Modyford Papers, 1667–1676

OXFORD

Bodleian Library, University of Oxford

Deposited Deeds

Ashurst

c. 1 Letter Book and Account Book of Henry Ashurst, 1674–1701

Rawlinson Letters

66 Letter Book of Joseph Cruttenden, 1710–1717

Rawlinson Manuscripts

C. 934 Papers Relating to the New England Company, 1649–1656

Rhodes House Library, University of Oxford

Richard Pares Transcripts

Diary of William Senhouse, 1750–1800

TAUNTON, SOMERSET

Somerset Record Office

Muniments of the Dickinson Family of Kingweston (DD/DN)

Tudway-Wells Manuscripts (DD/TD)

Helyar of Coker Court Documents and Muniments (DD/WHh)

EDINBURGH

National Library of Scotland

Steuart Papers (MS 5028-5040)

Scottish Record Office

Collections Deposited by Messrs. Tods, Murray, and Jamieson, W.S. (Gift and Deposit No. 237)

Alexander Nisbett Journal, 1727–1730 (Box 10, pt. 4)

Account Book of Charleston (Port Tobacco), Maryland, Merchant, 1740–1741 (Box 10, pt. 4)

Mead Plantation Accounts, 1723–1729

Collections Deposited by Messrs. John C. Brodie, W.S. (Gift and Deposit No. 247)

Letter Books and Correspondence of William Cuninghame and Company, 1761–1789 (Box 58)

PENCAITLAND, EAST LOTHIAN

Personal Collection of Sir David J. W. Ogilvy, Winton House

Tullideph Papers

Letter Books of Dr. Walter Tullideph, 1734–1767

Guadeloupe

BASSE-TERRE

Archives Départmentales

Minutes notariales

Netherlands

AMSTERDAM

Gemeentelijke Archiefdienst

Notarieel Archief

THE HAGUE

Algemeen Rijksarchief

Koloniale Archieven

Archieven van de Eerste West-Indische Compagnie, 1621–1674

MIDDELBURG

Rijksarchief in Zeeland

Middelburgse Commercie Compagnie Archieven, 1720–1789

Norway

OSLO

Rigsarkivet

Personalia

Thomas Fearnley Kopibog, 1753–1769 (nr. 38.2.2)

Index

This index combines the usual substantive headings with entries for each of the sources used in the writing of the handbook (as explained in the note preceding the Bibliography). Some of the entries incorporate lists of the names of places that exchanged with one another; two conventions serve to shorten such lists. Where London is one of the places (e.g., under the rate of exchange between London and Paris), the entry will always be under the other place name. Second, to avoid repeating both names in each pair, the entry will only appear under the name of the place that comes first in the alphabet (e.g., the discussion of the rate of exchange between Dublin and Belfast is indexed only under Belfast).

In accordance with the editorial style of the Institute of Early American History and Culture, this index follows English alphabetical usage; that is, the presence of diacritical marks does not affect the order. German *ü*, as in *Büsch*, for example, is alphabetized as *u*, not *ue*. The reader should notice that library catalogs do not follow this system and would alphabetize *Büsch* as *Buesch*.

Decimal equivalents of currencies. *See* Currency
Defiance (brig), 275n
Defriez. See *Isaac v. Defriez*
Delaware: relationship of, with Pennsylvania, 175, 181–182; money and exchange of, 181–182. *See also* Exchange; Monetary units, British
Delaware River Valley: as focal point of economic region, 122–123, 189; Pennsylvania currency in, 175, 192. *See also* Delaware; Maryland; New Jersey; Pennsylvania; Virginia
Demerara. *See* Essequibo and Demerara
Denier (French monetary unit), 88
Denmark: coins of, 4, 9–12; calendar changes of, 25, 25n; colonies of, 80, 280; monetary problems in colonies of, 118, 297–299; laws concerning colonies of, 298–299. *See also* Copenhagen; Monetary units, Danish; West India Company, Danish; West Indies, Danish
Denucé, Jan, *Koopmansleerboeken*, 44n
Depression, periods of economic. *See* Periods
Derby, earl of. *See* Stanley, William
Dering v. Packer, 135n
Dermigny, Louis, "Circuits de l'argent," 283nn
Desaguliers, Henri, *General Treatise of the Exchanges*, 44n, 107n
Devaluation, currency: in general, 117–119, 118n; in colonies, 118, 125–126, 131–133, 176–177, 185, 205, 215, 220, 227, 235, 239, 256–258, 276, 281, 291, 301, 302. *See also* Coins; Exchange, par of; individual colonies by place name
Devonshire, Reeve, and Lloyd (Bristol): letter to, 122n
Dexter, Franklin Bowditch, "Correspondence of Jared Ingersoll," 121n; *Itineraries of Ezra Stiles*, 152n, 155n
Dick, James, and Anthony Stewart (Maryland): letters of, 191n
Dicker, Michael Lee (Exeter): payee of bill of exchange, 178; letter to, 180n
Dickinson, Caleb (Jamaica): letter to, 118n
Dickinson, Caleb (England): journal of, 254n
Dickinson, Jonathan (Pennsylvania): letters from, 118n, 187n, 224n
Dickson, Peter G. M., *Financial Revolution in England*, 31n
Diedenhoven, Pieter (Curaçao), 293, 293n; letter to, 295n
Digges, John (Maryland): account book of, 200n, 203n
Dillen, Johannes G. van, "Bank of Amsterdam," 43nn; *Principal Public Banks*, 43nn, 44n, 61n–62n, 64n, 68n, 119n; "Effectenkoersen aan de Amsterdamsche beurs,"

51n; *Geschiedenis der wisselbanken*, 51n. *See also* Phoonsen, Johannes
Dinwiddie, Robert (Bermuda; Barbados): letters from, 245n, 276n, 279n
Disallowance, of colonial laws by Privy Council. *See* Great Britain, Privy Council
Discourse concerning the Currencies of the British Plantations. *See* Douglass, William
Distilling and distillers, 117, 137. *See also* Rum
Dixon. *See* Purdie and Dixon
Dixon, Edward (Virginia): papers of, 213n, 245n
Doblon (pistole) (Spanish monetary unit), 5, 6n, 11, 100
Dobra (Portuguese monetary unit), 5, 6, 6n, 12, 291, 293n, 299n, 300
Dobrão (Portuguese monetary unit), 12, 107
Dobson, Narda, *History of Belize*, 275n
"Dog dollar." *See* Leeuwendaalder
Dolbeare, Thomas (Jamaica), 248; letter from, 123n, 248nn, 255n, 288n
Dollar. *See* Peso
Dominica, 272n, 273; money and exchange of, 272–273; captured by French, 272. *See also* Exchange; Monetary units, British
Dominican Republic. *See* Santo Domingo
Doncken, Jacob von (St. Eustatius): drawer of bill of exchange, 294
Donnan, Elizabeth, *History of the Slave Trade*, 145n, 226n, 245n, 254n, 255n, 267n, 298n, 301n, 328
Dorchester County (Maryland), 187n, 191n, 196n, 200n, 203n, 245n, 263n
Dottin, James (Barbados): letter from, 239n
Doty, Richard G. *See* Newman, Eric P., and Richard G. Doty
Double doblon (four-pistole piece). *See* Doblon
Douglass, William, 169, 275, 291; *Discourse concerning currencies*, 8n, 120n, 134n, 144n, 170nn, 171n, 187n, 203nn, 219n, 230n, 231n, 239n, 275n, 276n, 285n; *Essay, concerning Silver and Paper Currencies*, 120n, 144n, 187n, 203n, 213n, 283n, 291n; *Present State of the British Settlements*, 144n, 152n, 155n, 219n, 263n, 267n
Doursther, Horace, *Dictionnaire universel des poids et mesures*, 7n, 8n
Drawee, of bill of exchange, 20
Drawer, of bill of exchange, 20
Drawing, of bills of exchange. *See* Exchange, negotiation of

Drinker, Henry. *See* James, Abel, and Henry Drinker
Drysdale, Hugh (gov., Virginia): letter from, 212n
Dublin (Ireland), 23n, 35
Ducado de cambio (Spanish monetary unit), 99
Ducat (Danish monetary unit), 11
Ducat (Dutch monetary unit), 11
Ducat (German monetary unit), 11
Ducatoon (Dutch monetary unit), 4, 9
Dudley, Joseph (Massachusetts): letter to, 143n
Du Hamel, Guillaume, *Hamburger Wechsel-Cours*, 64n
Dulany family (Maryland): papers of, 201n
Dunbar, Charles (Antigua): letters from, 258n, 263n
Dunbar, William (Antigua): 258n; letters from, 258n, 259n
Duncan, Thomas Bentley, *Atlantic Islands*, 301n
Dunster, Charles (London): letter from, 173n
Durant, Cornelius (St. Croix): account of, 298n
Dutch. *See* Netherlands
"Dutch and English Price Current," 324n
"Dutch Bills," at Antigua, 259
Dutch West India Company. *See* West India Company, Dutch
Dutch West Indies. *See* West Indies, Dutch
Dwight, Theodore. *See* Knight, Sarah Kemble

E
Earl of Bellomont. *See* Richard Coote
Earthquake, St. Domingue, 287
Eastern Shore. *See* Maryland
"East-Hampton Book of Laws," 157n
East India Company, 325n
Eaton, Isaac (St. Domingue): letter from, 287n
Ebeling, Christoph D. *See* Büsch, Johann G., and Christoph D. Ebeling; *also* Büsch, Johann G., *Über Banken und Münzwesen*
Echagoyn, Philippe de, *Tablas de reduciones de monedas*, 299n
Economic cycles. *See* Periods, economic and political
Economic regions. *See* Regions
Ecu (French monetary unit), 4, 9, 27, 87, 88
Eddy, Mr. (Rhode Island), 117n
Edenton (North Carolina), 219n
Edgar, Walter B., *Letterbook of Robert Pringle*, 221nn, 225n, 228n, 295n
Edinburgh, 34
Édits concernant le Canada, 282n
Edward, Thomas (Massachusetts), 152n

*See the introduction to this Index.

Exchange (cont.)
   by extralegal means, 296; between Denmark and
   Danish colonies, 297–298; between Spain and Spanish
   colonies, 299–300; between Cuba and London, 300;
   between Portugal and Portuguese colonies, 301;
   between Gold Coast and London, 329; shared by group
   of colonies, see Regions

   rate of: in general, 18–23, 27, 29, 31, 32, 107, 121,
   122–123, 124, 125; causes of fluctuations in, 19–22, 27,
   116, 121–122, 131–132, 134n, 159, 171, 180, 207,
   220–221, 227, 240, 284, 299 (see also Arbitrage;
   Damages; Usance); estimates of, 27, 29, 107; form of
   expression of, 120, 133, 280, 299n; attempts to
   manipulate, 131, 205; artificial, 124–125, 161, 196;
   between* Amsterdam and Archangel, 42n, and
   Copenhagen, 80, and London, 26, 31n, 52–60, 55n,
   305–311, and New York, 160, and St. Petersburg, 42n,
   and Stockholm, 64n, and Surinam, 296; between
   Antigua and London, 258, 259n, 260–262, 319–321;
   between Antwerp and London, 23n, 42n; between
   Bahamas and London, 275; between Barbados and
   London, 240n, 241–244, 318–321, and Martinique,
   288n; between Belfast and Dublin, 35, and London, 35;
   between Bermuda and London, 276, 278–279, 320–321;
   between Brazil and Portugal, 301; between Bristol and
   Pennsylvania, 177; between Buenos Aires and Cadiz,
   299; between Cadiz and Lima, 299, and London,
   99n–100n, 101–106, 305–311, and Mexico City, 299;
   between Chile and Seville, 299n; between Copenhagen
   and Danzig, 81, and Hamburg, 80, and London, 82–86,
   305–311, and Lübeck, 81, and Königsberg, 81, and
   Paris, 81, and Stockholm, 81; between Cork and
   London, 35; between Dominica and London, 272–273;
   between Dublin and London, 23n, 31, 35, 37–41,
   305–311; between Edinburgh and London, 31, 32–34,
   33n, and Paris, 34, 34n; between Georgia and London,
   229, 317; between Glasgow and Virginia, 207n;
   between Grenada and London, 272, 274, 321; between
   Hamburg and London, 30–31n, 69–79, 305–311, and
   St. Petersburg, 42n, and Stockholm, 64n; between
   Jamaica and London, 248, 248n, 250–253, 318–321;
   between Lisbon and London, 23n, 30–31n, 108–114,
   108n, 305–311, and São Thomé, 301n; between

Exchange (cont.)
   Louisbourg and London, 231n; between Martinique and
   Maryland, 288n; between Maryland and London, 191,
   197–199, 202–203, 315–317, and Ireland, 195n, and St.
   Eustatius, 293n; between Massachusetts and London,
   123n, 132, 136, 137n, 138–142, 146, 150, 313, 317, and
   Nova Scotia, 134; between Mexico City and Seville,
   299n; between Montreal and London, 232; between
   Montserrat and London, 258; between Nevis and
   London, 258, 259n, 269–271, 219–221; between New
   Hampshire and London, 136n; between New Jersey
   and London, 172–173, 315–317; between Newry and
   London, 35; between New York and London, 123n,
   158n, 162–165, 314–317, and St. Domingue, 287n;
   between North Carolina and London, 216, 217–219,
   315–317; between Nova Scotia and London, 231n;
   between Panama and Seville, 299n; between Paris and
   London, 23n, 29, 30n, 34, 34n, 88–97, 283, 305–311,
   and St. Domingue, 286n, 289, 290, 321, and St.
   Petersburg, 42n; between Pennsylvania and London,
   123n, 177, 183–186, 314–317, and St. Domingue, 20, 26;
   between Peru and Seville, 299n; between Quebec and
   London, 232; between Rhode Island and London,
   136–137n; between St. Christopher and London, 258,
   259n, 265–267, 319, 321; between St. Eustatius and
   London, 293n; between St. Petersburg and London,
   42n; between St. Vincent and London, 273; between
   Santo Domingo and Seville, 299n; between South
   Carolina and London, 222–224, 314–317; between
   Stockholm and London, 64n; between Virginia and
   London, 209–212, 314–317; between Waterford and
   London, 35

Exchange brokers, 19, 20n, 30n, 122, 122n
Exeter (England), 32, 178, 180n

F
Falmouth (Virginia), 188n, 201n
Faneuil, Peter: papers of, 144n; letter to, 221n
Fanfani, Amintore, 42n
Farr, Richard. See Atkins, Michael, Richard Farr, and Son
Farthing (British monetary unit), 35
Fauquier, Francis (gov., Virginia): letter from, 213n
Fearnley, Thomas (Norway): letter from, 32n
Feavearyear, Albert E., Pound Sterling, 8n
Felt, Joseph B., Historical Account of Massachusetts
   Currency, 133n, 152n

Feltham, John, Tour through the Isle of Man, 32n
Ferguson, Elmer James, 125; Papers of Robert Morris, 7n;
   "Colonial Finance," 118n, 125n
Fergusson, Murdock, and Co. (Madeira), 301; letters
   from, 301nn
Fernow, Berthold, "Coins and Currency of New-York,"
   156n, 157nn, 158nn; Records of New Amsterdam, 159n.
   See also O'Callaghan, Edmund B., and Berthold Fernow
Fetter, Frank Whitson, Irish Pound, 33n, 34n, 35nn
Fettsplace, Edward, Jr.: letter to, 288n
Fiering, Myron B., "Use of Correlation to Augment
   Data," 24n
Filing, of coin, 8
Financial Times, 29
Fish: as commodity money, 230
Fishbourne, William (Pennsylvania): letter from, 180
Fisher, Harold E. S., Portugal Trade, 22n, 31n, 108n
Fisher, Joshua, and Sons (Pennsylvania): letter from,
   188n
Fishing industry, Newfoundland, 230
"Fish pay," at Newfoundland, 230–231
Fitch, Thomas (Massachusetts): papers of, 144n
Fitzhugh, William (Maryland): ledgers of, 193n, 194n,
   200n, 204n, 214n, 277n, 279n
Fitzhugh, William (Virginia): letter from, 208n
Fitzwilliam, Richard (gov., Bahama Islands): letter from,
   275n
Flanders, Henry. See Mitchell, James T., and Henry
   Flanders
Fleming, Horace A., "Halifax Currency," 231n
Fleming, R. Harvey, "Phyn, Ellice and Company," 122n,
   123n
Fleming v. Lynde, 136n
Fletcher, Benjamin (gov., New York): letters from, 165nn
Fletcher, John (London): letter to, 255n
Flexney, Daniel, and Jacob Chitty (London): payees of bill
   of exchange, 236–237, 238
Flora (snow), 276n
Florida, as British colony: Georgia paper money in, 228;
   money and exchange of, 230. See also Exchange;
   Mobile; Monetary units, British; St. Augustine
Florida, as Spanish colony: money and exchange of, 230
   (see also 299–300); government subsidies to, 284. See also
   Monetary units, Spanish
Florijn (florin). See Gulden
Flour: price of, 24

Treasury. *See* Great Britain, Treasury

Treher, Matthias (Amsterdam): payer of bill of exchange, 294

Trelawney, Edward (gov., Jamaica): letter from, 254n

Trelawney, Edward (Massachusetts): letter from, 132n

Trelawney, Robert (Plymouth): letter to, 132n

Trent, William (Pennsylvania): ledgers of, 187n, 244n

Trenton (New Jersey), 119n, 167n, 171n

Trott, Nicholas, *Laws of the British Plantations*, 219n

Trumbull, James H., and Charles J. Hoadly, *Public Records of the Colony of Connecticut*, 132n, 135n, 143n

Trustees of Georgia. *See* Georgia, Trustees of

Tucker, Henry, and Sons (Bermuda): letter from, 277, 279n

Tucker, Robert (Virginia): letter to, 24

Tullideph, Walter (Antigua; Scotland), 259, 293; letter books of, 200n, 258n, 259n, 263n

Turks Islands: money and exchange of, 275–276; attacked by French force, 304. *See also* Exchange; Monetary units, British

Turner. *See* Mead and Ingram v. Turner

Two Letters to Mr. Wood. See Smith, Wavel

Two-pound (£2) piece (Scottish monetary unit), 10

Tyzack, John (London): report of, 275n

U

United Kingdom. *See* England; Scotland

United Provinces. *See* Netherlands

United States, Department of Commerce, Bureau of the Census, *Historical Statistics of the United States*, 180–181n, 189n, 194n

United States Congress, president of: letter to, 228n

Upper Marlboro (Maryland), 201n

Usance: in general, 20–21, 21n, 36, 121–122, 121n; in the colonies, 21, 121n, 158, 177, 195, 207, 220–221, 240, 240n, 248–249, 259, 273, 285–286, 296

Usher, Abbott Payson, *Early History of Deposit Banking*, 19n

Usher, Hezekiah (Massachusetts): payer of bill of exchange, 127

V

Vallette, Elie, *Deputy Commissary's Guide*, 194, 196n

Vance, Hugh, *Inquiry into the Nature and Uses of Money*, 121n, 203n

Van Colen and de Groot (Antwerp): handbook of, 44n

Van der Wee, Herman, *Growth of the Antwerp Market*, 42n

Van Laer, Arnold J. F., *New York Historical Manuscripts*, 159n

Vaz, Joaquín Ferraro, *Catálogo das moedas portuguesas*, 13n, 107n

Vázquez de Prada Vallejo, Valentín, *Lettres marchandes d'Anvers*, 29n, 42n, 108n; "Moneda y cambia," 42n

Vellon. *See* Moneda de vellon

Venice, 189

Venus (snow): account book of, 254n

Verelst, Harman (London): letters from, 225nn

Vernon, Samuel and William (Rhode Island): papers of, 214n, 225n, 245n, 254n, 258n, 264n, 298n, 329n

Vestindisk courant, 297

Vestindisk-Guineisk Kompagni. *See* West India Company, Danish

Vibæk, Jens, *Dansk Vestindien*, 298n

Victualling Office. *See* Great Britain, Admiralty

Vilar, Pierre, *Or et monnaie*, 7n

Villiers, John A. J. *See* Storm van 's Gravesande, Laurens

Virginia, 123, 131, 212n, 213n, 214n, 276, 293n, 301; bills of, at Boston, 124; statute law of, 124n, 205n, 206n, 208nn; manipulation of rate of exchange in, 131n; relationship of, with Pennsylvania and Maryland, 175, 177, 189, 194–195; money and exchange of, 205–214, 239. *See also* Accokeek Furnace; Accomack County; Alexandria; Cabin Point, James River; Exchange; Falmouth; Frederick County; Gloucester County; Monetary units, British; New Kent County; Norfolk; Occoquan; Oxford; Rappahannock River; Spotsylvania; Spotsylvania County; Stafford County; Westmoreland County; Williamsburg; York County; Yorktown

Virginia Gazette, 145n, 213n

Voort, Johannes Petrus van de, *Westindische plantages*, 297n

Vossenberg. *See* Aschenbrenner and Vossenberg

W

Wailly, Natalis de, *Mémoire sur les variations de la livre tournois*, 87n, 283n

Walker, David (Maryland): letter to, 201n

Wallaby. *See* Williamson v. Wallaby

Wallace, David Duncan, *Life of Henry Laurens*, 225n; *History of South Carolina*, 225n

Wallace, Davidson, and Johnson (Maryland): journal of, 21n

Wall and Tardy (St. Domingue): price current of, 286n

Waller, Benjamin (Virginia): documents from, 213n

Wall Street Journal, 29

Waln, Robert (Pennsylvania): letters to, 123n, 221n

Walter v. Evans, 254n

Wampum currency, 157, 169

Wanton, Joseph, Jr. (Rhode Island): letter to, 160n

Ward, Richard (gov., Rhode Island): letter from, 154n

Ward v. Palmer, 165n

Warden, James (St. Croix): letter from, 298n

Wars. *See* Periods, economic and political

Washington, Augustine (Virginia), 130

Washington, George (Virginia), 130; letter to, 256n

Waterford (Ireland), 35

Waterhouse. See *Lilie v. Waterhouse*

Watkins, Joseph (Virginia): letter to, 194n

Watson. *See* Slayter and Watson

Watson, John F., *Annals of Philadelphia*, 122n

Watts, John (New York), 123, 159, 160, 196; letters from, 122n, 123n, 159nn. *See also* Barck, Dorothy C.

Watts, Robert (Barbados): letter to, 244n

Way, Benjamin (London): testimony of, 246–247n

Wechsel-Cours in Hamburg, 63n

Weeden, William B., *Economic and Social History of New England*, 145n

Weights and measures, 7, 25, 25n

Weiss, Roger W., "Colonial Monetary Standard of Massachusetts," 118n, 132n, 134n; "Paper Money in the American Colonies," 124n

Weld, Thomas (County Durham, England): letter from, 142n. *See* Scull, G. D.

Well's Register, 221n

Wentworth, Benning (gov., New Hampshire): letter to, 154n

Wentworth, Samuel (Boston): letter from, 144n

Werden, Isaac (Grenada): letter from, 273

Weskett, John, *Laws and Practice of Insurance*, 292n

Wesley, John (Georgia): letter from, 225n

West Africa: money and exchange of, 328–329. *See also* Gold Coast; Guinea Coast; Monetary units, West African; Whydah

Westergaard, Waldemar C., *Danish West Indies*, 297nn

"Western Design," 246

Westershall Plantation, Grenada, 274n

West Florida. *See* Florida

West India Company (Vestindisk-Guineisk Kompagni),